SERVICE MANAGEMENT FOR COMPETITIVE ADVANTAGE

James A. Fitzsimmons
Mona J. Fitzsimmons

GW00602018

McGRAW-HILL, INC.

New York St. Louis San Francisco Auckland Bogotá Caracas
Lisbon London Madrid Mexico City Milan Montreal New Delhi
San Juan Singapore Sydney Tokyo Toronto

SERVICE MANAGEMENT FOR COMPETITIVE ADVANTAGE
International Editions 1994

Exclusive rights by McGraw-Hill Book Co. - Singapore for manufacture and export. This book cannot be re-exported from the country to which it is consigned by McGraw-Hill.

3 4 5 6 7 8 9 0 CMO UPE 9 8 7 6 5

This book was set in Times Roman by ComCom, Inc.
The editors were Lynn Richardson and Dan Alpert;
the production supervisor was Paula Keller.
The cover was designed by Howard Leiderman.

Library of Congress Cataloging-in-Publication Data

Fitzsimmons, James A.
    Service management for competitive advantage / James A. Fitzsimmons and Mona J. Fitzsimmons.
        p.   cm.
    Includes bibliographical references and index.
    ISBN 0-07-021217-1
    1. Service industries-Management.   I. Fitzsimmons, Mona J.
    II. Title.
    HD9980.5.F549   1994
    658-dc20   93-35762

When ordering this title, use ISBN 0-07-113312-7

Printed in Singapore

ABOUT THE AUTHORS

JAMES A. FITZSIMMONS is the William H. Seay Professor of Business at the University of Texas. He received a B.S.E. in industrial engineering from the University of Michigan, an M.B.A. from Western Michigan University, and a Ph.D. with distinction from the University of California at Los Angeles. His principal research interest is in the area of service operations management, and he won the Stan Hardy Award in 1983 for the best paper published in the field of operations management. A computer methodology that he designed, referred to as CALL, has been used by major cities worldwide to plan emergency ambulance systems. Consulting assignments include the RAND Corporation; the U.S. Air Force; the cities of Los Angeles, Denver, Austin, Melbourne, and Auckland; the state of Texas; General Motors; La Quinta Motor Inns; Greyhound; and McDonald's. Teaching experience includes faculty appointments at Boston University, the University of California at Los Angeles, California State University at Northridge, California Polytechnic State University at San Luis Obispo, and the University of New Mexico. He has held positions at Corning Glass Works and Hughes Aircraft Company in the role of an industrial engineer with professional registration in the state of Michigan. He also served in the U.S. Air Force as an officer in charge of base construction projects. He has served eight years as the Department of Management Ph.D. graduate adviser at the University of Texas and been nominated for six teaching awards. He is a founding member and the first treasurer of the Operations Management Association, as well as the associate editor of *Management Science* and the developer and coauthor of *Service Operations Management,* the first textbook in the field. He has contributed to several books and is the author or coauthor of more than forty articles published in journals such as *Management Science, Journal of Operations Management, Interfaces, Socio-Economic Planning Sciences,* and *International Journal of Production Research.* Professor Fitzsimmons has participated in various grant-supported projects and research studies and most recently was elected at-large vice president of the Decision Sciences Institute.

MONA J. FITZSIMMONS, a graduate of the University of Michigan, received her undergraduate degree in journalism with major supporting work in chemistry and psychology. Her graduate work was in geology, and she taught in public and private schools and at the university level. She has done writing and editing for the Encyclopaedia Britannica Education Corporation and for various professional journals and organizations. She edited and indexed *Service Operations Management,* written by James A. Fitzsimmons and Robert S. Sullivan and published by McGraw-Hill in 1982. Her nonprofessional activities have included volunteer work for the Red Cross aquatics program and wildlife rehabilitation. Currently, she is a free-lance consumer activist who has particular interests in the areas of responsible environmental behaviors, the responsibilities of patients and physicians in the health care equation, and relief from the health and financial burdens that tobacco use places on society.

To Our Children:
Michael, Gary, and Constance

CONTENTS

PREFACE

This book represents a gauntlet—a challenge to those who administer, teach, and learn in our business schools. The future economic, social, and environmental prosperity of the nation depends on creative management of services.

Services touch the lives of every person in this country every day: food services, communication services, emergency services, to name only a few. Our welfare and the welfare of our economy is now based on services. The activities of manufacturing and agriculture will always be necessary, but we can eat only so much food and we can use only so many goods. Services, however, are largely experiential, and we will always have a limitless appetite for them.

So herein lies the challenge to be met in our business schools: First, we must have administrators who encourage and support faculty who are willing to move out of comfortable old niches and to learn and teach new materials and skills. Second, we must have faculty who are willing to grow and to serve first their most important customers, their students. Third, we must have students who come with enthusiasm, energy, thoughtfulness and, perhaps most important of all, open minds and curiosity.

Within the past decade, service operations management has been established as a field of study that embraces all service industries. For example, under the leadership of the senior author of this text, the discipline was recognized as an academic field and designated as a separate track by the Decision Sciences Institute beginning with its 1987 Boston meeting. Next, in 1989 the *International Journal of Service Industry Management* was inaugurated. Finally, the First International Service Research Seminar in Service Management was held in France in 1990, drawing participants from the fields of operations management, marketing, and organizational behavior. This conference recognized the multidisciplinary nature of services and dropped the adjective "operations" in order to emphasize the integrative nature of service management.

This book acknowledges and emphasizes the essential uniqueness of service management. These are some key features:

• The book is written in an engaging literary style, makes extensive use of examples, and is based on the research and consulting experience of the authors.

• The theme of managing services for competitive advantage is emphasized in each chapter and provides a focus for each management topic.

• The integration of marketing, operations, and human behavior is recognized as central to effective service management.

• To dispel the common belief that manufacturing management principles can be applied to services without recognition of the different operating environments, the role of services in society and the uniqueness of service delivery systems are stressed.

• New information technologies such as yield management and data envelopment analysis, developed only within the past few years, are included as illustrations of the strategic role of information in managing services.

• Emphasis is placed on the need for continuous improvement in quality and productivity in order to compete effectively in a global environment.

• To facilitate pedagogical flexibility, all quantitative models are contained in chapter supplements and in the final section of the book, Part VI.

• To motivate the reader, a vignette of a well-known company starts each chapter, illustrating the strategic nature of the topic to be covered.

• Each chapter has a preview, a closing summary, topics for discussion, exercises when appropriate, and one or more cases.

• The instructor's manual contains case analyses, exercise solutions, a video library, and supplementary cases and readings.

We were very fortunate to have our manuscript reviewed by several colleagues—all people of integrity, wit, and vision—who were equal to the challenge we issued. Their detailed comments, insights, and thought-provoking suggestions were gratefully received and incorporated in the text in many places. Special thanks and acknowledgment go to the following people for their valuable reviews: Mohammad Ala, California State University, Los Angeles; Joanna R. Baker, Virginia Polytechnic Institute and State University; Mark Davis, Bentley College; Maling Ebrahimpour, University of Rhode Island; Michael Gleeson, Indiana University; Ray Haynes, California Polytechnic State University at San Luis Obispo; Art Hill, the University of Minnesota; Sheryl Kimes, Cornell University; and Richard Reid, the University of New Mexico. We also wish to thank Melba L. Jett for her indexing expertise and encouragement throughout this project. The personal computer, printer, and software provided through the generosity of William H. Seay, who endowed the senior author's professorship, made the writing of this book a great pleasure.

We express special appreciation to all our friends who encouraged us and tolerated our social lapses while we produced this book. In particular, we are indebted for the support of Richard and Janice Reid, who have provided lively and stimulating conversations and activities over many years, and who generously allowed us the use of their mountain retreat. The first half of this book was written in the splendid isolation of their part of the Jemez Mountains of New Mexico. No authors could want for better inspiration.

James A. Fitzsimmons
Mona J. Fitzsimmons

OVERVIEW OF THE BOOK

Part I of this book begins with a discussion of the role of services in an economy. We first look at the evolution of societies based on economic activity, beginning with agriculture and moving to industrialization and finally to service economies. Next, we look at how services differ from manufacturing and the implications that these differences have for the management of services. This section sets the stage and examines the environment in which services now operate.

In Part II, we develop the central theme of the book: managing services for competitive advantage. The necessity of integrating marketing and operations in services is first realized when a market position is established and the competitive service strategy is formulated. For services, information plays a central strategic role by creating barriers to entry, generating revenue, being an asset, and being a source for productivity improvement.

Structuring the service enterprise to support the competitive strategy is the topic of Part III. The service delivery system is engineered through the use of a process flowcharting concept called *blueprinting* that explicitly recognizes the front office, where customer contact occurs, and the behind-the-scenes back-office operations. Questions concerning the facility design and layout are next addressed from the perspective of both customer participation and operations efficiency. Finally, the critical decision of where to locate the service facility is considered.

Management of day-to-day operations is addressed in Part IV. We begin with the notion of the service encounter, which describes the interaction between service provider and customer in the context of a service organization. A treatment of service quality follows naturally once we have established a customer service orientation. Because the nature of services provides a challenge in matching capacity with demand, strategies for managing demand and for managing supply are presented. Finally, the question of managing waiting lines is addressed from a psychological viewpoint.

In Part V, we look at strategies to achieve world-class service. The concept of continual improvement in quality and productivity is discussed in the context of technological innovation in services and the stages of service firm competitiveness. Growth and expansion strategies are explored, including the traditional franchising method and considerations for multinational development.

Part VI contains a selection of quantitative decision models with important service applications. This concluding part presents models used to forecast service demand, queuing models for capacity planning, and linear programming models with applications in services.

SERVICES AND THE ECONOMY

We begin our study of service management with an appreciation of the central role that services play in the economy of nations and world commerce. No economy can function without the infrastructure that services provide in the form of transportation and communications and without government services such as education and health care. However, as an economy develops, services become even more important, and soon the vast majority of the population is employed in service activities.

The management of services has unique challenges different from those found in manufacturing, which has been the traditional focus of management research and teaching. Thus, Chapter 2 will address the nature of service operations and identify their distinctive characteristics. Perhaps the most important characteristic of service operations is the presence of the customer in the service delivery system. Focusing on the customer and serving his or her needs has always been an important daily activity for service providers.

CHAPTER 1

THE ROLE OF SERVICES IN AN ECONOMY

Services lie at the very hub of economic activity in any society. Dorothy Riddle, in writing about the role of the service sector in world development, formulated the economic model shown in Figure 1.1. This model of the economy shows the flow of activity among the three principal sectors of the economy: extractive (mining and farming), manufacturing, and service, which is divided into five subgroups. All activity eventually leads to the consumer. Examples of services in each of the five subgroups are:

Business services. Consulting, finance, banking
Trade services. Retailing, maintenance and repair
Infrastructure services. Communications, transportation
Social/personal services. Restaurants, health care
Public administration. Education, government

Infrastructure services, such as transportation and communications, are the essential links between all sectors of the economy, including the final consumer. In a complex economy, infrastructure services and trade services function as intermediaries between the extractive and manufacturing sectors and as the channel of distribution to the final consumer. Infrastructure services are a prerequisite for an economy to become industrialized; therefore, no advanced society can be without these services.

In an industrialized economy, specialized firms can supply business services to manufacturing firms more cheaply and more efficiently than the manufacturing firms can supply the services for themselves. Thus, more and more often we find advertising, consulting, financing, testing, and other business functions being provided for the manufacturing sector by service firms.

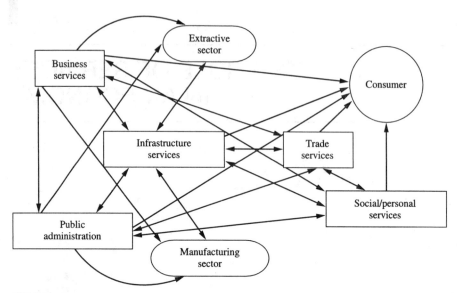

FIGURE 1.1
Interactive model of an economy. [*After Dorothy I. Riddle,* Service-Led Growth, *Praeger, New York, 1986, p. 27.*]

Except for basic subsistence living, where individual households are self-suffi-cient, service activities are absolutely necessary for the economy to function and to enhance the quality of life. Consider, for example, the importance of a banking industry to transfer funds and a transportation industry to move foods to areas that cannot produce them. Moreover, a wide variety of social and personal services such as restaurants, lodging, cleaning, and child care have been created to move former household functions into the economy.

Public administration plays a critical role in providing a stable environment for investment and economic growth. In communities and countries where public administrative services are weak or heavily skewed solely by political or idealistic concerns, essential services are inaccessible to many citizens.

Thus, it is imperative to recognize that services are not peripheral activities but, rather, integral parts of society. They are central to a functioning and healthy economy and lie at the heart of the economy. The service sector not only facilitates but also makes possible the goods-producing activities of the extractive and manufacturing sectors. Services are the crucial force for change toward a global economy.

CHAPTER PREVIEW

We begin with a discussion of economic evolution and find that modern industrialized economies are dominated by employment in the service sector

TABLE 1.1
STAGES OF ECONOMIC ACTIVITY

Primary (Extractive):	*Quaternary* (Trade and commerce):*
Agriculture	Transportation
Mining	Retailing
Fishing	Communications
Forestry	Finance and insurance
Secondary (Goods-producing):	Real estate
Manufacturing	Government
Processing	*Quinary* (Refining and extending human capacities):*
Tertiary (Domestic services):*	Health
Restaurants and hotels	Education
Barber- and beauty shops	Research
Laundry and dry cleaning	Recreation
Maintenance and repair	Arts

*Services.

industries. This represents a natural evolution of economies from preindustrial, to industrial, and finally to postindustrial societies. The economic activity of society determines the nature of how people live and how the standard of living is measured. The nature of the service sector is explored in terms of employment opportunities, contributions to economic stability, and source of economic leadership. Finally, the role of the service manager is discussed in terms of entrepreneurial innovation, opportunities for new services based on demographic trends, and the many managerial challenges in an expanding service economy.

ECONOMIC EVOLUTION

In the early 1900s, only three of every ten workers in the United States were employed in services. The remaining workers were active in agriculture and industry. By 1950, employment in services accounted for 50 percent of the workforce. Now services employ about eight out of every ten workers. During the past 90 years we have witnessed a major evolution in our society from being predominantly manufacturing-based to being predominantly service-based.

Economists studying economic growth are not surprised by these events. Colin Clark argues that as nations become industrialized, there is an inevitable shift of employment from one sector of the economy to another.[1] As productivity increases in one sector, the labor force moves into another sector. This observation, known as the *Clark-Fisher hypothesis,* leads to a classification of economies by noting the activity of the majority of the workforce.

Table 1.1 describes five stages of economic activity. Many economists, including Clark, limited their analyses to only three stages, of which the tertiary stage was

[1]Colin Clark, *The Conditions of Economic Progress,* 3d ed., The Macmillan Co., London, 1957.

TABLE 1.2
PERCENT EMPLOYMENT IN SERVICE JOBS
FOR SELECTED INDUSTRIALIZED NATIONS,
1980–1987

Country	1980	1987
United States	67.1	71.0
Canada	67.2	70.8
Belgium	64.3	70.1
Australia	64.7	69.7
United Kingdom	60.4	67.7
Israel	63.3	66.0
France	56.9	63.6
Finland	52.2	60.1
Japan	54.5	58.1
Italy	48.7	57.7

Source: 1987 *Statistical Yearbook,* Department of International Economic and Social Affairs Statistical Office, United Nations, New York, 1990, pp. 76–87.

simply services. We have taken the suggestion of Nelson N. Foote and Paul K. Hatt and subdivided the service stage into three categories.[2]

Today an overwhelming number of countries in the world are still in a primary stage of development. These economies are based on extracting natural resources from the land. Their productivity is low, and income is subject to fluctuations based on the prices of commodities such as sugar and copper. In Africa and Asia more than 70 percent of the labor force is engaged in farming.

However, many of the so-called advanced industrial nations would better be described as service economies based on the work activity of their populations. Table 1.2 is a partial list of industrialized countries in order of the percentage of those employed in service-producing jobs. This table contains some surprises, such as finding Canada and Australia (known for their mining industries) high on the list. Several observations can be made: global economic development is progressing in unanticipated directions, successful industrial economies are built on a strong service sector, and competition in services will become global just as it has in manufacturing. In fact, at present the ten largest commercial banks in the world are owned by the Japanese. However, trade in services remains a challenge because many countries erect barriers to protect domestic firms. For example, India and Mexico, among others, prohibit the sale of insurance by foreign companies.

As shown in Figure 1.2, the service sector in the United States now accounts for more than three-fourths of the total employment, which continues a trend that began more than one century ago. The United States can no longer be characterized as an industrial society; it is, instead, a postindustrial, or service, society. Of course,

[2]N. N. Foote and P. K. Hatt, "Social Mobility and Economic Advancement," *American Economic Review,* May 1953, pp. 364–378.

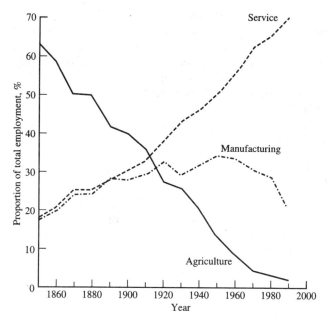

FIGURE 1.2
Trends in U.S. employment by sector, 1850–1990. [*From U.S.
Department of Commerce, Bureau of the Census,* Historical
Statistics of the United States, *1975, p. 137, and U.S. Department of
Commerce, Bureau of the Census,* Statistical Abstract of the U.S.,
1984, p. 421.]

this does not mean that manufacturing has lost its importance, but like agriculture,
it is not now an activity in which a large number of citizens participate.

STAGES OF ECONOMIC DEVELOPMENT

Describing where our society has been, its current condition, and its most likely
future is the task of social historians. Daniel Bell, a professor of sociology at
Harvard University, has written extensively on this topic. The material that follows
is based on his work.[3] To place the concept of a postindustrial society in
perspective, we need to compare its features with those of preindustrial and
industrial societies.

Preindustrial Society

The condition of most of the world's population today is one of subsistence. Life
is characterized as a game against nature. Working with muscle power and

[3]Daniel Bell, *The Coming of Post-Industrial Society: A Venture in Social Forecasting,* Basic Books,
Inc., New York, 1973.

tradition, the labor force is engaged in agriculture, mining, and fishing. Life is conditioned by the elements, such as the weather, the quality of the soil, and the availability of water. The rhythm of life is shaped by nature, and the work pace varies with the seasons. Productivity is low and bears little evidence of technology. Social life revolves around the extended household. The combination of low productivity and large population results in a high percentage of underemployment (workers not fully utilized). Many seek positions in services, but of the personal or household variety. Preindustrial societies are agrarian and structured around tradition, routine, and authority.

Industrial Society

The predominant activity is production of goods. The focus of attention is on making more with less. Energy and machines multiply the output per labor-hour and structure the nature of work. Division of labor is the operational "law" that creates routine tasks and the notion of the semiskilled worker. Work is accomplished in the artificial environment of the factory, and people tend the machines. Life becomes a game played against a fabricated nature—a world of cities, factories, and tenements. The rhythm of life is machine-paced and dominated by rigid working hours and time clocks.

An industrial society is a world of schedules and the acute awareness of the value of time. The standard of living becomes measured by the quantity of goods. But note that the complexity of coordinating the production and distribution of goods results in the creation of large bureaucratic and hierarchical organizations. These organizations are designed with certain roles for their members, and the operation tends to be impersonal, with persons treated as things. The individual is the unit of social life in a society that is considered the sum total of all the individual decisions being made in the marketplace. Of course, the unrelenting pressure of industrial life is softened by the countervailing force of labor unions.

Postindustrial Society

While an industrial society defines the standard of living by the quantity of goods, the postindustrial society is concerned with the quality of life, as measured by services such as health, education, and recreation. The central figure is the professional person because information, rather than energy or physical strength, is the key resource. Life now is a game played among persons. Social life becomes more difficult because political claims and social rights multiply. Society becomes aware that independent actions of individuals can combine to create havoc for everyone, as seen in traffic congestion and environmental pollution. The community rather than the individual becomes the social unit.

Bell suggests that the transformation from industrial to postindustrial society occurs in many ways. First, there is a natural development of services, such as transportation and utilities, to support industrial development. As labor-saving devices are introduced into the production process, more workers become engaged

TABLE 1.3
COMPARISON OF SOCIETIES

	Features					
Society	Game	Pre-dominant activity	Use of human labor	Unit of social life	Standard of living measure	Structure
Preindustrial	Against nature	Agriculture Mining	Raw muscle power	Extended household	Sub-sistence	Routine Traditional Authoritative
Industrial	Against fabricated nature	Goods production	Machine tending	Individual	Quantity of goods	Bureaucratic Hierarchical
Postindustrial	Among persons	Services	Artistic Creative Intellectual	Community	Quality of life in terms of health, education, recreation	Inter-dependent Global

in nonmanufacturing activities, such as maintenance and repair. Second, the growth of the population and mass consumption of goods increase wholesale and retail trade along with banking, real estate, and insurance. Third, as income increases, the proportion spent on the necessities of food and home decreases, and the remainder creates a demand for durables and then for services.

Christian Engel, a German statistician of the nineteenth century, explains the growth in personal services, such as those offered in restaurants, hotels, travel, and entertainment. However, a necessary condition for the "good life" is health and education. In our attempts to eliminate disease and increase the span of life, health services become a critical feature of modern society. Higher education becomes the condition for entry into a postindustrial society, which requires professional and technical skills of its population. Finally, the claims for more services and social justice lead to a growth in government. Concerns for environmental protection require government intervention and illustrate the interdependent and even global character of postindustrial problems. Table 1.3 summarizes the features that characterize these three stages of economic development—preindustrial, industrial, and postindustrial.

THE NATURE OF THE SERVICE SECTOR

For many people, *service* is synonymous with *servitude* and brings to mind workers flipping hamburgers and waiting on tables. However, the service sector that has grown significantly over the past 30 years cannot be accurately described as a sector composed only of low-wage or low-skill jobs in department stores and fast-food restaurants. Instead, as seen in Table 1.4, the fastest-growing jobs within

TABLE 1.4
RATE OF GROWTH OF U.S. JOBS, JANUARY 1982–JANUARY 1992

	Nonfarm jobs, Jan. 1982, in 1000s	Nonfarm jobs, Jan. 1982, %	Nonfarm jobs, Jan. 1992, in 1000s	Nonfarm jobs, Jan. 1992, %	Growth of nonfarm jobs, %
Service-producing:					
Finance, insurance, real estate	5,341	6.0	6,665	6.2	24.8
Miscellaneous services	19,036	21.3	28,577	26.4	50.1
State and local government	13,098	14.6	15,476	14.3	18.2
Wholesale trade	5,296	5.9	6,010	5.6	13.5
Retail trade	15,161	16.9	19,118	17.7	26.1
Transportation and utilities	5,082	5.7	5,746	5.3	13.1
Federal government	2,739	3.1	2,981	2.8	8.8
Total	65,753	73.5	84,573	78.3	
Goods-producing:					
Construction	3,905	4.4	4,587	4.2	17.5
Mining	1,127	1.3	657	0.6	–41.7
Manufacturing	18,781	21.0	18,283	16.9	–2.7
Total	23,813	26.7	23,527	21.7	
Total jobs	89,566		108,100		20.7

Source: Economic Indicators, prepared for the Joint Economic Committee by the Council of Economic Advisors, U.S. Government Printing Office, June 1992, p. 14.

the service sector are in finance, insurance, real estate, miscellaneous services (health, education, professional services, etc.), and retail trade. Note that the job areas whose growth rates were less than the rate of increase of total jobs (i.e., less than 20.7 percent) lost their market share, even though they showed gains in their absolute numbers. The exceptions are in mining and manufacturing, which lost in absolute numbers and thus showed negative growth rates. This trend should accelerate with the end of the cold war and subsequent downsizing of the military and defense industry.

Changes in the pattern of employment will have implications on where and how people live, on educational requirements, and consequently on the kinds of organizations that will be important to society. Industrialization created the need for the semiskilled worker who could be trained in a few weeks to perform the routine machine-tending tasks. The growth in the service sector has caused a shift to white-collar occupations. In the United States, the year 1956 was a turning point. For the first time in the history of industrial society, the number of white-collar workers exceeded the number of blue-collar workers, and the gap has been widening since then. The most interesting growth has been in the managerial and professional-technical fields, jobs that require a college education. Figure 1.3

shows the employment shift from an industrial society of machine operators to a postindustrial society of professional and technical workers.

Today service industries are the source of economic leadership. During the past 30 years more than 44 million new jobs have been created in the service sector to absorb the influx of women into the workforce and to provide an alternative to the lack of job opportunities in manufacturing. The service industries now account for approximately 70 percent of the national income in the United States. This should not be surprising, given that there is a limit to how many cars a consumer can use and to how much one can eat and drink. But the appetite for services, especially innovative ones, is insatiable. Among the services presently in demand are those that reflect an aging population, such as geriatric health care, and others reflecting the two-income family, such as day care.

FIGURE 1.3

Occupational distribution of the labor force. [*Computed from* Historical Statistics of the United States, Colonial Times to 1970, *part 1, U.S. Department of Commerce, Bureau of the Census, September 1975.*]

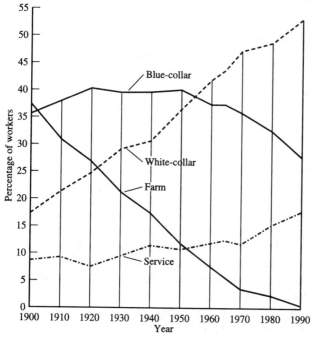

White-collar workers:
Professional and technical
Managers, officials, and proprietors
Clerical and kindred
Sales workers

Service workers:
Private household workers
Service, except private household

Blue-collar workers:
Craftsmen and foremen
Operatives
Laborers, except farm and mine

Farm workers:
Farmers and farm managers
Farm laborers and foremen

The growth of the service sector has produced a less cyclical national economy. During the past four recessions in the United States, employment by service industries has actually increased, while jobs were being lost in manufacturing. This suggests that consumers are willing to postpone the purchase of products but will not sacrifice service essentials like education, telephone service, banking, health care, and public services such as fire and police protection.

Several reasons can explain the recession-resistant nature of services. First, by their nature, services cannot be inventoried, as is the case for products. Because consumption and production occur simultaneously for services, the demand for services is more stable than that for manufactured goods. When the economy falters, many services continue to survive. Hospitals keep busy as usual, and commissions may drop in real estate, insurance, and security businesses, but employees need not be laid off.

Second, during a recession both consumers and business firms defer capital expenditures and, instead, fix up and make do with existing equipment. Thus, service jobs in maintenance and repair are created.

ROLE OF THE SERVICE MANAGER

The successful growth of the service sector will depend on entrepreneurial innovation and skilled management that will promote an ethic of continuous improvement in quality and productivity. An economy that has lost a significant industrial base to foreign competition does not have the luxury of allowing its service sector to follow manufacturing into decline.

Entrepreneurial Innovation

The following predictions for the year 2001 have been made by futurists:[4]

- Only 1 person in 50 will be promoted to top management, compared with 1 in 20 in 1987.
- Firms with fewer than 200 people will employ 85 percent of the workforce.
- The service sector will account for 88 percent of the workforce.
- An estimated 70 percent of U.S. homes will have computers, and an increasing volume of work will be done at home.
- About 63 percent of new entrants into the labor force will be women.
- The retirement age for social security eligibility will rise to 70.

These predictions are all consistent with a dynamic service-dominated society. We can add to these trends a source of entrepreneurial talent as mid-career professionals get squeezed out of the flattening management pyramid in large companies in response to the mergers and acquisitions of the late 1980s. However,

---

[4]Elsa C. Arnett, "Futurists Paint a Fascinating Picture of Life in the 21st Century," *The Washington Post,* July 24, 1989.

these ambitious entrepreneurs lack guidelines for the initiation of new service concepts.

The product development model that is driven by technology could be called a "push theory" of product innovation. A concept for a new product germinates in the laboratory with a new scientific discovery that becomes a solution looking for a problem. The 3M experience with Post-it notes is an example of this innovation process. The laboratory discovery was a poor adhesive that found a creative use as a glue for notes attached temporarily to objects without leaving a mark when removed.

For services, the Cash Management Account introduced by Merrill Lynch is an example of the "pull theory" of service innovation. During the high-interest period of the 1980s, a need arose to finance short-term corporate cash flows, and individual investors were interested in obtaining an interest rate that was higher than the rate currently available on passbook bank deposits.

The French Revolution provides another view of service formation, this time based on changing demographics. Before the revolution, only two restaurants were in existence in Paris, but shortly afterward there were more than 500. The dispossessed nobility had been forced to give up their private chefs, who found that opening their own restaurants was a logical solution to their unemployment.

For a manufacturing firm, product innovation is often driven by engineering-based research. However, for service firms, customers interact directly with the service process, and this focus on meeting customer needs drives service innovation and explains why marketing plays such a central role in service management.

The introduction of a new technology, however, does have an ancillary effect on service innovation. For example, the VCR has spawned a video rental business and created a renewed demand for old movies. Thus, the creation of an innovative service enterprise has many sources.

Service innovation can also arise from exploiting the information available from other activities. For example, records of sales by auto parts stores can be used to identify frequent failure areas in particular cars. This information has value both for the manufacturer, who can accomplish engineering changes, and for the retailer, who can diagnose customer problems. The creative use of information can also be a source of new services, or it can add value to existing services. For example, an annual summary statement of transactions furnished by one's financial institution has added value at income tax time.

Service innovators face a difficult problem in testing their service ideas. The process of product development includes building a laboratory prototype for testing prior to full-scale production. However, new services are seldom tested before they are launched in the marketplace, which provides a partial explanation for the observed high failure rate of service innovations, particularly for retailing and restaurants. At the present time new service concepts must usually prove themselves in the field instead of in a "laboratory" setting. Methods to simulate service delivery systems before their introduction need to be developed. One example of an effort in this direction is provided by Burger King, which acquired a warehouse in Miami to enclose a replica of its standard outlet. This mock restaurant was used to simulate changes in layout required for the introduction of new features such as drive-through window service and a breakfast menu. The marketing concept of a "focus group," consisting of customers selected to review service proposals in a roundtable discussion, is another means of evaluating new service ideas. The difficulty in service prototyping is the need to evaluate the service delivery system in operation where technology, service providers, and customers are integrated.

Social Trends

Three social trends will have a major influence on services: the aging of the U.S. population, the growth of two-income couples, and the increase in the number of single people. As the baby boom generation matures, the percentage of older people in America will increase greatly. Currently 6.2 million Americans are more than 80 years old; by the year 2000 this figure is projected to be 8 million, and by the year 2010 the number will be 21.1 million.[5] This aging of the population will create opportunities for retired people to take part-time work owing, in part, to fewer younger people entering the workforce. In the future, companies facing a labor shortage may, in fact, be forced to hire retired workers, at least on a temporary or part-time basis. That trend is already apparent. For example, The Travelers Insurance Company has developed a Retirement Job Bank of its retired employees that is used as a source of skilled labor to fill in during peak work times, absences, and vacations.[6] Also, elderly people are living longer and more active lives, with consequent demands on health care, public transportation, and leisure services.

The two-income family is fast replacing the traditional family of the 1950s, which consisted of a husband, a housewife, and two children. The new two-income family unit has created demands for services such as day care, pre-schooling, and "eating out" services. For two-income families, time becomes a premium; consequently, they are willing to pay for services that give them more free time. As a result, many new services have been created that now focus exclusively on saving time for these individuals. Examples include home delivery services and personal shopping services for everything from gifts to clothing. Increased disposable income from two wage earners may also translate into increased demands for leisure, entertainment, and tourism services.

The number of single people in America is growing, and the trend is expected to continue.[7] Recreational sports and other group-oriented activities will be in demand because they will offer the opportunity to meet other single people. Home food delivery services that now offer pizza may find a market for the delivery of gourmet meals to single people.

All these social trends support the notion that the home will become a sanctuary

---

[5]Susan B. Garland, "The Graying of America Spawns a New Crisis," *Business Week*, Aug. 17, 1987, pp. 60–62.

[6]Harold E. Johnson, "Older Workers Help Meet Employment Needs," *Personnel Journal*, May 1988, pp. 100–105.

[7]Edward Cornish, "The Coming of the Singles Society," *The Futurist*, July–August 1987, p. 2.

for people in the future, and that sanctuary will be supported by a communication system bringing video and electronic messages from the global community to the living room.

Management Challenges

Complacency in the management of service industries, inattention to quality, disregard for customer concerns, and exclusive attention to short-term financial orientation all threaten to undermine the service sector of the economy. It is important to realize that the service sector, under the pressures just mentioned, could become as vulnerable to foreign competition as has the manufacturing sector. The following discussion of the competitive challenges in services is based in part on a classic article by James Brian Quinn and Christopher E. Gagnon in which they caution the reader that services could follow manufacturing into decline.[8]

Quinn and Gagnon point out that the economic trends in services are undeniable and similar to the recent experience in manufacturing. The net positive trade balances in services have fallen steadily since the early 1980s. For example, a serious loss of market share has been experienced in international airline travel as the once powerful carriers, Pan Am and TWA, declared bankruptcy in the face of foreign competitors that upgraded their fleets and emphasized quality of service.

Purely domestic services are not immune to foreign competition either. Direct foreign investment in the U.S. service sector is substantial. Many famous names in services such as Twentieth Century–Fox, Stouffer's Hotels and Restaurants, Marshall Field, and Giant Foods are now foreign-owned. In California, Japanese banks are changing the nature of competition and winning accounts by taking a much longer view in making business loans to new ventures at very competitive interest rates.

The nature of competition in services is also changing because the forces of deregulation and new technologies have restructured service industries in recent years. Deregulation has caused significant restructuring in the domestic airline industry, with successful new regional carriers appearing (e.g., Southwest and Alaska) and old giants (e.g., Eastern and Braniff) declaring bankruptcy. New route networks have formed around the hub-and-spoke concept to provide service in a more cost-effective manner. The use of computer reservation systems has allowed the airlines to provide a variety of competitive fares based on preselling seats at a discount; thus, they can ensure high-load factors and profitable operations. Service managers need to understand these new competitive dimensions in order to take advantage of opportunities to improve service quality and performance, thereby creating barriers to entry from foreign and domestic competitors. Competing on the traditional dimensions of quality, price, and availability will always be important, but consider the following additional dimensions based on the use of information technologies, which are the source of the value added by service firms.

---

[8]J. B. Quinn and C. E. Gagnon, "Will Services Follow Manufacturing into Decline?" *Harvard Business Review,* November–December 1986, pp. 95–103.

Economies of Scale Economies of scale are realized when fixed costs in new technology are allocated over increased volume; the result is reduced cost per transaction. For example, the automation of the securities trading process changed the entire structure of the industry and made possible the handling of daily volumes in the millions of shares. The old system of transferring shares from seller to buyer manually has been replaced by an electronic clearinghouse. Without the use of a central electronic depository, Wall Street could not function as an efficient securities marketplace. New and expensive medical technology, such as the CAT scanner, has resulted in regional treatment centers and the concentration of medical services at these large hospitals. Thus, we find that the introduction of capital-intensive technology has resulted in the concentration of services and aggregation of demand.

Economies of Scope Economies of scope, a new and somewhat controversial concept, describes the benefits realized when entirely new service products move through established distribution networks with little added cost. For example, once the communications and information-handling technologies are in place, a much wider set of services can be distributed to a more diffuse customer base at low marginal costs. In addition, this information technology base can offer strategic benefits through more rapid product introduction and faster response to competitors' moves. Insurance companies that automated their back-office operations in the 1960s to improve premium billing and collections found themselves with a competitive advantage during the interest rate explosion of the 1980s. Companies had to alter their products rapidly to attract interest-sensitive new customers and to avoid the losses from current customers borrowing against their policies at low interest rates. Only those companies with the flexibility of computer information systems could design and deploy their products quickly enough to get a competitive edge. Some companies added new computer-intensive financial services such as cash management accounts to attract funds. A very common example of economies of scope can be found at the local convenience store that has added self-service gasoline and microwave meal service to its original grocery stocks.

Complexity Since deregulation, the domestic airline industry has witnessed an ever-changing fare structure so complex that fares can no longer be published in flight schedules. Computerized reservations systems allow airlines to analyze the status of flights and of customer buying behavior in such detail that they can optimize margins on each type of demand and meet competitors' responses. The ability to monitor hundreds of flights and make seat allocation decisions on an hourly basis is accomplished with significant computer support and software algorithms. This special use of computer information to manage perishable capacity and to maximize revenues is called *yield management,* a topic that will be treated in detail in Chapter 10.

Sophisticated use of information systems to manage complexity is also found in retail stores. Bar-code scanners of merchandise give instant feedback on sales and inventory movements, which results in a better match of inventory control to customers' needs. This information has enabled major chains to customize the stock featured at their stores so they can accommodate regional preferences and compete better with small specialty shops.

Boundary Crossing   Competition among services once thought to be in different industries is becoming commonplace. Some of the most striking examples are found in financial services. Many consumers now use their banks and brokers almost interchangeably because neither is seriously restricted in its scope of operations. Banks, insurance companies, and brokerage houses offer a similar range of financial products and services and now compete in one market without the traditional boundaries. As noted earlier, convenience stores now compete with fast-food restaurants as well as with service stations. Even manufacturing firms, such as GM and Ford, have entered the service arena by offering financing services to auto buyers. The ability of auto manufacturers to finance the sales of their cars has allowed them to offer reduced-interest loans as an incentive to buy their products. In fact, General Motors Acceptance Corporation is, at present, the nation's largest single holder of consumer debt. We can readily see that competition in services can come from any quarter.

International Competitiveness   Worldwide service trade is growing with the help of cheaper and more flexible transportation and communication capabilities. In the 1960s only 7 percent of the U.S. economy was exposed to foreign competition. However, in the 1980s that figure was greater than 70 percent, and it is still climbing. With the world heading toward a single economy, or "global village," this trend toward greater international competition is expected to continue for both manufacturing and service firms.[9] For example, the purchase of Flying Tigers has enabled Federal Express to guarantee delivery anywhere in the world in two days; as a result, it joins DHL and others for a share in the growing global package delivery business. Geographic distance is no longer a barrier between nations, however, and the challenges of ethnic diversity in the domestic market are multiplied by the difficulties of delivering a service in an international market with different cultural and language barriers.

SUMMARY

We have discovered that the modern industrial economies are, in fact, dominated by employment in the service sector. Just as farming was displaced by manufacturing in the nineteenth century as the center of economic activity, manufacturing has been displaced by services as the focus of activity in the final decade of the twentieth century. Chapter 2 will conclude our discussion of the role of services

[9]John Greenwald, "Down and Down the Dollar Goes," *Time*, Sept. 7, 1992, pp. 36–37.

in our new society and prepare us for developing new managerial skills by arguing that the distinctive characteristics of services require an approach to management that is significantly different from the approach found in manufacturing.

TOPICS FOR DISCUSSION

1. Illustrate how a person's lifestyle is influenced by the type of work he or she does. For example, contrast a farmer, a factory worker, and a schoolteacher.
2. Is it possible for an economy to be based entirely on services?
3. Speculate on the nature of the society that may evolve after the postindustrial society.
4. Explain why a manager of a service operation may face a more complex and difficult task than a manager of a manufacturing operation.
5. Comment on the role marketing plays in the service innovation process.

SELECTED BIBLIOGRAPHY

Bell, Daniel: *The Coming of Post-Industrial Society: A Venture in Social Forecasting,* Basic Books, Inc., New York, 1973.

Cook, James: "You Mean We've Been Speaking Prose All These Years?" *Forbes,* Apr. 11, 1983, pp. 143–149.

Cowell, Donald W.: *The Marketing of Services,* Heinemann, London, 1984.

Davis, Stanley M.: *Future Perfect,* Addison-Wesley, Reading, Mass., 1987.

Fuchs, Victor R.: *The Service Economy,* National Bureau of Economic Research, New York, 1968.

Gartner, A., and F. Riessman: *The Service Society and the Consumer Vanguard,* Harper & Row, Publishers, Inc., New York, 1975.

Gershung, J. I.: *After Industrial Society,* The Macmillan Co., New York, 1978.

Gersuny, C., and W. Rosengren: *The Service Society,* Schenkman Publishing Co., Cambridge, Mass., 1973.

Ginzberg, E., and G. Vojta: "The Service Sector of the U.S. Economy," *Scientific American,* vol. 244, no. 3, March 1981, pp. 48–55.

Guile, Bruce E., and James B. Quinn: *Managing Innovation: Cases from the Service Industries,* National Academy Press, Washington, D.C., 1988.

————: *Technology in Services: Policies for Growth, Trade, and Employment,* National Academy Press, Washington, D.C., 1988.

Heskett, J. L.: "Lessons in the Service Sector," *Harvard Business Review,* March–April 1987, pp. 118–126.

————: *Managing in the Service Economy,* Harvard Business School Press, Boston, 1986.

————, W. E. Sasser, Jr., and C. W. L. Hart: *Service Breakthroughs,* Free Press, New York, 1990.

Hirschhorn, L.: "The Post-Industrial Economy: Labour, Skills and the New Mode of Production," *The Service Industries Journal,* vol. 8, no. 1, 1988, pp. 19–38.

Johnston, R.: "Service Industries: Improving Competitive Performance," *The Service Industries Journal,* vol. 8, no. 2, 1988, pp. 202–211.

Kulonda, D. J., and W. H. Moates, Jr.: "Operations Supervisors in Manufacturing and Service Sectors in the United States: Are They Different?" *International Journal of Operations and Production Management,* vol. 6, no. 2, 1986, pp. 21–35.

Lewis, R.: *The New Service Society,* Longman, New York, 1973.

Lovelock, C. H.: "Business Schools Owe Students Better Service," *Managing Services,* Prentice-Hall, Englewood Cliffs, N.J., 1988, pp. 22–24.

——— and R. K. Shelp: "The Service Economy Gets No Respect," *Managing Services,* Prentice-Hall, Englewood Cliffs, N.J., 1988, pp. 1–5.

Quinn, J. B., and C. E. Gagnon: "Will Services Follow Manufacturing into Decline?" *Harvard Business Review,* November–December 1986, pp. 95–103.

Riddle, D. I.: *Service-Led Growth,* Praeger, New York, 1986.

Toffler, Alvin: *The Third Wave,* William Morrow and Co., Inc., New York, 1980.

CHAPTER 2

THE NATURE OF SERVICES

We explore the distinctive features of services in this chapter. The service environment is sufficiently unique to allow us to question the direct application of traditional manufacturing-based techniques to services without some modification, although many approaches are analogous. Ignoring the differences between manufacturing and service requirements will result in failure. But more importantly, the recognition of the special features of services will provide insights for enlightened and innovative management. Advances in service management cannot occur without an appreciation of the service system environment.

The distinction between a product and a service is difficult to make because the purchase of a product is accompanied by some facilitating service (e.g., installation), and the purchase of a service often includes facilitating goods (e.g., food at a restaurant). Each purchase includes a bundle of goods and services in varying proportions, as shown in Table 2.1.

In this chapter we are intentionally drawing the distinctions between manufacturing and services. However, many services have a clear front-office (e.g., bank teller interacting with a customer) and back-office (e.g., check-clearing operations) dichotomy in their operations. We would be foolish to ignore the substantial opportunities for applying manufacturing techniques to the isolated back-office operations. These opportunities will be explored in Chapter 5, where we consider the design of the service delivery system.

CHAPTER PREVIEW

The chapter begins with a classification of services based on the degree of customer interaction or customization and the degree of labor intensiveness. This classifi-

TABLE 2.1
PROPORTION OF GOODS AND SERVICES IN TYPICAL PURCHASE BUNDLE

	Goods				Services			
100%	75	50	25	0	25	50	75	100%
	Self-service gasoline............							
		Personal computer..............						
			Office copier..................					
				Fast-food restaurant............				
					Gourmet restaurant.............			
					Auto repair...................			
						Airline flight....................		
						Haircut.......................		

Source: Adapted from W. E. Sasser, R. P. Olsen, and D. D. Wyckoff, *Management of Service Operations,* Allyn and Bacon, Boston, 1978, p. 11.

cation allows us to focus on managerial issues that are found across similar service industries. An appreciation of the nature of services begins with a realization that a service is a package of explicit and implicit benefits performed within a supporting facility and using facilitating goods. These multiple dimensions of a service are central to the design and control of a service delivery system. The distinctive characteristics of service operations are discussed, and the implications for management are noted.

On the basis of these characteristics, the role of the service manager is viewed from an open-system perspective. That is, the service manager must deal with an environment in which the customers are present in the delivery system. This contrasts with manufacturing operations that are isolated or "buffered" from the customer by an inventory of finished goods. Thus, manufacturing has traditionally operated as a cost center, focusing on process efficiency. Service managers, who often operate as profit centers, must be concerned with both efficient and effective delivery of services.

SERVICE CLASSIFICATION

Concepts of service management should be generally applicable to all service organizations. Unfortunately, service firms have coalesced into industry groups that are seldom willing to appreciate management issues common to firms in another group. For example, hospital administrators could learn something about their own business from the restaurant and hotel trade. Professional services such as consulting, law, and medicine have management problems in common.

A service classification scheme can help organize our discussion of service management and break down the industry barriers to shared learning. In manufacturing, the classification of production processes as continuous flow (e.g., in an oil refinery), line flow (e.g., in an automobile plant), batch (e.g., in a brewery), job shop (e.g., in a printing shop), and project (e.g., in the construction of a space station) has been instrumental in building a body of knowledge in manufacturing. For example, the research on line balancing first undertaken by the automobile industry has found application in any firm that must assemble its products from discrete parts. In an effort to demonstrate that management problems are common across service industries, Roger Schmenner proposed the service process matrix shown in Figure 2.1.

In this matrix, services are classified across two dimensions that significantly affect the character of the service delivery process. The horizontal dimension is the degree of labor intensity, defined as the ratio of labor cost to capital cost. Thus, capital-intensive services such as airlines and hospitals are found in the upper row because of their considerable investment in plant and equipment relative to labor costs. Labor-intensive services such as schools and legal assistance are found in the bottom row because labor costs are high relative to capital requirements.

The vertical dimension measures the degree of customer interaction and customization. Customization is a marketing variable that describes the ability of the customer to affect personally the nature of the service delivered. Little interaction between customer and service provider is needed when the service provided is standardized rather than customized. For example, a meal at McDonald's, which is assembled from prepared items, is low in customization and is served with little interaction occurring between the customer and the service providers. In contrast, a doctor and her or his patient must interact fully in the diagnostic and treatment phases to achieve satisfactory results. Patients also expect to be treated as individuals and wish to receive medical care customized to their particular needs. However, the interaction that results from high customization creates potential problems for the management of the service delivery process.

The four quadrants of the service process matrix have been given names as defined by the two dimensions to describe the nature of the services illustrated. *Service factories* provide a standardized service with high capital investment, much

Degree of Labor Intensity	Degree of Interaction and Customization	
	Low	High
Low	*Service factory:* • Airlines • Trucking • Hotels • Resorts and recreation	*Service shop:* • Hospitals • Auto repair • Other repair services
High	*Mass service:* • Retailing • Wholesaling • Schools • Retail aspects of commercial banking	*Professional service:* • Doctors • Lawyers • Accountants • Architects

FIGURE 2.1
The service process matrix. [*From "How Can Service Businesses Survive and Prosper?" by Roger W. Schmenner,* Sloan Management Review, *vol. 27, no. 3, spring 1986, p. 25, by permission of publisher. Copyright 1986 by the Sloan Management Review Association. All rights reserved.*]

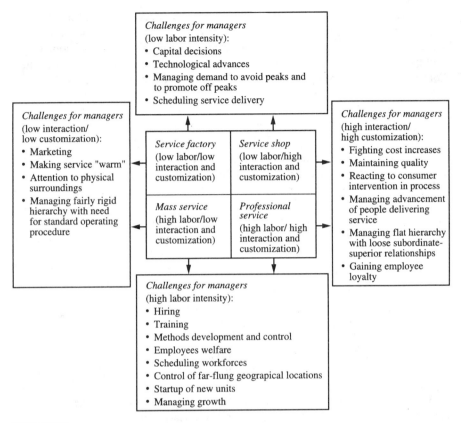

FIGURE 2.2
Challenges for service managers. [*From "How Can Service Businesses Survive and Prosper?" by Roger W. Schmenner,* Sloan Management Review, *vol. 27, no. 3, spring 1986, p. 27, by permission of publisher. Copyright 1986 by the Sloan Management Review Association. All rights reserved.]*

like a line-flow manufacturing plant.[1] *Service shops* permit more service customization, but they do so in a high-capital environment similar to that of a job shop. Customers of a *mass service* will receive an undifferentiated service in a labor-intensive environment, but those seeking a *professional service* will be given individual attention.

Managers of services in any category, whether service factory, service shop, mass service, or professional service, share similar challenges, as noted in Figure 2.2. Services with high capital requirements (low labor intensity), such as airlines and hospitals, require close monitoring of technological advances to remain competitive. The high capital investment also requires managers to schedule

---

[1]This concept of a service operated like a manufacturing factory is different from the more recent realization by manufacturing firms that operating a factory more like a service can achieve a competitive advantage. See R. B. Chase and D. A. Garvin, "The Service Factory," *Harvard Business Review,* vol. 67, no. 4, July–August 1989, pp. 61–69.

demand to maintain utilization of the equipment. Managers of high labor-intensive services, such as medical or legal professionals, must instead concentrate on personnel matters. The degree of customization affects the ability to control the quality of service delivered and the perception of the service by the customer. Approaches to addressing each of these challenges are topics that will be discussed in later chapters.

THE SERVICE PACKAGE

Service managers have difficulty in identifying their product. This problem is partly due to the intangible nature of services. But it is the presence of the customer in the process that creates a concern for the total service experience. Consider the following examples. For a sit-down restaurant, the atmosphere is just as important as the meal because many diners regard the occasion as a vehicle for getting together with friends. A customer's opinion of a bank can be formed quickly on the basis of a teller's cheerfulness or the length of the waiting line.

The service package is defined as a bundle of goods and services provided in some environment. This bundle consists of the following four features:

1. *Supporting facility.* The physical resources that must be in place before a service can be offered. Examples are a golf course, a ski lift, a hospital, and an airplane.

2. *Facilitating goods.* The material purchased or consumed by the buyer or items provided by the customer. Examples are golf clubs, skis, food items, replacement auto parts, legal documents, and medical supplies.

3. *Explicit services.* The benefits that are readily observable by the senses and consist of the essential or intrinsic features of the service. Examples are the absence of pain after a tooth is repaired, a smooth-running automobile after a tune-up, and the response time of the fire department.

4. *Implicit services.* Psychological benefits that the customer may sense only vaguely or extrinsic features of the service. Examples are the status of a degree from an Ivy League school, the privacy of a loan office, and worry-free auto repair.

The service package consists of the preceding four features, all of which are experienced by the customer and form the basis of his or her perception of the service. It is important that the service manager offer a total experience for the customer consistent with the desired service package. Take, for example, a budget hotel. The supporting facility is a concrete-block building with austere furnishings. Facilitating goods are reduced to the minimum of soap and paper. The explicit service is a comfortable bed in a clean room. Implicit services might include a friendly desk clerk and the security of a well-lighted parking area. Deviations from this service package, such as adding bellhops, would destroy the bargain image. Table 2.2 presents a list of criteria for evaluating the service package.

The importance of the facilitating goods in the service package can be used to classify services across a continuum from pure services to various degrees of mixed

TABLE 2.2
CRITERIA FOR EVALUATING THE SERVICE PACKAGE

Supporting facility

1. *Architectural appropriateness:*
   Renaissance architecture for university campus.
   Unique recognizable feature of blue tile roof.
   Massive granite facade of downtown bank.
2. *Interior decorating:*
   Is the proper mood established?
   Quality and coordination of furniture.

3. *Facility layout:*
   Is there a natural flow of traffic?
   Are adequate waiting areas provided?
   Is there unnecessary travel or backtracking?
4. *Supporting equipment:*
   Does the dentist use a mechanical or air drill?
   What type and age of aircraft does the charter airline use?

Facilitating goods

1. *Consistency:*
   Crispness of french fries.
   Portion control.
2. *Quantity:*
   Small, medium, or large pizza.
   Free checks.

3. *Selection:*
   Variety of replacement mufflers.
   Menu items available.
   Rental skis.

Explicit services

1. *Training of service personnel:*
   Is the auto mechanic NIASE-certified?
   (National Institute for Automotive Service Excellence)
   To what extent are paraprofessionals used?
   Are the physicians trained in American medical schools?
2. *Comprehensiveness:*
   Fast-food restaurant compared with cafeteria.
   General hospital compared with neighborhood clinic.
   College vs. university.
   Motel with meeting rooms, restaurant, and swimming pool.

3. *Consistency:*
   Airline's on-time record.
   Professional Standards Review Organization (PSRO) for doctors.
4. *Availability:*
   Twenty-four-hour banking service.
   Location of fire stations.
   Access to unemployment office by public transportation.

Implicit services

1. *Attitude of service personnel:*
   Cheerful flight attendant.
   Police officer issuing traffic citation with tact.
   Surly service person in restaurant.
2. *Privacy and security:*
   Attorney advising client in attorney's office.
   Magnetic key card for motel room.
3. *Convenience:*
   Use of appointments.
   Free parking.
4. *Atmosphere:*
   Restaurant decor.
   Use of standardized forms.
   Sense of confusion rather than order.

5. *Waiting:*
   Joining a drive-in banking queue.
   Telephoning someone and being placed on hold.
   Enjoying a martini in the restaurant bar.
6. *Status:*
   College degree from Ivy League school.
   Box seats at sports event.
7. *Sense of well-being:*
   Large commercial aircraft.
   Well-lighted parking lot.

services. For example, psychiatric counseling with no facilitating goods would be considered a pure service. Automobile maintenance usually requires more facilitating goods than does a haircut.

Making general statements about service management is difficult when there are such variations in the nature of services. However, an appreciation of the unique features of the service environment is important for understanding fully the challenges facing service managers.

DISTINCTIVE CHARACTERISTICS OF SERVICE OPERATIONS

In services a distinction must be made between inputs and resources. For services, inputs are the customers themselves. Customers typically arrive at their own discretion with unique demands on the service system. Resources are the facilitating goods, labor, and capital at the command of the service manager. Thus, in order to function, the service system must interact with the customers as inputs. An exception to this distinction occurs in self-service operations, where the customer is treated as a coproducer. This view of services is necessary because of the characteristics of services. A discussion of the characteristics of service operations and their implications for management follows. It should be noted that many of the unique characteristics of services are interrelated—for example, customer participation and perishability.

The Customer as a Participant in the Service Process

The presence of the customer as a participant in the service process requires an attention to facility design that is not found in manufacturing. The fact that automobiles are made in a hot, dirty, noisy factory is of no concern to the eventual buyers because they first see the product in the pleasant surroundings of a dealer's showroom. The presence of the customer on-site requires attention to the physical surroundings of the service facility that is not necessary for the factory. For the customer, service is an experience conducted in the environment of the service facility. The quality of service is enhanced if the service facility is designed from the customer's perspective. Attention to interior decorating, furnishings, layout, noise, and even color can influence the customer's perception of the service. Compare the feelings invoked by picturing yourself in a stereotypical bus station with those produced by imagining yourself in an airline terminal. Of course, passengers are not allowed in the terminal's back office (i.e., the luggage-handling area), which is operated in a factorylike environment. However, some innovative services have opened the back office to public scrutiny to promote confidence in the service (e.g., some restaurants provide a view into the kitchen, and some auto repair bays can be observed through windows in the waiting area).

An important consideration in providing a service is the realization that the customer can play an active part in the process. A few examples will illustrate that the knowledge, experience, motivation, and even honesty of the customer all directly affect the performance of the service system:

1. The popularity of supermarkets and discount stores is predicated on the fact that customers are willing to assume an active role in the retailing process.

2. The accuracy of a patient's medical record can greatly influence the effectiveness of the attending physician.

3. The education of a student is determined largely by the student's own effort and contributions.

This strategy is best illustrated by the fast-food restaurants that have significantly reduced the number of serving and cleaning personnel. The customer not only places the order directly from a limited menu but also is expected to clear the table after the meal. Naturally, the customer expects faster service and less expensive meals to compensate for these inputs. However, the service provider benefits in many subtle ways. First, there are fewer personnel who require supervision and such things as fringe benefits. Second, and more importantly, the customer provides the labor just at the moment it is required; thus, service capacity varies more directly with demand rather than being fixed by the size of the employed staff. The customer acts like a temporary employee, arriving just when needed to perform duties to augment the work of the service staff.

This strategy has received great acceptance in an educated society, such as the United States, where self-reliance is valued. The customer, instead of being a passive buyer, becomes a contributor to the gross national product.

Simultaneous Production and Consumption of Services

The fact that services are created and consumed simultaneously and thus cannot be stored is a critical feature in the management of services. The inability to inventory services precludes using the traditional manufacturing strategy of relying on inventory as a buffer to absorb fluctuations in demand. Inventory for a manufacturer serves as a convenient system boundary, separating internal operations of planning and control from the external environment. Thus, the manufacturing facility can be operated at a constant level of output that is most efficient. The factory is operated as a closed system, with inventory decoupling the productive system and customer demand. Services operate as open systems, with the full impact of demand variations transmitted to the system.

Inventory can also be used to decouple the stages in a manufacturing process. For services the decoupling is achieved through customer waiting. Inventory control is a major issue in manufacturing operations, whereas in services the corresponding problem is customer waiting, or queuing. The problems of selecting service capacity, facility utilization, and use of idle time are all balanced against customer waiting time.

The simultaneous production and consumption also eliminates many opportunities for quality control intervention. Unlike manufacturing, where the product is inspected before delivery, services must rely on other measures to ensure the consistency of output. In Chapter 9 the important subject of service quality is addressed.

Time-Perishable Capacity

A service is a perishable commodity. Consider an empty airline seat, an unoccupied hospital or hotel room, or an hour without a patient in the day of a dentist. In each case a lost opportunity has occurred. Because a service cannot be stored, it is lost forever when not used. The full utilization of service capacity becomes a management challenge because customer demand exhibits considerable variation, and unlike the situation in manufacturing, building inventory to absorb the fluctuations is not an option.

Consumer demand for services typically exhibits very cyclic behavior over short periods of time, with considerable variation between the peaks and valleys. The custom of eating lunch between noon and 1 p.m. places a burden on restaurants to accommodate the noon rush. The practice of day-end mailing by businesses contributes to the fact that 60 percent of all letters are received at the post office between 4 and 8 p.m.[2] The demand for emergency medical service in Los Angeles was found to vary from a low of 0.5 call per hour at 6 a.m. to a peak of 3.5 calls per hour at 6 p.m.[3] This peak-to-valley ratio of 7 to 1 was also true for fire alarms during an average day in New York City.[4]

For recreational and transportation services, seasonal variation in demand creates surges in activity. As many students know, flights home are often booked months in advance of spring break and the Christmas holidays.

Faced with variable demand and a perishable capacity to provide the service, the manager has three basic options:

1. Smooth demand by:
   a. Using reservations or appointments.
   b. Using price incentives (e.g., giving telephone discounts for evening and weekend calls).
   c. Demarketing peak times (e.g., advertising to shop early and avoid the Christmas rush).
2. Adjust service capacity by:
   a. Using part-time help during peak hours.
   b. Scheduling work shifts to vary workforce needs according to demand (e.g., telephone companies staff their operators to match call demand).
   c. Increasing the customer self-service content of the service.
3. Allow customers to wait.

[2] R. C. Cohen, R. McBridge, R. Thornton, and T. White, "Letter Mail System Performance Design: An Analytical Method for Evaluating Candidate Mechanization," Report R-168, Institute for Defense Analysis, Washington, D.C., 1970.

[3] James A. Fitzsimmons, "The Use of Spectral Analysis to Validate Planning Models," *Socio-Economic Planning Sciences,* vol. 8, no. 3, June 1974, pp. 123–128.

[4] E. H. Blum, "Urban Fire Protection: Studies of the New York City Fire Department," R-681, New York City Rand Institute, New York, January 1971.

This last option can be viewed as a passive contribution to the service process that carries the risk of losing a dissatisfied customer to a competitor. By waiting, the customer permits greater utilization of service capacity. The airlines explicitly recognize this by offering standby passengers a reduced price for their tickets.

Site Selection Dictated by Location of Consumers

Whereas products are shipped from the manufacturer to the wholesaler to the retailer, the service customer and provider must physically meet for a service to be performed. Either the customer comes to the service facility (restaurant), or the service provider goes to the customer (ambulance service). Of course, there are exceptions; banking by mail and taking university courses via television are examples. In fact, owing to advances in information technology, opportunities for innovation in service systems abound (e.g., American Airlines has a data processing center located in the Caribbean).

Travel time and costs are reflected in the economics of site selection (e.g., in the case of Domino's Pizza). The result is that many small service centers are located close to prospective consumers. Of course, the tradeoff is between the fixed cost of the facility and the travel costs of the customers. The more expensive the facility, the larger or more densely populated must be the market area. For example, many a major league baseball team has had trouble surviving in a medium-sized city.

The resulting small size of operation and the multisite locations of services create several challenges.

Limited Scale Economies Sizing a service to its immediate geographic market area removes the opportunity to gain the economies of scale found in manufacturing. The ability to distribute products over long distances permits the construction of large facilities with high-volume processes near the source of raw materials and/or cheap labor to achieve low unit costs. However, some services such as franchised food firms have centralized many of their common functions (e.g., purchasing, advertising, and food preparation) to achieve similar economies of scale.

Control of Decentralized Services Unlike manufacturing, services are performed in the field, not in the controlled environment of a factory. For example, fast-food restaurants maintain service consistency across multiple locations by standardization in the delivery process. The standardization may be achieved, for example, by designing special equipment (e.g., a french-fry scoop that measures the portion) or by offering a limited service (e.g., only burgers, fries, and shakes). More sophisticated services, such as health care, must rely on extensive training, licensing, and peer review.

For services that travel out to the customer (e.g., telephone installations, delivery services, and maintenance and repair services), the problems of routing, dispatching, and scheduling become important. These aspects are examined in the supplement to Chapter 5.

Labor Intensiveness

In most service organizations, labor is the important resource that determines the effectiveness of the organization. And like manufacturing, services have a problem of technological obsolescence. However, it is the skills of the labor force that age as new knowledge makes current skills obsolete. In an expanding organization, recruitment of new labor provides some of the benefits of the new knowledge. However, in a slow-growth or stable organization in which seniority is important, the only successful strategy may be continuous retraining. The problem of aging labor skills is particularly acute in the professional service organization, where extensive formal education is a prerequisite to employment.

The interaction between customer and employee in services creates the possibility of a more complete human work experience. The personal nature of services is in stark contrast to the depersonalization of work found in manufacturing. In services, work activity is oriented toward people rather than toward things. For example, the chef hidden in the kitchen must prepare a meal that satisfies a diner in taste as well as appearance. Even the introduction of automation may strengthen personalization by eliminating the relatively routine impersonal tasks, thereby permitting increased personal attention to the remaining work. At the same time, however, personal attention creates opportunities for variability in the service provided. This is not inherently bad unless customers perceive significant quality variation. A customer expects to be treated fairly and given the same service others receive. The development of standards and employee training in proper procedures is the key to ensuring consistency in the service provided. It is rather impractical to monitor the output of each employee except via customer complaints.

The direct customer-employee contact has implications for industrial (service) relations as well. Auto workers with grievances against the firm have been known to sabotage the product on the assembly line. Presumably, the final inspection will ensure that any such cars are corrected before delivery. However, a disgruntled service employee can do irreparable harm to the organization because the employee is the firm's sole contact with customers. The service manager, therefore, must be concerned about the employees' attitudes as well as their performance. J. Willard Marriott, founder of the Marriott Hotel chain, has said, "In the service business you can't make happy guests with unhappy employees."[5] Through training and genuine concern for employee welfare, the organizational goals can be internalized.

Intangibility

Services are ideas and concepts; products are things. It follows that service innovations are not patentable. To secure the benefits of a novel service concept, the firm must expand extremely rapidly and preempt competitors. Franchising has been the vehicle to secure market areas and establish a brand name. Franchising

[5]G. M. Hostage, "Quality Control in a Service Business," *Harvard Business Review*, vol. 53, no. 4, July–August 1975, pp. 98–106.

allows the parent firm to sell its idea to a local entrepreneur, thus preserving capital while retaining control and reducing risk.

The intangible nature of services also presents a problem for customers. When buying a product, the customer is able to see it, feel it, and test its performance before purchase. For a service the customer must rely on the reputation of the service firm. In many service areas the government has intervened to guarantee acceptable service performances. Through the use of registration, licensing, and regulation, the government can assure consumers that the training and test performance of some service providers meet certain standards. Thus, we find that public construction plans must be approved by a registered professional engineer, a doctor must be licensed to practice medicine, and the telephone company is a regulated utility. However, in its efforts ostensibly to protect the consumer, the government may be stifling innovation, raising barriers to entry, and generally reducing competition.

Difficulty in Measuring Output

Measuring the output of a service organization is a frustrating task for several reasons. For example, counting the number of customers served is seldom useful because it does not account for the quality of service performed. The problem of measurement is further complicated by the fact that not-for-profit service systems (e.g., hospitals, universities, and governments) do not have a single criterion, such as maximizing profit, on which to base an evaluation of their performance. More importantly, can a system's performance be evaluated on the basis of output alone when this assumes a homogeneous input? A more definitive evaluation of service performance is a measure of the change in each customer from input to output state, a process known as transactional analysis.

AN OPEN-SYSTEMS VIEW OF SERVICES

Service organizations are sufficiently unique in their character to require special management approaches beyond the simple adaptation of management techniques found in manufacturing a product. The distinctive characteristics suggest enlarging the system view to include the customer as a participant in the service process. The customer, as shown in Figure 2.3, is viewed as an input transformed by the service process into an output with some degree of satisfaction.

The role of the service operations manager includes the functions of both production and marketing in an open system with the customer as a participant. When considering services, the traditional manufacturing separation of the production and marketing functions, with finished-goods inventory as the interface, is neither possible nor appropriate. Marketing performs two important functions in daily service operations: (1) educating the consumer to play a role as an active participant in the service process and (2) promoting demand smoothing to match service capacity. This marketing activity must be coordinated with scheduling staff levels and controlling and evaluating the delivery process.

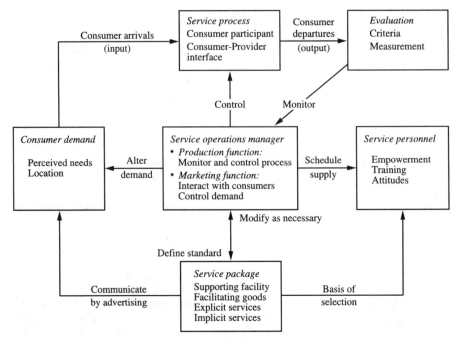

FIGURE 2.3
Open-systems view of service operations.

By necessity, the operations and marketing functions are integrated for service organizations.

For services, *the process is the product.* The presence of the customer in the service process negates the closed-system perspective taken in manufacturing. Techniques to control operations in an isolated factory producing a tangible good are inadequate for services. No longer is the process machine-paced and the output easily measured for compliance with specifications. Instead, customers arrive with different demands on the service; thus, multiple measures of performance are necessary. Service employees interact directly with the customer, with little opportunity for management intervention. This requires extensive training and empowerment of employees to act appropriately in the absence of direct supervision.

Furthermore, customer impressions of service quality are based on the total service experience, not just on the explicit service performed. A concern for employee attitudes and training becomes a necessity in service systems to ensure service quality. The entire service process, when viewed from the customer perspective, raises concerns ranging from the aesthetic design of the facility to pleasant diversions in waiting areas.

An open-system concept of services also allows one to view the customer as a resource. Permitting the customer to participate actively in the service process can be a method of increasing productivity, which, in turn, creates a competitive edge.

SUMMARY

The management of an open system requires techniques and sensitivities different from those of a closed system. Service managers are faced with nonroutine operations where only indirect control is possible. In services it is the human element that is central to effective operations. For example, the unavoidable interaction between service and consumer is a source of great opportunity, as in direct selling. However, this interaction can seldom be fully controlled; thus, service quality may suffer. For this reason, the attitude and appearance of personnel in service organizations are important considerations. For services the presence of the customer in the process materially alters what is viewed as the product. The unique characteristics of intangibility, perishability, and simultaneous provision and consumption introduce special challenges for service management. In many respects the service manager adopts a style of management different from that of his or her manufacturing counterpart.

As we move into Part II of this book, we will begin our examination of strategic implications for services with a look at a classification system and at positioning the service in a competitive environment.

TOPICS FOR DISCUSSION

1. In what ways would the management style of a service manager differ from that of a manufacturing manager?
2. What are some possible measures of performance for a fire department? for a fast-food restaurant?
3. Comment on why hospitals are classified as a service shop in Figure 2.1, given that they are so labor-intensive.
4. Select a service with which you are familiar, and identify the seven "distinctive characteristics of service operations" that it has.
5. What factors are important for a manager to consider when attempting to enhance the service organization's image?

CASE: VILLAGE VOLVO

Village Volvo is the "new kid in town." It represents an effort by two former authorized Volvo dealer mechanics to provide quality repair service on out-of-warranty Volvos at a reasonable cost. On the basis of their 22 combined years of training and experience with the local Volvo dealer, they have earned a respected reputation and a following of satisfied customers that make an independent service operation feasible. Village Volvo occupies a new Butler building (prefabricated metal structure) that has four work bays in addition to the office, waiting area, and storage room.

The owners feel they have designed their operation to provide clients with a "custom car care" service that is unavailable at the dealer. They have set aside specific times each week when clients may drive in for quick, routine services such as tune-ups and oil changes. But they encourage clients to schedule appointments for diagnosis and repair of specific problems.

At the time of the appointment, the mechanic who will be working on the vehicle and the client discuss the problems the client has noticed. On occasion, the mechanic may take a short test drive with the client to be certain both understand the area of concern.

Another source of information available to the mechanic is the Custom Care Vehicle Dossier (CCVD). Village Volvo maintains a continuing file on each vehicle it services. This history can help the mechanic diagnose problems and also provides a convenient record if a vehicle should be returned for warranty service on an earlier repair. The owners are considering the use of the CCVD as a way of "reminding" customers that routine maintenance procedures may be due.

After the mechanic has made a preliminary diagnosis, the service manager gives the vehicle owner an estimate of the cost and the approximate time the repair will be completed, if no unexpected problems arise. Company policy states that the owner will be consulted before any work other than the agreed-upon job is done. Although the customer may speak with the mechanic during the repair process, the service manager is the main point of contact. It is the service manager's responsibility to be sure the customer understands the preliminary diagnosis, to advise the customer of any unexpected problems and costs, and to notify the customer when the vehicle is ready for pickup.

Village Volvo has no provisions for "alternate transportation" for customers at this time. A "shuttle service" two or three times a day is being considered, because the owners think their suburban location may deter some clients. A waiting room is equipped with a television set, comfortable chairs, coffee, a soft-drink vending machine, magazines, and the local newspaper. This facility is used almost exclusively by clients who come during the "drop-in" times, 3 to 5 p.m. Wednesdays and 8 to 10 a.m. Thursdays, for quick, routine jobs such as tune-ups and buyer checks of used cars.

The owner-mechanics do no repairs between 7 and 8 a.m. and 5 and 6 p.m. because these are heavy "customer contact" hours. They believe it is just as important to discuss with the client the repairs that have been done as it is to discuss what problems exist before work is done. As repairs are done, the owner-mechanic makes note of any other problems that might need attention in the future (e.g., fan and alternator belts show some wear and may need to be replaced in about 6000 miles). These notes are brought to the customer's attention at pickup time and are also recorded in the CCVD for future use, perhaps in the form of a "reminder" postcard to the owner.

All small worn-out parts that have been replaced are placed in a clean box in the car. More cumbersome replaced parts are identified and set aside for the client's inspection. Care is taken throughout the repair process to keep the car clean, and the inside is vacuumed as a courtesy before pickup. After repairs are finished, the vehicle is taken for a short test drive; then it is parked, ready for pickup.

The Village Volvo owners see their responsibility as extending beyond immediate service to their clients. The owners have developed a network of other service providers, who assist in recycling used parts and waste products and to whom they can refer clients for work that is not part of Village Volvo's services, such as body work, alignments, and reupholstering. The owners are also considering the possibility of offering a minicourse one Saturday morning each month to teach clients what they can do to attain their 200,000-mile Volvo medals.

Questions

1. Describe Village Volvo's service package.

2. How are the distinctive characteristics of a service firm illustrated by Village Volvo?

3. How could Village Volvo manage its back office (repair operations) like a factory?

4. How can Village Volvo differentiate itself from Volvo dealers?

SELECTED BIBLIOGRAPHY

Collier, David A.: "Managing a Service Firm: A Different Management Game," *National Productivity Review,* winter 1983–84, pp. 36–45.

Killeya, J. C., and C. G. Armistead: "The Transfer of Concepts and Techniques between Manufacturing and Service Systems," *International Journal of Operations and Production Management,* vol. 3, no. 3, 1983, pp. 22–28.

Morris, B., and R. Johnston: "Dealing with Inherent Variability: The Difference between Manufacturing and Service?" *International Journal of Operations and Production Management,* vol. 7, no. 4, 1986, pp. 13–22.

Riddle, D. I.: *Service-Led Growth,* Praeger, New York, 1986.

Sasser, W. E., R. P. Olsen, and D. D. Wyckoff: *Management of Service Operations,* Allyn and Bacon, Inc., Boston, 1978.

Schmenner, Roger W.: "How Can Service Businesses Survive and Prosper?" *Sloan Management Review,* vol. 27, no. 3, spring 1986, pp. 21–32.

PART TWO

THE SERVICE CONCEPT AND COMPETITIVE STRATEGY

The foundation for the theme of the book is presented in this section. An effective competitive strategy is particularly important for service firms because they compete in an environment where there are relatively low barriers to entry. Consequently, the firms are always faced with new competition.

We begin in Chapter 3 with a service classification that focuses on the strategic opportunities available in the design of the service concept. The three generic competitive strategies—overall cost leadership, differentiation, and focus—are applied to services, and illustrations are provided. The elements of the strategic service concept are also developed and illustrated.

The strategic role of information is explored in Chapter 4. Successful service firms have discovered the strategic value of the information available from direct interaction with their customers. Using this information has proved effective in creating barriers to entry, increasing revenues, and increasing productivity.

CHAPTER 3

SERVICE STRATEGY AND MARKET POSITION

Most service firms compete in an economic environment that generally consists of a large number of small- and medium-sized firms, many of them privately owned. Of course, large service firms such as major airlines and hospitals also exist. In this type of economic environment, no firm has a significant market share; thus, no firm can dominate the industry (with the exception of government services, cable TV, and utilities). However, since the deregulation actions of government in the 1980s, there has been some service industry consolidation, particularly with airlines and financial institutions. In any event, a thorough understanding of the competitive dimensions and limitations of the industry is necessary before a firm can begin to formulate its service strategy.

CHAPTER PREVIEW

The diversity of firms in the service sector makes generalizations concerning strategy difficult. Five schemes are presented to classify services in ways that provide strategic insight and transcend narrow industry boundaries. These schemes can be used to think about the choices being made to position the service in relation to its competitors. *Positioning* is a marketing term used to describe the process of establishing and maintaining a distinctive place in the market.

Three generic strategies have been found successful in formulating strategies that allow a firm to outperform competitors. The strategies of overall cost leadership, differentiation, and market focus are approaches that both manufacturing and service firms have adopted in various ways to gain competitive advantage. However, with each of these strategies, management must not lose sight of the fact that only a focus on the customers and on satisfying their needs will result in a loyal customer base.

Winning customers in the marketplace means competing on several dimensions. Customers base their purchase decisions on many variables, such as price, convenience, reputation, and safety. The importance of a particular variable to a firm's success depends on the competitive marketplace and the preferences of individual customers.

The chapter concludes with a discussion of the strategic service concept that contains all the elements in the design of a competitive service. The service concept is divided into four structural elements: delivery system, facility design, location, and capacity planning. It is also divided into four managerial elements: service encounter, quality, managing capacity and demand, and information. These eight elements are each treated separately in the chapters that follow (Chapters 4 to 11), and all illustrate the theme of seeking competitive advantage for the service firm.

CLASSIFYING SERVICES FOR STRATEGIC INSIGHTS[1]

A general discussion of service strategy is complicated by the diversity of service firms in the economy and by their differing customer relationships. However, strategic insights that transcend industry boundaries are needed to avoid the myopic view, which is prevalent among service managers, that concepts do not translate from one industry to another. For example, competitive strategies in use by banking services could have application in laundry services because both deal with a customer's property. The new laundry drop-off and pickup service available at commuter rail stations is similar in concept to bank ATMs in supermarkets. The following classification schemes developed by Christopher Lovelock provide us with an appreciation of possible strategic dimensions that transcend industry boundaries.

Nature of the Service Act

As shown in Figure 3.1, the service act can be considered across two dimensions: who or what is the direct recipient of the service and the tangible nature of the service. This creates four classification possibilities: (1) tangible actions directed to the customer, such as passenger transportation and personal care; (2) tangible actions directed to the customer's possessions, such as laundry cleaning and janitorial services; (3) intangible actions directed at the customer's intellect; and (4) intangible actions performed on customer's assets, such as financial services.

This classification scheme raises questions about the traditional way services have been delivered. For example, does the customer need to be present physically throughout the service, only to initiate or terminate the transaction, or not at all? If customers need to be present physically, then they must travel to the service

[1]Adapted from Christopher H. Lovelock, "Classifying Services to Gain Strategic Marketing Insights," *Journal of Marketing,* vol. 47, summer 1983, pp. 9–20.

	Direct Recipient of the Service	
Nature of the Service Act	People	Things
Tangible actions	*Services directed at people's bodies:* Health care Passenger transportation Beauty salons Exercise clinics Restaurants Haircutting	*Services directed at goods and other physical possessions:* Freight transportation Industrial equipment repair and maintenance Janitorial services Laundry and dry cleaning Landscaping/lawn care Veterinary care
Intangible actions	*Services directed at people's minds:* Education Broadcasting Information services Theaters Museums	*Services directed at intangible assets:* Banking Legal services Accounting Securities Insurance

FIGURE 3.1
Understanding the nature of the service act. [*Reprinted with permission of the American Marketing Association: Christopher H. Lovelock, "Classifying Services to Gain Strategic Marketing Insights,"* Journal of Marketing, *vol. 47, summer 1983, p. 12.*]

facility and become part of the process, or the server must travel to the customer (e.g., ambulance service). This has significant implications for facility design and employee interaction because the impressions made will influence the perceptions of the service. In addition, questions are raised concerning the impact of facility location and business hours on customer convenience. It is not surprising that retail banks have embraced the automatic teller machine and other electronic communications alternatives to personal interaction.

Thinking creatively about the nature of the service may identify more convenient forms of service delivery or a product that can substitute for the service. For example, videotapes of lectures and compact-disk recordings of concerts represent a convenient substitute for physical attendance, and they also serve as permanent library records of the events.

Relationship with Customers

Service firms have the opportunity to build long-term relationships because service customers conduct their transactions directly with the provider, most often in person. In contrast, manufacturers have traditionally been isolated from the eventual end user by a distribution channel consisting of some combination of distributors, wholesalers, and/or retailers. Figure 3.2 contrasts the nature of the customer's "membership" with the nature of the service delivery. The value to the firm of customer membership is captured in this figure. A number of changes have occurred, however, since the article was published in 1983. For example, car rental firms and major hotel chains have joined airlines in offering discounts through

Nature of Service Delivery	Type of Relationship between Service Organization and Its Customers	
	"Membership" relationship	No formal relationship
Continuous delivery of service	Insurance Telephone subscription College enrollment Banking American Automobile Association	Radio station Police protection Lighthouse Public highway
Discrete transactions	Long-distance phone calls Theater series subscription Commuter ticket or transit pass Sam's Wholesale Club Egghead computer software	Car rental Mail service Toll highway Pay phone Movie theater Public transportation Restaurant

FIGURE 3.2
Relationships with customers. [*Reprinted with permission of the American Marketing Association: Christopher H. Lovelock, "Classifying Services to Gain Strategic Marketing Insights,"* Journal of Marketing, *vol. 47, summer 1983, p. 13.*]

frequent flyer programs. Another example is seen where some private toll highways offer annual passes that can be attached to one's car. These passes electronically trigger a debit so that the driver need not stop to pay a toll.

Knowing your customers is a significant competitive advantage to the service organization. Having a data base of customers' names and addresses and their service use permits target marketing and individual treatment of customers. Customers benefit from membership because of the convenience of annual fixed fees and the knowledge that they are valued customers with occasional perks (e.g., frequent flyer awards).

Customization and Judgment

An opportunity exists to tailor the service to the needs of the customer because services are created as they are consumed, and the customer is often a participant in the process. In Figure 3.3 we see that customization proceeds along two dimensions: either the character of the service permits customization, or the service personnel have the discretion to modify the service provided.

Selecting the quadrant of Figure 3.3 in which to position a service is a strategic choice. For example, traditional movie theaters offer only one screen and thus are appropriately located in the low-low quadrant. However, most new movie theaters are built with multiple screens, allowing some degree of customization. Burger King, among fast-food restaurants, advertises "Have it your way," permitting some customization of its "Whopper." Within a particular industry, every quadrant could be occupied by different segments of that industry, as illustrated by the various types of food service operations presented in Figure 3.3. However, a

Extent to Which Customer Contact Personnel Exercise Judgment in Meeting Individual Customer Needs	Extent to Which Service Characteristics Are Customized	
	High	Low
High	Professional services Surgery Taxi service Beautician Plumber Education (tutorials) Gourmet restaurant	Education (large classes) Preventive health programs College food service
Low	Telephone service Hotel services Retail banking (excl. major loans) Family restaurant	Public transportation Routine appliance repair Movie theater Spectator sports Fast-food restaurant

FIGURE 3.3
Customization and judgment in service delivery. [*Reprinted with permission of the American Marketing Association: Christopher H. Lovelock, "Classifying Services to Gain Strategic Marketing Insights,"* Journal of Marketing, *vol. 47, summer 1983, p. 15.*]

strategic choice of offering more customization and allowing service personnel to exercise judgment has implications for the service delivery system.

Nature of Demand and Supply

As noted in Chapter 2, the time perishability of service capacity creates a challenge for service managers because they lack the option available to manufacturers of producing and storing inventory for future sale. But the extent of demand and supply imbalances varies across service industries, as shown in Figure 3.4.

To determine the most appropriate strategy in each case, it is necessary to consider the following questions:

1. What is the nature of the demand fluctuation? Does it have a predictable cycle (e.g., daily meal demand at a fast-food restaurant) that can be anticipated?

2. What are the underlying causes of these fluctuations in demand? If the causes are customer habits or preference, could marketing effect a change?

3. What opportunities exist to change the level of capacity or supply? Can part-time workers be hired during peak hours?

Because managing capacity and demand is a central challenge to the success of a service firm, Chapter 10 is devoted entirely to this topic.

Method of Service Delivery

As shown in Figure 3.5, the method of service delivery has both a geographic component and a level of customer interaction component.

Services with multiple sites have significant management implications for

Extent to Which Supply Is Constrained	Extent of Demand Fluctuation over Time	
	Wide	**Narrow**
Peak demand can usually be met without a major delay	Electricity Natural gas Telephone Hospital maternity unit Police and fire emergencies	Insurance Legal services Banking Laundry and dry cleaning
Peak demand regularly exceeds capacity	Accounting and tax preparation Passenger transportation Hotels and motels Restaurants Theaters	Services similar to those above but with insufficient capacity for their base level of business

FIGURE 3.4
What is the nature of demand for the service relative to supply? [*Reprinted with permission of the American Marketing Association: Christopher H. Lovelock, "Classifying Services to Gain Strategic Marketing Insights,"* Journal of Marketing, *vol. 47, summer 1983, p. 17.*]

ensuring quality and consistency in the service offering. Detailed strategic implications of site location are the topic of Chapter 7. With advances in electronic communications, arm's-length transactions are becoming more common because they offer customer convenience and efficient service delivery. The strategic implications of a service delivery system design and its effect on the interaction between customer and service organization are the topics of Chapters 5 and 6.

The classification schemes described above are useful in suggesting strategic alternatives and avoiding industry myopia. However, before a service strategy can be formulated, an understanding of the competitive nature of the industry must be appreciated.

FIGURE 3.5
Method of service delivery. [*Reprinted with permission of the American Marketing Association: Christopher H. Lovelock, "Classifying Services to Gain Strategic Marketing Insights,"* Journal of Marketing, *vol. 47, summer 1983, p. 18.*]

Nature of Interaction between Customer and Service Organization	Availability of Service Outlets	
	Single site	**Multiple site**
Customer goes to service organization	Theater Barbershop	Bus service Fast-food chain
Service organization comes to customer	Lawn care service Pest control service Taxi	Mail delivery AAA emergency repairs
Customer and service organization transact at arm's length (mail or electronic communications)	Credit card company Local TV station	Broadcast network Telephone company

UNDERSTANDING THE COMPETITIVE ENVIRONMENT OF SERVICES

Service industries compete in an economic environment that is difficult because of the following fundamental reasons:

- *Relatively low overall entry barriers.* Service innovations are not patentable, and in most cases services are not capital-intensive.
- *Minimal opportunities for economies of scale.* Many services are dispersed at multiple sites serving a local geographic area and have only marginal opportunities for scale economies from shared purchasing or advertising.
- *High transportation costs.* Because of the simultaneous production and consumption of services, the customer must travel to the service facility, or the service must travel to the customer. Both of these alternatives limit the market area.
- *Erratic sales fluctuations.* Service demand varies as a function of the time of day and day of the week (and sometimes seasonally), with random arrivals.
- *No advantage of size in dealing with buyers or suppliers.* The small size of many service firms places them at a disadvantage in bargaining with powerful buyers or suppliers. Many exceptions should come to mind, such as McDonald's buying beef and Marriott buying mattresses.
- *Product substitution.* Product innovations can be a substitute for services (e.g., home pregnancy test kit).
- *Customer loyalty.* Established service firms using personalized service create a loyal customer base, which becomes a barrier to entry for new services. For example, a hospital supply firm may place its own ordering computer terminals in its customer's site. These terminals then facilitate the placement of new orders to the extent that competitors are effectively excluded.
- *Exit barriers.* Marginal service firms may continue to operate despite low or even nonexistent profits. For example, a privately held firm may have employment of family members rather than substantial profits as its goal. Some service firms, such as antique stores or scuba diving shops, have a hobby or romantic appeal that provides owners with enough job satisfaction to offset low financial compensation. Profit-motivated competitors would thus find it difficult to drive these privately held firms from the market.
- *Government regulation.* Regulation in services is pervasive and represents a significant barrier to entry. But such regulation can also stifle innovation. For example, before Federal Express could begin operations, an exemption from the Civil Aeronautics Board was sought to permit air transport service to any city in the United States without filing for a certificate of "public convenience and necessity." By selecting a fleet of small Dassault Fanjet Falcons with a cargo capacity of less than 75,000 pounds, Federal Express was classified as an "air-taxi" operator and avoided the necessity of filing for these permits for each city pair served.

For any particular service industry, there are firms that have overcome the above competitive difficulties and prospered. For example, McDonald's has achieved a dominant position in the fast-food industry by overcoming many of the difficulties listed above. However, new entrants must develop a service strategy that will address the important competitive features of their respective industries. There are three generic strategies that have been successful in providing a competitive advantage. Illustrations of how service firms have used these strategies will be our next topic.

COMPETITIVE SERVICE STRATEGIES [2]

Michael Porter has argued persuasively that there are three generic competitive strategies: overall cost leadership, differentiation, and market focus.[3] Each of these strategies will be described in turn, with examples of how service firms use the strategy to outperform their competition.

Overall Cost Leadership

Cost leadership requires efficient-scale facilities, tight cost and overhead control, and often, also, innovative technology. Having a low-cost position provides a defense against competition, because less efficient competitors will suffer first in the face of competitive pressures. Implementing a low-cost strategy usually requires high capital investment in state-of-the-art equipment, aggressive pricing, and start-up losses to build market share. A cost leadership strategy can sometimes revolutionize an industry, as illustrated by the success of McDonald's, Wal-Mart, and Federal Express. Moreover, service firms have been able to achieve low-cost leadership using a variety of approaches such as the following.

Seeking Out Low-Cost Customers   Some customers cost less to serve than others and can be targeted by the service provider. For example, United Services Automobile Association (USAA) occupies a preeminent position among automobile insurers because it serves only military officers, a group that presents a lower-than-average risk of problems requiring compensation. This group also entails lower cost because its members, who are relatively nomadic, are willing to do business by telephone or mail and are accustomed to doing so. Consequently, USAA can conduct all business transactions by phone and mail, which eliminates the need for the expensive sales force employed by traditional insurers. Another example of this strategy is provided by low-cost retailers, such as Sam's Wholesale Club and Price Club, that target customers who are willing to buy in quantity, do without any frills, and serve themselves.

Standardizing a Custom Service   Typically, income tax preparation is considered a customized service. However, H. & R. Block has been successful serving

---

[2]Adapted from James L. Heskett, "Positioning in Competitive Service Strategies," *Managing in the Service Economy*, chap. 3, Harvard Business School Press, Boston, 1986.

[3]Michael E. Porter, "Generic Competitive Strategies," *Competitive Strategy*, chap. 2, Free Press, New York, 1980.

customers nationwide when only routine tax preparation is required. Storefront legal services and family health care centers are attractive means of delivering routine professional services at low cost. The key word here is *routine!*

Reducing the Personal Element in Service Delivery   This potentially high-risk strategy can be accepted by customers if increased convenience results. For example, convenient access to automatic teller machines (ATMs) has weaned customers from personal interaction with live tellers and consequently has reduced transaction costs for the bank.

Reducing Network Costs   Unusual start-up costs are encountered by service firms that require a network to knit together providers and customers. Electric utilities, which have substantial fixed costs in transmission lines, provide the most obvious example. Federal Express conceived a unique approach to reducing network costs by using a hub-and-spoke network. By locating a hub in Memphis with state-of-the-art sorting technology, the overnight air package carrier was able to serve the United States with no direct routes between the cities it served. Each time a new city is added to the network, Federal Express needs to add only one more route to the hub instead of adding routes between all cities served. The efficiency of the hub-and-spoke network strategy has not been lost on the passenger airline operators.

Taking Service Operations Off-Line   Many services, such as haircutting and passenger transportation, are inherently "on-line" because they can only be performed with the customer present. For services in which the customer need not be present physically, the service transaction can be "decoupled," with some content performed "off-line." This is particularly true of data-based services using electronic communication. L.L. Bean, using a money-back guarantee, is the model of efficient catalog sales nationwide. Performing services "off-line" represents significant cost savings owing to economies of scale, low-cost facility location (e.g., American Airlines has one of its 800-number reservations centers located in the Caribbean), and absence of the customer in the system. In short, the decoupled service operation is run like a factory.

Differentiation

The essence of the differentiation strategy lies in creating a service that is perceived as being unique. Approaches to differentiation can take many forms: brand image (McDonald's golden arches), technology (Sprint's fiber optics), features (American Express's complete travel services), customer service (Nordstrom's reputation among department stores), dealer network (Century 21's nationwide real estate presence), and other dimensions. A differentiation strategy does not ignore costs, but the primary thrust of the strategy lies in creating customer loyalty. As illustrated below, differentiation to enhance the service is often achieved at some cost that the targeted customer is willing to pay.

Making the Intangible Tangible Services, by their very nature, are often intangible and leave the customer with no physical reminder of the purchase. Recognizing the need to remind customers of their stay, many hotels now provide complimentary toiletry items with the hotel name prominently affixed. The Hartford Steam Boiler Inspection and Insurance Company writes insurance on industrial power plants but has enhanced its service to include regular inspections and recommendations to management for avoiding potential problems.

Customizing the Standard Product Providing a customized touch may endear a firm to its customers at very little cost. A hotel operator able to address a resident by name can make an impression that translates into repeat business. Our earlier example of Burger King's effort to differentiate itself from McDonald's is accomplished at the cost of customer delay associated with a made-to-order policy instead of making hamburgers to stock.

Reducing Perceived Risk Lack of information about the purchase of a service creates a sense of risk taking in many customers. Customers lacking knowledge or self-confidence about such services as auto repair will seek out providers who take the extra time to explain the work to be done, present a clean and organized facility, and guarantee their work (e.g., Village Volvo). Customers often see the "peace of mind" engendered when this trusting relationship is developed as being worth the extra expense.

Giving Attention to Personnel Training Investment in personnel development and training that results in enhanced service quality is a competitive advantage that is difficult to replicate. Firms that lead in their industries are known among competitors for the quality of their training programs. In some cases the firms have established collegelike training centers (e.g., Arthur Andersen's facility in St. Charles, Illinois, and McDonald's Hamburger University near Chicago).

Controlling Quality Delivering a consistent level of service quality at multiple sites with a labor-intensive system is a significant challenge. Firms have approached the problem in a variety of ways, including personnel training, explicit procedures, technology, limits on the scope of the service, direct supervision, and peer pressure, among others. For example, to ensure consistency, the Magic Pan chain of restaurants designed a foolproof machine to produce its famous crepes. The question of service quality is further complicated by the potential gap between customers' expectations and experiences. Influencing customer quality expectations thus becomes an issue. Chapter 9 is devoted to a detailed look at this important topic of managing service quality.

Focus

The focus strategy is built around the idea of serving a particular target market very well by addressing the customers' specific needs. The target market could be

Target	Strategic Advantage	
	Low cost	Uniqueness
Entire market	Overall cost leadership	Differentiation
Market segment	Focus	

FIGURE 3.6
Market position of generic strategies.
[*Adapted with the permission of The Free Press, a Division of Macmillan, Inc., from* COMPETITIVE STRATEGY: Techniques for Analyzing Industries and Competitors *by Michael E. Porter. Copyright © 1980 by The Free Press.*]

a particular buyer group (USAA and military officers), segment of the market (Shouldice Hospital and patients with inguinal hernias, Motel 6 and budget travelers, Federal Express and people who need guaranteed overnight package delivery), or geographic market (Wal-Mart and rural retail buyers, Southwest Airlines and other regional airlines). The focus strategy rests on the premise that the firm can serve its narrow target market more effectively and/or efficiently than other firms can that are trying to serve a broad market. As a result, the firm achieves differentiation in its narrow target market by meeting customer needs better and/or by lowering costs.

Davidow and Uttal argue how important customer selection is to achieving a successful focus strategy.[4] They relate how one bank in Palo Alto, California, targets wealthy individuals and discourages others by such policies as closing an account after two checks have bounced. Davidow and Uttal's three-step approach to focus includes segmenting the market to design core services, classifying customers according to the value they place on service, and setting expectations slightly below perceived performance.

The focus strategy is, thus, the application of overall cost leadership and/or differentiation to a particular market segment. The relationship of the three generic strategies to market position is shown in Figure 3.6. We conclude this chapter with discussions of winning customers in the marketplace and of the elements that form the strategic service concept.

WINNING CUSTOMERS IN THE MARKETPLACE

Depending on the competition and personal needs, customers select a service provider using criteria listed below. This list is not intended to be complete, because the very addition of a new dimension by a firm represents an attempt to engage in a strategy of differentiation. For example, the initiation of the frequent flyer program "AAdvantage" by American Airlines was an attempt to add the dimension of loyalty to competition in air travel.

• *Availability.* How accessible is the service? The use of ATM machines by banks has created 24-hour availability of some banking services, i.e., service beyond

---

[4]W. H. Davidow and B. Uttal, "Service Companies: Focus or Falter," *Harvard Business Review,* July–August 1989, pp. 77–85.

the traditional "banker's hours." The use of 800 numbers by many service firms facilitates access after normal working hours.

• *Convenience.* The location of the service defines convenience for customers who must travel to the service. Gasoline stations, fast-food restaurants, and dry cleaners are examples of services that must select locations on busy streets in order to succeed.

• *Dependability.* How reliable is the service? Once the exterminator is gone, how soon do the bugs return? A major complaint of automobile repair service is the failure to fix the problem on the first visit.

• *Personalization.* Are you treated as an individual? For example, hotels have discovered that repeat customers respond to being greeted by their name. The degree of customization allowed in providing the service, no matter how slight, can be viewed as more personalized service.

• *Price.* Competing on price is not as effective in services as it is with products because it is often difficult to compare the costs of services objectively. It may be easy to compare costs in the delivery of routine services such as an oil change, but in professional services competition on price might be considered counterproductive because price is often viewed as a surrogate for quality.

• *Quality.* Service quality is a function of the relationship between a customer's prior expectations of the service and his or her perception of the service experience during and after the fact. Unlike the quality of a product, service quality is judged by both the process of service delivery and the outcome of the service.

• *Reputation.* The uncertainty associated with the selection of a service provider is often resolved by talking with others about their experiences before a decision is made. Unlike a product, a poor service experience cannot be exchanged or returned for a different model.

• *Safety.* Well-being and security are important considerations because in many services, such as air travel and medicine, the customers are putting their lives in the hands of others.

• *Speed.* How long must I wait for service? For emergency services such as fire and police protection, response time is the major criterion of performance. In other services, waiting may sometimes be considered a tradeoff for receiving more personalized service, reduced rates, etc.

Terry Hill, when writing about manufacturing strategy, used the term *order-winning criteria* to refer to competitive dimensions that sell products.[5] He further suggested that some criteria could be called *qualifiers* because the presence of these dimensions is necessary for a product to enter the marketplace. Finally, Hill said some qualifiers could be considered *order-losing sensitive.*

We will use the following terms in a similar manner to classify competitive criteria for services.

---

[5]Terry Hill, *Manufacturing Strategy,* Irwin, Homewood, Ill., 1989, pp. 36–46.

Service Winners

These are dimensions such as price, convenience, or reputation that are used by a customer to make a choice among competitors. Depending on the needs of the customer at the time of purchase, the service winner may vary. For example, seeking a restaurant for lunch may be based on convenience, but a dinner date could be influenced by reputation.

Qualifiers

Before a service can be taken seriously as a competitor in the market, it must attain a certain level for each service-competitive dimension, as defined by the other market players. For example, in airline service we would name safety, as defined by the airworthiness of the aircraft and by the rating of the pilots, as an obvious qualifier. In a mature market such as fast foods, established competitors may define a level of quality, such as cleanliness, that new entrants must at least match to be viable contenders. For fast food, a dimension that once was a service winner, such as a drive-in window, could, over time, become a qualifier because some customers will not stop otherwise.

Service Losers

Failure to deliver at or above the expected level for a competitive dimension can result in a dissatisfied customer who is lost forever. For various reasons, the dimensions of dependability, personalization, and speed are particularly vulnerable to becoming service losers. Some examples might be the failure of an auto dealer to repair a mechanical problem (dependability), rude treatment by a doctor (personalization), or the failure of an overnight delivery service to deliver a package on time (speed).

STRATEGIC SERVICE CONCEPT

A house begins in the mind's eye of the architect and is translated onto paper in the form of engineering drawings for all the building's systems: foundation, structural, plumbing, and electrical. An analog to this design process is the strategic service concept with the system elements outlined below. All these elements must be engineered to create a consistent service offering that achieves the strategic objectives. The service concept becomes a blueprint that communicates to customers and employees alike what service they should expect to give and receive.

Structural:

Delivery system. Front office and back office, automation, customer participation.

Facility design. Size, aesthetics, layout.

Location. Customer demographics, single or multiple sites, competition, site characteristics.

Capacity planning. Managing queues, number of servers, accommodating average demand or peak.

Managerial:

Service encounter. Service culture, motivation, selection and training, empowerment.

Quality. Measurement, monitoring, methods, expectations vs. perceptions, service guarantee.

Managing capacity and demand. Strategies for altering demand and controlling supply, queue management.

Information. Competitive resource, data collection.

A successful hospital located in Toronto, Canada, that performs only inguinal hernia operations will be used to illustrate how each element of the service concept contributes to the strategic mission. Shouldice Hospital is privately owned and uses a special operating procedure to correct inguinal hernias that has resulted in an excellent reputation. Its success is measured by the recurrence rate, which is twelve times lower than that of its competitors.[6]

The *structural* elements of Shouldice's service concept that support its strategy to target customers suffering from inguinal hernias are discussed below.

• *Delivery system.* A hallmark of the Shouldice approach is patient participation in all aspects of the process. For example, patients shave themselves before the operation, walk from the operating table to recovery, and are encouraged the evening after surgery to discuss the experience with newcomers to alleviate the new patients' preoperative fears.

• *Facility design.* The facility is intentionally designed to encourage exercise and rapid recovery within four days, approximately one-half the time at traditional hospitals. Hospital rooms are devoid of amenities, and patients must walk to lounges, showers, and the cafeteria. The extensive hospital grounds are landscaped to encourage strolling, and the interior is carpeted and decorated to avoid any hospital associations.

• *Location.* Locating in a large metropolitan community with excellent air service gives Shouldice access to a worldwide market. The large local population also provides a source of patients who can be scheduled on short notice to fill in canceled bookings.

• *Capacity planning.* Because hernia operations are elective, patients can be scheduled in batches to fill the operating time available; thus, capacity is utilized to its maximum. This ease in scheduling operations allows Shouldice to operate like a fully occupied hotel. Thus, the supporting activities such as housekeeping and food service can also be kept fully employed.

The *managerial* elements of the Shouldice service concept also support the strategy of delivering a quality medical procedure.

[6]Harvard Business School case, "Shouldice Hospital Limited," ICCH no. 9-683-068, 1983, p. 3.

- *Service encounter.* Only doctors willing to abide by the Shouldice Method are recruited. All employees are trained to help counsel patients and encourage them to achieve rapid recovery. A service culture fostering a family-type atmosphere is reinforced by communal dining for both workers and patients.
- *Quality.* The most important quality feature is the adherence of all physicians to the Shouldice Method of hernia repair, which results in the low recurrence rate. In addition, patients with difficulties are referred back to the doctor who performed the procedure. Perceived quality is enhanced by the Shouldice experience, which is more like a short holiday than a hospital stay.
- *Managing capacity and demand.* Patients are screened by means of a mail-in questionnaire and admitted by reservation only. Thus, the patient demand in terms of timing and appropriateness can be controlled effectively. As mentioned above, walk-in patients or local residents who are on a waiting list are used to fill in vacancies created by canceled reservations; thus, full use of capacity is ensured.
- *Information.* A unique feature of the Shouldice service is the annual alumni reunion, which represents a continuing relationship with its patients. Keeping information on patients allows Shouldice to build a loyal customer base that is an effective word-of-mouth advertising medium. Providing free annual checkups also allows Shouldice to build a unique data base on its procedure.

SUMMARY

The topic of service strategy began with a number of schemes to classify service industries with the intent of gaining insights into possible strategic opportunities that transcend industry boundaries. Our discussion then turned to the economic nature of competition in the service sector. The fragmented nature of service industries populated with many small- to medium-sized firms suggests a rich environment for the budding entrepreneur.

The three generic competitive strategies of overall cost leadership, differentiation, and focus were used to outline examples of creative service strategies. Because of the transferability of concepts among service firms, successful strategies observed in one industry may find application in firms seeking a competitive advantage in another service industry.

Next we looked at several dimensions of service competition and examined the concepts of service winners, qualifiers, and losers as competitive criteria.

The chapter concluded with a discussion of the strategic service concept as a blueprint for implementing the service. The application of the service concept to Shouldice Hospital illustrated how all eight elements support the service strategy. Chapter 4 will look at how information contributes to a successful service strategy.

TOPICS FOR DISCUSSION

1. What are the characteristics of services that will be affected most by the emerging electronic and communications technologies?

2. When does collecting information through service membership become an invasion of privacy?

3. What are some of the management problems associated with allowing service employees to exercise judgment in meeting customer needs?
4. In what way did United Airlines experience a loss of focus when it acquired hotels?
5. Give examples of service firms that use both the strategy of focus and differentiation and the strategy of focus and overall cost leadership.
6. Apply the strategic service concept to a service of your choice, and illustrate how all eight elements support the service strategy.

CASE: AMERICA WEST AIRLINES

America West Airlines was established in Phoenix as an employee-owned organization that served ten cities in the southwestern region of the United States with a fleet of new MD-80 aircraft. Since then it has grown to include 60 cities and has extended its range westward to Hawaii and eastward to Boston.

The neophyte company showed remarkable daring by choosing to enter an arena where the majors, American Airlines and Delta Air Lines, were already firmly entrenched and Southwest Airlines was digging in. Even more daring, some would say foolhardy, was the timing: deregulation was threatening to swallow up small airlines faster than they could refuel their planes.

But America West came into the game prepared with a skilled and creative management team, well-trained support personnel, and an effective inside pitch. Obviously, the fledgling company did not have the resources to provide the nationwide coverage, much less the worldwide coverage, that American and Delta provided. Its smaller region, however, allowed it to do something the majors couldn't: America West established a major hub in Phoenix and offered more flights per day at lower cost between its cities than could the two larger competitors. In many cases America West offered direct routing and, consequently, relatively short flight times between destinations. American and Delta, "burdened" with serving everywhere from Tallahassee to Seattle, were able to schedule flights between America West destinations, but with longer layovers and at premium prices because they were major carriers. For example, consider travel from Austin, Texas, to Los Angeles. America West has four flights scheduled each day, each taking approximately 4.5 hours and requiring one layover of 30 minutes in Phoenix, and its least expensive fare is $238. American Airlines offers eight flights each day, each lasting at least 5 hours, and the traveler has a 60-minute layover in Dallas but spends $298 for American's least expensive flight.

When America West passengers must lay over, it is almost always at the Phoenix hub. (America West has a "sub-hub" in Las Vegas, where layovers are usually overnight, an appeal not lost on many travelers.) Consequently, America West's "accommodations" at the Phoenix airport are as comfortable as one could hope for in a place that hosts such a large number of people each day. The waiting areas are spacious, with banks of well-padded seats placed farther apart than the seats in most airports. Television monitors are mounted in several places throughout the facility. And because the concessions are run by nationally known fast-food franchises, the traveler has ample reason to "feel at home."

Southwest Airlines presented a competitive challenge somewhat different from that of American and Delta. Southwest was serving the same general region as America West and was also offering frequent, low-cost flights, but with older Boeing 737 aircraft. Thus, it would seem that these two airlines were meeting head to head and might be destined to "flight"-to-the-finish of one of them.

Southwest established its hub at Love Field in Dallas, thereby offering its passengers easier access to and from the city, which is especially attractive to commuters. (Landing at Love Field does, however, present a problem for those who must make connections in the Dallas–Fort Worth International Terminal.) Southwest began as the "fun airline," the one with attendants in hot pants and the snappy commercials on television. Since then, it has met the competitive challenge by offering its frequent, low-cost, no-frills service. It generally has just two fares, peak and off-peak, and so it isn't necessary to call at 1 a.m. "to see if fares have changed in the past ten hours." Reservations for flights may be made by phone, but they must be paid for either through a travel agent or in person at an airport desk. There are no preassigned seats; seating is done on a first-come, first-served basis according to a numbered boarding pass handed to the passenger at check-in time. On-board amenities are usually limited to free soft drinks, juice, and peanuts. Prepackaged cookies and crackers with cheese or peanut butter are available on long flights. Alcoholic beverages are available for a price. Except for short commuter flights, routing frequently involves several lengthy layovers, and it is not always possible to check baggage clear through to one's destination.

America West has thus far managed to meet Southwest's challenge in a variety of ways. The traveler can make reservations and pay for them with a credit card number by telephone, a very real convenience for many people. Pre-assigned seating can also be done by telephone. Also, in contrast with Southwest's ticketing policy, travel agents can ticket passengers using the SABRE reservation system. On-board amenities include complimentary copies of *USA Today* and *The Wall Street Journal,* free beverages and peanuts, and, on longer trips, an uncooked snack such as a sandwich, salad, cheese, fruit, and dessert. Baggage can be checked on all flights.

Clearly, America West's strategies have kept it in the game, although in recent times it has been struggling with some financial problems, and so the battle is still engaged.

Questions

1. What generic competitive strategy has America West chosen to enter the air passenger market? What are the dangers of this strategy?

2. Identify the service winners, qualifiers, and service losers in America West's market.

3. How has America West addressed the eight elements in its strategic service concept?

4. Marketing analysts use market position maps to display visually the customers' perceptions of a firm in relation to its competitors with regard to two attributes. Prepare a market position map for America West comparing it with American, Delta, and Southwest, using the differentiation attributes of "cabin service" and "preflight service." You will need to define the endpoints on each scale to anchor the relative positioning of the airlines along the attribute (e.g., for cabin service one extreme is no amenities). The actual position is subjective because no precise measurements are available.

SELECTED BIBLIOGRAPHY

Davidow, W. H., and B. Uttal: "Service Companies: Focus or Falter," *Harvard Business Review,* July–August 1989, pp. 77–85.

Heskett, James L.: *Managing in the Service Economy,* Harvard Business School Press, Boston, 1986.

Hill, Terry: *Manufacturing Strategy,* Irwin, Homewood, Ill., 1989.

Hisrich, R. D., and M. P. Peters: *Entrepreneurship,* Irwin, Homewood, Ill., 1989.

Lovelock, Christopher H.: "Classifying Services to Gain Strategic Marketing Insights," *Journal of Marketing,* summer 1983, pp. 9–20.

————: *Services Marketing,* Prentice-Hall, Englewood Cliffs, N.J., 1984.

Porter, Michael E.: *Competitive Strategy,* Free Press, New York, 1980.

Roth, A. V., and M. van der Velde: "Operations as Marketing: The Key to Effective Service Delivery Systems," Boston University Press, Boston, 1989.

Shostack, Lynn G.: "Service Positioning through Structural Change," *Journal of Marketing,* January 1987, pp. 34–43.

Thomas, Dan R. E.: "Strategy Is Different in Service Business," *Harvard Business Review,* July–August 1978, pp. 158–165.

Zeithaml, Valarie A.: "How Consumer Evaluation Processes Differ between Goods and Services," in James H. Donnelly and William R. George (eds.), *Marketing of Services,* American Marketing Association, Chicago, 1984.

————, A. Parasuraman, and L. L. Berry: "Problems and Strategies in Services Marketing," *Journal of Marketing,* spring 1985, pp. 33–46.

CHAPTER 4

STRATEGIC ROLE OF THE INFORMATION RESOURCE

As manufacturing technology once changed an agricultural economy into an industrial economy, today's information technology is transforming our industrial economy into a service economy. The availability of computers and global communications has created industries for the collecting, processing, and communicating of information. It is possible for everyone on the globe to be in instant communication with everyone else, and this revolution is changing world society in many ways. Consider the impact of the emerging private satellite network industry that provides uplinks and downlinks for personnel training, product introductions, credit checks, billing, financial exchanges, and overall telecommunications.

K mart was among the first retail giants to establish a private satellite network using the new small-dish antenna VSAT (Very Small Aperture Terminal) placed on store roofs for receiving and transmitting masses of data. The VSAT at each K mart store is linked to the company's Troy, Michigan, data center via a satellite transponder leased from GTE Spacenet. The communication network has allowed K mart to coordinate its multisite operations better and to realize substantial benefits such as improved data transmission about rate of sales, inventory status, product updates, and, most importantly, credit authorizations for customers. The instant accessibility to credit histories can significantly lower the risk of nonpayment that the credit-card companies face, thus lowering the discount rate that reverts back to the retailer. This savings alone will eventually pay for the cost of the satellite network.[1]

[1]From Bernie Ward, "Microspace, Maxiprofits," *Sky,* December 1990, pp. 22–31.

Strategic Focus	Competitive Use of Information	
	On-line (Real time)	Off-line (Analysis)
External (Customer)	*Creation of barriers to entry:* Reservation system Frequent user club Switching costs	*Data base asset:* Selling information Development of services Micromarketing
Internal (Operations)	*Revenue generation:* Yield management Point of sales Expert systems	*Productivity enhancement:* Inventory status Data envelopment analysis (DEA)

FIGURE 4.1
Strategic roles of information in services. [*Adapted from James A. Fitzsimmons, "Strategic Role of Information in Services,"* Perspectives in Operations Management: Essays in Honor of Elwood S. Buffa, *Rakesh V. Sarin (ed.), Kluwer Academic Publishers, Norwell, Mass., 1993, p. 103.*]

CHAPTER PREVIEW

In this chapter a framework for viewing the contribution of information to the competitive strategy of the service firm is presented. Using the dimensions of strategic focus (either external or internal) and competitive use of information (either on-line or off-line), four strategic roles of information are identified.

The four roles are creation of barriers to entry, revenue generation, data base asset, and productivity enhancement. For each role examples from industry are used to illustrate how firms have effectively used information in each case. The chapter concludes with a discussion of the limits in the use of information, dealing with the questions of privacy and anticompetitive behavior.

THE COMPETITIVE ROLE OF INFORMATION IN SERVICES [2]

For service management, information technology is helping to define the competitive strategy of successful firms. Figure 4.1 captures the different roles in which information technology can support a service firm's competitive strategy. We shall explore each of these roles in turn with illustrations from successful applications.

Creation of Barriers to Entry

As noted in Chapter 3, services exist in a market with low entry barriers. However, James L. Heskett has argued that barriers to entry can be created by using economies of scale, using market share, creating switching costs, investing in networks, and using data bases and information technology to strategic advantage.[3]

---

[2] Adapted from James A. Fitzsimmons, "Strategic Role of Information in Services," *Perspectives in Operations Management: Essays in Honor of Elwood S. Buffa,* Rakesh V. Sarin, ed., Kluwer Academic Publisher, Norwell, Mass., 1993.

[3] James L. Heskett, "Operating Strategy—Barriers to Entry," *Managing in the Service Economy,* chap. 6, Harvard Business School Press, Boston, 1986.

We will discuss three uses of information for creating barriers to entry: reservation systems, "frequent flyer" or similar programs to gain customer loyalty, and development of customer relationships to increase switching costs.

Reservation Systems   A barrier to entry can be created by developing on-line reservations systems that are provided for sales intermediaries such as travel agents. American Airlines's SABRE System is an example of the economy of information that is created by a comprehensive information system. United and Delta have duplicated this reservations system at great cost, but most smaller carriers use these systems for a fee. The competitive importance of on-line reservations systems became evident in late 1982. At this time the Civil Aeronautics Board (CAB) and the Department of Justice began a joint investigation of possible antitrust violations by airline reservations systems. In this investigation, Frontier Airlines filed charges accusing United Airlines of unfairly restricting competition in the use of its Apollo computerized reservations system.[4]

Frequent User Club   It was a small step for American Airlines, given its massive reservations system, to add passenger accounts to accumulate travel credit for frequent flyer awards. These programs, which award free trips and several ancillary benefits, create strong brand loyalty among travelers, particularly business travelers who are not paying their own way. Thus, discount fares of a new competitor have no appeal to these travelers, as People Express learned. A travel consultant has been quoted as saying, "It's one of the most anticompetitive programs ever erected."[5]

Alfred Kahn, the father of deregulation, headed the CAB in the late 1970s and did not foresee how airlines would create reservations systems and frequent flyer plans to stifle competition. He is quoted as saying, "Nobody recognized all the ways in which a carrier could insulate itself from competition."[6]

Switching Costs   Information technology in the form of on-line computer terminals has been used in the medical supplies industry to link hospitals directly to the suppliers' distribution networks. Both American Hospital Supply and McKesson, the drug distributor, have installed their on-line terminals in hospitals so that supplies and drugs can be purchased as the need arises. Significant switching costs are built into this arrangement because the hospital is able to reduce inventory-carrying costs and has the convenience of on-line ordering for replenishments. The supplier benefits by a reduction in selling costs because it is difficult for a competitor to entice away a customer who is already co-opted into its system.[7]

---

[4]For specific allegations, see "Frontier Airlines, Inc. (A)," Harvard Business School Case no. 9-184-041, HBS Case Services, 1983.

[5]R. L. Rose and J. Dahl, "Skies Are Deregulated, but Just Try Starting a Sizable New Airline," *The Wall Street Journal,* July 19, 1989, p. A1.

[6]Ibid., p. A8.

[7]From Harold S. Bott, "Information for Competitive Advantage," *Operations Management Review,* fall 1985, p. 35.

Revenue Generation

Real-time information technologies with a focus on internal operations can play a competitive role in increasing revenue opportunities. The concept of yield management is best understood as a revenue-maximizing strategy to make full use of service capacity. Advances in microcomputers have created opportunities for innovative point-of-sale devices. And the use of expert systems tied to 1-800 numbers allows increased customer service.

Yield Management   American Airlines, through the use of its SABRE reservations system, was the first to realize the potential of what is now called *yield management*. By constantly monitoring the status of its upcoming flights and the status of its competitors' flights on the same route, American makes pricing and allocation decisions on unsold seats. Thus, the number of Supersaver fares allocated to a flight can be adjusted to ensure that remaining empty seats have a chance of being sold, but not at the expense of a full-fare seat. This real-time pricing strategy maximizes the revenue for each flight by ensuring that no seat goes empty for want of a bargain-seeking passenger while holding some seats in reserve for the late arrivals willing to pay full fare.[8]

Thus, yield management is the application of information to improve the revenue generated by a time-perishable resource (airline seats, hotel rooms, etc.). The success of yield management for American has not gone unnoticed by other service industries. For example, Marriott Hotels has installed a nationwide yield management system to increase occupancy rates. American Airlines is capitalizing on its innovation by selling the yield management software to noncompetitive industries such as the   French national railroad. The topic of yield management is covered in more detail in Chapter 10.

Point of Sale   Wal-Mart has discovered a new toy for the discount shopper: the VideOcart. As the shopper pushes the VideOcart through the store, information about the department at hand flashes on the video screen attached to the cart. The cart also helps customers find items in the store by listing hundreds of products by department and then displaying a map of the store for ease in location. The company supplying the cart claims that it has increased sales by $1 per visit in trials at supermarkets.[9] For another example, consider the use of the palm-sized microcomputer transmitter. With this device, a server in a restaurant can transmit an order directly to the kitchen monitor and the bill to the cashier at the same time. This saves unnecessary steps and allows more time for suggestive selling.

Expert Systems   Otis Elevator Company puts an expert system together with laptop computers in the hands of its maintenance staff to speed repair in the field. Collecting information on the behavior of its elevators over the years has led to

---

[8]Barry C. Smith, J. F. Leimkuhler, and R. M. Darrow, "Yield Management at American Airlines," *Interfaces,* vol. 22, no. 1, January–February 1992, pp. 8–31.

[9]From Kevin Helliker, "Wal-Mart's Store of the Future Blends Discount Prices, Department-Store Feel," *The Wall Street Journal,* May 17, 1991, p. B1.

a knowledge base incorporated into the expert system. A repair person in the field using a laptop computer can call up the system and receive diagnostic help in identifying the source of a problem. The result is that elevators are placed back in service quickly, and fewer repair people are needed. Some of the earlier applications of expert systems have been in the medical field, and conceivably the systems could be accessed by physicians for a fee. And an oil exploration expert system was able to identify promising drilling sites for a major oil company.

Data Base Asset

James L. Heskett observed that the data base a service firm possesses can be a hidden asset of strategic importance. The expense of assembling and maintaining a large data base is itself a barrier to entry for competitors. But more importantly, the data base can be mined for profiles of customers' buying habits, and these present opportunities for developing new services.[10]

Selling Information Dun & Bradstreet created a business of selling access to its data base of business credit information. American Home Shield, a provider of service contracts for individual home heating, plumbing, and electrical systems, discovered it had a valuable asset in its data base, accumulated over many years of repair experience. Manufacturers are now invited to access this data base to evaluate the performance patterns of their products. American Express has detailed access to the spending habits of its card holders and now offers breakdowns of customer spending patterns to its retail customers.

Developing Services Sears, Roebuck and Co. became a financial services giant by exploiting its customer data base. Unlike American Express, Sears was in a position to use its credit card and customer buying pattern data base for the delivery of new services. It has had a long presence in the insurance industry with its Allstate division, and more recently it has had firms such as Dean Witter & Company and Coldwell Bankers to establish itself as a "one-stop financial services center with retail hours." It must be noted, however, that at present Sears is divesting itself of a portion of its financial services in a partial attempt to shore up its flagging retail facilities.

Micromarketing Today we can see a truly focused service strategy that can target customers at the micro level. Bar coding and checkout scanner technology creates a wealth of consumer buying information that can be used to target customers with precision. As shown in Table 4.1, analysis of this data base allows marketers to pinpoint their advertising and product distribution. To increase sales, Borden Inc. has used such information to select stores in which to feature its premium pasta sauce. Kraft USA saw its sales of cream cheese increase when it targeted its flavors to the tastes of a particular store's shoppers.[11]

[10]Heskett, op. cit., p. 44.
[11]Michael J. McCarthy, "Marketers Zero in on Their Customers," *The Wall Street Journal*, Mar. 18, 1991, p. B1.

TABLE 4.1
EXAMPLE OF MICROMARKETING ANALYSIS

Hitting the Bull's-Eye
Micromarketers can now target a product's best customers and the stores where they're most likely to shop. Here's one company's analysis of three products' best targets in the New York area.

Brand	Heavy user profile	Life-style and media profile	Top 3 stores
Peter Pan peanut butter	Households with kids headed by 18–54 year olds, in suburban and rural areas	• Heavy video renters • Go to theme parks • Below average TV viewers • Above average radio listeners	**Foodtown Super Market** 3350 Hempstead Turnpike, Levittown, NY **Pathmark Supermarket** 3635 Hempstead Turnpike, Levittown, NY **King Kullen Market** 598 Stewart Ave., Bethpage, NY
Stouffers Red Box frozen entrees	Households headed by people 55 and older, and upscale suburban households headed by 35–54 years old	• Go to gambling casinos • Give parties • Involved in public activities • Travel frequently • Heavy newspaper readers • Above average TV viewers	**Dan's Supreme Super Market** 69-62 188th St., Flushing, NY **Food Emporium** Madison Ave. & 74th St., NYC **Waldbaum Super Market** 196-35 Horace Harding Flushing, NY
Coors light beer	Head of household, 21–34, middle to upper income, suburban and urban	• Belong to a health club • Buy rock music • Travel by plane • Give parties, cookouts • Rent videos • Heavy TV sports viewers	**Food Emporium** 1498 York Ave., NYC **Food Emporium** First Ave. & 72nd St., NYC **Gristedes Supermarket** 350 E. 86th St., NYC

Source: Michael J. McCarthy, "Marketers Zero in on Their Customers," *Wall Street Journal,* March 18, 1991, p. B1. Reprinted by permission of The Wall Street Journal, © 1991, Dow Jones & Company, Inc. All Rights Reserved Worldwide.

Productivity Enhancement

New developments in the collection and analysis of information have increased our ability to manage multisite service operations. Through the use of laptop or notebook computers, retail inventory can be managed on a daily basis to make better use of shelf space by matching products with sales. Information collected on the performance of multisite units can be used to identify the most efficient producers. Productivity is enhanced systemwide when the sources of these successes are shared with other sites. The foundation for a learning organization is then established.

Inventory Status   Using a handheld computer, Frito-Lay sales representatives have eliminated paper forms; they download the data collected on their routes each day via telephone to the Plano, Texas, headquarters. The company then uses this data to keep track of inventory levels, pricing, product promotions, and stale or returned merchandise. These daily updates on sales, manufacturing, and distribution keep fresh products moving through the system, matching consumer demands. For a perishable product like potato chips, having the right product at the right place and in the proper amount is critical to Frito-Lay's success. A Frito-Lay spokesperson said the company saved more than $40 million in its first year owing to reduced paperwork, reduced losses from stale products, and route consolidation.[12]

Data Envelopment Analysis   DEA is a linear programming technique developed by A. Charnes, W. W. Cooper, and E. Rhodes to evaluate nonprofit and public sector organizations. It has subsequently found applications in for-profit service organizations. DEA compares each service delivery unit with all other service units for a multisite organization and computes an efficiency rating based on the ratio of resource inputs to outputs. Multiple inputs (i.e., labor-hours, materials, etc.) and multiple outputs (sales, referrals, etc.) are possible and desirable in measuring a unit's efficiency. Taking this information, the linear programming model determines the efficiency frontier on the basis of those few units producing at 100 percent efficiency. Areas for improvement can be identified by comparing the operating practices of efficient units with those of less efficient units. Sharing management practices of efficient units with less efficient units provides an opportunity for the latter's improvement and total system productivity enhancement. Repeated use of DEA can establish a climate of organizational learning that fuels a competitive strategy of cost leadership.

Banker and Morey applied DEA to a 60-unit fast-food restaurant chain and found 33 units to be efficient.[13] In the analysis, three outputs (food sales for breakfast, lunch, and dinner) and six inputs (supplies and materials, labor, age of store, advertising expenditures, urban vs. rural location, and existence of a drive-in window) were used. It is interesting to note that the inputs included both discretionary and uncontrollable variables (e.g., the demographic variable of urban/rural locations and whether or not the unit had a drive-in window). The topic of data envelopment analysis is covered in more detail as a supplement to Chapter 12.

---

[12]Peter H. Lewis, "Looking beyond Innovation, an Award for Results," *The New York Times,* June 23, 1991, p. 8.

[13]R. D. Banker and R. C. Morey, "Efficiency Analysis for Exogenously Fixed Inputs and Outputs," *Operations Research,* vol. 34, no. 4, July–August 1986, pp. 518–519.

LIMITS IN THE USE OF INFORMATION

So far only the benefits of using information as a competitive strategy have been addressed. Some of the strategies raise questions of fairness, invasion of privacy, and anticompetitiveness. Also, if these strategies were abused, the result could harm consumers.

In an attempt to create barriers to entry, the use of reservation systems and frequent user programs has been identified as potentially anticompetitive. For example, how should a frequent flyer's free-trip award be considered, particularly when the passenger has been traveling on business at corporate expense? The IRS is considering taxing the free trip as income in kind, and corporations believe the free tickets are theirs. However, the long-run implication is the removal of price competition in air travel.

Perhaps the easiest way to start a riot is to ask passengers on a flight how much their tickets cost. Under yield management, ticket prices can change every hour; therefore, the price paid is a moving target, and the ticketing process becomes a lottery. At the extreme, is yield management fair and equitable to the public? Or has every service price always been negotiable, and are customers only now becoming aware of their buying power?

The concept of micromarketing has the potential to create the most violent backlash from consumers because of the perceived invasion of privacy. When a record of your every purchase at the local supermarket is shared with eager manufacturers, very manipulative sales practices could result. Lotus Development Corporation recently felt the sting of consumer displeasure after announcing the availability of its MarketPlace household data base to anyone with a PC and modem. Lotus received more than 30,000 requests from irate persons wanting to be removed from the data base. Lotus subsequently withdrew its offer of general availability, but it still sells access to the data base to large corporations.[14]

SUMMARY

The strategic role of information in service strategies is organized into four categories: creation of barriers to entry, revenue generation, data base asset, and productivity enhancement. Information-based competitive strategies were illustrated for each category.

Yield management, pioneered by American Airlines, is the most comprehensive use of information for strategic purposes and best illustrates the integrated nature of services. Using forecasting methods from operations management, pricing strategies from marketing, and consumer psychology from organizational behavior, American Airlines has developed a computer-based method to sell airline seats at various prices to maximize the revenue for any given flight. This innovation directly attacks the classic service dilemma of matching supply and demand. The discussion of the limits to information use suggests that service managers again

---

[14]"How Did They Get My Name?" *Newsweek*, June 3, 1991, p. 41.

must always be sensitive to the perceptions of their actions on the public they serve.

Thus far we have explored the concept of services in Part I and various strategies important to services in Part II. Part III, which begins with the next chapter, will examine ways of structuring services in a competitive market.

TOPICS FOR DISCUSSION

1. Will the widespread use of yield management eventually erode the concept of fixed prices for any service?
2. What possible negative effects does yield management have on customer relations?
3. What are the ethical issues associated with micromarketing?
4. Do you agree with the travel consultant's statement about frequent flyer awards that "It's one of the most anticompetitive programs ever erected"?
5. For each of the three generic strategies (cost leadership, differentiation, and focus), which of the four competitive uses of information is most powerful?

CASE: THE BEST LITTLE COOKIE HOUSE AROUND[15]

A chocolate chip cookie is a pretty straightforward thing—a bit of flour, a bit of sugar, a bit of shortening, a whole lot of chocolate chips, and not much more. Given those humble beginnings, one might not expect the stir created in 1992. We refer, of course, to the national controversy over who bakes the better cookie, Barbara Bush or Hillary Clinton.

Each of those stunning ladies undoubtedly makes superb creations that would grace any schoolkid's lunchbox. But, the truth be told, there has been a major revolution in the chocolate chip cookie industry that overshadows their efforts. This revolution was brought about by a young woman, Debbi Sivyer Fields, whose chocolate chip history goes back to her early years, when she baked just for family and friends.

Mrs. Fields (yes, *that* Mrs. Fields!) opened her first cookie shop in Palo Alto, California, in 1977. By 1980 she had established shops in other cities in northern California and in Hawaii. Throughout this expansion, she maintained control and personal involvement in all of them, and her success was a tribute as much to the personal relationship she felt with her customers and her natural business savvy as to the quality of her cookies.

As she began her expansion to other parts of the country, however, it became apparent that conventional methods of conducting a far-flung business would not allow her to maintain the personal control and involvement in day-to-day

---

[15]Information for this case was gathered from several sources including the following: Keri Ostrofsky, "Mrs. Fields Cookies," *Harvard Business School Case No. 9-189-056,* 1989; Tom Richman, "Mrs. Fields' Secret Ingredient," *Inc.,* October 1987, pp. 65–69; Jack Schember, "Mrs. Fields' Secret Weapon," *Personnel Journal,* September 1991, vol. 70, no. 9, pp. 56–58; and personal communication from Nina Macheel of Fields Software Group Inc.

operations that she wanted. At that time she felt that franchising, for example, would involve transferring a degree of authority to others and a concomitant loss of control over the quality of the cookies and the service. That situation was unacceptable to Mrs. Fields. So, initially, the challenge became one of cooking up an organizational and operational structure to meet Mrs. Fields's requirements.

Enter Mr. Fields. Yes, folks, there is a Mr. Fields behind the cookie dough, too. Randy Fields is an economist, and together the Fieldses have developed a business that, in February 1993, according to a company spokesperson, included 348 domestic Mrs. Fields cookie stores, 23 Mrs. Fields Bakeries, 94 La Petite Boulangerie bakeries, 36 international cookie stores, and, bowing to the exigencies of the prevailing economic climate, 34 franchise operations.

The Fieldses solved the early problem of retaining direct control over their far-flung enterprises by developing a very flat organizational structure and an effective information system.

Organizational Structure

Each outlet, for example, has only one administrative person, a store manager. A district store manager (DSM) supervises several store managers and reports to a regional director of operations (RDO). The RDOs report to two directors of operations who, in turn, report to Mrs. Fields. The regional and district managers make marketing decisions for the stores, and store controllers at the headquarters in Park City, Utah, manage the financial affairs.

Each day the store controllers look at the computer reports of sales at each store. They also note the trends and any problems that have occurred during that time. Within 24 hours, the controllers relay their findings to Mrs. Fields via a vice president.

Operational Support

The MIS (Management Information Systems) people at Mrs. Fields's implement and support the personal computer arrangement in each store, develop financial software, and manage telecommunications equipment and a voice-mail system. Each day a single corporate data base tracks sales in all the outlets and produces reports that allow corporate management personnel to spot and resolve problems quickly.

Before a proposed system is accepted, it is subjected to a cost/benefit analysis and then justified according to one of three criteria: (1) Does it offer an economic advantage? (2) Will it promote new sales? (3) Does it have any strategic importance? Mr. Fields sees information systems as a way for the company to grow without incurring the cost of expanding the staff. We also note that the original MIS for Mrs. Fields's has evolved into a "spin-off" business in its own right, Fields Software Group headed by Mr. Fields, which markets its software product ROI (Retail Operations Intelligence) to other multi-unit retail and service organizations.

MIS in the Trenches

The computer system that is installed in each store has many applications. For example, it is used to monitor the financial records, schedule operations in the store, provide marketing support, make hourly sales projections, record employee work hours, track inventory, interview applicants, and support electronic mail.

At the beginning of each workday, the store manager enters into the computer the information for that day, such as the day of the week, a special event in the area that might influence sales, and weather conditions. The computer program responds with specific questions and then uses a mathematical model to outline the day's schedule. For example, it tells the manager how many sales per hour to expect and how many cookies per hour to bake. Next, the manager enters the types of cookies to be made that day, and the system prescribes the number of batches to mix, the times when the batches are to be mixed, and the times when any unused dough must be discarded.

Sales are entered into the computer throughout the day, and the system adjusts its projections and the mixing schedules accordingly. The system also makes suggestions, such as "offer samples" or "increase suggestive selling" when sales lag. Managers, however, are not obligated to follow the suggestions. Inventory is also tracked by the system, which then generates orders for supplies.

Mrs. Fields's information system plays an integral part in the hiring of employees. The information submitted by a job applicant is entered into a program that compares the applicant's qualifications with those of Mrs. Fields's employees. The program looks for a "fit" with the corporate culture and then advises the manager whether to call the applicant back for a follow-up interview, which is conducted interactively with the computer. The program once again recommends whether or not to hire the applicant, but the manager may appeal the recommendation directly to the personnel department.

In addition to the Day Planner and Interview applications, the capabilities of the information system most frequently used by the store managers include the following: Form Mail, a menu-driven application used primarily for messages between the manager and staff; Labor Scheduler, an expert system that schedules the staff; Skills Test, a set of multiple-choice tests for employees being considered for raises and promotions; and Time Clock, a program that enables staff to punch in and out, and that also facilitates the payroll process.

Questions

1. In what way has the management information system created a competitive advantage for Mrs. Fields?

2. How might the management information system contribute to the reported 100 percent turnover of store managers?

3. Will the management information system support or inhibit the expansion of Mrs. Fields's outlets? Why?

SELECTED BIBLIOGRAPHY

Banker, Rajiv D., and R. C. Morey, "Efficiency Analysis for Exogenously Fixed Inputs and Outputs," *Operations Research,* vol. 34, no. 4, July–August 1986, pp. 513–521.

Bott, Harold S.: "Information for Competitive Advantage," *Operations Management Review,* fall 1985, pp. 30–42.

Heskett, James L.: *Managing in the Service Economy,* Harvard Business School Press, Boston, Mass., 1986.

———, W. E. Sasser, and C. W. L. Hart: *Service Breakthroughs,* The Free Press, New York, 1990.

McFarlan, Warren F.: "Information Technology Changes the Way You Compete," *Harvard Business Review,* May–June 1984, pp. 98–103.

Porter, E. Michael: *Competitive Strategy,* The Free Press, New York, 1980.

———, and V. E. Millar: "How Information Gives You Competitive Advantage," *Harvard Business Review,* July–August 1985, pp. 149–160.

Sherman, David H.: "Improving the Productivity of Service Businesses," *Sloan Management Review,* spring 1984, pp. 41–43.

Smith, Barry C., J. F. Leimkuhler, and R. M. Darrow: "Yield Management at American Airlines," *Interfaces,* vol. 22, no. 1, January–February 1992, pp. 8–31.

PART THREE

STRUCTURING THE SERVICE ENTERPRISE

Now that the service concept and competitive strategy have been articulated, our attention is directed to issues of service design. We begin by introducing a method of service process diagramming called *blueprinting* that can be used to evaluate existing or proposed service delivery designs much as an engineer uses drawings of a product to showcase a design. Several generic approaches to service design are discussed. A walk-through audit of a restaurant illustrates how to validate a design from a customer perspective.

Questions of facility design such as aesthetics are important elements for creating the appropriate environment to support the service concept. Consideration is also given to the psychological need to avoid customer disorientation in an unfamiliar setting. The concepts of product layout and process layout used in manufacturing are adapted for service layout applications. The issue of facility location is addressed, beginning with an estimation of spatial demand, the use of appropriate location models, and final site selection considerations. Finally, several marketing innovations are discussed that question our assumptions concerning the role of location in service delivery.

THE SERVICE DELIVERY SYSTEM

Designing a service delivery system is a creative process. It begins with a service concept and strategy to provide a service with features to differentiate it from the competition. The various alternatives for achieving these objectives must be identified and analyzed before decisions can be made. Designing a service system involves issues such as location, facility design and layout for effective customer and work flow, procedures and job definitions for service providers, measures to ensure service quality, extent of customer involvement, equipment selection, and adequate service capacity. The design process is never finished. Once the service becomes operational, modifications in the delivery system are introduced as conditions warrant.

For an example of innovative service system design, consider Federal Express. The concept of guaranteed overnight airfreight delivery of packages and letters was the subject of a college term paper written by the founder, Frederick W. Smith. As the story is told, the term paper received a C because the idea was so preposterous, but the business is now a model for the industry.

Traditionally, airfreight has been slow and unreliable, an ancillary service provided by airlines primarily interested in passenger service. The genius of Smith, an electrical engineer, was recognizing the analogy between freight transport and an electrical network connecting many outlets through a junction box. From this insight was born the "hub-and-spoke" network of Federal Express, with Memphis serving as the hub and sorting center for all packages. Planes arriving at night from cities throughout the United States would unload their packages and wait approximately two hours before returning to their home cities with packages ready for delivery the next morning. Thus, a package from Los Angeles destined for San Diego would travel from Los Angeles to Memphis on one plane and from Memphis to San Diego on another. With the exception of severe weather grounding an aircraft or of a sorting error, the network design guaranteed that a package would reach its destination overnight. Thus, the design of the service delivery system itself contained the strategic advantage that differentiated Federal Express from the existing airfreight competitors.

Today Federal Express has expanded to several hubs (e.g., Newark and Los Angeles) and uses trucks to transport packages between nearby large urban centers (e.g., Boston and New York).

CHAPTER PREVIEW

Our discussion begins with the concept of *blueprinting,* which is an effective technique to describe the service delivery process in visual form. Using a *line of visibility,* we will differentiate between the front-office and back-office portions of the service delivery system. The front-office portion of the system is where customer contact occurs, with concern for ambience and effectiveness (e.g., a bank lobby). The back-office portion of the system is hidden from the customer and often is operated as a factory for efficiency (e.g., the check-sorting operations of a bank).

The analysis of structural alternatives in the system design will be considered in the context of the strategic objectives. Linking the concepts of production efficiency and sales opportunity will illustrate the necessity of integrating marketing and operations in service management.

Following a taxonomy for service process design, three generic approaches for viewing service system design are presented. Each approach—the production-line approach, customer participation, and customer contact—advocates a particular philosophy. The features of these approaches will be examined.

Finally, a walk-through audit is presented as a method for service managers to assess the effectiveness of their service from the viewpoint of the customer. A chapter supplement treats the vehicle routing problem that occurs when a service makes deliveries to customer locations.

SERVICE BLUEPRINTING[1]

Developing a new service based on the subjective ideas contained in the service concept can lead to costly trial-and-error efforts to translate the service concept into reality. In the development of a building, the design is captured on architectural drawings called *blueprints,* because the reproduction is printed on special paper, creating blue lines. These blueprints show what the product should look like and all the specifications needed for its manufacture. G. Lynn Shostack has proposed that a service delivery system can be captured in a visual diagram (i.e., a service blueprint) and used in a similar manner for the design of services. As we explore the blueprint for a bank installment lending operation shown in

[1]Adapted from G. Lynn Shostack, "Designing Services That Deliver," *Harvard Business Review,* January–February 1984, pp. 133–139.

Figure 5.1, many uses for this diagram will become apparent. First we see that the blueprint is a map or flowchart (called a *process chart* in manufacturing) of all the transactions that constitute the service delivery process. Some activities are processing information, others are interactions with customers, and still others are decision points. The decision points are shown as a diamond to highlight these important steps, such as providing protocols to avoid mistakes, for special consideration. Studying the blueprint could suggest opportunities for improvement and also the need for further definition of certain processes (e.g., the step "print payment book" contains many activities, such as printing booklet, preparing check, addressing and mailing envelope).

The *line of visibility* separates activities of the front office, where customers obtain tangible evidence of the service, from the back-office processing, which is out of customer view. The high- and low-contact parts of the service delivery process are kept physically separate, but they remain linked by communications. This separation does highlight the need to give special attention to operations above the line,

FIGURE 5.1
Blueprint for bank installment lending operation. [*Reprinted with permission of the American Marketing Association: G. Lynn Shostack, "Service Positioning through Structural Change,"* Journal of Marketing, *vol. 51, January 1987, p. 36.*]

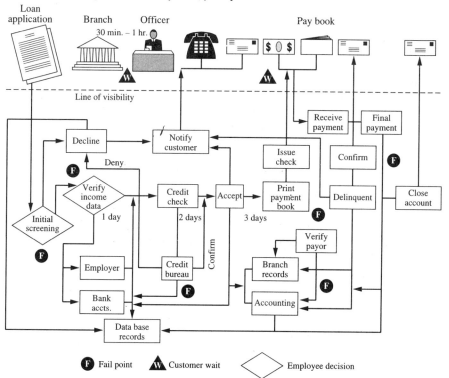

where customer perceptions of the service's effectiveness are formed. A full treatment of this service encounter is the subject of Chapter 8. The physical setting, the decor, employees' interpersonal skills, and even printed material all make a statement about the service. The subject of facility design and layout is discussed in Chapter 6. Designing an efficient process is the goal of the back office, but indirectly the back-office operations have an effect on the customer owing to delays and errors.

The blueprinting exercise also gives managers the opportunity to identify potential *fail points* (F) and design "foolproof" (*poka-yoke* is the term borrowed from Japan) procedures to avoid their occurrence, thus ensuring the delivery of high-quality service. In the installment lending example most customer contact is by mail after the initial loan application. To avoid errors several verification points are included in the back-office activities.

For critical operations that are performance determinants of the service, we find *standard execution times* displayed. Some execution times will be represented as a range to account for the discretion necessary in some transactions (e.g., 30 minutes to 1 hour to apply for a loan). These standard times will also be useful in making capacity decisions and setting expectations (e.g., loan check received six days after the application is approved).

A triangle is used to identify places in the process where customer waiting could be anticipated. Thus, customers waiting to see a loan officer will need a pleasant and adequate seating area with amenities such as coffee and reading material. The subject of managing queues is discussed in Chapter 11. Separating the activity of preparing the payment book from issuing the loan check could significantly reduce the time a customer must wait for the check.

In summary, a blueprint is a precise definition of the service delivery system that allows management to test the service concept on paper before final commitments are made. The blueprint also facilitates problem solving and creative thinking by identifying potential points of failure and highlighting opportunities to enhance customers' perceptions of the service.

STRATEGIC POSITIONING THROUGH PROCESS STRUCTURE

Preparing the service blueprint is the first step in developing a service process structure that will position the firm in the competitive market. Decisions still remain on the degree of complexity and divergence desired in the service. G. Lynn Shostack defined these concepts and used them to show how a service firm can position itself on the basis of process structure.[2]

The steps and sequences in the process captured by the service blueprint and measured by the number and intricacy of the steps represent the *degree of complexity* of the service delivery structure. For example, the preparation of a take-out order at a fast-food restaurant is less complex than the preparation of a gourmet dinner at a fine French restaurant. The amount of discretion or freedom

[2]G. Lynn Shostack, "Service Positioning through Structural Change," *Journal of Marketing,* vol. 51, January 1987, pp. 34–43.

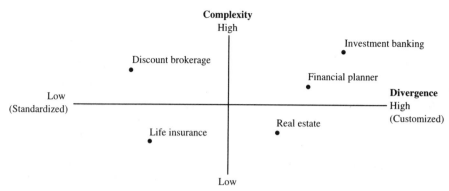

FIGURE 5.2
Structural positioning of financial services.

permitted the server to customize the service is the *degree of divergence* allowed at each service process step. For example, the activities of an attorney, as contrasted with those of a paralegal, are highly divergent because the interaction with the client requires judgment, discretion, and situational adaptation.

The two dimensions of complexity and divergence, for example, allow us to create a market-positioning chart for the financial services industry as shown in Figure 5.2. In all service industries we can see movement in every direction of the process structure chart as firms position themselves in relation to their competitors.

Firms like H & R Block have sought high-volume, middle-class taxpayers by creating a *low-divergence* tax service for those seeking help preparing standard tax returns. With low divergence, the service can be provided with narrowly skilled employees performing routine tasks, and the result is consistent quality at reduced cost.

A hair-styling salon for men represents a *high-divergence* strategy reshaping the traditional barbering industry. High divergence is characterized as a niche strategy that seeks out customers willing to pay extra for the personalization.

Narrowing the scope of a service by specializing is a focused strategy that results in *low complexity*. Retailing has recently seen an explosion of specialty shops selling only one product such as ice cream, cookies, or coffee. For such a strategy to succeed, the service or product must be perceived as unique or of very high quality.

In order to gain greater market penetration or to maximize the revenue from each customer, a strategy of adding more services can be embarked on, thereby creating a structure with *high complexity*. For example, supermarkets have evolved into superstores through the addition of banking services, pharmacies, flower shops, books, movie video rental, and food preparation.

Repositioning need not be limited to changes in only one dimension of the process structure (i.e., level of divergence or level of complexity). For a family restaurant seeking a strategy combining changes in levels of both complexity and divergence, consider Table 5.1.

TABLE 5.1
STRUCTURAL ALTERNATIVES FOR FAMILY RESTAURANT

Lower complexity/divergence	Current process	Higher complexity/divergence
No reservations.	Take reservation.	Specific table selection.
Self-seating; menu on blackboard.	Seat guests, give menus.	Recite menu: describe entrees and specials.
Eliminate.	Serve water and bread.	Assortment of hot breads and hors d'oeuvres.
Customer fills out form.	Take orders.	At table; taken personally by maitre d?.
	Prepare orders:	
Preprepared: no choice.	Salad (4 choices)	Individually prepared at table.
Limit to 4 choices.	Entree (15 choices)	Expand to 20 choices: add flaming dishes; bone fish at table; prepare sauces at table.
Sundae bar: self-service.	Dessert (6 choices)	Expand to 12 choices.
Coffee, tea, milk only.	Beverage (6 choices)	Add exotic coffees; wine list; liqueurs.
Serve salad and entree together, bill and beverage together.	Serve orders.	Separate-course service: sherbet between courses; hand-grind pepper.
Cash only: pay when leaving.	Collect payment.	Choice of payment, including house accounts; serve mints.

Source: Reprinted with permission of the American Marketing Association: G. Lynn Shostack, "Service Positioning through Structural Change," *Journal of Marketing,* vol. 51, January 1987, p. 41.

TAXONOMY FOR SERVICE PROCESS DESIGN

Service processes can be classified using the concept of divergence, the object toward which the service activity is directed, and the degree of customer contact. In Table 5.2 services are broadly divided into low divergence (standardized service) and high divergence (customized service). Within these two categories the object of the service process is identified as goods, information, or people. The degree of customer contact ranges from no contact, to indirect contact, to direct contact (divided further into self-service and personal interaction with the service worker).

Degree of Divergence

A standardized service (low divergence) is designed for high volumes with a narrowly defined and focused service. The tasks are routine and require a workforce with relatively low levels of technical skills. Because of the repetitive nature of the service, opportunities for the substitution of automation for labor abound (e.g., use of vending machines, automatic car wash). Reducing the discretion of service workers is one approach to achieving consistent service quality, but with possible negative consequences. These concepts will later be referred to as the "production-line" approach to service design.

For customized services (high divergence), more flexibility and judgment are required to perform the service tasks. In addition, more information is exchanged between the customer and service worker. These characteristics of customized services require high levels of technical and analytic skills because the service process is unprogrammed and not well defined (e.g., counseling, landscaping). To achieve customer satisfaction, decision making is delegated to service workers,

TABLE 5.2
TAXONOMY OF SERVICE PROCESSES

		Low divergence (standardized service)			High divergence (customized service)		
		Processing of goods	Processing of information or images	Processing of people	Processing of goods	Processing of information or images	Processing of people
No customer contact		Dry cleaning Restocking a vending machine	Check processing Billing for a credit card		Auto repair Tailoring a suit	Computer programming Designing a building	
Indirect customer contact			Ordering groceries from a home computer Phone-based account balance verification			Supervision of a landing by an air controller Bidding at a TV auction	
Direct customer contact	No customer–service worker interaction (self-service)	Operating a vending machine Assembling premade furniture	Withdrawing cash from an automatic bank teller Taking pictures in a photo booth	Operating an elevator Riding an escalator	Sampling food at a buffet dinner Bagging of groceries	Documenting medical history at a clinic Searching for information in a library	Driving a rental car Using a health club facility
	Customer–service worker interaction	Food serving in a restaurant Car washing	Giving a lecture Handling routine bank transactions	Providing public transportation Providing mass vaccination	Home carpet cleaning Landscaping service	Portrait painting Counseling	Haircutting Performing a surgical operation

Source: Reprinted with permission from Urban Wemmerlov, "A Taxonomy for Service Process and Its Implications for System Design," *International Journal of Service Industry Management,* vol. 1, no. 3, 1990, p. 29.

who can perform their tasks with some autonomy and discretion (i.e., the workers are empowered).

Object of the Service Process

When goods are processed, a distinction must be made between goods that belong to the customer and goods that are provided by the service firm *(facilitating goods)*. For services such as dry cleaning or auto repair, the service is performed on the property of the customer. In this case, the property must be secured from damage or loss. Other services such as restaurants supply facilitating goods as a significant part of the service package. Appropriate stock levels and the quality of these facilitating goods become a concern, as illustrated by McDonald's attention to the purchase of food items.

Processing information (i.e., receiving, handling, and manipulating data) occurs in all service systems. In some cases this is a back-office activity, such as check processing at a bank. For other services the information is communicated indirectly by electronic means, as with telephone-based account balance verification. Service workers in these situations may spend hours before a video screen performing routine tasks, and motivation becomes a challenge. However, there are services, such as counseling, where information is processed in direct interactions between customer and service worker. For the highly skilled employees in these services, the challenge of dealing with unstructured problems is important to job satisfaction.

Processing people involves physical changes (e.g., a haircut or a surgical operation) or geographic changes (e.g., a bus ride or a car rental). Because of the "high-touch" nature of these services, service workers must possess interpersonal skills in addition to technical skills. Attention also must be paid to service facility design and location, because the customer is physically present in the system. These topics are covered in Chapters 6 and 7.

Type of Customer Contact

Customer contact with the service delivery system can occur in three basic ways. First, the customer can be physically present and interact *directly* with the service providers in the creation of the service. In this instance the customer has full sensory awareness of the service surroundings. Second, the contact may be *indirect* and occur via electronic media from the customer's home or office. Finally, some service activities can be performed with *no* customer contact at all. Banking provides an example where all three customer contact options occur. Making an application for an automobile loan requires an interview with a loan officer; payment on the loan can be accomplished by the electronic transfer of funds; and the financial record keeping for the loan is conducted in a back office of the bank.

Direct customer contact is subdivided into two categories: no interaction with service workers (self-service) and customer interaction with service workers. Often, self-service is particularly attractive because customers provide the necessary labor at the time it's needed. Many cost-effective applications of technology in services, such as direct dialing and ATMs, have relied on a market segment of customers willing to learn how to interact with machines. When customers desire direct interaction with service providers, all the issues addressed above concerning the processing of people (i.e., training in interpersonal skills and facility issues of location, layout, and design) become important to ensure a successful service experience. When customers are in the service process physically, additional management problems arise, such as managing queues to avoid creating a negative image. The topic of customer waiting is discussed in Chapter 11, and the related issues of managing customer demand and scheduling service capacity are discussed in Chapter 10.

Service processes with indirect customer contact or with no customer contact need not be constrained by the issues above that arise from the physical presence of the customer in the system. Because the customer is decoupled from the service delivery system, a more manufacturing type of approach can be taken. Decisions on site location, facility design, work scheduling, and the training of employees can all be driven by efficiency considerations. In fact, the no-customer contact and goods-processing combination creates a category normally thought of in manufacturing. For example, dry cleaning is a batch process, and auto repair is a job shop.

This taxonomy of service processes presents a way to organize the various types of processes encountered in service systems and helps in our understanding of the design and management of services. The taxonomy also serves as a strategic positioning map for service processes and, thus, as an aid in the design or redesign of service systems.

GENERIC APPROACHES TO SERVICE SYSTEM DESIGN

In Chapter 2, we defined the service package as a bundle of attributes that a customer experiences. This bundle consists of four features: supporting facility, facilitating goods, explicit services, and implicit services. With a well-designed service system, all of these features are harmoniously coordinated in light of the desired service package. Consequently, the definition of the service package is the key to designing the service system. This design can be approached in one of several ways.

At one extreme, we can deliver services by way of a production-line approach. With this approach, routine services are provided in a controlled environment to ensure consistent quality and efficiency of operation. Another approach for service system design is to encourage active customer participation in the process. Allowing the customer to take an active role in the service process can result in many benefits to both consumer and provider. An intermediate approach divides the service into high- and low-customer-contact operations. This allows the low-contact operations to be designed as a technical core, isolated from the customer. It should be noted that combinations of these approaches can be used. For example, banks isolate their check-processing operation, use self-serve automatic tellers, and provide personalized loan service.

Production-Line Approach

We tend to see service as something personal: it is performed by individuals directly for other individuals. This humanistic perception can be overly constraining and can, therefore, impede innovative service system design. For example, we might sometimes benefit from a more technocratic service delivery system. Manufacturing systems are designed with control of the process in mind. The output is often machine-paced. Jobs are designed with explicit tasks to perform. Special tools and machines are supplied to increase worker productivity. A service taking this production-line approach could gain a competitive advantage with a cost leadership strategy.

McDonald's provides the quintessential example of this manufacturing-in-the-field approach to service.[3] Raw materials, such as the hamburger patties, are measured and prepackaged off-site, leaving the employees with no discretion as to size, quality, or consistency. Furthermore, the storage facilities are expressly for the predetermined mix of products. No extra space is available for foods and beverages not called for in the service.

The production of french fries illustrates the attention to design detail. The fries come precut, partially cooked, and frozen. The fryer is sized to cook a correct quantity of fries. This is an amount that will be not so large as to create an inventory of soggy fries or so small as to require making new batches very frequently. The fryer is emptied onto a wide, flat tray near the service counter. This setup prevents fries from an overfilled bag from dropping to the floor, which would result in wasted food and an unclean environment. A special wide-mouthed scoop with a funnel in the handle is used to ensure a consistent measure of french fries. The thoughtful design ensures that employees never soil their hands or the fries, the floor remains clean, and the quantity is controlled. Furthermore, a generous-looking portion of fries is delivered to the customer by a speedy, efficient, and cheerful employee.

The entire system is engineered from beginning to end, from prepackaged hamburgers to highly visible trash cans that encourage customers to clear their table. Every detail is accounted for through careful planning and design of the entire system. The production-line approach to service system design attempts to translate a successful manufacturing concept into the service sector. There are several features of this approach that contribute to its success.

Limited Discretionary Action of Personnel　A worker on an automobile assembly line is given well-defined tasks to perform, along with the tools to accomplish them. Employees with discretion and latitude might produce a more personalized car, but with loss of uniformity from one car to the next. Standardization and quality (defined as consistency in meeting specifications) are the hallmarks of a production line. For standardized routine services, consistency in service performance would be valued by customers. For example, specialized services like muffler replacement and pest control are advertised as having the same high-quality service

[3]Theodore Levitt, "Production-Line Approach to Service," *Harvard Business Review,* September–October 1972, pp. 41–52.

at any franchised outlet. Thus, the customer can expect identical service at any location of a particular franchise operation (one Big Mac is as desirable as another), just as one product from a manufacturer is indistinguishable from another. However, if a more personalized service is desired, the concept of employee empowerment becomes appropriate. The idea of giving employees more freedom to make decisions and to assume responsibility is discussed in Chapter 8.

Division of Labor   The production-line approach suggests that the total job be broken down into groups of tasks. Task grouping permits specialization of labor skills. Not everyone at McDonald's needs to be a cook. Furthermore, the division of labor allows one to pay only for the skill required to perform the task. Consider, for example, a new concept in health care called the *automated multiphasic testing laboratory*. Patients are processed through a fixed sequence of medical tests, which are part of the diagnostic workup. Tests are performed by medical technicians using sophisticated equipment. Because the entire process is divided into routine tasks, the examination can be accomplished without the need for an expensive physician.

Substitution of Technology for People   The systematic substitution of equipment for people has been the source of progress in manufacturing. This approach also can be used in services, as seen by the acceptance of automatic teller machines in lieu of bank tellers. But a great deal can be accomplished by means of the soft technology of systems. Consider, for example, the use of mirrors placed in an airplane galley. This benign device provides a reminder and an opportunity for flight attendants to maintain a pleasant appearance in an unobtrusive manner. Another example is the greeting card display that has a built-in inventory replenishment and reordering feature. When the stock gets low, a colored card appears to signal a reorder. Using a portable printer, insurance agents can personalize their recommendations and illustrate the accumulation of cash values. Data about the client are inputted to a distant computer by telephone to calculate the projections.

Service Standardization   The limited menu at McDonald's guarantees a fast hamburger. Limiting the service options creates opportunities for predictability and preplanning. The service becomes a routine process with well-defined tasks and an orderly flow of customers. Standardization also helps provide uniformity in service quality because the process is easier to control. Franchise services take advantage of standardization to build national organizations and thus overcome the problem of demand being limited only to the immediate region around a service location.

Customer Participation

For most service systems, the customer is present when the service is being performed. Instead of being a passive bystander, the customer represents productive labor just at the moment it is needed. Opportunities exist for increasing productivity by shifting some of the service activities onto the customer. Furthermore, customer participation can increase the degree of customization. For example, Fuddrucker's, a chain of fast-food restaurants, has a self-service condiment bar that allows customers the opportunity to choose specific items and amounts as desired. Thus, involving the customer in the service process can support a competitive strategy of cost leadership with limited customization if focused on a self-serve customer market.

Depending on the degree of customer involvement, a spectrum of service delivery systems is possible, from self-service to complete dependence on a service provider. For example, consider the services of a real estate agent. A homeowner has the option of selling the home personally, as well as the option of staying away from any involvement by engaging a real estate agent for a significant commission. An intermediate alternative is the "Gallery of Homes" approach. For a flat fee, say $500, the homeowner lists the home with the Gallery. Home buyers visiting the Gallery are interviewed concerning their needs and are shown pictures and descriptions of homes that might be of interest. Appointments for visits with homeowners are made, and an itinerary is developed. The buyers provide their own transportation, and the homeowners show their own homes. The Gallery agent conducts the final closing and arranges financing as usual. Productivity gains are achieved by a division of labor. The real estate agent concentrates on duties requiring special training and expertise, while the homeowner and buyer share the remaining activities.

The following features illustrate some of the contributions customers can make in the delivery of services.

Substitution of Consumer Labor for Provider Labor   The increasing minimum wage has hastened the substitution of consumer labor for personalized services. Hotel bellhops are now seen less often than they used to be, and more buffets are being served in restaurants. Airlines are encouraging passengers to use carry-on luggage. Technology has also helped to facilitate customer participation. Consider, for example, the use of automatic teller machines at banks and the use of long-distance direct dialing. The modern customer has become a coproducer, receiving benefits for his or her labor in the form of lower-cost services.

Smoothing of Service Demand   Service capacity is a time-perishable commodity. For example, in a medical setting it is more appropriate to measure capacity in terms of physician-hours available rather than in terms of the number of doctors on the staff. This approach emphasizes the permanent loss to the service provider of capacity whenever the server is idle owing to a lack of customer demand. However, the nature of demand for service is one of pronounced variation by the hour of the day (restaurants), day of the week (theaters), or season (ski resorts). If variations in demand can be smoothed, the required service capacity will be reduced, and fuller, more uniform utilization of capacity can be realized. The result is improved service productivity.

To implement a demand-smoothing strategy, the participation of customers is required. They must adjust the timing of their demand to match service availability. Typical means of accomplishing this are appointments and reservations. In compensation, customers expect to avoid waiting for the service. Customers may also be induced to acquire the service during off-peak hours by price incentives (e.g., reduced telephone rates after 5 p.m. or midweek discounts on lift tickets at ski resorts).

If attempts to smooth demand fail, high utilization of capacity may still be accomplished by requiring customers to wait for service. Thus, customer waiting contributes to productivity by permitting greater utilization of capacity. Perhaps a sign such as the following should be posted in waiting areas: "Your waiting allows us to offer bargain prices!"

We would expect customers to be compensated for this input to the service process through lower prices. But what about "free" or prepaid government service? In this situation, waiting is a surrogate for the price that might otherwise be charged the user. The results are a rationing of the limited public service among users and high utilization of capacity. However, using customers' waiting time as an input to the service process may be criticized on the grounds that individual customers value their time differently.

The customer may need to be "trained" to assume a new and, perhaps, more independent role as an active participant in the service process. This education role of the provider is a new concept in services. Traditionally the service provider has kept the consumer ignorant and, thus, dependent on the server.

As services become more specialized, the customer must also assume a diagnostic role. For example, does the loud noise under my car need the attention of AAMCO (transmission) or Midas (muffler)? Furthermore, an informed customer may also provide a quality-control check, which has been particularly lacking in the professional services. Thus, the key to increased service productivity may depend on an informed and self-reliant customer. A more detailed discussion of demand smoothing is found in Chapter 10.

Customer Contact

The manufacture of products is conducted in a controlled environment. The process design is totally focused on creating a continuous and efficient conversion of inputs into products without consumer involvement. Using inventory, the production process is decoupled from the variations in customer demand and thus can be scheduled to operate at full capacity.

How can service managers design their operations to achieve the efficiencies of manufacturing when customers are participating in the process? Richard B. Chase has argued persuasively that service delivery systems can be separated into high- and low-contact customer operations.[4] The low-contact, or back-office, operation is then run as a plant, where all the production management concepts and automation technology are brought to bear. This separation of activities can result

---

[4]Richard B. Chase, "Where Does the Customer Fit in a Service Operation?" *Harvard Business Review*, November–December 1978, pp. 137–142.

in a customer perception of personalized service while, in fact, achieving economies of scale through volume processing.

The success of this approach depends on the required amount of customer contact in the creation of the service and on the ability to isolate a technical core of low-contact operations. In our taxonomy of service processes, this approach to service design would seem most appropriate for the processing-of-goods category—for example, dry cleaning, where the service is performed on the customer's property.

Degree of Customer Contact   *Customer contact* refers to the physical presence of the customer in the system. The degree of customer contact can be measured by the percentage of time the customer is in the system relative to the total service time. In the high-contact services, the customer determines the timing of demand and the nature of the service by direct participation in the process. The perceived quality of service is determined to a large extent by the customer's experience. Consumers have no direct influence on the production process of low-contact systems because they are not present. Even if a service falls into the high-contact category, it may still be possible to seal off some operations to be run as a factory. For example, the maintenance operations of a public transportation system and the laundry of a hospital are plants within a service system.

Separation of High- and Low-Contact Operations   When service systems are decoupled into high- and low-contact operations, each area can be designed separately to achieve improved performance. The different considerations in the design of the high- and low-contact operations are listed in Table 5.3. Notice that high-contact operations require personnel with excellent public relations skills. The service tasks and activity levels are uncertain because customers dictate the timing of demand and, to some extent, the service itself. Note that low-contact operations can be physically separated from customer contact operations. These back-office operations can be scheduled like a factory to obtain high utilization of capacity.

Airlines have effectively used this approach in their operations. Airport reservation clerks and flight attendants wear uniforms designed in Paris and attend training sessions on the proper way to serve passengers. Baggage handlers are seldom seen, and aircraft maintenance is performed at a distant depot and run like a factory.

Sales Opportunity and Service Delivery Options   The commonly held view that organizations are information processing systems is evident when considering information content requirements as a variable in designing service tasks. The service design matrix developed by Richard B. Chase, shown in Figure 5.3, illustrates the relationship between production efficiency and sales opportunity as a function of service delivery options.[5]

---

[5]R. B. Chase and N. J. Aquilano, "A Matrix for Linking Marketing and Production Variables in Service System Design," *Production and Operations Management,* 6th ed., Irwin, Homewood, Ill., 1992.

TABLE 5.3
MAJOR DESIGN CONSIDERATIONS FOR HIGH- AND LOW-CONTACT OPERATIONS

Design consideration	High-contact operation	Low-contact operation
Facility location	Operations must be near the customer.	Operations may be placed near supply, transportation, or labor.
Facility layout	Facility should accommodate the customer's physical and psychological needs and expectations.	Facility should enhance production.
Product design	Environment as well as the physical product define the nature of the service.	Customer is not in the service environment, so the product can be defined by fewer attributes.
Process design	Stages of production process have a direct, immediate effect on the customer.	Customer is not involved in the majority of processing steps.
Scheduling	Customer is in the production schedule and must be accommodated.	Customer is concerned mainly with completion dates.
Production planning	Orders cannot be stored, so smoothing production flow will result in loss of business.	Both backlogging and production smoothing are possible.
Worker skills	Direct workforce makes up a major part of the service product and so must be able to interact well with the public.	Direct workforce need only have technical skills.
Quality control	Quality standards are often in the eye of the beholder and hence variable.	Quality standards are generally measurable and hence fixed.
Time standards	Service time depends on customer needs, and therefore time standards are inherently loose.	Work is performed on customer surrogates (e.g., forms), and time standards can be tight.
Wage payment	Variable output requires time-based wage systems.	Fixable output permits output-based wage systems.
Capacity planning	To avoid lost sales, capacity must be set to match peak demand.	Storable output permits setting capacity at some average demand level.
Forecasting	Forecasts are short-term, time-oriented.	Forecasts are long-term, output-oriented.

Source: Used by permission of the *Harvard Business Review.* Exhibit from "Where Does the Customer Fit in a Service Operation," by Richard B. Chase (November–December 1978). Copyright © 1978 by the president and fellows of Harvard College; all rights reserved.

The service delivery options are ordered from left to right in increasing richness of information transfer. As discussed above, production efficiency is related to the degree of customer contact with the core service operations. Sales opportunity is a measure of the probability of making add-on sales and increasing the revenue

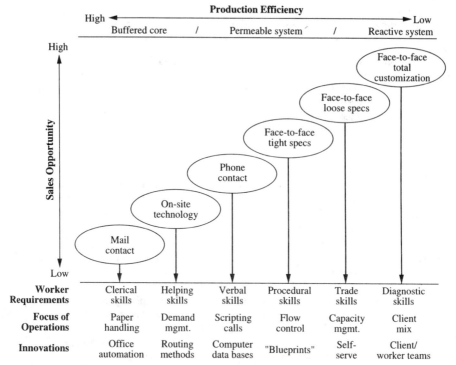

FIGURE 5.3
Sales opportunity and service system design. [*Reprinted with permission from R. B. Chase and N. J. Aquilano, "A Matrix for Linking Marketing and Production Variables in Service System Design,"* Production and Operations Management, *6th ed., Richard D. Irwin, Inc., Homewood, Ill., 1992, p. 123.*]

generated from each customer. The matrix permits the explicit consideration of the tradeoffs made between marketing and production considerations when selecting the service delivery option.

We should not conclude that only one service delivery option must be selected. In order not to eliminate certain market segments, multiple channels of service should be considered. For example, gas stations have both full-service and self-service pumps, and most banks still have live tellers in addition to ATMs.

WALK-THROUGH AUDIT[6]

The delivery of a service should conform to customers' expectations from the beginning to the end of the experience, because the customer is a participant in the service process, and his or her impression of the service quality is influenced by many observations. An environmental audit can be a useful management tool for the systematic evaluation of a customer's view of the service provided.

[6]From J. A. Fitzsimmons and G. B. Maurer, "A Walk-through-Audit to Improve Restaurant Performance," *The Cornell H.R.A. Quarterly,* February 1991, pp. 95–99.

Such a walk-through audit was developed by Fitzsimmons and Maurer for sit-down restaurants in which the customer is served. The audit consisted of 42 questions spanning the restaurant dining experience, beginning with approaching the restaurant from the parking area, then walking into the restaurant and being greeted, waiting for a table, being seated, ordering and receiving food and drinks, and finally receiving the check and paying the bill. Sample questions from the walk-through audit are shown in Figure 5.4. The questions span nine categories of variables: (1) maintenance items, (2) person-to-person service, (3) waiting, (4) table and place settings, (5) ambience, (6) food presentation, (7) check presentation, (8) promotion and suggestive selling, and (9) tipping.

The audit was mailed to the owners or managers of 250 restaurants throughout

FIGURE 5.4
Sample questions from the walk-through audit. [*J. A. Fitzsimmons and Gavin Maurer, "A Walk-Through-Audit to Improve Restaurant Performance," The Cornell HRA Quarterly, vol. 31, no. 4, February 1991, p. 97. © Cornell HRA Quarterly. Used by permission. All rights reserved.*]

Presented below are representative examples from among the 42 questions included in the audit used in our study.

Please answer all questions as they relate to your restaurant. There are no right or wrong answers. For each question, circle the number that best represents your restaurant for that item. Please check "Not Applicable" when the item does not apply to your restaurant's service.

1.	How often is the parking area cleaned of trash items? (Not Applicable ____)	**Less than daily**				**At least hourly**
		1	2	3	4	5
		Time in minutes				
		Less than 15	**15–29**	**30–44**	**45–59**	**60 or more**
8.	During busy periods, the wait before being seated is: (Not Applicable ____)					
	a. Weekdays	1	2	3	4	5
	b. Weekends	1	2	3	4	5
	Are drinks served to customers who are waiting? Yes ___ No ___					
10.	Once seated inside, the lighting level is: (Not Applicable ____)	**Like Candlelight**				**Brighter than a sunny day**
		1	2	3	4	5
22a.	The average level of suggestive selling of appetizers is: (Not Applicable ____)	**Less than $2.00**	**$2–2.99**	**$3–3.99**	**$4–4.99**	**$5.00 or more**
		1	2	3	4	5
29.	After the entree is served, what is the average number of visits to the table by the servers? (Not Applicable ____)	**1 or 2**	3	4	5	**6 or more**
		1	2	3	4	5
		Time in minutes				
		0 min.	**1 min.**	**2 min.**	**3 min.**	**4 or more**
40.	Within how many minutes after the meal is finished is the final check presented? (Not Applicable ____) Before meal is finished = 0	1	2	3	4	5
		Percentage				
		8 or less	**9–11**	**12–14**	**15**	**Over 15**
41.	What is the average tip as a percentage of the bill? (Not Applicable ____)	1	2	3	4	5

Texas to study the relationship of tipping behavior to environmental variables. Many of the comparisons within the study relate directly to the level of tipping as a percentage of the total bill. It is believed that tipping is a good measure of customer satisfaction; clearly, however, some customers can be satisfied and still leave relatively low tips, and other customers will tip at a given level regardless of the service they perceive. Within this study, the tipping percentage ranged from less than 8 percent to more than 15 percent. Questions that relate to tipping behavior are grouped into the following categories: (1) person-to-person service, (2) service delays, (3) ambience, (4) check presentation, and (5) promotion and suggestive selling.

Person-to-Person Service

It was anticipated that high levels of person-to-person service would relate to high satisfaction among customers, and therefore to large tips. This was confirmed by the study.

Several variables are shown to have a strong positive relationship to the size of the tip: (1) the time the server spends at the table doing extra food preparation, (2) the number of visits to the table by the server after the entree has been served, and (3) the average number of times the server refills coffee cups or drink glasses during the dessert portion of the meal. This indicates that extra attention at the table seems to generate greater tips, possibly owing to greater customer satisfaction.

An important implication of these findings for management is that the initial training of servers should emphasize visits to the table as one strategy for achieving higher tip levels. Restaurants that promote high customer-server interaction may enjoy an additional competitive advantage because (1) customers are more satisfied and will be likely to return and (2) the prospect of higher tips may attract and retain a better serverstaff.

Service Delays

The audit indicates that tipping is high when customers are served drinks while waiting to be seated. This suggests that customers do not want to be ignored once they have arrived and that they have more positive perceptions of the dining experience if they receive some level of service before they are seated. This may point out an opportunity for restaurants to benefit by offering other activities or services to waiting customers. For more discussion of the effects of waiting during the service process, see Chapter 11.

Ambience Variables

The ambience, or aesthetic atmosphere, of a restaurant is one of the most important environmental variables for competitive differentiation. Four ambience variables— lighting level, music level, color scheme, and presence of cooking smells—were included in the study. However, only lighting levels proved to have a significant correlation with tipping behavior; a low light level was associated with large tips.

The level of light is also associated with other variables that have similar effects on tipping. For example, nearly two-thirds of the restaurants that use tablecloths and full place settings report having "candlelight" or slightly brighter lighting. Thus, tipping behavior may be associated with the complexity of the dining experience, where a complex dining experience is defined as one in which overt sensory stimulation gives way to subtle appeals, such as those found in very "elegant" restaurants.

The extent to which cooking smells can be noticed also supports this dining complexity dimension. Cooking smells are very closely associated with brighter light levels and homey or earth-tone color schemes. When comparing cooking smells with lighting, it appears that lower light levels are associated with low levels of cooking smells. Restaurants whose cooking smells are less noticeable also tend to use color schemes that utilize pastels, while restaurants with "very noticeable" cooking smells utilize homey or earth-tone color schemes. This indicates that the homey or earth-tone color scheme is associated with less complex dining experience, while pastels appear to be the fashion in restaurants that offer full table settings, tablecloths, and more complex dining experiences.

The creation and maintenance of the restaurant ambience has management implications. The selection of lighting levels and color schemes and the control of cooking smells must present an ambience consistent with the desired customer experience.

Check Presentation

The study shows that there are two distinct ways of presenting the check, depending on whether the management wants fast turnover of customers or encourages diners to linger after the meal is finished. Both strategies may be positively perceived by customers and result in better tips.

One way to achieve fast turnover is to combine the clearing of each plate as the diner finishes and the presentation of the check as closely as possible following the meal. This strategy did not necessarily mean lower tips, and it may lead to higher tips when customers want quick, efficient service without too many frills. In some cases, however, delayed presentation of the check is also associated with higher tipping. Unlike other service interactions that indicate that long waiting times carry negative perceptions of service, a delay in presenting the check can carry a positive perception. In the study, a group of restaurants reported that customers are given the bill no sooner than three minutes after the meal is finished. A majority of these restaurants reported higher-than-average tipping levels, provided the wait did not exceed four minutes.

Again, tip percentage is greater than for the sample as a whole, indicating that there are some restaurants in which the customers expect to be able to linger and will show their appreciation by tipping relatively higher than the sample. This may indicate that there is a point at which customers' perceptions change from pleasurable lingering to dissatisfied waiting.

Promotion and Suggestive Selling

Promotion variables include suggestive selling, as well as promoting food and drink items at special prices. Promotional activity is found to have a positive effect on the dining experience, as suggested by higher tips. Furthermore, suggestive selling has a multiplier effect on tips resulting from the added personal service and increased dollar amount of the bill. Thus, management can provide suggestive-selling vehicles as a way to increase both restaurant and server revenues.

Implications for Management

This study has demonstrated the importance of a walk-through audit as an opportunity to evaluate the service experience from a customer's perspective, because customers often become aware of cues the owners and managers may have overlooked. There is no inherently superior service design. There are, instead, designs that are consistent and that provide a signal to customers about the service they can expect. Providing tangibility in a service involves giving the customer verbal, environmental, sensory, and service cues that define the service for the customer and encourage repeat visits.

SUMMARY

We found that a service delivery system design can be captured in a visual diagram called a *service blueprint*. The line of visibility in this diagram introduced the concept of a front-office and back-office partition of the service system. Competitive positioning of the service delivery system was accomplished using the dimensions of complexity and divergence to measure structural differentiation. We also looked at classifying services according to the concept of divergence, the object of the service, and the degree of customer contact. Three generic approaches to the design of service delivery systems were considered: production-line approach, customer participation, and customer contact. These approaches and their combinations provide many opportunities for innovative designs. Finally, a walk-through audit for restaurants was provided as an example of a management tool for ensuring that the service delivery system is meeting customer expectations.

Our look at the structuring of services will continue in Chapter 6 with a consideration of how designs and layouts contribute to a competitive advantage.

TOPICS FOR DISCUSSION

1. Shostack's "line of visibility" on a service blueprint divides the service into front-office and back-office operations. How can this be useful to managers?
2. Select a service and prepare a "blueprint" identifying fail points, decision points, customer wait points, and the line of visibility.
3. What are the limits to the production-line approach to service?
4. Give an example of a service where isolation of the technical core would be inappropriate.

5. What are some drawbacks of increased customer participation in the service process?
6. What ethical issues are involved in the promotion of sales opportunities in a service transaction?
7. Select a service and prepare a list of questions and measures for a walk-through audit.

CASE: 100 YEN SUSHI HOUSE[7]

Sang M. Lee tells of a meeting with two Japanese businessmen in Tokyo to plan a joint U.S.-Japanese conference to explore American and Japanese management systems. As lunchtime drew near, his hosts told him with much delight that they wished to show him the "most productive operation in Japan."

Lee describes the occasion: "They took me to a sushi shop, the famous 100 Yen Sushi House, in the Shinzuku area of Tokyo. Sushi is the most popular snack in Japan. It is a simple dish, vinegared rice wrapped in different things, such as dried seaweed, raw tuna, raw salmon, raw redsnapper, cooked shrimp, octopus, fried egg, etc. Sushi is usually prepared so that each piece will be about the right size to be put into the mouth with chopsticks. Arranging the sushi in an appetizing and aesthetic way with pickled ginger is almost an art in itself.

"The 100 Yen Sushi House is no ordinary sushi restaurant. It is the ultimate showcase of Japanese productivity. As we entered the shop, there was a chorus of 'Iratsai,' a welcome from everyone working in the shop—cooks, waitresses, the owner, and the owners' children. The house features an ellipsoid-shaped serving area in the middle of the room, where inside three or four cooks were busily preparing sushi. Perhaps 30 stools surrounded the serving area. We took seats at the counters and were promptly served with a cup of 'Misoshiru,' which is a bean paste soup, a pair of chopsticks, a cup of green tea, a tiny plate to make our own sauce, and a small china piece to hold the chopsticks. So far, the service was average for any sushi house. Then, I noticed something special. There was a conveyor belt going around the ellipsoid service area, like a toy train track. On it I saw a train of plates of sushi. You can find any kind of sushi that you can think of—from the cheapest seaweed or octopus kind to the expensive raw salmon or shrimp dishes. The price is uniform, however, 100 yen per plate. On closer examination, while my eyes were racing to keep up with the speed of the traveling plates, I found that a cheap seaweed plate had four pieces, while the more expensive raw salmon dish had only two pieces. I sat down and looked around at the other customers at the counters. They were all enjoying their sushi and slurping their soup while reading newspapers or magazines.

"I saw a man with eight plates all stacked up neatly. As he got up to leave, the cashier looked over and said, '800 yen, please.' The cashier had no cash register, since she can simply count the number of plates and then multiply by 100 yen. As the customer was leaving, once again we heard a chorus of 'Arigato Gosaimas' (thank you) from all the workers."

[7]Reprinted with permission from Sang M. Lee, "Japanese Management and the 100 Yen Sushi House," *Operations Management Review,* winter 1983, pp. 46–48.

Lee continues his observations of the sushi house operations: "In the 100 Yen Sushi House, Professor Tamura [one of his hosts] explained to me how efficient this family-owned restaurant is. The owner usually has a superordinate organizational purpose such as customer service, a contribution to society, or the well-being of the community. Furthermore, the organizational purpose is achieved through a long-term effort by all the members of the organization, who are considered 'family.'

"The owner's daily operation is based on a careful analysis of information. The owner has a complete summary of demand information about different types of sushi plates, and thus he knows exactly how many of each type of sushi plates he should prepare and when. Furthermore, the whole operation is based on the repetitive manufacturing principle with appropriate 'just-in-time' and quality control systems. For example, the store has a very limited refrigerator capacity (we could see several whole fish or octopus in the glassed chambers right in front of our counter). Thus, the store uses the 'just-in-time' inventory control system. Instead of increasing the refrigeration capacity by purchasing new refrigeration systems, the company has an agreement with the fish vendor to deliver fresh fish several times a day so that materials arrive 'just in time' to be used for sushi making. Therefore, the inventory cost is minimum.

". . . In the 100 Yen Sushi House, workers and their equipment are positioned so close that sushi making is passed on hand to hand rather than as independent operations. The absence of walls of inventory allows the owner and workers to be involved in the total operation, from greeting the customer to serving what is ordered. Their tasks are tightly interrelated and everyone rushes to a problem spot to prevent the cascading effect of the problem throughout the work process.

"The 100 Yen Sushi House is a labor-intensive operation, which is based mostly on simplicity and common sense rather than high technology, contrary to American perceptions. I was very impressed. As I finished my fifth plate, I saw the same octopus sushi plate going around for about the 30th time. Perhaps I had discovered the pitfall of the system. So I asked the owner how he takes care of the sanitary problems when a sushi plate goes around all day long, until an unfortunate customer eats it and perhaps gets food poisoning. He bowed with an apologetic smile and said 'Well, sir, we never let our sushi plates go unsold longer than about 30 minutes.' Then he scratched his head and said, 'Whenever one of our employees takes a break, he or she can take off unsold plates of sushi and either eat them or throw them away. We are very serious about our sushi quality.'"

Questions

1. Prepare a service blueprint for the 100 Yen Sushi House operation.

2. What features of the 100 Yen Sushi House service delivery system differentiate it from the competition, and what competitive advantages do they offer?

3. How has the 100 Yen Sushi House incorporated the just-in-time system into its operation?

4. Suggest other services that could adopt the 100 Yen Sushi House service delivery concepts.

SELECTED BIBLIOGRAPHY

Bartholdi, J. J. III, L. K. Platzman, R. L. Collins, and W. H. Warden III: "A Minimal Technology Routing System for Meals on Wheels," *Interfaces,* vol. 13, no. 3, June 1983, pp. 1–8.

Chase, Richard B.: "Where Does the Customer Fit in a Service Operation?" *Harvard Business Review,* November–December 1978, pp. 137–142.

———: "The Customer Contact Approach to Services: Theoretical Bases and Practical Extensions," *Operations Research,* vol. 29, no. 4, July–August 1981, pp. 698–706.

——— and N. J. Aquilano: "A Matrix for Linking Marketing and Production Variables in Service System Design," *Production and Operations Management,* 6th ed., Irwin, Homewood, Ill., 1992.

———, G. B. Northcraft, and G. Wolf: "Designing High-Contact Service Systems: Application to Branches of a Savings and Loan," *Decision Sciences,* vol. 15, no. 4, 1984, pp. 542–556.

——— and D. A. Tansik: "The Customer Contact Model for Organization Design," *Management Science,* vol. 29, no. 9, 1983, pp. 1037–1050.

Cook, T., and R. Russell: "A Simulation and Statistical Analysis of Stochastic Vehicle Routing with Timing Constraints," *Decision Sciences,* vol. 9, no. 4, October 1978, pp. 673–687.

Fitzsimmons, James A.: "Consumer Participation and Productivity in Service Operations," *Interfaces,* vol. 15, no. 3, 1985, pp. 60–67.

Heskett, J. L.: "Operating Strategy: Barriers to Entry," *Managing in the Service Economy,* Harvard Business School Press, Boston, 1986, chap. 6.

Hill, Arthur V.: "An Experimental Comparison of Dispatching Rules for Field Service Support," *Decision Sciences,* vol. 23, no. 1, January–February 1992, pp. 235–249.

———, V. A. Mabert, and D. W. Montgomery: "A Decision Support System for the Courier Vehicle Scheduling Problem," *Omega,* vol. 16, no. 4, July 1988, pp. 333–345.

Johnston, B., and B. Morris: "Monitoring Control in Service Operations," *International Journal of Operations and Production Management,* vol. 5, no. 1, 1985, pp. 32–38.

Lee, Sang M.: "Japanese Management and the 100 Yen Sushi House," *Operations Management Review,* winter 1983, pp. 45–48.

Lele, M. M.: "How Service Needs Influence Product Strategy," *Sloan Management Review,* fall 1986, pp. 63–70.

Levitt, Theodore: "Production-Line Approach to Service," *Harvard Business Review,* September–October 1972, pp. 41–52.

———: "The Industrialization of Service," *Harvard Business Review,* September–October 1976, pp. 63–74.

Lovelock, C. H., and R. F. Young: "Look to Customers to Increase Productivity," *Harvard Business Review,* May–June 1979, pp. 168–178.

Mills, P. K., R. B. Chase, and N. Margulies: "Motivating the Client/Employee System as a Service Production Strategy," *Academy of Management Review,* vol. 8, no. 2, 1983, pp. 301–310.

Orloff, C. S.: "Routing a Fleet of M-Vehicles to/from a Central Facility," *Networks,* vol. 4, 1974, pp. 147–162.

Russell, Robert: "An Effective Heuristic for the M-Tour Traveling Salesman Problem with Some Side Conditions," *Operations Research,* vol. 25, no. 3, May–June 1977, pp. 517–525.

Schmenner, Roger: "How Can Service Business Survive and Prosper?" *Sloan Management Review,* spring 1986, pp. 21–32.

Shostack, G. L.: "Designing Services That Deliver," *Harvard Business Review,* January–February 1984, pp. 133–139.

————: "Service Positioning through Structural Change," *Journal of Marketing,* vol. 51, January 1987, pp. 34–43.

————: "How to Design a Service," *European Journal of Marketing,* vol. 16, no. 1, 1982, pp. 49–63.

CHAPTER 5 SUPPLEMENT: Vehicle Routing

Delivery of some services requires travel to the customer's location. In these cases, a method to develop vehicle routes quickly that minimizes time and distance traveled becomes an important consideration in service design. An algorithm to perform this task will be developed and illustrated.

On a typical Saturday, a college student may need to accomplish several tasks: work out at the gym, do some research in the library, go to the laundromat, and stop at a food market. Assuming that there are no constraints on when these tasks may be done, the student faces no great obstacle in determining an itinerary that will require the least amount of time and distance traveled. The solution is straightforward and can be formulated in one's head.

Many services must likewise develop itineraries, but in these cases the solutions may not be as obvious as the college student's. Examples range from Federal Express's ground transportation pickup and delivery routes, to bread deliveries at your supermarket, to the schedule for a telephone repairperson's route each day. Clearly, in these cases we would like a useful tool to determine acceptable routing and scheduling without a great deal of hassle.

Enter G. Clarke and J. W. Wright, who, in the 1960s, developed the Clarke-Wright (C-W) algorithm to schedule vehicles operating from a central depot and serving several outlying points.[8] In practice the C-W algorithm is applied to a problem through a series of iterations until an acceptable solution is obtained. Practical applications of the algorithm, in fact, may not necessarily be optimal, but the short amount of time and the ease with which it can be applied to problems that are not elementary and straightforward make it an extremely useful tool. The logic of this algorithm, which involves a *savings* concept, serves as the basis for more sophisticated techniques that are available in many commercial software programs.

The C-W savings concept considers the savings that can be realized by linking pairs of "delivery" points in a system composed of a central depot that serves the outlying sites. As a very simple example, consider Bridgette's Bagel Bakery. Bridgette bakes her bagels during downtime at her brother Bernie's Beaucoup Bistro. She must then transport her bagels to two sidewalk concession stands run by her sisters, Bernadette and Louise. Each stand is

---

[8]G. Clarke and J. W. Wright, "Scheduling of Vehicles from a Central Depot to a Number of Delivery Points," *Operations Research,* vol. 12, no. 4, July–August 1964, pp. 568–581.

located 5 miles from the Bistro, but they are 6 miles apart. The layout may be represented graphically as follows:

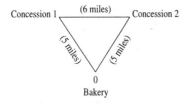

Concession 1 ____(6 miles)____ Concession 2

(5 miles)   (5 miles)

0
Bakery

In this situation the C-W algorithm first looks at the cost of driving from the bakery to one concession and back to the bakery, and then to the second concession and back to the bakery. The total cost, therefore, is equal to the sum of the costs (in miles) of driving from 0 to 1 and returning ($2C_{01}$) and driving from 0 to 2 and returning ($2C_{02}$), or

$$\text{Total cost} = 2C_{01} + 2C_{02}$$

Bridgette's total cost for following this route is 2×5 (miles) $+ 2 \times 5$ (miles), or 20 miles. The C-W algorithm next considers the savings that can be realized by driving from the bakery to one concession, then to the second concession, and finally back to the bakery. This route saves Bridgette the cost of one trip from concession 1 back to the bakery and of one trip from the bakery to concession 2, but it adds the cost of the trip from concession 1 to concession 2. The net savings S_{ij} gained by linking any two locations i and j into the same route is expressed as

$$S_{ij} = C_{0i} + C_{0j} - C_{ij}$$

Bridgette would realize a net savings of 4 miles from linking the two concessions by creating one trip from the bakery to concession 1 and then traveling to concession 2 and returning to the bakery.

$$S_{12} = C_{01} + C_{02} - C_{12}$$
$$= 5 + 5 - 6 = 4$$

Admittedly, this example can easily be solved by inspection and does not require a sophisticated heuristic, but it does serve as a convenient illustration of the savings concept that forms the basis of the C-W algorithm.

USING THE C-W ALGORITHM IN A SYSTEM WITH NO CONSTRAINTS

The application of the C-W algorithm to a less obvious situation proceeds through five steps, which will be described as we put them to work helping Bridgette, who is expanding her bagel service to four concessions in outlying areas. The distances related to each of these concessions and the bakery are given in Exhibit 1.

    1. *Construct a shortest-distance half-matrix; i.e., the matrix will contain the shortest distance between each pair of sites, including the starting location. A half-matrix is sufficient*

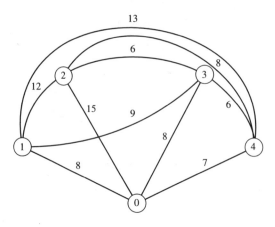

EXHIBIT 1
Network of bakery and four
concessions with distances in miles.

for this use because travel distance or time is the same in both directions. The shortest-distance
half-matrix for Bridgette's bakery and the four outlying concessions is shown in Exhibit 2.
[*Note:* for very large problems, the shortest distances may not be obvious. In these cases,
computer software programs to make these calculations are available.]

2. *Develop an initial allocation of one round-trip to each destination.* Note in the diagram
below that each concession is linked to the bakery by double lines with direction arrows.
Four round-trips are represented.

Routes

3. *Calculate the net savings for each pair of outlying locations, and enter them in a net
savings half-matrix.* These net savings for each pair of outlying locations are calculated
using equation (1) just as we did in Bridgette's initial problem. In this example, the net
savings from linking concessions 1 and 2 is 8 + 15 − 12 = 11. Similar calculations are made
for each of the other possible pairs, and the values are then entered into a net savings
half-matrix, as shown in Exhibit 3.

EXHIBIT 2
Shortest-distance half-matrix:
miles between bakery and
concessions.

		Concessions			
		1	2	3	4
Bakery	0	8	15	8	7
	1		12	9	13
Concessions	2			6	8
	3				6

EXHIBIT 3
Net savings between all concession
pairs.

		Concessions			
		1	2	3	4
Bakery	0	. . .	. . .	. . .	. . .
	1		11	7	2
Concessions	2			17	14
	3				9

4. *Enter values for a special trip indicator* T *into appropriate cells of the net savings half-matrix.* Our net savings calculation for linking each pair is based on how much is saved relative to the cost of the vehicle making a *round-trip* to each member of the pair. We will add to our net savings half-matrix the indicator *T*, which will show if two locations in question—for example, *i* and *j* or 0 (which represents the point of origin) and *j*—are directly linked. *T* may have one of three values, as given below:

$T = 2$ when a vehicle travels from the point of origin (Bridgette's bakery in our example) to location *j* (concession 1, 2, 3, or 4 in our example) and then returns. This is designated as $T_{0j} = 2$ and will appear only in the first row of the half-matrix. The appropriate value of *T* is entered into the net savings half-matrix and circled to distinguish it from the savings value. Remember, $T = 2$ indicates a *round-trip.*

$T = 1$ when a vehicle travels *one way directly* between two locations *i* and *j*. This is designated as $T_{ij} = 1$ and can appear anywhere in the half-matrix. Remember, $T = 1$ indicates a *one-way* trip.

$T = 0$ when a vehicle does *not* travel *directly* between two particular locations *i* and *j*. Accordingly, this is designated as $T_{ij} = 0$. Remember, $T = 0$ indicates that *no* trip is made between that pair of locations.

By convention the $T = 0$ value is not entered; a cell without a *T* value of 1 or 2 noted in the matrix is understood to have a $T = 0$. It is important to recognize that for each location *x*, the sum of the *T* values in column *x* plus the sum of the *T* values in row *x* must equal 2 (i.e., for every location served a vehicle must arrive and depart).

Exhibit 4A shows Bridgette's net savings half-matrix for her four new concessions, with the appropriate *T* value of 2 listed in the cells representing round-trips between the bakery and each of the concession locations. Note that the directional lines on the graphical depiction of this initial solution indicate a round-trip to each location.

5. *Identify the cell in the net savings half-matrix that contains the maximum net savings.* If the maximum net savings occurs in cell *(i, j)* in the half-matrix, then locations *i* and *j* can be linked if, and only if, the following conditions are met:

a. T_{0i} and T_{0j} must be greater than zero.
b. Locations *i* and *j* are not already on the same route, or loop.
c. Linking locations *i* and *j* does not violate any system constraints, which will be discussed later.

If all three of the conditions above *are* met, set $T_{ij} = 1$. In Bridgette's case, cell (2, 3) has the highest net savings, 17. T_{02} and T_{03} are each greater than zero, locations 2 and 3 are

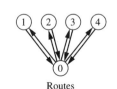

EXHIBIT 4A
Initial solution.

Routes

Routes: First trip: 0–1–0
Second trip: 0–2–0
Third trip: 0–3–0
Fourth trip: 0–4–0

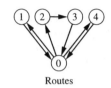

Routes: First trip: 0–1–0
        Second trip: 0–2–3–0
        Third trip: 0–4–0

EXHIBIT 4B
First iteration.

not already on the same route, and at present there are no constraints to linking locations 2 and 3; thus, all the conditions are met, and we may enter a T value of 1 in cell (2, 3), as shown in Exhibit 4B. This $T_{23} = 1$ in the cell indicates a *one-way* trip between concessions 2 and 3. At the same time that we have established the one-way trip between locations 2 and 3, we have eliminated a one-way trip from location 2 back to the bakery (0) and another one-way trip from the bakery to location 3. Therefore, it is necessary to reduce the $T = 2$ values in cells (0, 2) and (0, 3) to $T = 1$ in each. Exhibit 4B shows the appropriate T values for this new iteration, and the graphical depiction indicates the three new one-way routes.

If any one of the conditions—5a, 5b, or 5c—is *not* met, then identify the cell with the next highest savings, and repeat step 5. Repeat this inspection, if necessary, until you have identified the cell with the highest savings that satisfies all three conditions, and set its T value equal to 1 (remember to reduce the appropriate $T = 2$ or $T = 1$ values in row 0). If no cell meets the conditions, then the algorithm ends. [The algorithm also ends when all locations are linked together on a single route, which we will discover as we proceed with Bridgette's problem.]

This first application of the C-W algorithm has saved Bridgette 17 miles, but still more savings can be realized by subjecting her data to another iteration of step 5. Looking again at Exhibit 4B, we can identify cell (2, 4) as having the next highest net savings value, 14. T_{02} and T_{04} are each greater than zero, locations 2 and 4 are not at present on the same route, and there are no constraints against having locations 2 and 4 on the same route; therefore, we can link these two locations. Enter $T = 1$ in cell (2, 4), and reduce each of the T values in cells (0, 2) and (0, 4) by one trip, as shown in Exhibit 4C. Notice in the graphical

EXHIBIT 4C
Second iteration.

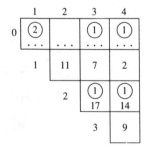

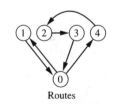

Routes

Routes: First trip: 0–1–0
        Second trip: 0–4–2–3–0

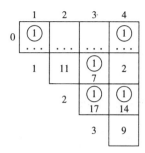

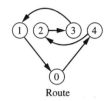

Route

Route: Single trip: 0–4–2–3–1–0

EXHIBIT 4D
Final solution.

depiction that the trips from the bakery to concession 2 and from concession 4 back to the bakery have been eliminated, requiring an adjustment of the directional arrows.

Is further improvement possible? The next highest net savings is 11, found in cell (1, 2). In this situation T_{01} is greater than zero, but T_{02} is not, and so linking these two locations would violate condition 5a. Cell (3, 4) has the next highest net savings. The T_{03} and T_{04} values are each greater than zero, but concessions 3 and 4 are already on the same route, which violates condition 5b. Therefore, we must look at the next highest net savings, which is 7, in cell (1, 3). Here, T_{01} and T_{03} are each greater than zero, concessions 1 and 3 are not already on the same route, and no constraints exist; therefore, we may link these two locations. We enter $T = 1$ in cell (1, 3) and reduce the T values in cells (0, 1) and (0, 3) by 1 each, as shown in Exhibit 4D. We have removed one trip between the bakery and concession 1 and one trip from concession 3 to the bakery. The directional arrows suggest that a counterclockwise route be used, but our assumption of equal time or distance traveling in either direction would permit the final route to be traversed in either direction.

USING THE C-W ALGORITHM IN A SYSTEM WITH CONSTRAINTS

Suppose Bridgette's Bagel Bakery business booms and Bridgette decides to supply four new franchise operations. These franchises are located according to the schematic shown in Exhibit 5. Unfortunately, Bridgette cannot carry enough bagels in her Blue Bagel Beamer to supply all the new locations on a single route such as we constructed in the previous section. Each franchise requires 500 bagels per day, and she can transport a maximum of 1000 bagels at one time. How can we use the C-W algorithm to solve Bridgette's problem? In general, the introduction of a constraint such as Bridgette's capacity limit or a delivery-time window does not alter the method of applying the algorithm. We need only account for the constraint so it does not violate step 5c.

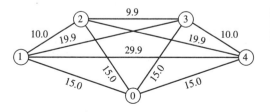

EXHIBIT 5
Network representation of a single bakery and four concessions.

	1	2	3	4
Bakery 0	15.0	15.0	15.0	15.0
	1	10.0	19.9	29.9
		2	9.9	19.9
			3	10.0

EXHIBIT 6
Shortest-distance half-matrix: miles between pairs of
locations.

In our present example our first step once again is to construct a shortest-distance half-matrix containing the distance between each pair of locations, as shown in Exhibit 6.

Next we construct the net savings half-matrix and enter the appropriate $T = 2$ values for the initial solution, as shown in Exhibit 7A. (Note that we have not included graphical depictions of the individual trips and their directional arrows in this example, but some readers may find it helpful to add such sketches.)

We note that cell (2, 3) has the largest net savings and satisfies all the conditions under step 5 of the C-W algorithm. Therefore, we can link locations 2 and 3. Enter the $T = 1$ value in cell (2, 3), and reduce the T values in cells (0, 2) and (0, 3) to 1, as shown in Exhibit 7B.

The route just established from the bakery to franchise 2 to franchise 3 and back to the bakery (0-2-3-0) cannot have any more links added because additional links would exceed Bridgette's capacity (a violation of condition 5c). Therefore, we must eliminate the following links: (1, 2), (1, 3), (2, 4) and (3, 4). The only link that remains possible is between locations 1 and 4. Adding the $T = 1$ value to cell (1, 4) and reducing the T values in cells (0, 1) and (0, 4) yields the final solution, shown in Exhibit 7C.

Exhibit 8 shows the final routes we have just constructed. The total mileage to be driven is 99.8. However, Exhibit 9 shows an alternate route devised from inspection that does the job in only 80 miles! As we noted earlier, the C-W algorithm does not *guarantee* an optimal solution every time. In this simple case, in fact, the solution with the algorithm is about 25 percent poorer than the optimal solution. In general, however, the algorithm is highly effective. It does yield very acceptable results, which, combined with its simplicity of use, makes it a very useful tool for developing vehicle routes.

EXHIBIT 7A
Initial solution.

	1	2	3	4
Bakery 0	②	②	②	②
	1	20.0	10.1	0.1
		2	20.1	10.1
			3	20.0

Routes: First trip: 0–1–0
Second trip: 0–2–0
Third trip: 0–3–0
Fourth trip: 0–4–0

EXHIBIT 7B
First iteration.

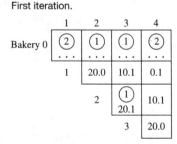

	1	2	3	4
Bakery 0	②	①	①	②
	1	20.0	10.1	0.1
		2	① 20.1	10.1
			3	20.0

Routes: First trip: 0–1–0
Second trip: 0–2–3–0
Third trip: 0–4–0

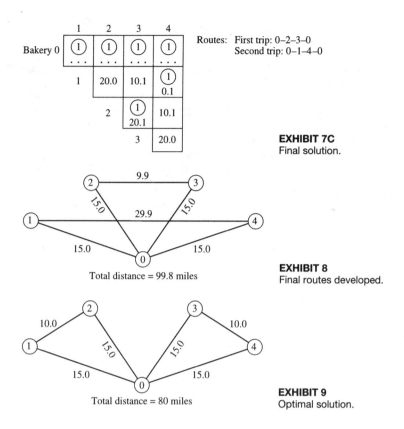

Routes: First trip: 0–2–3–0
Second trip: 0–1–4–0

EXHIBIT 7C
Final solution.

Total distance = 99.8 miles

EXHIBIT 8
Final routes developed.

Total distance = 80 miles

EXHIBIT 9
Optimal solution.

USE OF A "MINIMAL TECHNOLOGY ROUTING SYSTEM"

Bartholdi et al. have reported using a very clever manual method for routing vehicles that deliver Meals on Wheels (MOW) for Senior Citizens Services, Inc., in Atlanta, Georgia.[9] This program involved delivering a very large number of lunchtime meals to people located in a widely dispersed pattern in the city. This fact alone could daunt the most intrepid vehicle scheduler, but consider an added complication: the clientele being served in this program were incapacitated, mostly by age and/or illness, which resulted in a high turnover of clients and in routes that had to be changed accordingly. Moreover, the sponsoring organization did not have funding for sophisticated computers or skilled people to operate them. In fact, at the time of this study, one person was responsible for all administrative aspects of the program.

[9]Adapted from J. J. Bartholdi, III, L. K. Platzman, R. L. Collins, and W. H. Warden, III, "A Minimal Technology Routing System for Meals on Wheels," *Interfaces,* vol. 13, no. 3, June 1983, pp. 1–8.

So, MOW needed a way of routing and scheduling that could accommodate the following constraints:

1. A large and frequently changing clientele made it necessary to be able to add and remove clients and locations easily.

2. It was necessary to allot the delivery work equally because the meals were delivered by four drivers who were paid by the hour, and each was anxious to have his or her fair share of the work.

3. The program had to be utilized without computer support.

4. The program could be utilized by an "unskilled" scheduler.

Very simply, Bartholdi's solution was first to assign each location on a grid of the Atlanta city map a Θ (theta) value. This part was done by the researchers using a traveling-salesperson heuristic based on a "space-filling curve" concept. The resulting Θ map would form a reference sheet for the MOW manager to use in scheduling the routes and vehicles. Next, two Rolodex cards were made out for each client; the client's cards contained his or her name and address and the Θ value of the address. One card was inserted in one Rolodex alphabetically, and the other card was filed in a second Rolodex according to increasing values of Θ.

Using the system was an exercise in elegance and simplicity. First the Θ file, which was organized according to Θ location, was manually divided into four relatively equal parts, and each part was assigned to a delivery person. Accommodating changes in clientele was equally easy. As a person was removed from the service, his or her card was pulled from the alphabetical file, the Θ value was noted, and the corresponding card was pulled from the Θ file. This "automatically" updated the route. Similarly, when a client was added to the service, his or her cards were added to the files, and again, the routing was automatically updated. In practice, this system proved to work exceedingly well.

Obviously, many methods exist to facilitate vehicle routing and scheduling, and it would not be possible to explore each and every one of them in this space. We have, however, looked at one of the most widely used methods, the Clarke-Wright algorithm, and at a method that is charming in its simplicity and usefulness.

EXERCISES

5.1. Double Star Beer has five distribution centers and one central brewery. Below are the distances in miles between all nodes. Set up the net savings matrix for this problem, and determine which two nodes would be linked in the first-iteration solution matrix.

0–1	10 mi	1–2	7 mi	2–4	20 mi
0–2	10 mi	1–3	16 mi	2–5	19 mi
0–3	14 mi	1–4	13 mi	3–4	6 mi
0–4	12 mi	1–5	8 mi	3–5	18 mi
0–5	13 mi	2–3	5 mi	4–5	6 mi

5.2. For the following distance matrix, find the final-solution matrix and the recommended route.

	1	2	3	4
0	6	7	9	8
1		12	13	12
2			8	9
3				14

5.3. For the following net savings matrix, find the recommended route.

	1	2	3	4
0	...	...	...	...
1		2	4	3
2			5	7
3				2

5.4. A Double Star Beer distributor makes deliveries to four taverns from a central warehouse, as shown in the accompanying figure. Distances are given in miles.
  a. Construct a shortest-route matrix for travel between all pairs of locations.
  b. Set up a net savings matrix.
  c. Recommend a delivery route to minimize distance traveled.

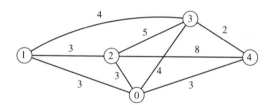

5.5. The city refuse collection department uses a fleet of small trucks that collect trash around the city and make periodic deliveries to four staging sites. Currently two dump trucks transport the trash from these staging sites to an incinerator. One truck is assigned to service sites 1 and 2 and the other to sites 3 and 4. The network in the accompanying figure gives the miles between the staging sites and the incinerator, shown as node 0.

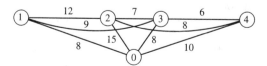

a. What is the cost per day to operate this two-truck system if gasoline is $1.50 per gallon and the trucks average 5 miles per gallon and make 10 trips to each staging site per day? Truck drivers are paid $80 per day.

b. A proposal has been made to purchase one large diesel truck with enough capacity to visit all four staging sites on one trip. What should be its route to minimize distance traveled?

c. If diesel fuel costs $1 per gallon and the truck averages 10 miles per gallon, determine the daily savings in operating costs.

CASE: THE DALEY MONTHLY CAR POOL[10]

Alice Daley, owner and publisher of the local periodical, *The Daley Monthly,* has a staff of six people writing articles. Currently, employees drive in each morning from their homes, as shown in the accompanying figure.

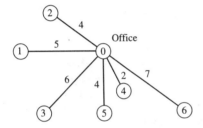

Because of increasing gasoline prices, the employees have approached Ms. Daley with a suggestion to use the company's nine-passenger van as a vehicle for a car pool. In considering this idea, Ms. Daley collected the additional data shown below on mileage between all pairs of employee locations.

1–2	2 mi	2–3	5 mi	3–5	5 mi
1–3	4 mi	2–4	6 mi	3–6	10 mi
1–4	6 mi	2–5	7 mi	4–5	3 mi
1–5	6 mi	2–6	11 mi	4–6	5 mi
1–6	12 mi	3–4	6 mi	5–6	5 mi

An alternative to using the company van is using an economy car. However, the compact can hold only three passengers, so it would call for two trips. But the average of 26 miles per gallon for the compact compared with the 12 miles per gallon for the van makes this option worth considering, particularly when gasoline is averaging 90 cents per gallon.

One final consideration is traffic congestion. The average speed possible is 30 miles per hour before 8 a.m. and 15 miles per hour between 8 and 9 a.m.

---

[10]Prepared by Roland Bressler and Raymond Matthews under the supervision of Professor James A. Fitzsimmons.

Questions

1. What is the total gasoline cost per day under the current arrangement of employees driving their own cars? Assume that fuel economy is 10 miles per gallon.

2. Find the least costly route for a car pool using the nine-passenger van. What would be the gasoline cost per day for this arrangement?

3. What time would the van need to leave the office in order to return with all employees by 8 a.m.? 9 a.m.?

4. If the employee living at location 6 offered to keep the van overnight, does this change the route?

5. If the compact car were used, what routes would you recommend to minimize gasoline expense? What would be the daily gasoline cost of this proposal?

6. At what time would the compact car need to leave the office to begin its pickups in order to be finished by 8 a.m.? 9 a.m.?

7. Would your routes be modified if employees living at locations 2 and 5 volunteered to use their compact cars and left from home to begin pickups?

8. What advantages and disadvantages are there to starting work at 8 a.m.?

CASE: AIRPORT SERVICES, INC.[11]

Airport Services, Inc., is planning to implement a remote shuttle service among five terminals and the Port Welkin Airport. Mr. Kelly Mist has been given the task of developing the routing and service schedules for the proposed operation to use in the franchise application to the Port Welkin City Council. Mrs. Janet Rush, Mr. Mist's supervisor, asks him to create schedules which have low operating costs for each round trip. Mrs. Rush states that with the locations it has in mind for terminal sites, Airport Services may have to run five buses, one between each terminal and the airport. She is hopeful, however, that fewer buses can be used.

Assignments

1. Mr. Mist is given the following information on which his analysis must be based:

Average operating cost: $0.455 per kilometer
Average operating speed: 60 kilometers per hour
Average layover time per stop: 9 minutes

From a city map, he develops a distance matrix for all the proposed service locations, designating the airport as site 0; all distances are given in kilometers.

	1	2	3	4	5
0	10	4	5	5	7
1		7	11	15	6
2			8	9	8
3				6	4
4					9

[11]Prepared by James Vance under the supervision of Professor James A. Fitzsimmons.

Using the Clarke-Wright algorithm, recommend the best routing schedule under Mrs. Rush's least-cost objective.

2. Mrs. Rush's initial reaction to Mr. Mist's work is very favorable; however, she has just been informed by the Port Welkin mayor that the city will require each bus to have a round-trip time (to and from the airport) of 40 minutes or less, excluding the loading and unloading time at the airport only. Although Mrs. Rush realizes that this will offer the shuttle users faster service, she is sure that it will cost the company more money.

Develop a new routing schedule that will meet this new time constraint yet still keep Airport Services' costs low.

3. The Port Welkin Council awarded Airport Services a shuttle franchise on the basis of Mr. Mist's latest routing plan, and Mrs. Rush feels that initiation of service has gone about as well as could be expected. Mr. Mist informs her that they are experiencing a recurring shortage of capacity at terminal 3; that is, more people board the bus than there are seats available. Mrs. Rush decides to seek a solution that meets the franchise conditions but doesn't require people to stand or use any more vehicles, even though the operating costs may rise slightly. Mr. Mist has analyzed the normal average boarding and alighting volumes at each remote terminal, as shown below. Also, he knows that Airport Services is using 48-passenger vehicles, which are usually full when leaving the airport on a multistop route.

Terminal	Avg. no. boarding	Avg. no. alighting
1	28	30
2	20	18
3	18	14
4	21	26
5	30	32

Develop a routing schedule that will incorporate the additional capacity constraint. How does this final solution compare with the previous two solutions with respect to operating costs and round-trip time?

CHAPTER 6

SERVICE FACILITY DESIGN AND LAYOUT

Subtle differences in facility design are important! Consider customers' perceptions of the two leading discount giants, K mart and Wal-Mart. In several independent surveys, shoppers say they are more satisfied with Wal-Mart and generally view Wal-Mart with higher esteem than K mart.[1] The companies offer similar merchandise at almost identical prices and operate stores that appear to be similar. What could explain this difference in customer perceptions?

Upon closer scrutiny we find subtle differences in store decor and layout. At Wal-Mart the main aisles are wider than those at K mart. Fluorescent lighting is recessed into the ceiling, creating a softer impression than the glare from the exposed fixtures at K mart. The apparel departments are carpeted in a warm, autumnal orange, while K mart's are tiled in off-white. Together, such features signal consumers that Wal-Mart is more upscale and that it carries merchandise of a little better quality than K mart's. Wal-Mart's attention to facility design details has helped shape shoppers' attitudes by striking that delicate balance needed to convince customers that its prices are low without making people feel cheap.

Wal-Mart has successfully used facility design to differentiate itself from its competitors. Using facility design as part of a differentiation strategy is very common. For example, the A-frame structure and blue roof of IHOP (International House of Pancakes) attract travelers to a pancake breakfast, just as the "golden arches" of McDonald's signal a hamburger lunch.

Using a standard, or "formula," facility is an important feature in the overall cost leadership strategy. Major gasoline retailers have perfected the design of their

---

[1]Francine Schwadel, "Little Touches Spur Wal-Mart's Rise," *The Wall Street Journal,* Sept. 22, 1989, p. B1.

gasoline stations to facilitate their construction (often completed within two weeks), to lower costs, and to create a consistent image awareness that will attract customers.

For theme restaurants and bars (e.g., a western bar or an Irish pub), the facility design is central to their focus strategy of targeting a particular market and creating a unique ambience. However, tradition still reigns in retail banking, except for an innovative bank with headquarters in Columbus, Ohio, called Banc One. Banc One has designed branches that look more like mini–shopping malls than banks, with glass atriums, "boutiques" offering special services, signs of blue neon, comfortable seating areas, and fresh coffee. Banc One, with its community focus, even has branches open on Saturdays and Sundays.[2]

CHAPTER PREVIEW

This chapter begins with a discussion of the issues to be considered in facility design. Facility layout is addressed with attention to traffic flow, space planning, and the need to avoid unnecessary travel. The concept of process flow analysis used by industrial engineers is modified for service operations and illustrated by a restaurant study in which a new credit card processing procedure is evaluated.

The traditional product and process layouts from manufacturing are shown to have service counterparts and can be studied using the techniques of assembly-line balancing and relative location analysis. Finally, the topic of disorientation caused by poor layouts is treated from an environmental psychology viewpoint, and the importance of signage is stressed.

DESIGN

Service operations can be directly affected by the facility design. A restaurant with inadequate ventilation for nonsmoking diners may discourage many customers. A physical fitness center that has easy wheelchair access may be able to enlarge its services to include a new clientele.

Design and layout represent the supporting facility component of the *service package.* Together they influence how a service facility is used and, sometimes, if it is used at all. Consider again Toronto's Shouldice Hospital, mentioned in Chapter 3. A good portion of its success in repairing inguinal hernias results from thoughtful design and layout. For example, the operating rooms are grouped together so that surgeons may easily consult with each other during procedures. Because early ambulation promotes faster healing, the hospital is designed to provide ample pleasant places to walk and even to climb a few steps. Meals are served only in community dining rooms rather than in patient rooms, which requires more walking and, as an added benefit, allows patients to get together and "compare notes." Patient rooms, while functional and comfortable, are not equipped with "extras" such as television sets that might encourage patients to "lie around."

[2]Steve Lohr, "The Best Little Bank in America," *The New York Times,* July 7, 1991, sec. 3, p. 1.

Other factors of design and layout can be "urgent." Consider the generally inadequate supply of rest-room facilities for women in most public buildings, especially during mass entertainment events. During intermission at your next concert or play, observe how long it takes individual females and males to use the rest rooms. Do you see any evidence of "potty parity" designed into the building? Count the number of rest rooms for men and the number for women in your classroom building. Chances are there are equal numbers for each gender, which does not necessarily ensure equality of access.

Clearly, good design and layout of a service enhance the service, from attracting customers, to making them more comfortable, to ensuring their safety (e.g., adequate lighting, fire exits, proper location of dangerous equipment). But also, the facility design has an impact on the implicit service component of the service package—in particular, on criteria like privacy and security, atmosphere, and sense of well-being.

Several factors influence design: (1) the nature and objectives of the service organization, (2) land availability and space requirements, (3) flexibility, (4) aesthetic factors, and (5) the community and environment.

Nature and Objectives of Service Organizations

The nature of the core service should dictate the parameters of its design. For example, a fire station must have a structure large enough to house its vehicles, its on-duty personnel, and its maintenance equipment. A bank must be designed to accommodate some type of vault. Physicians' offices come in many shapes and sizes, but they must all be designed to afford patients some privacy.

Beyond such fundamental requirements, however, design can contribute much more to defining the service. Design can engender immediate recognition, as in the case of McDonald's arches or IHOP's blue roof. External design can also give a clue as to the nature of the service inside. One would expect to see well-manicured grounds, freshly painted or marble columns, and perhaps a fountain in front of a funeral home. A school, on the other hand, might have colorful tiles on its facade and certainly a playground or athletic field nearby.

Appropriateness of design is also important. A gasoline service station can be constructed of brightly colored prefabricated sheet metal. However, would you deposit money in a bank that was using a trailer on wheels for a temporary branch?

Land Availability and Space Requirements

The land that is available for a service facility often comes with many constraints, such as costs, zoning requirements, and actual area. Good design must accommodate all of these constraints. In an urban setting, where land is at a premium, buildings can only be expanded upward, and organizations must often exhibit great creativity and ingenuity in their designs to use a relatively small space efficiently. For example, in some urban areas McDonald's has incorporated a second-floor loft for eating space (e.g., in Copenhagen).

Suburban and rural areas frequently offer larger, more affordable parcels of land that ameliorate the space constraints on urban facilities. However, many sites, especially urban ones, may have strict zoning laws on land usage and ordinances governing the exterior appearance of the structure. Space for off-street parking is also a necessary requirement. In any event, space for future expansion should always be considered.

Flexibility

Successful services are dynamic organizations that are able to adapt to changes in the quantity and nature of demand. How well a service can adapt depends greatly on the flexibility that has been designed into it. Flexibility might also be called "designing for the future." Questions to address during the design phase might be: How can this facility be designed to allow for later expansion of present services? How can we design this facility to accommodate new and different services in the future? For example, many of the original fast-food restaurants built for walk-in traffic have had to make facility modifications to accommodate customer demands for drive-through window service.

Several airports face facility problems today because the designers failed to anticipate either the tremendous growth in the numbers of people flying or the advent of the "hub-and-spoke" airline network following deregulation. Consequently, passengers often have to tote carry-on luggage through a maze of stairways and long passageways to reach the departure gate of their connecting flights. And consider the frustrations facing passengers trying to retrieve checked luggage from a baggage-handling operation that was designed for circa 1960s air travelers!

Designing for the future often can translate into financial savings. Take, for example, a church that locates in a developing community but does not have the resources to build the sanctuary it would like to have plus the necessary ancillary facilities it will need. Good design might lead the congregation to build a modest structure that can be used as a temporary sanctuary but that later can be adapted easily and economically to serve as a fellowship hall, a Sunday school, and even a day care facility to meet the needs of a growing community.

In other instances, designing for the future may require additional expenses initially, but it will save financial resources in the long run—and it may, in fact, provide for growth that might not otherwise be possible. For example, cities often invest in oversized water and wastewater treatment plants, anticipating future growth.

Aesthetic Factors

Let's compare two shopping trips to successful upscale clothing stores. First, we'll go to an upscale department store such as Nordstrom's. As we enter the women's fine dresses department, we are aware of the carpeting beneath our feet, the ample space between clothing racks, the lack of crowding of dresses on the racks, the complimentary lighting, and, most certainly, the very well groomed salesperson who is ready to serve us immediately. The fitting rooms are located in an area separate from the display area; they are roomy and carpeted, and they have mirrors on three sides so you can appreciate every aspect of your appearance. Everything in the department is designed to give us a sense of elegance and attention to our needs.

Our second trip takes us to an Eddie Bauer Factory Outlet store. Within just a few steps of the entrance, we are confronted with tables piled high with a vast assortment of clothing. Along the walls and among the tables are racks packed as full as possible with more clothing. Only a maze of narrow pathways is visible around the floor. Salespersons are stationed at cash register counters and are available to help when you seek them out. The fitting rooms are small "stalls" on the showroom floor and are equipped with only one mirror. (It helps to shop here with a companion who can give you the advantage of "hindsight!") This is a large warehouse type of store rather than a modest-sized, serene, elegant place to shop. But the outlet store offers great bargains in exchange for sacrificing plushness and lots of personal attention.

Both stores offer attractive, quality clothing, but we feel very differently in each one, and their respective designs have played an important part in shaping our attitudes. Clearly, the aesthetic aspects of a design have a marked effect on the consumer's perceptions and behaviors, but they also impact the employees and the service they provide. Lack of attention to aesthetic factors during the design phase can lead to surly service rather than to "service with a smile."

The Community and Environment

The design of a service facility may be of greatest importance where it impacts the community and its environment. Will the planned church allow enough space for parking, or will neighbors find it impossible to enter or exit their properties during church activities? Can Priscilla Price design a boarding kennel facility that will not hound neighboring businesses with undue noise and odor? How can a community design a detention facility that will provide adequately for the inmates' health and welfare and still ensure the safety of the town's residents? Has the local dry cleaner designed his or her facility to keep hazardous chemicals out of the local environment?

These questions illustrate how crucial the facility design can be in gaining community acceptance of the service. Zoning regulations and many public interest groups can also provide guidance in designing service facilities that are compatible with their communities and environment.

LAYOUT

In addition to facility design, the layout, or arrangement, of the service delivery system is important for the convenience of the customer as well as the service provider. No customer should be subjected to unnecessary aggravation from a poorly planned facility. Furthermore, a poor layout can be costly in time wasted when service workers are engaged in unproductive activity. Consider the following experience of a citizen attempting to secure a building permit.

Suppose you want to build the "home of your dreams." You have ordered plan #1006BHG from Columbia Design Group, Portland, Oregon, for its "Cozy Cottage." You have found just the right spot of land overlooking the lake and are eager to get that hammer in your hand. All set to go? Well, not quite. There is just one small detail—a building permit. You make a quick phone call to the county's building inspection department and are advised that it's very easy: "Just come downtown to our office and pay $200, and we'll take care of you." No problem; you can handle that.

You arrive at the county services building, check in hand. (You did park in a legal spot, didn't you?) A check of the black felt signboard in the front lobby tells you that the building inspection department is in Office 3 1. (Is that supposed to be 31, or has a little white number fallen off?) Office 31 is on this floor, so you check there first. No, it turns out to be a rest room. You ride up to the third floor and find the office across from the elevator—Building Inspector's Office, a small, dark, dingy, windowless room with a high counter just inside the doorway. A surly old man levers himself out of a protesting chair behind a desk piled with pink, turquoise, beige, and yellow papers. A coffee pot and a mountain of multihued papers are strewn on a table along one wall. He hobbles over to the counter to help you. (At least there aren't 20 people in line ahead of you.) After hearing what you want, he tells you that you are in the WRONG office, that he just assigns inspectors to issue permits for occupancy at the end of construction. You have to go to "the other wing," he says.

"The other wing" requires a return to the lobby, a check of the black felt board, and a ride in another elevator—if it were working. Just inside the door of Office 333 is a sign: "Take a number and sit." Your number is 21, and there are eight chairs facing a high counter. The room is well lit and has ten desks arranged in three rows behind the counter. There are two doors to back rooms on the east wall, and file cabinets line the west wall. Large maps are posted on the back wall. While waiting you observe (many times) the typical interaction between an employee and a customer: they exchange pleasantries; then the employee goes to the first back room and returns with a packet of papers. The papers are shuffled back and forth between the employee and the customer, each signing or making notations in turn. The packet is taken to the other back room and replaced by yet another packet, and the little miniwaltz of fluttering papers and flying pens is repeated to the tune of subdued murmurs. This packet is reassembled and returned to the first office. The employee then retrieves a form from one of the file cabinets, fills it out on a typewriter at one of the desks (three pages in triplicate), places two copies in other file cabinets, and, finally, hands the customer the treasured "Building Permit."

After you witness 20 variations on the same "song and dance," it is your turn. You ask for your building permit. The employee goes to the first back room and returns empty-handed, saying "I can't seem to find your other permits." "What other permits?" you ask. "Why, electrical connection, water connection, and sewage connection permits, of course." You explain that you are building by the lake and will not be on a community water or sewage system; you are going to have a well and a septic tank. "Oh, then you will need to file a geologist's report, a ground percolation test report, and permits to install a septic tank and a leachfield before we can issue your building permit—and you'll still need to get the electrical permit. I can tell you where to go, if you like."

The episode above illustrates the effect of design and layout on service providers and consumers. Providers' attitudes and responsiveness can be profoundly influenced by their surroundings and the work patterns imposed on them by the layout of their work space.

Sometimes solutions are relatively easy. In our example above, consider your first stop, the building inspection office. With adequate lighting and rearrangement of the furniture so that applicants could approach the employee's desk, the employee might be disposed to tell the customer how to find the building permit office—and also that preliminary permits and reports are necessary before a building permit can be issued.

We can see other opportunities to improve the service described above. Rearrangement of the work space in the building permit office might allow more efficient service by saving steps and time. These savings would translate into employees who provide service more quickly and, consequently, with more equanimity because they would not have to deal with applicants who have grown surly during interminable waiting. The service could be further improved by posting signs at the front desk detailing what preliminary permits and reports must be filed before the building permit can be issued. This simple measure would benefit the provider and the customer alike.

A larger-scale improvement in layout could be considered. The building inspector's office, the building permit office, and other allied permit offices could be relocated in close proximity to each other within the building. Perhaps some offices could even be combined physically, allowing easier communication between employees on related matters. Here again, customers would reap the benefits of more efficient service, reduced travel time between offices, and reduced waiting time.

Many improvements can be effected with little cost either to the service provider or to the consumer. In other situations, the layout of a service organization may involve significant expense, which would necessitate a critical analysis before implementation. Consider the following discussion and examples of process flowcharting, product layout analysis, and process layout analysis.

Process Flowcharting

A process flowchart is a visual aid used by industrial engineers to analyze production systems to identify opportunities for improvement in process efficiency. The process flowchart is similar in concept to the service blueprint discussed in Chapter 5, except that process flowcharting focuses on employee or customer travel

TABLE 6.1
SERVICE PROCESS CHART CATEGORIES AND SYMBOLS

Category	Symbol	Description
Operation	O	An operation performed by the server off-line or customer self-service. A possible service failure point.
Customer contact	▲	An occasion when server and customer interact. An opportunity to influence customer service perceptions.
Travel	→	The movement of customers, servers, or information between operations.
Delay	D	Delay resulting in a queue and a need for waiting space for customers.
Inspection	■	An activity by customer or server to measure service quality.

distance and the times associated with activities such as delays, inspections, travel, and operations. Thus, the focus is on layout efficiency measured in time and distance traveled.

For manufacturing layout analysis, the production process is broken down into the underlying sequence of operations, with times for each recorded and the distance measured when material is moved between operations. Delays, inspection activity, and storage of material are also noted. A description of the process in visual form helps identify areas where efficiency can be improved by eliminating unnecessary activities—e.g., by reducing the distance material is moved or by combining operations.

Because the customer is part of the process in services, the traditional industrial process chart is modified for use in studying service processes by redefining the customary symbols, as shown in Table 6.1.

Service process flowcharting begins with the observation of the service to identify the sequence of steps in the service. Each step in the sequence is classified according to the five categories in Table 6.1 and listed in order. Draw the process flowchart by connecting the symbols, and note the time associated with each step and the distance traveled for movements.

Example 6.1: Credit Card Processing

For restaurants the credit card transaction is time-consuming for both guests and servers. A new procedure for processing credit card transactions has been suggested, and the benefits to server and guest will be compared with the current procedure. The process flow analysis contained in Figures 6.1 and 6.2 comparing the procedures was reported by Kimes and Mutkoski; it has been slightly modified to use the service process categories shown in Table 6.1.[3]

[3]S. E. Kimes and S. A. Mutkoski, "The Express Guest Check: Saving Steps with Process Design," *The Cornell H.R.A. Quarterly,* vol. 30, no. 2, August 1989, p. 23.

Distance	Time		Activity
			Customer requests check
30 ft.	0.5 min.	O ▶ D ▽ □	Server walks
	0.5 min.	O ▶ D ▽ □	Server prepares check
30 ft.	0.5 min.	O ▶ D ▽ □	Server walks
	0.25 min.	O ▶ D ▽ □	Server presents check
30 ft.	0.5 min.	O ▶ D ▽ □	Server walks
	0.5 min.	O ▶ D ▽ □	Customer inspects, puts card out
30 ft.	0.5 min.	O ▶ D ▽ □	Server returns to table
	0.25 min.	O ▶ D ▽ □	Server picks up card
30 ft.	0.5 min.	O ▶ D ▽ □	Server walks to process
	0.5 min.	O ▶ D ▽ □	Server fills out slip
	0.5 min.	O ▶ D ▽ □	Server processes slip
	1.0 min.	O ▶ D ▽ □	Server obtains preauthorization
30 ft.	0.5 min.	O ▶ D ▽ □	Server walks
	0.25 min.	O ▶ D ▽ □	Server presents slip
30 ft.	0.5 min.	O ▶ D ▽ □	Server walks
	0.5 min.	O ▶ D ▽ □	Customer signs (leaves)
30 ft.	0.5 min.	O ▶ D ▽ □	Server walks
	0.25 min.	O ▶ D ▽ □	Server picks up slip
30 ft.	0.5 min.	O ▶ D ▽ □	(Customer leaves) Server walks

Total time
Server: 9 min. (270 ft.)
Customer: 7.75 min.

FIGURE 6.1
Current credit card processing procedure. [*S. E. Kimes and S. A. Mutkoski, "The Express Guest Check: Saving Steps with Process Design,"* The Cornell HRA Quarterly, *August 1989, p. 23.* © Cornell HRA Quarterly. Used by permission. All rights reserved.]

FIGURE 6.2
Proposed credit card processing procedure. [*S. E. Kimes and S. A. Mutkoski, "The Express Guest Check: Saving Steps with Process Design,"* The Cornell HRA Quarterly, *August 1989, p. 23.* © Cornell HRA Quarterly. Used by permission. All rights reserved.]

Distance	Time		Activity
			Customer requests check
30 ft.	0.5 min.	O ▶ D ▽ □	Server walks
	0.5 min.	O ▶ D ▽ □	Server prepares check
	0.5 min.	O ▶ D ▽ □	Server fills out slip
30 ft.	0.5 min.	O ▶ D ▽ □	Server walks
	0.25 min.	O ▶ D ▽ □	Server presents check and slip
30 ft.	0.5 min.	O ▶ D ▽ □	Server walks
	0.5 min.	O ▶ D ▽ □	Customer inspects, puts card out, signs slip
30 ft.	0.5 min.	O ▶ D ▽ □	Server returns to table
	0.25 min.	O ▶ D ▽ □	Server picks up card and slip
30 ft.	0.5 min.	O ▶ D ▽ □	Server walks
	0.5 min.	O ▶ D ▽ □	Server processes slip and card
	1.0 min.	O ▶ D ▽ □	Server obtains authorization
30 ft.	0.5 min.	O ▶ D ▽ □	Server walks
	0.25 min.	O ▶ D ▽ □	Server presents card and receipt
30 ft.	0.5 min.	O ▶ D ▽ □	Server walks
		O ▶ D ▽ □	Customer leaves

Total time
Server: 7.5 min. (210 ft.)
Customer: 6.75 min.

From a comparison of the process flowcharts, we find that the proposed card processing procedure has saved the server one trip to the table and, thus, 270 − 210 = 60 feet of walking. The server and the guest both benefit from savings in time to perform the transaction, 1.5 and 1.0 minutes, respectively.

Product Layout and the Line-Balancing Problem

Some standard services can be divided into an inflexible sequence of steps or operations that all customers must experience. This is an example of a product layout most often associated with manufacturing assembly lines, where a product is assembled in a fixed sequence of steps. The most obvious analogy is to a cafeteria, where diners push their trays along as they assemble their meal. Staffing such a service requires an allocation of tasks among servers to create jobs requiring nearly equal time. The job requiring the most time per customer creates a "bottleneck" and defines the capacity of the service line. Any change in the capacity of the service line requires attention to the bottleneck activity. Several options are available: adding another worker to the job, providing some aid to reduce the activity time, or regrouping the tasks to create a new line balance with different activity assignments. A well-balanced line would have all jobs of nearly equal duration to avoid unnecessary idleness and inequity in work assignments. A service line approach has the additional advantage of allowing for division of labor and the use of dedicated special equipment, as illustrated by Example 6.2.

Example 6.2: Automobile Driver's License Office

The state automobile driver's license office is under pressure to increase productivity to accommodate 120 applicants per hour with the addition of only one clerk to its present staff. The license renewal process is currently designed as a service line, with customers processed in the fixed sequence listed in Table 6.2. Activity 1, review application for correctness, must be performed first, and activity 6, issue temporary license, must be the last step and by state policy must be handled by a uniformed officer. Step 5, photograph applicant, requires an expensive instant camera. The process flow diagram for the current

TABLE 6.2
LICENSE RENEWAL PROCESS TIMES

Activity	Description	Time, s
1	Review application for correctness	15
2	Process and record payment	30
3	Check for violations and restrictions	60
4	Conduct eye test	40
5	Photograph applicant	20
6	Issue temporary license (state trooper)	30

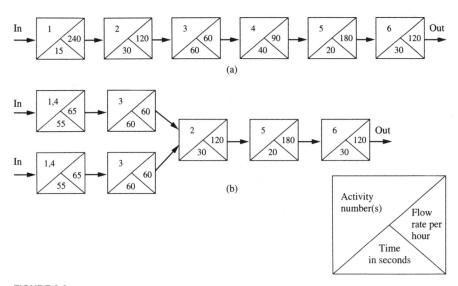

FIGURE 6.3
(a) Present and (b) proposed flow diagrams.

arrangement, as shown in Figure 6.3a, identifies the bottleneck activity as step 3, check for violations and restrictions; this limits the current capacity to 60 applicants per hour. The proposed process design, shown in Figure 6.3b, is able to achieve the desired capacity of 120 applicants per hour because the activities have been regrouped to balance better the work load among the staff. Can you think of another process design that meets the capacity goal but could be viewed by customers and employees as offering more personalized service?

Process Layout and the Relative Location Problem

The building permit example is an illustration of a process layout because service personnel performing similar functions or having the same responsibility were grouped into departments. A process layout allows the customers to define the sequence of service activities to meet their needs and thus affords some degree of customization. The process layout also allows the service to be tailored to the customer's specifications, thereby delivering personalized services. The ability to customize the service requires more highly skilled service providers with discretion to personalize the service to the customers' needs. Professional services such as law, medicine, and consulting are organized into specialties.

From the service provider's perspective, the flow of customers appears to be intermittent, and so there is a need for a waiting area in each department. The variability in demand at each department results when customers choose different sequences of services and place different demands on the service provided.

Customers, upon arriving at a particular department, will often find it busy and will then need to join a queue, which usually operates on a first-come, first-served (FCFS) basis.

A dramatic and physical example of a service process layout is a university campus with buildings dedicated to the various disciplines, giving students the flexibility of choosing classes among them. The relative location problem can be seen in the layout of the university campus. For student and faculty convenience, we would expect selected departments such as engineering and the physical sciences to be in close proximity to each other, while perhaps economics and business would be located together in another area. The library and administration offices would be located in a central part of the campus. One possible objective for selecting a layout would be minimization of the total distance traveled by faculty, staff, and students between all pairs of departments. However, many different layouts are possible. In fact, if we have identified n departments to be assigned to n locations, then there are n factorial possible layouts (i.e., 3,628,800 layouts for 10 departments). Because finding the best layout among all these possibilities is beyond complete enumeration, we will use a heuristic approach to finding a good layout in Example 6.3.

Example 6.3: Ocean World Theme Park

The architect for Ocean World is beginning to formulate plans for the development of property outside Waco, Texas, for the opening of a second marine theme park after the success of its Neptune's Realm on the West Coast. Because of the hot and humid Texas weather during the summer months, consideration is being given to minimizing the visitors' total travel distance between attractions. Data showing a typical day's flow of visitors between attractions at San Diego are given in Table 6.3 and will be used in the layout planning.

TABLE 6.3
DAILY FLOW OF VISITORS BETWEEN ATTRACTIONS, HUNDREDS*

Flow matrix:

	A	B	C	D	E	F
A		7	20	0	5	6
B	8		6	10	0	2
C	10	6		15	7	8
D	0	30	5		10	3
E	10	10	1	20		6
F	0	6	0	3	4	

Net flow →

Triangularized matrix:

	A	B	C	D	E	F
A		15	30	0	15	6
B			12	40	10	8
C				20	8	8
D					30	6
E						10
F						

*Description of attractions: A = killer whale, B = sea lions, C = dolphins, D = water skiing, E = aquarium, F = water rides.

(*a*) **Intial layout**

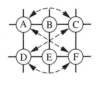

Dept.	Flow distances
AC	$30 \infty 2 = 60$
AF	$6 \infty 2 = 12$
DC	$20 \infty 2 = 40$
DF	$6 \infty 2 = 12$
	————
Total	124

(*b*) **Move C close to A**

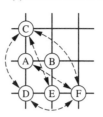

Dept.	Flow distances
CD	$30 \infty 2 = 40$
CF	$8 \infty 2 = 16$
DF	$6 \infty 2 = 12$
AF	$6 \infty 2 = 12$
CE	$8 \infty 2 = 16$
	————
Total	96

(*c*) **Exchange A and C**

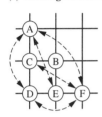

Dept.	Flow distances
AE	$15 \infty 2 = 30$
CF	$8 \infty 2 = 16$
AF	$6 \infty 2 = 12$
AD	$0 \infty 2 = 0$
DF	$6 \infty 2 = 12$
	————
Total	70

(*d*) **Exchange B and E and move F**

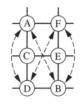

Dept.	Flow distances
AB	$15 \infty 2 = 30$
AD	$0 \infty 2 = 0$
FB	$8 \infty 2 = 16$
FD	$6 \infty 2 = 12$
	————
Total	58

FIGURE 6.4
Relative locations developed using operations sequence analysis.

A heuristic called *operations sequence analysis* will be used to identify a good layout for this relative location problem.[4] The method uses as input the matrix of flows between departments and a grid showing the geographic center location for department assignments. In Table 6.3 we have created a triangularized form of the original flow matrix to sum the flows in either direction because we are interested only in the total.

The heuristic begins with an initial layout, shown on the grid in Figure 6.4*a*. This initial layout is arbitrary but could be based on judgment or on past experience. For *nonadjacent* attractions, the flow between them is multiplied by the number of grids separating the attractions. Note that we have assumed that diagonal separation is approximately equal to the distance of a grid side instead of using the Pythagorean theorem. These products are summed to arrive at a total flow distance of 124 for this initial layout. Considering the large contribution made to this sum by the separation of attractions A and C, we decide to move C adjacent to A to form the revised layout shown in Figure 6.4*b*. The revised layout shown in Figure 6.4*c* is the result of exchanging attractions A and C. The final layout in Figure 6.4*d* is created by exchanging attractions B and E and moving attraction F to form a rectangular space. By making high-flow attractions adjacent, we have reduced total nonadjacent flow distance to a value of 58 for our final layout as shown in Figure 6.5.

[4]Elwood S. Buffa, "Sequence Analysis for Functional Layouts," *Journal of Industrial Engineering,* vol. 6, no. 2, March–April 1955, pp. 12–13.

FIGURE 6.5
Final site plan for Ocean World theme park. [*Map by Kate O'Brien, Desert Tale Graphics.*]

The departmental exchange logic of operations sequence analysis was incorporated into a computer program known as CRAFT (Computerized Relative Allocation of Facilities Technique).[5] CRAFT requires the following inputs: an interdepartmental flow matrix, a cost matrix (cost/unit/unit distance moved), and an initial layout with exact departmental dimensions filling the space available. CRAFT can incorporate some constraints such as fixing the location of a department. The program logic depicted in Figure 6.6 shows the incremental nature of the heuristic, which selects at each iteration the two departments that, if exchanged, will yield the most improvement in flow distance reduction. This process layout program can be found in personal computer software such as *QS: Quantitative Systems, Version 3.0.*[6]

As can be seen in the bibliography at the end of this chapter, reports indicate the extensive use of CRAFT in service organization layout planning—for example, in insurance offices, hospitals, movie studios, and universities.

An objective other than minimization of travel distance could be appropriate for designing the layout of a service. For example, if we had a core business with several

---

[5]E. S. Buffa, G. C. Armour, and T. E. Vollmann, "Allocating Facilities with CRAFT," *Harvard Business Review,* vol. 42, no. 2, March–April 1964, pp. 136–159.

[6]Yih-Long Chang and Robert S. Sullivan, *QS: Quantitative Systems, Version 3.0,* Prentice-Hall, Englewood Cliffs, N.J., 1993.

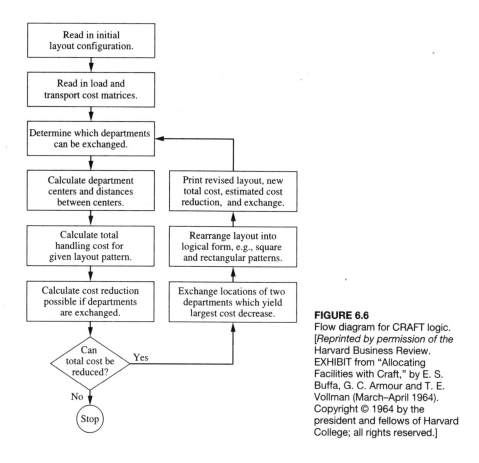

FIGURE 6.6
Flow diagram for CRAFT logic.
[*Reprinted by permission of the* Harvard Business Review. EXHIBIT from "Allocating Facilities with Craft," by E. S. Buffa, G. C. Armour and T. E. Vollman (March–April 1964). Copyright © 1964 by the president and fellows of Harvard College; all rights reserved.]

ancillary businesses, we would want a layout that encouraged customers to browse in these other areas. Consider the layout of a gambling casino. Hotel guests must walk through corridors lined with trendy shops and must always pass through the slot machine area to reach the front door or to gain entrance to the restaurant.

ENVIRONMENTAL PSYCHOLOGY AND ORIENTATION

Orientation is the first behavioral need of an individual upon entering a place. It includes questions of place orientation such as "Where am I?" as well as questions of function orientation, such as "How does this organization work, and what do I do next?" Upon entering a physical setting, customers gain control when they can use spatial cues, along with previous experience, to identify where they are, where they should go, and what they need to do. Anxiety and a sense of helplessness can result if spatial cues are not present or if previous experience cannot be drawn on to avoid disorientation.

Richard E. Wener argues that the causes of disorientation in service settings can be reduced by a facility design that incorporates the following: previous experience, design legibility, and orientation aids.[7]

Franchised services, using formula facilities, have effectively removed the anxiety of disorientation so that customers know exactly what to do. Holiday Inn took this concept a step further by advertising that a guest will find no surprises at any of its inns. The business is capitalizing on the need for familiarity to attract repeat customers.

Orientation can be aided by facility designs that allow customers to see into and through the space. Layouts for banks and hotels often use an entrance atrium that allows the plan to be viewed and conceptualized at a glance. Such a layout also allows customers to observe the actions of others for behavioral cues.

Orientation aids and signage such as "You Are Here" maps, if properly aligned with the user's perspective (i.e., "up" on the sign equates to straight ahead to the user) and complete with environmental landmarks, can be effective. Strategically located plants and artwork can also act as points of reference. Color-coded subway routes with corresponding color-coded connecting arrows represent an excellent use of signage to assist in self-service and to promote smooth traffic flow.

SUMMARY

The strategic importance of facility design and layout was demonstrated by the reported perceptions of Wal-Mart and K mart by their customers. Facility design using aesthetics and decor must be consistent with the objectives of the service package. With modification for service operations, process flowcharting was shown to be useful in the analysis of service layouts to identify unnecessary activities, to highlight points of potential service failure and customer contact, and to identify space needs for waiting customers. Analytical approaches developed for product and process production systems were applied to the analysis of service facility layouts. Finally, the psychological implications of poor service layout were addressed, along with the need for effective signage and thoughtful facility design to avoid customer disorientation.

Chapter 7 will examine other aspects of facility location and its impact on creating a competitive advantage.

TOPICS FOR DISCUSSION

1. Compare the attention to aesthetics in waiting rooms that you have visited. How was your mood affected by the different environments?
2. For Example 6.3, the Ocean World theme park, make an argument for not locating popular attractions next to each other.

---

[7]Richard E. Wener, "The Environmental Psychology of Service Encounters," in J. A. Czepiel, M. R. Solomon, and C. F. Surprenant (eds.), *The Service Encounter,* Lexington Books, Lexington, Mass., 1985, pp. 101–113.

3. Select a service, and discuss how the design and layout of the facility meet the five factors: nature and objectives of the organization, land availability and space requirements, flexibility, aesthetics, and the community and environment.
4. Give examples of service designs and layouts that accentuate the service concept and examples that detract from the service concept. Explain the successes and failures.
5. The CRAFT program is an example of a heuristic programming approach to problem solving. Why may CRAFT not find the optimal solution to a layout problem?

EXERCISES

6.1. The registration procedures for students at many American universities are similar. The pattern generally involves obtaining name cards, health clearances, class cards, ID photos, etc. On the basis of your own experience of the procedure and times involved, draw a process chart for the registration procedure.

6.2. Getting a physical examination at a physician's office involves a series of steps. The table below lists the activities and their average times. The activities can occur in any order, but the doctor's consultation must be the last activity. Three nurses are assigned to perform activities 1, 2, and 4.

Activity	Average time, min
1. Blood pressure, wt., temp.	6
2. Medical history	20
3. Doctor's checkup	18
4. Lab work	10
5. Doctor's consultation	12

   a. What is the bottleneck activity and the maximum number of patients that can be seen per hour?
   b. Suggest a reallocation of nursing and/or doctor activities that would result in increased service capacity. Draw a process flow diagram. What is the capacity of your improved system?

6.3. A school cafeteria is operated by five persons performing the activities below in the average times shown.

Activity	Average time, sec.
1. Serve salad and dessert	10
2. Pour drinks	30
3. Serve entree	60
4. Serve vegetables	20
5. Tally and collect payment	40

   a. What is the bottleneck activity and the maximum service capacity per hour?
   b. Suggest a reallocation of activities that would increase capacity and use only four employees. Draw a process flow diagram. What is the capacity of the improved system?

c. Recommend a way to maintain the serving capacity found in part **b** using only three employees.

6.4. The Second Best Discount Store is considering rearranging its stockroom to improve customer service. Stock pickers are given customer orders to fill from six warehouse areas. The movement between these areas is noted in the flow matrix below.

	A	B	C	D	E	F
A	...	1	4	2	0	3
B	0	...	2	0	2	1
C	2	2	...	4	5	2
D	3	4	2	...	0	2
E	1	0	3	1	...	4
F	4	3	1	2	0	...

Using the initial layout below, perform an operations sequence analysis to determine a layout that minimizes total flow between nonadjacent departments. Calculate your flow improvement.

6.5. A convenience store is considering making a change in its layout to encourage impulse buying. The triangular flow matrix below gives the measure of association between different product groups (e.g., beer, milk, and magazines). A plus sign (+) indicates a high association, such as between beer and peanuts; a minus sign (–) indicates a repulsion, such as between beer and milk; and a zero (0) indicates no association.

	A	B	C	D	E	F
A		+	+	0	0	–
B	.		+	0	–	–
C				+	+	0
D					+	+
E						0
F						

Using an operations sequence analysis, determine a layout that will encourage impulse buying by placing high-association product groups close to one another.

CASE: HEALTH MAINTENANCE ORGANIZATION (A)

In January 1991, Joan Taylor, the administrator of the Life-Time Insurance Company HMO in Buffalo, New York, was pleased with the Austin, Texas, location selected for a new ambulatory health center. (The process used to select this site will be discussed in Chapter 7.) The center would serve not only as a clinic for the acutely ill but also as a center for preventive health services.

An important goal of the HMO was to offer programs that would encourage members to stay healthy. Various programs had already been planned. These included programs on smoking cessation, proper nutrition, and diet, as well as exercise.

The clinic portion of the health center would be quite large. However, certain constraints in the layout would be necessary. Acutely ill patients would need to be separated from well patients. In addition, local safety regulations prohibited the x-ray department from being adjacent to the main waiting room.

It was very important to Ms. Taylor to minimize the walking distance for both the patients and the HMO personnel. The matrix below provides the expected flow between the departments, based on 40 patients per day.

		A	B	C	D	E	F
Reception	A	. . .	30	0	5	0	0
Waiting room	B	10	. . .	40	10	0	0
Examination	C	15	20	. . .	15	5	5
Laboratory	D	5	18	8	. . .	6	3
X-ray	E	0	4	1	2	. . .	4
Minor surgery	F	2	0	0	0	1	. . .

Note: Waiting room and x-ray cannot be adjacent owing to safety regulations regarding possible radiation leakage.

Suggest various layouts, and determine which layout would minimize the walking distance between the different areas in the clinic.

CASE: HEALTH MAINTENANCE ORGANIZATION (B)

The administrator of the Life-Time Insurance Company HMO, Ms. Taylor, was anxious to solve potential problems before the clinic opened in Austin. In Buffalo, where the original clinic is located, the pharmacy had been extremely busy from the beginning. Long waiting times for prescriptions presented a very real problem.

The Buffalo HMO pharmacy was modern, spacious, and well designed. The peak time for prescriptions was between 10 a.m. and 3 p.m. During this period, prescriptions would back up, and the waiting time would increase. After 5 p.m. the staff would be reduced to one pharmacist and one technician. The two had no trouble providing very timely service throughout the evening.

Ms. Taylor became acutely aware of the long waiting times because several complaints had been lodged. Each person stated that the waiting time had exceeded one hour. However, the pharmacy always maintained a minimum of five persons on duty until 5 p.m.

Ms. Taylor personally studied the tasks of all the pharmacy personnel. She noted the time required to accomplish each task, as shown in the study results below. Because the prescriptions were filled in an assembly-line fashion, each person performed only one task.

Activity	Rate per hour
Receive prescriptions	150
Type labels	30
Fill prescriptions	60
Check prescriptions	90
Dispense prescriptions	120

Note: The activities of filling, checking, and dispensing prescriptions must be performed by a registered pharmacist.

Identify the bottleneck activity, and suggest ways in which the capacity can be increased.

CASE: ESQUIRE DEPARTMENT STORE

Esquire Department Store, established by Arthur Babbitt, Sr., in 1971, has shown a recent decline in sales. The store manager, young Arthur Babbitt, Jr., has noticed a decrease in the movements of customers between departments. He believes customers are not spending enough time in the department store. This may be due to the present layout, which is based on the concept of locating related departments close to each other. Babbitt, Sr., is not convinced. He argues that he has been in business for about 20 years and that the loyal customers are not likely to quit shopping here simply because of the layout. He believes they are losing customers because the new factory outlet mall outside of town seems to attract them away with discount prices.

Babbitt, Jr., explains that the greater the distance the customer travels between departments, the more products the customer will see. Customers usually have something specific in mind when they go shopping, but exposure to more products may stimulate additional purchases. Thus, it seems to Babbitt, Jr., that the best answer to this problem is to change the present layout so the customer is exposed to more products. He feels that the environment now is different from the environment of 1971 and that the company must display products better and encourage impulse buying.

At this point Babbitt, Sr., interrupts to say, "Son, you may have a point here about the store layout. But before I spend money on tearing this place up, I need to see some figures. Develop a new layout, and show me how much you can increase the time customers spend in the store."

Babbitt, Jr., returns to his office and pulls out some information that he has gathered about revising the store layout. He has estimated that there are 57

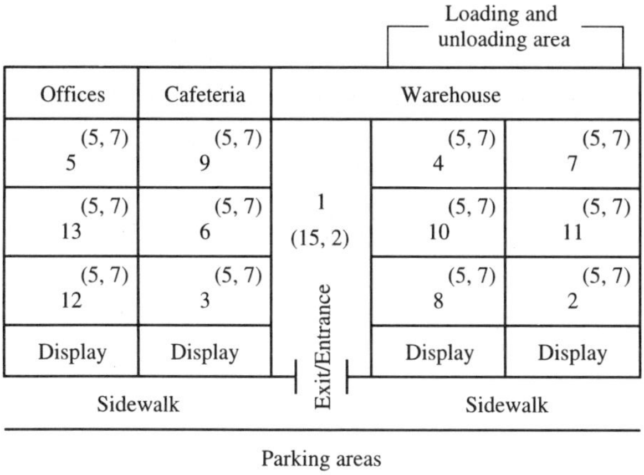

FIGURE 6.7
Current layout of Esquire.
(Figures in parentheses refer to rows and columns.)

customers entering the store per hour on the average. The store operates 10 hours a day for 200 days a year. He has a drawing of the present layout, which is shown in Figure 6.7, and a chart depicting the flow of customers between departments, which is shown in Table 6.4.

TABLE 6.4
FLOW OF CUSTOMERS BETWEEN DEPARTMENTS, IN THOUSANDS

	1	2	3	4	5	6	7	8	9	10	11	12	13
1	0	32	41	19	21	7	13	22	10	11	8	6	10
2	17	0	24	31	16	3	13	17	25	8	7	9	12
3	8	14	0	25	9	28	17	16	14	7	9	24	18
4	25	12	16	0	18	26	22	9	6	28	20	16	14
5	10	12	15	20	0	18	17	24	28	30	25	9	19
6	8	14	12	17	20	0	19	23	30	32	37	15	21
7	13	19	23	25	3	45	0	29	27	31	41	24	16
8	28	9	17	19	21	5	7	0	21	19	25	10	9
9	14	8	13	15	22	18	13	25	0	33	27	14	19
10	18	25	17	19	23	15	25	27	31	0	21	17	10
11	29	28	31	16	29	19	18	33	26	31	0	16	16
12	17	31	25	21	19	17	19	21	31	29	25	0	19
13	12	25	16	33	14	19	31	17	22	15	24	18	0

1 Exit-entrance	6 Cosmetics	11 Ladies' lingerie
2 Appliances	7 Ladies' ready-to-wear	12 Shoes
3 Audio-stereo-TV	8 Men's ready-to-wear	13 Furniture
4 Jewelry	9 Boy's clothing	
5 Housewares	10 Sporting goods	

Questions

1. Use the CRAFT program as found in the personal computer software *QS: Quantitative Systems, Version 3.0* to develop a layout that will maximize customer time in the store.

2. What percentage increase in customer time spent in the store is achieved by the proposed layout?

3. What other consumer behavior concepts should be considered in the relative location of departments?

SELECTED BIBLIOGRAPHY

Armour, G. C.: "A Heuristic Algorithm and Simulation Approach to Relative Location of Facilities," *Management Science,* vol. 9, no. 1, September 1963, pp. 294–309.

Atkinson, G. A., and R. J. Phillips: "Hospital Design: Factors Influencing the Choice of Shape," *The Architects' Journal Information Library,* April 1964, pp. 851–855.

Bitner, Mary Jo: "Evaluating Service Encounters: The Effects of Physical Surroundings and Employee Responses," *Journal of Marketing,* vol. 54, April 1990, pp. 69–82.

Buffa, Elwood S.: "Sequence Analysis for Functional Layouts," *Journal of Industrial Engineering,* vol. 6, no. 2, March–April 1955, pp. 12–13.

———, G. C. Armour, and T. E. Vollmann: "Allocating Facilities with CRAFT," *Harvard Business Review,* vol. 42, no. 2, March–April 1964, pp. 136–159.

Chang, Yih-Long, and R. S. Sullivan: *QS: Quantitative Systems, Version 3.0,* Prentice-Hall, Englewood Cliffs, N.J., 1993.

Elshafei, Alwalid N.: "Hospital Layout as a Quadratic Assignment Problem," *Operational Research Quarterly,* vol. 28, no. 1, 1977, pp. 167–179.

Francis, R. L., and J. A. White: *Facility Layout and Location: An Analytical Approach,* Prentice-Hall, Inc., Englewood Cliffs, N.J., 1974.

Kimes, S. E., and S. A. Mutkoski, "The Express Guest Check: Saving Steps with Process Design," *The Cornell H.R.A. Quarterly,* vol. 30, no. 2, August 1989, pp. 21–25.

Lew, P., and P. M. Brown: "Evaluation and Modification of CRAFT for an Architectural Methodology," in G. T. Moore (ed.), *Emerging Methods in Environmental Design and Planning,* The M.I.T. Press, Cambridge, Mass., 1970, pp. 151–161.

Markin, R. J., C. M. Lillis, and C. L. Narayana: "Social-Psychological Significance of Store Space," *Journal of Retailing,* spring 1976, pp. 43–54.

Muther, R., and K. McPherson: "Four Approaches to Computerized Layout Planning," *Industrial Engineering,* vol. 2, 1970, pp. 39–42.

Norman, D. A.: *The Psychology of Everyday Things,* Basic Books, New York, 1988.

Nugent, C. E., T. E. Vollmann, and J. Ruml: "An Experimental Comparison of Techniques for the Assignment of Facilities to Locations," *Operations Research,* vol. 16, no. 1, January–February 1968, pp. 150–173.

Sommers, M. S., and J. B. Kernan: "A Behavioral Approach to Planning, Layout and Display," *Journal of Retailing,* winter 1965–1966, pp. 21–26, 62.

Volgyesi, A. S.: "Toronto General: The Hospital That a Computer Built," *Computer Decisions,* September 1969.

Vollmann, T. E., C. E. Nugent, and R. L. Zartler: "A Computerized Model for Office Layout," *Journal of Industrial Engineering,* vol. 19, no. 7, July 1968, pp. 321–327.

―――― and E. S. Buffa: "The Facilities Layout Problem in Perspective," *Management Science,* vol. 12, no. 10, June 1966, pp. 450–468.

Wener, Richard A.: "The Environmental Psychology of Service Encounters," in J. A. Czepiel, M. R. Solomon, and C. F. Surprenant (eds.), *The Service Encounter,* Lexington Books, Lexington, Mass., 1985, pp. 101–113.

SERVICE FACILITY LOCATION

In addition to the traditional role of creating entry barriers and generating demand, location also has an impact on the strategic dimensions of flexibility, competitive positioning, demand management, and focus.

Flexibility of a location is a measure of the degree to which the service can react to changing economic situations. Because location decisions are long-term commitments with capital-intensive aspects, it is essential to select locations that can be responsive to future economic, demographic, cultural, and competitive changes. For example, a strategy of locating sites in a number of states could reduce the overall risk of financial crisis from regional economic downturns. This portfolio approach to multisite location could be augmented by the selection of individual sites near inelastic demand (e.g., locating a motel near a convention center).

Competitive positioning refers to methods by which the firm can establish itself relative to its competitors. Multiple locations can serve as a barrier to competition by building a firm's competitive position and establishing a market awareness. Acquiring and holding prime locations before the market has developed can keep the competition from gaining access to these desirable locations and create an artificial barrier to entry analogous to a product patent.

Demand management is the ability to control the quantity, quality, and timing of demand. For example, hotels cannot manipulate capacity effectively because of the fixed nature of the facility. However, a hotel can control demand by locating near a diverse set of market generators that supply a steady demand regardless of the economic condition, day of the week, or season.

Focus can be developed by offering the same narrowly defined service at many locations. Many multisite service firms develop a standard, or formula, facility that can be duplicated at many locations. While this "cookie-cutter" approach makes expansion easier, a problem can occur when sites are located in close proximity and siphon business from each other. This problem of demand cannibalization can be avoided if a firm establishes a pattern of desired growth for its multisite expansion.

Location decisions have traditionally been based on intuition, with a considerable range of success. Although site selection is often based on opportunistic factors such as site availability and favorable leasing, a quantitative analysis can be useful to avoid a serious mistake. For example, being the only store in a deserted shopping mall offers no advantage, regardless of how low the rent may be.

CHAPTER PREVIEW

This chapter begins with an overview of the problem structure, including travel time models, site selection, decision-making criteria, and the estimation of spatial demand. Facility location models for both single- and multiple-facility systems are also explored. These models are illustrated with both public and private sector examples. The models are oriented toward the selection of a site for a physical facility but could be used to deploy mobile units such as ambulances, police cars, and repair vehicles for field service.

We have assumed that the consumer and provider must be together physically for a service to be performed. However, alternatives do exist if one is willing to substitute communication for transportation or to use marketing intermediaries. Such alternatives will be explored as possible methods of extending services beyond their immediate geographic area.

LOCATION CONSIDERATIONS

Many factors enter into the service facility location decision. Figure 7.1 presents a classification of location problems. The broad categories are geographic representation, number of facilities, and optimization criteria. Let's take a look at each one of these categories in more detail.

Geographic Representation

The traditional classification of location problems is based on how the geography is modeled. The location options and travel distance can be represented either on a plane or on a network. Location on a plane, or flat surface, is characterized by a solution space that has infinite possibilities. Facilities may be located anywhere on the plane and are identified by an xy cartesian coordinate (or in a global context by latitudes and longitudes), as shown in Figure 7.2. Distance between locations is measured at the extremes in one of two ways. One method is the *euclidian* metric, or vector, travel distance (remember the Pythagorean theorem), defined as follows:

$$d_{ij} = [(x_i - x_j)^2 + (y_i - y_j)^2]^{1/2} \tag{1}$$

where d_{ij} = distance between points i and j
  x_i, y_i = coordinates of the ith point
  x_j, y_j = coordinates of the jth point

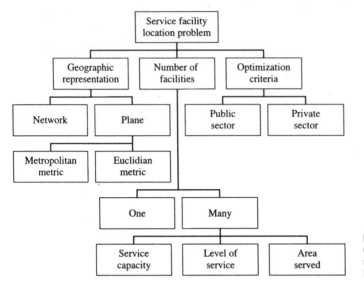

FIGURE 7.1
Classification of service facility location problems.

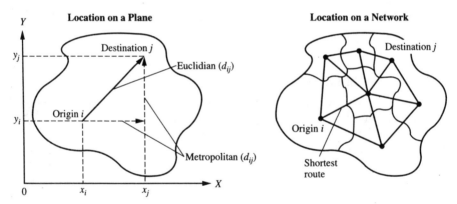

FIGURE 7.2
Geographic structure.

For example, if

$$x_i, y_i = 2, 2 \quad \text{and} \quad x_j, y_j = 4, 4$$

then

$$d_{ij} = [(2 - 4)^2 + (2 - 4)^2]^{1/2} = 2.83$$

The other method is the *metropolitan* metric, or rectangular displacement, travel distance (i.e., north-south and east-west travel in urban areas), defined as follows:

$$d_{ij} = |x_i - x_j| + |y_i - y_j| \tag{2}$$

Using the same example from above for the metropolitan metric:

$$d_{ij} = |2 - 4| + |2 - 4| = 4.0$$

Location on a network is characterized by a solution space that is restricted to the nodes of a network. For example, a highway system could be considered a network with major highway intersections as nodes. The arcs of the network represent travel distance (time) between pairs of nodes, calculated using the shortest route.

The selection of geographic representation and distance metric is often dictated by the economics of the data collection effort and the problem environment. Networks can more accurately represent the geographic uniqueness of an area (e.g., the travel restrictions caused by a river with few bridges or by mountainous terrain). Unfortunately, the cost of gathering the travel times between nodes on a network can be prohibitive. When locating is done on a plane that represents an urban area, the metropolitan metric often is used because streets for some cities are arranged in an east-west and north-south pattern. Both the metropolitan and euclidian metrics require an estimate of average speed to convert distance traveled to time.

Number of Facilities

The location of a single facility can generally be treated mathematically with little difficulty. Unfortunately, the methods used to site a single facility do not guarantee optimal results when modified and applied to multisite location problems. Finding a unique set of sites is complicated by the problem of assigning demand nodes to sites (i.e., defining service areas for each site). The problem is further complicated if the capacity at each site varies. In addition, for some services such as health care, a hierarchy of service exists. Private physicians and clinics offer primary care, general hospitals provide primary care plus hospitalization, and health centers add special treatment capabilities. Thus, the selection of services provided may also be a variable in multisite location studies.

Optimization Criteria

Private and public sector location problems are similar in that they share the objective of maximizing some measure of benefit. However, the location criteria chosen differ because the "ownership" is different. Within the private sector, the location decision is governed by either the minimization of cost (e.g., in the case of distribution centers) or the maximization of profit (e.g., in the case of retail locations). In contrast, we like to think that public facility decisions are made in response to the needs of society as a whole. The objective for public decision making is to maximize a societal benefit that may be difficult to quantify.

Private Sector Criteria Traditional private sector location analysis focuses on a tradeoff between the cost of building and operating facilities and the cost of transportation. Much of the literature has addressed this problem, which is appropriate for the distribution of products (i.e., the warehouse location problem). However, these models may find some applications in services when the services are delivered to the customers (e.g., consulting, auditing, janitorial, and lawn care services).

For the case when the consumer travels to the facility, no direct cost is incurred by the provider. Instead, distance becomes a barrier restricting potential consumer demand for the service. Facilities, such as retail shopping centers, are therefore located to attract the maximum number of customers.

Public Sector Criteria Location decisions in the public sector are complicated by the lack of agreement on goals and the difficulty of measuring benefits in dollars in order to make tradeoffs with facility investment. Because the benefits of a public service are difficult to define or to quantify directly, surrogate, or substitute, measures of utility are used.

Average distance traveled by users to reach the facility is a popular surrogate. The smaller this quantity, the more accessible the system is to its users. The problem becomes one of minimizing total average distance traveled, with a constraint on the number of facilities. The problem is additionally constrained by some maximum travel distance for the user. Another possibility is the creation of demand. Here the user population is not considered fixed but is determined by the location, size, and number of facilities. The greater the demand created or drawn, the more efficient the system is in filling the needs of the region.

These utility surrogates are optimized with constraints on investment. Cost-effectiveness analysis is usually performed to examine the tradeoffs between investment and utility. The tradeoffs for the surrogates are (1) the decrease in average distance traveled per additional thousand-dollar investment and (2) the increase in demand per additional thousand-dollar investment.

Effect of Criteria on Location The selection of optimization criteria influences service facility location. For example, William J. Abernathy and John C. Hershey studied the location of health centers for a three-city region.[1] As part of the study they noted the effect of health-center locations with respect to the following criteria:

1. *Maximize utilization.* Maximize the total number of visits to the centers.

2. *Minimize distance per capita.* Minimize the average distance per capita to the closest center.

3. *Minimize distance per visit.* Minimize the average per-visit travel distance to the nearest center.

The problem was structured so that each city had a population with a different mix of health care consumption characteristics. These characteristics were meas-

[1]W. J. Abernathy and J. C. Hershey, "A Spatial-Allocation Model for Regional Health-Services Planning," *Operations Research,* vol. 20, no. 3, May–June 1972, pp. 629–642.

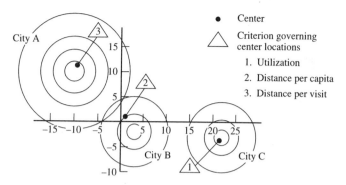

FIGURE 7.3
Location of one health center for three different criteria. [*W. J. Abernathy
and J. C. Hershey, "A Spatial-Allocation Model for Regional Health-
Services Planning." Reprinted with permission from* Operations Research,
*vol. 20, no. 3, 1972, p. 637, Operations Research Society of America.
No further reproduction permitted without the consent of the copyright
owner.*]

ured along two dimensions: (1) the effect of distance as a barrier to health care
use and (2) the utilization rate at immediate proximity to a health care center.
Figure 7.3 shows a map of the three cities and the location of a single health care
center under each of the three criteria. The three criteria yield entirely different
locations because of the different behavioral patterns of each city. For criterion 1
(maximize utilization), the center is located at city C because this city contains a
large number of individuals for whom distance is a strong barrier. City B is selected
for criterion 2 (minimize distance per capita) because it is centrally located between
the two larger cities. City A is the largest population center and has the most
mobile and frequent users of health care. Criterion 3 (minimize distance per visit)
logically selects this city.

ESTIMATION OF SPATIAL DEMAND

The quality of service facility location analysis rests on an accurate assessment of
spatial demand for the service (i.e., demand by geographical area). This requires
the selection of some geographic unit that partitions the area to be served and of
some method of predicting demand from each of these partitions. Census tracts
or their smaller divisions, the block or block groups, are used. In many cases the
demand for service is collected empirically by searching past records for addresses
of users and tallying these by district. The steps that define spatial demand will
be illustrated by an example of a day care center.[2]

---

[2]From L. A. Brown, F. B. Williams, C. Youngmann, J. Holmes, and K. Walby, "The Location of
Urban Population Service Facilities: A Strategy and Its Application," *Social Science Quarterly,* vol.
54, no. 4, March 1974, pp. 784–799.

Define the Target Population

The characteristics that define the target population must be established. For example, if a system of day care centers for all families were being established, the target population might consist of families with children under 5 years and an employable adult. A private system might also include the ability to pay. In this example the target population is defined as families that receive Aid to Dependent Children (ADC) support with children under 5 years and an employable or trainable parent.

Select a Unit of Area

For purposes of accuracy, geographical units should be as small as practicable. There are two limits: (1) the area unit must be large enough to contain a sample size sufficient for estimating demand, and (2) the number of area units must not exceed the computational capacity of computers and facility location techniques. A census tract is often selected as the area unit because demographic data on the residents are readily available on computer tapes from the U.S. Census Bureau. In this study, block groups were selected as geographical units because census tracts were too large and single blocks too small.

Estimate Spatial Demand

Demographic data on block-group residents were analyzed statistically using linear regression to develop equation (3), which predicts the percentage of ADC families in each block group.

$$Y_i = 0.0043X_{1i} + 0.0248X_{2i} + 0.0092X_{3i} \qquad (3)$$

where Y_i = percentage of ADC families in block group i

X_{1i} = percentage of persons in block group i who are under 18 and living in a housing unit with more than 1.5 persons per room

X_{2i} = percentage of families in block group i with a single male head and children younger than 18 years

X_{3i} = percentage of families in block group i with a single female head and children younger than 18 years

Once Y_i, a percentage, was estimated for each block group, it was multiplied by both the number of families in the block group and the average number of children younger than 5 per family. This figure became the estimate of the number of children requiring day care service from each block group.

Map Spatial Demand

The block-group demand can be mapped to provide a visual representation of the spatial distribution of day care needs. The spatial demand map is useful in indicating neighborhoods of concentrated demand that are possible candidates as sites for day care centers. Furthermore, many facility location techniques require an initial set of locations that are successively improved on.

FACILITY LOCATION TECHNIQUES

An understanding of the facility location problem can be gained from the results of locating a single facility. For example, consider the problem of locating a beach mat concession along the beachfront at Waikiki. Suppose you wish to find a location that would minimize the average walk to your concession from anywhere on the beach. Furthermore, you have data showing the density of bathers along the beachfront, which is related to the size and location of hotels. This problem is shown schematically in Figure 7.4. The objective is as follows:

$$\text{Minimize} \qquad Z = \sum_{i=0}^{s} w_i(s - x_i) + \sum_{i=s}^{n} w_i(x_i - s) \qquad (4)$$

where w_i = relative weight of demand attached to the ith location on the beach
x_i = location of the ith demand point on the beach in feet from the origin, taken, in this case, to be the west end of the beach
s = site of the beach mat concession

The total-distance function Z is differentiated with respect to s and set equal to zero. This yields

$$\frac{dZ}{ds} = \sum_{i=0}^{s} w_i - \sum_{i=s}^{n} w_i = 0$$

or

$$\sum_{i=0}^{s} w_i = \sum_{i=s}^{n} w_i \qquad (5)$$

The above result suggests that the site should be located at the median with respect to the density distribution of bathers. That is, the site is located such that 50 percent of the potential demand is to each side. We probably should have expected

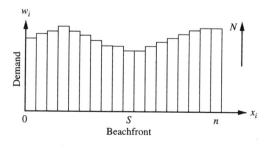

FIGURE 7.4
Locating a single facility along a line.

this because the median has the property of minimizing the sum of the absolute deviations from it.

The result for locating a site along a line can be generalized for locating a site on a plane if we use the metropolitan travel metric. Total travel distance will be minimized if the coordinates of the site correspond to the intersection of the x and y medians for their respective density distributions.

The selection of a solution technique is determined by the characteristics of the problem, as outlined in Figure 7.1. Our discussion of location techniques is not exhaustive, but a few techniques are discussed to illustrate approaches to the problem. The selected techniques are also representative of approaches that deal with the various problem characteristics: single-facility versus multiple-facility location, location on a plane or network, and public vs. private optimization criteria.

Single Facility

Metropolitan Metric   The location of a single facility on a plane to minimize the weighted travel distances by means of the metropolitan travel metric is straightforward. The objective is as follows:

Minimize
$$Z = \sum_{i=1}^{n} w_i \left\{ |x_i - x_s| + |y_i - y_s| \right\} \tag{6}$$

where w_i = weight attached to the ith point (e.g., population)
   x_i, y_i = coordinates of the ith demand point
   x_s, y_s = coordinates of the service facility
   n = number of demand points served

Notice that the objective function may be restated as two independent terms.

Minimize
$$Z = \sum_{i=1}^{n} w_i |x_i - x_s| + \sum_{i=1}^{n} w_i |y_i - y_s| \tag{7}$$

Recall from our beach mat example that the median of a discrete set of values is such that the sum of absolute deviations from it is a minimum. Thus, our optimum site will have coordinates such that x_s is at the median value for w_i ordered in the x direction and y_s is at the median value for w_i ordered in the y direction. Because x_s or y_s or both may be unique or lie within a range, the optimal location may be at a point, on a line, or within an area.

Example 7.1: Copying Service

A copying service has decided to open an office in the central business district of a city. The manager has identified four office buildings that will generate a major portion of its business. Figure 7.5 shows the location of these demand points on an xy coordinate system. Weights are attached to each point and represent potential demand per month in hundreds of orders. Because of the

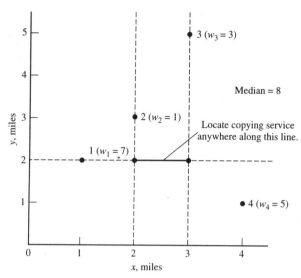

FIGURE 7.5
Locating a copying service.

urban location, a metropolitan travel metric is appropriate. The manager would like to determine a location that will minimize the total weighted travel distance of customers.

A site located at the intersection of the x and y medians will solve this location problem. The median is calculated as follows:

$$\text{Median} = \sum_{i=1}^{n} \frac{w_i}{2} \qquad (8)$$

From Figure 7.5 we find that the median has a value of $(7 + 1 + 3 + 5)/2 = 8$. To identify the x-coordinate median for x_s, we sum the values of w_i in the x direction both left to right and right to left. In the top half of Table 7.1 we have ordered the demand points from left to right, as they appear in Figure 7.5 (i.e., 1, 2, 3, 4). The weights attached to each demand point are summed in order until the median value of 8 is reached or exceeded. The x_i value of 2 is circled to indicate the median location. This procedure is repeated with demand points ordered from right to left, as shown in the bottom half of Table 7.1 (i.e., 4, 3, 2, 1). The x_i value of 3 is circled as the median location from this direction. Table 7.2 illustrates the same procedure for identifying the y-coordinate median for y_s. In this case the y_i value of 2 is circled when approached from either direction. This procedure ensures that if a range of locations is appropriate, it will be readily identified. In this case the location that minimizes total travel distance is a line defined as

$$2 \leq x_s \leq 3$$
$$y_s = 2$$

TABLE 7.1
MEDIAN VALUE FOR x_s

Point i	Location x_i	Σw_i
	Ordering left to right	
1	1	7　= 7
2	②	7 + 1 = 8
3	3	
4	4	
	Ordering right to left	
4	4	5　= 5
3	③	5 + 3 = 8
2	2	
1	1	

TABLE 7.2
MEDIAN VALUE FOR y_s

Point i	Location y_i	Σw_i
	Ordering bottom to top	
4	1	5　= 5
1	②	5 + 7 = 12
2	3	
3	5	
	Ordering top to bottom	
3	5	3　= 3
2	3	3 + 1　= 4
1	②	3 + 1 + 7 = 11
4	1	

Euclidian Metric Changing the geographic structure to the straight-line distance between points complicates the location problem. The objective now becomes:

Minimize
$$Z = \sum_{i=1}^{n} w_i[(x_i - x_s)^2 + (y_i - y_s)^2]^{\frac{1}{2}} \tag{9}$$

Taking the partial derivatives with respect to x_s and y_s and setting them equal to zero results in two equations. Solving these equations for x_s and y_s yields the following pair of equations that identify the optimal location.

$$x_s = \frac{\displaystyle\sum_{i=1}^{n} \frac{w_i x_i}{d_{is}}}{\displaystyle\sum_{i=1}^{n} \frac{w_i}{d_{is}}} \tag{10}$$

$$y_s = \frac{\displaystyle\sum_{i=1}^{n} \frac{w_i y_i}{d_{is}}}{\displaystyle\sum_{i=1}^{n} \frac{w_i}{d_{is}}} \tag{11}$$

where $d_{is} = [(x_i - x_s)^2 + (y_i - y_s)^2]^{\frac{1}{2}}$.

Unfortunately, these equations have no direct solution because x_s and y_s appear on both sides of the equality (i.e., they are contained in the d_{is} term). The solution procedure begins with trial values of x_s and y_s. The formulas are used to calculate

TABLE 7.3
EUCLIDIAN METRIC CALCULATIONS FOR TRIAL LOCATION

Customer (i)	1	2	3	4
Location (x, y)	(1, 2)	(2, 3)	(3, 5)	(4, 1)
Weight (w_i)	7	1	3	5
Distance (d_{is})	1.0	1.0	3.16	2.24

revised values of x_s and y_s. The process is continued until the difference between successive values of x_s and y_s is negligible.[3]

Using the copying service example shown in Figure 7.5, the calculations shown in Table 7.3 were made to find an optimal location, assuming for now that a euclidian metric is appropriate. Beginning with a trial location of ($x_s = 2, y_s = 2$) and using equation (10), we find the revised value for $x_s = 20.78/11.19 = 1.857$. Using equation (11), we find the revised value for $y_s = 23.98/11.19 = 2.143$. Time and patience permitting, we could continue until successive values of x_s and y_s were nearly identical and declare an optimal solution. The euclidian location will always result in a point and only by accident will agree with the metropolitan metric location.

The logic of the euclidian metric single-location model was not lost on Federal Express in its original selection of Memphis as the only hub of its air package delivery network that serves the entire United States. Memphis was considered close to the "center of gravity" for package movements in the United States.

Locating a Retail Outlet

When locating a retail outlet, such as a supermarket, the objective is to maximize profit. In this case a discrete number of alternative locations need to be evaluated to find the most profitable site.

A gravity model is used to estimate consumer demand. This model is based on the physical analog that the gravitational attraction of two bodies is directly proportional to the product of their masses and inversely proportional to the square of the distance that separates them. For a service, the attractiveness of a facility may be expressed by equation (12).

$$A_{ij} = \frac{S_j}{T_{ij}^{\lambda}} \tag{12}$$

where A_{ij} = attraction to facility j for consumer i
S_j = size of the facility j
T_{ij} = travel time from consumer i's location to facility j
λ = parameter estimated empirically to reflect the effect of travel time on various kinds of shopping trips (e.g., where a discount store may have a $\lambda = 2$, convenience stores would have a larger value for λ)

---

[3]This form of the problem is referred to as the *generalized Weber problem* after Alfred Weber, who first formulated the problem in 1909.

David L. Huff developed a retail location model, using this gravity model to predict the benefit a customer would have for a particular store size and location.[4] Knowing that customers would also be attracted to other competing stores, he proposed the ratio P_{ij}. For n stores, this ratio measures the probability of a customer from a given statistical area i traveling to a particular shopping facility j.

$$P_{ij} = \frac{\dfrac{S_j}{T_{ij}}}{\sum\limits_{j=1}^{n} \dfrac{S_j}{T_{ij}^{\lambda}}} \tag{13}$$

An estimate of E_{jk}, the total annual consumer expenditures for a product or product class k at a prospective shopping facility j, can then be calculated as below:

$$E_{jk} = \sum\limits_{i=1}^{m} (P_{ij} C_i B_{ik}) \tag{14}$$

where P_{ij} = probability of a consumer from a given statistical area i traveling to a shopping facility j, calculated by means of equation (13)
C_i = number of consumers at area i
B_{ik} = average annual amount budgeted by consumer at area i for a product class k
m = number of statistical areas

An estimate of M_{jk}, the market share captured by facility j of product or product class k sales, can be calculated using the ratio below:

$$M_{jk} = \frac{E_{jk}}{\sum\limits_{i=1}^{m} (C_i B_{ik})} \tag{15}$$

An iterative procedure is used to calculate the expected annual profit for each potential site for various possible store sizes at the site. Net operating profit before taxes is calculated as a percentage of sales adjusted for the size of the store. The result is a list of potential sites, with the store size at each that maximizes profit. All that remains is to negotiate a real estate deal for the site that comes closest to maximizing annual profit.

Returning to Example 7.1: Copying Service

Let us assume that a copying service is currently located at $(x = 2, y = 2)$, as shown by the dot in Figure 7.5 at the far left end of the optimal line. Further, assume that each customer order represents an expenditure of approximately

[4]David L. Huff, "A Programmed Solution for Approximating an Optimum Retail Location," *Land Economics*, August 1966, pp. 293–303.

$10. Because convenience would be an important customer criterion, let us assume that $\lambda = 2$. If we wish to open a new store at location $(x = 3, y = 2)$ (i.e., at the far right dot on the optimal line), but with twice the capacity of the existing copying center, how much market share would we expect to capture? Using the Huff model, the calculations shown in Tables 7.4 to 7.7 are made.

TABLE 7.4
TRAVEL DISTANCE IN MILES (T_{ij}) [USING METROPOLITAN METRIC]

	Customer location (i)			
Site (j)	1	2	3	4
Proposed (3, 2)	2	2	3	3
Existing (2, 2)	1	1	4	3

TABLE 7.5
ATTRACTION (A_{ij})

	Customer location (i)			
Site (j)	1	2	3	4
Proposed $(S_1 = 2)$	0.5	0.5	0.222	0.5
Existing $(S_2 = 1)$	1.0	1.0	0.0625	0.111
Total attraction	1.5	1.5	0.2845	0.611

TABLE 7.6
PROBABILITY (P_{ij})

	Customer location (i)			
Site (j)	1	2	3	4
Proposed	.33	.33	.78	.82
Existing	.67	.67	.22	.18

TABLE 7.7
MONTHLY EXPENDITURES (E_{jk}) AND MARKET SHARE (M_{jk})

	Customer expenditures					
Site	1	2	3	4	Monthly total	Market share
Proposed	$2,333	$ 333	$2,340	$4,100	$ 9,106	0.57
Existing	4,667	667	660	900	6,894	0.43
Totals	$7,000	$1,000	$3,000	$5,000	$16,000	1.00

This example illustrates the result of an aggressive location strategy used by well-financed national retail chains. For example, Blockbuster Video, as the name might imply, has a reputation of moving into a community with supersized stores and driving out small, locally operated video rental establishments.

Multiple Facilities

Location Set Covering Problem The difficulty of evaluating public facility location decisions has resulted in a search for surrogate, or substitute, measures of the benefit of the facility location. One such measure is the distance that the most distant customer would have to travel to reach the facility. This is known as the *maximal service distance.* We want to find the minimum number and location of facilities that will serve all demand points within some specified maximal service distance. This is known as the *location set covering problem.*

Example 7.2: Rural Medical Clinics

A state department of health is concerned about the lack of medical care in rural areas. A group of nine communities has been selected for a pilot program in which medical clinics will be opened to serve primary health needs. It is hoped that every community will be within 30 miles of at least one clinic. The planners would like to determine the number of clinics required and their locations. Any community can serve as a potential clinic site except community 6 because facilities are unavailable there. Figure 7.6 shows a network identifying the cities as numbered circles. Lines drawn between the sites show the travel distances in miles.

The problem is approached by first identifying for each community the other communities that can be reached from it within the 30-mile travel limit. Beginning with community 1, we see from Figure 7.6 that communities 2, 3, and 4 can be reached within the 30-mile travel distance limit. The results of similar inspections for each community are reported in the second column of Table 7.8 as the set of communities served from each site. An equivalent

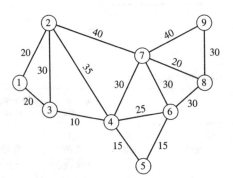

FIGURE 7.6
Travel network for rural area.

TABLE 7.8
RANGE OF SERVICE FOR POTENTIAL SITES

Community	Set of communities served from site	Potential sites that could serve the community*
1	1, 2, 3, 4	1, 2, 3, 4
2	1, 2, 3	(1, 2, 3)†
3	1, 2, 3, 4, 5	1, 2, 3, 4, 5
4	1, 3, 4, 5, 6, 7	1, 3, 4, 5, 7
5	3, 4, 5, 6	(3, 4, 5)†
6	4, 5, 6, 7, 8	4, 5, 7, 8
7	4, 6, 7, 8	(4, 7, 8)†
8	6, 7, 8, 9	7, 8, 9
9	8, 9	(8, 9)†

*Community 6 cannot serve as a clinic site.
†Subsets of potential sites.

statement could be made that this set, less any communities that could not serve as a site, represents the set of sites that could cover the community in question with service within 30 miles. Thus, for community 5, a clinic located at site 3, 4, or 5 meets the maximal travel limit.

The third column of Table 7.8 represents the set of potential sites that could cover a given community. Several of these sets have been placed in parentheses because they represent subsets of other potential locations. For example, because community 2 can only be served by sites 1, 2, and 3, one of these sites must then be selected for a clinic location. Identifying these subsets reduces the problem size while ensuring that the restrictions are satisfied.

Notice that any site common to two or more of these subsets is an excellent candidate for selection because of our desire to minimize the number of clinics to cover all the communities. In this case, sites 3, 4, and 8 are candidates. From inspection we see that if sites 3 and 8 are selected, all subsets are accounted for; thus, all communities can be covered with just these two clinics. We also have identified the service region for each clinic. The clinic located at community 3 will serve communities 1 to 5, and the clinic located at community 8 will serve communities 6 to 9.

The location set covering problem often can yield more than one solution. For example, if the maximal travel distance were set at 40 miles, the following five pairs of clinic site locations would provide coverage: (3, 8), (3, 9), (4, 7), (4, 8), and (4, 9).

Maximal Covering Location Problem A variation of the location set covering problem is *maximal covering*. This problem is based on a very appealing objective: maximize the population covered within a desired service distance.

A travel network, such as the one shown in Figure 7.6, would now be augmented with information on the user population of each community. Richard Church and

TABLE 7.9
SITE SELECTION CONSIDERATIONS

1. *Access:* Convenient to freeway exit and entrance ramps Served by public transportation	4. *Parking:* Adequate off-street parking
2. *Visibility:* Set back from street Sign placement	5. *Expansion:* Room for expansion 6. *Environment:* Immediate surroundings should complement the service
3. *Traffic:* Traffic volume on street that may indicate potential impulse buying Traffic congestion that could be a hindrance (e.g., fire stations)	7. *Competition:* Location of competitors 8. *Government:* Zoning restrictions Taxes

Charles ReVelle developed a greedy adding (GA) algorithm for solving this problem that builds on the location set covering analysis.[5] The algorithm starts with an empty solution set and then adds to this set the best facility sites one at a time. The first facility selected covers the largest population. Additional sites are selected that cover the greatest amount of the remaining uncovered population until all the population is covered or the limit on the number of sites is reached.

For example, recall from Example 7.2 that sites 3, 4, and 8 were identified as candidates for the set covering problem. If we assume that each community has an equal population, then the GA algorithm would select site 4 as the first site to maximize population coverage. From Table 7.8 we see that site 4 covers communities 1, 3, 4, 5, 6, and 7. This exceeds the number of communities covered by either site 3 or site 8. Site 8 would be selected next because it covers the uncovered communities 8 and 9, while site 3 would only cover the uncovered community 2.

SITE CONSIDERATIONS

Selection of the actual site requires other considerations beyond minimization of travel distance. Available real estate represents a major constraint on the final selection of the site. However, as indicated by Table 7.9, many considerations enter into the final site selection decision.

BREAKING THE RULES

Before we leave the topic of service facility location, some caveats need to be mentioned. Several creative exceptions to the assumed logic of the location models presented need to be discussed. Our location objective up to this point has been

---

[5]R. Church and C. ReVelle, "The Maximal Covering Location Problem," *Papers of the Regional Science Association,* vol. 32, fall 1974, pp. 101–118.

focused on customer convenience as measured in distance traveled to the planned facility. The success of the specialty mail-order business of L.L. Bean, located in Freeport, Maine, calls into question the necessity of always finding a location that is convenient for customers' physical access.

In the following discussion we will consider a marketing concept called *competitive clustering* that is used for shopping goods. A strategy called *saturation marketing* that defies the curse of cannibalization has been successful for some urban retailers. A concept of *marketing intermediaries* is used to extend the service market well beyond the confines of geography. And finally, the opportunity to substitute electronic communication for transportation is explored.

Competitive Clustering

The marketing concept called *competitive clustering* is a reaction to observed consumer behavior. When shopping for items such as new automobiles or used cars, customers like to make comparisons and, for convenience, seek out that part of town where many dealers are concentrated (the so-called motor mile).

Motel chains such as La Quinta have observed that inns located in areas with many competitors nearby experience higher occupancy rates than those located in isolation. It is surprising that locating near the competition is a strategy with profitable counterintuitive results for some services. Furthermore, many motels are located at an interstate highway interchange because their market is not the local population but, instead, businesspeople and others traveling by car.

Saturation Marketing

Au Bon Pain, a café known for its gourmet sandwiches, French bread, and croissants, has embraced the unconventional strategy of saturation marketing popularized in Europe. The idea is to group outlets tightly in urban and other high-traffic areas. Au Bon Pain has clustered 16 cafés in downtown Boston alone, with many of them less than 100 yards apart. In fact, one group of five shops operates on different floors of Filene's department store. Although modest cannibalization of sales has been reported, the advantages of reduced advertising, easier supervision, and customer awareness taken together overwhelm the competition and far outweigh the drawbacks. An explanation of this approach is the realization of micromarkets based on customer movement patterns. The strategy works best in high-density, downtown locations, where shops can intercept the hordes of impulse customers with little time to shop or eat.[6]

Marketing Intermediaries

The idea that services are created and consumed simultaneously does not seem to allow for the "channel-of-distribution" concept developed for goods. Because

[6]Suzanne Alexander, "Saturating Cities with Stores Can Pay," *The Wall Street Journal,* Sept. 11, 1989, p. B1.

services are intangible and thus cannot be stored or transported, the geographic area for service would seem to be restricted. However, service channels of distribution have evolved that use separate organizational entities as intermediaries between the producer and consumer.

James H. Donnelly provides a number of examples that illustrate how some services have created unlimited geographic service areas.[7] The retailer who extends a bank's credit to its customers is an intermediary in the distribution of credit. The fact that Bank of America is a California bank does not limit the use of the VISA card, which is honored worldwide. The health maintenance organization (HMO) performs an intermediary role between the practitioner and patient by increasing the availability and convenience of "one-stop" shopping. Group insurance written through employers and labor unions is an example of how the insurance industry uses intermediaries to distribute its service.

Substitution of Communication for Transportation

An appealing alternative to moving people from one place to another is the use of telecommunications. One proposal that has met with some success is the use of telemetry to extend health care into remote regions. Paramedics or nurse practitioners can use communication with a distant hospital to provide health care without the need to transport the patient. The banking industry has been promoting direct payroll deposit, which permits employees to have their pay deposited directly into their checking accounts. By authorizing employers to deposit salaries, the employees save trips to the bank. Bankers also benefit by reduced check-processing paperwork and less congestion at their drive-in teller facilities.

A study by David A. Lopez and Paul Gray illustrates how an insurance company in Los Angeles decentralized its operations by using telecommunications and locating satellite offices strategically.[8] An examination was made of the benefits and costs to the insurance firm when work was moved to the workers, rather than when workers moved to their work. Insurance companies and other information-based industries are good candidates for employer decentralization because members of their office staff perform routine clerical tasks using the firm's computer data bases. The proposed plan replaced the centralized operation in downtown Los Angeles with a network of regional satellites located in the suburbs where the workers live.

The analysis included a location study to determine the size, location, and number of satellites that would minimize the variable costs associated with employee travel and the fixed costs of establishing the satellites. The decentralization plan yielded several benefits to the company: (1) reduced staff requirements,

[7]James H. Donnelly, "Marketing Intermediaries in Channels of Distribution for Services," *Journal of Marketing*, vol. 40, January 1976, pp. 55–70.

[8]D. A. Lopez and P. Gray, "The Substitution of Communication for Transportation: A Case Study," *Management Science*, vol. 23, no. 11, July 1977, pp. 1149–1160.

(2) reduced employee turnover and training, (3) reduced salaries for clerical employees, (4) elimination of a lunch program, and (5) increased income from the lease of the headquarters site. Employees whose travel to work was reduced by at least $5\frac{1}{2}$ miles realized a net benefit over their reduced salary and loss of subsidized lunch. This employee benefit is important in light of increasing energy expenses for transportation.

It was found that the work of underwriting life insurance and servicing insurance policies could be performed by means of a computer terminal. Phone communications were usually sufficient for personal contacts, and few face-to-face meetings were needed. These findings substantiate other studies in Britain and Sweden which indicate that individuals require face-to-face contacts only for initial meetings and periodic refreshing. They do not require continual face-to-face contact to reach decisions and to conduct routine business.

SUMMARY

Facility location plays an important role in the strategy of the service firm by its influence on the competitive dimensions of flexibility, competitive positioning, demand management, and focus. The approach to service facility location began with a discussion of issues that must be considered, such as geographic representation, number of facilities, and optimization criteria and their effect on the location selected. The first step in the facility location analysis is estimating spatial demand. This requires a definition of the target population, selection of the areal unit, and often the use of regression analysis.

The discussion of facility location techniques began with the single-facility problem. Two simple models were presented that identified an optimal location for minimizing total distance traveled using the two most common travel patterns (metropolitan or euclidian). The location of a single retail outlet to maximize profit is an important decision that has been studied by David Huff, using a gravity model to predict customer attractiveness to a store based on size and location. For the multiple-facility location problem, the concept of location set covering is central to understanding the many approaches to identifying multiple-site locations.

A section on breaking the rules presents several location strategies that appear counterintuitive in comparison with the analytical models presented earlier. Strategies such as competitive clustering are common for shopping goods, and saturation marketing has been successful for some small retail outlets. The use of marketing intermediaries can decouple the provider from the consumer. Finally, if the requirement for face-to-face interaction between server and consumer is relaxed, then the advantages of substituting communication for transportation become possible.

This chapter concludes our look at the factors relating to structuring services for competitive advantage. Chapter 8 begins Part IV of the book, where we will turn our attention to aspects of managing service operations.

TOPICS FOR DISCUSSION

1. Pick a particular service, and identify shortcomings in its site selection.

2. How would you proceed to estimate empirically the parameter λ in the Huff retail location model for a branch bank?

3. Why do you think set covering is an attractive approach to public sector facility location?

4. What are the characteristics of a service that would make communication a good substitute for transportation?

5. What are the benefits of using intermediaries in the service distribution channel?

EXERCISES

7.1. A temporary-help agency wants to open an office in a suburban section of a large city. It has identified five large corporate offices as potential customers. The locations of these offices on an xy coordinate grid in miles for the area are as follows: $c_1 = (4, 4)$, $c_2 = (4, 11)$, $c_3 = (7, 2)$, $c_4 = (11, 11)$, and $c_5 = (14, 7)$. The expected demand for temporary help from these customers is weighted as follows: $w_1 = 3$, $w_2 = 2$, $w_3 = 2$, $w_4 = 4$, and $w_5 = 1$. The agency reimburses employees for travel expenses incurred by their assignments. Recommend a location (xy coordinates) for the agency that will minimize the total weighted metropolitan distance for job-related travel.

7.2. Four hospitals located in a county are cooperating to establish a centralized blood-bank facility to serve them all. On an xy coordinate grid of the county, the hospitals are found at the following locations: $H_1 = (5, 10)$, $H_2 = (7, 6)$, $H_3 = (4, 2)$, and $H_4 = (16, 3)$. The expected number of deliveries per month from the blood bank to each respective hospital is estimated at 450, 1200, 300, and 1500. Using the metropolitan metric, recommend a location for the blood bank that will minimize total distance traveled.

7.3. A small city airport is served by four airlines. The terminal is rather spread out, with boarding areas located on an xy coordinate grid at $A = (1, 4)$, $B = (5, 5)$, $C = (8, 3)$, and $D = (8, 1)$. The number of flights per day of approximately equal capacity is $A = 28$, $B = 22$, $C = 36$, and $D = 18$. A new central baggage claim area is under construction.

    a. Using the metropolitan metric, recommend a location for the new baggage claim area that will minimize the total weighted distance from boarding areas.

    b. Using the result found in part **a** as an initial solution and the euclidean metric, find the optimum location.

7.4. A locally owned department store samples two customers in each of five geographic areas to draw an estimate of consumer spending in its home appliances department. It is estimated that these customers are a good sample of the 10,000 customers whom the store thinks it serves. The number of customers in each area is $N_1 = 1500$, $N_2 = 2500$, $N_3 = 1000$, $N_4 = 3000$, and $N_5 = 2000$. It is found that the two consumers have the following budgets in dollars for home appliances per year: $C_{11} = 100$, $C_{12} = 150$; $C_{21} = 75$, $C_{22} = 100$; $C_{31} = 125$, $C_{32} = 125$; $C_{41} = 100$, $C_{42} = 120$; and $C_{51} = 120$, $C_{52} = 125$. Using the Huff retail location model, estimate annual home appliance sales for the store.

7.5. Bull's-Eye, a chain department store, opens a branch in a shopping complex near the store mentioned in Exercise 7.4. The Bull's-Eye branch is three times larger than the locally owned store. The travel times in minutes from the five areas to the two stores ($j = 1$ for the

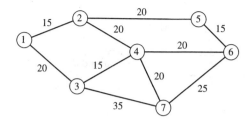

FIGURE 7.7
Service area network.

locally owned store, $j = 2$ for Bull's-Eye) are as follows: $T_{11} = 20$, $T_{12} = 15$; $T_{21} = 35$, $T_{22} = 20$; $T_{31} = 30$, $T_{32} = 25$; $T_{41} = 20$, $T_{42} = 25$; and $T_{51} = 25$, $T_{52} = 25$. Use the Huff retail location model to estimate the annual consumer expenditures in the home appliance section of each store, assuming that $\lambda = 1$.

7.6. Recall the rural medical clinics in Example 7.2 in the text. Suppose that each community were required to be 25 miles at most from the nearest clinic. How many clinics would now be needed, and what would be their locations? Give all possible location solutions.

7.7. A rural volunteer fire department has just purchased two used fire engines that a nearby city auctioned off. The time in minutes to travel between communities in the service area is shown on the network in Figure 7.7.
   a. Select all possible pairs of communities in which the fire engines should be located to ensure that all communities can be reached in 30 minutes or less.
   b. What additional consideration could be used to make the final site selection from the community pairs found in part **a**?

7.8. You have been asked to help locate a catering service in the central business district of a city. The locations of potential customers on an xy coordinate grid are as follows: $P_1 = (4, 4)$, $P_2 = (12, 4)$, $P_3 = (2, 7)$, $P_4 = (11, 11)$, and $P_5 = (7, 14)$. The expected demand is weighted as follows: $W_1 = 4$, $W_2 = 3$, $W_3 = 2$, $W_4 = 4$, and $W_5 = 1$. Recommend a location that will minimize the total weighted metropolitan distance traveled.

7.9. A community is currently being served by a single self-serve gas station with six pumps. A competitor is opening a new facility with twelve pumps across town. Table 7.10 shows the travel times in minutes from the four different areas in the community to the sites and the number of customers in each area.
   a. Using the Huff retail location model and assuming that $\lambda = 2$, calculate the probability of a customer traveling from each area to each site.
   b. Estimate the proportion of the existing market lost to the new competitor.

TABLE 7.10
TRAVEL TIMES TO GAS STATIONS

Area	1	2	3	4
Old station	5	10	9	15
New competitor	20	8	12	6
No. of customers	100	150	80	50

TABLE 7.11
ESTIMATED NUMBER OF POTENTIAL ENROLLEES PER CENSUS TRACT

Census tract	Enrollees, in thousands	Census tract	Enrollees, in thousands
1	5	13.02	4
2	4	14	5
3	3	15.01	6
4	1	15.02	4
5	2	15.03	5
6	1	16.01	3
7	4	16.02	2
8	1	18.03	5
9	2	20	2
10	4	21.01	4
11	2	21.02	3
12	2	23.01	4
13.01	3		

CASE: HEALTH MAINTENANCE ORGANIZATION (C)

As indicated in a case in Chapter 6, Joan Taylor, the administrator of Life-Time Insurance Company, based in Buffalo, New York, was charged with establishing a health maintenance organization (HMO) satellite clinic in Austin, Texas. The HMO concept would offer Austinites an alternative to the traditional fee-for-service medical care. Individuals could enroll in the HMO voluntarily and, for a fixed fee, be eligible for health services. The fee would be paid in advance.

Ms. Taylor had carefully planned the preliminary work required to establish the new clinic in Austin. When she arrived, most of the arrangements had been completed. However, the location of the ambulatory health center (clinic) had not been selected.

Preliminary data on the estimated number of potential enrollees in the HMO had been determined by census tract. These data are presented in Table 7.11. Determine the location of the clinic, using the census-tract map in Figure 7.8.

CASE: ATHOL FURNITURE, INC.[9]

Athol Furniture, Inc. (AFI) is a growing regional chain of discount furniture and large-appliance stores. Management has targeted the small city of Bluff Lake as the next location for a new retail outlet. Although the total population is currently 21,000, Bluff Lake is expected to grow during the next decade because of increased mining in the surrounding hills.

---

[9]This case was prepared by James H. Vance under the supervision of Professor James A. Fitzsimmons.

FIGURE 7.8
Census-tract map of Austin, Texas.

AFI's marketing department did a general analysis of the potential of market expansion into Bluff Lake, but the task of locating the best site for a store has been given to Mr. Carlos Gutierrez. After obtaining the market data on Bluff Lake, Mr. Gutierrez decides that it would be very appropriate to utilize the Huff location model in developing a recommendation for the company's management because there are existing competitors and several potential sites under consideration.

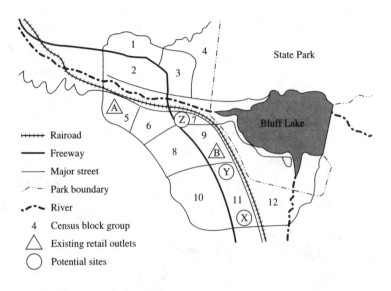

FIGURE 7.9
Bluff Lake.

Figure 7.9 is a map of Bluff Lake showing major streets and highways, the railway (AFI will ship its merchandise into the city by rail from a regional warehouse 800 miles away), Crystal River, Bluff Lake, and the census block groups, which are numbered 1 through 12. Table 7.12 gives the number of households, average annual income per household, and average annual furniture/large-appliance expenditure per household for each census block group.

TABLE 7.12
MARKET DATA

Census block group	Number of households	Avg annual income	Avg. annual furniture/large-appliance expenditures per household
1	730	$12,000–$12,500	$180
2	1130	8,500–9,000	125
3	1035	19,500–20,000	280
4	635	25,000–over	350
5	160	4,500–5,000	75
6	105	4,000–4,500	50
7	125	4,000–4,500	60
8	470	8,000–8,500	115
9	305	6,000–6,500	90
10	1755	18,500–19,000	265
11	900	15,000–15,500	215
12	290	25,000–over	370
	7640		

TABLE 7.13
COMPETITORS' STORE SIZES

Store	Sales area, sq ft
A	10,000
B	15,000

TABLE 7.14
MAXIMUM SIZE LIMIT OF AFI SITES

Site	Maximum sales area, sq ft
X	15,000
Y	20,000
Z	10,000

In Figure 7.9, the letters A and B show the locations of AFI's existing competitors, and Table 7.13 indicates the sizes of these existing stores to the nearest 5000 square feet of sales area. The letters X, Y, and Z in Figure 7.10 show the possible sites which Mr. Gutierrez feels AFI could use for a retail store. The maximum size limit (sales area) of each potential location is given in Table 7.14.

On the basis of average speeds for the main streets and the highways obtained from the city's planning department, Mr. Gutierrez has developed a matrix of travel times between the existing and potential retail sites and the center of each census block group. These travel times in minutes can be found in Table 7.15.

From experience with other AFI locations, Mr. Gutierrez has developed a fairly accurate portrayal of the relationship of the store size (sales area) to margin on sales, expenses, and net operating profit before taxes. This information is shown in Table 7.16.

TABLE 7.15
MINIMUM TRAVEL TIME BETWEEN POTENTIAL AND EXISTING SITES
AND BLOCK GROUPS, MIN

Site	Census block group											
	1	2	3	4	5	6	7	8	9	10	11	12
A	7	5	5	9	1	3	4	5	7	10	14	17
B	10	8	8	10	7	3	3	2	1	2	2	5
X	16	14	14	16	13	8	7	6	4	4	2	2
Y	12	10	10	12	9	5	4	3	2	4	2	5
Z	7	5	5	7	4	2	1	4	3	10	10	13

TABLE 7.16
RELATIONSHIP OF SIZE OF STORE TO MARGIN ON SALES, EXPENSES,
AND NET OPERATING PROFIT, % OF SALES

Sales area, sq ft	Operating data		
	Margin on sales	Expenses	Net operating profit before taxes
10,000	16.2	12.3	3.9
15,000	15.6	12.0	3.6
20,000	14.7	11.8	2.9

Questions

1. Utilizing a spreadsheet version of the Huff location model (with $\lambda = 1.00$), recommend a store size and location for AFI that will maximize expected net operating profit before taxes. Assuming that AFI does not wish to consider a store smaller than 10,000 square feet, assess the store sizes, based on increments of 5000 square feet up to the maximum allowable sales area for each potential site.

2. What is the expected annual net operating profit before taxes for the outlet you have recommended?

3. Try two other values of λ (e.g., 0.5 and 5.0) to measure the sensitivity of customer travel propensity on your recommended location.

4. Briefly state any shortcomings you may perceive in this model.

SELECTED BIBLIOGRAPHY

Abernathy, W. J., and J. C. Hershey: "A Spatial-Allocation Model for Regional Health-Services Planning," *Operations Research,* vol. 20, no. 3, May–June 1972, pp. 629–642.

Ardalan, Alireza: "A Comparison of Heuristic Methods for Service Facility Locations," *International Journal of Operations and Production Management,* vol. 8, no. 2, pp. 52–58.

Brown, L. A., F. B. Williams, C. Youngmann, J. Holmes, and K. Walby: "The Location of Urban Population Service Facilities: A Strategy and Its Application," *Social Science Quarterly,* vol. 54, no. 4, March 1974, pp. 784–799.

Church, R., and C. ReVelle: "The Maximal Covering Location Problem," *Papers of the Regional Science Association,* vol. 32, fall 1974, pp. 101–118.

Craig, C. S., A. Ghosh, and S. McLafferty: "Models of the Retail Location Process: A Review," *Journal of Retailing,* vol. 60, no. 1, spring 1984, pp. 5–36.

Daniels, P. W.: "Technology and Metropolitan Office Location," *The Service Industries Journal,* vol. 7, no. 3, 1982, pp. 276–291.

Donnelly, James H.: "Marketing Intermediaries in Channels of Distribution for Services," *Journal of Marketing,* vol. 40, January 1976, pp. 55–70.

Fitzsimmons, James A.: "A Methodology for Emergency Ambulance Deployment," *Management Science,* vol. 19, no. 6, February 1973, pp. 627–636.

―――― and L. A. Allen: "A Warehouse Location Model Helps Texas Comptroller Select Out-of-State Audit Offices," *Interfaces,* vol. 13, no. 5, September–October 1983, pp. 40–46.

―――― and S. E. Kimes: "Selecting Profitable Hotel Sites at La Quinta Motor Inns," *Interfaces,* vol. 20, no. 2, March 1990, pp. 12–20. Reprinted in *Cases and Readings in Production and Operations Management,* Allyn and Bacon, Boston, 1991.

―――― and B. N. Srikar: "Emergency Ambulance Location Using the Contiguous Zone Search Routine," *Journal of Operations Management,* vol. 2, no. 4, August 1982, pp. 225–237.

Gelb, B. D., and B. M. Khumawala: "Reconfiguration of an Insurance Company's Sales Regions," *Interfaces,* vol. 14, no. 6, 1984, pp. 87–94.

Huff, David L.: "A Programmed Solution for Approximating an Optimum Retail Location," *Land Economics,* August 1966, pp. 293–303.

Jain, A. K., and V. Mahajan: "Evaluating the Competitive Environment in Retailing Using Multiplicative Competitive Interactive Model," *Research in Marketing,* vol. 2, 1979, pp. 217–235.

Khumawala, B. M.: "An Efficient Algorithm for the p-Median Problem with Maximum Distance Constraint," *Geographical Analysis,* vol. 5, no. 4, October 1973, pp. 309–321.

Lopez, D. A., and P. Gray: "The Substitution of Communication for Transportation: A Case Study," *Management Science,* vol. 23, no. 11, July 1977, pp. 1149–1160.

Mahajan, V., S. Sharma, and D. Srinivas: "An Application of Portfolio Analysis for Identifying Attractive Retail Locations," *Journal of Retailing,* vol. 61, no. 4, winter 1985, pp. 19–34.

Mandell, Marvin B.: "Modelling Effectiveness-Equity Trade-offs in Public Service Delivery Systems," *Management Science,* vol. 37, no. 4, April 1991, pp. 467–482.

Price, W. L., and M. Turcotte: "Locating a Blood Bank," *Interfaces,* vol. 16, no. 5, 1986, pp. 17–26.

Quelch, J. A., and H. Takeuchi: "Nonstore Marketing: Fast or Slow?" *Harvard Business Review,* July–August 1981, pp. 75–84.

Rosenberg, L. J., and E. C. Hirschman: "Retailing without Stores," *Harvard Business Review,* July–August 1980, pp. 103–112.

Savas, E. S.: "On Equity in Providing Public Services," *Management Science,* vol. 24, no. 8, April 1978, pp. 800–808.

MANAGING SERVICE OPERATIONS

The day-to-day operation of a service is a constant challenge because the objectives of the organization, the needs of the customer, and attention to service providers must all be managed simultaneously in an ever-changing environment. We begin by exploring how to manage the encounter between customer and service provider within the context of meeting organizational objectives. This discussion leads naturally to the issue of service quality, which is measured by the gap between customer expectations and perceptions of the service. The important topic of service quality is addressed by illustrating a number of approaches to managing service quality, including measurement issues, quality service by design, service process control, and personnel programs for quality improvement.

The inability of services to inventory output, as in manufacturing, creates a management challenge to match customer demand with service capacity. This challenge illustrates the inseparability of marketing and operations in service management. Marketing approaches that can influence customer demand are explored, including a continuation of our earlier discussion of the concept of yield management pioneered by American Airlines. Adjusting service capacity to match demand is accomplished by workshift scheduling methods and the use of part-time employees. However, a perfect match is seldom possible, and this results in waiting customers. Thus, the management of queues becomes an important skill to avoid customer perceptions of a poor service experience.

THE SERVICE ENCOUNTER

Most services are characterized by an encounter between a service provider and a customer. Recall from Chapter 5 that this encounter occurs above the "line of visibility" on the service blueprint. This interaction, which defines the quality of the service in the mind of the customer, has been called a "moment of truth" by Richard Normann.[1] The encounter, often brief, is a moment in time when the customer is evaluating the service and forming an opinion of its quality. A customer experiences many encounters with a variety of service providers, and each of these moments of truth is an opportunity to influence the customer's perceptions of the service quality. For example, an airline passenger experiences a series of encounters, beginning with the purchase of the ticket from a telephone reservation clerk and continuing with baggage check-in at the airport, in-flight service, baggage claim upon arrival, and, finally, the award of frequent flyer credit.

Realizing that such moments of truth are critical in achieving a reputation for superior quality, Jan Carlzon, the CEO of Scandinavian Airlines System, focused on these encounters in the reorganization of SAS to create a distinctive and competitive position in quality of service. According to Jan Carlzon's philosophy, the organization exists to serve the front-line workers who have direct customer contact. His revolutionary thinking stood the old organization chart on its head, placing the customer encounter personnel (formerly at the bottom) at the top of the chart. It then became everyone else's responsibility to serve those front-line personnel who served the customer. Changing the organization chart signaled a move to refocus on satisfying the customer and managing the moments of truth. It is interesting that the implementation required dividing the company into various

[1]Richard Normann, *Service Management,* John Wiley & Sons, New York, 1984, pp. 8–9.

profit centers down to the route level and allowing managers, now close to the customers, the authority to make decisions on their own.[2]

CHAPTER PREVIEW

In this chapter the service encounter is depicted as a triangle of interacting interests of the customer, the service organization, and contact personnel. Each participant in the service encounter attempts to exert control over the service transaction, leading to the need for flexibility and empowerment of contact personnel. A discussion of service organization culture follows, with examples of how founders of successful service firms have established a set of values and expectations that encourages their employees to focus on delivering exceptional service.

The activities of selecting and training contact personnel are addressed next. Then the many expectations and attitudes of customers are explored, as well as the concept of the customer as a coproducer. The high correlation of service quality perceptions shared by contact personnel and customers leads to a discussion of management's contribution to creating a customer service orientation among its employees. A chapter supplement addresses the topic of work measurement.

THE SERVICE ENCOUNTER TRIAD

One of the unique characteristics of services is the active participation of the customer in the service production process. Every moment of truth involves an interaction between a customer and a service provider in which each has a role to play in an environment staged by the service organization. Figure 8.1, adapted from John Bateson, captures the relationships between the three parties in the service encounter and suggests possible sources of conflict.

The managers of a for-profit service organization have an interest in delivering service as efficiently as possible to protect their margins and to remain price-competitive. Nonprofit service organizations might substitute effectiveness for efficiency, but they must still operate under the limits imposed by a budget. In an effort to control service delivery, managers tend to impose rules and procedures on the contact personnel to limit their autonomy and discretion in serving the customer. These same rules and procedures are also intended to limit the extent of service provided for the customer and the resulting lack of customization that might result in a dissatisfied customer. Finally, the interaction between contact personnel and the customer has the element of perceived control by both parties. The contact people want to control the behavior of the customer to make their own work more manageable and less stressful. At the same time, the customer is attempting to gain control of the service encounter to derive the most benefit from the encounter.

Ideally, the three parties gain much by working together to create a beneficial

[2]Jan Carlzon, *Moments of Truth,* Ballinger, Cambridge, Mass., 1987.

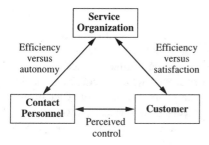

FIGURE 8.1
The service encounter triad. [*Adapted from John E. G. Bateson, "Perceived Control and the Service Encounter," in J. A. Czepiel, M. R. Solomon, and C. F. Surprenant (eds.),* The Service Encounter, *Lexington Books, Lexington, Mass., 1985, chap. 5, p. 76.*]

service encounter. However, the moment of truth can be dysfunctional when one party dominates the interaction by focusing solely on his or her own control of the encounter. The following examples illustrate the conflict that arises when each party in turn dominates control of the encounter.

Encounter Dominated by the Service Organization

In an attempt to be efficient and perhaps to follow a cost leadership strategy, an organization may standardize the service delivery by imposing strict operating procedures and, thus, severely limiting the discretion of the contact personnel. Customers are presented with a few standard service options from which to choose, and personalized service is not available. Many franchise services such as McDonald's, Jiffy Lube, and H & R Block have been successful with a structural organization and environment that dominates the service encounter. Much of their success has been the result of teaching customers what not to expect from their service. However, much of the frustration customers experience with other institutions, labeled pejoratively as "bureaucracies," is the result of contact personnel having no autonomy to deal with individual customer needs. Contact personnel in such organizations may sympathize with the customer, but they are forced to "go by the book," and their job satisfaction is diminished in the process.

Contact Personnel–Dominated Encounter

When the contact personnel are placed in an autonomous position, they may perceive themselves as having a significant degree of control over customers. The customer is expected to place considerable trust in the contact person's judgment because of the perceived expertise of the service provider. The relationship between physician and patient best illustrates the shortcomings of the contact personnel–dominated encounter. The patient, not even referred to as a customer, is placed in a subordinate position with no control over the encounter. Furthermore, an allied organization, such as a hospital in this case, is subjected to tremendous demands placed on it by individual staff physicians with no regard for matters of efficiency.

Customer-Dominated Encounter

The extremes of standardized and customized services represent opportunities for customers to control the encounter. For a standardized service, self-service is an option that gives customers complete control over the limited service provided. For example, at a self-service gasoline station equipped with a credit card reader, the customer need not interact with anyone. The result can be very efficient and satisfying to the customer who needs or desires very little service. However, for a customized service such as legal defense in a criminal case, all of the organization's resources may be needed, at great cost in efficiency.

A satisfactory and effective service encounter should balance the need for control of the three participants. The organization's need for efficiency to remain economically viable can be satisfied when contact personnel are properly trained and the customer's expectations and role in the delivery process are communicated effectively. Our discussion of approaches to managing the service encounter begins with the service organization.

THE SERVICE ORGANIZATION

The service organization establishes the environment for the service encounter. The interaction between customer and contact personnel occurs within the context of an organization's culture as well as its physical surroundings.

Culture

The founders and/or senior managers of a service organization establish, purposely or unintentionally, a climate or culture that prescribes a norm of behavior or set of values to guide employee decision making in the firm. Take, for example, ServiceMaster, a very profitable company that provides hospitals with housekeeping services. Writing about ServiceMaster, Carol Loomis discovered that the company's name embodied its value of "Service to the Master."

> Founded by a devout Baptist, the late Marion E. Wade, the company has always described itself as driven by religious principle. The first of its corporate objectives is "to honor God in all we do." The cafeteria wall at ServiceMaster's suburban headquarters proclaims that "Joy cometh in the morning," and although there are no "Cleanliness is next to Godliness" signs around, the neatness and shine of the office project the thought.[3]

Choice of language is another approach to communicate values, as illustrated by Disney Corporation. At Disney theme parks, show business terms are used because they are in the entertainment business. Instead of Personnel there is Casting. Employees are referred to as cast members to instill the appropriate frame of mind. Cast members work either "onstage" or "backstage," but both kinds of employees are required to put on the show.

The above examples illustrate how an organization's values, when consistently

---

[3]Carol J. Loomis, "How the Service Stars Managed to Sparkle," *Fortune,* June 11, 1984, p. 117.

communicated by management, permit contact personnel to act with considerable autonomy because their judgment is founded on a shared set of values. The values are often communicated by stories and legends about individual risk-taking on behalf of the organization and its customers. Federal Express, with a motto of "absolutely positively overnight," has many stories of extraordinary employee feats to safeguard that service guarantee. Consider, for example, the pickup driver who was faced with a collection box he was unable to open. Instead of leaving it standing on the street corner until someone could come out to repair it, he wrestled the entire box into his vehicle so that the packages it contained could be liberated and delivered the next day.

The organization benefits from a shared set of values because contact personnel are empowered to make decisions without the need for the traditional level of supervision which assumes that only management is vested with authority to act on behalf of the organization.

Empowerment

For years McDonald's has served as the model of efficient service delivery. Incorporating the traditional mass-production philosophy of industry, McDonald's has been successful in delivering a consistent meal to billions of customers, using an organization that could be described as "manufacturing in the field." The discretion of contact personnel is limited by procedures and design (e.g., the french fry scoop that guarantees portion control). Most of the employees are minimum-wage teenagers, and high turnover is the norm. The organization's structure is pyramid-shaped, with layers of supervision from assistant store manager, store manager, and regional manager to corporate "consultants," to ensure consistency of service delivery across all locations.

A new model of service organization is emerging now that has a structure best described as an inverted T. In this organization, the layers of supervision are drastically reduced because contact personnel are trained, motivated, and supplied with timely computer-based information that enables them to manage the service encounter at the point of delivery.

It perhaps comes as a surprise that Taco Bell has become the new service model of "employee empowerment." Other firms adopting this new model include ServiceMaster, Marriott, and Dayton Hudson. Senior managers of these firms all share a belief that people want to do good work and will do so if given the opportunity. Consequently, they have made the following commitments: (1) to invest in people as much as or more than in machines, (2) to use technology to support contact personnel rather than to monitor or replace them, (3) to consider the recruitment and training of contact personnel to be critical to the firm's success, and (4) to link compensation to performance for employees at all levels. In this type of organization a much reduced middle management no longer has the traditional supervisory role; instead, middle managers become facilitators for the front-line, or contact, personnel. More importantly, investment in computer information systems is necessary to supply the front-line personnel with the ability to resolve problems as they arise and to ensure a quality service encounter.[4]

Empowered contact personnel must be motivated, informed, competent, committed, and well trained. Front-line personnel should exhibit the ability to take responsibility, manage themselves, and respond to pressure from customers.

CONTACT PERSONNEL

Ideally, customer contact personnel should have personality attributes that include flexibility, tolerance for ambiguity, an ability to monitor behavior and change it on the basis of situational cues, and empathy for customers. The last attribute, empathy for customers, has been found to be more important than age, education, sales-related knowledge, sales training, and intelligence.

Some individuals may find front-line service boring and repetitive, while others see the job as providing an opportunity to meet and interact with a variety of people. People with the necessary interpersonal skills may gravitate toward high-contact service jobs, but a selection process is still required to ensure high-quality moments of truth.

Selection

No reliable tests exist to measure a person's service orientation; however, a variety of interviewing techniques have proved useful. Abstract questioning, the situational vignette, and role playing have all been used in evaluating potential front-line employees.

Abstract Questioning The questions asked in the abstract interview are open-ended. They provide insights into an applicant's ability to relate the immediate service situation to information collected from past experience. An example of a question that assesses an applicant's attention to the environment would be "From your past work experience, what type of customer was most difficult for you to deal with and why?" In order to determine if an applicant actively collects information, a questioner might ask, "What was the customer's primary complaint or negative characteristic?" Some final questions to evaluate the applicant's interpersonal style could be "How did you handle the customer? What would be the ideal way to deal with that type of customer?"

Abstract questioning can also be used to reveal a person's willingness to adapt. An effective employee will take notice of details in his or her personal life as well as on the job. People who take the time to consider the happenings around them and who can describe the significance of those events are usually able to learn more and faster.

Because of their nature and preparation for the interview, some applicants will be better able than others to talk extensively about their past experiences. Careful

[4]L. A. Schlesinger and J. L. Heskett, "The Service-Driven Service Company," *Harvard Business Review*, September–October 1991, p. 72.

listening and probing by the interviewer for the substance of an answer to an abstract question will lessen the possibility of being deceived with puffery. Finally, it must be noted that there is no assurance that the ability to reflect on past events will necessarily guarantee that perceptiveness and flexibility will transfer to the job.

Situational Vignette   A situational vignette interview requires the applicant to answer questions regarding a specific situation. For example, consider the following situational vignette:

> The day after a catering service has catered a large party, a customer returns some small cakes, claiming that they were stale. Even though the man is demanding a refund, he is so soft-spoken and timid that you can hardly hear him across the counter. You know that your business did not make those cakes, because they don't look like your chef's work. What would you do?

Presenting a situation like this may reveal information regarding an applicant's instincts, interpersonal capabilities, common sense, and judgment. In order to gain more information about a candidate's adaptability, further questions about the situation can be asked: "How would you handle the man if, suddenly, he were to become irate and insistent? What steps would you take to remedy the situation?"

Situational vignettes provide an opportunity to determine whether applicants are able to "think on their feet." However, an applicant with good communication skills still may not indicate clearly a genuine desire to serve customers and an empathic nature. Again, the interviewer must pay close attention to the substance of an applicant's response in addition to the way it is delivered.

Role Playing   This interviewing technique requires applicants to participate in a simulated situation and to react as if this service environment were real. Role playing is often used in the final phase of recruitment, and others in the organization are asked to cooperate by posing as "actors" for the situation.

Role playing provides a way for an interviewer to observe an applicant under stress. Interviewers using the role-playing technique may probe and change the situation as the session progresses. This method allows for more realistic responses than does either the abstract questioning or situational vignette interview. Applicants are required to use their own words and react to the immediate situation instead of describing them.

Although role playing provides an excellent opportunity to observe a candidate's strengths and weaknesses in a realistic customer encounter, direct comparison of applicants is difficult. Role playing does require careful scripting, and the "actors" need to rehearse their roles prior to the interview session.

Training

Most training manuals and employee handbooks for customer contact personnel are devoted to explaining the technical skills needed to perform the jobs. For

TABLE 8.1
DIFFICULTIES WITH INTERACTIONS BETWEEN CUSTOMERS AND
CONTACT PERSONNEL

Unrealistic customer expectations	Unexpected service failure
1. Unreasonable demands	1. Unavailable service
2. Demands against policies	2. Slow performance
3. Unacceptable treatment of employees	3. Unacceptable service
4. Drunkenness	
5. Breaking of societal norms	
6. Special-needs customers	

Source: Adapted from J. D. Nyquist, M. J. Bitner, and B. H. Booms, "Identifying Communication Difficulties in the Service Encounter: A Critical Incident Approach," in J. A. Czepiel, M. R. Solomon, and C. F. Surprenant (eds.) *The Service Encounter,* Lexington Books, Lexington, Mass., 1985, chap. 13, pp. 195–212.

example, they often detail explicitly how to fill out guest reports, use cash registers, dress properly, and enforce safety requirements, but customer interaction skills are dismissed with a comment to be pleasant and smile.

Research has found that difficulties with interactions between customers and contact personnel fall into two major groups and nine categories, as shown in Table 8.1.

Unrealistic Customer Expectations Approximately 75 percent of the reported communication difficulties arise from causes other than a breakdown in the technical service delivery. These difficult encounters involve customers who hold unrealistic expectations that cannot be met by the service delivery system. Examples include passengers who bring oversize luggage aboard an airplane or diners who snap fingers and yell at servers. The unrealistic customer expectations can be broken down into the following six categories:

1. *Unreasonable demands.* Services that the firm cannot offer or customer demands that require inappropriate time and attention. ("I want to carry all my luggage on board" or "Please sit with me; I'm afraid of flying.")

2. *Demands against policies.* Requests that are impossible to fulfill because of safety regulations, laws, or company policies. ("We've been waiting an hour for takeoff, and I must have my smoke" or "Our party of ten wants separate checks for the meal.")

3. *Unacceptable treatment of employees.* Mistreatment of employees with verbal or physical abuse. ("You idiot! Where is my drink?" or a diner pinching a waitress.)

4. *Drunkenness.* Intoxicated customer requiring special attention. ("Bring me another drink!" or an intoxicated passenger who requires assistance to get off the plane.)

5. *Breaking of societal norms.* Customers breaking societal norms in general. ("We can't sleep because of the loud TV in the next apartment" or guests swimming nude in the pool.)

6. *Special-needs customers.* Special attention to customers with psychological, medical, or language difficulties. ("My wife is hemorrhaging" or "Wieviel kostet das?")

Unexpected Service Failure A failure in the service delivery system places a communication burden on the contact personnel. Service failures provide a unique opportunity for contact personnel to demonstrate innovation and flexibility in their recovery. Three categories of service failures can be identified:

1. *Unavailable service.* Services that are normally available or expected are lacking. ("I reserved a table by the window" or "Why is the ATM out of order?")

2. *Slow performance.* Service is unusually slow, creating excessive customer waiting. ("Why hasn't our plane arrived?" or "We've been here for an hour, and no one has taken our order.")

3. *Unacceptable service.* Service does not meet acceptable standards. ("My seat doesn't recline" or "Eeegads, there's a hair in my soup!")

Unavoidable communication difficulties with customers require contact personnel whose training and interpersonal skills can keep a bad situation from becoming worse. Programs can be developed to train contact personnel to use prescribed responses in given situations. For example, when faced with unreasonable demands, as illustrated above for category 1 difficulties, the server can appeal to the customer's sense of fairness by pointing out that the needs of other customers will be jeopardized. Actual scripts can be developed and rehearsed for each anticipated situation. For example, in response to "I want to carry all my luggage on board," the employee need only say, "I'm very sorry, but federal safety regulations permit a passenger only two carry-on pieces small enough to be stored under the seat or overhead. May I check your larger pieces all the way to your final destination?"

Another approach involves general training in communication skills. This approach should help contact personnel to anticipate the types of exchanges they might encounter, to expand their repertoire of possible responses, and to develop decision rules for choosing appropriate responses to a given situation. Role playing can provide an ideal setting for gaining this communication experience. Contact personnel who are well trained will be able to control the service encounter in a professional manner, and the result will be increased satisfaction for the customer and decreased stress and frustration for the provider.

THE CUSTOMER

Every purchase is an event of some importance for the customer, while the same transaction usually is routine for the service provider. The emotional involvement associated with the routine purchase of gasoline at a self-serve station or an overnight stay at a budget hotel is minor. But consider the very personal and dramatic roles played by a customer taking an exotic vacation or seeking medical treatment. Unfortunately, it is very difficult for the bored contact personnel, who see hundreds of customers a week, to maintain a corresponding level of emotional commitment.

Expectations and Attitudes

Service customers are motivated to look for a service much as they would for a product, and similarly, their expectations govern their shopping attitudes. Gregory Stone developed a now famous topology in which shopping-goods customers were classified into four groups. The definitions that follow have been modified for the service customer.[5]

The economizing customer. This customer wants to maximize the value obtained for expenditures of time, effort, and money. He or she is a demanding and sometimes fickle customer who looks for value that will test the competitive strength of the service firm in the market. Loss of these customers serves as an early warning of potential competitive threats.

The ethical customer. This customer feels a moral obligation to patronize some particular group or firm. Service firms that have developed a reputation for community service can create such a loyal customer base. For example, the Ronald McDonald House program for families of hospitalized children has helped the image of McDonald's.

The personalizing customer. This customer wants interpersonal gratifications, such as recognition and conversation, from the service experience. Greeting customers on a first-name basis has always been a staple of the neighborhood family restaurant, but computerized customer files can generate a similar personalized experience when used skillfully by front-line personnel in many other businesses.

The convenience customer. This customer has no interest in shopping for the service; convenience is the secret to attracting him or her. Convenience customers often are willing to pay extra for personalized or hassle-free service. For example, supermarkets that provide home delivery may appeal to these customers.

The attitude of customers with respect to their need for control of the service encounter was the subject of a study investigating customers' decision-making processes when they were confronted with the choice between a self-service option and the traditional full-service approach.[6] Customers who were interviewed appeared to be using the following dimensions in their selection of service options: (1) amount of time involved, (2) customer's control of the situation, (3) efficiency of the process, (4) amount of human contact involved, (5) risk involved, (6) amount of effort involved, and (7) customer's need to depend on others.

It is not surprising that customers interested in the self-service option found the second dimension, customer's control of the situation, to be the most important in choosing this option. The study was conducted over a variety of services ranging from banks and gas stations to hotels and airlines. Services competing on a cost leadership strategy can make use of this finding by engaging the customer as a *coproducer* to reduce costs.

[5]Gregory P. Stone, "City Shoppers and Urban Identification: Observations on the Social Psychology of City Life," *American Journal of Sociology,* July 1954, pp. 36–43.

[6]John E. G. Bateson, "The Self-Service Consumer: Empirical Findings," in L. Berry, L. Shostack, and G. Upah (eds.), *Marketing of Services,* American Marketing Association, Chicago, 1983, chap. 5, pp. 76–83.

The Customer as Coproducer[7]

In the service encounter both the provider and the customer have roles to play in transacting the service. Society has defined specific tasks for service customers to perform, such as the procedure required for cashing a check at a bank. Diners in some restaurants may assume a variety of productive roles, such as assembling their meals and carrying them to the table in a cafeteria, serving themselves at a salad bar, or busing their tables. In each case the customer has learned a set of behaviors that is appropriate for the situation. The customer is participating in the service delivery as a partial employee with a role to play, following a script that is defined by societal norms or implied by the particular design of the service offered.

Customers possess a variety of scripts that are learned for use in different service encounters. Following the appropriate script allows the customer and service provider to predict the behavior of each other as they play out their respective roles. Thus, each participant expects some element of perceived control in the service encounter. Difficulties can arise when new technology requiring a new or redefined script is introduced into the service encounter.

Customer resistance to new forms of service transactions—such as the introduction of Universal Product Codes in supermarkets, which removed the need for item pricing, and automated teller machines (ATMs) in banking, which eliminated the need for human interaction—may be explained by the need to learn a radically new script. What once had been a "mindless" routine service encounter now requires some effort to learn a new role. The adoption of a new customer role can be facilitated if the transition becomes a logical modification of past behavior. For example, the ATM could be designed to function in a manner similar to a live teller's using computer-generated voice commands and a keypad similar to a calculator. The acceptance of the Windows operating system for IBM and IBM-compatible personal computers (and the earlier Macintosh computer by Apple) can be attributed to the fact that all applications share the same interface; thus, only one script needs to be learned.

CREATING A CUSTOMER SERVICE ORIENTATION[8]

A study of 23 branch banks revealed a high correlation between customers' and employees' perceptions of service quality. Each dot in Figure 8.2 represents data from a different branch bank. Employees were asked: "How do you think the customers of your bank view the general quality of the service they receive in your branch?" Customers were given the following question: "Describe the general quality of the service received in your branch." Both groups graded service on the same six-point scale.

---

[7]Adapted from M. R. Solomon, C. F. Surprenant, J. A. Czepiel, and E. G. Gutman, "A Role Theory Perspective on Dyadic Interactions: The Service Encounter," *Journal of Marketing,* vol. 49, winter 1985, pp. 99–111.

[8]Adapted from Benjamin Schneider, "The Service Organization: Climate Is Crucial," *Organizational Dynamics,* autumn 1980, pp. 52–65.

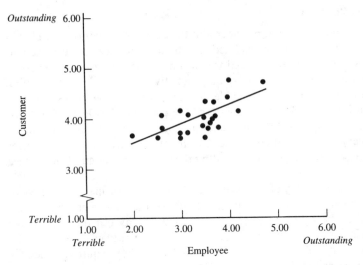

FIGURE 8.2
Relationship between customer and employee perceptions of customer
service. [*After Benjamin Schneider, "The Service Organization: Climate Is
Crucial,"* Organizational Dynamics, *autumn 1980, p. 62. Copyright by
Benjamin Schneider. All rights reserved.*]

Further analysis showed that customers perceived better service in branches
where employees reported the following:

1. There is a more enthusiastic service emphasis.
2. The branch manager emphasizes service as personnel carry out their roles.
3. There is an active effort to retain all customer accounts, not just large-account
holders.
4. The branch is staffed with sufficient well-trained tellers.
5. Equipment is well maintained, and supplies are plentiful.

In addition, when employees described their branch as one in which the manager
emphasized customer service, customers reported not only that service was superior
but also, more specifically, that:

1. Tellers were courteous and competent.
2. Staffing levels were adequate.
3. The branch appeared to be administered well.
4. Teller turnover was low.
5. The staff had positive work attitudes.

From this study it appears that when employees perceive a strong service
orientation, the customers report superior service. Creating a customer service
orientation results in superior service practices and procedures that are observable
by customers and, furthermore, seem to fit employee views of the appropriate style
for dealing with customers. Thus, even though employees and customers view

service from different perspectives, their perceptions of organizational effectiveness are positively related.

A lesson for management is also suggested by this study. The way management relates to the contact personnel (or internal customers) is reflected in how the external customers are treated.

However, as shown in Figure 8.3, some discrepancies between employee and management perceptions of service goals were also evident in this same study. This

FIGURE 8.3
Discrepancies between employee and management perceptions of service delivery goals.
[*After Benjamin Schneider, "The Service Organization: Climate Is Crucial," Organizational Dynamics, autumn 1980, p. 64. Copyright by Benjamin Schneider. All rights reserved.*]

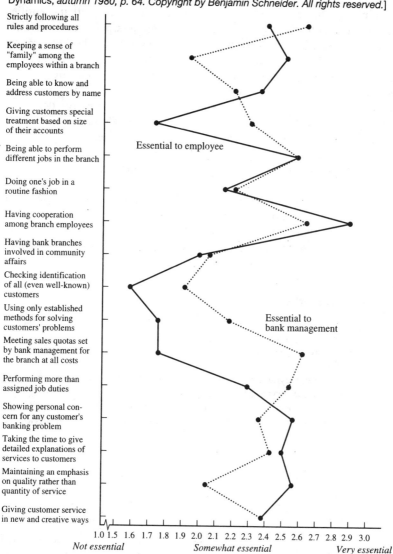

lack of congruence between employees and management eventually affects customer perceptions of service quality because management emphasis in a service organization cannot be hidden from those who are served.

SUMMARY

The service encounter is viewed as a triad, with the customer and contact personnel both exercising control over the service process in an environment defined by the service organization. The importance of flexibility in meeting customer needs has resulted in many service organizations empowering their contact personnel to exercise more autonomy.

Giving employees more discretion requires a selection process that identifies applicants with the potential for adaptability in their interpersonal behaviors. Communication difficulties with customers will arise even in the best of circumstances. Unrealistic customer expectations and unexpected service failures must be dealt with by the contact personnel as they arise. Training to anticipate possible situations and developing "scripts" to respond to problems are two important measures that can contribute to the professionalism of the service providers.

Customers can be classified by their service expectations. Those with a need for control are candidates for self-service options. Viewing customers as coproducers returns us to the concept of "scripts"; in this case, customers follow scripts to facilitate the service, and the scripts provide some behavioral predictability in the encounter.

Finally, the concept of creating a customer service orientation was discussed with reference to a study of branch banks. In this study it was discovered that customers and contact personnel share similar views of the quality of service delivered.

Another aspect of the service encounter is service quality, which will be explored in Chapter 9.

TOPICS FOR DISCUSSION

1. How does the historical image of service as servitude affect today's customer expectations and service employee behavior?
2. What are the organizational and marketing implications of considering a customer as a "partial employee"?
3. Comment on the different dynamics of one-on-one service and group service in regard to perceived control of the service encounter.
4. How is the use of a "service script" related to service quality?
5. If the roles played by customers are determined by cultural norms, how can services be exported?

CASE: AMY'S ICE CREAM[9]

Amy's Ice Cream is a local Austin, Texas, business that presently has six locations in town. When asked about the driving force behind the business, Phil Clay, the

[9]Prepared by Bridgett Gagne, Sandhya Shardanand, and Laura Urquidi under the supervision of Professor James A. Fitzsimmons.

production manager, explained that "while the product is of excellent quality and does come in some unique flavors, ultimately ice cream is ice cream. One can just as easily go to Swensen's or the Marble Slab to get great ice cream. Service is what differentiates Amy from other ice cream stores and keeps customers coming back again and again." And indeed, the service at Amy's is unique.

Amy Miller, the owner and founder, got her start in the ice cream business when she worked for Steve's Ice Cream in Boston, a store whose gimmick was mashing toppings into ice cream. She recalls how Harvard and M.I.T. graduates would work at the store, obviously for reasons other than the great salary and fringe benefits. She quickly realized that this was a business which instantly made its customers happy. Working in an ice cream store was a "feel-good" occupation, a phenomenon that lured such bright workers who could easily make much more money working almost anywhere else.

When she opened the first Amy's Ice Cream in Austin in October 1984, she had two philosophies, one that an employee should enjoy what he or she does and another that the service, as well as the ice cream, should make the customer smile. These philosophies have provided the foundation for a business that is firmly established and thriving almost one decade later.

In the beginning, theater majors and artists were often hired as servers because the idea of enjoying what they were doing was just as appealing to them as making money! These outgoing and creative employees were very skilled at projecting their colorful personalities across the counter. They joked with the customers and interacted with them while filling their orders. Customers were drawn to the fun and variety of the service, which might be described as "ice cream theater." And once drawn, the customers returned again and again for repeat performances.

How does Amy's recruit employees who are up to "performing"? Originally, the employment application form was rather casual, just handwritten and mimeographed. Mr. Clay recalls one day, however, that he was out of forms when a very large man asked for one. The man became somewhat belligerent at being told there were none available, so Mr. Clay whipped out a white paper bag, which was the only writing surface under the counter, and offered it as an "alternate" form. The applicant was satisfied and carried away his form to complete! When Mr. Clay relayed this story to Amy, she said the white paper bag would work just fine, and it became the new official application form. In fact, it has proven to be a very good indicator of whether or not an applicant is willing and able to express herself or himself easily and creatively. A person who uses the bag just to write down the usual biographical information (name, address, Social Security number, etc.) probably will not be as entertaining a scooper as the one who makes a puppet or hot air balloon out of it. Getting "the sack" at Amy's takes on a whole new meaning. Applicants who pass the sack test are then interviewed.

New employees go through an on-the-job training process. One part of the training concerns ice cream procedures so the servers can deliver a consistent product. The other part of the training teaches them to express themselves from behind the counter, which includes recognizing which customers enjoy the revelry and which ones just want to be left alone, and how far the kidding can be taken with different customers. In general, employees are free to interact theatrically with those customers who want to do so.

Amy's operates on an approximate three percent profit margin. Consequently, the servers are minimum-wage, and about 80 percent of them are part-time workers who receive no additional benefits. In fact, most managers make less than $15,000 per year, and there is a $30,000 cap for all employees, including Amy. In view of the low remuneration, how is Amy's Ice Cream always able to recruit the high-quality help that translates into satisfied customers? Well, they do get Amy's Ice Cream T-shirts at cost and all the ice cream they can eat!

But perhaps the major reason is that Amy's is freedom-oriented rather than rules-oriented. The only "uniform" an employee must wear is an apron, whose primary function is to project a sense of continuity behind the counter. A hat is also de rigueur, but the employee is free to choose any hat as long as it effectively restrains the hair. The employee may also wear any clothing that suits his or her mood of the day as long as it is not soiled, political, or excessively revealing.

Employees can bring their own music to play in their stores, keeping in mind their type of clientele. For example, an Amy's located in a downtown nightspot district draws a young, exuberant crowd that would appreciate lively music, whereas an Amy's located in an upscale shopping mall attracts a clientele whose musical tastes might be a bit quieter.

The design of each store and the artwork displayed in each tend to be colorful and eclectic. But here again, the employees are free to make contributions. Amy's employs a local artist to decorate all the stores; still, the individual managers have considerable say in what they feel is desirable for their own stores. Often, the artwork is an exhibition of local artists' efforts.

Everyone does everything that needs to be done in the store. If the floor needs cleaning, the manager is just as likely to do it as a scooper. There is a very strong sense of teamwork and camaraderie. Employee meetings are usually held at 1 a.m., after the last Amy's Ice Cream has closed for the night. Door prizes are offered to encourage attendance.

Apparently, it is a lifestyle choice to work for Amy's. These employees are people who do not want a "real job" where they would have to wear certain clothes and work certain hours, and where they would not have nearly as much fun. Obviously, money is not the major motivation, and it may be that the lack of big money is one of the unifying forces among employees.

Amy's Ice Cream has created what is definitely a "non-mainstream environment," which many feel is responsible for the legions of happy customers who keep the business merrily dipping along.

Questions

  1. Describe the service organization culture at Amy's Ice Cream.
  2. What are the personality attributes of employees sought by Amy's Ice Cream?
  3. Design a personnel selection procedure for Amy's Ice Cream using abstract questioning, a situational vignette, and/or role playing.

SELECTED BIBLIOGRAPHY

Albrecht, Karl: "Achieving Excellence in Service," *Training and Development Journal,* vol. 39, no. 12, December 1985, pp. 64–67.

Bateson, J.: "Perceived Control and the Service Encounter," in J. A. Czepiel, M. R. Solomon, and C. F. Surprenant (eds.), *The Service Encounter,* Lexington Books, Lexington, Mass., 1985, chap. 5, pp. 76–83.

Berry, L. L.: "The Employee as Customer," *Journal of Retailing Banking,* vol. 3, no. 1, March 1981, pp. 33–40.

Bitner, Mary Jo: "Evaluating Service Encounters: The Effects of Physical Surroundings and Employee Responses," *Journal of Marketing,* vol. 54, no. 2, April 1990, pp. 69–82.

Bitran, Gabriel R., and Johannes Hoech: "The Humanization of Service: Respect at the Moment of Truth," *Sloan Management Review,* vol. 31, no. 2, winter 1990, pp. 89–96.

Bowen, D. E., and B. Schneider: "Boundary-Spanning-Role Employees and the Service Encounter: Some Guidelines for Management and Research," in J. A. Czepiel, M. R. Solomon, and C. F. Surprenant (eds.), *The Service Encounter,* Lexington Books, Lexington, Mass., 1985, chap. 9, pp. 129–147.

Carlisle, A. E., and K. Carter: "*Fortune* Service and Industrial 500 Presidents: Priorities and Perceptions," *Business Horizons,* vol. 31, no. 2, March–April 1988, pp. 77–83.

Carlzon, Jan: *Moments of Truth,* Ballinger, Cambridge, Mass., 1987.

Chase, R. B.: "The 10 Commandments of Service System Management," *Interfaces,* vol. 15, no. 3, May–June 1985, pp. 68–72.

Cowell, D.: "People and Services," *The Marketing of Services,* Heinemann, London, 1984, chap. 11.

Davidson, David S.: "How to Succeed in a Service Industry: Turn the Organization Chart Upside Down," *Management Review,* vol. 67, no. 4, April 1978, pp. 13–16.

Gronroos, Christian: *Service Management and Marketing,* Lexington Books, Lexington, Mass., 1990.

Hales, C.: "Quality of Working Life, Job Redesign and Participation in a Service Industry: A Rose by Any Other Name?" *The Service Industries Journal,* vol. 7, no. 3, 1987, pp. 253–273.

Heskett, J. L.: "People and the Service Culture," *Managing in the Service Economy,* Harvard Business School Press, Boston, 1986, chap. 7, pp. 117–134.

Hobson, C. J., R. B. Hobson, and J. J. Hobson: "People Skills: A Key to Success in the Service Sector," *Supervisory Management,* vol. 29, no. 10, October 1984, pp. 3–9.

Hollander, S. C.: "A Historical Perspective on the Service Encounter," in J. A. Czepiel, M. R. Solomon, and C. F. Surprenant (eds.), *The Service Encounter,* Lexington Books, Lexington, Mass., 1985, chap. 4, pp. 49–65.

Kulonda, D. J., and W. H. Moates, Jr.: "Operations Supervisors in Manufacturing and Service Sectors in the United States: Are They Different?" *International Journal of Operations and Production Management,* vol. 6, no. 2, 1986, pp. 21–35.

Nyquist, J. D., M. J. Bitner, and B. H. Booms: "Identifying Communication Difficulties in the Service Encounter: A Critical Incident Approach," in J. A. Czepiel, M. R. Solomon, and C. F. Surprenant (eds.), *The Service Encounter,* Lexington Books, Lexington, Mass., 1985, chap. 13, pp. 195–212.

Schlesinger, Leonard A.: "Enfranchisement of Service Workers," *California Management Review,* summer 1991, pp. 83–101.

———: "Breaking the Cycle of Failure in Services," *Sloan Management Review,* spring 1991, pp. 17–28.

————, and J. L. Heskett: "The Service-Driven Service Company," *Harvard Business Review*, September–October 1991, pp. 71–81.

Schneider, Benjamin, and Daniel Schechter: "Development of a Personnel Selection System for Service Jobs," in S. W. Brown, E. Gummesson, B. Edvardsson, and B. Gustavsson (eds.), *Service Quality: Multidisciplinary and Multinational Perspectives*, Lexington Books, Lexington, Mass., 1991.

Shiffler, R. E., and R. W. Coye: "Monitoring Employee Performance in Service Operations," *International Journal of Operations and Production Management*, vol. 8, no. 2, 1988, pp. 5–13.

Solomon, M. R.: "Packaging the Service Provider," *The Service Industries Journal*, vol. 5, no. 1, 1985, pp. 65–72.

————, C. F. Surprenant, J. A. Czepiel, and E. G. Gutman: "A Role Theory Perspective on Dyadic Interactions: The Service Encounter," *Journal of Marketing*, vol. 49, winter 1985, pp. 99–111.

Surprenant, C. F., and M. R. Solomon: "Predictability and Personalization in the Service Encounter," *Journal of Marketing*, vol. 51, April 1987, pp. 86–96.

Voss, C. A.: "The Service Dispatcher/Receptionist Role," *International Journal of Operations and Production Management*, vol. 3, no. 3, 1983, pp. 35–39.

Wehrenberg, Stephen B.: "Front-line Interpersonal Skills a Must in Today's Service Economy," *Personnel Journal*, vol. 66, no. 1, January 1987, pp. 115–118.

CHAPTER 8 SUPPLEMENT: Work Measurement

TIME STUDY

This technique of work measurement is used to develop standards of performance. Management can use these standard times for many purposes, such as determining staffing needs, allocating tasks to jobs, developing standard costs, evaluating employee performance, and establishing wage payment plans. Recall the standard times attached to critical operations on the service blueprint.

Time study involves identifying and measuring the individual work *elements* of multipart repetitive jobs. These repetitive jobs are also called work *cycles*. For example, consider the responsibilities of the person who serves salads at your local cafeteria. A particular work *cycle* for this server might include the *elements* of retrieving a dish, filling the dish, adding a dressing, and handing the dish to the diner.

Measurements are made with a stopwatch, and the time when each element is completed is recorded on an observation sheet, such as that shown in Table 8.2. The variability of the element times and the level of confidence or accuracy that is desired provide a statistical basis for determining the number of cycles to observe.

Our example worksheet contains a record of the observations of a server who wraps silverware into napkins and repeats the sequence, or cycle, ten times. Each column represents one finished place setting. The stopwatch is started as the server begins positioning the napkin. The first reading (R), in hundredths of a minute on the watch, is noted when the server reaches for the silverware. The second reading is made after the last piece of silverware is placed on the napkin, and the third reading is noted after the napkin is rolled around the silverware. The final reading for cycle 1 is made after the rolled napkin is placed in a box. In our example, the actual readings for elements 1 through 4 in cycle 1 are noted at

TABLE 8.2
TIME STUDY OBSERVATION SHEET
Activity: _Folding silverware into napkins_

Began timing: _2:32_   Study no. _13_   Observer _C.C._   Date: _1/10/94_
Ended timing: _2:35_   Std time _0.326 min/item_

Element description		1	2	3	4	5	6	7	8	9	10	Sum	Avg. time	Rating	Normal time
						Cycles									
1 Position napkin	T	0.03	0.05	0.05	0.06	0.06	0.06	0.05	0.05	0.05	0.04	0.50	0.050	1.10	0.055
	R	3	28	65	95	25	57	85	13	42	67				
2 Group knife, fork, and spoon	T	0.05	0.08	0.09	0.08	0.08	0.07	0.08	0.09	0.06	0.08	0.76	0.076	1.00	0.076
	R	8	36	74	103	33	64	93	22	48	75				
3 Roll silverware	T	0.07	0.15	0.06	0.06	0.07	0.06	0.06	0.06	0.07	0.07	0.73	0.073	0.90	0.065
	R	15	51	80	9	40	70	99	28	55	82				
4 Place in box	T	0.08	0.09	0.09	0.10	0.11	0.10	0.09	0.09	0.08	0.09	0.92	0.092	1.05	0.097
	R	23	60	89	19	51	80	208	37	63	91				
5	T														
	R														
6	T														
	R														
7	T														
	R														
8	T														
	R														
9	T														
	R														

Foreign elements:

Normal cycle time 0.293
÷ [1-Allowance (10%)] 0.9
=
Standard time 0.326

Note: T = time
R = reading

179

3, 8, 15, and 23 one-hundredths of a minute, respectively, after the stopwatch is started. After the server is timed through nine more repetitions of the work cycle, each elapsed time (T) is calculated. For example, the time the server took between the end of the first element and the end of the second element in cycle 1 is 8 − 3 = 5 one-hundredths of a minute, written in the chart as 0.05.

The next step in using the time study sheet is to find the sum of the elapsed times for each element across all the cycles and then to calculate the average time for each element. These average times provide information for this particular server, but if this server were significantly faster or slower than an average server, management would not want to base decisions on such times. Therefore, the values are adjusted by means of a *performance rating* to reflect what may reasonably be expected of an "average" worker.

A performance rating represents a subjective judgment of the person conducting the time study. Expert analysts are trained to estimate rates of efficiency by viewing films of people working at different rates. For example, a poor worker might work at what the analyst would consider to be 90 percent of normal, and the average time would be adjusted downward by a factor of 0.9; a very fast worker might be rated at 110 percent of normal, and the average time would then be adjusted upward by a factor of 1.10. The adjusted times are called *normal element times* and are derived according to the following formula:

$$NT_i = R_i(OT_i) \tag{1}$$

where NT_i = normal time of the ith work element
OT_i = average observed time of the ith work element
R_i = proficiency rating of the employee in performing the ith work element, expressed as a decimal percentage (e.g., 0.90 for 90 percent of normal)

In our example, therefore, the server's normal time for the first element, position napkin, is

$$NT_i = 1.10(0.050)$$
$$= 0.055$$

Similar calculations are made to obtain normal times for the remaining elements. It should be noted that because of their subjective nature, performance ratings as used in the example above can be a source of contention.

The sympathetic reader may already recognize the need to qualify the normal element times that have just been calculated. The server cannot be expected to fold silverware into napkins in a robotlike manner for a solid eight hours during a working day. Allowances must be made for breaks, personal needs, and perhaps other interruptions, such as obtaining more napkins and silverware. These allowances are figured as a percentage of the job time (i.e., a 10 percent allowance would translate into six minutes every working hour). The resulting adjusted times, the *standard element times*, and their sum, the *standard cycle time*, are calculated according to the following formulas:

$$ST_i = \frac{NT_i}{1 - A} \tag{2}$$

$$CT = \sum_{i=1}^{n} ST_i \tag{3}$$

where ST_i = standard time for the ith work element

A = allowance, expressed as a decimal percentage (e.g., 0.10 for 10 percent)

CT = standard cycle time

n = number of work elements in the work cycle

We complete our example time study sheet by adding the normal element times to get a normal cycle time of 0.293. This result is adjusted by an allowance of 10 percent, or 0.10, to yield a standard cycle time of 0.326. Note that the sample time study sheet has a space to record foreign elements observed, such as setting aside a dirty fork. These random occurrences are not included explicitly in the work cycle but are accounted for in selecting the allowance when deriving standard times. The standard cycle time can now be used by management to assign a server sufficient time to prepare enough folded silverware and napkins for the next mealtime.

WORK SAMPLING

Time studies are used to determine how long it takes to complete a task; work sampling is used to determine how people allocate their time among various types of activities. Suppose we are interested in the proportion of time an employee spends at various activities that occur at random times during the workday. Tallying observations of worker activity noted at random times during the day would lead to our desired proportions.

Consider, for example, a server at a Red Lobster franchise restaurant. This server must take drink orders and food orders, serve drinks, dish up and serve salads, grind fresh pepper on the salads, serve biscuits, serve entrees, take dessert orders, serve desserts, and present the check, and throughout, the server must be clearing away dirty dishes and refilling drinks as required. Obviously, there is much variation in the server's duties: one diner may require information on how particular foods are prepared before the order can be taken, another diner may drink water as fast as the glass is filled, some diners may eat quickly and require little attention beyond the basic service, and other diners may request much extra service.

In order to study worker activity as complex and seemingly random as we have just described, we can use a method called *work sampling*. Work sampling is concerned with the proportion of time a worker is engaged in different activities rather than with the actual time spent performing an activity. This technique is most useful in the design and redesign of contact personnel jobs because of the non-programmed nature of direct customer contact activities.

Work sampling involves seven steps, as described by Sheryl E. Kimes and Stephen A. Mutkoski.[10]

1. *Define the activities.* Divide the work into as few categories as possible and into categories that do not overlap.

2. *Design the observation form.* The form should be designed with ease of use and ease of future analysis in mind.

3. *Determine the length of the study.* The study must be long enough to provide a random sample of activities.

4. *Test the form.* Try it in actual practice to see if the categories are well defined and if

[10]S. E. Kimes and S. A. Mutkoski, "Customer Contact in Restaurants: An Application of Work Sampling," *The Cornell H.R.A. Quarterly,* May 1991, pp. 82–88.

it is easy to use and accurate. Does the test application suggest any changes that need to be made in the definition of the categories or the design of the form?

5. *Determine the sample size and observation pattern.* Common statistical methods can be used to select the size of a sample to study and an observation schedule. In general, the larger the sample size, the more accurate and representative the sample will be. A formula can be used to determine how many observations must be made to achieve the desired level of confidence, or accuracy, and a schedule for making those observations must be devised. Details of the statistical methods involved are described later in this supplement in the section called "Sample Size."

6. *Conduct the study.* Observers must be trained to use the form properly. Kimes and Mutkoski also point out the importance of considering the effect that the study can have on the behavior of those being observed. They suggest two approaches to mediate any adverse effect on the subjects: one is to inform them and assure them that they are not being evaluated, and the other is to make very discreet, unobtrusive observations without informing them. In addition, data for the first day or two could be discarded to allow the workers to feel at ease with the data collection process.

7. *Analyze the data.* Again, common statistical methods can be used to calculate the information required by management. In simplest terms, it is necessary only to total the number of observations in each category and calculate the percentage of time spent on that activity.

Kimes and Mutkoski describe an application of work sampling in a study of servers in two different types of restaurants, family and "mid-scale." The major difference between the two restaurant types for the purposes of their study was in the nature and amount of customer-server interaction: they hypothesized that the emphasis in the family restaurants "would be on efficiency with an eye toward increasing table turnover, while in a mid-scale restaurant, the emphasis would be more on guest service with the idea of increasing 'add-on' sales and guest satisfaction."

Their sampling plan, above all, had to provide "a good random representative sample" of servers' activities. Therefore, they selected six different family restaurants and six different mid-scale restaurants and conducted their studies during the peak lunch and dinner times. They observed two servers at each restaurant for at least $1\frac{1}{2}$ hours.

For this study, the servers' activities were divided into the following eight categories:

1. *Guest contact.* Any interaction with the customer.
2. *Walk—empty.* Walking without carrying anything.
3. *Walk—full.* Walking while carrying food, beverages, or dirty dishes.
4. *Bus.* Clearing a vacated table.
5. *Prepare.* Preparing food and beverages before service.
6. *Can't see.* Server is out of sight.
7. *Check.* Delivering or processing the check.
8. *Rest.* Server's break time.

These categories were listed on the form shown in Table 8.3, which was to be used by the student observers. The observers visited each restaurant anonymously to minimize any effect they might have on the subjects. Observations of activities were recorded at one-minute intervals: one server was checked on the minute, and the other server was checked on the half minute. Because observations made at such regular intervals are not random, the researchers compensated by drawing a random sample of the student observations at each restaurant for the final analysis.

TABLE 8.3

WORK SAMPLING FORM FOR RESTAURANT STUDY

Restaurant _____ Lunch _____ Dinner_____
Date _____ Time _____

Key OB#	Guest Contact	Walk— Empty	Walk— Full	Bus	Prepare	Can't See	Check	Rest	Key OB#
1		√							1
2	√								2
3	√								3
4		√							4
5						√			5
6						√			6
34						√			34
35						√			35
36						√			36
37			√						37
38	√								38
39		√							39
40							√		40
Sum									Sum

By noting what the server is doing once each minute, an observer can obtain a sampling of which tasks occupy the server's time. The 40 observation points indicated in the above form would not constitute a sufficient sample by themselves, but would be part of a lengthier study.

Kimes and Mutkoski suggest ways in which management can use the information from their study: if servers are spending more or less time with customers than desired, perhaps the jobs can be redesigned to increase or decrease the customer contact time; if servers are spending too much time on busing tables, for example, perhaps more bus help could be employed; if servers are off the floor too much, perhaps a type of "front-waiter, back-waiter" system would be helpful.

Sample Size

Consider the following situation. The nursing supervisor at a major hospital must make up a new work schedule for her staff and needs information on which to base her decisions. Therefore, she is interested in determining the actual proportion of time nurses (RNs) spend in direct patient care. She believes the RNs spend approximately 20 percent of their time in direct patient care, but she wants to conduct a work sampling study to validate her estimate. For the study she wants to be 95 percent confident that the resulting estimate will be within 5 percent of the true proportion.

Given the desired confidence defined above, we can calculate the size of the sample required for the study. The size of the sample, or number of observations, depends on an estimate of the proportion of time spent in a particular activity and the accuracy that is desired. The formula for calculating the sample size is

$$N = \frac{Z^2 P\ (1-P)}{E^2} \tag{4}$$

where N = sample size
Z = standard normal deviate for desired level of confidence
P = assumed proportion, expressed as a decimal percentage
E = maximum error allowed, expressed as a decimal percentage

In actual practice, an estimate of the proportion of time spent on a particular activity (P) can be made by conducting small initial studies or by assigning a conservative value of 50 percent, or 0.5 (which will guarantee that the sample size is large enough to achieve the desired level of confidence). A third way of estimating P is to make a reasonable assumption based on experience, as did the supervisor in our hospital example above when she set P equal to 0.2 (20 percent). For this example, $E = 0.05$ and $Z = 1.96$ (for a two-tailed 0.95 confidence level, as found in the end-of-book Appendix table, Areas of a Standard Normal Distribution). Substituting these values in equation (4) yields

$$N = \frac{(1.96)^2(0.2)(1 - 0.2)}{(0.05)^2} = 246 \text{ observations}$$

The supervisor now needs to construct a schedule of random observations. Also, the observations should be made over a period of time long enough to ensure adequate representation of all activities. For this example, assume that the study will be conducted for 20 weekdays. This means that 13 observations per day ($246/20 = 12.3$) are to be made. These observations should be made at random times during each workday, and the hour and minute for each observation can be determined using a random-number table.

WORK METHODS CHARTS

The flow of work activities and the interactions between customers and workers can be represented graphically. The most commonly used graphic tools are *worker-customer charts* and *activity charts.*

Worker-Customer Charts

When the server's work cycle time is shorter than that required by the supply of customers, the interaction can be shown on a time scale. The resulting worker-customer chart can be used to schedule work activities so that one employee can serve more than one customer at a time.

Figure 8.4 shows a worker-customer chart for a bank where one drive-in teller serves two lanes. We simplify this example by using average times and ignoring randomness. On the average, a customer takes 15 seconds to approach the service area, 48 seconds to be served, and 9 seconds to depart. Note that the customer's average cycle time is 72 seconds, but the teller's average cycle time is 48 seconds. You can also see that while the teller is occupied with the first customer, a second customer has entered the system and is waiting for service in the second lane.

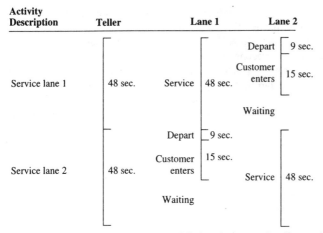

Activity Description	Teller	Lane 1	Lane 2

Service lane 1 — Teller: 48 sec. — Lane 1: Service 48 sec. — Lane 2: Depart 9 sec., Customer enters 15 sec.

Waiting

Service lane 2 — Teller: 48 sec. — Lane 1: Depart 9 sec., Customer enters 15 sec., Waiting — Lane 2: Service 48 sec.

Total cycle time: 96 seconds   Idle-lane time per cycle: 48 seconds
Idle-teller time per cycle: 0   Working-lane time per cycle: 144 seconds
Working-teller time per cycle: 96 seconds

FIGURE 8.4
Worker-customer chart: teller serving two lanes of a drive-in bank.

Activity Charts

The worker-customer chart described above is a useful tool in simple situations. But a situation involving multiple servers and many customers may benefit from the use of a more complex graphical depiction called an activity chart. An activity chart also uses a time scale, as shown in Figure 8.5. In this example two tellers at a drive-in bank are located

FIGURE 8.5
Activity chart: two tellers serving three lanes of a drive-in bank.

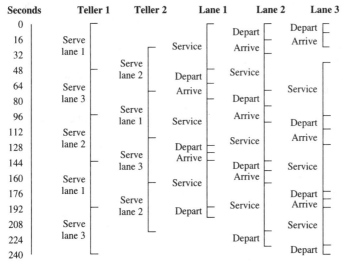

in a single station. The bank has three lanes, one served directly from the teller station window and the other two from pneumatic tubes that transfer materials to and from the teller station. The average service time at each position is 48 seconds per customer. Each customer requires an average of 15 seconds to enter the service area and an average of 9 seconds to depart. We can see from this chart that the system is operating efficiently; that is, the system quickly adapts to avoid waiting by customers and idle time for tellers. Also note that we have created a two-server queuing system with a single waiting line in spite of the physical need for multiple lanes. For a complete discussion of queuing systems, see Chapters 11 and 15.

EXERCISES

8.1 We want to estimate the proportion of time when a car wash facility is unused. It is known that the facility is busy for at least 80 percent of the day. A study is conducted for one week. If we need an estimate within ±5 percent at a 90 percent confidence level, how many observations are required each day?

8.2 One station attendant serves a full-service gas station that has a total of three pumps. On the average, a car takes 10 seconds to pull up to a pump; the attendant takes 15 seconds to find out customer needs and to begin pumping gas. It takes 40 seconds for the gas to be pumped (the attendant is free during this time), and cleaning the windshield takes 15 seconds. Finally, it takes 30 seconds to replace the nozzle on the pump and for payment to be made. Customers enter the station every 60 seconds (deterministic). Draw a worker-customer chart for a five-minute observation of this scenario. (A customer goes to an empty pump if available or to any pump otherwise.)

8.3 One of the cleaning staff at the Last Resort Motel was observed making beds at an average rate of eight minutes per bed. The proficiency rating of the staff person is estimated to be 90 percent.
  a. What is the normal time for this task?
  b. If the allowance for fatigue and personal needs is 10 percent, what is the standard time for this task?

8.4 The cleaning staff at the Last Resort Motel has complained about overwork. Management has decided to conduct a work sampling study to verify its contention that the staff is busy only about 60 percent of the time. The study should yield an estimate of idle time with a ±5 percent degree of accuracy at a 95 percent confidence level.
  a. How many random observations should be made?
  b. Explain how you would select each observation time during a typical eight-hour day (the study will be conducted for ten days).

CASE: COUNTY GENERAL HOSPITAL[11]

County General is a large public hospital serving a major metropolitan area in the growing Sunbelt region of the United States. A significant portion of the hospital's budget is consumed by labor costs, and the total number of employees is broken down as follows:

[11]Prepared by James Vance under the supervision of Professor James A. Fitzsimmons.

Administrative and management	18
Professional:	
MDs	67
RNs	145
LVNs	196
Support	368
Total	794

The hospital's top management has been concerned for some time that the labor costs for professional staff, particularly the registered nurses, have not been kept under control as closely as the annual operating plan had envisioned at its inception. In attempting to see how the nursing staff can be utilized better, management has decided to undertake a work sampling study of the registered nurses to see what proportions of their time are actually spent on various tasks.

In designing the study, management established eight general categories of activities for defining the registered nurse's typical workday: (1) direct patient care, (2) indirect patient care (preparation of medicine, equipment, etc.), (3) paperwork, (4) communication and teaching, (5) escorting and errands, (6) housekeeping, (7) travel, and (8) nonproductive (idle time, mealtime, etc.).

Observers who perform the actual sampling will be given lists of specific duties that would define each category and would also ensure that the study has a high degree of consistency in the allocation of a nurse's daily duties to the correct categories. On the basis of a pilot study, County General's management estimates that the proportions of time spent in each of the above categories are 15, 12, 10, 40, 5, 3, 5, and 10 percent, respectively. The study will be conducted during a 14-day period from each of three workshifts, and management wants to ensure that the estimates come within ±2 percent of the true proportions with a 98 percent confidence level.

Questions

1. How many observations will be required to make sure that all the categories have enough data collected to meet the established parameters for accuracy? Assume that there is a normal distribution.

2. The study was accomplished as designed, and the hospital management team was given the summary data shown below:

Category	% of time	Category	% of time
1	13.8	5	3.1
2	12.3	6	4.5
3	11.9	7	3.1
4	39.7	8	11.6

On the basis of your knowledge of hospital functions and the general goal of providing a high level of service to patients, suggest at least one or two strategies that management might apply to utilize better the time of the registered nursing staff. Describe the effects your strategies might have on the time requirements for other staff groups and on the general level of health care in County General.

CHAPTER 9

SERVICE QUALITY

Service with a smile used to be enough to satisfy most customers, but now some service firms are differentiating themselves in the marketplace by offering a "service guarantee." Unlike a product warranty, which promises to repair or replace the faulty item, service guarantees typically offer the dissatisfied customer a refund, a discount, or free service.

Take, for example, the First Interstate Bank of California. After interviewing its customers, management discovered that they were annoyed by a number of recurring problems, such as inaccurate statements and broken automatic teller machines. Account retention improved after the bank began to pay customers $5 for reporting each such service failure. What is surprising is that the service guarantee had a motivating effect on the employees. When an automatic teller machine failed at a branch, the employees, out of pride, decided to keep the branch open until the machine was repaired at 8:30 p.m. Another hidden benefit of a guarantee is customer feedback. Now customers have a reason and motivation to talk to the company instead of just to their friends.

The service guarantee, in addition to advertising the firm's commitment to quality, focuses employees by defining performance standards explicitly and, more importantly, builds a loyal customer base. The experience of Hampton Inns, an early adopter of a "100 percent satisfaction guarantee," illustrates that superior quality is a competitive advantage. In a survey of 300 guests who invoked the guarantee, more than 100 had already stayed again at a Hampton Inn. The hotel chain figures it has received eight dollars in revenue for every dollar paid to a disgruntled guest.[1]

---

[1]Daniel Pearl, "More Firms Pledge Guaranteed Service," *The Wall Street Journal*, July 17, 1991, p. B1.

CHAPTER PREVIEW

Service quality is a complex topic, as seen by the need for a definition containing five dimensions: reliability, responsiveness, assurance, empathy, and tangibles. Using these dimensions, the concept of a service quality gap is introduced; it is based on the difference between a customer's expectations of a service and the perceptions of the service as delivered. A survey instrument that measures service quality, called SERVQUAL, is based on implementing the service quality gap concept. The discussion of measurement also includes the concept of benchmarking, which is a process of comparing one's service delivery system with the systems of other firms that have a reputation of being best in class.

However, quality begins with the design of the service delivery system. Thus, concepts borrowed from manufacturing—such as Taguchi methods, *poka-yoke,* and quality function deployment—are applied to service delivery system design. In addition, applications of statistical process control to services are illustrated with the construction of quality-control charts. Achieving service quality through the use of quality tools is illustrated by the example of Midway Airlines.

Finally, programs to improve quality and create an organization focused on providing excellence in quality are discussed. The teachings of Deming and Crosby, the concept of an unconditional service guarantee, and the Malcolm Baldrige National Quality Award are all explored.

DEFINING SERVICE QUALITY

For services, the assessment of quality is made during the service delivery process, which usually takes place with an encounter between a customer and a service contact person, as discussed in Chapter 8. Customer satisfaction with service quality can be defined by comparing perceptions of service received with expectations of service desired. When expectations are exceeded, service is perceived to be of exceptional quality and also to be a pleasant surprise. When expectations are not met, service quality is deemed unacceptable. When expectations are confirmed by perceived service, quality is satisfactory. As shown in Figure 9.1, these expectations are based on several sources, including word of mouth, personal needs, and past experience.

Dimensions of Service Quality

The dimensions of service quality shown in Figure 9.1 were identified by marketing researchers studying several different service categories: appliance repair, retail banking, long-distance telephone service, securities brokerage, and credit card companies. They identified five principal dimensions that customers use to judge service quality. These dimensions—reliability, responsiveness, assurance, empathy, and tangibles—are listed in order of declining relative importance to customers:[2]

---

[2]A. Parasuraman, V. A. Zeithaml, and L. L. Berry, "SERVQUAL: A Multiple-Item Scale for Measuring Consumer Perceptions of Service Quality," *Journal of Retailing,* vol. 64, no. 1, spring 1988, pp. 12–40.

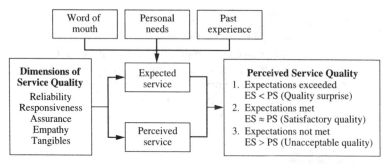

FIGURE 9.1
Perceived service quality. [*Reprinted with permission of the American Marketing Association: adapted from A. Parasuraman, V. A. Zeithaml, and L. L. Berry, "A Conceptual Model of Service Quality and Its Implications for Future Research,"* Journal of Marketing, *vol. 49, Fall 1985, p. 48.*]

Reliability. The ability to perform the promised service dependably and accurately. Reliable service performance is a customer expectation and means that the service, every time, is accomplished on time, in the same manner, and without errors. For example, receiving mail at approximately the same time each day is important to most people. Reliability extends into the back office, where accuracy in billing and record keeping is expected.

Responsiveness. The willingness to help customers and to provide prompt service. Keeping customers waiting, particularly for no apparent reason, creates unnecessary negative perceptions of quality. In the event of a service failure, the ability to recover quickly with professionalism can create very positive perceptions of quality. For example, serving complimentary drinks on a delayed flight can turn a potentially poor customer experience into one that is remembered favorably.

Assurance. The knowledge and courtesy of employees and their ability to convey trust and confidence. The assurance dimension includes the following features: competence to perform the service, politeness and respect for the customer, effective communication with the customer, and the general attitude that the server has the customer's best interests at heart.

Empathy. The provision of caring, individualized attention to customers. Empathy includes the following features: approachability, sense of security, and the effort to understand the customer's needs.

Tangibles. The appearance of physical facilities, equipment, personnel, and communication materials. The condition of the physical surroundings is tangible evidence of the care and attention to details exhibited by the service provider. This assessment dimension can extend to the conduct of other customers in the service, such as a noisy guest in the next room at a hotel.

Customers use the five dimensions described above to form their judgments of service quality, which are based on a comparison of expected service and perceived service. The gap between expected service and perceived service is a measure of service quality; satisfaction is either negative or positive.

Gaps in Service Quality

Measurement of the gap between expected service and perceived service is a routine customer feedback process practiced by leading service companies. For example, Club Med, an international resort hotel operating villages worldwide, uses the questionnaire shown in Figure 9.2. This questionnaire is mailed to all guests immediately after their departure from a Club Med vacation to assess the quality of their experience. Note that the first question explicitly asks the guest to evaluate the gap between his or her expectations and the actual Club Med experience.

In Figure 9.3 the gap between customer expectations and perceptions is defined as GAP 5 and is shown to depend on the size and direction of the four gaps associated with the delivery of the service.

The first gap is the discrepancy between customer expectations and management perceptions of these expectations. GAP 1 arises from management's lack of a full understanding of how customers formulate their expectations on the basis of a number of sources: advertising, past experience with the firm and its competitors, personal needs, and communications with friends. Strategies for closing this gap could include improving market research, fostering better communication between management and its contact employees, and reducing the levels of management that distance the customer.

The second gap results from management's inability to formulate target levels of service quality to meet perceptions of customer expectations and to translate these into workable specifications. GAP 2 may result from a lack of management commitment to service quality or a perception of the infeasibility of meeting customers' expectations. However, setting goals and standardizing service delivery tasks can close this gap.

The third gap is referred to as the service performance gap because actual delivery of the service does not meet the specifications set by management. GAP 3 can arise for a number of reasons, such as lack of teamwork, poor employee selection, inadequate training, and inappropriate job design.

Customer expectations of the service are formed by media advertising and other communications from the firm. GAP 4 is the discrepancy between service delivery and external communications in the form of exaggerated promises and lack of information provided for contact personnel.

The remainder of this chapter will address ways of closing these gaps in service quality. We begin by considering approaches to measuring service quality.

MEASURING SERVICE QUALITY

Measuring service quality is a challenge because customer satisfaction is determined by many intangible factors. Unlike a product with physical features that can be objectively measured (e.g., the fit and finish of a car), service quality contains many psychological features (e.g., the ambience of a restaurant). Service quality often extends beyond the immediate encounter because, as in the case of health

G.M. Questionnaire

Club Med Village: _____

Dates of your stay: From: _____ to: _____
                         Month/Day/Year   Month/Day/Year

Name: _____ Member # _____

Address: _____

City: _____ State: _____ Zip: _____

1. Did Club Med meet your expectations?
   □ Far below expectations □ Surpassed expectations
   □ Fell short of expectations □ Far surpassed expectations
   □ Met expectations

2. If this was not your first Club Med, how many other times have you been to a Club Med village? _____

3. How did you make your Club Med reservations?
   □ Through a travel agent □ Through Club Med Reservations

4. Quality of your reservations handling (pre-travel information):
   □ Very poor □ Poor □ Fair □ Good □ Excellent

5. Which one factor was most important in your choosing Club Med for your vacation?
   □ Previous stay with us □ Advertisement □ Editorial Article
   □ Travel Agent Recommendation □ Friend/Relative Recommendation

6. Kindly indicate your age bracket:
   □ Under 25 □ 25-34 □ 35-44 □ 45-54 □ 55 or over

7. Kindly indicate your marital status: □ Married □ Single

8. Would you vacation with Club Med again? □ Yes □ No

9. If you answered yes to question 8, where would you like to go on your next Club Med vacation?
   □ U.S.A. □ Mexico □ French West Indies □ Caribbean □ Europe
   □ Other: _____

	OVERALL IMPRESSION	ORGANIZATION	TEAM OF G.O.s	FOOD	BAR	SPORTS	DAYTIME AMBIANCE	EVENING ENTERTAINMENT	MUSIC AND DANCE	MINI CLUB	EXCURSIONS	ACCOMMODATIONS	CLUB FLIGHTS AND TRANSFERS	CLEANLINESS
EXCELLENT	6	6	6	6	6	6	6	6	6	6	6	6	6	6
VERY GOOD	5	5	5	5	5	5	5	5	5	5	5	5	5	5
GOOD	4	4	4	4	4	4	4	4	4	4	4	4	4	4
FAIR	3	3	3	3	3	3	3	3	3	3	3	3	3	3
POOR	2	2	2	2	2	2	2	2	2	2	2	2	2	2
VERY POOR	1	1	1	1	1	1	1	1	1	1	1	1	1	1

Your Comments: _____
_____
_____

FIGURE 9.2
Customer satisfaction questionnaire. [After Club Med, 40 West 57 Street, New York, NY 10019.]

Customer

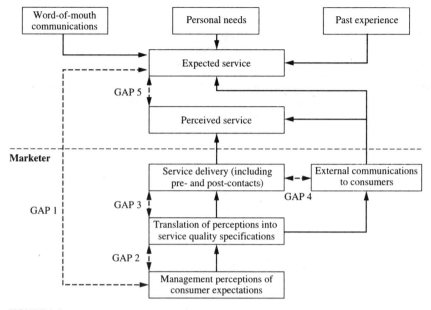

FIGURE 9.3
Service quality gap model. [*Reprinted with permission of the American Marketing Association: V. A. Zeithaml, L. L. Berry, and A. Parasuraman, "Communication and Control Processes in the Delivery of Service Quality,"* Journal of Marketing, *vol. 52, April 1988, p. 36.*]

care, it has an impact on a person's future quality of life. The multiple dimensions of service quality are captured in the SERVQUAL instrument, which is an effective tool for surveying customer satisfaction that is based on the service quality gap model.

SERVQUAL[3]

The authors of the service quality gap model shown in Figure 9.3 developed a multiple-item scale called SERVQUAL for measuring the five dimensions of service quality: reliability, responsiveness, assurance, empathy, and tangibles. This two-part instrument, shown in Table 9.1, has an initial section to record customer expectations for a class of services (e.g., budget hotels) followed by a second section to record a customer's perceptions for a particular service firm. The 22 statements in the survey describe aspects of the five dimensions of service quality.

A score for the quality of service is calculated by computing the differences between the ratings that customers assign to paired expectation and perception

[3]From A. Parasuraman, V. A. Zeithaml, and L. L. Berry, "SERVQUAL: A Multiple-Item Scale for Measuring Consumer Perceptions of Service Quality," *Journal of Retailing,* vol. 64, no. 1, spring 1988, pp. 12–40.

TABLE 9.1
THE SERVQUAL INSTRUMENT*

DIRECTIONS: This survey deals with your opinions of _____ services. Please show the extent to which you think firms offering _____ services should possess the features described by each statement. Do this by picking one of the seven numbers next to each statement. If you strongly agree that these firms should possess a feature, circle the number 7. If you strongly disagree that these firms should possess a feature, circle 1. If your feelings are not strong, circle one of the numbers in the middle. There are no right or wrong answers—all we are interested in is a number that best shows your expectations about firms offering _____ services.

E1.   They should have up-to-date equipment.
E2.   Their physical facilities should be visually appealing.
E3.   Their employees should be well dressed and appear neat.
E4.   The appearance of the physical facilities of these firms should be in keeping with the type of services provided.
E5.   When these firms promise to do something by a certain time, they should do so.
E6.   When customers have problems, these firms should be sympathetic and reassuring.
E7.   These firms should be dependable.
E8.   They should provide their services at the time they promise to do so.
E9.   They should keep their records accurately.
E10. They shouldn't be expected to tell customers exactly when services will be performed. (–)†
E11. It is not realistic for customers to expect prompt service from employees of these firms. (–)
E12. Their employees don't always have to be willing to help customers. (–)
E13. It is okay if they are too busy to respond to customer requests promptly. (–)
E14. Customers should be able to trust employees of these firms.
E15. Customers should be able to feel safe in their transactions with these firms' employees.
E16. Their employees should be polite.
E17. Their employees should get adequate support from these firms to do their jobs well.
E18. These firms should not be expected to give customers individual attention. (–)
E19. Employees of these firms cannot be expected to give customers personal attention. (–)
E20. It is unrealistic to expect employees to know what the needs of their customers are. (–)
E21. It is unrealistic to expect these firms to have their customers' best interests at heart. (–)
E22. They shouldn't be expected to have operating hours convenient to all their customers. (–)

DIRECTIONS: The following set of statements relate to your feelings about XYZ. For each statement, please show the extent to which you believe XYZ has the feature described by the statement. Once again, circling a 7 means that you strongly agree that XYZ has that feature, and circling a 1 means that you strongly disagree. You may circle any of the numbers in the middle that show how strong your feelings are. There are no right or wrong answers—all we are interested in is a number that best shows your perceptions about XYZ.

P1.   XYZ has up-to-date equipment.
P2.   XYZ's physical facilities are visually appealing.
P3.   XYZ's employees are well dressed and appear neat.
P4.   The appearance of the physical facilities of XYZ is in keeping with the type of services provided.
P5.   When XYZ promises to do something by a certain time, it does so.
P6.   When you have problems, XYZ is sympathetic and reassuring.
P7.   XYZ is dependable.
P8.   XYZ provides its services at the time it promises to do so.
P9.   XYZ keeps its records accurately.

TABLE 9.1
(Continued)

P10.	XYZ does not tell customers exactly when services will be performed. (–)
P11.	You do not receive prompt service from XYZ's employees. (–)
P12.	Employees of XYZ are not always willing to help customers. (–)
P13.	Employees of XYZ are too busy to respond to customer requests promptly. (–)
P14.	You can trust employees of XYZ.
P15.	You feel safe in your transactions with XYZ's employees.
P16.	Employees of XYZ are polite.
P17.	Employees get adequate support from XYZ to do their jobs well.
P18.	XYZ does not give you individual attention. (–)
P19.	Employees of XYZ do not give you personal attention. (–)
P20.	Employees of XYZ do not know what your needs are. (–)
P21.	XYZ does not have your best interests at heart. (–)
P22.	XYZ does not have operating hours convenient to all their customers. (–)

*A seven-point scale ranging from "Strongly Agree" (7) to "Strongly Disagree" (1), with no verbal labels for the intermediate scale points (i.e., 2 through 6), accompanied each statement. Also, the statements were in random order in the questionnaire. A complete listing of the 34-item instrument used in the second stage of data collection can be obtained from the first author.

†Ratings on these statements were reverse-scored prior to data analysis.

Source: Reprinted with permission of the Journal of Retailing from A. Parasuraman, V. A. Zeithaml, and L. L. Berry, "SERVQUAL: A Multiple-Item Scale for Measuring Consumer Perceptions of Service Quality," *Journal of Retailing,* vol. 64, no. 1, spring 1988, pp. 38–40.]

statements. This score is referred to as GAP 5, shown in Figure 9.3. Scores for the other four gaps can also be calculated in a similar manner.

The instrument has been designed and validated for use in a variety of service encounters. The authors have suggested many applications for SERVQUAL, but its most important function is to track service quality trends through periodic customer surveys. For multisite services, SERVQUAL could be used by management to determine if any unit has poor service quality (indicated by a low score); if so, management can direct attention to correcting the source of customers' poor perceptions. SERVQUAL could be used in marketing studies to compare a service with a competitor's service and again identify the dimensions of superior or inadequate service quality.

Benchmarking

The measure of the quality of a firm's performance can be made by comparison with the performance of other companies known for being "best in class." For example, Singapore Airlines has a reputation for outstanding cabin service, Federal Express for consistent overnight delivery, Hampton Inns for clean rooms, and Nordstrom's department store for attentive salespersons. For every quality dimension, some firm has earned the reputation for being "best in class" and thus is a benchmark for comparison. However, benchmarking involves more than comparing statistics. It also includes visiting the leading firm to learn firsthand how management has achieved the outstanding performance. For obvious proprietary reasons, this often requires going outside one's own field. Some manufacturers, for example, have visited the pit stops at automobile races to learn methods of reducing the time for production-line changeovers. Other manufacturers have visited Domino's Pizza to understand how it delivers customized products within 30 minutes.

For a typical example, consider an electronics company looking to improve its purchasing function. It formed a study team that visited Ford to learn how Ford reduced the number of its suppliers, talked to Toyota about vendor relationships, and observed the buying process at Reliance Electric. The team returned with quantifiable measures that benchmarked the superior performance of these leading firms and with knowledge of how the gains were accomplished.[4]

Scope of Service Quality

A comprehensive view of the service system is necessary to identify the possible measures of service quality. We will use health care delivery as our example service and view quality from five perspectives: content, process, structure, outcome, and impact. For health care, it is obvious that the scope of service quality extends beyond the quality of care provided for the patient; it also includes the impact on the family and community. This comprehensive view of service quality need not be limited to health care, as demonstrated by the negative economic impact of failed savings and loan institutions on their customers as well as on the community as a whole.

Content   Are standard procedures being followed? For example, is the dentist following accepted dental practices in extracting a tooth? For routine services, standard operating procedures generally are developed, and service personnel are expected to follow these established procedures. In health care, a formal peer review system, called Professional Standards Review Organization (PSRO), has been developed as a method of self-regulation. Under this system, physicians in a community or speciality establish standards for their practices and meet regularly to review peer performance so that compliance is assured.

Process   Is the sequence of events in the service process appropriate? The primary concern here is the maintenance of a logical sequence of activities and a well-coordinated use of service resources. The interactions between the customer and the service personnel are monitored. Also of interest are the interactions and communications among the service workers. Check sheets (see Table 9.2) are common measurement devices. For emergency services, such as fire and ambulance, disaster drills in a realistic setting are used to test a unit's performance. Problems with coordination and activity sequencing can be identified and corrected through these practice sessions.

---

[4]A. Steven Walleck, "A Backstage View of World-Class Performers," *The Wall Street Journal,* Aug. 26, 1991, p. A10.

TABLE 9.2
QUALITY-CONTROL CHECK SHEET FOR AN EMERGENCY ROOM

Head injuries

Date of visit: _____   MRN: _____
Nurse: _____   Physician: _____
Nurse reviewer initials: _____   Physician reviewer initials: _____

Nursing criteria	Yes	No	N/A
1. Are the patient's vital signs assessed upon arrival?	☐	☐	☐
2. Does the triage note include time and mechanism of injury?	☐	☐	☐
3. Does the triage note include history of loss of consciousness and presence/absence of associated symptoms (nausea/vomiting/focal neurologic complaints)?	☐	☐	☐
4. Does the triage note include a brief neurologic assessment (Glasgow scale)?	☐	☐	☐
5. Does the triage list patient's current medications, including time of last dose recorded?	☐	☐	☐
6. Does triage note include past medical history?	☐	☐	☐
7. Is the patient's cervical spine immobilized?	☐	☐	☐
8. If history of LOC > 5 minutes or neurologic findings present is supplemental O2 applied, cardiac monitor applied, i.v. line established, and physician notified immediately?	☐	☐	☐
9. Is the patient's mental status reassessed every 30 minutes?	☐	☐	☐
10. Are the discharge instructions reviewed with the patient and other responsible adult?	☐	☐	☐

Physician assessment criteria			
1. Is the chief complaint including time, mechanism of injury, and loss of consciousness recorded?	☐	☐	☐
2. Does the note include presence/absence of other injuries?	☐	☐	☐
3. Is a HEENT exam noting: scalp lacerations or contusions, pupil size and reactivity, tympanic membranes, and neck exam recorded?	☐	☐	☐
4. Is Chest, Lung, Heart and Abdominal exam recorded?	☐	☐	☐
5. Is a Neurologic exam including: Glasgow scale, motor and sensory examination, and gait recorded?	☐	☐	☐

Physician action criteria			
1. Is a CAT scan obtained if there is a history of LOC or neurologic findings?	☐	☐	☐
2. Is a CAT scan obtained if there is a history of blood clotting disorder, thrombocytopenia, lethargy, or patient taking coumadin?	☐	☐	☐
3. Are x-rays of the c-spine obtained?	☐	☐	☐
4. If the patient is discharged is the mental status at the time of discharge recorded?	☐	☐	☐
5. Are discharge instructions including indications for return to the ED, aftercare plan, and referral for follow-up care given to patient and other responsible adult?	☐	☐	☐

Patient outcome criteria			
1. Does the patient and responsible adult verbalize understanding of signs and symptoms indicating need to return?	☐	☐	☐
2. If the CAT scan reveals emergent intracranial hematoma is surgical intervention initiated within 2 hours?	☐	☐	☐
3. Did the patient require second visit due to missed diagnosis?	☐	☐	☐

Structure   Are the physical facilities and organizational design adequate for the service? The physical facilities and support equipment are only part of the structural dimension. The qualifications of the personnel and the organizational design are also important quality dimensions. For example, the quality of medical care in a group practice can be enhanced by an on-site laboratory and x-ray facilities. But more importantly, the organization may facilitate consultations among the participating physicians. Group medical practice also provides the opportunity for peer pressure to control the quality of care provided by its members.

The adequacy of the physical facilities and equipment can be determined by comparison with set standards for quality conformance. A well-known fast-food restaurant is recognized for its attention to cleanliness. Store managers are subjected to surprise inspections in which they are held responsible for the appearance of the parking lot and sidewalk, as well as for the restaurant's interior. Personnel qualifications for hiring, promotion, and merit increases are also matters of meeting standards. University professors seldom are granted tenure unless they have published, because the ability to publish in a refereed journal is considered to be independent evidence of research quality. A measure of organizational effectiveness in controlling quality would be the presence of active self-evaluation procedures and members' knowledge of their peers' performances.

Outcome   What change in status has the service effected? The ultimate measure of service quality is a study of the end result. Is the consumer satisfied? We are all familiar with the cards placed at restaurant tables requesting our comments on the quality of service. Complaints by consumers are one of the most effective measures of the quality outcome dimension. For public services, the assumption is often made that the status quo is acceptable, unless the level of complaints begins to rise. The concept of monitoring output quality by tracking some measure like the number of complaints is widely used. For example, the performance of a hospital is monitored by comparing certain measures against industry norms. The infection rate per 1000 surgeries might be used to identify hospitals that may be using substandard operating room procedures.

Clever approaches to measuring outcome quality often are employed. For example, the quality of trash pickup in a city can be documented by taking pictures of the city streets after the trash vehicles have made their rounds. One often-forgotten measure of outcome quality is the satisfaction of empowered service personnel with their own performance.

Impact   What is the long-range effect of the service on the life of the consumer? Are the citizens of a community able to walk the streets at night with a sense of security? The result of a poll asking that question would be a measure of the impact of police performance. The overall impact of health care is often measured by life expectancy or the infant mortality rate, and the impact of education is often measured by literacy rates and performance on nationally standardized tests.

However, it should be noted that the impact also must include a measure of service and accessibility, usually quoted as population served per unit area. Health

TABLE 9.3
MEASURING SERVICE QUALITY FOR A HEALTH CLINIC

Quality perspective	Description	Possible measures
Content	Evaluation of medical practice	Review medical records for conformance with national standards of medical care.
Process	The sequence of events in the delivery of care and the interactions between patients and medical staff	Use checklists to monitor conformance with procedures. Conduct exit interviews with patients.
Structure	The physical facilities, equipment, staffing patterns, and qualifications of health personnel	Record times patients wait to see a doctor. Note ratio of doctors to registered nurses on duty. Record utilization of equipment.
Outcome	The change in the patient's health status as a result of care	Record deaths as a measure of failures. Note the level of patient dissatisfaction by recording the number of complaints. Record the number of diseased organs removed in surgery.
Impact	Appropriateness, availability, accessibility, and overall effect on the community of the health clinic	Note number of patients turned away because of lack of insurance or financial resources. Record the mode of travel and distance patients travel to reach the clinic.

care in the United States is criticized for the financial barriers to patient accessibility in general, but especially in rural and large inner-city areas. As a result, this country's impact measures of life expectancy and infant mortality are far worse than in all other industrial countries and in several third world countries. In a similar fashion, literacy rate is a measure of the impact of the education system, and again the United States lags many other nations. Health care and education are, perhaps, the two most essential services in the United State today, and clearly, they are in great need of managers who can devise and implement excellent and innovative service operations strategies.

A commercial example of an impact measurement is the number of hamburgers sold, which used to be displayed in neon lights by McDonald's. A bank's lending rate for minorities could be a measure of that institution's economic impact on a community.

Table 9.3 illustrates how this service quality perspective can be applied to measuring the quality of service delivered by a health clinic.

QUALITY SERVICE BY DESIGN

Quality can neither be inspected into a product nor somehow added on, and this same observation applies to services. A concern for quality begins with the design of the service delivery system. How can quality be designed into a service? One approach is to focus on the four dimensions of the service concept that we explored in Chapter 2.

Incorporation of Quality in the Service Concept

Consider the example of a budget hotel competing on overall cost leadership.

1. *Supporting facility.* Architecturally, the building is designed to be constructed of materials, such as concrete blocks, that are maintenance-free. The grounds are watered by an automated underground sprinkler system. The air-conditioning and heating system is decentralized by using individual room units to confine any failure to just one room.

2. *Facilitating goods.* Room furnishings are durable and easy to clean (e.g., bedside tables are supported from the wall to facilitate carpet cleaning). Disposable plastic cups are used instead of glass. Glasses are more expensive and require cleaning and thus would detract from the budget image.

3. *Explicit services.* Maids are trained to clean and make up rooms in a standard manner. Every room has the same appearance, including such "trivial" matters as the opening of the drapes.

4. *Implicit services.* Individuals with a pleasant appearance and good interpersonal skills are recruited as desk clerks. Training in standard operating procedures (SOPs) ensures uniform and predictable treatment for all guests. An on-line computer keeps track of guest billing, reservations, and registration processing. This system allows guests to check out quickly and automatically notifies the cleaning staff when a room is free to be made up.

Table 9.4 illustrates how the budget hotel has taken these design features and implemented a quality system to maintain conformance to the design requirements. This approach is based on Philip Crosby's definition of quality as "conformance to requirements."[5] This example illustrates the need to define explicitly, in measurable terms, what constitutes conformance to requirements. Quality is seen as an action-oriented activity requiring corrective measures when nonconformance occurs.

Taguchi Methods

The example above illustrates the application of ideas from Genichi Taguchi, who advocated "robust design" of products to ensure their proper functioning under adverse conditions.[6] The idea is that for a customer, the proof of a product's quality is in its performance when abused. For example, a telephone is designed

---

[5]Philip B. Crosby, *Quality Is Free: The Art of Making Quality Certain,* McGraw-Hill Book Company, New York, 1979.

[6]G. Taguchi and D. Clausing, "Robust Quality," *Harvard Business Review,* January–February 1990, pp. 65–75.

TABLE 9.4
QUALITY REQUIREMENTS FOR BUDGET HOTEL

Service concept feature	Attribute or requirement	Measurement	Nonconformance corrective action
Supporting facility	Appearance of building	No flaking paint	Repaint unit
	Grounds	Green grass	Water
	Air-conditioning and heating	Temperature maintained at 68° ± 2°	Repair or replace
Facilitating goods	TV operation	Reception clear in daylight	Repair or replace
	Soap supply	Two bars per bed	Restock
	Ice	One full bucket per room	Restock from ice machine
Explicit services	Room cleanliness	Stain-free rug	Shampoo
	Swimming-pool water purity	Marker at bottom of deep end visible	Change filter
	Room appearance	Drapes drawn to width of 3 ft	Instruct maid
Implicit services	Security	All perimeter lights working	Replace defective bulbs
	Pleasant atmosphere	Telling departing guests "Have a nice day"	Instruct desk clerk
	Waiting for room	No customer having to wait for a room	Review room cleaning schedule

to be far more durable than necessary because more than once it will be pulled off a desk and dropped on the floor. In our budget hotel example, the building is constructed of concrete blocks and furnished with durable furniture.

Taguchi also applied the concept of robustness to the manufacturing process. For example, the recipe for caramel candy was reformulated to make plasticity or chewiness less sensitive to the cooking temperature. Similarly, our budget hotel uses an on-line computer to notify the cleaning staff automatically when a room has been vacated. Keeping the maids posted on which rooms are available for cleaning allows this task to be spread throughout the day and thereby avoids a rush in the late afternoon, which could result in quality degradation.

Taguchi believed that product quality was achieved by consistently meeting design specifications. He measured the cost of poor quality by the square of the deviation from the target, as shown in Figure 9.4. Once again, notice the attention to standard operating procedures (SOPs) used by the budget hotel to promote uniform treatment of guests and consistent preparation of the rooms.

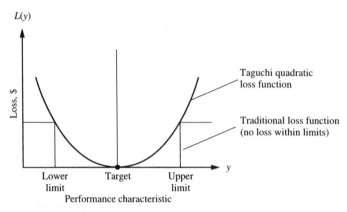

FIGURE 9.4
Taguchi quality loss function.

Poka-yoke

Shigeo Shingo believed that low-cost, in-process quality-control mechanisms and routines used by employees in their work could achieve high quality without costly inspection. He observed that errors occurred not because employees were incompetent but, rather, because of lapses in attention. He advocated the adoption of *poka-yoke* methods, which can be roughly translated as "foolproof" devices. The *poka-yoke* methods use checklists or manual devices that do not let the employee make a mistake.[7]

For an example, recall McDonald's use of the french fry scoop, which measures out a consistent serving of potatoes. This *poka-yoke* device also enhances cleanliness and, hence, the aesthetic quality of the service as well. The emergency room check sheet shown in Table 9.2 is another *poka-yoke* device; it reminds workers of steps often forgotten in hurrying to satisfy patients in a timely manner. Limiting employee discretion by physical design or by the institution of SOPs is an important strategy in service quality control. Because it is difficult for management to intervene in the service process and impose a quality appraisal system (inspection and testing), limiting discretion and incorporating *poka-yoke* methods facilitate mistake-free service. It is interesting to note how these unobtrusive design features channel service behavior without the slightest hint of coercion.

Quality Function Deployment

In an effort to provide customer input at the product design stage, a process called *quality function deployment* (QFD) was developed in Japan and used extensively

[7]Shigeo Shingo, *Zero Quality Control: Source Inspection and the Poka-Yoke System,* Productivity Press, Stamford, Conn., 1986.

What? How?	(2) Service company facets
(1) Customer quality criteria	(3) Relationship grid
Reliability Responsiveness Assurance Empathy Tangibles	✳ strong relationship ● medium relationship ▲ weak relationship

FIGURE 9.5
Service quality relationship grid. [*After Ravi S. Behara and Richard B. Chase, "Service Quality Deployment: Quality Service by Design," in Rakesh V. Sarin (ed.),* Perspectives in Operations Management: Essays in Honor of Elwood S. Buffa, *Kluwer Academic Publishers, Norwell, Mass., 1993.*]

by Toyota and its suppliers. The process results in a matrix, referred to as a "house of quality," for a particular product that relates customer attributes to engineering characteristics. The central idea of QFD is the belief that products should be designed to reflect customers' desires and tastes; thus, the functions of marketing, design engineering, and manufacturing need to work together. The "house of quality" provides a framework for the translation of customer satisfaction into identifiable and measurable conformance specifications for product or service design.[8]

Ravi Behara and Richard Chase have adapted the concept of quality function deployment for service firms. They have used the SERVQUAL instrument to incorporate customer input into the service design process by focusing on the five dimensions of service quality. In addition to designing quality into a new service process, the approach is useful in the redesign of existing services and as a diagnostic tool for continuous quality improvement.[9]

The foundation of their "house of service" is the service quality relationship grid. As seen in Figure 9.5, this grid consists of three elements: (1) customer quality criteria, consisting of the five dimensions of service quality; (2) service company facets, which are the planning, procedures, and personnel aspects of the service delivery system; and (3) a relationship grid, which measures the strength of the relationship between the customer and the service facet.

A section of a completed grid for an auto-service firm is shown in Figure 9.6. The primary service dimension, reliability, has been disaggregated into secondary and tertiary quality determinants on the basis of the statements from SERVQUAL. The primary company facets have also been disaggregated into secondary factors. The strength of the relationship between customer criteria and company facets is subjectively noted by symbols: * (strong), ○ (medium), and △ (weak).

A schematic of a complete "house of service" is shown in Figure 9.7, with the sections labeled and numbered from 1 to 9. When the "house of service" is finished,

[8]J. R. Hauser and D. Clausing, "The House of Quality," *Harvard Business Review,* May–June 1988, pp. 63–73.

[9]R. S. Behara and R. B. Chase, "Service Quality Deployment: Quality Service by Design," in Rakesh V. Sarin (ed.), *Perspectives in Operations Management: Essays in Honor of Elwood S. Buffa,* Kluwer Academic Publisher, Norwell, Mass., 1993.

Strength of relationship: ✳ Strong ● Medium ▲ Weak

Service company facets (How?) — grouped under **Planning**, **Procedures**, **Personnel**

Customer quality criteria (What?) — **Reliability** (Primary)

Secondary	Tertiary	Relative importance	Layout	Resources (eqpt.)	Resources (pers.)	Systems capacity	Housekeeping	Customer handling	Car handling	Information handling	Routine/nonroutine situations	Inventory	Job/personnel scheduling	Selection	Skills training tech/interpersonal	Attitude/morale
Accuracy	Correct problem diagnosis			✳	✳						●			●	✳	▲
Accuracy	Work right first time			✳	●					✳	●		✳	●	✳	▲
Accuracy	Correct billing			●						✳					✳	
Maintaining records	Clear statement of work done			●						✳	●				✳	
Maintaining records	Update maintenance book									✳					✳	●
Honoring promises	Do work mentioned by customer			✳	✳			✳		✳		▲		▲	●	▲
Honoring promises	Car ready at promised time			✳	✳	✳				▲		▲	✳		▲	●
Honoring promises	Keep promises/appointments							✳		✳					✳	●

FIGURE 9.6 Section of relationship grid for auto-service firm. [After Ravi S. Behara and Richard B. Chase, "Service Quality Deployment: Quality Service by Design," in Rakesh V. Sarin (ed.), Perspectives in Operations Management: Essays in Honor of Elwood S. Buffa, Kluwer Academic Publisher, Norwell, Mass., 1993.]

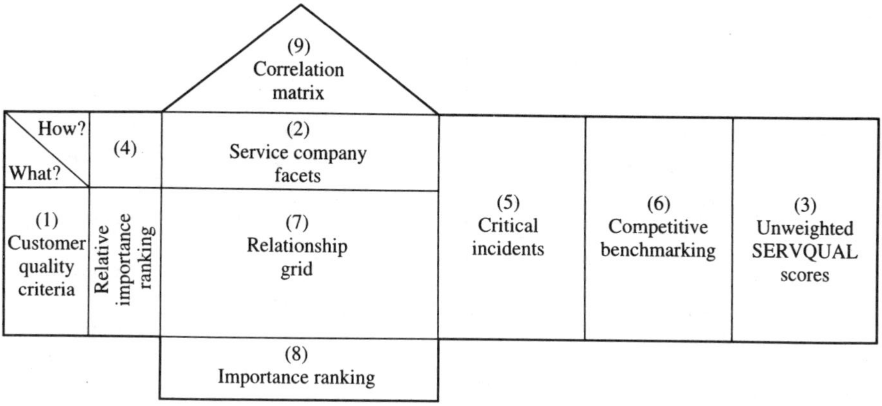

FIGURE 9.7
House of service. [*After Ravi S. Behara and Richard B. Chase, "Service Quality Deployment: Quality Service by Design," in Rakesh V. Sarin (ed.),* Perspectives in Operations Management: Essays in Honor of Elwood S. Buffa, *Kluwer Academic Publisher, Norwell, Mass., 1993.*]

the symbols in the relationship grid will be replaced by numerical scores to highlight the important relationships. The components of the "house of service" are defined below.

1. *Customer quality criteria.* The five dimensions of service quality disaggregated into second and third levels.

2. *Service company facets.* The planning, procedures, and personnel elements in the service delivery system design disaggregated one level.

3. *Unweighted SERVQUAL scores.* The average GAP 5 scores for all tertiary quality criteria.

4. *Relative importance ranking.* The five dimensions are ranked in importance, from reliability (5) to tangibles (1).

5. *Critical incidents.* The number of customer complaints of service failure for a given period.

6. *Competitive benchmarking.* The difference in score between the service and its best-in-class competitor.

7. *Relationship grid.* The symbolic grid is quantified according to the following scale: a strong relationship is 9, medium is 3, and weak is 1.

8. *Importance ranking.* The rank of the total weighted score for each company facet.

9. *Correlation matrix.* The strength of the relationship between company facets to indicate the importance of cooperation among different departments.

A completed section of the quantified "house of service" is shown in Figure 9.8. As shown by the importance ranking, information handling is the most important design issue related to customer perception of service reliability.

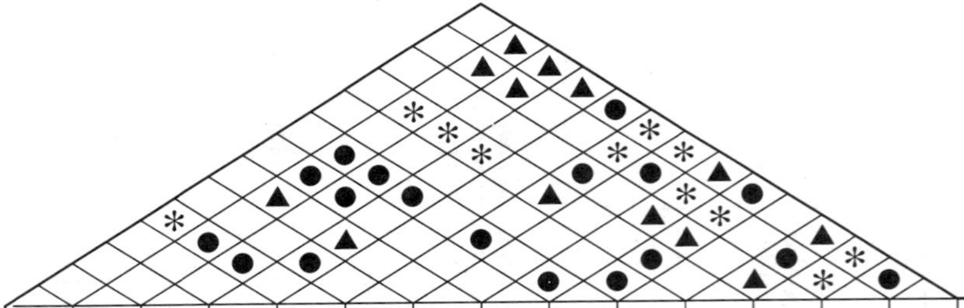

Figure 9.8 — Partial house of service for auto-service firm (House of Quality matrix).

Pr.	Secondary	Tertiary	Relative importance	Layout	Resources (eqpt.)	Resources (pers.)	Systems capacity	Housekeeping	Consumer handling	Car handling	Information handling	Routine/nonroutine situations	Inventory	Job/personnel scheduling	Selection	Skills training tech/interpersonal	Attitudes/morale	Critical incidents	Competitive benchmarking	SERVQUAL scores
Reliability	Accuracy	Correct problem diagnosis	5		76	76									25	76	8	2	3	-.28
		Work right first time	5		917	306					917	306		917	306	917	102	7	8	-.37
		Correct billing	5		130						389					389		6	3	-.48
	Maintaining records	Clear statement of work done	5		138						414	138				414		5	4	-.46
		Update maintenance book	5								77					77	26	3	1	-.57
	Honoring promises	Do work mentioned by customer	5			558			558		558		62		62	186	62	7	3	-.59
		Car ready at promised time	5		149	149	149				17		17	149		17	50	5	3	-.22
		Keep promised appointments	5						478		478					478	159	6	3	-.59
		Absolute importance		1968	1089	149		1036		2850	469	79	1060	393	2554	407				
		Relative importance		3	4	10		6		1	7	11	5	9	2	8				

What? / Customer quality criteria. How? / Service company facets.

FIGURE 9.8

Partial house of service for auto-service firm. Cell value = (relative importance) × (strength of relationship from Figure 9.6) × (critical incidents) × (competitive benchmarking) × (SERVQUAL score). Sample cell value calculation for row 1, column 2 of relationship grid [value for "Correct problem diagnosis" and "Resources (eqpt.)"]: 5 × (* = 9) × 2 × 3 × .28 = 76. [After Ravi S. Behara and Richard B. Chase, "Service Quality Deployment: Quality Service by Design," in *Service Quality Deployment: Quality Service by Design*, in Honor of Elwood S. Buffa, Kluwer Academic Publisher, Norwell, Mass., 1993.] Rakesh V. Sarin (ed.), Perspectives in Operations Management: Essays in Honor of Elwood S. Buffa, Kluwer Academic Publisher, Norwell, Mass., 1993.]

206

ACHIEVING SERVICE QUALITY

Services are difficult for the customer to evaluate before the fact because, as we have already noted, they are intangible and consumed simultaneously with production. This presents a challenge to the service manager because quality inspection intervention between the customer and the contact employee is not an option as in manufacturing (e.g., no slip of paper can be placed in the box by inspector number 12).

Cost of Quality

Caveat emptor, let the buyer beware, has become obsolete. Impersonal service, faulty products, and broken promises all carry a price—as American businesses discovered in the late 1980s and early 1990s. A very visible example of this reality is the prominent part that liability concerns and insurance play in almost every service imaginable today. Poor quality can lead to bankruptcy: a gourmet soup company, for example, was forced out of business when its vichyssoise was found to contain poison-producing botulism organisms. Announcements of automobile recalls for correcting defects are commonplace. Products can be returned, exchanged, or fixed, but what of faulty service?

What recourse does the customer of a faulty service have? Legal recourse! Medical malpractice lawsuits have been notorious for their large settlements. Although some cases of abuse by the legal system have surely occurred, the possibility of malpractice litigation does promote a physician's sense of responsibility to the patient. The threat of a negligence suit might induce a responsible doctor to take more time in an examination, seek more training, or give up performing a procedure for which he or she is not competent. Unfortunately, as evidenced by the frequent claims of physicians that extra testing is necessary to defend against potential malpractice claims, the cost of care may increase without an improvement in quality.

No service has immunity from prosecution. For example, a Las Vegas hotel was sued for failing to provide proper security when a guest was assaulted in her room. An income tax preparer can be fined up to $500 per return if a taxpayer's liability is understated because of the preparer's negligence or disregard of Internal Revenue Service rules and regulations.

A noted quality expert, Joseph M. Juran, advocated a cost-of-quality accounting system to convince top management of the need to address quality issues.[10] He identified four categories of costs: internal failure costs (from defects discovered before shipment), external failure costs (from defects discovered after shipment), detection costs (for inspection of purchased materials and during manufacture), and prevention costs (for keeping defects from occurring in the first place). Juran found that in most manufacturing companies, external and internal failure costs together accounted for 50 to 80 percent of the total cost of quality. Thus, to

---

[10]J. M. Juran and F. M. Gryna, Jr., *Quality Planning and Analysis,* McGraw-Hill Book Company, New York, 1980.

TABLE 9.5
COSTS OF QUALITY FOR SERVICES

Failure costs	Detection costs	Prevention costs
External failure:	Process control	Quality planning
Customer complaints	Peer review	Training program
Warranty charges	Supervision	Quality audits
Liability insurance	Customer comment card	Data acquisition and analysis
Legal judgments	Inspection	Preventive maintenance
Loss of repeat service		Supplier evaluation
Internal failure:		Recruitment and selection
Scrap		
Rework		
Recovery:		
Expedite		
Labor and materials		

minimize the total cost of quality, he advocated that more attention should be paid to prevention.

In Table 9.5 we have adapted Juran's cost-of-quality accounting system for use by service firms. In the prevention column, recruitment and selection of service personnel is viewed as a way to avoid poor quality. Identifying people with the appropriate attitudes and interpersonal skills can result in hiring contact persons with the natural instincts needed to serve customers well.

Inspection is included in the detection column but is generally impractical except in the back-office operations of a service.

The inclusion of "recovery" in the failure column represents a unique opportunity for services to make things right while the customer is still in the service system. For example, airlines offer free drinks to boarded passengers when the plane's departure is delayed. More heroic efforts become legends, such as the story of a Federal Express employee who hired a helicopter to repair a downed telephone line during a snowstorm. Expenses incurred to accomplish a recovery are "pennies on the dollar" compared with the higher external failure costs that result from not going the extra mile in the customer's eyes.

Because service is an experience for the customer, any failure or recovery becomes a story to tell others. Service managers need to recognize that dissatisfied customers will not only take their future business elsewhere but also tell others about the unhappy experience; thus, a significant loss of future business can result.

Tools for Achieving Service Quality

Service Process Control   The control of service quality can be viewed as a feedback control system. In a feedback system the output is compared with a standard. The deviation from the standard is communicated back to the input, and adjustments then are made to keep the output within a tolerable range. The thermostat in a home is a common example of feedback control. Room temperature is monitored continually; when the temperature drops below some preset value, the furnace is activated, and it will continue to operate until the correct temperature is restored.

Figure 9.9 shows the basic control cycle applied to service process control. The service concept establishes a basis for setting goals and defining measurements of system performance. Output measures are taken and monitored for conformance to requirements. Nonconformance to requirements is studied to identify its causes and determine corrective action.

Unfortunately, it is difficult to implement an effective control cycle for service systems. Problems begin with the definition of service performance measures. While the intangible nature of services makes direct measurement difficult, it is not impossible. There are many surrogate measures of service quality. For example, the waiting time of customers might be used as a measure of service quality. In some public services, the number of complaints received is used to measure quality.

Monitoring service performance is frustrated by the simultaneous nature of production and consumption. This close interface between customer and provider prevents any direct intervention in the service process to observe conformance to requirements. Consequently, consumers may be asked to express their impression of service quality "after the fact" by filling out questionnaires. But monitoring only the final customer impressions of service quality may be too late to avoid losing future sales. These difficulties of controlling service quality may be addressed by focusing on the delivery process itself and employing a technique borrowed from manufacturing called statistical process control.

FIGURE 9.9
Service process control.

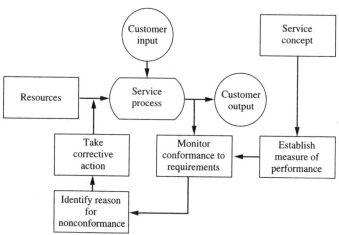

Statistical Process Control   The performance of a service is often judged by some key indicators. For example, the educational performance of a high school is measured by the Scholastic Aptitude Test (SAT) scores of its students. The effectiveness of a police department's crime prevention program is judged by the crime rate, and a bank teller's performance is judged by the accuracy of his or her end-of-day balances.

What happens if the service process is not performing as expected? Generally, an investigation is conducted to identify the cause of the problem and suggest corrective action. However, performance variations may be the result of random occurrences and may not have a specific cause. The decision maker wants to detect true degradation in service performance and avoid the failure costs associated with poor service. On the other hand, making an unnecessary change in a system that is performing correctly should be avoided. Thus, there are two types of risks involved in controlling quality, as shown in Table 9.6. These risks have been given names to identify the injured party. If a process is deemed out of control when, in fact, it is performing correctly, a Type I error has occurred, which is the *producer's risk*. If a process is deemed to be functioning properly when, in fact, it is out of control, a Type II error has occurred, which is the *consumer's risk*.

In manufacturing, a visual display called a *control chart* is used to plot measurements of a critical dimension from a process operation (e.g., the diameter of a machined part) to determine if the process is in control (i.e., the part is conforming to specifications). A similar device can be used in services also. For example, Figure 9.10 shows a control chart used to monitor emergency ambulance response time. This control chart is a daily plot of mean response time that permits monitoring performance for unusual deviations from the norm. When a measurement falls outside the control limits—i.e., above the upper control limit (UCL) or below the lower control limit (LCL)—the process is considered out of control. Consequently, the system is in need of attention. For our ambulance example, day 4 signaled a need for investigation by the supervisor. Why was there an excessive mean response time for that day? This was explained by the fact that a nearby ambulance was out of commission and our vehicle needed to travel longer distances. Since day 4, ambulance performance has remained within the control limits, and so no action is required.

Constructing a control chart is similar to determining a *confidence interval* for the mean of a sample. Recall from statistics that sample means tend to be normally

TABLE 9.6
RISKS IN QUALITY-CONTROL DECISIONS

	Quality-control decision	
True state of service	Take corrective action	Do nothing
Process in control	Type 1 error (producer's risk)	Correct decision
Process out of control	Correct decision	Type II error (consumer's risk)

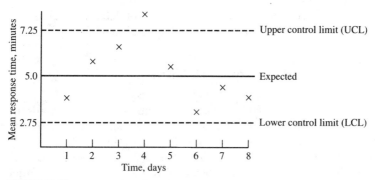

FIGURE 9.10
$\bar{X}$ chart for ambulance response.

distributed as per the central-limit theorem (i.e., although the underlying statistic may be distributed in any manner, mean values drawn from this statistic have a normal distribution). We know from standard normal tables that 99.7 percent of the normal distribution falls within ±3 standard deviations of the mean. Using representative historical data, the mean and standard deviations for some system performance measure are calculated. These are used to construct a 99.7 percent confidence interval for the mean calculated from samples. We expect future sample means to fall within this confidence interval. If they do not, then we conclude that the process has changed and the true mean has shifted.

The steps in constructing and using a quality-control chart are summarized below:

   I. Decide on some measure of service system performance.
  II. Collect representative historical data from which estimates of the population mean and variance for the system performance measure can be made.
 III. Using the standard normal tables, select a confidence level on the basis of the desired Type I error.
 IV. Decide on a sample size, and using the estimates of population mean and variance, calculate the control limits on the basis of the desired Type I error.
  V. Graph the control chart as a function of sample means versus time.
 VI. Plot current sample means on the chart, and interpret the results as:
   A. Process in control
   B. Process out of control
      1. Evaluate the situation.
      2. Take corrective action.
      3. Evaluate the corrective action.
VII. Update the control chart on a periodic basis, and incorporate recent data.

Control charts for means fall into two categories based on the type of performance measure. A variable control chart ($\bar{X}$ chart) records measurements that permit fractional values, such as length, weight, or time. An attribute control chart (*p* chart) records discrete data, such as the number of defects or number of errors as a percentage. An example of each type of control chart follows.

Example 9.1: Control Chart for Variables ($\bar{X}$ Chart)

The quality-control chart for mean ambulance response time, shown in Figure 9.10, is an example of a variable measure. Assume that past records of ambulance system performance yield an estimate of population mean response time of 5.0 minutes, with an estimated standard deviation of 1.5 minutes. Furthermore, it has been decided to take a random sample of four ambulance calls each day to calculate a sample mean response time for monitoring performance. The usual confidence level of ±3 standard deviations is selected to guarantee a Type I error of less than 0.3 percent. Thus, there is a 0.3 percent chance of committing the error of taking corrective action when, in fact, the process is in control. This occurs because, for a normal distribution, 0.3 percent of the sample values fall beyond ±3 standard deviations from the mean. Appropriate formulas for calculating the control limits for an $\bar{X}$ chart are given below:

$$\text{UCL} = \mu + Z_\alpha \sigma_{\bar{X}} \tag{1}$$

$$\text{LCL} = \mu - Z_\alpha \sigma_{\bar{X}} \tag{2}$$

where μ = population mean
σ = population standard deviation
Z_α = standard normal deviate for Type I error of α percent
n = size of periodic sample
$\sigma_{\bar{X}} = \sigma/\sqrt{n}$ standard error of the mean

For the ambulance response time control chart shown in Figure 9.10, the control limits are calculated as follows:

$$\text{UCL} = 5.0 + 3(1.5/\sqrt{4}) = 5.0 + 3(0.75) = 7.25$$
$$\text{LCL} = 5.0 - 3(1.5/\sqrt{4}) = 5.0 - 3(0.75) = 2.75$$

Example 9.2: Control Chart for Attributes (*p* Chart)

In some cases, system performance is classified as either good or bad. Of primary concern is the percentage of bad performance. For example, consider the operator of a mechanized sorting machine in a post office. The operator must read the ZIP code on a parcel and, knowing its location in the city, divert the package by conveyor to the proper route truck. From past records, the error rate for skilled operators is about 5 percent, or a fraction defective of 0.05. Management wants to develop a control chart to monitor new operators with 95 percent assurance that personnel unsuited for the job can be identified. The following formulas are used to construct a percentage, or *p*, chart:

$$UCL = p + Z_\alpha \sigma_p \qquad (3)$$
$$LCL = p - Z_\alpha \sigma_p \qquad (4)$$

where p = population fraction defective
Z_α = standard deviate for Type I error of α percent
n = size of periodic sample
$\sigma_p = [p(1 - p)]/n$ standard error of the percentage

The p chart control limits for the sorting operation will be calculated on the basis of random samples of 100 parcels drawn from the route trucks. The selection of 1.96 for the Z_α value is found in the end-of-book Appendix table, with the restriction that half of α must be in each tail. Note that if the calculation of an LCL results in a negative number, the LCL is set equal to zero.

$$UCL = 0.05 + 1.96 \frac{(0.05)(0.95)}{100} = 0.05 + 1.96(0.0218) = 0.093$$

$$LCL = 0.05 - 1.96 \frac{(0.05)(0.95)}{100} = 0.05 - 1.96(0.0218) = 0.007$$

The p chart for this operation is shown in Figure 9.11. Given this nine-day probationary experience for the new employee, would you conclude that the person is suitable for the sorting position? What might you conclude if an operator's mean error rate fell below the 0.007 LCL?

Statistical Process Control at Midway Airlines[11]   Midway Airlines was once a successful regional carrier, with a major hub at the Midway Airport in Chicago and with service to other midwestern and northeastern cities. Midway was unable

---

[11]Adapted from D. Daryl Wyckoff, "New Tools for Achieving Service Quality," *The Cornell H.R.A. Quarterly,* November 1984, pp. 78–91.

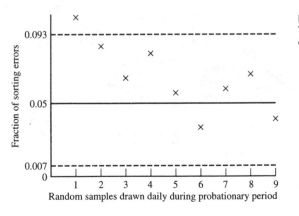

FIGURE 9.11
The p chart for a sorting operation.

to compete with the major carriers and eventually filed for bankruptcy, but not for lack of attention to quality. It used the hub-and-spoke network developed by budget carriers after deregulation required on-time departures that would avoid delays, which compromised the efficient transfer of passengers during their multileg journeys. Figure 9.12 shows a control chart used by Midway's employees to monitor this important measure of schedule performance. It is interesting to note that just the effort of tracking the percentage of on-time departures resulted in marked improvement for the early months of 1982. However, in November and December the on-time performance was severely eroded.

Additional study was deemed necessary to determine the underlying causes of late departures. Midway turned to a cause-and-effect tool called *fishbone analysis,* or an Ishikawa chart, which was so named after its originator. Figure 9.13 shows a fishbone analysis that identifies possible causes of flight departure delays. The analysis begins with the problem at the head and traces major categories of causes back along the spine. The usual causes are labeled under the broad categories: Personnel, Procedure, Equipment, Material, and Other. From personal experience, Midway's employees suggested specific causes of late departures, as noted below each broad category. Following a discussion of the completed chart, a consensus was reached that "acceptance of late passengers" was a probable cause. Typically, flights were held for late passengers because the company's policy on handling such passengers was vague.

Next, data were collected to determine how significant late arrivals were as a cause of departure delays. Midway used a technique called *Pareto analysis* that arranges data so that causes of a problem are ordered in descending frequency of occurrence. Pareto, a nineteenth-century Italian economist, observed that 80 percent of the country's wealth resided with 20 percent of its citizens. This principle, known as the *80/20 rule,* has been observed in many situations. For example, 80 percent of a retailer's sales are generated by 20 percent of the customers. Applying this rule to Midway, 80 percent of the departure delays should be accounted for by 20 percent of the causes. As seen in Table 9.7, approximately 90 percent of the departure delays were explained by four causes.

Accommodating late passengers proved to be the number one cause of departure

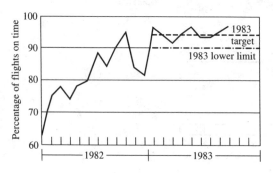

FIGURE 9.12
Control chart of Midway Airlines departure delays. [D. Daryl Wyckoff, *"New Tools for Achieving Service Quality,"* The Cornell HRA Quarterly, November 1984, p. 87. © Cornell. HRA Quarterly. Used by permission. All rights reserved.]

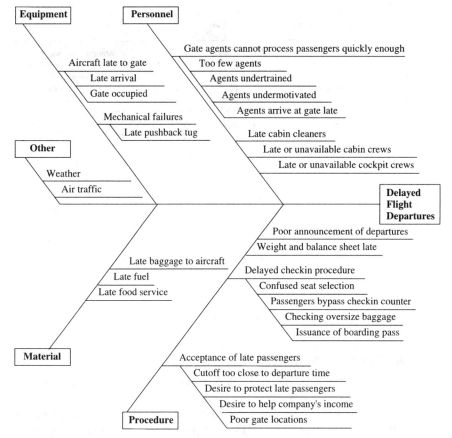

FIGURE 9.13
Portion of Midway Airlines fishbone analysis: causes of flight departure delays. [*D. Daryl Wyckoff, "New Tools for Achieving Service Quality,"* The Cornell HRA Quarterly, *November 1984, p. 89. © Cornell HRA Quarterly. Used by permission. All rights reserved.*]

delays. Because gate agents were anxious to avoid losing the fares of latecomers, they delayed flight departures and thus inconvenienced punctual passengers. Midway established a policy of on-time departure, and soon thereafter the number of late arrivals declined. The other causes of delays, such as waiting for "pushback" and a cabin-cleaning problem at Newark, were then addressed.

In January 1983, once the flight departure process was under control, the company set a target of 95 percent on-time departure and a lower control limit of 90 percent. The experience of Midway illustrates the reason why statistical process control is successful in improving service quality. The collection, recording, and analysis of data are accomplished by employees, who view the activity as an opportunity for self-improvement and learning.

TABLE 9.7
PARETO ANALYSIS OF FLIGHT DEPARTURE DELAYS

All stations, except hub		Newark		Washington (national)	
Percentage of incidences	Cumulative percentage	Percentage of incidences	Cumulative percentage	Percentage of incidences	Cumulative percentage
Late passengers 53.3	53.3	Late passengers 23.1	23.1	Late passengers 33.3	33.3
Waiting for pushback 15.0	68.3	Waiting for fueling 23.1	46.2	Waiting for pushback 33.3	66.6
Waiting for fueling 11.3	79.6	Waiting for pushback 23.1	69.3	Late weight and balance sheet 19.0	85.6
Late weight and balance sheet 8.7	88.3	Cabin cleaning and supplies 15.4	84.7	Waiting for fueling 9.5	95.1

Source: D. Daryl Wyckoff, "New Tools for Achieving Service Quality," *The Cornell HRA Quarterly,* November 1984, p. 89. © Cornell HRA Quarterly. Used by permission. All rights reserved.

PROGRAMS FOR SERVICE QUALITY IMPROVEMENT

Service quality begins with people! All our measurements to detect noncon-formance by means of statistically based control charts do not produce a quality service. Instead, quality begins with the development of positive attitudes among all people in the organization. How is this accomplished? Positive attitudes can be fostered through a coordinated program that begins with employee selection and progresses through training, initial job assignments, and other aspects of career advancements. To avoid complacency, an ongoing quality improvement program is required. These programs emphasize preventing poor quality, taking personal responsibility for quality, and building an attitude that quality can be made certain.

Personnel Programs for Quality Assurance

Multiunit service firms face special problems of maintaining consistent service across all units. For example, customers expect the same service from a hotel unit in Chicago that they found previously at a New Orleans unit of the same chain. In fact, the idea of "finding no surprises" is used as a marketing feature.

G. M. Hostage[12] believes that the success of the Marriott Corporation is due in part to personnel programs that stress training, standards of performance, career development, and rewards. He finds that service quality is enhanced by the

[12]G. M. Hostage, "Quality Control in a Service Business," *Harvard Business Review,* vol. 53, no. 4, July–August 1975, pp. 98–106.

attitude the company takes toward its employees. The following eight programs have been the most effective.

1. Individual development. Using programmed instruction manuals, new management trainees acquire the skills and technical knowledge needed for the entry-level position of assistant manager. For a geographically dispersed organization, these manuals ensure that job skills are being taught in a consistent manner.

2. *Management training.* Management personnel through the middle levels attend one management development session each year. A variety of professional management topics are addressed at two- and three-day seminars attended by lower-level managers from various operating divisions.

3. *Human resources planning.* The kinds of people needed to fill key company positions in coming years are identified. An inventory of good prospects is created for future promotion. A key element of the plan is a periodic performance review of all management personnel.

4. Standards of performance. A set of booklets was developed to instruct employees in how to conduct themselves when dealing with guests and, in some cases, even in how to speak. The Marriott Bellman stresses how to make a guest feel welcome and special. The Switchboard Operator tells in detail how to speak with a guest and how to handle a variety of specific situations. The Housekeeper tells precisely how a room is to be made up, down to the detail of placing the wrapped soap bar on the proper corner of the washbasin with the label upright. In many cases booklets are accompanied by an audiovisual film or a videotape to demonstrate proper procedures. Adherence to these standards is checked by random visits from a flying squad of inspectors.

5. *Career progression.* A job advancement program with a ladder of positions of increasing skill and responsibility gives employees the opportunity to grow with the company.

6. *Opinion surveys.* An annual rank-and-file opinion survey is conducted by trained personnel at each unit. Subsequently, the results are discussed at a meeting. This survey has acted as an early warning system to head off the buildup of unfavorable attitudes.

7. Fair treatment. Employees are provided with a handbook of company expectations and obligations to its personnel. The formal grievance procedure includes access to an ombudsperson to help resolve difficulties.

8. *Profit sharing.* A profit-sharing plan recognizes that employees are responsible for much of the company's success and that they deserve more than a paycheck for their efforts.

Quality-Improvement Program to Achieve Zero Defects

Philip Crosby, a former vice president for quality at ITT and now a sought-after quality-management consultant, advocates a 14-step zero-defects quality-improvement program.[13] His program has been implemented at a number of service firms, such as the Paul Revere Insurance Company. This program has the following 14 sequential steps:

1. *Management commitment.* The need for quality improvement is first discussed with members of management to gain their commitment. This raises the level of visibility and concern for quality at the highest levels and ensures everyone's cooperation.

2. *Quality-improvement team.* Representatives from each department are selected to form a team. This team runs the quality-improvement program and ensures each department's participation.

3. *Quality measurement.* The status of quality throughout the organization is audited. This requires that quality measurements be reviewed and established where they do not exist. Once quality becomes measurable, an objective evaluation is made to identify nonconformance and monitor corrective action. Developing quality measures for services is a difficult task, but it represents an opportunity for worker participation. Service personnel most often respond with enthusiasm and pride when asked to identify quality measures for their work.

4. *Cost-of-quality evaluation.* To avoid any bias in the calculations, the comptroller's office identifies the cost of quality. The cost of quality is composed of items such as litigation, rework, engineering changes, and inspection labor. Measuring the cost of quality provides an indication of where corrective action will be profitable for an organization.

5. *Quality awareness.* The cost of poor quality is communicated to supervisors and employees through the use of booklets, films, and posters. This helps change attitudes about quality by providing visible evidence of the concern for quality improvement.

6. *Corrective action.* A systematic process of facing problems, talking about them, and resolving them on a regular basis is needed. The habit of identifying quality problems and correcting them at the local level is encouraged.

7. *Establishment of a zero-defects program.* Three or four members of the team are selected to investigate the zero-defects concept and to implement the program. The committee should understand the literal meaning of the phrase *zero defects.* The idea that everyone should do his or her work right the first time must be communicated to all employees.

8. *Supervisor training.* A formal orientation is conducted for people at all levels of management to enable them to explain the program to their people.

9. *Zero-defects day.* An event is created that employees can recognize as a turning point in the organization's attitude toward quality. From this day on, zero defects will be the performance standard of the organization.

[13]Philip B. Crosby, *Quality Is Free: The Art of Making Quality Certain,* McGraw-Hill Book Company, New York, 1979.

10. *Goal setting.* Employees are encouraged to think in terms of establishing improvement goals for themselves and for their groups. Supervisors should help their employees set specific and measurable goals.

11. Error-cause removal. People are asked to describe on a simple one-page form any problem that keeps them from performing error-free work. The appropriate department is asked to respond to the problem expeditiously.

12. *Recognition.* Award programs are established to recognize those who meet their goals. With genuine recognition of performance, continued support for the program will result.

13. *Quality councils.* The quality professionals are brought together on a regular basis to discuss actions necessary for program improvement.

14. *Do it over again.* A typical program takes more than one year, and by then, employee turnover necessitates a new educational effort. The repetition makes the program a permanent part of the organization.

Deming's 14-Point Program

W. Edwards Deming is generally credited with initiating the highly successful Japanese quality revolution. In Deming's view, management was responsible for 85 percent of all quality problems and therefore had to provide the leadership in changing the systems and processes that created them. Management needed to refocus attention on meeting customer needs and on continuous improvement to stay ahead of the competition. His philosophy is captured in a 14-point program:[14]

1. *Create constancy of purpose for improvements of product and service.* Management must stop the preoccupation solely with the next quarter and build for the future. Innovation in all areas of business should be expected.

2. *Adopt the new philosophy.* Refuse to allow commonly accepted poor levels of work, delays, and lax service.

3. *Cease dependence on mass inspection.* Inspection comes too late and is costly. Instead, focus on improving the process.

4. *End the practice of awarding business on price tag alone.* Purchasing should buy on the basis of statistical evidence of quality, not on the basis of price. Reduce the number of vendors, and reward high-quality suppliers with long-term contracts.

5. *Constantly and forever improve the system of production and service.* Search continually for problems in the system, and seek ways for improvement. Waste must be reduced and quality improved in every business activity, front-office and back-office.

6. *Institute modern methods of training on the job.* Restructure training to define acceptable levels of work. Use statistical methods to evaluate training.

---

[14]W. Edwards Deming, *Quality, Productivity, and Competitive Position,* MIT Center for Advanced Engineering Study, Cambridge, Mass., 1982.

7. *Institute modern methods of supervising.* Focus supervision on helping workers do a better job. Provide the tools and techniques to promote pride in one's work.

8. *Drive out fear.* Eliminate fear by encouraging communication of problems and expression of ideas.

9. *Break down barriers between departments.* Encourage problem solving through teamwork and the use of quality-control circles.

10. *Eliminate numerical goals for the workforce.* Goals, slogans, and posters cajoling workers to increase productivity should be eliminated. Such exhortations cause worker resentment because most of the necessary changes are outside of their control.

11. *Eliminate work standards and numerical quotas.* Production quotas focus on quantity, and they guarantee poor quality in their attainment. Quality goals such as acceptable percentage of defective items do not motivate workers toward improvement. Use statistical methods for continuing improvement of quality and productivity.

12. *Remove barriers that hinder the hourly workers.* Workers need feedback on the quality of their work. All barriers to pride in one's work must be removed.

13. *Institute a vigorous program of education and training.* Because of changes in technology and turnover of personnel, all employees need continual training and retraining. All training must include basic statistical techniques.

14. *Create a structure in top management that will push every day on the above 13 points.* Clearly define management's permanent commitment to continuous improvement in quality and productivity.

Unconditional Service Guarantee[15]

Whenever you buy a product, a warranty to guarantee its performance is expected. But to guarantee a service, impossible! Not so, according to Christopher Hart, who writes that service guarantees exist and have five important features:

1. *Unconditional.* Customer satisfaction is unconditional, without exceptions. For example, L.L. Bean, a Maine mail-order house, accepts all returns without question and provides a replacement, a refund, or a credit.

2. *Easy to understand and communicate.* Customers should know precisely what to expect from a guarantee in measurable terms. For example, Bennigan's promises that if a lunch is not served within 15 minutes, the diner receives a free meal.

3. *Meaningful.* The guarantee should be important to the customer in financial terms as well as in service expectations. Domino's Pizza guarantees that if a pizza is not delivered within 30 minutes, the customer gets $3 off rather than a free pizza because its customers consider a rebate more desirable.

---

[15]From Christopher W. L. Hart, "The Power of Unconditional Service Guarantees," *Harvard Business Review,* July–August 1988, pp. 54–62.

4. *Easy to invoke.* A dissatisfied customer should not be hassled with filling out forms or writing letters to invoke a guarantee. Cititravel, a subsidiary of Citicorp, guarantees the lowest airfares or a refund of the difference. A toll-free call to an agent is all that is necessary to confirm a lower fare and get a refund.

5. *Easy to collect.* The best guarantees are resolved on the spot, as illustrated by Domino's Pizza and Bennigan's.

A service guarantee has obvious marketing appeal. But more importantly, the service guarantee can redefine the meaning of service for an industry by setting quality standards. For example, Federal Express defined small-parcel delivery with its overnight delivery guarantee. A service guarantee promotes organization effectiveness in several ways:

1. *Focuses on customers.* A guarantee forces a company to identify its customers' expectations. In a survey of its passengers, British Airways found that they judged its service on four dimensions: care and concern, initiative, problem solving, and—to the airline's surprise—recovery when things go wrong.

2. *Sets clear standards.* A specific, unambiguous guarantee for the customer also sets clear standards for the organization. The Federal Express delivery guarantee of "absolutely positively by 10:30 a.m." defines the responsibilities of all employees.

3. *Guarantees feedback.* Customers invoking a guarantee provide valuable information for quality assessment. Dissatisfied customers now have an incentive to complain and to get management's attention.

4. *Promotes an understanding of the service delivery system.* Before a guarantee is made, managers must identify the possible failure points in their system and the limits to which these can be controlled. Federal Express adopted a hub-and-spoke network to ensure that all packages would be brought to Memphis in the evening for sorting and flown out that very night for delivery by 10:30 a.m.

5. *Builds customer loyalty.* A guarantee reduces the customer's risk and builds market share by retaining dissatisfied customers who otherwise would leave for the competition.

Malcolm Baldrige National Quality Award

The Malcolm Baldrige National Quality Award was created by Congress on August 20, 1987. The award is named for Malcolm Baldrige, who served as Secretary of Commerce from 1981 until his death in a rodeo accident in 1987. The award is given annually to recognize U.S. companies that excel in quality achievement and quality management. There are three eligibility categories of the award: manufacturing companies, service companies, and small businesses.

Award recipients by year and category since its inception are given in the following table.

Manufacturing	Service	Small business
1988		
Motorola Inc. Schaumburg, Ill. Westinghouse Commercial Nuclear Fuel Division Pittsburgh, Pa.		Globe Metallurgical Inc. Cleveland, Ohio
1989		
Milliken & Company Spartanburg, S.C. Xerox Business Products and Systems Stamford, Conn.		
1990		
Cadillac Motor Car Company Detroit, Mich. IBM Rochester Rochester, Minn.	Federal Express Corporation Memphis, Tenn.	Wallace Co., Inc. Houston, Tex.
1991		
Solectron Corp. San Jose, Calif. Zytec Corp. Eden Prairie, Minn.		Marlow Industries Dallas, Tex.
1992		
AT&T Network Systems Group—Transmissions Business Unit Morristown, N.Y. Texas Instruments Defense Systems & Electronics Group Dallas, Tex.	AT&T Universal Card Services Jacksonville, Fla. The Ritz-Carlton Hotel Co. Atlanta, Ga.	Granite Rock Co. Watsonville, Calif.

Each company participating in the award process submits an application, which includes an Award Examination; sample examination items and point values are listed below. The Award Examination is designed not only to serve as a reliable basis for making awards but also to permit a diagnosis of the applicant's overall quality management. All award applicants receive feedback prepared by teams of U.S. quality experts. Because of this quality audit aspect of the award, Motorola requires all its vendors to apply for the award.

1993 EXAMINATION ITEMS AND POINT VALUES

1993 Examination Categories/Items	Point Values

1.0 Leadership — 95
- 1.1 Senior executive leadership 45
- 1.2 Management for quality 25
- 1.3 Public responsibility and corporate citizenship 25

2.0 Information and analysis — 75
- 2.1 Scope and management of quality and performance data and information 15
- 2.2 Competitive comparisons and benchmarking 20
- 2.3 Analysis and uses of company-level data 40

3.0 Strategic quality planning — 60
- 3.1 Strategic quality and company performance planning process 35
- 3.2 Quality and performance plans 25

4.0 Human resource development and management — 150
- 4.1 Human resource planning and management 20
- 4.2 Employee involvement 40
- 4.3 Employee education and training 40
- 4.4 Employee performance and recognition 25
- 4.5 Employee well-being and satisfaction 25

5.0 Management of process quality — 140
- 5.1 Design and introduction of quality products and services 40
- 5.2 Process management: product and service production and delivery processes 35
- 5.3 Process management: business processes and support services 30
- 5.4 Supplier quality 20
- 5.5 Quality assessment 15

6.0 Quality and operational results — 180
- 6.1 Product and service quality results 70
- 6.2 Company operational results 50
- 6.3 Business process and support service results 25
- 6.4 Supplier quality results 35

7.0 Customer focus and satisfaction — 300
- 7.1 Customer expectations: current and future 35
- 7.2 Customer relationship management 65
- 7.3 Commitment to customers 15
- 7.4 Customer satisfaction determination 30
- 7.5 Customer satisfaction results 85
- 7.6 Customer satisfaction comparison 70

Total points — 1000

Source: "1993 Award Criteria," *The Malcolm Baldrige National Quality Award,* Managed by United States Department of Commerce, Technology Administration, National Institute of Standards and Technology, Gaithersburg, Md.; Administered by American Society for Quality Control, Milwaukee, Wis., p. 15.

SUMMARY

We began our study of quality issues in services by noting that customers are the ultimate judges of a service's value. Market researchers have identified five principal dimensions that customers use to judge service quality. Customers use those dimensions to make their assessments, which are based primarily on a comparison of their expectations for the service desired with their perceptions of the service delivered. We then looked at the different types of gaps that can occur when customers' expectations do not meet their perceptions of the service.

Next we turned to the problem of measuring service quality and discussed five aspects concerning the scope of services, i.e., their content, process, structure, outcome, and impact. Benchmarking and SERVQUAL are two useful approaches that can be used to measure quality in a variety of services.

We noted the necessity of "designing in" quality and examined the Taguchi, *poka-yoke,* and quality function deployment methods of quality by design.

The costs of quality are categorized as failure costs, detection costs, and prevention costs. We illustrated the application of statistical process control to avoid high failure costs in service operations.

Finally, we considered the most important aspect of service quality—people—and looked at several programs, such as Crosby's zero-defects program and Deming's 14-point program, that are designed to ensure that service providers will always strive for excellence. Recent efforts to foster quality in services include unconditional guarantee programs and the Malcolm Baldrige National Quality Award.

In Chapter 10 we will look at the implications of supply and demand for service managers.

TOPICS FOR DISCUSSION

1. How do the five dimensions of service quality differ from those of product quality?
2. Why is the measurement of service quality so difficult?
3. Illustrate the four components in the cost of quality for a service of your choice.
4. Why do service firms hesitate to offer a service guarantee?
5. How can the recovery from a service failure be a blessing in disguise?

EXERCISES

9.1. In recent months several complaints have been sent to the police department of Gotham City regarding the increasing incidence of congestion on the city's streets. The complaints attribute the cause of these traffic tie-ups to the lack of synchronization of the traffic lights. The lights are controlled by a main computer system, and adjusting the program is costly. Therefore, the controllers are reluctant to change the situation unless there is a clear need to do so.

The police department began a study of 1000 intersections that were reported to have congestion in the past nine months. For a sample size of 1000, the data are as listed in the following table:

Month	Congestion incidence
January	14
February	18
March	14
April	12
May	16
June	8
July	19
August	12
September	14
October	7
November	10
December	18

a. Construct a control chart based on the above data.

b. If, during the next three months, the reports of congestion at these 1000 intersections indicate the following, should the system be modified?

Month	Congestion incidence
January	15
February	9
March	11

9.2. The Speedway Clinical Laboratory is a scientific blood-test laboratory that receives samples of blood from local hospitals and clinics. The blood samples are passed through several automated tests, and the results are printed out through a central computer that reads and stores the information about each sample of blood tested.

Management is concerned with the quality of the services it is providing and wants to establish quality-control limits as a measure of the quality of the tests given. Such managerial practice is viewed as significant, because an incorrect analysis of a sample can lead to a wrong diagnosis by the physician, which may cost the life of the patient. For this reason, 100 of the blood samples were collected after they had gone through the testing. After the tests were performed manually on this sample size of 100, the results were as follows:

Day	Bad samples	Day	Bad samples
1	8	11	4
2	3	12	6
3	1	13	5
4	0	14	10
5	4	15	2
6	2	16	1
7	9	17	0
8	6	18	6
9	3	19	3
10	1	20	2

a. Construct a control chart to be used in assessing the quality of the service described above.

b. On the average, what is the expected number of samples that were tested and had wrong results?

c. Later, another sample size of 100 was taken. After the accuracy of the tests was inspected, ten samples were found to have been analyzed incorrectly. What is your conclusion about the quality of the service?

9.3. The Long Life Insurance Company receives applications to buy insurance from its salespeople, who are specially trained in selling insurance to new customers. After the applications are received, they are processed through a computer. The computer is programmed in such a way that it can print out messages whenever it runs through an item that is not consistent with company policies. The company is concerned with the accuracy of the training that its salespeople receive. It contemplates recalling them for more training if the quality of their performance is below certain limits. Five samples of 20 applications that were received from specific market areas were collected and inspected. The results are as follows:

Sample	No. applications with errors
1	2
2	2
3	1
4	3
5	2

a. Estimate the standard deviation for the percentage of applications that need rework, from samples of size 20.

b. Determine the upper and lower control limits for a p chart with a sample size of 20.

c. After the control limits were established, a sample size of 20 was taken. Four applications were found to have mistakes. What can we conclude from this?

9.4. The management of the Diners Delight franchised restaurant chain is in the process of establishing quality-control charts for the time that its service people give to each customer. Management thinks that the length of time each customer is given should remain within certain limits to enhance the quality of the service. A sample of six service people was selected, and the customer service they provided was observed four times. The activities that the service people were performing were identified, and the time to service one customer was recorded:

	Service time, sec.			
Service person	Sample 1	Sample 2	Sample 3	Sample 4
1	200	150	175	90
2	120	85	105	75
3	83	93	130	150
4	68	150	145	175
5	110	90	75	105
6	115	65	115	125

a. Determine the upper and lower control limits of an X chart with a sample size of 6.

b. After the control chart was established, a sample of six service people was observed, and the following customer service times, in seconds, were recorded: 180, 125, 110, 98, 156, and 190. Is corrective action called for?

CASE: Clean Sweep, Inc.

Clean Sweep, Inc. (CSI) is a custodial-janitorial services company specializing in contract maintenance of office space. Although it is not a large company in comparison with its primary competitors, CSI does have several major contracts to service some of the state government's offices. In order to enter and stay in the custodial service business, CSI adopted the strategy of having a small workforce that performs high-quality work at a reasonably rapid pace. At present, CSI's management feels that it has a staff that is more productive on an individual basis than the staff of its competition. Management recognizes that this single factor is the key to the company's success, and so maintaining a high level of worker productivity is critical.

Within the staff, the organizational structure is divided into four crews, each of which is composed of a crew leader and six to nine other crew members, and all crews are under the direction of a single crew supervisor. Within the state building complex, there are nine buildings included in CSI's contracts, and the custodial assignments have been distributed as shown in Table 9.8 to balance the work-load distribution among the crews (on the basis of gross square feet of floor space per member).

TABLE 9.8
CUSTODIAL ASSIGNMENTS

Crew	No. of members*	Buildings assigned and gross ft²	Total ft² assigned
1	6	Bldg. A, 30,000; Bldg. C, 45,000; Bldg. F, 35,000	110,000
2	8	Bldg. B East, 95,000; Bldg. H, 55,000	150,000
3	9	Bldg. B West, 95,000; Bldg. G, 85,000	180,000
4	8	Bldg. D, 40,000; Bldg. E, 75,000; Bldg. I, 42,000	157,000

*Excludes crew leader.

The responsibilities of each crew involve the following general tasks, listed in no order of importance: (1) vacuum carpeted floors, (2) empty trash cans and place trash in industrial waste hoppers, (3) dry-mop and buff marble floors, (4) clean rest rooms, (5) clean snack bar area(s), and (6) dust desk tops.

Each crew works an $8\frac{1}{2}$-hour shift, during which it gets two 15-minute paid rest breaks and one 30-minute lunch break (unpaid). However, there is some variation among the crews in choosing break and lunch times, primarily owing to the personalities of the crew leaders. The leaders of crews 2 and 3 are the strictest in their supervision, while the leaders of crews 1 and 4 are the least strict, according to the crew supervisor.

CSI's management is aware that the department of the state government that oversees the custodial service contracts makes periodic random inspections and rates the cleaning jobs CSI does. This department also receives any complaints about the custodial service from office workers. Table 9.9 contains the monthly ratings and number of complaints received (by building) during CSI's current contracts. Because the time for renegotiation of CSI's contracts is several months away, company management would like to maintain a high quality level during the remaining months to improve its competitive stance.

As is typical with other custodial service operations, employee turnover in CSI's staff has been fairly high, but it is still lower than the turnover experienced by many of CSI's competitors. Management attributes this to the higher pay scale CSI offers, relative to that of the competition. Even though individual staff costs are higher, the greater productivity levels of a smaller-than-average workforce have resulted in greater-than-average profits for the company. Nevertheless, there are problems reported by the crew supervisor, as well as complaints voiced by the crew members. These complaints fall into two general categories: (1) inequity in crew leaders' attitudes and performance expectations and (2) lack of opportunities for personal advancement. Table 9.10 shows a historical distribution of monthly complaints from each crew according to these two categories for the same period covered by the ratings reported in Table 9.9.

TABLE 9.9
COMPLAINTS ABOUT AND RATINGS OF CLEANING CREWS*

Month	Building									
	A	Be	Bw	C	D	E	F	G	H	I
1	2	5	7	3	2	3	2	4	3	4
	7	5	3	6	7	5	6	5	4	5
2	1	6	8	2	1	1	2	3	2	5
	7	5	3	6	6	5	6	5	5	4
3	0	6	8	1	0	2	2	4	0	1
	8	5	4	6	8	5	6	6	6	7
4	1	5	4	1	0	1	1	4	1	3
	7	5	5	8	8	6	7	5	6	6
5	1	3	2	2	0	1	1	3	1	2
	6	6	6	7	8	6	7	5	6	6
6	2	5	3	0	1	0	0	2	1	0
	7	6	6	7	7	8	6	5	5	7
7	0	4	2	1	0	0	0	0	0	1
	8	7	7	6	6	8	8	6	7	7
8	1	2	4	2	1	0	1	2	1	1
	6	6	5	7	7	8	7	5	6	7
9	1	2	4	1	1	0	1	1	3	0
	7	7	5	6	7	8	6	5	5	8

*First-row numbers for each month represent total number of complaints. Second-row numbers for each month represent ratings on a 1-to-10 scale; any rating under 5 is felt to be poor, and 8 or above is good.

TABLE 9.10
JOB-RELATED COMPLAINTS FROM CREW MEMBERS

	Crew 1		Crew 2		Crew 3		Crew 4	
Month	Ineq- uity	No advance- ment	Ineq- uity	No advance- ment	Ineq- uity	No advance- ment	Ineq- uity	No advance- ment
1	0	1	3	3	4	3	0	2
2	0	0	2	1	1	1	0	1
3	1	0	2	1	2	2	1	2
4	0	0	1	2	3	1	0	2
5	1	1	3	1	2	1	0	2
6	1	0	1	2	2	1	0	1
7	0	1	1	1	1	3	0	1
8	0	0	2	2	1	2	1	1
9	0	0	2	1	2	2	0	2

Questions

1. Given the facts of the case and your conception of the custodial service industry, assess the service quality of CSI's crews.

2. Discuss possible ways to improve service quality.

3. Describe some potential strategies for reducing CSI's staffing problems.

CASE: The Complaint Letter

Most service problems are solved by direct communication between the server and the customer at the moment of service. Occasionally, however, a customer may be motivated to communicate some thoughtful and detailed feedback to a service provider after the encounter, as illustrated in the following letter:

THE COMPLAINT LETTER

October 13, 1986
123 Main Street
Boston, Massachusetts

Gail and Harvey Pearson
The Retreat House on Foliage Pond
Vacationland, New Hampshire

Dear Mr. and Mrs. Pearson:

This is the first time that I have ever written a letter like this, but my wife and I are so upset by the treatment afforded by your staff that we felt compelled to let you know what happened to us. We had dinner reservations at the Retreat House for a party of four under my wife's name, Dr. Elaine Loflin, for Saturday evening, October 11. We were hosting my wife's brother and his wife, visiting from Atlanta, Georgia.

We were seated at 7:00 p.m. in the dining room to the left of the front desk. There were at least four empty tables in the room when we were seated. We were immediately given menus, a wine list, ice water, dinner rolls, and butter. Then we sat for 15 minutes until the cocktail waitress asked us for our drink orders. My sister-in-law said, after being asked what she would like, "I'll have a vodka martini straight-up with an olive." The cocktail waitress responded immediately, "I'm not a stenographer." My sister-in-law repeated her drink order.

Soon after, our waiter arrived, informing us of the specials of the evening. I don't remember his name, but he had dark hair, wore glasses, was a little stocky, and had his sleeves rolled up. He returned about ten minutes later, our drinks still not having arrived. We had not decided upon our entrees, but requested appetizers, upon which he informed us that we could not order appetizers without ordering our entrees at the same time. We decided not to order appetizers.

Our drinks arrived and the waiter returned. We ordered our entrees at 7:30. When the waiter asked my wife for her order, he addressed her as "young lady." When he served her the meal, he called her "dear."

At ten minutes of eight we requested that our salads be brought to us as soon as possible. I then asked the waiter's assistant to bring us more rolls (each of us had been served one when we were seated). Her response was, "Who wants a roll?," upon which, caught off guard, we went around the table saying yes or no so she would know exactly how many "extra" rolls to bring to our table.

Our salads were served at five minutes of eight. At 25 minutes past the hour we requested our entrees. They were served at 8:30, one and one-half hours after we were seated in a restaurant which was one-third empty. Let me also add that we had to make constant requests for water refills, butter replacement, and the like.

In fairness to the chef, the food was excellent, and as you already realize, the atmosphere was delightful. Despite this, the dinner was a disaster. We were extremely upset and very insulted by the experience.

Your staff is not well trained. They were overtly rude, and displayed little etiquette or social grace. This was compounded by the atmosphere you are trying to present and the prices you charge in your dining room.

Perhaps we should have made our feelings known at the time, but our foremost desire was to leave as soon as possible. We had been looking forward to dining at the Retreat House for quite some time as part of our vacation weekend in New Hampshire.

We will be hard-pressed to return to your establishment. Please be sure to know that we will share our experience at the Retreat House with our family, friends, and business associates.

Sincerely,
Dr. William E. Loflin

Source: Martin R. Moser, "Answering the Customer's Complaint: A Case Study," *The Cornell HRA Quarterly,* May 1987, p. 10. © Cornell HRA Quarterly. Used by permission. All rights reserved.

Experience has shown that complaint letters receive "mixed reviews." That is, some letters bring immediate positive responses from the providers while other letters bring no response or resolution. The restaurateur's response to the complaint letter in this case follows:

THE RESTAURATEUR'S REPLY

The Retreat House on Foliage Pond
Vacationland, New Hampshire
November 15, 1986

Dr. William E. Loflin
123 Main Street
Boston, Massachusetts

Dear Dr. Loflin:

My husband and I are naturally distressed by such a negative reaction to our restaurant, but very much appreciate your taking the time and trouble to apprise us of your recent dinner here. I perfectly understand and sympathize with your feelings, and would like to tell you a little about the circumstances involved.

The Lakes Region for the past four or five years has been notorious for its extremely low unemployment rate and resulting deplorable labor pool. This year local businesses found that the situation had deteriorated to a really alarming nadir. It has been virtually impossible to get adequate help, competent or otherwise! We tried to overhire at the beginning of the season, anticipating the problems we knew would arise, but were unsuccessful. Employees in the area know the situation very well and use it to their advantage, knowing that they can get a job anywhere at any time without references, and knowing they won't be fired for incompetency because there is no one to replace them. You can imagine the prevailing attitude among workers and the frustration it causes employers, particularly those of us who try hard to maintain high standards. Unhappily, we cannot be as selective about employees as we would wish, and the turnover is high. Proper training is not only a luxury, but an impossibility at such times.

Unfortunately, the night you dined at the Retreat House, October 11, is traditionally one of the busiest nights of the year, and though there may have been empty tables at the time you sat down, I can assure you that we served 150 people that night, despite the fact that no fewer than four members of the restaurant staff did not show up for work at the last minute, and did not notify us. Had they had the courtesy to call, we could have limited reservations, thereby mitigating the damage at least to a degree, but as it was, we, our guests, and the employees who were trying to make up the slack all had to suffer delays in service far beyond the norm!

As to the treatment you received from the waitress and waiter who attended you, neither of them is any longer in our employ, and never would have been had the labor situation not been so desperate! It would have indeed been helpful to us had you spoken up at the time—it makes a more lasting impression on the employees involved than does our discussing it with them

after the fact. Now that we are in a relatively quiet period we have the time to properly train a new and, we hope, better waitstaff.

Please know that we feel as strongly as you do that the service you received that night was unacceptable, and certainly not up to our normal standards.

We hope to be able to prevent such problems from arising in the future, but realistically must acknowledge that bad nights do happen, even in the finest restaurants. Believe me, it is not because we do not care or are not paying attention!

You mentioned our prices. Let me just say that were you to make a comparative survey, you would find that our prices are about one half of what you would expect to pay in most cities and resort areas for commensurate cuisine and ambience. We set our prices in order to be competitive with other restaurants in this particular local area, in spite of the fact that most of them do not offer the same quality of food and atmosphere and certainly do not have our overhead!

I hope that this explanation (which should not be misconstrued as an excuse) has shed some light, and that you will accept our deep regrets and apologies for any unpleasantness you and your party suffered. We should be very glad if someday you would pay us a return visit so that we may provide you with the happy and enjoyable dining experience that many others have come to appreciate at the Retreat House.

Sincerely,
Gail Pearson

Source: Martin R. Moser, "Answering the Customer's Complaint: A Case Study," *The Cornell HRA Quarterly,* May 1987, p. 11. © Cornell HRA Quarterly. Used by permission. All rights reserved.

Questions

1. Briefly summarize the complaints and compliments in Dr. Loflin's letter.
2. Critique the letter of Gail Pearson in reply to Dr. Loflin. What are the strengths and weaknesses of the letter?
3. Prepare an "improved" response letter from Gail Pearson.
4. What further action should Gail Pearson take in view of this incident?

SELECTED BIBLIOGRAPHY

Behara, R. S., and R. B. Chase: "Service Quality Deployment: Quality Service by Design," in Rakesh V. Sarin (ed.), *Perspectives in Operations Management: Essays in Honor of Elwood S. Buffa,* Kluwer Academic Publisher, Norwell, Mass., 1993.

Berry, L. L., V. A. Zeithaml, and A. Parasuraman: "Five Imperatives for Improving Service Quality," *Sloan Management Review Association,* vol. 31, no. 4, summer 1990, pp. 29–38.

Berry, L. L., V. A. Zeithaml, and A. Parasuraman: "Quality Counts in Services, Too," *Business Horizons,* Foundation for the School of Business at Indiana University, May–June 1985, pp. 44–52.

Collier, David A.: "The Customer Service and Quality Challenge," *The Service Industries Journal,* vol. 7, no. 1, 1987, pp. 77–90.

Crosby, Philip B.: *Quality Is Free: The Art of Making Quality Certain,* McGraw-Hill Book Company, New York, 1979.

Deming, W. Edwards: *Quality, Productivity, and Competitive Position,* M.I.T. Center for Advanced Engineering Study, Cambridge, Mass., 1982.

Garvin, David A.: "Competing on the Eight Dimensions of Quality," *Harvard Business Review,* November–December 1987, pp. 101–109.

Hart, Christopher W. L.: "The Power of Unconditional Service Guarantees," *Harvard Business Review,* July–August 1988, pp. 54–62.

Hauser, J. R., and D. Clausing: "The House of Quality," *Harvard Business Review,* May–June 1988, pp. 63–73.

Haywood-Farmer, John: "Towards a Conceptual Model of Service Quality," *International Journal of Operations and Production Management,* vol. 8, no. 6, 1988, pp. 19–29.

Hostage, G. M.: "Quality Control in a Service Business," *Harvard Business Review,* vol. 53, no. 4, July–August 1975, pp. 98–106.

Klaus, Peter G.: "Quality Epiphenomenon: The Conceptual Understanding of Quality in Face-to-Face Service Encounters," in J. A. Czepiel, M. R. Solomon, and C. F. Surprenant (eds.), *The Service Encounter,* Lexington Books, Lexington, Mass., 1985, chap. 2, pp. 17–35.

Lees, J., and B. G. Dale: "Quality Circles in Service Industries: A Study of Their Use," *The Service Industry Journal,* vol. 8, no. 2, 1988, pp. 143–154.

Parasuraman, A., V. A. Zeithaml, and L. L. Berry: "A Conceptual Model of Service Quality and Its Implications for Future Research," *Journal of Marketing,* vol. 49, fall 1985, pp. 41–50.

———, V. A. Zeithaml, and L. L. Berry: "SERVQUAL: A Multiple-Item Scale for Measuring Consumer Perceptions of Service Quality," *Journal of Retailing,* vol. 64, no. 1, spring 1988, pp. 12–40.

Reichheld, F. F., and W. E. Sasser: "Zero Defections: Quality Comes to Services," *Harvard Business Review,* September–October 1990, pp. 105–111.

Taguchi, G., and D. Clausing: "Robust Quality," *Harvard Business Review,* January–February 1990, pp. 65–75.

Takeuchi, H., and J. A. Quelch: "Quality Is More than Making a Good Product," *Harvard Business Review,* vol. 61, no. 4, July–August 1983, pp. 139–145.

Tribus, Myron: "Deming's Way," *Mechanical Engineering,* vol. 10, no. 1, January 1988, pp. 26–30.

Wyckoff, D. D.: "New Tools for Achieving Service Quality," *The Cornell H.R.A. Quarterly,* vol. 25, no. 3, November 1984, pp. 78–91.

Zeithaml, V. A., L. L. Berry, and A. Parasuraman: "Communication and Control Processes in the Delivery of Service Quality," *Journal of Marketing,* vol. 52, April 1988, pp. 35–48.

CHAPTER 10

MANAGING SUPPLY AND DEMAND

After fixed capacity investment decisions have been made (e.g., number of hotel rooms to be built or aircraft to be purchased) using the approaches described in Chapter 15, the hotel beds must be filled or airline seats sold to make the daily operations profitable. The subject of this chapter is the challenge faced by managers of matching service supply with customer demand on a daily basis in a dynamic environment.

Service capacity is a perishable commodity. For example, a plane flying with empty seats has lost forever the revenue opportunity of flying with one more passenger. American Airlines was the first in its industry to address this problem and to realize the potential of using what is now called *yield management,* which was discussed briefly in Chapter 4 and will be addressed in more detail in this chapter. The use of information technology to support yield management was not lost on Mr. Donald Burr, CEO of People Express, whose failing airline was bought by Texas Air in 1986. He is quoted as saying, "I'm the world's leading example of a guy killed by a computer chip."[1]

Unlike products that are stored in warehouses for future consumption, a service is an intangible personal experience that cannot be transferred from one person to another. Instead, a service is produced and consumed simultaneously. Whenever the demand for a service falls short of the capacity to serve, the results are idle servers and facilities. Furthermore, the variability in service demand is quite pronounced. In fact, our culture and habits contribute to these fluctuations. For example, most of us eat our meals at the same hours and take our vacations in

---

[1]R. L. Rose and J. Dahl, "Skies Are Deregulated, but Just Try Starting a Sizable New Airline," *The Wall Street Journal,* July 19, 1989, p. 1.

July and August. Studies of hospitals indicate low utilization in the summer and fall months. These natural variations in service demand create periods of idle service at some times and periods of consumer waiting at other times.

CHAPTER PREVIEW

In this chapter, we shall explore operating strategies that can increase capacity utilization by better matching the supply of and demand for services. We begin our discussion with marketing-oriented strategies that can alter and smooth customer demand, such as using price incentives and promotion to stimulate off-peak demand. Another common strategy is creating complementary services to balance the total demand among several services. The controversial practice of overbooking is examined in the context of making better use of perishable service capacity.

We will also look at operations-oriented strategies to control the level of service supply, such as scheduling workshifts, using part-time employees, and cross-training customer contact personnel in order to be more flexible in response to changes in customer demand. In conclusion, the new concept of yield management pioneered by the airlines will be explored as a comprehensive approach using many of these strategies in a sophisticated on-line information system.

STRATEGIES FOR MANAGING DEMAND

Excessive fluctuations in demand for service need not be accepted as inevitable. Service systems can smooth their demand by using both active and passive measures. With *smoothed demand,* the cyclical variation has been reduced. While the arrival of consumers will still occur at random intervals, the average rate of arrivals will be more stable over time. We shall discuss several strategies that might be used for demand smoothing. Figure 10.1 summarizes the strategies commonly used to manage service capacity.

Partitioning Demand

Demand for a service is seldom derived from a homogeneous source. Instead, it is often grouped into random arrivals and planned arrivals. For example, a drive-in bank can expect visits from its commercial accounts on a regular daily basis and at approximately the same time. It can also expect random arrivals of its personal account holders.

An analysis of health clinic demand done by E. J. Rising, R. Baron, and B. Averill showed that the greatest number of walk-in patients arrived on Monday and that fewer numbers arrived during the remaining weekdays.[2] While walk-in demand is uncontrollable, appointments are controllable. Therefore, why not make appointments in the latter part of the week to level demand? Using data for the

---

[2] E. J. Rising, R. Baron, and B. Averill, "A Systems Analysis of a University Health-Service Outpatient Clinic," *Operations Research,* vol. 21, no. 5, September 1973, pp. 1030–1047.

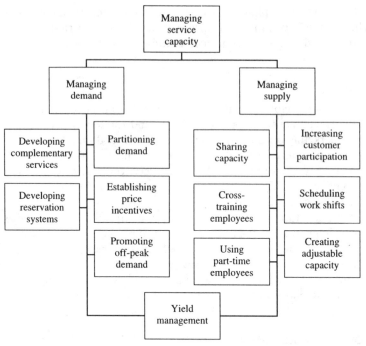

FIGURE 10.1
Strategies for matching supply of and demand for services.

same week in the previous year, the researchers noted the number of walk-in patients for each weekday. Subtracting these walk-in patients from daily physician capacity gives the number of appointment patients needed each day to smooth demand. For the sample week shown in Figure 10.2, this procedure yielded the number of appointment periods per day shown in Table 10.1.

The daily smoothing of demand was further refined by scheduling appointments at appropriate times during the day. After a two-month shakedown period, smoothing demand yielded the following benefits:

1. The number of patients seen by physicians increased by 13.4 percent.
2. The increase in patient demand was met, even though 5.1 percent fewer physician hours were scheduled.
3. The overall time physicians spent with patients increased 5.0 percent because of an increase in the number of appointments.
4. The average waiting time for patients remained the same.
5. A team of sociologists concluded that physician morale increased.

Offering Price Incentives

There are many examples of differential pricing. Consider the following:

1. Weekend and night rates for long-distance telephone calls.

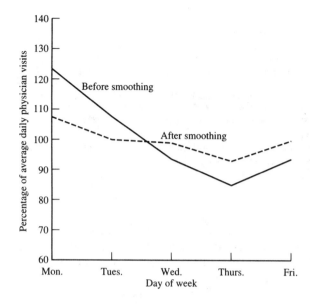

FIGURE 10.2
Effect of smoothing physician visits. [*E. J. Rising, R. Baron, and B. Averill, "A Systems Analysis of a University Health-Service Outpatient Clinic." Reprinted with permission from* Operations Research, *vol. 21, no. 5, Sept.–Oct. 1973, p. 1035,* Operations Research Society of America. No further reproduction permitted without the consent of the copyright owner.]

2. Matinee or reduced prices before 6 p.m. at movie theaters.
3. Off-season hotel rates at resort locations.
4. Peak-load pricing by utility companies.

Differential pricing has been suggested for federal campsites to encourage better use of this scarce resource. For example, J. C. Nautiyal and R. L. Chowdhary developed a discriminatory pricing system that ensures that camping fees will accurately reflect the marginal benefit of the last campsite on any given day.[3]

They identified four different camping experiences on the basis of days and weeks of the camping season. Table 10.2 contains a schedule of daily fees by experience type.

[3]J. C. Nautiyal and R. L. Chowdhary, "A Suggested Basis for Pricing Campsites: Demand Estimation in an Ontario Park," *Journal of Leisure Research,* vol. 7, no. 2, 1975, pp. 95–107.

TABLE 10.1
Smoothing Demand by Appointment Scheduling

Day	Appointments
Monday	84
Tuesday	89
Wednesday	124
Thursday	129
Friday	114

TABLE 10.2
SUGGESTED DISCRIMINATORY FEE SCHEDULE

Experience type	Days and weeks of camping season	No. of days	Daily fee
1	Saturdays and Sundays of weeks 10 to 15, plus Dominion Day and civic holidays	14	$6.00
2	Saturdays and Sundays of weeks 3 to 9 and 15 to 19, plus Victoria Day	23	2.50
3	Fridays of weeks 3 to 15, plus all other days of weeks 9 to 15 that are not in experience type 1 or 2	43	0.50
4	Rest of camping season	78	Free

The experience groupings were made on the basis of total daily occupancy in the park, under the assumption that occupancy is directly affected by available leisure time and climate. Campers in each experience group were interviewed to determine their travel costs. It was assumed that the marginal visitor was the camper who had incurred the highest cost in coming to the recreation site. This information was used to develop a demand curve for each experience type. Given the available number of campsites, the campsite fee was determined by means of these demand curves. Table 10.3 shows a comparison of the revenues generated under the existing system with those estimated when using discriminatory fees.

Additional benefits of discriminatory pricing can also be realized. For experience type 4, which is free, no regular staff need be maintained at the campsites. However, for the arrangement to work effectively in altering demand, it must be well advertised and include an advance booking system for campsites.

Note the projected increase in demand for experience type 3 because of the substantially reduced fee. The result of off-peak pricing is to tap a latent demand for campsites instead of redistributing peak demand to off-peak times. Thus, discriminatory pricing fills in the valleys (periods of low demand) instead of leveling off the peaks. The result is overall better utilization of a scarce resource and, for

TABLE 10.3
COMPARISON OF EXISTING REVENUE AND PROJECTED REVENUE FROM DISCRIMINATORY PRICING

Experience type	Existing fee of $2.50		Discriminatory fee	
	Campsites occupied	Revenue	Campsites occupied (est.)	Revenue
1	5,891	$14,727	5,000	$30,000
2	8,978	22,445	8,500	21,250
3	6,129	15,322	15,500	7,750
4	4,979	12,447	....	....
Total	25,977	$64,941	29,000	$59,000

a private-sector firm, a potential for increased profit, assuming that fees cover variable costs. However, private firms would also want to avoid directing high-paying customers to low rate schedules. For example, airlines exclude the business traveler from discount fares by using restrictions such as requiring passengers to remain at their destination over a weekend.

Promoting Off-Peak Demand

Creative use of off-peak capacity results from seeking out different sources of demand. An example is the use of a resort hotel during the off-season as a retreat location for business or professional groups. A mountain ski resort becomes a staging area for backpacking during the summer. Telephone companies offer lower rates to encourage long-distance dialing at night or on weekends, when switching equipment is underutilized. Figure 10.3 shows such a schedule for one of the long-distance carriers.

The strategy of promoting off-peak demand can be used to discourage overtaxing the facility at other times. A department store's appeal to "shop early and avoid the Christmas rush" and a supermarket's offer of double coupons on Wednesdays are examples.

Developing Complementary Services

Restaurants have discovered the benefits of complementary services by adding a bar. Diverting waiting customers into the lounge during busy periods can be profitable to the restaurant, as well as soothing to anxious consumers. Movie theaters have traditionally sold popcorn and soft drinks. But now they also include video games in their lobbies. These examples illustrate complementary services offered to occupy waiting consumers.

Convenience stores have expanded their services to include self-service gas pumps and fast-food meals. The concept of holistic medicine, which combines

FIGURE 10.3
Rate schedule for Sprint PLUS.

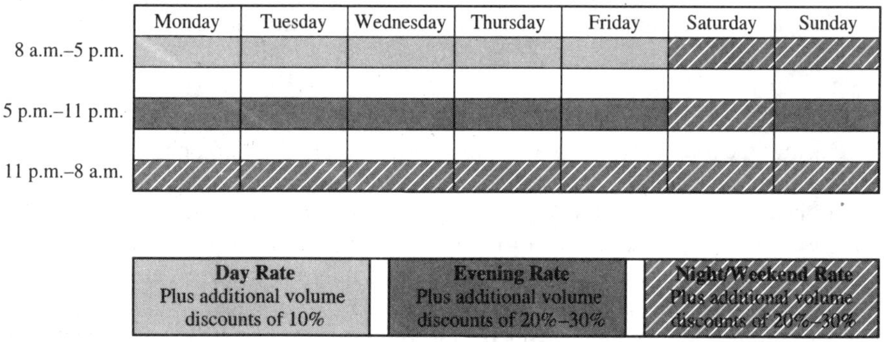

	Monday	Tuesday	Wednesday	Thursday	Friday	Saturday	Sunday
8 a.m.–5 p.m.							
5 p.m.–11 p.m.							
11 p.m.–8 a.m.							

Day Rate	Evening Rate	Night/Weekend Rate
Plus additional volume discounts of 10%	Plus additional volume discounts of 20%–30%	Plus additional volume discounts of 20%–30%

traditional medical attention with nutritional and psychiatric care, is a further example. Developing complementary services is a natural way of expanding one's market. It is particularly attractive if the new demands for service are contra-cyclical and result in a more uniform aggregate demand (i.e., when the new service demand is high, the original service demand is low). This explains why nearly all heating contractors also perform air-conditioning services.

Using Reservation Systems and Handling the Overbooking Problem

Taking reservations presells the potential service. As reservations are made, additional demand is deflected to other time slots at the same facility or to other facilities of the same organization. Hotel chains with national reservation systems regularly book customers in nearby hotels within their chain when the customer's first choice is not available.

Reservations also benefit consumers by reducing waiting and guaranteeing service availability. However, problems do arise when customers fail to honor their reservations (these customers are referred to as no-shows). Usually, customers are not held financially liable for their unkept reservations. This can lead to undesirable behavior, such as when passengers make several flight reservations to cover contingencies. This was a common practice of business passengers, who didn't know exactly when they would be able to depart. With multiple reservations, they would be assured of a flight out as soon as they were able to leave. But all unused reservations result in empty seats unless the airline is notified in advance of the cancellations. To control no-shows among discount flyers, airlines now issue nonrefundable tickets.

Airlines, faced with flying empty seats because of the no-shows, adopted a strategy of overbooking. By accepting reservations for more than the available seats, airlines hedge against significant numbers of no-shows. However, the airlines risk turning away passengers with reservations if they overbook too many seats. Because of overbooking abuses, the Federal Aviation Administration instituted regulations requiring airlines to reimburse overbooked passengers and to find them space on the next available flight. Similarly, many hotels place their overbooked guests in a nearby hotel of equal quality at no expense to the guests. A good overbooking strategy should minimize the expected opportunity cost of idle service capacity and the expected cost of turning away reservations.

Example 10.1: Surfside Hotel

During the past tourist season, Surfside Hotel did not achieve very high occupancy in spite of a reservation system designed to keep the hotel fully booked. Prospective guests apparently were making reservations that, for one reason or another, they failed to honor. A review of front-desk records during the current peak period, when the hotel was fully booked, revealed the record of no-shows given in Table 10.4.

A room that remains vacant owing to a no-show results in an opportunity loss of the $40 room contribution. From Table 10.4, the expected number of

TABLE 10.4
SURFSIDE HOTEL NO-SHOW EXPERIENCE

No-shows d	Probability P(d)	Critical fractile P(d < x)
0	.07	0
1	.19	.07
2	.22	.26
3	.16	.48
4	.12	.64
5	.10	.76
6	.07	.86
7	.04	.93
8	.02	.97
9	.01	.99

no-shows is calculated to be 3.04. This yields an expected opportunity loss of 3.04 × \$40, or \$121.60, per night. In order to avoid some of this loss, management is considering an overbooking policy. However, if a guest holding a reservation is turned away owing to overbooking, other costs are incurred. Surfside has made arrangements with a nearby hotel to pay for the rooms of guests it cannot accommodate. Furthermore, there is a penalty associated with the loss of customer goodwill and the impact this has on future business. Management estimates this total loss to be approximately \$100 per guest "walked" (a term used by the hotel industry). A good overbooking strategy must strike a balance between all these costs. The best overbooking strategy should minimize the expected loss in the long run. Table 10.5 displays the loss associated with each possible overbooking alternative.

TABLE 10.5
OVERBOOKING LOSS TABLE

No-shows	Prob-ability	Reservations overbooked									
		0	1	2	3	4	5	6	7	8	9
0	.07	0	100	200	300	400	500	600	700	800	900
1	.19	40	0	100	200	300	400	500	600	700	800
2	.22	80	40	0	100	200	300	400	500	600	700
3	.16	120	80	40	0	100	200	300	400	500	600
4	.12	160	120	80	40	0	100	200	300	400	500
5	.10	200	160	120	80	40	0	100	200	300	400
6	.07	240	200	160	120	80	40	0	100	200	300
7	.04	280	240	200	160	120	80	40	0	100	200
8	.02	320	280	240	200	160	120	80	40	0	100
9	.01	360	320	280	240	200	160	120	80	40	0
Expected loss, \$	....	121.60	91.40	87.80	115.00	164.60	231.00	311.40	401.60	497.40	560.00

For each overbooking strategy, the expected loss is calculated by multiplying the loss for each no-show possibility by its probability of occurrence and adding the products. For example, for a policy of overbooking by two rooms, the following calculations are made:

.07($200) + .19($100) + .22($0) + .16($40) + .12($80) + .10($120)
    + .07($160) + .04($200) + .02($240) + .01($280) = $87.80

Table 10.5 indicates that a policy of overbooking by two rooms will minimize the expected loss in the long run. If this policy is adopted, front-desk personnel will need to be trained to handle overbooked guests in a gracious manner!

In Chapter 15, the critical fractile model below is derived:

$$P(d < x) \le \frac{C_u}{C_u + C_o} \tag{1}$$

This model, based on marginal analysis, also can be used to identify the best overbooking strategy. Let C_o be the $100 opportunity loss associated with not having a room available for an overbooked guest (i.e., the number of no-shows was *overestimated*), and let C_u be the forgone $40 room contribution when a reservation is not honored (i.e., the number of no-shows was *underestimated*). Let d be the number of no-shows based on past experience and x the number of rooms overbooked. Then the number of rooms overbooked should just cover the cumulative probability of no-shows calculated below and no more:

$$P(d < x) \le \frac{\$40}{\$40 + \$100} \le .28$$

From Table 10.4, a strategy of overbooking by two rooms satisfies the critical fractile, confirming our earlier decision above.

STRATEGIES FOR MANAGING SUPPLY

For many services, demand cannot be smoothed very effectively. Consider, for example, the demand for telephone operators shown in Figure 10.4. These data are the half-hourly call rates during a typical 24-hour day for a metropolitan telephone company. We see that peak volume (2500 calls) occurs at 10:30 a.m. and that the minimum volume (20 calls) occurs at 5:30 a.m. The peak-to-valley variation is 125 to 1. No inducements are likely to change this demand pattern substantially. Therefore, control must come from adjusting service supply to match demand. We shall discuss several strategies that can be used to control service supply.

Using Daily Workshift Scheduling

By scheduling workshifts carefully during the day, the profile of service supply can be made to approximate demand. Workshift scheduling is an important staffing problem for many service organizations faced with cyclical demand, such as telephone companies, hospitals, banks, and police departments.

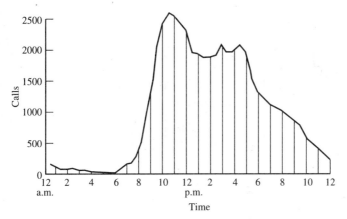

FIGURE 10.4
Daily demand for telephone operators. [*E. S. Buffa, M. J. Cosgrove, and*
B. J. Luce, "An Integrated Work Shift Scheduling System," Decision
Sciences, *vol. 7, no. 4, October 1976, p. 622. Reprinted with permission*
from Decision Sciences Institute, Georgia State University.]

The general approach begins with a forecast of demand by hour that is converted
to hourly service staffing requirements. The time interval could be less than an
hour; for example, 15-minute intervals are used by fast-food restaurants to schedule
work during meal periods. Next, a schedule of tours, or shifts, is developed to
match the staffing requirements profile as closely as possible. Finally, specific
service personnel are assigned to tours, or shifts. The telephone operator staffing
problem will be used to demonstrate the analysis required for each step. However,
the approach can be generalized to any service organization.

Forecast Demand   Daily demand is forecast in half-hour intervals, as shown
in Figure 10.4, and must account for weekday and weekend variations, as well as
seasonal adjustments. The Saturday and Sunday call load was found to be
approximately 55 percent of the typical weekday load. Summer months were found
to be generally lower in demand. Special high-demand days, such as Mother's Day
and Christmas, were taken into account.

Convert to Operator Requirements   A profile of half-hour operator requirements is developed on the basis of the forecasted daily demand and call
distribution. A standard service level, defined by the Public Utilities Commission,
requires that 89 percent of the time, an incoming call must be answered within 10
seconds. The half-hour operator requirements are thus determined by means of a
conventional queuing model to ensure that the service level is achieved for each
half hour.[4] The result is a profile of operators required by half hour, as shown in
Figure 10.5.

[4]The $M/M/c$ queuing model as described in Chapter 15 is used. This model permits the calculation
of probabilities for having a telephone caller wait for different numbers of operators.

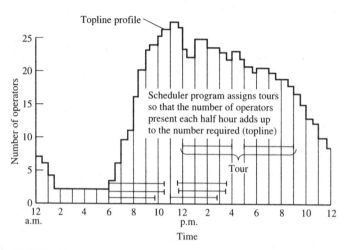

FIGURE 10.5
Profile of operator requirements and tour assignments. [*E. S. Buffa, M. J. Cosgrove, and B. J. Luce, "An Integrated Work Shift Scheduling System,"* Decision Sciences, *vol. 7, no. 4, October 1976, p. 626. Reprinted with permission from Decision Sciences Institute, Georgia State University.*]

Schedule Shifts Tours need to be assigned so that they aggregate to the top-line profile, shown in Figure 10.5. Each tour consists of two working sessions separated by a rest pause or meal period. The set of possible tours is defined by state and federal laws, union agreements, and company policy. A heuristic computer program chooses tours from the permissible set such that the absolute difference between operator requirements and operators assigned is minimized when summed over all "n" half-hour periods. If R_i is the number of operators required in period i and W_i is the number of operators assigned in period i, then the objective can be stated as follows:

Minimize
$$\sum_{i=1}^{n} |R_i - W_i| \tag{2}$$

The schedule-building process is shown schematically in Figure 10.6. At each iteration, one tour at a time is selected from all possible tours. The tour selected at each step is the one that best meets the criterion stated in expression (2) above. Because this procedure favors shorter tours, the different shift lengths are weighted in the calculation. The result is a list of tours required to meet the forecasted demand, as well as a schedule of lunch and rest periods during the tours.

Assign Operators to Shifts Given the set of tours required, the assignment of operators to these tours is complicated because of the 24-hour, 7-days-per-week operation. Questions of equity arise regarding the timing of days off and the assignment of overtime work, which involves extra pay. Another computer program makes operator assignments according to policies, such as "give at least

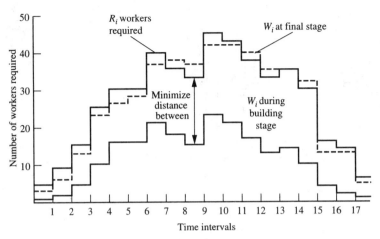

FIGURE 10.6
Schedule building process. [*E. S. Buffa, M. J. Cosgrove, and B. J. Luce, "An Integrated Work Shift Scheduling System,"* Decision Sciences, *vol. 7, no. 4, October 1976, p. 622. Reprinted with permission from Decision Sciences Institute, Georgia State University.*]

one day off per week and maximize consecutive days off." The actual assignment of operators to shifts also takes into account employee shift preferences. The result of this final step is a feasible schedule of employees assigned to tours.

Using Weekly Workshift Scheduling with Days-Off Constraint

As noted above, developing tours to match the profile of daily demand is only part of the problem. Many services such as police and fire protection operate on a seven-days-per-week basis. Employees working five days a week need to be scheduled for time off, usually for two consecutive days each week. Management is interested in developing these work schedules and meeting the varying employee requirements for weekdays and weekends with the smallest number of staff members possible.

This problem can be formulated as an integer linear programming (ILP) model. To begin, the desired staffing levels are determined for each day in the week. The problem then becomes one of determining the minimum number of employees required for assignment to each of seven possible tours. Each of the tours consists of five days on and two consecutive days off, and each will begin on a different day of the week and last for five consecutive working days. Consider the following general formulation of this problem as an integer linear programming model.

Variable definitions:

$x(i)$ = number of employees assigned to tour i, where day i begins two consecutive days off [e.g., employees assigned to x_1 have Sunday and Monday off]

b_j = desired staffing level for day j

Objective function:
Minimize $x_1 + x_2 + x_3 + x_4 + x_5 + x_6 + x_7$

Constraints:

Sunday	$x_2 + x_3 + x_4 + x_5 + x_6$	$\geq b_1$
Monday	$x_3 + x_4 + x_5 + x_6 + x_7 \geq b_2$	
Tuesday	$x_1 \qquad\quad + x_4 + x_5 + x_6 + x_7 \geq b_3$	
Wednesday	$x_1 + x_2 \qquad\quad + x_5 + x_6 + x_7 \geq b_4$	
Thursday	$x_1 + x_2 + x_3 \qquad\quad + x_6 + x_7 \geq b_5$	
Friday	$x_1 + x_2 + x_3 + x_4 \qquad\quad + x_7 \geq b_6$	
Saturday	$x_1 + x_2 + x_3 + x_4 + x_5 \qquad\qquad \geq b_7$	
	$x_i \geq 0$ and integer	

Example 10.2: Computer Center Operations

The university computer center is operated on a 24-hour, 7-days-per-week schedule. The day is divided into three 8-hour shifts. The total number of operators required during the day shift is shown below:

Day	Su	M	Tu	W	Th	F	Sa
Operators	3	6	5	6	5	5	5

The computer center director is interested in developing a workforce schedule that will minimize the number of operators required to staff the facility. Employees work five days a week and are entitled to two consecutive days off each week.

The ILP model above was used with the appropriate right-hand-side constraint values, and it yielded the following results: $x_1 = 1$, $x_2 = 1$, $x_3 = 2$, $x_4 = 0$, $x_5 = 3$, $x_6 = 0$, $x_7 = 1$. The corresponding staffing schedule is shown in the table below.

Operator	Schedule matrix, x = day off						
	Su	M	Tu	W	Th	F	Sa
1	x	x	. . .	. . .	. . .	. . .	. . .
2	. . .	x	x	. . .	. . .	. . .	. . .
3	. . .	. . .	x	x	. . .	. . .	. . .
4	. . .	. . .	x	x	. . .	. . .	. . .
5	. . .	. . .	. . .	. . .	x	x	. . .
6	. . .	. . .	. . .	. . .	x	x	. . .
7	. . .	. . .	. . .	. . .	x	x	. . .
8	x	. . .	. . .	. . .	. . .	. . .	x
Total	6	6	5	6	5	5	7
Required	3	6	5	6	5	5	5
Excess	3	0	0	0	0	0	2

These scheduling problems typically result in multiple optimal solutions. For example, in this case the solution $x_1 = 1$, $x_2 = 1$, $x_3 = 1$, $x_4 = 1$, $x_5 = 1$, $x_6 = 1$, $x_7 = 2$ is feasible and also requires eight operators. Why might this second solution be preferred to the schedule shown in the table above?

Increasing Consumer Participation

This strategy is best illustrated by the fast-food restaurants that have eliminated personnel who serve food and clear tables. The customer (now a coproducer) not only places the order directly from a limited menu but also is expected to clear the table after the meal. Naturally, the customer expects faster service and less expensive meals to compensate for the help. However, the service provider benefits in many subtle ways. Of course, there are fewer personnel to supervise and to pay. But more importantly, the customer as a coproducer provides the labor just at the moment it is required; thus, capacity to serve varies more directly with demand rather than being fixed.

Some drawbacks to self-service do exist because the quality of labor is not completely under the service manager's control. A self-service gas customer may fail to check tire pressure and the oil level regularly, which can lead to problems eventually. Self-service of "bulk" foods (such as cereals, grains, honey, and peanut butter) in markets can lead both to contamination of the product in the bulk container and to waste because of spillage.

Creating Adjustable Capacity

Through design, a portion of capacity can be made variable. Airlines routinely move the partition between first class and coach to meet the changing mix of passengers. An innovative restaurant, Benihana of Tokyo, arranged its floor plan to accommodate eating areas serving two tables of eight diners each. Chefs are assigned to each area, and they prepare the meal at the table in a theatrical manner with flashing knives and animated movements. The restaurant can thus effectively adjust its capacity by having only the number of chefs on duty that is needed.

Capacity at peak periods can be expanded by the effective use of slack times. Performing supportive tasks during slower periods of demand allows employees to concentrate on essential tasks during rush periods. This strategy requires some cross-training of employees to allow performance of non-customer-contact tasks during slow-demand periods. For example, servers at a restaurant can wrap silverware in napkins or clean and tidy up the premises when demand is low; thus they are free of these tasks during the rush period.

Sharing Capacity

A service delivery system often requires a large investment in equipment and facilities. During periods of underutilization, it may be possible to find other uses for the capacity. Airlines have cooperated in this manner for years. At small airports, airlines share the same gates, ramps, baggage-handling equipment, and ground personnel. It is also common for some airlines to lease their aircraft to other airlines during the off-season. The lease agreement includes painting on appropriate insignia and refurbishing the interior.

Cross-Training Employees

Some service systems are made up of several operations. Sometimes when one operation is busy, another operation may be idle. Cross-training employees to perform tasks in several operations creates flexible capacity to meet localized peaks in demand.

The gains from cross-training employees can be seen at supermarkets. When queues develop at the cash registers, the manager calls on stockers to operate registers until the surge is over. Likewise, during slow periods some of the cashiers are busy stocking shelves. This approach can also help build an esprit de corps and give employees relief from monotony. For fast-food restaurants, cross-trained employees create capacity flexibility because tasks can be reassigned to fewer employees during slow periods (temporarily enlarging the job) and become more specialized during busy periods (division of labor).

Using Part-Time Employees

When peaks of activity are persistent and predictable, such as we see at mealtimes in restaurants or on paydays at banks, part-time help can supplement regular employees. If the skills and training required are minimal, a ready part-time labor pool is available from high school and college students and others interested in supplementing their primary source of income.

Another source of part-time help is off-duty personnel placed on standby. Airlines and hospitals often pay their personnel to be on standby. Standbys are paid some nominal fee to restrict their activities and to be ready for work if needed.

Scheduling Part-Time Tellers at a Drive-in Bank[5]

Drive-in banks experience predictable variations in activity for different days of the week. Figure 10.7 shows the teller requirements for a typical week based on customer demand variations. The bank usually employed enough tellers to meet peak demands on Friday. However, this policy created considerable idle teller time on the low-demand days, particularly Tuesday and Thursday. In order to reduce teller costs, management decided to employ part-time tellers and reduce the full-time staff to a level that just meets the demand for Tuesday. Furthermore, to provide equity in hours worked, it was decided that a part-time teller should work at least two but no more than three days in a week.

[5]From V. A. Mabert and A. R. Raedels, "The Detail Scheduling of a Part-Time Work Force: A Case Study of Teller Staffing," *Decision Sciences,* vol. 8, no. 1, January 1977, pp. 109–120.

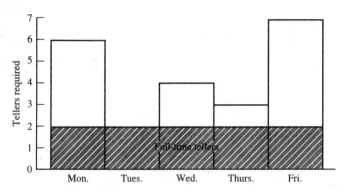

FIGURE 10.7
Teller requirements.

A primary objective of scheduling part-time workers is to meet requirements with the minimum number of teller days. A secondary objective is to have a minimum number of part-time tellers. The approach is illustrated using bank tellers, but the same procedure can be used for scheduling part-time employees for many other services.

Determine the Minimum Number of Part-Time Tellers Needed   Figure 10.8 shows that with two full-time tellers, 12 teller days remain to be covered during the week. Using three-day schedules, we see that five tellers on Friday determines the feasible minimum in this case.

Develop a Decreasing-Demand Histogram   From Figure 10.7, note the daily part-time teller requirements. Resequence the days in order of decreasing demand, as shown in Figure 10.8.

Assign Tellers to the Histogram   Starting with the first part-time teller, assign that individual to the first block on Friday, the second teller to block two, and so forth, as shown in Figure 10.8. Repeat the sequence with Monday, and carry over the remaining tellers into Wednesday. Table 10.6 summarizes the resulting daily part-time work schedule, which consists of two 3-day schedules and two 2-day schedules.

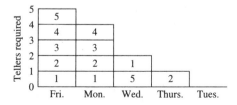

FIGURE 10.8
Decreasing part-time teller demand histogram.

TABLE 10.6
DAILY PART-TIME WORK SCHEDULE, X = workday

Teller	Mon.	Tues.	Wed.	Thurs.	Fri.
1	X	....	X	....	X
2	X	....	....	X	X
3, 4	X	....	....	....	X
5	....	....	X	....	X

YIELD MANAGEMENT[6]

Since deregulation permitted airlines to set their own prices, a new approach to revenue maximization has emerged, called *yield management.* You will see that yield management is actually a comprehensive system that incorporates many of the strategies discussed earlier in this chapter (e.g., reservation systems, overbooking, and partitioning demand).

Because of the perishable nature of airline seats (i.e., once a flight has departed, the potential revenue from an empty seat is lost forever), offering a discount on fares to fill the aircraft became attractive. However, selling all seats at a discount would preclude the possibility of selling some at full price. Yield management attempts to allocate the fixed capacity of seats on a flight to match potential demand in various market segments (e.g., coach, tourist, and supersaver) in the most profitable manner. Although the airlines were the first to develop yield management, other capacity-constrained service industries such as hotels, rental-car firms, and cruise lines are also adopting the practice.

Yield management is most appropriate for service firms that exhibit the following characteristics:

Relatively fixed capacity. Service firms with a substantial investment in facilities, such as hotels and airlines, can be considered capacity-constrained. Once all the seats on a flight are sold, further demand can be met only by booking passengers on a later flight. However, motel chains with multiple inns in the same city have some capacity flexibility because guests attempting to find room at one site can be diverted to another location within the same company.

Ability to segment markets. For yield management to be effective, the service firm must be able to segment its market into different customer classes. By requiring a Saturday night stay for a discounted fare, the airlines are able to discriminate between a time-sensitive business traveler and a price-sensitive customer. Developing various price-sensitive classes of service is a major marketing challenge for a firm using yield management. Figure 10.9 shows how a resort hotel might segment its market into three customer classes and adjust the allocation of available rooms to each class on the basis of the seasons of the year.

[6]From Sheryl E. Kimes, "Yield Management: A Tool for Capacity-Constrained Service Firms," *Journal of Operations Management,* vol. 8, no. 4, October 1989, pp. 348–363.

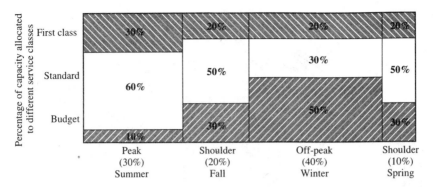

FIGURE 10.9
Seasonal allocation of rooms by service class for resort hotel. [*After Christoper H. Lovelock, "Strategies for Managing Demand in Capacity-Constrained Service Organizations,"* Service Industries Journal, *vol. 4, no. 3, November 1984, p. 23.*]

Perishable inventory. For capacity-constrained service firms, each room or seat is referred to as a unit of inventory to be sold (actually rented). As noted above for the airlines, the revenue from an unsold seat is lost forever. Airlines attempt to minimize this spoiled inventory by encouraging standbys. Given this time-perishable nature of an airline seat, what is the cost to the airline when a passenger is awarded a free ticket on a flight that has at least one empty seat?

Product sold in advance. We have seen that reservation systems are adopted by service firms to sell capacity in advance of use. However, managers are faced with the uncertainty of when to accept an early reservation at a discount price or when to wait and hope to sell the inventory unit to a higher-paying customer. In Figure 10.10 a demand control chart (recall quality-control charts from Chapter 9) is drawn for a hotel on the basis of past bookings for a particular day of the week and season of the year. Because some variation in demand is expected, an acceptable range (in this case ± 2 standard deviations) is drawn around the expected reservation accumulation curve. If demand is higher than expected, budget-rate classes are closed and only reservations at standard rates are accepted. If the accumulation of reservations falls below the acceptable range, then reservations for rooms at budget rates are accepted.

Fluctuating demand. Using demand forecasting, yield management allows managers to increase utilization during periods of slow demand and to increase revenue during periods of high demand. By controlling the availability of budget rates, managers can maximize total revenue for the constrained service. Yield management is implemented in real time by opening and/or closing reserved sections, even on an hourly basis if desired.

Low marginal sales costs and high marginal capacity change costs. The cost of selling an additional unit of inventory must be low, such as the negligible cost of a snack for an airline passenger. The marginal cost of capacity additions is large

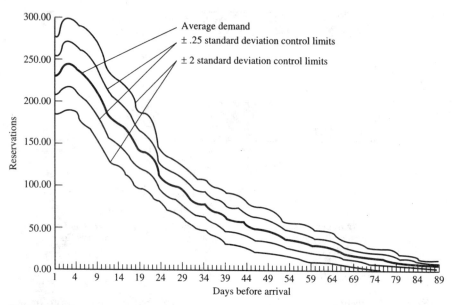

FIGURE 10.10
Demand control chart for a hotel. [*Sheryl E. Kimes, "Yield Management: A Tool for Capacity-Constrained Service Firms,"* Journal of Operations Management, *vol. 8, no. 4, October 1989, p. 359. Reprinted with permission, The American Production and Inventory Society.*]

because of the necessary lumpy facility investment (i.e., a hotel addition must be at least an increment of 100 rooms).

Example 10.3: Blackjack Airline

During the recent economic slump Blackjack has found that airplanes on its Los Angeles–to–Las Vegas route have been flying more empty seats than usual. In an effort to stimulate demand, marketing has decided to offer a special nonrefundable 14-day advance-purchase "gamblers fare" for only $49 one-way based on a round-trip ticket. The regular full-fare coach ticket costs $69 one-way. The MD-80 used by Blackjack has a capacity of 150 passengers in coach, and management wants to limit the number of seats sold at the discount fare in order to sell full-fare tickets to passengers who have not made advance travel plans. Considering recent experience, the demand for full-fare tickets appears to have a normal distribution, with a mean of 60 and a standard deviation of 15.

Phillip E. Pfeifer[7] observed that this yield management problem can be

---

[7]Phillip E. Pfeifer, "The Airline Discount Fare Allocation Problem," *Decision Sciences,* vol. 20, winter 1989, p. 155.

analyzed with the critical fractile model used earlier in the chapter [equation (1)] for analyzing the overbooking problem.

$$P(d < x) \leq \frac{C_u}{C_u + C_o}$$

where x = seats reserved for full-fare passengers.

d = demand for full-fare tickets.

C_u = lost revenue associated with reserving too few seats at full fare (*u*nderestimated demand). The lost opportunity is the difference between the fares (\$69 − \$49 = \$20) because we assume that the nonshopper passenger, willing to pay full fare, purchased a seat at the discount price.

C_o = cost of reserving one too many seats for sale at full fare (*o*verestimated demand). We assume that the empty full-fare seat could have been sold at the discount price. However, C_o takes on two values, depending on the buying behavior of the passenger who would have purchased the seat if not reserved for full fare.

$$C_o = \begin{cases} \$49 & \text{if passenger is a shopper} \\ -(\$69 - \$49) & \text{if passenger is a nonshopper} \end{cases}$$

For the nonshopper case, the cost is reduced by the difference between the fares because the airline profits from the fact that the nonshopper, who did not make the purchase, pays full fare rather than a discount fare. However, to establish an expected value for C_o, we need the proportion p of passengers who are shoppers. In this case, market research determined that approximately 90 percent of the passengers are discount seekers. Thus, the expected value for the cost of overage becomes

$$C_o = (0.9)(\$49) - (1 - 0.9)(\$69 - \$49) = \$42.10$$

The critical fractile value $P(d < x)$ = \$20/(\$20 + \$42.10) = .32 From the end-of-book Appendix table, Areas of a Standard Normal Distribution, the z value for a cumulative probability of .32 is −.47. Thus the number of full-fare seats to reserve is found as follows:

$$\begin{aligned} \text{Reserved full-fare seats} &= \mu + z\sigma \\ &= 60 + (-.47)(15) \\ &= 52 \end{aligned}$$

Substituting symbols for the values used in the example above, we can derive a simple expression for determining the number of full-fare seats to reserve.

$$P(d < x) \leq \frac{(F - D)}{p \cdot F} \tag{3}$$

where x = seats reserved for full-fare passengers
d = demand for full-fare tickets
F = price of full fare
D = price of discount fare
p = probability that a passenger is a shopper

SUMMARY

The inherent variability of demand creates a challenge for managers trying to make the best use of service capacity. The problem can be approached from two perspectives. One strategy focuses on smoothing consumer demand, which permits fuller utilization of a fixed service capacity. Various alternatives for managing demand are available, such as partitioning demand, offering price incentives, promoting off-peak use, and developing complementary services and reservation systems.

Another strategy considers the problem from the supply side. Many alternatives have been proposed to adjust service capacity to match demand. Elaborate procedures for workshift scheduling have been developed to adjust capacity to demand. When possible, part-time employees can be used to create variable capacity. Increasing consumer participation in the service process shifts some of the service tasks to the consumer and reduces part of the burden during peak-demand periods. Other possibilities include sharing capacity with others, as airlines do by leasing their aircraft during off-season periods. Occasionally, capacity can be adjusted—for example, by opening and closing dining areas in a restaurant. Cross-training employees can also provide flexible capacity by enabling employees to assist one another during busy periods.

The strategies are presented as two separate views of the problem, one from the demand side and the other from the supply side. Of course, this should not preclude the use of mixed strategies that attempt to mediate the problem from both perspectives. Yield management as practiced by American Airlines is considered such a mixed strategy, because the company integrates supply and demand management using the power of information contained in its computer reservation system. The result is the real-time ability to sell a class of service to the right customer at the appropriate time, and at the most competitive price.

TOPICS FOR DISCUSSION

1. Explain, from a consumer participation point of view, why airlines find it profitable to offer reduced fares for standby passengers.
2. What are some noneconomic incentives that might encourage banking customers to use the drive-in window at off-peak times?
3. It has been suggested that the price of airline tickets should be variable, with the cost becoming higher as one approaches the time of departure. Comment.
4. What are some of the organizational problems that can arise from the use of part-time employees?

5. How can computer-based reservation systems be used to increase service capacity utilization?
6. Illustrate how a particular service has successfully implemented strategies for managing both demand and supply.
7. What are some possible dangers associated with developing complementary services?

EXERCISES

10.1 Reconsider the Surfside Hotel example, given that rising costs have resulted in a $100 opportunity loss owing to a no-show. Assume that the no-show experience has not significantly changed and that the loss that results when a guest is overbooked is still $100. Should Surfside revise its no-show policy?

10.2 An outpatient clinic has kept a record of walk-in patients during the past year. The table below shows the expected number of walk-ins by day of the week.

Day	Mon.	Tues.	Wed.	Thurs.	Fri.
Walk-ins	50	30	40	35	40

The clinic has a staff of five physicians, and each can examine 15 patients a day on the average.
   a. What is the maximum number of appointments that should be scheduled for each day if it is desirable to smooth out the demand for the week?
   b. Why would you recommend against scheduling appointments at their maximum level?
   c. If the majority of the walk-ins arrive in the morning, when should the appointments be made to avoid excessive waiting?

10.3. A commuter airline overbooks its flights by one passenger (i.e., the ticket agent will take seven reservations for an airplane that has only six seats). The no-show experience for the past 20 days is shown below:

No-shows	0	1	2	3	4
Frequency	6	5	4	3	2

Using the relationship $P(d < x) \leq C_u/(C_u + C_o)$, find the maximum implied overbooking opportunity loss C_o if the revenue C_u from a passenger is $20.

10.4. Crazy Joe operates a canoe rental on the Guadalupe River. He currently leases 15 canoes from a dealer in the nearby city at a cost of $10 per day. On weekends, when the water is high, he picks up the canoes and drives to a launching point on the river, where he rents canoes to white-water enthusiasts for $30 per day. Lately, canoeists have complained about the unavailability of canoes. Crazy Joe records the demand for canoes and finds the experience below for the past 20 days.

Daily demand	10	11	12	13	14	15	16	17	18	19	20
Frequency	1	1	2	2	2	3	3	2	2	1	1

Recommend an appropriate number of canoes to lease.

10.5. The sheriff has been asked by the county commissioners to increase the weekend patrols in the lake region during the summer months. The sheriff has proposed the following weekly schedule, shifting deputies from weekday assignments to weekends:

Day	Sun.	Mon.	Tues.	Wed.	Thurs.	Fri.	Sat.
Assignments	6	4	4	4	5	5	6

Develop a complete schedule of duty tours, providing two consecutive days off per week for each officer. Formulate the problem as an integer linear programming model to minimize the number of officers needed. Solve using a personal computer software package such as *QS: Quantitative Systems, Version 3.0.*[8]

10.6. An airline serving Denver's Stapleton Airport and Steamboat Springs, Colorado, is considering overbooking its flights to avoid flying empty seats. For example, the ticket agent is thinking of taking seven reservations for an airplane that has only six seats. During the past month, the no-show experience has been as follows:

No-shows	0	1	2	3	4
Percentage	30	25	20	15	10

The operating costs associated with each flight are as follows: pilot, $150; first officer, $100; fuel, $30; landing fee, $20.

What would be your overbooking recommendation if a one-way ticket sells for $80 and the cost of not honoring a reservation is a free lift ticket worth $50 plus a seat on the next flight? What is the expected profit per flight for your overbooking choice?

CASE: RIVER CITY NATIONAL BANK

River City National Bank has been in business for ten years and is a fast-growing community bank. The bank president, Gary Miller, took over his position five years ago in an effort to get the bank on its feet. He is one of the youngest bank presidents in the southwest, and his energy and enthusiasm explain his rapid advancement. Mr. Miller has been the key factor behind the bank's increase in status and maintenance of high standards. One of the reasons for this is that the bank customers come first in Mr. Miller's eyes. To him, one of the bank's main objectives is to serve its customers better.

The main bank lobby has one commercial teller and three paying-and-receiving teller booths. The lobby is designed to have room for long lines, should they occur. Attached to the main bank are six drive-in lanes (one is commercial only) and one walk-up window to the side of the drive-in. Owing to the bank's rapid growth, the drive-in lanes and the lobby have been constantly overcrowded, although the bank has some of the longest banking hours in town. The lobby is open from 9 a.m. until 2 p.m., Monday through Saturday, and reopens from 4 to 6 p.m. on Friday. The drive-in is open from 7 a.m. until midnight, Monday through Friday, and on

[8]Yih-Long Chang and R. S. Sullivan, *QS: Quantitative Systems, Version 3.0*, Prentice-Hall, Englewood Cliffs, N.J., 1993.

Saturday from 7 a.m. until 7 p.m. But several old and good customers had complained. They did not like the long wait in line and also felt that the tellers were becoming quite surly.

This was very disheartening to Mr. Miller, despite the fact that the cause of the problem was the increase in business the bank was doing. Thus, it was with his strong recommendation that the board of directors finally approved the building of a remote drive-in bank just down the street. The drive-in can be approached from two directions and has four lanes on either side, as seen in Figure 10.11. The first lane on either side is commercial only, and the last lane on each side has been built but is not yet operational. The banking hours for this facility are 7 a.m. to 7 p.m., Monday through Saturday.

The bank employs both full-time and part-time tellers. The lobby tellers and the morning tellers (7 a.m. to 2 p.m.) are considered full-time employees, whereas the tellers on the afternoon shift (2 p.m. to 7 p.m.) and the night owl shift (7 p.m. to midnight) are considered part-time. The tellers perform normal banking services: they cash checks, receive deposits, verify deposit balances, sell money orders and traveler's checks, and cash government savings bonds.

At the present time, the overcrowding for the most part has been eliminated. The hardest problem in resolving that situation was making customers aware of the new facility. The tellers at the remote drive-in, after six months, are still hearing customers say, "I didn't realize ya'll were over here. I'm going to start coming here more often!"

Now, instead of facing an overcrowding situation, the bank is finding that it is having problems with fluctuating demand. River City National rarely experienced this problem until the extra capacity of tellers and drive-in lanes was added at the new remote facility.

Two full-time and four part-time tellers are employed at the remote drive-in Monday through Friday. Scheduling on Saturdays is no problem, as all six tellers take turns rotating, with most working every other Saturday. On paydays and

FIGURE 10.11
Layout of remote drive-in.

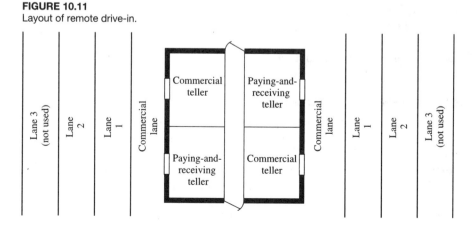

on Fridays, the lanes at the remote drive-in have cars lined up out to the street. A high demand for money and service from the bank is the main reason for this dilemma but certainly not the only one. Many customers are not ready when they get to the bank. They need a pen or a deposit slip, or they do not have their check filled out or endorsed yet. This, of course, creates idle time for the tellers. There are also other problems with customers that take time, such as explaining that their accounts are overdrawn and that their payroll checks must therefore be deposited instead of cashed. In addition, there is usually a handful of noncustomers trying to cash payroll checks or personal checks. These people can become quite obstinate and take up a lot of time when they find that their checks cannot be cashed. Transactions take 30 seconds on the average. Transaction times range from 10 seconds for a straight deposit to 90 seconds for cashing a bond to about 3 minutes for making out traveler's checks. (The latter occurs very rarely.)

Compared with the peak banking days, the rest of the week is very quiet. The main bank stays busy but is not crowded. On the other hand, business at the remote drive-in is unusually slow. Mr. Miller's drive-in supervisor, Ms. Shang-ling Chen, did a study on the number of transactions the tellers at the remote facility made on the average. The figures for a typical month are shown in Table 10.7.

Once again customers are complaining. When the tellers at the remote drive-in close out at 7 p.m. on Fridays, they are always turning people away while they are in the process of balancing. These customers have asked Mr. Miller to keep the new drive-in open at least until 9 p.m. on Friday. The tellers are very much against the idea, but the board of directors is beginning to favor it. Mr. Miller wants to keep his customers happy but feels there must be some other way to resolve this situation. Therefore, he calls in Ms. Chen and requests that she please look into the problem and make some recommendations for a solution.

Assignment

As Ms. Chen's top aide, you are assigned the task of providing an analysis of the situation and recommending a solution. This is your opportunity to serve your company and community as well as to make yourself "look good" and earn points toward your raise and promotion.

CASE: GATEWAY INTERNATIONAL AIRPORT[9]

Gateway International Airport (GIA) has experienced a substantial growth in both commercial and general aviation operations during the past several years (an operation is a landing or a takeoff). Because of the initiation of new commercial service at the airport (scheduled for several months in the future), the Federal Aviation Administration (FAA) has concluded that this increase in

[9]Prepared by James H. Vance under the supervision of James A. Fitzsimmons.

TABLE 10.7
TRANSACTIONS FOR TYPICAL MONTH AT REMOTE DRIVE-IN

Day of week	First week		Second week	
	Morning shift	Afternoon shift	Morning shift	Afternoon shift
Monday	. . .	. . .	175	133
Tuesday	. . .	. . .	120	85
Wednesday	200	195	122	115
Thursday	156	113	111	100
Friday	223*	210	236*	225
Saturday	142	127	103	98

Day of week	Third week		Fourth week	
	Morning shift	Afternoon shift	Morning shift	Afternoon shift
Monday	149	120	182	171
Tuesday	136	77	159	137
Wednesday	182	186	143	103
Thursday	172	152	118	99
Friday	215*	230	206*	197
Saturday	147	150	170	156

Day of week	Fifth week	
	Morning shift	Afternoon shift
Monday	169	111
Tuesday	112	89
Wednesday	92	95
Thursday	147	163
Friday	259*	298

*Most of these transactions occurred after 10 a.m.

operations and the associated change in the hourly distribution of takeoffs and landings will require an entirely new work schedule for the current air traffic control (ATC) staff. The FAA feels that GIA may have to hire additional ATC personnel because the present staff of five probably will not be enough to handle the expected demand.

After examining the various service plans each commercial airline submitted for the next six-month period, the FAA staff developed an average hourly demand forecast of total operations (Figure 10.12) and a weekly forecast of variation from the average daily demand (Figure 10.13). An assistant to the manager for operations has been delegated the task of developing workforce requirements and schedules for the ATC staff so as to maintain an adequate level of operational safety with a minimum of excess ATC "capacity."

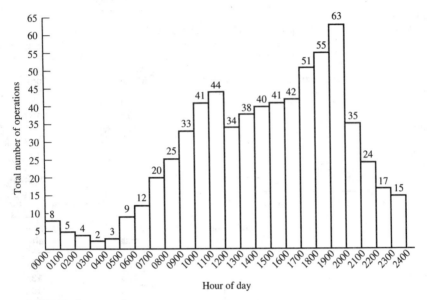

FIGURE 10.12
Hourly demand for operations.

The various constraints are as follows:

1. Each controller will work a continuous eight-hour shift (ignoring any lunch break), which will always begin at the start of an hour at any time during the day (i.e., any and all shifts begin at X:00), and the controller must have at least 16 hours off duty before resuming duty.

2. Each controller will work exactly five days per week.

3. Each controller is entitled to two consecutive days off, with any consecutive pair of days being eligible.

4. FAA guidelines will govern GIA's workforce requirements so that the ratio of total operations to number of available controllers in any hourly period cannot exceed 16.

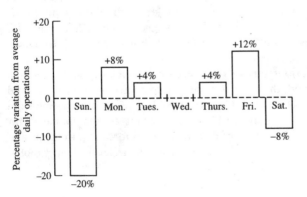

FIGURE 10.13
Daily demand variation from average.

Questions

1. Assume that you are the assistant to the manager for operations at the FAA. Use the techniques of workshift scheduling to develop an analysis of the total workforce requirements and days-off schedule. For the primary analysis, you may assume that:

   a. Operator requirements will be based on a shift profile of demand (i.e., eight hours).

   b. There will be exactly three separate shifts each day, with no overlapping of shifts.

   c. The distribution of hourly demand shown in Figure 10.12 is constant for each day of the week, but the levels of hourly demand vary during the week according to Figure 10.13.

2. On the basis of your primary analysis, discuss the potential implications for workforce requirements and days-off scheduling if assumptions **a** and **b** above are relaxed so that analysis can be based on the hourly demand without the constraints of a preset number of shifts and no overlapping of shifts. In other words, discuss the effects of analyzing hourly demand requirements on the basis of each ATC position essentially having its own shift, which can overlap with any other ATC shift to meet that demand.

3. Do you feel that this would result in a larger or smaller degree of difficulty in meeting the four general constraints? Why?

4. What additional suggestions could you make to the manager of operations that might tend to minimize the workforce requirements level and days-off scheduling difficulty?

CASE: TOWN AND COUNTRY RENT-A-CAR[10]

Town and Country has experienced a substantial increase in its business volume as a result of the recent fare wars between major air carriers. Town and Country operates a single office at a major international airport with a fleet of 60 compact and 30 midsize cars. The recent developments have prompted management to rethink the company's reservation policy. The table below contains data on the rental experience of Town and Country.

Car	Rental rate	Discount rate	Discount seekers, %	Daily demand	Standard deviation
Compact	$30	$20	80	50	15
Midsize	$45	$30	60	30	10

The daily demand appears to follow a normal distribution. However, it has been observed that midsize-car customers do not choose to rent a compact car when there is no midsize car available. The discount rate is available to persons

[10]Prepared by Selcuk Karabati under the supervision of James A. Fitzsimmons.

who are willing to reserve a car at least 14 days in advance and agree to pick up the car within 2 hours after their flight arrives. Otherwise, a nonrefundable deposit against their credit card will be forfeited. The current reservation policy is as follows: 40 of the compact cars are held for customers willing to pay the full rate, and 25 midsize cars are held for full-rate-paying customers.

Questions

1. Determine the lost revenue associated with reserving one too few cars at the full rate (C_u) for both compact and midsize cars.
2. Determine the cost of reserving one too many cars at the full rate (C_o) for both compact and midsize cars.
3. What is the optimal reservation policy if expected profit is to be maximized?
4. Given your optimal reservation policy determined above, would you consider a fleet expansion?
5. Discuss the effect on your reservation policy if customers rent a car for more than one day at a time.

SELECTED BIBLIOGRAPHY

Abernathy, W. J., N. Baloff, and J. C. Hershey: "The Nurse Staffing Problem: Issues and Prospects," *Sloan Management Review*, fall 1971, pp. 87–99.

——, ——, ——, and S. Wandel: "A Three Stage Manpower Planning and Scheduling Model—A Service Sector Example," *Operations Research*, vol. 21, no. 3, May–June 1973, pp. 693–710.

Antle, D. W., and R. A. Reid: "Managing Service Capacity in an Ambulatory Care Clinic," *Hospital & Health Services Administration*, vol. 33, no. 2, summer 1988, pp. 201–211.

Baker, K. R., and M. J. Magazine: "Workforce Scheduling with Cyclic Demands and Day-Off Constraints," *Management Science*, vol. 24, no. 2, October 1977, pp. 161–167.

Bechtold, S. E.: "Implicit Optimal and Heuristic Labor Staffing in a Multiobjective, Multilocation Environment," *Decision Sciences*, vol. 19, no. 2, spring 1988, pp. 353–372.

—— and L. W. Jacobs: "The Impact of Labor Scheduling with Flexible Rest Periods on Productivity in Service Operations: An Implicit Optimal Modeling Approach," *Proceedings of the OMA-UK Annual International Conference*, Coventry, England, Jan. 6–7, 1988, pp. 42–61.

—— and M. J. Showalter: "A Methodology for Labor Scheduling in a Service Operating System," *Decision Sciences*, vol. 18, no. 1, winter 1987, pp. 89–107.

Belobaba, Peter P.: "Application of a Probabilistic Decision Model to Airline Seat Inventory Control," *Operations Research*, vol. 37, no. 2, March–April 1989, pp. 183–197.

Buffa, E. S., M. J. Cosgrove, and B. J. Luce: "An Integrated Work Shift Scheduling System," *Decision Sciences*, vol. 7, no. 4, October 1976, p. 622.

Collier, D. A.: "A Managerial Guide for the Service Capacity-Scheduling Decision," *Service Management: Operating Decisions*, Prentice-Hall, Englewood Cliffs, N.J., 1987, pp. 51–55.

Drake, A. W., R. L. Keeney, and P. N. Morse: "Improving the Effectiveness of New York City's 911," *Analysis of Public Systems*, M.I.T. Press, Cambridge, Mass., 1972, chap. 9.

Glover, F., R. Glover, J. Lorenzo, and C. McMillan: "The Passenger-Mix Problem in the Scheduled Airlines," *Interfaces,* vol. 12, no. 3, June 1982, pp. 73–80.

Kimes, Sheryl E.: "Yield Management: A Tool for Capacity-Constrained Service Firms," *Journal of Operations Management,* vol. 8, no. 4, October 1989, pp. 348–363.

————: "The Basics of Yield Management," *The Cornell H.R.A. Quarterly,* November 1989, pp. 14–19.

Lovelock, C. H.: "Strategies for Managing Demand in Capacity-Constrained Service Organizations," *Service Industries Journal,* vol. 4, no. 3, November 1984, pp. 12–30.

Mabert, V. A., and A. R. Raedels: "The Detail Scheduling of a Part-Time Work Force: A Case Study of Teller Staffing," *Decision Sciences,* vol. 8, no. 1, January 1977, pp. 109–120.

Nautiyal, J. C., and R. L. Chowdhary: "A Suggested Basis for Pricing Campsites: Demand Estimation in an Ontario Park," *Journal of Leisure Research,* vol. 7, no. 2, 1975, pp. 95–107.

Northcraft, G. B., and R. B. Chase: "Managing Service Demand at the Points of Delivery," *Academy of Management Review,* vol. 10, no. 1, 1985, pp. 66–75.

Pfeifer, Phillip E.: "The Airline Discount Fare Allocation Problem," *Decision Sciences,* vol. 20, winter 1989, pp. 149–157.

Relihan, Walter J. III: "The Yield-Management Approach to Hotel-Room Pricing," *The Cornell H.R.A. Quarterly,* May 1989, pp. 40–45.

Rising, E. J., R. Baron, and B. Averill: "A Systems Analysis of a University Health-Service Outpatient Clinic," *Operations Research,* vol. 21, no. 5, September 1973, pp. 1030–1047.

Rose, R. L., and J. Dahl: "Skies Are Deregulated, but Just Try Starting a Sizable New Airline," *The Wall Street Journal,* July 19, 1989, p. 1.

Sasser, Earl W.: "Match Supply and Demand in Service Industries," *Harvard Business Review,* November–December 1976, pp. 133–140.

Snyder, C. A., J. F. Cox, and R. R. Jesse, Jr.: "A Dependent Demand Approach to Service Organization Planning and Control," *Academy of Management Review,* vol. 7, no. 3, 1982, pp. 455–465.

Warner, D. M., and J. Pranda: "A Mathematical Programming Model for Scheduling Nursing Personnel in a Hospital," *Management Science,* vol. 19, no. 4, December 1972, pp. 411–422.

Williams, Fred E.: "Decision Theory and the Innkeeper: An Approach for Setting Hotel Reservation Policy," *Interfaces,* vol. 7, no. 4, August 1977, pp. 18–30.

Zeithaml, V. A., A. Parasuraman, and L. L. Berry: "Problems and Strategies in Services Marketing," *Journal of Marketing,* vol. 49, spring 1985, pp. 33–46.

11

CHAPTER

MANAGING QUEUES

The management of queues at Burger King represents an evolving process of refinement. When its stores first opened, a "conventional" lineup was used. That arrangement required customers to line up in single file behind a single cash register, where orders were taken. Assemblers prepared the orders and presented them to customers at the far end of the counter. This conventional style of lineup is often called the "snake," as mentioned in this *Wall Street Journal* article.[1]

Louis Kane hates snakes.

The restaurant executive means the single lines that feed customers one at a time to a group of cashiers. He thinks snakes are much too "institutional." Besides, he says, he would rather try to guess which line will move the fastest. But surveys show that customers prefer snakes to multiple lines because they hate "getting stuck behind some guy ordering nine cappuccinos, each with something different on top," says Mr. Kane, co-chairman of the Boston-based Au Bon Pain soup-and-sandwich chain.

The customers have won. Over the past couple of years, Au Bon Pain has instituted snakes at every restaurant that has enough room. But the debate lives on. "We talk about this a great deal," Mr. Kane says.

The issue is queues. Experts suggest that no aspect of customer service is more important than the wait in line to be served. The act of waiting—either in person or on the phone—"has a disproportionately high impact" on customers, says David Maister, a Boston consultant who has studied the psychology of waiting. "The wait can destroy an otherwise perfect service experience."

A customer waiting in line is potentially a lost customer. According to one study, up to 27% of customers who can't get through on the telephone will either buy elsewhere

---

[1]Reprinted with permission. Amanda Bennett, "Their Business Is on the Line," *The Wall Street Journal,* Dec. 7, 1990, p. B1.

or skip the transaction altogether, says Rudy Oetting, a senior partner at Oetting & Co., a New York company that consults on telephone use. Adds Russell James, an official at Avis Rent a Car Inc.: "You can't be out-lined by a competitor or you will lose business."

Today's customers are also more demanding than ever. "The dramatic difference between 1980 and 1990 can be described in one word: speed," says N. Powell Taylor, manager of GE Answer Center, a General Electric Co. operation that fields three million calls a year. "People expect quicker answers. No one has the time any more."

In the past few years particularly, many companies have stepped up efforts to shorten waits—or at least make them more tolerable. Here are some of the methods they are trying:

Animate

Some contend that a wait isn't a wait if it's fun. At Macy's in New York now, the line to see Santa Claus wends its way through displays of dancing teddy bears, elves and electric trains. "It's part of the adventure of going to see Santa Claus," says Jean McFaddin, a vice president at the big department store, where 300,000 people see Santa in 30 days.

At Disneyland and Walt Disney World, the waits—which can be up to 90 minutes long—are planned along with the attractions themselves. Visitors waiting for rides that board continuously pass animated displays that are designed to be viewed as people walk along. Waits for theater shows include such attractions as singers and handicraft displays aimed at audiences that will be waiting in one place as long as 30 minutes. Indeed, the waits themselves are called "preshows." Says Norman Doerges, executive vice president of Disneyland, "that's what makes the time pass, is the entertainment."

At the Omni Park Central Hotel in New York, when a line exceeds six people, assistant managers are dispatched to the hotel restaurant to bring out orange and grapefruit juice to serve to the people in line. "We are trying to tell the guest 'we know you are here,'" says Philip Georgas, general manager and regional vice president.

Still, not all diversions are suitable. Many callers don't like listening to recordings while they're on hold. GE plays its corporate theme for customers while they wait, but it draws the line at playing recorded advertising. "We tend to stay away from commercials," says Mr. Taylor, because of the fear that customers will think company employees "are probably sitting there doing nothing," making customers wait so they will have to listen to the commercials.

Discriminate

"The key thing is not just moving people out of the line," says Mr. James at Avis. "The key is who you move out of the line." For the past two years, high-volume renters at Avis have been able to sign a permanent rental agreement in advance and be driven directly to their cars when they arrive at many Avis locations. Somewhat less-frequent renters check in at a kiosk near the car park. Other car rental concerns are offering similar preferential services.

Such service is increasingly common in the travel, banking and credit-card industries. But "one needs a great deal of creativity in this area" lest less-favored customers be offended, says Mr. Maister. "Those businesses that want to serve priority customers faster are best advised to do it out of sight of the regular customers." He cites some airlines that locate first-class check-in counters away from the economy counters. "You don't want to rub the noses of the economy passengers in it."

Automate

While assembly-line techniques can accelerate manufacturing operations, they often slow the delivery of services. When callers must speak to several different people to get a complete answer, "crew interference" sets in, says Warren Blanding, editor of Customer Service Newsletter in Silver Spring, Md. "The most efficient way to do a job is to have one person do it."

So Employers Health Insurance, Green Bay, Wis., has assembled a complex computer data base of scripts that employees can read to customers on the telephone. The employee keys in the caller's name, location and type of health insurance question. The computer then pops up a question-and-answer format that can be read verbatim.

"We know that 75% of the calls we get in are standard questions," says Sterling L. Phaklides, an assistant vice president in the claims division. "Because people are sticking to the scripts, they are giving up-to-date information" without consulting technicians, he says. But callers who ask questions that aren't covered in the scripts can be referred to specialists at any point. "It does save telephone time, the official says. The claims area handles 3,700 calls a day; only about 1% of callers hang up before they are connected—which is better than average, he says.

Obfuscate

Mr. Maister says the perceived wait is often more important than the actual wait. In a paper on the psychology of waiting, he notes that some restaurants deliberately announce longer waiting times, thus pleasing customers when the wait is actually shorter. At Disneyland in Anaheim, Calif., lines snake around corners, Mr. Maister says. Thus people focus more on how fast the line is moving than on how long the line is.

Disneyland says its aim isn't to deceive. It posts waiting times at the start of each line. "A big danger in disguising a line is that people don't know what they are getting into," says Mr. Doerges. "If you do it without proper preparation, people get frustrated."

Still, some think that even that information will be too depressing. Technology is available that will announce a caller's place in line, but Penny Rohde, vice president, customer service, at First Gibralter Bank in Dallas, chose not to use it. "I felt like . . . focusing on the positive, rather than perhaps saying that there are 14 callers ahead of you."

Under First Gibralter's system, after $1\frac{1}{2}$ minutes a phone voice offers the caller the option of continuing to wait or leaving a message. Since it started the system in October, the bank has averaged about 100 messages a day out of between 3,000 and 3,200 calls.

Dissatisfaction with the slowness of the single-line arrangement led Burger King to try the "hospitality" lineup. With the hospitality lineup, cash registers are evenly spaced along the counter, and customers select a line, in effect betting on which of several lines will move the fastest. In this arrangement the cashier who takes an order also assembles the order. Although the hospitality lineup proves to be very flexible in meeting peak-period demand, it does tend to be more labor-intensive than the conventional lineup. Consequently, Burger King made yet another change, this time to what is called a "multiconventional" lineup. This is a hybrid of both earlier systems. The restaurant returned to a single line, but now a new cash register allows up to six orders to be recorded at the same time. Assemblers prepare the orders and distribute them at the end of the counter. Returning to a single line has guaranteed fairness because customers are served in the order of their arrival. In addition, the customers have enough time to make their meal selection without slowing the order-taking process.

Burger King's concern with reducing customer waiting time represents a trend toward providing faster service. Speed of delivery is viewed, in many cases, as a competitive advantage in the marketplace. For example, many hotels today will total your bill and slide it under your room door during the last night of your stay, thereby achieving "zero waiting time" at the checkout counter.

Fluctuations in demand for service are difficult to cope with because consumption and production of services occur simultaneously. Customers typically arrive at random and place immediate demands on the available service. If service capacity is fully utilized at the time of arrival, the customer is expected to wait patiently in line. Varying arrival rates and service time requirements result in the formation of queues (i.e., lines of customers waiting their turn for service). The management of queues is a continuing challenge for service managers.

CHAPTER PREVIEW

Our understanding of waiting lines begins with a definition of queuing systems and the inevitability of waiting. The implications of asking people to wait are further studied from a psychological perspective. We shall discover that the perception of waiting is often more important to the consumer than is the actual time spent waiting. This suggests that innovative ways should be found to reduce the negative aspects of waiting. The economic value of waiting as a cost for the provider and currency for the consumer is also considered. Finally, the essential features of a service system are discussed in terms of a schematic queuing model, and queuing terminology is defined.

QUEUING SYSTEMS

A *queue* is a line of waiting customers who require service from one or more servers. The queue need not be a physical line of individuals in front of a server. Instead, it might be students sitting at computer terminals scattered around a college campus or a person being placed on "hold" by a telephone operator. Servers are typically considered individual stations where customers receive service. The stereotypical queue—people waiting in a formal line for service—is seen at the checkout counters of a supermarket and the teller windows in a bank. Yet queuing systems occur in a variety of forms. Consider the following variations:

1. Servers need not be limited to serving one customer at a time. Transportation systems, such as buses, airplanes, and elevators, are bulk services.

2. The consumer need not always travel to the service facility; in some systems the server actually comes to the consumer. This approach is illustrated by urban services such as fire and police protection and ambulance service.

3. The service may consist of stages of queues in a series or of a more complex network of queues. For example, consider the haunted-house attraction at amusement parks like Disneyland, where the queues are staged in sequence so that visitors can be processed in batches and entertained during the waiting periods, first outside on the walk, then in the vestibule, and finally on the ride itself.

In any service system, a queue forms whenever current demand exceeds the existing capacity to serve. This occurs when the servers are so busy that arriving consumers cannot receive immediate service. Such a situation is bound to occur in any system in which arrivals occur at varying times and service times also vary.

THE INEVITABILITY OF WAITING

Waiting is a part of everyone's life; it can involve an incredible amount of time! For example, a typical day might include waiting at several stoplights, waiting for someone to answer the telephone, waiting for your meal to be served, waiting for the elevator, waiting to be checked out at the supermarket—the list goes on and on.

In the "old Russia" and even in the new unified countries that have formed since the recent breakup of the Communist nation, we find dramatic examples of the role that queuing can play in people's daily lives. A noted Russian scholar, Hedrick Smith, observed that the queue in that country is a national pastime. He has written:

> Personally, I have known of people who stood in line 90 minutes to buy four pineapples, three hours for a two-minute roller coaster ride, three and a half hours to buy three large heads of cabbage only to find the cabbages were gone as they approached the front of the line, 18 hours to sign up to purchase a rug at some later date, all through a freezing December night to register on a list for buying a car, and then waiting 18 more months for actual delivery, and terribly lucky at that. Lines can run from a few yards long to half a block to nearly a mile, and usually they move at an excruciating creep.[2]

He found that there was also a matter of line etiquette. Line jumping by serious shoppers was accepted only for ordinary items but not for scarce ones. Smith continues:

> "People know from experience that things actually run out while they are standing in line," advised one young blonde. "So if the line is for something really good and you leave it for very long, people get very upset. They fly off the handle and curse you and try to keep you from getting back in when you return. It's up to the person behind you to defend your place in line. So it's serious business asking someone to hold your place.

[2]Hedrick Smith, *The Russians,* Quadrangle Press, New York, 1975, pp. 64–65.

They take on a moral obligation not only to let you in front of them later on but to defend you. You have to be stubborn yourself and stand your ground in spite of the insults and the stares. And when you get to the front of the line, if the sales clerks are not limiting the amount, you can hear people, maybe six or eight places back, shouting at you not to take so much, that you are a person with no scruples or that you have no consideration for other people. It can be rather unpleasant."[3]

Since Smith made his observations, perestroika has brought about many changes in the former Soviet Union, but it has yet to affect the queues that are still so much a part of daily life there. The Russian queuing experience is far more severe than that found in the United States. However, in any service system, waiting is bound to occur. A complete absence of waiting would only be possible in a situation in which consumers are asked to arrive at fixed intervals and in which service times are deterministic (e.g., a psychiatrist schedules patients every hour for 50-minute sessions). Later we will demonstrate that waiting is caused by both the fluctuations in arrival rates and the variability in service times. Thus, delays can be encountered even when arrivals are by appointment, as long as service times vary. This is a common experience for patients waiting in a physician's office. Waiting also occurs at fast-food restaurants where the variability of service times has been reduced by offering a short menu but where customers arrive at random. Therefore, waiting is inevitable, and service operations managers must consider how customers in queue are to be treated.

THE PSYCHOLOGY OF WAITING[4]

If, as noted above, waiting is such an integral and ordinary part of our lives, why does it cause us so much grief? David H. Maister offers some interesting perspectives on this subject.

He suggests two "Laws of Service." The first law deals with the customer's expectations versus his or her perceptions. If a customer receives better service than he or she expects, then the customer departs a happy, satisfied person, and the service may benefit from a trickle-down effect; i.e., the happy customer will tell friends about the good service. Note that the trickle-down effect can work both ways: a service can earn a bad reputation in the same manner (and create more interesting stories to pass along!).

Maister's second law states that it is "hard to play 'catch-up ball.' " By this he means that first impressions can influence the rest of the service experience; thus, the service that requires its customers to wait would be advised to make the wait period a pleasant experience. To do the "impossible"—i.e., to make waiting at least tolerable and, at best, pleasant and productive—a creative and competitive service management must consider the following aspects of the psychology of waiting.

---

[3] Ibid., p. 67.
[4] Adapted from David H. Maister, "The Psychology of Waiting Lines," in J. A. Czepiel, M. R. Solomon, and C. F. Surprenant (eds.), *The Service Encounter*, Lexington Press, Lexington, Mass., 1985, chap. 8, pp. 113–123.

That Old Empty Feeling

Just as "nature abhors a vacuum," people dislike "empty time." Empty, or unoccupied, time feels awful. It keeps us from other productive activities; frequently it is physically uncomfortable; it makes us feel powerless and at the mercy of servers, whom we may perceive as uncaring about us; and perhaps worst of all, it seems to last forever. The challenge to the service organization is obvious: fill the time in a positive way. It may require no more than comfortable chairs and a fresh coat of paint to cheer up the environment. Furnishings in a waiting area can indirectly affect the perception of waiting. The fixed benchlike seating in bus and rail terminals discourages conversation. The light, movable table-and-chair arrangement found in a European sidewalk café brings people together and provides opportunities for socializing. In another situation, a music recording may be enough to occupy a telephone caller on hold and at the same time reassure the caller that he or she has not been disconnected.

Perhaps the strategy most widely noted in the literature is that of installing mirrors near elevators. Hotels, for example, record fewer complaints about excessive waits for elevators that are surrounded by mirrors. The mirrors allow people to occupy their time by checking their grooming and surreptitiously observing others who are waiting.

But services can often make waiting times productive as well as pleasurable. Instead of treating the telephone caller mentioned above to the strains of Mozart or Madonna, the service can air some commercials. Such a practice involves some risk, however, because some people resent being subjected to this tactic when they are being held captive. Or consider The Olive Garden restaurants. Diners who are waiting for tables can spend their time in the bar, which benefits the restaurant with added sales, or they can wait in the lobby and watch a chef prepare fresh pastas, which certainly stimulates appetites. No need to play "catch-up ball" here. Each diner reaches the table happily anticipating an agreeable experience rather than sourly grumbling "it's about time!"

Services that consist of several stages, such as one might find at a diagnostic clinic, can conceal waiting by asking people to walk between successive stages. There are innumerable other ways to fill time: with reading matter, television monitors, even live entertainment, posters, artwork, toys to occupy children, and cookies and pots of coffee. The diversions are limited only by management's imagination and desire to serve the customer effectively.

A Foot in the Door

As noted above, some diversions merely fill time so that waiting doesn't seem so long, and other diversions can also provide the service organization with some ancillary benefits. Happy customers are more likely to be profitable customers than are unhappy customers. But another aspect of diversions is important.

Maister points out that "service-related" diversions themselves, such as handing out menus to waiting diners or medical history forms (and paper cups!) to waiting patients, "convey a sense that service has started." One's level of anxiety subsides considerably once service has started. In fact, people generally can tolerate longer waits, within reason, if they feel service has begun better than they can tolerate such waits if service has not started. Another view is that customers become dissatisfied more quickly with an initial wait than with subsequent waits after the service has begun.

The Light at the End of the Tunnel

There are many anxieties at work before service begins. Have I been forgotten? Did you get my order? This line doesn't seem to be moving; will I ever get served? If I run to the rest room, will I lose my turn? When will the plumber get here? Will the plumber get here at all? Whether rational or not, anxieties may be the single biggest factor influencing the waiting customer.

Managers must recognize these anxieties and develop strategies to alleviate them. In some cases, the strategy may be a simple matter of having an employee acknowledge the customer's presence. At other times, telling the customer how long he or she will have to wait will be sufficient reassurance that the wait will end sometime. Signs can serve this purpose as well. For example, as you approach the Port Aransas, Texas, ferry landing, you see signs posted along the road noting the number of minutes you have left to wait if you are stopped in line at that point.

Scheduling appointments, where appropriate, is one strategy to reduce waiting time, but it is not foolproof. Unforeseen events might interfere, or prior appointments may require more time than expected. If the appointed time comes and goes, the anxiety of not knowing how long the wait will be then sets in, along with some measure of irritation at the "insult" of being stood up. However, a simple explanation and apology for the delay will usually go a long way in reestablishing goodwill.

Excuse Me, but I Was Next

Uncertain and unexplained waits create anxieties and, as noted above, occasionally some resentment in customers. But the moment a customer sees a later arrival being served first, anxiety about how long the wait will be is transformed into downright anger about the unfairness of it all. This can lead to a testy, if not explosive, situation, and the service provider is just as likely to be the target of the anger as is the usurper.

A simple strategy for avoiding violations of the first-come, first-served (FCFS) queuing policy is a take-a-number arrangement. For example, customers entering a meat market take a number from a dispenser and wait for it to be called. The number currently being served may be displayed so that the new customer can see how long the wait will be. With this simple measure, management has relieved the customer's anxiety over the length of the wait and the possibility of being treated unfairly. As an ancillary benefit, it encourages "impulse buying" by allowing the customer to wander about the shop instead of protecting a place in line. This system, as equitable as it is, is not totally free from producing anxiety; it does require the customer to stay alert to the numbers being called or risk losing his or her place in line.

Another simple strategy for fostering FCFS service when there are multiple servers is the use of a single queue. Banks, post offices, and airline check-in counters commonly employ this technique. A customer who enters one of these facilities joins the back of the line. The first person in line is served by the next available server; anxiety is relieved because there is no fear that later arrivals will "slip" ahead of their rightful place.[5] Often, customers who have been "guaranteed" their place in line in this way will relax and enjoy a few pleasantries with others in the line. Note that such comradery also occupies the customer's empty time and makes the waiting time seem shorter. Queue configurations are examined in more detail later in this chapter.

Not all services lend themselves to such a straightforward prioritization. Police service is one example; for obvious reasons an officer on the way to a call about a "noisy dog next door" will change priorities when told to respond to a "robbery-in-progress" call. In this case, the dispatcher can ameliorate the "noisy-dog" caller's wait anxiety by explaining the department's response policy and providing the caller with a reasonable expectation of the time when an officer will arrive.

Other services may wish to give preferential treatment to special customers; consider the express check-in for "high rollers" at Las Vegas hotels or for first-class passengers at airline check-in counters. But such special "perks" can also engender irritation among the unfavored who are standing in long lines nearby. A management sensitive to the concerns of *all* its customers will take measures to avoid an image of obvious discrimination. In the example just mentioned, one solution might be to "conceal" the preferential treatment by locating it in an area separate from the regular service line.

They Also Serve, Who Sit and Wait

Management must keep in mind that one of the most important parts of its service package is its attention to the needs of its customers during the wait process. The customer who is subjected to unnecessary anxiety or aggravation during the wait period is likely to be a demanding and difficult customer—or to become a former customer.

THE ECONOMICS OF WAITING

The economic cost of waiting can be viewed from two perspectives. For a firm, the cost of keeping an employee (internal customer) waiting may be measured by

---

[5]For a discussion of "slips" and "skips," see Richard C. Larson, "Perspectives on Queues: Social Justice and the Psychology of Queuing," *Operations Research,* vol. 35, no. 6, November–December 1987, pp. 895–905.

unproductive wages. For external customers, the cost of waiting is the forgone alternative use of time. To this are added the costs of boredom, anxiety, and other psychological distresses.

In a competitive market, excessive waiting or the expectation of long waits can lead to lost sales. How often have you driven by a filling station, observed many cars lined up at the pumps, and then decided not to stop? One strategy to avoid lost sales is to conceal the queue from arriving customers. In the case of restaurants, this is often achieved by diverting people into the bar, a tactic that frequently results in increased sales. Amusement parks, such as Disneyland, require people to pay for their tickets outside the park, where they are unable to observe the waiting lines inside. Casinos "snake" the waiting line for nightclub acts through the slot machines area to hide its true length and foster impulsive gambling.

The consumer can be considered a resource with the potential to participate in the service process. For example, a patient waiting for a doctor can be asked to complete a medical history record and thereby save valuable physician time (service capacity). The waiting period also can be used to educate the person in good health habits. This can be achieved by making available health publications or filmstrips. For another example, restaurants are quite innovative in their approaches to engaging the customer directly in providing the service. In many restaurants, after giving your order to a waiter, you are asked to go to the salad bar and prepare your own salad, which you eat while the cook prepares your meal.

Consumer waiting may be viewed as a contribution to productivity by permitting greater utilization of limited capacity. The situation of customers waiting in line for a service is analogous to work-in-process inventory for a manufacturing firm. The service firm is actually inventorying customers in order to increase the overall efficiency of the process. In service systems, higher utilization of facilities is purchased at the price of customer waiting. Prominent examples can be found in public services such as post offices, medical clinics, and welfare offices, where high utilization is achieved with long queues.

Yoram Barzel reports the following event[6] to illustrate the economic value of waiting:

On June 14, 1972, the United States of America Bank (of Chicago) launched an anniversary sale. The commodity on sale was money, and each of the first 35 persons could "buy" a $100 bill for $80 in cash. Those farther down the queue could each obtain similar but declining bonuses: the next 50 could gain $10 each; 75, $4 each; 100, $2 each; and the following 100, $1 each. Each of the next 100 persons could get a $2 bill for $1.60 and, finally 800 (subsequently, it seems, expanded to 1800) persons could gain $0.50 each. The expected waiting time in such an unusual event was unpredictable; on the other hand, it was easy to assess the money value of the commodity being distributed.

First in line were four brothers aged 16, 17, 19, and 24. Because the smallest was 6'2", their priority was assured. "I figured," said Carl, the youngest brother, "that we spent 17 hours to make a $20 profit. That's about $1.29 an hour."

[6]Yoram Barzel, "A Theory of Rationing by Waiting," *The Journal of Law and Economics,* vol. 17, no. 1, April 1974, p. 74.

"You can make better than that washing dishes," added another of the brothers. Had they been better informed they could have waited less time. The 35th person to join the line arrived around midnight, had to wait just 9 hours, and was the last to earn $20—$2.22 per hour. To confirm her right, she made a list of all those ahead of her in the line.

"Why am I here?" she asked. "Well, that $20 is the same as a day's pay to me. And I don't even have to declare it on my income tax. It's a gift, isn't it?"

The experience described above demonstrates that those in line considered their waiting time as the cost of securing a "free" good.

While waiting can have a number of economic interpretations, its true cost is always difficult to determine. For this reason the tradeoff between the cost of waiting and the cost of providing service is seldom made explicit. Yet service providers must consider the physical, behavioral, and economic aspects of the consumer waiting experience in their decision making.

ESSENTIAL FEATURES OF QUEUING SYSTEMS

Figure 11.1 depicts the essential features of queuing systems. These are (1) calling population, (2) arrival process, (3) queue configuration, (4) queue discipline, and (5) service process.

Services obtain customers from a *calling population.* The rate at which they arrive is determined by the *arrival process.* If servers are idle, then the customer is immediately attended. Otherwise, the customer is diverted to a queue, which can have various configurations. At this point, some customers may *balk* when confronted with a long or slow-moving waiting line and seek service elsewhere. Other customers, after joining the queue, may consider the delay intolerable, and so they *renege,* which means that they leave the line before service is rendered. When a server does become available, a customer is then selected from the queue, and service begins. The policy governing the selection is known as the *queue discipline.* The service facility may consist of no servers (self-service), one or more servers, or complex arrangements of servers in series or in parallel. After the service has been rendered, the customer departs the facility. At that time, the customer

FIGURE 11.1
Queuing system schematic.

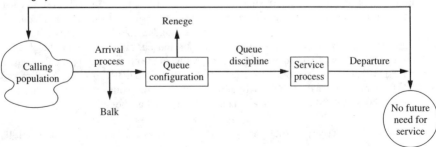

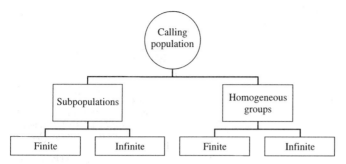

FIGURE 11.2
Classification of calling population.

may either rejoin the calling population for future return or exit with no intention of returning.

We shall now discuss in more detail each of these five essential features of queuing systems.

Calling Population

The calling population need not be homogeneous but may consist of several subpopulations. For example, the arrivals at an outpatient clinic can be divided into walk-in patients, patients with appointments, and emergency patients. Each patient class will place different demands on services; but more importantly, the waiting expectations of each will differ significantly.

It is possible in some queuing systems for the source of calls to be limited to a finite number of people. Take, for example, the demands made on an office copier by a staff of three secretaries. In this case the probability of future arrivals depends on the number of persons currently in the system seeking service. For instance, the probability of a future arrival becomes zero once the third secretary joins the copier queue. But unless the population is quite small, an assumption of independent arrivals or infinite population usually suffices. In Figure 11.2 a classification of calling population is shown.

Arrival Process

Any analysis of a service system must begin with a complete understanding of the temporal and spatial distribution of demand for the service. Typically, data are collected by recording the actual time of arrivals. These data are then used to calculate interarrival times. Many empirical studies indicate that the distribution of interarrival times will be exponential. The shape of the curve in Figure 11.3 is typical of the exponential distribution. Note the high frequency at the origin and the long tail that tapers off to the right. The exponential distribution can also be recognized by noting that the mean and standard deviation are theoretically equal ($\mu = 2.4$ and $\sigma = 2.6$ for Figure 11.3).

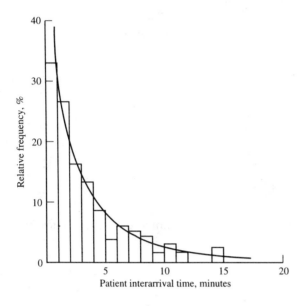

FIGURE 11.3
Distribution of patient interarrival times for a university health clinic. [*E. J. Rising, R. Baron, and B. Averill, "A Systems Analysis of a University Health-Service Outpatient Clinic." Reprinted with permission from* Operations Research, *vol. 21, no. 5, Sept.–Oct. 1973, p. 1038, Operations Research Society of America. No further reproduction permitted without the consent of the copyright owner.*]

The exponential distribution has a continuous probability density function of the form

$$f(t) = \lambda e^{-\lambda t} \qquad t \geq 0 \tag{1}$$

where λ = average arrival rate within a given interval of time (e.g., minutes, hours, days)

t = time between arrivals

e = base of natural logarithms (2.718 . . .)

mean = $1/\lambda$

variance = $1/\lambda^2$

The cumulative distribution function is

$$F(t) = 1 - e^{-\lambda t} \qquad t \geq 0 \tag{2}$$

Equation (2) gives the probability that the time between arrivals will be t or less. Note that λ is the inverse of the mean time between arrivals. Thus, for Figure 11.3, the mean time between arrivals is 2.4 minutes, which implies that λ is 1/2.4 = 0.4167 arrival per minute (an average rate of 25 patients per hour). Substituting 0.4167 for λ, the exponential distribution for the data displayed in Figure 11.3 is

$$f(t) = 0.4167 e^{-0.4167t} \qquad t \geq 0 \tag{3}$$

and
$$F(t) = 1 - e^{-0.4167t} \qquad t \geq 0 \tag{4}$$

Equation (4) can now be used to find the probability that, if a patient has already arrived, another will arrive in the next 5 minutes. We simply substitute 5 for t, and so $F(5) = 1 - e^{-0.4167(5)} = 1 - 0.124 = 0.876$, or an 87.6 percent chance.

Another distribution, known as the Poisson, has a unique relationship to the exponential distribution. The Poisson distribution is a discrete probability function of the form

$$f(n) = \frac{(\lambda t)^{n_e - \lambda t}}{n!} \qquad n = 0, 1, 2, 3, \ldots \tag{5}$$

where λ = average arrival rate within a given interval of time (e.g., minutes, hours, days)

t = number of time periods of interest (usually $t = 1$)

n = number of arrivals (0, 1, 2, . . .)

e = base of natural logarithms (2.718 . . .)

mean = λt

variance = λt

The Poisson distribution gives the probability of n arrivals during the time interval t. For the data of Figure 11.3, substituting for $\lambda = 25$, an equivalent description of the arrival process is

$$f(n) = \frac{25^{n_e - 25}}{n!} \qquad n = 0, 1, 2, \ldots \tag{6}$$

This gives the probability of 0, 1, 2, . . . patients arriving during any one-hour interval. Note that we have taken the option of converting $\lambda = 0.4167$ arrival per minute to $\lambda = 25$ arrivals per hour.

Figure 11.4 shows the relationship between the Poisson distribution (arrivals per hour) and the exponential distribution (minutes between arrivals). As can be seen, they represent alternative views of the same process. Thus, an exponential distribution of interarrival times with a mean of 2.4 minutes is equivalent to a Poisson distribution of number of arrivals per hour with a mean of 25 (i.e., 60/2.4).

Service demand data are often collected automatically (e.g., by trip wires on

FIGURE 11.4
Poisson and exponential equivalence.

Poisson distribution of number of arrivals per hour (top view)

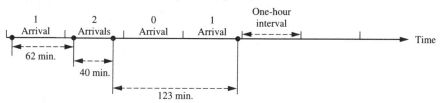

Exponential distribution of time between arrivals in minutes (bottom view)

highways), and the number of arrivals over a period of time is divided by the number of time intervals to arrive at an average rate per unit of time. The demand rate during the unit of time should be stationary with respect to time [i.e., lambda (λ) is a constant]. Otherwise, the underlying fluctuations in demand rate as a function of time will not be accounted for. This dynamic feature of demand is illustrated in Figure 11.5 for hours in a day, in Figure 11.6 for days of the week, and in Figure 11.7 for months of the year.

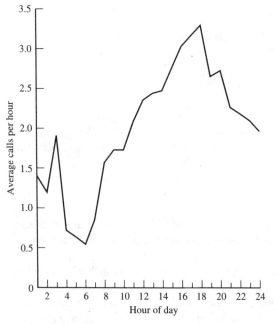

FIGURE 11.5
Ambulance calls by hour of day. [*Reprinted with permission from James A. Fitzsimmons, "The Use of Spectral Analysis to Validate Planning Models,"* Socio-Economic Planning, *vol. 8, no. 3, June 1974, p. 127. Copyright © 1974, Pergamon Press Ltd.*]

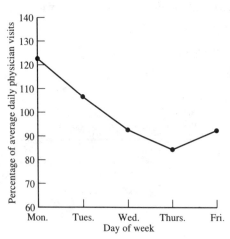

FIGURE 11.6
Patient arrivals at health clinic by day of week. [*E. J. Rising, R. Baron, and B. Averill, "A Systems Analysis of a University Health-Service Outpatient Clinic." Reprinted with permission from* Operations Research, *vol. 21, no. 5, Sept.–Oct. 1973, p. 1035, Operations Research Society of America. No further reproduction permitted without the consent of the copyright owner.*]

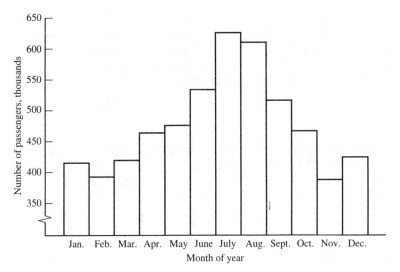

FIGURE 11.7
International airline passengers by month of year. [*FAA Statistical Handbook of Civil Aviation, 1960.*]

Variation in demand intensity directly affects the requirements for service capacity. When possible, service capacity is adjusted to match changes in demand, perhaps by varying the staffing levels. Another strategy is to smooth demand by asking customers to make appointments or reservations. Differential pricing is used by the telephone company to encourage callers to use off-peak hours. Movie theaters provide ticket discounts for patrons arriving before 6 p.m. Smoothing demand and adjusting supply are important topics and are covered in depth in Chapter 10. Figure 11.8 presents a classification of arrival processes.

FIGURE 11.8
Classification of arrival processes.

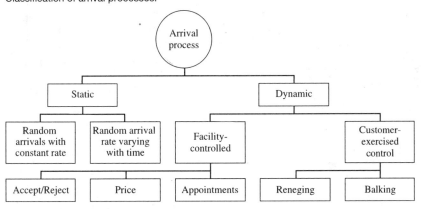

Although our discussion has focused on the frequency of demand as a function of time, the spatial distribution of demand may also vary. This is particularly true of emergency ambulance demand in an urban area, which has a spatial shift in demand owing to the temporary population movements from residential areas to commercial and industrial areas during working hours.

Queue Configuration

Queue configuration refers to the number of queues, their locations, their spatial requirement, and their effect on customer behavior. Figure 11.9 illustrates three alternative waiting configurations for a service, such as a bank, a post office, or an airline counter, where multiple servers are available.

For the multiple-queue alternative shown in Figure 11.9a, the arriving customer must decide which queue to join. The decision need not be irrevocable, because one may switch to the end of another line. This line-switching activity is called *jockeying*. In any event, watching the line next to you move faster is a source of aggravation. However, the multiple-queue configuration does have the following advantages:

1. The service provided can be differentiated. The use of express lanes in supermarkets is an example. Shoppers with small demands on service can be isolated and processed quickly, thereby avoiding long waits for little service.

2. Division of labor is possible. For example, drive-in banks assign the more experienced teller to the commercial lane.

3. The customer has the option of selecting a particular server of preference.

FIGURE 11.9
Alternative waiting-area configurations.

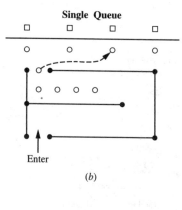

4. Balking behavior may be deterred. When arriving customers see a long single queue snaked in front of a service, they often interpret this as evidence of a long wait and decide not to join the line.

Figure 11.9*b* depicts the common arrangement of brass posts with red velvet ropes strung between them, forcing arrivals to join one sinuous queue. Whenever a server becomes available, the first person in line moves over to the service counter. This is a popular arrangement found in bank lobbies, post offices, and amusement parks. Its advantages are as follows:

1. The arrangement guarantees fairness by ensuring that a first-come, first-served rule applies to all arrivals.

2. There is a single queue; thus, no anxiety is associated with waiting to see if one selected the fastest line.

3. With only one entrance at the rear of the queue, the problem of cutting in is resolved, and reneging is made difficult.

4. Privacy is enhanced because the transaction is conducted with no one standing immediately behind the person being served.

5. This arrangement is more efficient in terms of reducing the average time customers spend waiting in line.

Figure 11.9*c* illustrates a variation on the single queue in which the arriving customer takes a number to indicate his or her place in line. With the use of such numbers to indicate positions in a queue, there is no need for a formal line. Customers are free to wander about, strike up a conversation, relax in a chair, or pursue some other diversion. Unfortunately, as we noted earlier, they must remain alert to hear their numbers being called or risk missing their turns for service. Bakeries make subtle use of the "take-a-number" system in order to increase impulse sales. Customers given the chance to browse among the tantalizing pastries often find that they purchase more than the loaf of fresh bread for which they came.

If the waiting area is inadequate to accommodate all the customers desiring service, then they are turned away. This condition is referred to as a *finite queue.* Restaurants with limited parking may experience this problem to a certain extent. However, a public parking garage is a classic example. Once the last stall is taken, future arrivals are rejected with the word *FULL* until a car is retrieved.

Figure 11.10 shows a classification of queue configurations.

Finally, concealment of the waiting line itself may deter customers from balking. Amusement parks often process waiting customers by stages. The first stage is a line outside the concession entrance, the second is the wait in an inside vestibule area, and the final stage is the wait for an empty vehicle to convey a party through the attraction.

Queue Discipline

The queue discipline is a policy established by management to select the next customer from the queue for service. The most popular service discipline is the

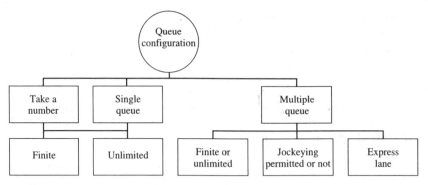

FIGURE 11.10
Classification of queue configurations.

first-come, first-served (FCFS) rule. This represents an egalitarian approach to serving waiting customers because all customers are treated alike. The rule is considered static because no information other than position in line is used to identify the next customer for service.

Dynamic queue disciplines are based on some attribute of the customer or status of the waiting line. For example, computer installations typically give first priority to waiting jobs with very short processing times. This shortest-processing-time (SPT) rule has the important feature of minimizing the average time a customer spends in the system.[7] This rule is seldom used in its pure form, because jobs with long operation times would be continually set aside for more recent arrivals with shorter times. By selecting next the job with the shortest service time, excessive delays result for jobs with long service times. Typically, arrivals are placed in priority classes on the basis of some attribute, and the FCFS rule is used within each class. An example is the express checkout counter at supermarkets, where orders of ten or fewer items are processed. This allows large stores to segment their customers and thereby compete with the neighborhood convenience stores, which provide prompt service. In a medical setting, the procedure known as triage is used to give priority to those who would benefit most from immediate treatment.

The most responsive queue discipline is the preemptive priority rule. Under this rule, the service currently in process for a person is interrupted to serve a newly arrived customer with higher priority. This rule is usually reserved for emergency services, such as fire or ambulance services. An ambulance on the way to a hospital to pick up a patient for routine transfer will interrupt this mission to respond to a suspected-cardiac-arrest call.

The queue discipline can have an important effect on the likelihood that a waiting customer will renege. For this reason, information on the expected waiting time might be made available to the arriving customer and updated periodically

[7]R. W. Conway, W. L. Maxwell, and L. W. Miller, *Theory of Scheduling,* Addison-Wesley Publishing Company, Reading, Mass., 1967, p. 27.

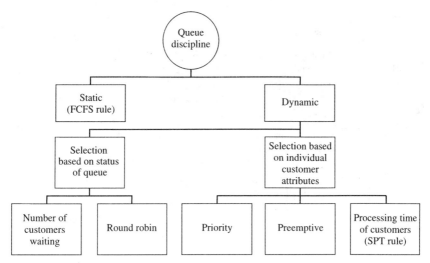

FIGURE 11.11
Classification of queue disciplines.

for each waiting customer. This information is usually available to computer center users interested in the status of their jobs waiting in queue to be processed.

Some fast-food chains, like Wendy's, take a more direct approach to avoid customer reneging. When long lines begin to form, a service person begins to take orders while customers are still waiting in line. Taking this idea further is the concept of round-robin service used by time-shared computer systems. In these systems, a customer is given partial service, and then the server moves on to the next waiting customer. Thus, customers alternate between waiting and being served. Figure 11.11 shows a classification of queue disciplines.

Service Process

The distribution of service times, the arrangement of servers, management policies, and server behavior all contribute to service performance. Figure 11.12 contains histograms of several service time distributions in an outpatient clinic. As can be seen, the distribution of service times may be of any form. Conceivably, the service time could be a constant, such as the time to process a car through an automated car wash. However, when the service is brief and simple to perform (e.g., preparing orders at a fast-food restaurant, collecting tolls at a bridge, or checking out items at a supermarket), the distribution of service times frequently is exponential (see Figure 11.3). The histogram for second-service times, Figure 11.12c, most closely approximates an exponential distribution. The second-service times represent those brief encounters in which, for example, the physician prescribes a medication or goes over your test results with you. The distribution of service times is a reflection of the variations in customer needs and server performances.

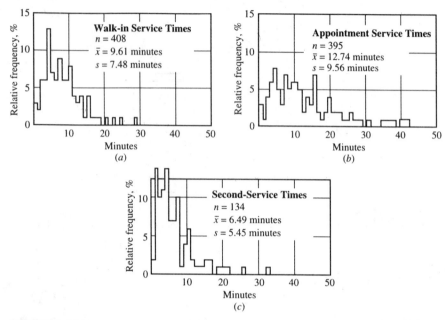

FIGURE 11.12
Histograms of outpatient-clinic service times. [*E. J. Rising, R. Baron, and B. Averill, "A Systems Analysis of a University Health-Service Outpatient Clinic." Reprinted with permission from* Operations Research, *vol. 21, no. 5, Sept.–Oct. 1973, p. 1039, Operations Research Society of America. No further reproduction permitted without the consent of the copyright owner.*]

Table 11.1 illustrates the variety of service facility arrangements that are possible. With servers in parallel, management gains flexibility in meeting the variations in demand for service. Management can effectively vary the service capacity by opening and closing service lines to meet changes in demand. At a bank, additional teller windows are opened when the length of queues becomes excessive. Cross-training employees adds to this flexibility. For example, at supermarkets, stockers are often used as cashiers when lines become long at the checkout counters. A final advantage of parallel servers is that they provide redundancy in case of equipment failures.

TABLE 11.1
SERVICE FACILITY ARRANGEMENTS

Service facility	Server arrangement
Parking lot	Self-serve
Cafeteria	Servers in series
Toll booths	Servers in parallel
Supermarket	Self-serve, first stage; parallel servers, second stage
Hospital	Many service centers in parallel and series, not all used by each patient

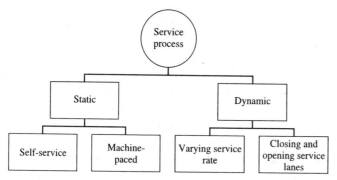

FIGURE 11.13
Classification of service processes.

The behavior of service personnel toward customers is critical to the success of the organization. Under the pressure of long waiting lines, a server may speed up and spend less time with each customer. Unfortunately, a gracious and leisurely manner then becomes curt and impersonal. Sustained pressure to hurry may increase the rate of customer processing, but it also sacrifices quality. This behavior on the part of a pressured server can have a detrimental effect on other servers in the system. For example, a busy emergency telephone operator may dispatch yet another patrol car before properly screening the call for its critical nature. In this situation, the operator should have spent more time than usual to ensure that the limited resources of patrol cars were being dispatched to the most critical cases. Figure 11.13 suggests a classification of service processes.

SUMMARY

An understanding of the queuing phenomenon is necessary before creative approaches to the management of service systems can be considered. An appreciation of the behavioral implications of keeping customers waiting reveals that the perception of waiting is often more important than the actual delay. Waiting also has economic implications for both the service firm and its customers.

A schematic queuing model identified the essential features of queuing systems: calling population, arrival process, queue configuration, queue discipline, and service process. We have discovered that an understanding of each feature provides insights and identifies management options for improving customer service.

In Chapter 15 we will explore applications of several analytical queuing models that are useful for predicting customer waiting times. These models will suggest further insights that will be helpful in capacity planning and scheduling decisions.

TOPICS FOR DISCUSSION

1. Suggest some strategies for controlling the variability in service times.
2. Suggest diversions that could make waiting less painful.

3. Select a bad and good waiting experience, and contrast the situations with respect to the aesthetics of the surroundings, diversions, the people waiting, and the attitude of servers.
4. Suggest ways that service management can influence the arrival times of customers.
5. At some fast-food restaurants, when the line becomes long, an order taker will walk along the line taking orders. What are the benefits of this policy?

CASE: THRIFTY CAR RENTAL

Thrifty Car Rental has become one of the southwest's major rental agencies, even though it competes with several national agencies. It is definitely the largest regional company, with offices and outlets in 19 cities and 5 states, and it operates primarily off-site from the airport terminals of those major cities. Thrifty's rental fleet consists almost entirely of fuel-efficient compact and subcompact automobiles. Its clientele utilizes the vehicles for tourism and business purposes, obtaining service at any location with or without prior arrangements. Although Thrifty does lose customers on occasion when the desired vehicles are unavailable at a given location, this "stockout" situation occurs less than 10 percent of the time.

The service counter where customers are processed by Thrifty's personnel has a simple design. In the "old days" it varied only in the number of cubbyholes used to keep various forms within easy reach of the servers. Today, the cubbies and forms have given way to computer terminals for more streamlined service. The number of servers varies with the size of the local market and the level of demand at specific times. In the smaller markets, Thrifty may need only three people at one time behind the counter, but in the largest markets, this number could be as high as eight when demand is heaviest. Usually these peak-demand times reflect the airport's inbound-outbound flight schedule, and as they occur, one or more attendants may deal exclusively with clients who have made prior arrangements to pick up a vehicle or with those who are returning vehicles. When this situation exists, these attendants hang appropriate messages above their chosen stations to indicate their special service functions to clientele. Because the speed of customer service is an important factor in maintaining Thrifty's competitive edge, management and service personnel have worked very hard to ensure that each client is processed without unnecessary delay.

Another important factor in Thrifty's competitive stance is its ability to turn incoming vehicles around and have them quickly prepared for new clients. The following steps are necessary to process a vehicle for turnaround from incoming delivery to outgoing delivery: (1) confirmation of odometer reading, (2) refueling and confirmation of fuel charge, (3) visual damage inspection, (4) priority assessment, (5) interior cleaning, (6) maintenance assessment, (7) maintenance and checkout, (8) exterior cleaning and polishing, (9) refueling and lot storage, and (10) delivery to customer.

When a client returns a vehicle to any location, one of Thrifty's crew will confirm the odometer reading, drive about 200 meters to the service lot, and confirm any fuel charge necessary to refill the car's tank. In some cases the crew member may be able to process all this information on a hand-held computer, and the customer can be on her or his way without having to queue up in the office. In less streamlined locations, the crew member will immediately relay the information to all attendants so that the client may complete payment inside and be released as soon as possible. (If the crew member notices any interior or exterior damage to the vehicle, the attendant will notify the manager on duty; the client must clarify his or her responsibility in the circumstances and may be delayed while this is occurring.) After the damage inspection step, the fleet supervisor assigns a priority status to incoming cars on the basis of the company's known (certain) demand and reserve policy (for walk-up clients): high-priority treatment for those cars needed within the next six-hour period and normal treatment for everything else. Vehicles assigned a high priority get preferential treatment for servicing.

After the vehicle's interior is thoroughly cleaned and sprayed with a mild air freshener, a mechanic examines the vehicle's maintenance record, gives the vehicle a test drive, and notes on a form any maintenance actions deemed necessary. Thrifty has certain policies covering periodic normal maintenance, like oil and filter changes, tire rotation and balancing, lubrication, coolant replacement, and engine tune-ups. Major special maintenance actions, such as brake repair, transmission repair or adjustment, or air-conditioning and heating repair, are performed as needed.

Typically, a garage in Thrifty's system has a standard side-by-side three-bay design: two of the bays are always used for normal maintenance, and the third is used for either normal or special maintenance. About 20 percent of the time is spent on special maintenance in this third bay. In general, Thrifty uses a team of five mechanics for its garages: one master mechanic (who is the garage manager), two journeyman mechanics, and two apprentices. The apprentices are responsible for all normal maintenance tasks except the engine tune-up; they are stationed to service every vehicle in each outside bay, and they alternate on vehicles placed in the middle bay. The journeyman mechanics are responsible for all other maintenance, and they also alternate on servicing vehicles in the middle bay.

After servicing, the vehicle is moved outside, where the car wash is located, and a team of two people washes, rinses, and buffs the exterior to ensure that it has a good appearance. Because part of the rinse cycle contains a wax-type liquid compound, the vehicle does not usually require a time-consuming wax job. From this point, the vehicle's fuel tank is again topped off, and the vehicle is placed in the lot for storage. When the vehicle is called for by an attendant, a driver will take it to the rental area of the facility for the client to pick up.

Assignment

On the basis of your experience and the description of Thrifty's operations, describe the five essential features of the queuing systems at the customer counter, the garage, and the car wash.

CASE: EYE'LL BE SEEING YOU[8]

Mrs. F arrives fifteen minutes early for a 1:30 p.m. appointment with her Austin, Texas, ophthalmologist, Dr. X. The waiting room is empty, and all the prior names on the sign-in sheet are crossed out. The receptionist looks up but does not acknowledge her presence. Mrs. F, unaware of the drama about to unfold, happily anticipates that she may not have to wait long beyond her scheduled time and settles into a chair to read the book she has brought with her. Large windows completely surround three sides of the waiting room. The receptionist sits behind a large opening in the remaining wall. Attractive artwork decorates the available wall space, and trailing plants have been placed on a shelf above the receptionist's opening. It is an appealing, comfortable waiting room.

At 1:25 another patient, "Jack," arrives. Mrs. F knows his name must be Jack because the receptionist addresses him by first name, and the two share some light-hearted pleasantries. Jack takes a seat and starts looking through a magazine. At 1:40, a very agitated woman enters and approaches the receptionist. She explains that she is very sorry she missed her 1 o'clock appointment and asks if it would be possible for Dr. X to see her anyway. The receptionist replies very coldly, "You're wrong. Your appointment was for 11." "But I have 1 o'clock written down!" responds the patient, whose agitation has now changed to distress. "Well, you're wrong." "Oh dear, is there any way I can be worked in?" pleads the patient. "We'll see. Sit down."

Mrs. F and her two "companions" wait until 1:50, when staff person number 2 (SP2) opens the door between the waiting room and the hallway leading to the various treatment areas. She summons Jack, and they laugh together as she leads him to the back. Mrs. F thinks to herself, "I was here first, but maybe he just arrived late for an earlier appointment"; then she goes back to her book. Five minutes later, Ms. SP2 appears at the door and summons the distressed patient. At this point, Mrs. F walks to the back area (she's a long-time patient and knows the territory), seeks out Ms. SP2, and says, "I wonder if I've been forgotten. I was here before those two people who have just been taken in ahead of me." Ms. SP2 replies very brusquely, "Your file's been pulled. Go sit down."

Once again occupying an empty waiting room, Mrs. F returns to her reading. At 2:15 (no patient has yet emerged from a treatment area), Ms. SP2 finally summons Mrs. F and takes her to room 1, where she uses two instruments to make some preliminary measurements of Mrs. F's eyes. This is standard procedure in Dr. X's practice. Also standard is measuring the patient's present eyeglass prescription on a third instrument in room 1. Mrs. F extends her eyeglasses to Ms. SP2, but Ms. SP2 brushes past her and says curtly, "This way." Mrs. F is

---

[8]This case, sad to say, is true in its entirety. The names of the physician and his staff have been omitted, not to protect them but because this kind of treatment of patients is so pervasive in the American health care system that it serves no purpose to identify them. We offer the case for two reasons: first, because it is so wonderfully instructive regarding important material in this chapter, and second, because we wish to point out that customers and providers must work together in our emerging service society. Service providers must be sensitive to the needs of customers, and customers must demand and reward good service.

then led to a seat in the "dilating area," although no drops have been put in her eyes to start dilation.

The light in the dilating area is dimmed to protect dilating eyes, but Mrs. F is able to continue reading her book. No one else is seated in the dilating area. At 2:45, Ms. SP2 reappears, says "this way" (a woman of very few words, our Ms. SP2), and marches off to examining room 3. "Wait here," she commands and leaves Mrs. F to seat herself in the darkened room.

Mrs. F can hear Dr. X and Jack laughing in the next examining room. At 2:55 she hears the two men saying good-bye and leaving the room. Mrs. F expects Dr. X to enter her room shortly. But at 3:15, when he still has not appeared, she walks forward and interrupts Ms. SP2, the receptionist, the bookkeeper, and Ms. SP3, who are socializing. "Excuse me, but have I been forgotten?" she asks. Ms. SP2 turns her head from her companions and replies, "No, he's in the line. Go sit down." Mrs. F wonders what that means but returns to her assigned place. She is here, after all, for a particular visual problem, not just for a routine checkup.

However, all good things, including Mrs. F's patience and endurance of abusive treatment, eventually end. At 4 p.m., Mrs. F does some marching of her own—to the front desk, where she announces to the assembled Mss. SP1 through SP4 that she has been waiting since 1:30, that she has been sitting in the back for 2 ½ hours, and that not once during that time has one member of the staff come to let her know what the problem is, how much longer she can expect to wait, or, indeed, that she has not been forgotten. She adds that she will wait no longer, and she feels forced to seek the services of a physician who chooses to deliver health care. There are several patients seated in the waiting room at the time.

There is an epilogue to this case. Mrs. F went directly home and wrote the following letter to Dr. X informing him of the treatment she had (not) received at his office and stating that she and her family would seek care elsewhere:

January 5, 1989

_____ , M.D.

Austin, Texas

Dear Dr. _____ :

It is with very real regret that I am transferring our eye care to another physician, and I want you to know the reason for my decision.

It is 4:22 p.m., and I have just returned home from a 1:30 p.m. appointment with(out) you. The appointment was made because I had received an adverse report from Seton Hospital's recent home vision test. I was kept waiting in the dilation area and in examining room 3 for more than two-and-one-half hours, during which time not one single member of your staff gave me any explanation for the delay or assured me I had not been forgotten. When I finally asked if I were forgotten, I was treated with a very bad attitude ("how dare I even ask!") and still was given no reason for the delay or any estimate of how much longer I would have to wait. Consequently, I left without seeing you.

As I stated above, I make this change with very real regret because I value your expertise and the treatment you personally have given the four of us during these past many years. But I will not tolerate the callous treatment of your staff.

Sincerely yours,

Mrs. _____

Questions

1. In this chapter, we referred to Maister's First and Second Laws of Service. How do they relate to this case?

2. What features of a good waiting process are evident in Dr. X's practice? List the shortcomings that you see.

3. Do you think that Mrs. F is typical of most people waiting for a service? How so? How not?

4. If Dr. X were concerned with keeping the F family as patients, how could he have responded to Mrs. F's letter? Write a letter on Dr. X's behalf to Mrs. F.

5. How could Dr. X prevent such incidents in the future?

6. List constructive ways in which customers can respond when services fall seriously short of their requirements or expectations.

SELECTED BIBLIOGRAPHY

Barzel, Yoram: "A Theory of Rationing by Waiting," *The Journal of Law and Economics,* vol. 17, no. 1, April 1974, pp. 73–94.

Budnick, F. S., R. Mojena, and T. E. Vollmann: *Principles of Operations Research for Management,* Richard D. Irwin, Inc., Homewood, Ill., 1977.

Davis, Mark M., and M. J. Maggard: "An Analysis of Customer Satisfaction with Waiting Times in a Two-Stage Service Process," *Journal of Operations Management,* vol. 9, no. 3, August 1990, pp. 324–334.

Fitzsimmons, James A.: "The Use of Spectral Analysis to Validate Planning Models," *Socio-Economic Planning,* vol. 8, no. 3, June 1974, pp. 123–128.

Hall, Edward T.: *The Hidden Dimension,* Doubleday and Co., Inc., Garden City, N.Y., 1969.

Katz, K. L., B. M. Larson, and R. C. Larson: "Prescription for the Waiting-in-Line Blues: Entertain, Enlighten, and Engage," *Sloan Management Review,* vol. 32, no. 2, winter 1991, pp. 44–53.

Larson, Richard C.: "Perspectives on Queues: Social Justice and the Psychology of Queuing," *Operations Research,* vol. 35, no. 6, November–December 1987, pp. 895–905.

Maister, D. H.: "The Psychology of Waiting Lines," in J. A. Czepiel, M. R. Solomon, and C. F. Surprenant (eds.), *The Service Encounter,* Lexington Press, Lexington, Mass., 1985, chap. 8, pp. 113–123.

Rising, E. J., R. Baron, and B. Averill: "A Systems Analysis of a University Health-Service Outpatient Clinic," *Operations Research,* September 1973, pp. 1030–1047.

Schwartz, Barry: *Queuing and Waiting,* University of Chicago Press, Chicago, 1975.

Smith, Hedrick: *The Russians,* Quadrangle Press, New York, 1975.

TOWARD
WORLD-CLASS SERVICE

Competition in services has become global, as Federal Express has discovered in its attempt to expand overseas. The danger of services following the decline in competitiveness experienced by manufacturing is possible because no market is isolated in today's global economy. Only by promoting a culture of continuous improvement in productivity and quality can a service firm reach world-class status. In this regard, the application of Deming's philosophy of continuous service process improvement is recalled from Chapter 9 and explored further. Some of the improvements will come from managing the process of adopting new technology, which is a challenge because both employees and customers are affected. A new technique called data envelopment analysis (DEA), mentioned briefly in Chapter 4, will be used in Part V to measure service productivity as the ratio of resource inputs to service outputs of a service unit. Using DEA to compare units allows management to identify efficient producers.

Service expansion strategies can be described in the context of being multisite or multiservice. The traditional multisite service expansion strategy of franchising is explored with a discussion of the issues that arise between the franchisee and franchisor. For services considering multinational expansion, additional considerations arise such as cultural transferability and host government policies.

PRODUCTIVITY AND QUALITY IMPROVEMENT

Increasing productivity is important if a nation's standard of living is to rise. For a company to remain competitive in the global economy, wages can only be raised if they are matched by increased productivity. For the past decade, as shown in Figure 12.1, productivity as measured by output per hour has steadily increased for manufacturing while the output per hour for services has remained relatively flat. There are many explanations given for this lack of productivity improvement: the service sector was absorbing the baby boomers entering the labor force, and thus workers were young and inexperienced; capital investment per worker was (and still is) much lower in services than in manufacturing; automation was displacing workers in manufacturing; service output was (and remains) difficult to quantify; and training of service workers was neglected.

Changing demographics in the 1990s and the anticipated future labor shortage will force services to become more productivity-conscious. Consider the labor-saving ideas incorporated by the new Sleep Inn chain to reduce the labor costs needed to operate a hotel unit. For example, clothes washers and dryers are located behind the front desk so that the night clerk can load and unload laundry while on duty. To help reduce housekeeping chores, the nightstands are bolted to the wall so that maids need not vacuum around legs, and the shower stall is round to prevent dirt from collecting in corners. The computerized electronic security system has eliminated room keys: guests use their own credit cards to enter their rooms. Also, to reduce energy costs, heat or air-conditioning is turned on or off automatically when the guest checks in or out. In addition, the computer keeps track of the time maids spend cleaning each room. As seen in this example, creative facility design,

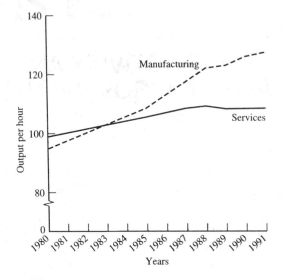

FIGURE 12.1
Productivity in manufacturing and services. [*After "Productivity and Related Measures: 1960 to 1991,"* Statistical Abstract of the U.S., *U.S. Department of Commerce, Economics and Statistics Administration, Bureau of the Census, 1992, table no. 647, p. 409.*]

effective use of labor, and innovative use of computers can have a major impact on increasing service productivity.[1]

CHAPTER PREVIEW

The focus of this chapter is on continuous improvement in service organizations through productivity and quality initiatives. Productivity is more than a design issue; it also represents an ongoing commitment to improving the operations and customer service. Because of customer participation in the service delivery process, any changes in the service delivery process raise the issue of customer acceptance. This issue is more critical when the automation of services extends from the back office to the front desk.

Continuous improvement is a way of thinking that needs to be incorporated into the firm's culture. Continuous improvement can be demonstrated by the analogy of queue reduction in services and inventory reduction in manufacturing using the just-in-time (JIT) philosophy. The Deming philosophy of continuous improvement will also be presented using the experience of Florida Power and Light, the first non-Japanese firm to win the prestigious Deming Prize.

Finally, a new linear programming model referred to as Data Envelopment Analysis (DEA) will be introduced as a method of measuring the efficiency of service delivery units. The comparative analysis of unit performance using DEA provides an opportunity to promote continuous improvement through shared learning.

---

[1]From David Wessel, "With Labor Scarce, Service Firms Strive to Raise Productivity," *The Wall Street Journal,* June 1, 1989, p. 1.

We begin our discussion with a framework that categorizes service firms according to their level of competitiveness with respect to key operational dimensions, all of which are sources of productivity and quality innovations.

STAGES IN SERVICE FIRM COMPETITIVENESS[2]

If a service firm is to remain competitive, continual improvement in productivity and quality must be part of its strategy and corporate culture. The framework shown in Table 12.1 was developed by Chase and Hayes to describe the role of operations in the strategic development of service firms. This framework is also useful as an illustration of the many sources of productivity and quality improvement (i.e., new technology is only one source). In addition, the framework provides a method to measure and evaluate a firm's progress in the development of its service delivery system. The framework organizes service firms into four different stages of development according to their competitiveness in service delivery. For each stage, the management practices and attitudes of the firm are compared across key operational dimensions.

It should be noted that services need not start at stage 1, but during their life cycle they could revert to stage 1 out of neglect. For example, one could argue that Federal Express began service as a stage 3 competitor because of its innovative hub-and-spoke network concept, whereby all sorting is accomplished at the single Memphis hub, thus guaranteeing overnight delivery.

Available for Service

Some service firms and often government services in particular fall into this category because they view operations as a necessary evil to be performed at minimum cost. There is little motivation to seek improvements in quality because the customers often have no alternatives. Workers require direct supervision because of their limited skills and because of the potential for poor performance that results from minimal investment in training. Investment in new technology is avoided until it is necessary for survival (e.g., consider the long-overdue adoption of Doppler radar by the FAA for air traffic control). These firms are essentially noncompetitive and exist only in this stage until challenged by competition.

Journeyman

After maintaining a sheltered existence in stage 1, a service firm may face competition and thus may be forced to reevaluate its delivery system. Operations managers must then adopt industry practices to maintain parity with the new competitors and avoid a significant loss of market share. For example, if all successful airlines were flying the same kind of plane, then a fledgling airline just

---

[2]Adapted from R. B. Chase and R. H. Hayes, "Operations' Role in Service Firm Competitiveness," *Sloan Management Review,* vol. 33, no. 1, fall 1991, pp. 15–26.

TABLE 12.1
FOUR STAGES OF SERVICE FIRM COMPETITIVENESS

	1. Available for service	2. Journeyman	3. Distinctive competence achieved	4. World-class service delivery
	Customers patronize service firm for reasons other than performance.	Customers neither seek out nor avoid the firm.	Customers seek out the firm on the basis of its sustained reputation for meeting customer expectations.	The company's name is synonymous with service excellence. Its service doesn't just satisfy customers; it *delights* them and thereby expands customer expectations to levels its competitors are unable to fulfill.
	Operations is reactive, at best.	Operations functions in a mediocre, uninspired fashion.	Operations continually excels, reinforced by personnel management and systems that support an intense customer focus.	Operations is a quick learner and fast innovator; it masters every step of the service delivery process and provides capabilities that are superior to competitors.
Service quality	Is subsidiary to cost, highly variable.	Meets some customer expectations; consistent on one or two key dimensions.	Exceeds customer expectations; consistent on multiple dimensions.	Raises customer expectations and seeks challenges; improves continuously.

Back office	Counting room.	Contributes to service, plays an important role in the total service, is given attention, but is still a separate role.	Is equally valued with front office; plays integral role.	Is proactive, develops its own capabilities, and generates opportunities.
Customer	Unspecified, to be satisfied at minimum cost.	A market segment whose basic needs are understood.	A collection of individuals whose variation in needs is understood.	A source of stimulation, ideas, and opportunity.
Introduction of new technology	When necessary for survival, under duress.	When justified by cost savings.	When promises to enhance service.	Source of first-mover advantages, creating ability to do things your competitors can't do.
Workforce	Negative constraint.	Efficient resource; disciplined; follows procedures.	Permitted to select among alternative procedures.	Innovative; creates procedures.
First-line management	Controls workers.	Controls the process.	Listens to customers; coaches and facilitates workers.	Is listened to by top management as a source of new ideas. Mentors workers to enhance their career growth.

Source: Reprinted from "Operations' Role in Service Firm Competitiveness," by R. B. Chase and R. H. Hayes, *Sloan Management Review*, vol. 33, no. 1, fall 1991, p. 17, by permission of publisher. Copyright © 1991 by the Sloan Management Review Association. All rights reserved.

entering the market might also be inclined to use the very same plane. The contribution of operations in this hypothetical situation becomes competitive-neutral because all the firms in the industry have adopted similar practices and even look like each other (because they have purchased equipment from the same supplier).

When firms do not compete on operations effectiveness, they are often creative in competing along other dimensions, such as breadth of product line, peripheral services, and advertising. The workforce is disciplined to follow standard proce-dures and is not expected to take any initiative when unusual circumstances arise. These firms have not yet recognized the potential contribution of operations to a firm's competitiveness.

Distinctive Competence Achieved

Firms in this category are fortunate to have senior managers who have a vision of what creates value for the customer and who also understand the role that operations managers must play in delivering the service. For example, Jan Carlzon, CEO of Scandinavian Airlines (SAS), realized that recapturing the business traveler market that had been lost to aggressive competition required improving on-time departure performance. To achieve this goal, he had to provide a leadership role that fostered operations innovations, which would then improve the delivery system.[3]

Operations managers are the typical advocates of total quality management (TQM) for firms that take the lead in instituting service guarantees, worker empowerment, and service-enhancing technologies. Workers in these organizations are often cross-trained and encouraged to take the initiative when necessary to achieve operational goals that are clearly stated (e.g., overnight delivery for Federal Express). Firms in this category implement management strategies to achieve the corporate vision and thereby differentiate themselves from their competition.

World-Class Service Delivery

Not satisfied with just meeting customer expectations, world-class firms expand on these expectations to levels that competitors find difficult to meet. Management is proactive in promoting higher standards of performance and in identifying new business opportunities by listening to customers. World-class service firms such as Disney, Marriott, and American Airlines define the quality standards by which others are judged.

New technology is no longer viewed only as a means to reduce costs; it is considered a competitive advantage not easily duplicated. For example, Federal Express developed COSMOS (Customer Operations Service Master On-line System) to provide a system that tracks packages from the time of pickup until delivery. Customers can call at any time and receive information on the exact

---

[3]Jan Carlzon, *Moments of Truth,* Ballinger Publishing, Cambridge, Mass., 1987.

location of their packages. This communication system can also be used to tell a driver en route to make customer pickups.

Working at a world-class firm is considered something special, and employees are encouraged to identify with the firm and its mission. For example, a Disney trash collector is considered a cast member who helps visitors enjoy the experience.

Sustaining superior performance throughout the delivery system is a major challenge, but duplicating the service at multiple sites, in particular overseas, is the true test of being a world-class competitor.

TECHNOLOGICAL INNOVATION IN SERVICES

The great gains in productivity for agriculture and manufacturing have come from the substitution of technology for human effort. Technology need not be confined to hardware and machines. It also includes innovative systems, such as electronic funds transfer or automated multiphasic health testing. However, while in manufacturing, the introduction of technological innovations goes unnoticed by the consumer, such innovations become an integral part of the service provided for the customer. For example, many airlines have introduced automatic ticketing machines that accept credit cards and issue tickets according to a request entered by the passenger, who pushes appropriate buttons. At many filling stations, a credit card reader located on the pump facilitates the purchase of gasoline.

Challenges of Adopting New Technology in Services

Because customers participate directly in the service process, the success of technological innovations depends on customer acceptance. The impact on customers is not always limited to a loss of personal attention; customers may also need to learn new skills (e.g., how to operate an automatic teller machine or pump gasoline), or they may have to forgo some benefit (e.g., loss of float through the use of electronic funds transfer). The contribution of customers as active participants in the service process must be considered when making changes in the service delivery system.

Service process innovations also may be spurred by technological changes in the environment. The laundry and dry-cleaning service has changed in response to synthetic fabrics and "no-iron" sheets. Cleaning synthetic fabrics required new detergents and dry-cleaning solvents. These in turn required the development of a process of injection and metering. The no-iron sheets also led to the first sheet-folding machine.

Back-office innovation that does not directly affect the customer may raise complications of a different sort. For example, consider the use of magnetic-ink-character recognition equipment in banking. This technological innovation did not affect the customer at all but instead made the "hidden" check-clearing process more productive. However, the full benefits could not be realized until all banks agreed to imprint their checks using a universal character code. Without such an agreement, the checks of uncooperative banks would need to be sorted by hand, which would severely limit the effectiveness of the technology. When all banks in the United States finally agreed on the use of the same magnetic-ink-character imprints on checks, the check-clearing process became much more efficient. The Bank of America took a leadership role in gaining acceptance of the concept, but the self-interest of banks was a principle motivation for acceptance. The volume of check processing had exceeded manual sorting capacity.

Other examples of this need to standardize occurred in retailing with the acceptance of the Universal Product Code (UPC) by manufacturers. Retailers who have adopted the UPC can use laser scanners to read the bar code (a series of vertical stripes of different widths). Consequently, they can use a computer to register sales and update inventory levels simultaneously.

The incentive to innovate in services is hampered because many ideas cannot be patented. An example is the idea of self-serve retailing. Much of the potential for technological and organizational progress is in this area, but the prospective rewards for innovations are diminished because the innovations may be freely imitated and implemented quickly by the competition.

Automation in Services

The back office has been the most logical place to introduce automation in services because the operations there are often repetitive and routine and thus amenable to labor-saving devices. Many applications have been in the hard automation category, such as replacing human manual activity with a machine (e.g., an automatic lawn sprinkler system at a hotel). More advanced programmable robots have also found application in services, sometimes interacting with the customer (e.g., automated answering systems that route callers by means of touch-tone phones).

Thus, a classification of automation applications in services must go beyond the traditional categories used in manufacturing because of the opportunities for interaction with the customer. In the following automation categories first suggested by David Collier we include the "expert system," a form of mental automation (e.g., using a computer for reasoning and problem solving):[4]

Fixed-sequence robot (F). A machine that repetitively performs successive steps of a given operation according to a predetermined sequence, condition, and position and whose set information *cannot* be easily changed. Service example: automatic parking lot gate.

Variable-sequence robot (V). A machine that is the same as a fixed-sequence robot but whose set information *can* be changed easily. Service example: automated teller machine.

Playback robot (P). A machine that can produce operations from memory that were originally executed under human control. Service example: telephone answering machine.

[4]David A. Collier, "The Service Sector Revolution: The Automation of Services," *Long Range Planning,* vol. 16, no. 6, December 1983, p. 11.

Numerical controlled robot (N). A machine that can perform a given task according to a sequence, conditions, and a position, as commanded by stored instructions that can be reprogrammed easily. Service example: animated characters at an amusement park.

Intelligent robot (I). A machine with sensory perception devices such as visual or tactile receptors that can detect changes in the work environment or task by itself and has its own decision-making abilities. Service example: autopilot for a commercial airplane.

Expert system (E). A computer program that uses an inference engine (decision rules) and a knowledge base (information on a particular subject) to diagnose problems. Service example: maintenance trouble-shooting for elevator repair.

Totally automated system (T). A system of machines and computers that performs all the physical and intellectual tasks required to produce a product or deliver a service. Service example: electronic funds transfer.

To illustrate the extent of automation in services, Table 12.2 contains examples of automation by service industry, with each example classified according to the categories above.

The extent of automation in service industries as shown in Table 12.2 suggests that services are becoming more capital-intensive and that the old notion of the service sector as being a low-skilled, labor-intensive operation needs to be reconsidered. Service workers will need more sophisticated skills to program, operate, and maintain the automated systems. More importantly, employee flexibility will be a valued attribute as the nature of work is changed by new technology. For example, consider the many changes in the office that have occurred with the introduction of personal computers and word processing capabilities.

Automation does give management more opportunity to monitor employee performance, as illustrated by the example of the maids at Sleep Inn motels, but this capability may result in increased worker stress. On the other hand, computers and electronic communication have provided many service workers with the freedom of working at home.

Managing the New Technology Adoption Process

Innovation is a destroyer of tradition and thus requires careful planning to ensure success. The productivity benefits of new technology will, by necessity, change the nature of work. Thus, any introduction of new technology should include employee familiarization to prepare workers for new tasks and to provide input in the technology interface design (e.g., will typing skill be required, or will employees just point and click?). For services, the impact of new technology may not be limited to the back office but could require a change in the role customers play in the service delivery process. Customer reaction to the new technology, determined through focus groups or interviews, could also provide input in the design to avoid future problems of its acceptance (e.g., consider the need for surveillance cameras at automated teller machines).

TABLE 12.2
CATEGORIES AND EXAMPLES OF AUTOMATION IN SERVICE INDUSTRIES

Wholesale and retail trade, 23.1%*

F Dry cleaner's conveyor	V Point-of-sale electronic terminal
F Newspaper dispenser	I Self-serve grocery checkout
V Automatic car wash	T Automated distribution warehouse
V Automatic window washers	T Automated security systems
V Optical supermarket	T Telemarketing

Utilities and government services, 17.9%*

F Automated one-person garbage trucks	I Airborne warning and control systems
V Mail-sorting machine	I Doppler radar
V Optical mail scanner	T Electric power–generating plants
N IRS Form 1040EZ reader	T Electronic computer-originated mail

Health care services, 7.6%*

F Electronic beepers	I Automated medication-delivery systems
F Pacemakers	I Electronic ambulance-dispatching systems
V CAT and MRI scanners	I Medical information systems
V Dental chair system	E Diagnostic expert systems
V Fetal monitors	

Restaurants and food services, 6.0%*

F Assembly-line and rotating-service cafeterias	V Automatic french fryer
F Vending machines	

Financial services, 4.9%*

F Pneumatic delivery systems	V MasterCard II—the electronic checkbook
V Automated trust portfolio analysis	E Stock trading
V Automated teller machines	T Electronic funds transfer systems
V IBM 3890 encoded-check processor machine	

Transportation services, 4.9%*

F Automatic tollbooth	I France's TGV trains
I Air traffic control systems	I Ship navigation systems
I Autopilots	T Space shuttle
I Bay Area Rapid Transportation system (California)	

Communication and electronic services, 2.2%*

V Collating copying machines	T Teleconference phone and Picturephone
V Two-way cable television	T Telephone switching systems
P Telephone answering machines	

TABLE 12.2
(Continued)

Education services, 1.6%*	
F Audiovisual machine	P Language translation computers
V Electronic calculators	P Personal and home computers
V Speak-and-Spell, Speak-and-Read	T Library cataloging systems

Hotel and motel services, 1.5%*	
F Automatic sprinkler systems	V Electronic key and lock systems
F Elevator, escalator, and conveyor	T Electronic reservation systems

Leisure services, 1.4%*	
F Movie projectors	I Arcade and computer games
F Wave machines	T Disney World (Hall of Presidents, e.g.)
P Videodisc machines	

*Percentage of total workforce. Employment and Earnings, U.S. Department of Labor, Bureau of Labor Statistics, December 1991, Table B-2, pp. 52–62.

Source: Adapted with permission from David A. Collier, "The Service Sector Revolution: The Automation of Services," *Long Range Planning,* vol. 16, no. 6, December 1983, pp. 12–13. Copyright © 1983 Pergamon Press Ltd.

Robert Radchuck, in writing about his experiences installing computer systems, has developed a ten-step planning guide to manage the implementation process. A modified version of these ten steps to include the concerns for employees and customers follows:[5]

Step 1: Orientation and education. Become knowledgeable about the new technology and where it is headed. Gain the active involvement of senior management.

Step 2: Technology opportunity analysis. Undertake a feasibility study to define opportunities, estimate costs, and identify benefits.

Step 3: Application requirements analysis. Define the requirements for the new technology, and identify the products to be purchased in terms of hardware and software. Refine cost and benefit estimates.

Step 4: Functional specification. Define the operating characteristics of the application, including the inputs, outputs, operator interface, and type of equipment to be used. This working document will be used in interactions with users of the system and thus should be an explicit definition in nontechnical terms of how the system will work.

Step 5: Design specification. Produce a specific engineering design with inputs from users, both service employees and customers, to evaluate the effectiveness of

[5]Adapted from Robert P. Radchuck, "Step-by-Step into High Tech.," *CA Magazine,* vol. 115, no. 6, June 1982, pp. 72–73.

the system interfaces. For example, as noted in Chapter 1, Burger King has made a mock-up of a typical store in a Miami warehouse, where new technology ideas are tested in a simulated environment before their introduction in the marketplace.

Step 6: Implementation planning. Using project planning techniques such as PERT/CPM, develop a detailed implementation plan. The plan should account for all activities, such as personnel familiarization and training, facilities planning, prototype testing, and an initial operation in parallel with the current system until the new technology is debugged.

Step 7: Equipment selection and contract commitments. Contract for equipment purchases, and schedule the equipment for delivery as per the implementation plan.

Step 8: Implementation. Execute the implementation plan, and prepare progress reports for senior management.

Step 9: Testing of technology. Before committing to full-blown operations, test the technology. If simulation is not possible, the new technology could be introduced at one or more trial sites before the entire service network is committed. Specific tests need to be defined in advance to evaluate the system's response to anticipated demands.

Step 10: Review of results. Document information that has been learned from the implementation experience by comparing original expectations with actual results. This final step may be the most important, because expertise in managing new technology implementation can be a competitive advantage.

MAKING CONTINUAL IMPROVEMENT A COMPETITIVE STRATEGY[6]

The history of economic development is based on learning from experience and applying this knowledge to improve productivity. For example, Henry Ford has been credited with discovering the revolutionary concept of the moving assembly line, on which material is moved past workstations in a factory. However, this idea could have originated from an agricultural analogy where equipment is moved through stationary fields for planting and harvesting. This analogy could also be extended to service firms where customers are moved to or through a process at a fixed facility. Thus, it is possible for a productivity improvement in one sector of the economy, with proper translation, to be useful in another.

For the past decade we have all been students of the Japanese manufacturing philosophy. First, we observed the use of the Kanban card and concluded that this novel method of shop floor control must be the secret of success. Further study revealed the emphasis on inventory reduction, and we coined the phrase *just in time* (JIT) to describe the process of production with zero inventories. Our understanding of JIT led to an appreciation of its effect on quality improvement. To our surprise, we discovered a method of organizing production that yields high-quality products at low cost. This realization shattered our long-held assumption that there has to

[6]From James A. Fitzsimmons, "Making Continual Improvement a Competitive Strategy for Service Firms," *Service Management Effectiveness,* Bowen, Chase, Cummings and Associates, Jossey-Bass Publishers, San Francisco, 1990, pp. 284–295.

be a tradeoff between quality and cost. The production function itself has now become a strategic competitive weapon. The success of Japanese penetration into foreign markets is witness to the effectiveness of this competitive strategy.

Identifying inventory as undesirable because it hides mistakes and decouples workers allows us to see its most serious fault. With inventory buffers, management and, more importantly, workers are not motivated to engage in problem solving. When inventory is reduced, problems can no longer be buried or sent to a rework area; instead, they must be faced immediately by the workers themselves. A manufacturing culture is established where everyone is responsible for process and quality improvement. Reliance on a staff of industrial and manufacturing engineers to provide ideas for process improvements is not necessary. Instead, the workers dealing with the process every day are asked to use their minds as well as their hands. The competitive implications of the experience curve are well known, and the leading Japanese manufacturing firms have institutionalized the concept in their organizations through the use of JIT.

The concept of making continual improvements in the production process is central to a firm's competitive strength and to a nation's productive growth. Approximately 70 percent of the GNP of the world's leading economic nations is generated by the service sector; thus, a productivity improvement ethic for services is imperative to assure future prosperity.

Inventory and Waiting Line Analogy

In *manufacturing* the focus of attention is on *material* resources. JIT views idle material resources or inventory as an "evil" to be eliminated or at least reduced. In *services* the focus of our attention is on *human* resources. The "evils" to be eliminated or reduced are customer waiting lines and idle staff. Thus, the analogy between inventory in manufacturing and waiting lines in services can be made.

As shown in Table 12.3, inventory and waiting lines share some common features. The cost of a customer waiting in line is an opportunity forgone, which is generally difficult to quantify. Unlike investment in inventory, which can be

TABLE 12.3
INVENTORY AND WAITING LINE ANALOGY

Feature	Inventory	Waiting line
Costs	Opportunity cost of capital	Opportunity cost of time
Space	Warehouse	Waiting area
Quality	Poor quality hidden	Negative impression
Decoupling	Promotes independence of production stages	Allows division of labor and specialization
Utilization	Work in process keeps machines busy	Waiting customers keep servers busy
Coordination	Detailed scheduling not necessary	Avoids matching supply and demand

quantified in financial terms, the cost of keeping customers waiting for service is subjective but can be very high. For example, a business executive kept waiting in his doctor's office sued the physician for his lost time and won the case. Thus, real costs can be associated with customer waiting, the most important being loss of future business. Storing inventory requires space and the associated investment in a protective facility. Waiting lines also create the need for otherwise unproductive space, which should, in addition, be attractively furnished. Banks have been known to devote one-half of their expensive real estate to drive-in banking facilities, with most of the area being used for a driveway.

Inventory is an excellent place to hide poor quality. The intangibility of service makes it difficult for customers to judge quality. Thus, they use surrogates such as the length of time they are kept waiting in line to evaluate service performance. As noted in Chapter 11, excessive waiting can be considered psychological punishment, and the significant negative impression of the service that it creates is difficult to overcome.

Waiting lines also perform some of the same functions in the management of services that inventory did for manufacturing before the advent of JIT. The decoupling function of inventory has been used for years to simplify the management of production operations. Work-in-process inventory allows management to divide the production process into independent departments or stages that can be managed in a decentralized fashion with supervisors and other work leaders having centralized production control. Waiting lines serve a similar decoupling function by permitting division of labor and specialization. For example, lines forming before a commercial teller at a bank cannot be served by idle retail tellers or, heaven forbid, by a loan officer. Thus, management is able to create different job classifications and pay according to skill requirements, with high-customer-contact tellers being paid entry-level wages. This division of labor has its price in the loss of flexibility to respond to customer demands.

In manufacturing, work-in-process inventory has traditionally been used to reduce or eliminate machine or operator idle time. Keeping an inventory of inputs before an operation would ensure high labor and equipment utilization. Waiting customers are used in a similar role to keep service personnel busy and pressured to work at a productive rate. The post office is notorious for employing this strategy as a cost-saving measure, but physicians also keep their waiting rooms full to avoid being idle themselves. In job shops the level of inventory is quite high, which reflects the complex nature of coordinating the operation. Detailed scheduling of the operation taken as a whole is impossible, and inventory is used to decentralize the scheduling and to allow individual machine centers to focus on selecting jobs from their queue. For service managers, waiting lines are used to store excess demand when it is impossible to adjust service capacity. Restaurants have traditionally used the bar as a holding area for customers who walk in without reservations.

The presence of excessive inventory in a factory or long waiting lines at a service is an indictment of poor management. This reliance on idle resources (queues of people or material) to create a smooth operation reveals a lazy management unwilling to assume the responsibility of continual process and quality improvement. Organizations without such a competitive operations strategy will be handicapped in the marketplace.

Continual Improvement as Part of the Service Organization Culture

How can continual improvement in productivity and quality be made a part of the service organization culture? What is needed is a clear and visible signal that problem solving is required. An excessively long waiting line of customers or idle servers is an obvious indication that the service is not currently being deployed in an effective manner. Depending on the circumstance, a variety of responses is possible.

• Ask back-office personnel to come forward and open additional service stations in parallel. For example, have platform personnel at a bank open additional teller windows.

• Ask back-office personnel to assist in performing the service. For example, have stockers assist checkout clerks in bagging groceries in a supermarket.

In response to periods of front-office idleness, customer contact personnel can help in the back office. For example, in the banking case, tellers can help in preparing customer account statements for mailing. For the supermarket example, checkout clerks can help stock shelves during lull periods. In general, the response is a redeployment of personnel to serve the customer better while maintaining high utilization of human resources.

What can be learned from these experiences to improve the service process in the future? If queues of customers develop at the same time each day, then the redeployment can be instituted before the lines form instead of in reaction to them. Other ideas could follow, such as instituting an express lane during these busy periods or having the manager preapprove checks to avoid delays. Ideas should flow naturally because service employees are themselves service customers and know instinctively what solutions should guarantee reasonable results. In the banking example, instead of opening express lanes, a better approach might be to staff special desks for the time-consuming services such as selling traveler's checks and CDs. A host or hostess, or even a sign, could direct arriving customers to the appropriate server. In this way the large number of short transactions is expedited, and the congestion can be eliminated quickly. Customers who have minor requests, and who are often in a hurry, will be served promptly. Customers with more demanding requirements are usually more willing to wait because the ratio of service time to wait time meets their expectations.

The above example illustrates the need for improved real-time communication among service personnel. In the JIT environment this was accomplished by the use of Kanban cards and other simple devices. We are convinced that service firm employees will be able to create innovative methods to alert their coworkers to changing levels of customer demands and thus to initiate the necessary redeployment of resources. The resulting interconnectedness will promote a team approach to customer service.

A major distinction between the traditional manufacturing organization and JIT is the source (direction) of production control. Traditionally, work was released to the first stage of the production process and was *pushed* through the plant from one station to the next. In the JIT system, production orders originate at the final assembly station, and work is *pulled* from upstream stages as needed. Thus, the entire production system becomes interconnected, and work is focused on meeting the needs of final demand. Each workstation is both a customer for upstream stations and a server for downstream stations. The result is a chain of workers acting as one team. For services, the process flow is seldom as well defined as that in manufacturing, and thus there is a greater need for an innovative communication linkage between servers. In services, upstream stations such as the receptionist are the first to experience customer demand, unlike the situation in our JIT manufacturing analogy, where work is pulled by the final assembly station from upstream stations. Thus, these stations are in a position to provide advance warning to downstream stations to prepare for arriving customers. Ideally, when a customer enters a service system, a "greeter" identifies the particular needs and uses an internal communication system (Kanban) to alert downstream service providers. Just as in the JIT manufacturing system, the customer "pulls" resources into play as needed.

Examples of this approach already exist. When a long line develops at Burger King or Wendy's, a service person walks up the line taking orders to speed the transaction time at the counter and possibly to deter customer reneging. At a motor vehicle license and registration office, a greeter is stationed just inside the entry door to provide customers with forms and directions to the appropriate service counter. The most comprehensive example of the service pull philosophy is found at The Limited retail clothing stores. Sales trends collected immediately by electronic cash registers are sent directly to the huge Columbus, Ohio, warehouse for distribution. At the same time, factory orders are placed worldwide on the basis of the demand that is being monitored in real time.

As seen from the examples above, the customer automatically becomes the focus of attention when the service employees redeploy their efforts to reduce the waiting lines. Thus, even if new ways to improve service are not immediately discovered, at least the customer is aware that special efforts are being made on her or his behalf.

Management Implications

Allowing service employees this extra latitude of discretion to react to customer waiting lines in creative ways has many implications for management. Table 12.4 compares the work environment and dimensions of organizational structure for the traditional and world-class service organizations.

We begin with the assumption that a service organization operates as an open system in its environment. This does not suggest that some back-room activities cannot be treated as a buffered core (i.e., isolated from direct customer contact). However, for the customer contact personnel, we premise their job design on the

TABLE 12.4
ORGANIZATIONAL STRUCTURE AND WORK ENVIRONMENT OF TRADITIONAL AND
WORLD-CLASS SERVICE ORGANIZATIONS

Dimension	Traditional	World-class
System assumption	Closed system	Open system
Job design premise	Division of labor	Flexibility
Structure	Rigid	Fluid
Relation to others	Individual	Team player
Employee orientation	Task	Customer
Management	Supervisor	Coach and facilitator
Technology	Replace human effort	Assist service delivery
Information	Efficiency	Effectiveness

need for flexibility. Adam Smith's concept of "division of labor," although appropriate for the closed systems found in manufacturing, can be counterproductive in an open service environment, where servers are in direct contact with customers. Flexibility for service jobs means cross-training, with the ability either to step in and perform another's task or to help facilitate the activities of another employee. Cross-training implies an increased organizational commitment to its personnel and thus a change in attitude about the desirability of high turnover and the use of minimum-wage labor. This should translate into improved employee relations because workers are treated with the same respect due customers.

The organizational structure must be fluid to permit the redeployment of all personnel to meet fluctuations in customer demand. Back-office personnel must, on occasion, share the task of serving customers directly. However, if the restrictive union work rules found in manufacturing were applied to services, they would prevent the realization of the competitive advantage of this operations strategy of fluidity. With this strategy, working as a team becomes the norm, and attention is focused on serving the customer instead of on just completing a task. The role of management changes from the traditional supervisor or checker to a coach and team builder.

Technology becomes more important as a method to assist in the delivery of the service rather than as a method to replace human contact. An exception to this approach is the promotion of self-service via devices such as automated tellers or airline ticket machines. For example, Southwest Airlines offers a free cocktail to customers who use their credit cards to purchase tickets at a self-service machine. This role of the customer as a participant in the service process to increase productivity is an important feature of services. Computerized information processing will play a central role in high-tech, high-touch service delivery systems. The creative use of information is central to the effective delivery of service by acting as the Kanban to permit the prepositioning of service delivery activities in a "pull" work-scheduling environment.

It is interesting to note the implications of a service "pull" philosophy based on ·corporate flexibility and real-time information processing, as well as the implications of the traditional mass-marketing "push" philosophy as practiced by most manufacturers, such as automobile firms. In a service "pull" environment the operations function becomes critical instead of being taken for granted, as in the "push" environment, where marketing is critical. With the exception of some group services such as lectures, sports events, or the theater, services are not batched but instead are performed on the individual. Thus, there is no setup involved as found in manufacturing, and consequently, the implementation of a service "pull" system can be accomplished with ease. Customer experience with service "pull" systems will provide the incentive for manufacturers to adopt a more service-oriented approach. Eventually, we should witness the transformation from a *push* economy to a *pull* economy.

AN APPLICATION OF DEMING'S PHILOSOPHY OF CONTINUAL IMPROVEMENT: THE CASE OF FLORIDA POWER AND LIGHT[7]

In 1985, John Hudiburg, CEO and chairman of the board of Florida Power and Light (FPL), announced a companywide effort to win the Deming Prize. The Deming Prize, a bronze medal, is named after W. Edwards Deming, a nonagenarian American statistician whose pioneering ideas about quality control were adopted eagerly by the Japanese when Deming fixed their fouled-up telephone service after World War II. In the spring of 1990, Florida Power and Light was the first non-Japanese company to win the prestigious prize created by the Japanese several decades ago in Deming's honor.

Foundations of the Quality-Improvement Program

The quality improvement program at FPL was based, as noted, on the teachings and philosophy of W. Edwards Deming. The foundations of the program consisted of four principles: customer satisfaction, management by facts, Deming's wheel, and respect for people.

Customer Satisfaction The entire program is focused on satisfying customers' needs. This requires an attitude of putting the customer first and a belief that this principle is the object of one's work.

Management by Facts This means that objective data must be collected and presented to management for decision making. This approach requires formal data gathering and statistical analysis of the data by the company's quality-improvement teams.

Deming's Wheel Deming's approach to quality emphasizes that checking or inspecting for quality is just one stage in the quality-improvement process.

[7]Adapted from Gary Dessler and D. L. Farrow, "Implementing a Successful Quality Improvement Programme in a Service Company: Winning the Deming Prize," *International Journal of Service Industry Management*, vol. 1, no. 2, 1990, pp. 45–53.

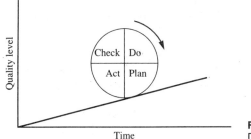

FIGURE 12.2
Deming's quality-improvement wheel.

Deming's approach consists of four steps: *plan* what to do; *do,* or carry out, the plan; *check* what was done; and *act* to prevent error or improve the process. As shown in Figure 12.2, the Deming wheel is a repetitive cycle that consists of the four steps: plan, do, check, act (PDCA). Implicit in the Deming PDCA approach is that quality improvements result from continuous incremental turns of the wheel.

Respect for People A companywide quality-improvement program assumes that all employees have a capacity for self-motivation and for creative thought. Employees are given support, and their ideas are solicited in an environment of mutual self-respect.

Phases of the Quality-Improvement Program

The quality-improvement program was implemented at FPL in three phases: (1) policy deployment, (2) development of quality-improvement teams, and (3) instituting a quality-in-daily-work program for individual employees.

Policy Deployment The policy deployment process was initiated by top management to concentrate the company's resources on a few priority issues. The motivation was a recognition that changes were occurring in the marketplace that could eventually undermine the company's performance. Objectives that emerged from the customer-needs assessment included (1) reduce the number of complaints to the Florida Public Service Commission, and (2) strengthen fossil unit reliability. These objectives were translated into more measurable terms and distributed to all employees for direction in their quality-improvement efforts.

Quality-Improvement Teams Key team members underwent extensive training in statistical quality-control techniques, PDCA cycle philosophy, and group decision-making techniques. The concept of the "customer-next process" was introduced to help focus the work group on who their customers were, either inside or outside the company.

The teams were taught to present their quality-improvement suggestions in a seven-step "story": (1) reason for improvement; (2) current situation, including data collected; (3) analysis using fishbone charts and Pareto diagrams; (4)

countermeasures, including analyses of barriers and aids; (5) results of meeting the target; (6) standardization of countermeasures for replication in other departments; and (7) future plans.

Quality in Daily Work   In the final phase of the quality-improvement program, the quality-improvement team approach was extended to individual workers. Individuals were thus encouraged to take a quality-improvement approach to their work. For example, using this approach, meter readers were able to reduce reading errors by 50 percent.

SUMMARY

Productivity and quality improvement are an important part of an organization's development and determine the level of a firm's competitiveness. Technological innovation plays an important part in advancing a firm in its stages of competitiveness. However, introducing new technology in services is a challenge because both employees and customers are often affected personally by the need to adapt to new ways of doing things. Automation of services has followed the lead of manufacturing in replacing manual tasks with machines but has also gone further in the application of computers to assist in problem-solving and decision-making tasks.

Making continual improvement a competitive strategy was explored by considering an analogy between JIT in manufacturing and reduction of queues in services. Finally, an application of Deming's philosophy of continual improvement was illustrated by the Florida Power and Light experience.

In Chapter 13 we will consider another challenge that services face in the global market: growth and expansion.

TOPICS FOR DISCUSSION

1. As services are automated, what types of new demands are placed on the marketing function? Give an example to illustrate your answer.
2. What emerging technologies will have a significant effect on the delivery of services in the future?
3. What are the dangers of using manufacturing analogies for application in the management of service firms?

CASE: MEGA BYTES RESTAURANT[8]

Mega Bytes is a restaurant that caters to business travelers and has a self-service breakfast buffet. In order to measure customer satisfaction, the manager constructs a survey and distributes it to diners during a three-month period. The results,

[8]Reprinted and selectively adapted with permission from M. Gaudard, R. Coates, and L. Freeman, "Accelerating Improvement," *Quality Progress,* vol. 24, no. 10, October 1991, pp. 81–88.

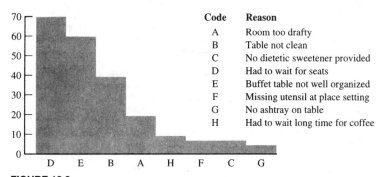

FIGURE 12.3
Pareto chart of complaints. [*Reprinted with permission from M. Gaudard, R. Coates, and L. Freeman, "Accelerating Improvement,"* Quality Progress, *vol. 24, no. 10, October 1991, p. 83.*]

summarized in the Figure 12.3 Pareto chart, indicate that the restaurant's major problem is that customers must wait too long to be seated.

A team of employees is formed to work on resolving the problem. The team members decide to use the Seven Step Method (SSM), a structured approach to problem solving and process improvement originally developed by Joiner Associates, Inc., of Madison, Wisconsin. The SSM leads a team through a logical sequence of steps that force a thorough analysis of the problem, its potential causes, and possible solutions. The structure imposed by the Seven Step Method helps the team to focus on the correct issues and to avoid diffusing its energy on tangential or counterproductive efforts. The Seven Step Method is directed at analytic studies rather than at enumerative studies. In general, analytic studies are interested in cause and effect and in making predictions, where enumerative studies are focused on an existing population.

The steps in this method are shown in Table 12.5 and applied here to the case of Mega Bytes:

Step 1: Define the project. The results of the survey taken of Mega Bytes customers indicate that customers must wait too long to be seated. Most of the customers are business travelers who want to be served promptly or they want an opportunity to discuss business during their meal. The team considers several questions such as "When does the wait start? When does it end? How is it measured?" and then arrives at an operational definition of the problem it must solve as "waiting to be seated."

Step 2: Study the current situation. The team collects baseline data and plots them as shown in Figure 12.4. At the same time, a flowchart for seating a party is developed. The team also diagrams the floor plan of Mega Bytes as shown in Figure 12.5.

The baseline data indicate that the percentage of people who must wait is higher early in the week than it is late in the week. This finding is expected because most Mega Bytes customers are business travelers. The size of the party does not appear

TABLE 12.5
THE SEVEN STEP METHOD

Step 1 Define the project.
1. Define the problem in terms of a gap between what is and what should be. (For example, "Customers report an excessive number of errors. The team's objective is to reduce the number of errors.")
2. Document why it is important to be working on this particular problem:
   - Explain how you know it is a problem, providing any data you might have that supports this.
   - List the customer's key quality characteristics. State how closing the gap will benefit the customer in terms of these characteristics.
3. Determine what data you will use to measure progress:
   - Decide what data you will use to provide a baseline against which improvement can be measured.
   - Develop any operational definitions you will need to collect the data.

Step 2 Study the current situation.
1. Collect the baseline data and plot them. (Sometimes historical data can be used for this purpose.) A run chart or control chart is usually used to exhibit baseline data. Decide how you will exhibit these data on the run chart. Decide how you will label your axes.
2. Develop flowcharts of the processes.
3. Provide any helpful sketches or visual aids.
4. Identify any variables that might have a bearing on the problem. Consider the variables of what, where, to what extent, and who. Data will be gathered on these variables to localize the problem.
5. Design data collection instruments.
6. Collect the data and summarize what you have learned about the variables' effects on the problem.
7. Determine what additional information would be helpful at this time. Repeat substeps 2 through 7 until there is no additional information that would be helpful at this time.

Step 3 Analyze the potential causes.
1. Determine potential causes of the current conditions:
   - Use the data collected in step 2 and the experience of the people who work in the process to identify conditions that might lead to the problem.
   - Construct cause-and-effect diagrams for these conditions of interest.
   - Decide on most likely causes by checking against the data from step 2 and the experience of the people working in the process.

2. Determine whether more data are needed. If so, repeat substeps 2 through 7 of step 2.
3. If possible, verify the causes through observation or by directly controlling variables.

Step 4 Implement a solution.
1. Develop a list of solutions to be considered. Be creative.
2. Decide which solutions should be tried:
   - Carefully assess the feasibility of each solution, the likelihood of success, and potential adverse consequences.
   - Clearly indicate why you are choosing a particular solution.
3. Determine how the preferred solution will be implemented. Will there be a pilot project? Who will be responsible for the implementation? Who will train those involved?
4. Implement the preferred solution.

Step 5 Check the results.
1. Determine whether the actions in step 4 were effective:
   - Collect more data on the baseline measure from step 1.
   - Collect any other data related to the conditions at the start that might be relevant.
   - Analyze the results. Determine whether the solution tested was effective. Repeat prior steps as necessary.
2. Describe any deviations from the plan and what was learned.

Step 6 Standardize the improvement.
1. Institutionalize the improvement:
   - Develop a strategy for institutionalizing the improvement and assign responsibilities.
   - Implement the strategy and check to see that it has been successful.
2. Determine whether the improvement should be applied elsewhere and plan for its implementation.

Step 7 Establish future plans.
1. Determine your plans for the future:
   - Decide whether the gap should be narrowed further and, if so, how another project should be approached and who should be involved.
   - Identify related problems that should be addressed.
2. Summarize what you learned about the project team experience and make recommendations for future project teams.

Source: Reprinted with permission from M. Gaudard, R. Coates, and L. Freeman, "Accelerating Improvement," *Quality Progress,* vol. 24, no. 10, October 1991, p. 82.

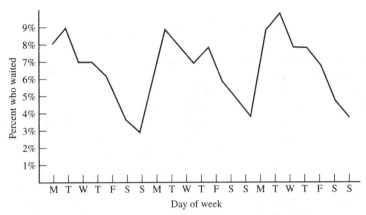

FIGURE 12.4
Run chart of percent of customers waiting more than one minute to be seated.
[*Reprinted with permission from M. Gaudard, R. Coates, and L. Freeman,
"Accelerating Improvement,"* Quality Progress, *vol. 24, no. 10, October 1991,
p. 83.*]

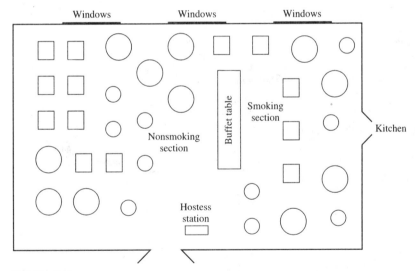

FIGURE 12.5
Restaurant floor plan. [*Reprinted with permission from M. Gaudard, R. Coates, and L.
Freeman, "Accelerating Improvement,"* Quality Progress, *vol. 24, no. 10, October 1991,
p. 83.*]

to be a factor. No surprises are shown in a histogram of the number of people
waiting in excess of one minute plotted against the time of the morning: more
people wait during the busy hours than wait during the slow hours.

The reason for the waiting is interesting, however. Most people are kept waiting
either because no table is available or because no table in the area of their

preference is available. Customers seldom have to wait because a host or hostess is not available to seat them or because others in their party have not yet arrived. At this point it would be easy to jump to the conclusion that the problem could be solved just by adding more staff early in the week and during busy hours.

But the team members decide they need additional information on why the tables are not available and on how seating preferences affect waiting time. Subsequent data indicate that "unavailable" tables are usually unavailable because they need to be cleared, not because they are occupied by diners. The data also show that most people who wait are those who have a preference for the nonsmoking section.

Step 3: Analyze the potential causes. A cause-and-effect diagram is constructed for "why tables are not cleared quickly" as shown in Figure 12.6. The team concludes that the most likely cause of both problems (uncleared tables and waits for nonsmoking tables) may be attributed to the distance between the tables and the kitchen and, perhaps, the current ratio of smoking-to-nonsmoking tables.

Step 4: Implement a solution. The team develops a list of possible solutions. Because the team cannot verify its conclusion by controlling variables, it chooses a solution that can be tested easily: set up temporary work stations in the nonsmoking area. No other changes are made, and data on the percentage of people now waiting longer than one minute to be seated are collected.

FIGURE 12.6
Cause-and-effect diagram describing why tables are not cleared quickly. [*Reprinted with permission from M. Gaudard, R. Coates, and L. Freeman, "Accelerating Improvement,"* Quality Progress, *vol. 24, no. 10, October 1991, p. 84.*]

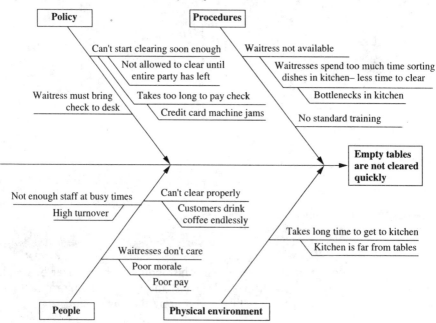

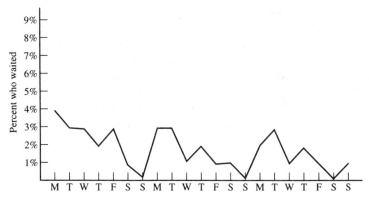

FIGURE 12.7
Run chart of percent of customers waiting more than one minute to be seated after implementation of solution. [*Reprinted with permission from M. Gaudard, R. Coates, and L. Freeman, "Accelerating Improvement,"* Quality Progress, *vol. 24, no. 10, October 1991, p. 85.*]

Step 5: Check the results. The team analyzes the results of the data collected for one month in step 4 of the study. As shown in Figure 12.7, the improvement is dramatic.

Step 6: Standardize the improvement. The temporary work stations are replaced with permanent ones.

Step 7: Establish future plans. The team decides to address the next highest bar in the Pareto chart of customer complaints; that is, the buffet table is not well organized.

The authors of the article on which our Mega Bytes case is based report that managers who used the SSM in various situations found the method's focus and restraint to be valuable because it provided organization, logic, and thoroughness. The managers were also impressed with the method's use of data instead of opinions and credited this factor with reducing territorial squabbles and promoting cooperation and trust among team members.

The Seven Step Method, while very valuable, does entail some difficulties. For instance, project teams have found that several concepts in the first two steps were very difficult to formulate. In particular, a team may have trouble developing a problem statement because the tendency is to frame a solution as a problem. In the case of Mega Bytes, the team had to avoid identifying the problem as "There are too few servers," "There aren't enough tables," or "The servers need to work faster." The real problem, however, was identified correctly as "The customers must wait too long."

Another concept that has been difficult for study teams is localization, a process of focusing on smaller and smaller vital pieces of the problem. This concept proved difficult initially because team members had not yet internalized the idea that improvement should be driven by customer requirements.

Some study teams experienced an assortment of other difficulties. Occasionally, team members could not see the benefit of collecting data accurately or they did not understand how baseline data would be used to validate a solution. Some members had trouble keeping an open mind and consequently resisted investigating the effects of variables that they felt were irrelevant. In some cases members had to learn new skills, such as how to obtain information in a nonthreatening way from workers in the system. And, finally, organizational problems, such as arranging meeting times and getting support from coworkers, had to be resolved.

Questions

1. How is the Seven Step Method different from Deming's plan-do-check-act (PDCA) cycle?

2. Prepare a cause-and-effect or fishbone diagram for a problem such as "why customers have long waits for coffee." Your fishbone diagram should be similar to Figure 12.6, using the main sources of cause: policy, procedure, people, and physical environment.

3. How would you resolve the difficulties that study teams have experienced when applying the Seven Step Method?

SELECTED BIBLIOGRAPHY

Baker, Edward M., and H. L. Artinian: "The Deming Philosophy of Continuing Improvement in a Service Organization: The Case of Windsor Export Supply," *Quality Progress,* vol. 18, no. 6, June 1985, pp. 61–69.

Banker, Rajiv D., and R. C. Morey: "Efficiency Analysis for Exogenously Fixed Inputs and Outputs," *Operations Research,* vol. 34, no. 4, July–August 1986, pp. 513–521.

———, A. Charnes, and W. W. Cooper: "Some Models for Estimating Technical and Scale Inefficiencies in Data Envelopment Analysis," *Management Science,* vol. 30, no. 9, September 1984, pp. 1078–1092.

———, ———, ———, J. Swarts, and D. A. Thomas: "An Introduction to Data Envelopment Analysis with Some of Its Models and Their Use," *Research in Government and Nonprofit Accounting,* vol. 5, 1989, pp. 125–163.

———, R. B Conrad, and R. P. Strauss: "A Comparative Application of Data Envelopment Analysis and Translog Methods: An Illustration Study of Hospital Production," *Management Science,* vol. 32, no. 1, January 1986, pp. 30–44.

Berg, Sanford V.: "Determinants of Technological Change in the Service Industries," *Technological Forecasting and Social Change,* vol. 5, no. 3, 1973, pp. 407–421.

Berry, L. L., V. A. Zeithaml, and A. Parasuraman: "Five Imperatives for Improving Service Quality," *Sloan Management Review,* vol. 31, no. 4, summer 1990, pp. 29–38.

Blois, Keith J.: "Productivity and Effectiveness in Service Firms," *The Service Industries Journal,* vol. 4, no. 3, 1984, pp. 47–60.

Charnes, A., W. W. Cooper, and E. Rhodes: "Evaluating Program and Managerial Efficiency: An Application of Data Envelopment Analysis to Program Follow Through," *Management Science,* vol. 27, no. 6, June 1981, pp. 668–697.

———, ———, and ———: "Measuring the Efficiency of Decision Making Units," *European Journal of Operations Research,* vol. 2, no. 6, November 1978, pp. 429–444.

Collier, David A.: "The Management of New Technology," *Service Management: The Automation of Services,* Reston Publishing Company, Reston, Va., 1985.

————: "The Service Sector Revolution: The Automation of Services," *Long Range Planning,* vol. 16, no. 6, December 1983, pp. 10–20.

Dessler, Gary, and D. L. Farrow: "Implementing a Successful Quality Improvement Programme in a Service Company: Winning the Deming Prize," *International Journal of Service Industry Management,* vol. 1, no. 2, 1990, pp. 45–53.

Fitzsimmons, James A.: "Making Continual Improvement a Competitive Strategy for Service Firms," *Service Management Effectiveness,* Bowen, Chase, Cummings and Associates, Jossey-Bass Publishers, San Francisco, 1990, pp. 284–295.

Fletcher, J., and H. Snee: "The Need for Output Measurements in the Service Industries," *The Service Industries Journal,* vol. 5, no. 1, 1985, pp. 73–78.

Lewin, Arie Y., R. C. Morey, and T. J. Cook: "Evaluating the Administrative Efficiency of Courts," *OMEGA,* vol. 10, no. 4, 1982, pp. 401–411.

McLaughlin, Curtis P., and Sydney Coffy: "Measuring Productivity in Services," *International Journal of Service Industry Management,* vol. 1, no. 1, 1990, pp. 46–64.

Mehra, S., and R. A. Inman: "JIT Implementation within a Service Industry: A Case Study," *International Journal of Service Industry Management,* vol. 1, no. 3, 1990, pp. 53–61.

Mills, P. K., and D. J. Moberg: "Perspectives on the Technology of Service Operations," *Academy of Management Review,* vol. 7, no. 3, 1982, pp. 467–478.

Quinn, James Brian, J. J. Baruch, and P. C. Paquette: "Technology in Services," *Scientific American,* vol. 257, no. 6, December 1987, pp. 50–58.

Roach, Stephen S.: "Services under Siege—The Restructuring Imperative," *Harvard Business Review,* September–October 1991, pp. 82–91.

Seiford, Lawrence M.: "A Bibliography of Data Envelopment Analysis (1978–1990)," Dept. of IE and OR, University of Massachusetts, Amherst, MA 01003, April 1990, 24 pp.

Sherman, David H.: "Improving the Productivity of Service Business," *Sloan Management Review,* vol. 25, no. 3, spring 1984, pp. 11–23.

Talukdar, R., and C. P. McLaughlin: "Monitoring and Improving the Productivity of Semi-autonomous Human Service Units," *Journal of Operations Management,* vol. 5, no. 4, 1985, pp. 375–393.

CHAPTER 12 SUPPLEMENT: Data Envelopment Analysis (DEA)

How can corporate management evaluate the productivity of a fast-food outlet, a branch bank, a health clinic, or an elementary school? The difficulties in measuring productivity are three-fold. First, what are the appropriate inputs to the system and the measures of those inputs? Second, what are the appropriate outputs of the system and the measures of the outputs? Third, what are the appropriate ways of measuring the relationship between inputs and outputs?

MEASURING SERVICE PRODUCTIVITY

The measure of the productivity of an organization, if viewed from an engineering perspective, is similar to a measure of a system's efficiency and could be stated as a ratio of outputs to inputs (e.g., miles per gallon for an automobile).

For example, to evaluate the operational efficiency of a branch bank, an accounting ratio such as cost per teller transaction might be used. A branch with a high ratio in comparison with the ratios of other branches would be considered less efficient. But the higher ratio could be due to a more complex mix of transactions. For example, a branch opening new accounts and selling CDs would require more time per transaction than another branch engaged only in simple transactions such as accepting deposits and cashing checks. The problem with using simple ratios is that the mix of outputs is not considered explicitly. This same criticism can be made concerning the mix of inputs. For example, some branches may have ATM machines in addition to live tellers, and this use of technology could affect the cost per teller transaction.

Broad-based measures such as profitability or return on investment are highly relevant as overall performance measures, but they are not sufficient to evaluate the operating efficiency of a service unit. For instance, one could not conclude that a profitable branch bank is necessarily efficient in its use of personnel and other inputs. A higher-than-average proportion of revenue-generating transactions could be the explanation, rather than cost-efficient use of resources.

THE DEA MODEL

Fortunately, a technique has been developed that has the ability to compare the efficiency of multiple service units providing similar services by explicitly considering their use of multiple inputs (resources) to produce multiple outputs (services). The technique, referred to as *Data Envelopment Analysis* (DEA), circumvents the need to develop standard costs for each service that is provided because it can incorporate multiple inputs and multiple outputs into both the numerator and the denominator of the efficiency ratio without the need to convert them to a common dollar basis. Thus, the DEA measure of efficiency explicitly accounts for the mix of inputs and outputs and consequently is more comprehensive and reliable than a set of operating ratios or profit measures.[9]

DEA is a linear programming model that attempts to maximize a service unit's efficiency, expressed as a ratio of outputs to inputs, by comparing a particular unit's efficiency with the performance of a group of similar service units delivering the same service. In the process some units achieve 100 percent efficiency and are referred to as the "relatively efficient units," while other units with efficiency ratings of less than 100 percent are considered inefficient units.

Corporate management can thus use DEA to compare a group of service units in order to identify relatively inefficient units, to measure the magnitude of the inefficiencies, and, by comparing the inefficient units with the efficient ones, to discover ways to reduce the inefficiencies.

The DEA linear programming model is formulated as follows.

Definition of Variables

Let E_k, with $k = 1, 2, \ldots, K$, be the efficiency ratio of unit k, where K is the total number of units being evaluated.

Let u_j, with $j = 1, 2, \ldots, M$, be a coefficient for output j, where M is the total number of output types considered.

[9]A. Charnes, W. W. Cooper, and E. Rhodes, "Measuring the Efficiency of Decision Making Units," *European Journal of Operations Research*, November 1978, pp. 429–444.

Let v_i, with $i = 1, 2, \ldots, N$, be a coefficient for input i, where N is the total number of input types considered.

Let O_{jk} be the number of observed units of output j generated by service unit k during one time period.

Let I_{ik} be the number of actual units of input i used by service unit k during one time period.

Objective Function

The objective is to find the set of coefficient u's associated with each output and v's associated with each input that will give the service unit being evaluated the highest possible efficiency.

$$\text{max } E_e = \frac{u_1 O_{1e} + u_2 O_{2e} + \cdots + u_M O_{Me}}{v_1 I_{1e} + v_2 I_{2e} + \cdots + v_N I_{Ne}} \tag{1}$$

where e is the index of the unit being evaluated.

This function is subject to the constraint that when the same set of input and output coefficients (u_j's and v_i's) is applied to all other service units being compared, no service unit will exceed 100 percent efficiency.

Constraints

$$\frac{u_1 O_{1k} + u_2 O_{2k} + \cdots + u_M O_{Mk}}{v_1 I_{1k} + v_2 I_{2k} + \cdots + v_N I_{Nk}} \leq 100\% \qquad k = 1, 2, \ldots, K \tag{2}$$

where all coefficient values are positive and nonzero.

To solve this fractional linear programming model using standard linear programming software requires a reformulation. Note that both the objective function and all the constraints are ratios rather than linear functions. The objective function in equation (1) is restated as a linear function by arbitrarily scaling the inputs for the unit under evaluation to a sum of 1.0.

$$\text{max } E_e = u_1 O_{1e} + u_2 O_{2e} + \cdots + u_M O_{Me} \tag{3}$$

subject to the constraint that

$$v_1 I_{1e} + v_2 I_{2e} + \cdots + v_N I_{Ne} = 1 \tag{4}$$

For each service unit, the constraints in equation (2) are similarly reformulated, as shown below:

$$u_1 O_{1k} + u_2 O_{2k} + \cdots + u_M O_{Mk} - 100(v_1 I_{1k} + v_2 I_{2k} + \cdots + v_N I_{Nk}) \leq 0 \qquad k = 1, 2, \ldots, K \tag{5}$$

where $u_j \geq 0 \qquad j = 1, 2, \ldots, M$
$ v_i \geq 0 \qquad i = 1, 2, \ldots, N$

A question of sample size is often raised concerning the number of service units required, compared with the number of input and output variables selected in the analysis. The following relationship relating the number of service units K used in the analysis and the number of input N and output M types considered is based on empirical findings and the experience of DEA practitioners:

$$K \geq 2 (N + M) \tag{6}$$

Example 12.1: Burger Palace

An innovative drive-in-only burger chain has established six units in several different cities. Each unit is located in a strip shopping center parking lot. Only a standard meal consisting of a burger, fries, and a drink is available. Management has decided to use DEA as an approach to improving productivity by identifying the units that are using their resources most efficiently and then sharing their experience and knowledge with less efficient units. Table 12.6 contains a summary of data for two inputs, labor-hours and material dollars consumed during a typical lunch-hour period to generate an output of 100 meals sold. Normally, the output will vary among the service units, but in this example we have made the outputs equal to allow for a graphical presentation of the units' productivity. As shown in Figure 12.8, service units S_1, S_3, and S_6 have been joined to form an efficient-production frontier of alternative methods of using labor-hours and material resources to generate 100 meals. As can be seen, these efficient units have defined an envelope that contains all the inefficient units—thus the reason for calling the process *data envelopment analysis*.

For this simple example, we can identify efficient units by inspection and see the excess inputs used by inefficient units (e.g., S_2 would be as efficient as S_3 if it used $50 less in materials). However, to gain an understanding of DEA, we will proceed to formulate the linear programming (LP) problems for each unit and solve each of them to determine efficiency ratings and other information.

We begin by illustrating the LP formulation for the first service unit, S_1, using equations (3), (4), and (5) above.

$$
\begin{aligned}
\max \; E(S_1) = {} & 100u_1 \\
\text{subject to } 100u_1 - {} & 200v_1 - 20000v_2 \leq 0 \\
100u_1 - {} & 400v_1 - 15000v_2 \leq 0 \\
100u_1 - {} & 400v_1 - 10000v_2 \leq 0 \\
100u_1 - {} & 600v_1 - 10000v_2 \leq 0 \\
100u_1 - {} & 800v_1 - 8000v_2 \leq 0 \\
100u_1 - {} & 1000v_1 - 5000v_2 \leq 0 \\
& 2v_1 + 200v_2 = 1 \\
& u_1, v_1, v_2 \geq 0
\end{aligned}
$$

TABLE 12.6
SUMMARY OF OUTPUTS AND INPUTS FOR BURGER PALACE

Service unit	Meals sold	Labor-hours	Material dollars
1	100	2	200
2	100	4	150
3	100	4	100
4	100	6	100
5	100	8	80
6	100	10	50

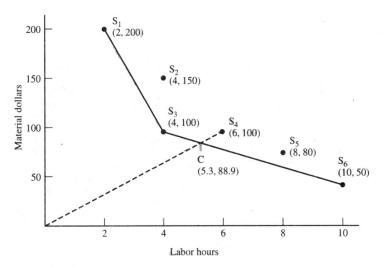

FIGURE 12.8
Productivity frontier for Burger Palace.

Similar linear programming problems are formulated (or better, the S_1 LP problem above is edited) and solved for each of the other service units by substituting the appropriate output function for the objective function and by substituting the appropriate input function for the last constraint. Constraints 1 through 6, which restrict all units to no more than 100 percent efficiency, remain the same in all problems.

This set of six LP problems was solved with the *QS: Quantitative Systems, Version 3.0* personal computer software in less than 5 minutes by editing the input data file between each run.[10] The LP results for each of the six units are shown in Table 12.7 and summarized in Table 12.8.

In Table 12.8 we find that DEA has identified the same units shown in Figure 12.8 as being efficient. Units S_2, S_4, and S_5 are all inefficient in varying degrees. Also shown in Table 12.8, associated with each inefficient unit, is an *efficiency reference set*. Each inefficient unit will have a set of efficient units associated with it that defines its productivity. As shown in Figure 12.8 for inefficient unit S_4, the efficient units S_3 and S_6 have been joined with a line defining the efficiency frontier. A dashed line drawn from the origin to inefficient unit S_4 cuts through this frontier and thus defines unit S_4 as inefficient. In Table 12.8 the value in parentheses associated with each member of the efficiency reference set (.7778 for S_3 and .2222 for S_6) represents the relative weight assigned to that efficient unit in the calculation of the efficiency rating for S_4. These relative weights are the shadow prices associated with the respective efficient-unit constraints in the LP solution (note in Table 12.7 that for unit 4, these weights appear as opportunity costs for S_3 and S_6).

The values for v_1 and v_2 associated with the inputs of labor-hours and materials, respectively, measure the relative increase in efficiency with each unit reduction of input value. For unit S_4, each unit decrease in labor-hours results in an efficiency increase of

[10]Yih-Long Chang and R. S. Sullivan, *QS: Quantitative Systems, Version 3.0*, Prentice-Hall, Englewood Cliffs, N.J., 1993.

TABLE 12.7
LP SOLUTIONS FOR DEA STUDY OF BURGER PALACE

Summarized results for unit 1							Page : 1
Variables		Solutions	Opportunity costs	Variables		Solutions	Opportunity costs
No.	Names			No.	Names		
1	U1	+1.0000000	0	6	S3	0	0
2	V1	+.16666667	0	7	S4	+33.333336	0
3	V2	+.00333333	0	8	S5	+60.000000	0
4	S1	0	+1.0000000	9	S6	+83.333336	0
5	S2	+16.666670	0	10	A7	0	+100.00000

Maximized objective function = 100   Iterations = 4

Summarized results for unit 2							Page : 1
Variables		Solutions	Opportunity costs	Variables		Solutions	Opportunity costs
No.	Names			No.	Names		
1	U1	+.85714287	0	6	S3	0	+.71428573
2	V1	+.14285715	0	7	S4	+28.571430	0
3	V2	+.00285714	0	8	S5	+51.428574	0
4	S1	0	+.28571430	9	S6	+71.428574	0
5	S2	+14.285717	0	10	A7	0	+85.714287

Maximized objective function = 85.71429   Iterations = 4

Summarized results for unit 3							Page : 1
Variables		Solutions	Opportunity costs	Variables		Solutions	Opportunity costs
No.	Names			No.	Names		
1	U1	+1.0000000	0	6	S3	0	+1.0000000
2	V1	+.06250000	0	7	S4	+12.500000	0
3	V2	+.00750000	0	8	S5	+10.000001	0
4	S1	+62.500000	0	9	S6	0	0
5	S2	+37.500008	0	10	A7	0	+100.00000

Maximized objective function = 100   Iterations = 3

5.55 percent. For unit S_4 to become efficient, it must increase its efficiency rating by 11.1 percentage points. This could be accomplished by reducing labor used by 2 hours (2 hours × 5.55% = 11.1%). Notice that with this reduction in labor-hours, unit S_4 becomes identical to efficient unit S_3. An alternative approach would be a reduction in materials used by $16.67 (i.e., 11.1/0.67 = 16.67). Any linear combination of these two measures would also move unit S_4 to the productivity frontier defined by the line segment joining efficient units S_3 and S_6.

Table 12.9 contains the calculations for a hypothetical unit C that is a composite reference unit defined by the weighted inputs of the reference set S_3 and S_6. As shown

TABLE 12.7
LP SOLUTIONS FOR DEA STUDY OF BURGER PALACE (*Continued*)

Summarized results for unit 4							Page : 1
Variables			Opportunity	Variables			Opportunity
No.	Names	Solutions	costs	No.	Names	Solutions	costs
1	U1	+.88888890	0	6	S3	0	+.77777779
2	V1	+.05555556	0	7	S4	+11.111112	0
3	V2	+.00666667	0	8	S5	+8.8888893	0
4	S1	+55.555553	0	9	S6	0	+.22222224
5	S2	+33.333340	0	10	A7	0	+88.888885

Maximized objective function = 88.88889   Iterations = 3

Summarized results for unit 5							Page : 1
Variables			Opportunity	Variables			Opportunity
No.	Names	Solutions	costs	No.	Names	Solutions	costs
1	U1	+.90909088	0	6	S3	0	+.45454547
2	V1	+.05681818	0	7	S4	+11.363637	0
3	V2	+.00681818	0	8	S5	+9.0909100	0
4	S1	+56.818180	0	9	S6	0	+.54545450
5	S2	+34.090916	0	10	A7	0	+90.909088

Maximized objective function = 90.90909   Iterations = 4

Summarized results for unit 6							Page : 1
Variables			Opportunity	Variables			Opportunity
No.	Names	Solutions	costs	No.	Names	Solutions	costs
1	U1	+1.0000000	0	6	S3	0	0
2	V1	+.06250000	0	7	S4	+12.500000	0
3	V2	+.00750000	0	8	S5	+10.000001	0
4	S1	+62.500000	0	9	S6	0	+1.0000000
5	S2	+37.500008	0	10	A7	0	+100.00000

Maximized objective function = 100   Iterations = 4

in Figure 12.8, this composite unit C is located at the intersection of the productivity frontier and the dashed line drawn from the origin to unit S_4. Thus, in comparison with this reference unit C, inefficient unit S_4 is using excess inputs in the amounts of 0.7 labor-hours and 11.1 material dollars.

We can see that DEA offers a multitude of opportunities for an inefficient unit to become efficient with respect to its reference set of efficient units. In practice, management would choose a particular approach on the basis of an evaluation of its cost, practicality, and feasibility. However, the motivation for change is clear; i.e., other units are *actually* able to achieve similar outputs with fewer resources.

TABLE 12.8
SUMMARY OF DEA RESULTS

Service unit	Efficiency rating (E)	Efficiency reference set	Relative labor-hour value (v_1)	Relative material value (v_2)
S_1	100.0	N.A.	.1667	.0033
S_2	85.7	S_1 (.2857)	.1428	.0028
		S_3 (.7143)		
S_3	100.0	N.A.	.0625	.0075
S_4	88.9	S_3 (.7778)	.0555	.0067
		S_6 (.2222)		
S_5	90.1	S_3 (.4545)	.0568	.0068
		S_6 (.5454)		
S_6	100.0	N.A.	.0625	.0075

TABLE 12.9
CALCULATION OF EXCESS INPUTS USED BY UNIT S4

Outputs and inputs	Reference set					Composite reference unit C	S4	Excess inputs used
	S_3			S_6				
Meals	(.7778)	×	100	+ (.2222)	×	100	=	100	100	0
Labor-hours	(.7778)	×	4	+ (.2222)	×	10	=	5.3	6	0.7
Material $	(.7778)	×	100	+ (.2222)	×	50	=	88.9	100	11.1

EXERCISES

12.1. For the Burger Palace example, perform a complete analysis of efficiency improvement alternatives for unit S_2, including the determination of a composite reference unit.

12.2. For the Burger Palace example, perform a complete analysis of efficiency improvement alternatives for unit S_5, including the determination of a composite reference unit.

12.3. For the Burger Palace example, what is the effect of removing an *inefficient* unit from the analysis (e.g., S_2)?

12.4. For the Burger Palace example, what is the effect of removing an *efficient* unit from the analysis (e.g., S_6)?

CASE: MID-ATLANTIC BUS LINES

Mid-Atlantic Bus Lines (MABL) was founded by a group of managers from Trailways when that company was acquired by Greyhound. They launched a first-class express bus service serving the major coastal cities from Philadelphia, Pennsylvania, to Jacksonville, Florida. By hiring laid-off Trailways drivers and leasing buses, they were able to establish franchises in each city with local entrepreneurs, who were given the right to operate a

TABLE 12.10
OUTPUTS AND INPUTS FOR MID-ATLANTIC BUS LINES

Bus depot	City served	Tickets sales	Freight sales	Labor-hours	Facility dollars
1	Philadelphia, Pa.	700	300	40	500
2	Baltimore, Md.	300	600	50	500
3	Washington, D.C.	200	700	50	400
4	Richmond, Va.	400	600	50	500
5	Raleigh, N.C.	500	400	40	400
6	Charleston, S.C.	500	500	50	500
7	Savannah, Ga.	800	500	40	600
8	Jacksonville, Fla.	300	200	30	400

Mid-Atlantic bus terminal. A percentage of the passenger ticket sales and freight sales would be kept by the terminal operator to cover his or her costs and profit.

After several months of operation, some terminal franchisees complained about inadequate profits and threatened to close their terminals. Because other franchisees were pleased with their experiences, a study of all the terminal operations in the system was undertaken. The information shown in Table 12.10 was collected over several weeks and represents a typical day's operation.

Questions

1. Use DEA to identify the efficient and inefficient terminal operations. Formulate the problem as a linear programming model, and solve using personal computer software such as *QS: Quantitative Systems, Version 3.0* that permits input file editing between runs.

2. Using the appropriate reference set of efficient terminals, make recommendations for changes in resource inputs for each inefficient terminal.

3. What recommendations would you have for the one seriously inefficient terminal in regard to increasing its outputs?

4. Discuss any shortcomings in the application of DEA to Mid-Atlantic Bus Lines.

CHAPTER 13

GROWTH AND EXPANSION

In June 1991 a guest and an employee were found dead after being electrocuted by a faulty underwater light in the swimming pool of a Days Inn in Orange, Texas.[1] This tragic incident is part of the story of a once successful motel chain that was taken over in a leveraged buyout in 1984. Cecil B. Day founded the chain in 1970 and operated it for years on the principle of strict adherence to exacting standards of excellence. Day, a high-minded man, prohibited the sale of alcohol on his properties, kept a chaplain on call 24 hours a day at each unit, and established a security department that was the envy of the industry. To maintain standards and consistency, the company owned at least half of its motels and granted franchises sparingly, rejecting more than 90 percent of the franchise applicants.

Twenty-two years after its founding, Days Inn does not own a single motel. After the leveraged buyout, Days Inn became an organization that merely sells its sign and its reservation and marketing services, and claims to be the fastest-growing motel chain. Franchise revenue became all that mattered, with each inn in the chain paying Days Inn 6 to 10 percent of its sales revenue. Lack of attention to the properties has resulted in stained walls, worn furniture, and broken air conditioners. More importantly, guests now appear to be at some risk from lax security and deferred maintenance, as illustrated by the electrocution incident.

Unlike competitors that require a new franchisee to build an inn from the ground up to exacting specifications, the post takeover Days Inn would erect its sign on a franchisee's existing property and ask for compliance later. This practice resulted in inconsistent quality throughout the chain. Note that the major selling

---

[1]From Kevin Helliker, "How a Motel Chain Lost Its Moorings after 1980's Buy-Out," *The Wall Street Journal,* May 26, 1992, p. 1.

point of most motel chains is consistent quality. Days Inn's willingness at this time to accept any existing motel as part of the chain has not been lost on Red Roof Inns, which advertises that its competition has "no two . . . alike" while touting its own inns as being corporate-owned and -operated. By selling off all company-owned units, Days Inn also deviated from accepted franchising practice. Without daily involvement in operations, it is generally believed that a franchisor will be less effective in dealing with franchisee problems. Former company insiders and industry experts point to Days Inn as an example of the dangers of rapid franchising.

CHAPTER PREVIEW

This chapter begins with a look at service growth and expansion in the context of multisite and multiservice expansion strategies. Using these dimensions, we put services into four classifications: focused service, focused network, clustered service, and diversified network.

Franchising can be an effective multisite expansion strategy for a well-defined service concept. We will explore the benefits to the franchisee and the responsibilities of the franchisor in an organizational arrangement held together by a contract.

Because our world has become "borderless," service expansion can no longer end with development of the domestic market. However, expansion overseas presents challenges, such as the cultural transferability of the service and discriminatory practices of foreign governments to protect their own domestic services from competition.

GROWTH AND EXPANSION STRATEGIES

The expectation of an entrepreneurial innovation is initial acceptance of the service concept followed by increasing customer demand. The need to expand a successful innovative service is often thrust upon the owner by the pressure of market potential and the desire to protect the service concept from competitors by building barriers to entry. To understand better the various ways in which a firm can expand its concept, consider Figure 13.1, which shows the fundamental expansion strategies available to service firms. We shall explore each of these growth strategies in turn and follow each with a discussion of the risks involved and the implications for management.

Focused Service

Typically, a service innovation begins at a single location with an initial service concept. This initial service concept is usually a well-defined vision focused on delivering a new and unique service. For example, Fred Smith's vision for Federal Express was the use of a single hub-and-spoke network to guarantee overnight delivery of packages.

	Single Service	Multiservice
	Focused service:	*Clustered service:*
Single Location	• Dental practice • Retail store • Family restaurant	• Stanford University • Mayo Clinic • USAA Insurance
	Focused network:	*Diversified network:*
Multisite	• Federal Express • McDonald's • Red Roof Inns	• Nations Bank • American Express • Arthur Andersen

FIGURE 13.1
Multisite and multiservice expansion strategies.

Success leads to increased demand, which requires capacity expansion at the site. Typically, the facility is then expanded, and personnel are added.

The successful firm will also attract competition and need to build a preferred position among as many customers as possible in the local market area. Adding ancillary services is one approach to penetrating the market or holding market share against the competition. Examples of peripheral services for a restaurant would include the addition of a salad bar or a drive-through window. However, the core service for a successful restaurant is usually excellent cuisine.

The risks associated with a single service location include being captive to the future economic growth of the area and being vulnerable to competition that can move in and capture market share. However, management and control of the enterprise is much simpler than in any of the other growth strategies.

Many examples of successful focused services exist. Consider particularly fine restaurants such as Chez Panisse in Berkeley or Antoine's in New Orleans. A focused service is often limited to a single site because of talented personnel, such as an award-winning chef or a nationally recognized heart surgeon. If the site is a key element of the service, such as a sheltered cove for a marina, it may not be easily duplicated elsewhere.

Focused Network

A service firm that must be readily accessible to customers, such as a fast-food restaurant, must consider adding sites to achieve significant growth. For firms such as McDonald's, a focused network allows management to maintain control which ensures consistency of service across all locations. It should be noted that for some services, such as Federal Express and other transportation or communications firms, the existence of a network is required merely to enable the service to function. Also, an entrepreneurial firm that has a successful, well-defined service concept and wants to reach a mass market can prevent imitation from competitors by capturing premium locations in different geographical areas.

However, the service concept must be well focused and thus easy to duplicate with rigorous control of service quality and costs. Frequently, the "cookie-cutter" concept of replicating service units is employed in facility construction, operating manuals, and personnel training. Franchising is often used to achieve the objective of rapid growth, with investment capital from franchisees and the motivation of independent operators. A more complete discussion of franchising is found later in this chapter.

For a single site, the founder is physically present to manage the firm's resources, market the service, train personnel, and ensure the integrity of the service concept. Expansion, especially in the beginning, can occur on an incremental basis. Initially, as the number of locations grows, managerial control slowly shifts from being informal to being formal so that the owner can control operations effectively even though he or she is absent from the additional sites.

But managing a network of service locations requires different management skills and involves challenges using sophisticated communications and control. Above all, the service concept must be rationalized and communicated to unit managers and staff, who must then execute the service consistently on a daily basis. Much planning must precede a multisite expansion, including preparing training and operations manuals, branding the concept, and launching a national marketing effort.

Service growth using the multisite strategy is very attractive because of its ability to reach the mass market quickly, but the risks of overexpansion and loss of control have resulted in many failures. However, the miles of "franchise rows" found in almost every city attest to the success of delivering a focused service through a multisite network.

Finally, having multiple sites in different geographic locations reduces the financial risk to the firm from severe localized economic downturns. A longitudinal study of occupancy at La Quinta Motor Inns during the 1980s dramatically illustrates the benefit of geographic risk containment. Founded in Texas, La Quinta Motor Inns had become a major presence statewide, with inns in all the major cities by 1980. During the oil and gas boom of the early 1980s, La Quinta embarked on an expansion strategy of following the exploration activity into the oil-producing states of Colorado, Louisiana, Oklahoma, and Wyoming. When the oil and gas boom bubble burst in the mid-1980s, the occupancy of many of the new inns and some of the inns in Texas plummeted. However, a financial disaster for the firm was avoided because other La Quinta inns not associated with the oil and gas industry continued to prosper.[2]

Clustered Service

Service firms with large fixed facilities often decide to grow by diversifying the service they offer. For example, during the 1970s many small colleges expanded into four-year regional universities to accommodate the increasing demand for a university degree. United Services Automobile Association (USAA) was originally founded to provide automobile insurance for military officers by direct mail.

[2]J. A. Fitzsimmons and S. E. Kimes, "Selecting Profitable Hotel Sites at La Quinta Motor Inns," *Interfaces,* vol. 20, no. 2, March 1990, pp. 12–20.

Located in San Antonio, Texas, USAA is now a major employer, and the physical facility is situated in a campuslike setting of several acres. Today, the services offered by USAA have been expanded to include banking, mutual funds, auto and homeowners' insurance, travel services, and a buying service. Large medical complexes such as the Mayo Clinic, M.D. Anderson, and Massachusetts General Hospital are examples of classic multiservice, single-site facilities. All these examples share the common feature that their service market is not defined by their location. For some services, such as medical centers and colleges, customers are willing to travel to the service location and spend considerable time at the facility (years for college students). For other services, such as USAA, travel is unnecessary because business is conducted without the need for physical interaction with the customer.

A major risk of service diversification is the potential loss of focus and neglect of the core service. For example, a ski resort may decide to make use of idle facilities during the summer by attracting conference business. However, the accommodations and food and beverage facilities suitable for skiers may be inadequate for hosting a conference. One saving grace in this situation is that at least the different market segments are separated by the seasons. Facility management becomes extremely complex when an attempt is made to serve more than one market segment concurrently. For example, hotels serving both tourists and business customers may have difficulty satisfying both markets.

To avoid the risk of loss of focus, a strategy of "concentric diversification" has been advocated.[3] Concentric diversification limits expansion to services with synergistic logic around the core service. The evolution of the convenience store is an excellent example of concentric diversification. Beginning with a limited selection of convenience items that could be purchased in a hurry, the stores have added self-serve gasoline, video rental, an automatic car wash, and self-serve microwave lunches. Concentric diversification creates economies of scale because the additional services require only marginal increases in variable costs (e.g., no additional cashier is needed).

Diversified Network

Service firms that grow through acquisition often find themselves combining both the multisite and the multiservice strategies. Several years ago, United Airlines acquired hotels and car rental agencies in the belief that sufficient synergy existed through the use of its Apollo reservation system to direct the traveling customer to its several businesses. Anticipated revenues never materialized, and so United sold off the peripheral services and returned to its core airline business. Managing a diversified network is a very complex task, as United Airlines and many other firms have learned.

Success is more often realized when the services are offered under one brand

---

[3]J. M. Carman and Eric Langeard, "Growth Strategies for Service Firms," *Strategic Management Journal,* vol. 1, no. 1, January–March 1980, p. 19.

name that establishes a broad marketing image. American Express has been particularly successful managing a global service network offering financial and travel services with real synergy.

FRANCHISING

Franchising is an alternative to expanding by using internally generated profits or by seeking funds in the capital markets. Recall from Chapter 4 that Mrs. Fields's Cookies did not use franchising as a method of expansion until very recently. However, franchising is a common vehicle for duplicating a service geographically by attracting investors who become independent owner-operators bound by a contractual agreement. For multisite services, the incorporation of conformance quality in the service concept has been the hallmark of the franchising agreement. The franchisor guarantees a consistent service because the concept is standardized in design, operation, and pricing. Customers expect identical service from any outlet, just as they make no distinction between products of the same brand. All franchise outlets benefit from this consistency in service because customers develop brand loyalty that is not bound by geography. For example, an American tourist in Munich, Germany, is treated to a McDonald's french fries, burger, and Coke meal that is identical to that served in San Francisco, Tokyo, and now Moscow.

The Nature of Franchising

The International Franchise Association defines franchising as a system by which a firm (franchisor) grants to others (franchisees) the right and license (franchise) to sell a product or service and possibly use the business system developed by the firm.

The franchisee owns the business through the payment of a franchise fee and purchase of the facility and equipment and assumes responsibility for all the normal operating activities, including hiring the employees, making daily decisions, and determining local advertising. The initial investment will vary, depending on capital requirements. For example, an H & R Block franchise may cost only $5000, but a McDonald's franchise could require $500,000. The service franchisee is usually granted an exclusive right or license to deliver the service in a specific market region in order to protect the franchisee against dilution of sales from other franchisees of the same brand. For example, Hardee's, a fast-food restaurant, agrees not to license another Hardee's franchisee within $1\frac{1}{2}$ miles of existing locations.

The franchisor retains the right to dictate conditions: standard operating procedures must be followed, materials must be purchased from either the franchisor or an approved supplier, no deviation from the product line is permitted, training sessions must be attended, and continuing royalty fees (e.g., 4 percent of gross sales for Wendy's) must be paid.

Benefits to the Franchisee

As a franchisee, the owner relinquishes some personal independence and control in return for a relationship that is based on the expectation of greater gains through group membership. The franchisee is given the opportunity to own a small business with less risk of failure owing to the identification with an established service brand. Membership in the franchisor organization also includes many additional benefits.

Management Training Prior to opening a new outlet, many franchisors provide an extensive training program. For example, McDonald's franchisees must spend two weeks at Hamburger University in suburban Chicago learning the McDonald's way of food preparation and customer service. The training accomplishes two objectives. First, the franchisee becomes well prepared to operate a business profitably, and second, McDonald's ensures that its procedures will be followed to guarantee consistency across units. Subsequent training is often offered through videotapes and traveling consultants.

Brand Name The franchisee gains immediate customer recognition from the nationally known and advertised brand name. The result is more immediate increased customer draw, and thus the break-even point is reached sooner than in a traditional new-business venture.

National Advertising Although the franchisee must usually contribute approximately 1 percent of gross sales to the franchisor for national advertising, the results benefit all operations. Furthermore, for businesses such as fast-food restaurants and motels in particular, a significant proportion of sales are to customers arriving from outside the immediate geographic region.

Acquisition of a Proven Business Traditionally, independent owners face a high failure rate, which a franchisee can expect to avoid. The franchisor has a track record of selecting appropriate sites, operating a reliable accounting system, and, most importantly, delivering a service concept already accepted by the public.

Economies of Scale As a member of the franchisor network, the franchisee is able to benefit from centralized purchasing and to achieve cost savings on materials and equipment unavailable to the independent owner.

Issues for the Franchisor

Franchising is an alternative to internally generated expansion for a firm seeking to develop a focused network of geographically dispersed units. Franchising allows the firm to expand rapidly with minimum capital requirements by selling the business concept to prospective entrepreneurs. Thus, franchising relies heavily on the motivation of investor-owners and allows the firm to grow without the cost of developing key managers. Of course, the process of screening potential franchisees must go beyond the minimum requirement of having the necessary capital. For example, Benihana of Tokyo found that many early franchisees were unqualified to manage an authentic Japanese theme restaurant.

Other issues include decisions on the degree of franchisee autonomy, the nature of the franchise contract, and a process for conflict resolution.

Franchisee Autonomy A franchisee's autonomy is the amount of freedom that is permitted in the operation of the unit. The degree of autonomy is a function of the extent of operations programming dictated in the franchise contract and of the success of "branding" achieved by national advertising.

The extent of operations programming is important to guarantee compliance with uniform standards of quality and service throughout the entire chain. If some franchisees were allowed to operate at substandard levels, the image of the entire chain would suffer, as we saw in the Days Inn example. A highly programmed operation might include:

1. Franchisor specifications such as day-to-day operating procedures, site selection, facility design, accounting system, supplies used and their sources, pricing, and menu items for the restaurant
2. Frequent inspections of the facility
3. The right to repurchase the outlet for noncompliance

Branding reinforces operations programming by establishing rather clear customer expectations from which it is difficult for the individual franchisee to deviate. In addition, successful branding should lead to greater profit potential, reduced risk, and a more sought-after investment opportunity.

Franchise Contract Control and power tend to concentrate in the hands of the franchisor. This raises questions concerning the relationship between franchisor and franchisee and also the misuse of power. The franchise contract is the vehicle for providing this relationship on a continuing basis. Very often these contracts are written with specific obligations on the part of the franchisee, but they are ambiguous regarding the responsibilities of the franchisor, and often, no attention is given to the rights of the franchisee. For example, litigation has arisen from the following contract stipulations: establishment of the resale value of the franchise and binding agreements requiring the purchase of supplies from the franchisor.

The objective in writing franchise contracts should be to avoid future litigation that might prevent a cooperative relationship from developing. Franchise contracts should be prepared to protect both parties and preserve the competitive strength of the entire franchise organization.

Conflict Resolution An intelligent and fair franchise contract will be the most effective means to reduce potential conflict. However, conflict frequently arises over the following issues because of differing objectives of the franchisor and franchisee:

1. How should fees be established and profits distributed?
2. When should franchisee facilities be upgraded, and how are the costs to be shared?
3. How far should the franchisor go in saturating a single market area with outlets?

The franchise system is a superorganization requiring interorganizational management. Thus a critical task of the franchisor is development of policy and procedures to handle conflict before it becomes divisive and impairs the entire system.

MULTINATIONAL DEVELOPMENT

Because its customers increasingly wanted to send packages to Europe and Asia, Federal Express decided in 1988 to duplicate its service overseas. The overseas operations have been drawing red ink ever since, resulting in a first-ever quarterly operating loss in 1991. Unfortunately, Federal Express arrived well after the competition, in the form of DHL and TNT, which had been providing express service for about a decade, having imitated the Federal Express concept in the late 1970s. Also, Federal Express was unprepared for the government regulations and bureaucratic red tape used to protect established firms. For example, it took three years to get permission from Japan to make direct flights from the Memphis hub to Tokyo, a key link in the overseas system. Just days before that service was to begin, Federal Express was notified that no packages weighing more than 70 pounds could pass through Tokyo; this was a provision to protect local transport businesses. Federal's obsession with tight central control also contributed to the problems. For instance, until recently all shipping bills were printed in English, and the cutoff time for package pickups was 5 p.m., as is the practice in the United States (the Spanish typically work until 8 p.m. after a lengthy midday break). Federal is now relaxing its go-it-alone, centralized control method of business that was successful in the United States. Pickup times, weight standards, and technology will now vary from country to country, and joint ventures with local firms are being sought to handle deliveries and marketing.[4]

Another issue is the frequent lack of supporting infrastructure in some foreign countries. (We take infrastructure for granted in the United States.) For example, the opening of the first McDonald's in Moscow required substantial supplier development. Management not only had to build a commissary to prepare all the products for the restaurant but also had to show farmers how to plant and harvest crops that were needed, such as potatoes and lettuce.

[4]From Daniel Pearl, "Federal Express Finds Its Pioneering Formula Falls Flat Overseas," *The Wall Street Journal*, Apr. 15, 1991, p. 1.

The Nature of the Borderless World[5]

Kenichi Ohmae, who has written extensively on strategic management, argues that we now live in a borderless world where customers worldwide are aware of the best products and services and expect to purchase them with no concern for national origin. In his strategic view, all firms compete in an interlinked world economy, and to be effective, they must balance the five C's of strategic planning: customers, competitors, company, currency, and country.

Customers   When people vote with their pocketbooks, they are interested in quality, price, design, value, and personal appeal. Brand labels such as the "golden arches" are spreading all over the world, and news of performance is hard to suppress. The availability of information, particularly in the industrialized Triad markets of North America, Europe, and Japan, has empowered customers and stimulated competition.

Competitors   Nothing stays proprietary for long. Equipment and software vendors supply their products and services to a wide range of customers. The result is rapid dispersion of technology available to all firms. Two factors, time and being the first mover, have now become more critical as elements of strategy. Furthermore, a single firm cannot be on the cutting edge of all technologies. Thus, operating globally means operating with partners, a lesson Federal Express has learned.

Company   Automation during the past years has moved firms from a variable-cost environment to a fixed-cost environment. Management focus has thus changed from boosting profits by reducing material and labor costs to increasing sales to cover fixed costs. This is particularly true of many service firms (e.g., airlines and communications businesses), which, to a large extent, are fixed-cost activities with huge investments in facilities and equipment. The search for a larger market has driven these firms toward globalization.

However, the nature of a firm's corporate culture may determine how effectively its service will travel overseas. The domestic success of Federal Express was built on a go-it-alone attitude, on rewards for nonunion employees who propose cost-cutting ideas, and on direct access to Fred Smith with any complaints. In contrast, UPS, which works with a union labor force and strict work standards, has moved overseas with fewer problems.

Currency   Global companies have tried to neutralize their exposure to fluctuating currency exchange rates by matching costs to revenues and by becoming strong in all regions of the Triad, so that if one is negative, it may be offset by others that are positive. Companies have also employed international finance

[5]From Kenichi Ohmae, *The Borderless World*, Harper Business, New York, 1990, pp. 1–9.

techniques such as hedging and options. Thus, to become currency-neutral, a firm is forced into global expansion.

Country   Having a strong presence in all the Triad regions provides additional strategic benefits beyond currency considerations. First, as noted above, exposure to economic downturns in one region may be offset by operations in other economies. Second, selling in your competitor's domestic market neutralizes its option to employ a strategy of using excessive profits earned in a protected domestic market for expansion overseas. For example, with government cooperation, Japanese companies have exploited this strategy, and recently they have been criticized for this by their trading partners.

However, only truly global companies can achieve "global localization" (a term coined by Akio Morta of Sony) and thereby be accepted as a local company while maintaining the benefits of worldwide operations. To reach this level, a firm must become close to the customers in the foreign country and accommodate their unique service needs. For fast-food restaurants, discovering the drinking and eating habits of the host country is critical for success. Thus, instead of expecting the Germans to enjoy a Big Mac with a Coke, McDonald's added beer to the menu. Permitting local management to modify the service within limits to accommodate local tastes should be encouraged, even at the risk of introducing some inconsistency across locations. An extreme example is Mr. Donut's in Japan, which changed everything about its product and service except the logo.

Considerations in Planning Multinational Operations[6]

In true services, which exclude receipts and payments on investments and government transactions, the United States has been maintaining a trade surplus for the past 20 years. Leadership in the "knowledge-based" services such as software, telecommunications, and information services has proved to be very mobile. However, not all services travel equally well, and considerations of cultural transferability, network development, and host government policy must be taken into account.

Cultural Transferability   Commercial banking would seem to be culturally neutral because financial needs and the associated business transactions are relatively homogeneous worldwide. Of course, the exception is the Middle East, where paying interest on a loan is not recognized by the Muslim faith; thus, banks must adjust by creating service charges that include but do not mention interest costs. Customer services are faced with the obvious language barrier and behavioral customs that might affect the service delivery (e.g., the need for nonsmoking areas in U.S. restaurants).

---

[6]From James L. Heskett, "The Multinational Development of Service Industries," *Managing in the Service Economy*, Harvard Business School Press, Boston, 1986, chap. 8, pp. 140–152.

However, in food service, the desire is often to emulate the cultural experience of a foreign land. The success of Benihana of Tokyo in the United States is partly due to creating the illusion of a Japanese dining experience while still serving familiar food. Likewise, for many non-Americans, eating at McDonald's and drinking a Coke is an opportunity to experience something American.

Network Development As we found with Federal Express, many service firms reluctantly expand into global operations, forced by the desires of their customers. In the case of holders of the VISA card and MasterCard, customers expected to use their credit cards wherever they traveled. In both cases the original concept was designed for a domestic market, but the customers eventually insisted on a global network. Maintaining operations control and standards of quality becomes difficult, however, because staffing is usually accomplished with nationals of the host country, and thus there are inherent language and cultural differences.

Host Government Policy Governments around the world have played a significant role in restricting the growth of multinational services. This includes but is not limited to making it difficult to repatriate funds, that is, to take profits out of the host country. Discrimination has taken a number of creative forms: banning the sale of insurance by foreign firms, giving preferential treatment to local shippers, placing restrictions on the international flow of information, and creating delays in processing licensing agreements. A major reason for this situation is the continuing refusal of countries (with the exception of the United States) to recognize the importance of services in international trade.

In November 1982, for the first time, trade barriers on services were placed on the agenda at a meeting of the General Agreement on Tariffs and Trade (GATT), a group of 88 trading nations that for decades has been establishing codes of conduct for trading goods. In 1993 the GATT agreement considering financial services was held hostage by several Asian countries that wish to protect their domestic firms from global competition. For example, Korea has an outright prohibition on foreigners selling mutual funds to local investors, and Japan requires a multiyear application process with no clear objective criteria for approval.[7]

SUMMARY

A successful service innovation can grow in two fundamental ways: (1) duplication of the service in different geographical locations with a multisite strategy of becoming a "focused network" or (2) incorporation of different services at the original site using a multiservice strategy, thereby becoming a "clustered service." Although it is not necessarily a desirable objective, some mature service firms combine both strategies and become a "diversified network."

[7]From Robert C. Pozen, "Is America Being Shut Out Again?" *The New York Times,* Jan. 10, 1993, p. 13.

Franchising has become the most common method to implement a multisite strategy in a very rapid manner, using capital furnished by investor-owners. Franchising is attractive to prospective entrepreneurs because of the many advantages of buying into a proven concept, but most importantly, the risk of failure is diminished.

We are now living in a borderless world with information on products and services available to customers worldwide. For many services a global presence is no longer an option but a necessity if they wish to continue to serve their customers. Overseas expansion has its risks and challenges, depending on the cultural transferability of the service, network development in a foreign land, and government discrimination against foreign services.

Chapter 14 begins Part VI, which includes several quantitative methods that can be applied to service situations. Chapter 14 will look at ways of forecasting demand.

TOPICS FOR DISCUSSION

1. For service firms, how does the operations strategy differ from the marketing strategy?
2. Is the competitive role of operations more important for a service firm than for a manufacturing firm?
3. Do you agree that the effect of learning and experience on total unit cost (learning curve) has never been demonstrated in a service situation?
4. Manufacturing firms often grow through product innovation. Are there examples of service firms that practice the equivalent strategy?
5. What is your assessment of the multinational competition in services?

CASE: FEDERAL EXPRESS: TIGER INTERNATIONAL ACQUISITION[8]

What has become one of America's great success stories began operations almost two decades ago in Memphis, Tennessee. At that time those who knew of Frederick Smith's idea did not realize that his small company was about to revolutionize the air cargo industry.

In 1972 the Civil Aeronautics Board ruled that operators flying aircraft with an "all-up" weight less than 75,000 pounds could be classified as an "air taxi" and would not be required to obtain a certificate of "public convenience and necessity" to operate. This new rule made it possible for Federal Express (FedEx) to penetrate the heavily entrenched airfreight industry. FedEx ordered a fleet of 33 Dassault Falcon fan-jets in 1972 and commenced operations a year later. On April 17, 1973, the company delivered 18 packages, becoming the first to offer nationwide overnight delivery.

One of FedEx's fundamental principles was the use of a hub-and-spoke system, in which all packages were first flown to Memphis, sorted during the night, and then shipped to their destinations the following morning. This system allowed

FedEx to serve a large number of cities with a minimum number of aircraft. It also provided tight control and efficiency of ground operations and soon became increasingly important as package tracking systems were installed.

During the first two years of operations FedEx lost money, but revenues surpassed the $5 billion mark in fiscal year 1989, partly owing to the acquisition of Tiger International.

As shown in Table 13.1, FedEx began global expansion in 1984, when it purchased Gelco International. FedEx followed that expansion with its first scheduled flight to Europe in 1985 and established its European headquarters in Brussels, Belgium, in the same year.

Domestic operations were expanded as well. In 1986, regional hubs were established in Oakland, California, and in Newark, New Jersey. A year later a sorting facility was opened in Indianapolis, and Honolulu was chosen for the Far East headquarters. That same year, 1987, FedEx was granted the rights to a small cargo route to Japan, and the following year the company was making regularly scheduled flights to the Orient.

However, international expansion did not result in immediate international success for FedEx. In Asia, its planes were flying at half their capacity owing to treaty restrictions, and a lack of backup planes in its South American operations was jeopardizing guaranteed delivery when regular aircraft were grounded. To make matters worse, many managers of the companies acquired in Europe had quit.

TABLE 13.1
FEDERAL EXPRESS CORPORATION TIMELINE

1973	Began service with Falcon fan-jets to 25 cities from Memphis in April.
1977	Air cargo industry deregulated.
1978	Purchased its first Boeing 727 and became a publicly held corporation.
1980	Took delivery of first McDonnell Douglas DC10 and implemented computerized tracking system.
1981	Introduced Overnight Letter, a lower-cost document service. Opened greatly expanded Superhub in Memphis.
1982	Shortened overnight delivery commitment to 10:30 a.m. in all major markets.
1983	Opened first Business Service Center. Became first company to achieve annual revenues of $1 billion in ten years.
1984	Purchased Gelco International and made first scheduled trans-Atlantic flight to Europe. Established European headquarters in Brussels.
1986	Enhanced tracking and informational capabilities with introduction of SuperTracker. Acquired Lex Wilkinson Ltd. of United Kingdom and Cansica of Canada.
1987	Acquired Indianapolis hub. Was granted exclusive small-cargo route to Japan.
1988	Scheduled first trans-Pacific flight to Japan. Acquired nine offshore transportation companies. Announced plan to purchase Tiger International.
1989	Completed purchase of Tiger International and merged Flying Tigers into system, becoming the world's largest full-service all-cargo airline.

As a solution to the international bottlenecks, FedEx made a dramatic move in December of 1988: it announced plans to purchase Tiger International, the parent company of Flying Tigers, the world's largest heavy cargo airline. The purchase price was about $880 million.

This action catapulted FedEx to the forefront of the international cargo market, giving it landing rights in 21 additional countries. However, the addition of Tigers was not without challenges. For example, the leveraged acquisition more than doubled FedEx's long-term debt to approximately $2 billion. Moreover, FedEx had bought into the business of delivering heavy cargo, much of which was not sent overnight; this business, therefore, represented a significant departure from FedEx's traditional market niche. One of the largest dilemmas facing FedEx following the merger was how to integrate the two workforces.

Major Players in the Domestic Air Cargo Industry

Federal Express is the nation's largest overnight carrier, with more than 40 percent of the domestic market. United Parcel Service (UPS), Emery Air Freight, Airborne Express, DHL (an international carrier based in Brussels), and a few other carriers account for the remaining market share. FedEx had 1988 revenues of $3.9 billion and a 1988 net income of $188 million.[9] However, FedEx had lost approximately $74 million on its international business since 1985, prompting the carrier to purchase Tiger International. The acquisition, which gained U.S. government approval on January 31, 1989, gave FedEx a strong entry position into heavy cargo as well as access to 21 additional countries.

Price wars, which began with UPS's entry into the overnight business, have decreased FedEx's revenues per package by 15 percent since 1984. Another setback suffered by FedEx was its $350 million loss on Zapmail, which it dropped in 1986. Zapmail, a document transmission service that relayed information via satellite, was quickly made obsolete by facsimile machines.

However, FedEx does offer its customers several other benefits not matched by its competitors. For example, it offers a one-hour "on-call" pickup service, and through the use of its data base information system, COSMOS, FedEx guarantees that it can locate any package in its possession within 30 minutes. FedEx has found that this type of customer security can help to ensure continued growth.[10]

The Nature of the Competition

The air cargo industry has undergone a series of mergers as a result of recent price wars that rocked the industry. Also, marketing alliances have been formed between domestic and foreign carriers to take better advantage of the international trade and to create new routes and services (such as package tracking).

When UPS entered the overnight-package market in 1982, competition heated

---

[9]Dean Foust, "Mr. Smith Goes Global," *Business Week,* February 13, 1989, pp. 66–72.

[10]David A. Clancy, "Air Cargo Takes Off," *Transportation and Distribution,* January 1989, pp. 32–36.

up substantially, starting a series of price wars that hurt all the air cargo players. Federal Express's average revenue per package declined by 30.3 percent between 1983 and 1988.

Fortunately for the competitors, it appears that the price-cutting strategy may have finally run its course. When UPS, which created the price wars, announced another price cut in October of 1988, competitors refused to follow. And in January 1993, UPS announced its first price increase in almost six years, a 5 percent increase in its charges for next-day service.

However, several factors, such as continued overcapacity, low switching costs, and high exit barriers, will continue to make the air cargo industry extremely competitive.

Conclusions on the Air Cargo Environment

Although the situation may be improving, intraindustry competition and rivalry continue to be the main deterrent to the air cargo industry. With overcapacity in the industry, firms desperate to fill planes continue to realize declining yields on the packages they ship. Moreover, the fact that passenger airlines are reentering the air cargo market with increased vigor does not help the capacity situation. All these factors are leading current players to consolidate their operations, in hopes of achieving increased economies of scale.

Technology is acting as both friend and foe of the air cargo industry. Facsimile machines have carved a large niche out of the overnight-document segment but, on the other hand, improved data bases are enabling companies to provide their clients with another valuable service: improved tracking information on the status of important shipments.

Until now, the large number of shippers has enabled buyers to enjoy low rates, but owing to their wide dispersion, buyers are not able to control effectively the air cargo companies. Likewise, air cargo companies continue to have an advantage over their suppliers. The ability to purchase older planes keeps firms less dependent on aircraft manufacturers, and a large unskilled labor pool from which to choose helps keep hub labor costs down. However, a lack of available airport facilities presents a serious problem to commercial airfreight. Not only is the lack of landing slots a problem in the United States, but acquiring government-controlled access to crowded international hubs can present a formidable challenge.

Worldwide Distribution

As the globe continues to shrink and economies become more interdependent, customers are demanding new services to facilitate revamped production processes. One of the most publicized is the just-in-time system that many U.S. firms have been borrowing from their Japanese competitors. JIT systems argue for elimination of the traditional inventory stockpiles common to manufacturing, including the raw material, work-in-process, and finished goods inventories. Without question, such a scheme relies on having the right part at the right place at the right time.

Air express has been able to play a reliable role in delivering the needed materials on time. FedEx, as well as its competitors, has succeeded in contracting with manufacturers to supply the needed logistical expertise to support its JIT framework. Essentially, the planes have become flying warehouses. As this area grows, the Tiger addition to Federal should reap large yields with its ability to handle the heavier shipments associated with international manufacturing. For example, an increasing amount of parts made in Asia are being shipped to the United States for final assembly.

Powership

To facilitate further penetration into a customer's business, Federal Express developed Powership, a program that locates terminals on a client's premises and thus enables FedEx to stay abreast of the firm's needs. In simplifying the daily shipping process, an automated program tracks shipments, provides pricing information, and prints invoices. Such a device helps to eliminate the administrative need of reconciling manifests with invoices. Currently, more than 7000 of Federal's highest-volume customers are integrated into the Powership system.

At Federal Express, customer automation is expected to play an increasingly significant role. By tying technological innovations with reliable on-time delivery, FedEx is achieving its goal of getting close to the customer.

Corporate Culture

Many believe that FedEx could not have grown to its current magnitude had it been forced to deal with the added pressure of negotiating with a unionized workforce. Federal Express has never employed organized labor, but this is not to suggest that attempts by unions have not been made in the past. In 1976 the International Association of Machinists and Aerospace Workers tried to organize the company's mechanics, who rejected the offer. Likewise, FedEx's pilots rejected an offer by the Airline Pilots Association during the same period. In 1978, the Teamsters attempted to organize the hub sorters but could not get enough signatures for a vote.

Despite an admirable human resource track record, the outlook for FedEx to continue its past performance is hazy. Because of the Tiger International acquisition, FedEx had to conceive of a way to merge the Flying Tigers unionized workforce with its own union-free environment. Previously, the willingness of FedEx workers to go above and beyond in performing their duties had given the company a marked advantage over UPS, the nation's largest employer of members of the United Brotherhood of Teamsters. But as the FedEx-Tiger merger progressed, many questions were left to be answered.

Acquisition of Tiger International

In December of 1988 Federal Express announced its intent to purchase Flying Tigers and, in early 1989, more than 40 years of air cargo experience were merged with FedEx. Besides giving Federal Express entry into an additional 21 nations, the Tigers merger possessed several other advantages for the aggressive company. Almost overnight FedEx became owner of the world's largest full-service all-cargo airline, nearly three times the size of its nearest competitor. Because FedEx could use this large fleet on its newly acquired routes, it would no longer be forced into the position of contracting out to other freight carriers in markets not served previously.

The addition of heavy freight to the FedEx service mix was viewed as a boost to its traditional express package delivery business. The merger fit in neatly with the company's plans to focus on the higher-margin box business while shifting away from document service. During the preceding two years, box shipments had increased by 53 percent, generating as much as 80 percent of revenues and an estimated 90 percent of profits.

On the downside, as noted earlier, the $2 billion debt that was incurred as a result of the merger and the capital intensiveness of the heavy-cargo business made the company more vulnerable to economic swings. Although the merger meshed well into its plans, FedEx was still a newcomer to the heavy-cargo market.

Another hurdle was the fact that many Flying Tigers premerger customers were competitors that used Tigers to reach markets where they, like FedEx, had no service or could not establish service.

Finally, FedEx had to conceive a plan to integrate the 6500 unionized Tigers workers into the company. Although Flying Tigers was founded with much the same type of entrepreneurial spirit that was cherished at Federal Express, the carrier had seen its workforce become members of organized labor early in its existence.

At the time of the merger, the Tigers union ties were severed; and even though FedEx promised to find positions for all the employees, critics felt that the union background of Tigers workers would dilute the culture at Federal Express. Whether or not FedEx could continue its success story appeared to hinge on its ability to impart its way of life on the Tigers workers, and not vice versa.

Questions

1. Describe the growth strategy of Federal Express. How has this strategy differed from those of its competitors?

2. What risks are involved in the acquisition of Tiger International?

3. In addition to the question of unionizing the pilots, what other problems might you have anticipated in accomplishing this merger?

4. Suggest a plan of action that Frederick Smith could have used to address the potential acquisition problems given in your answer above.

SELECTED BIBLIOGRAPHY

Adam, E. E., Jr., and P. M. Swamidass: "Assessing Operations Management from a Strategic Perspective," *Journal of Management,* vol. 15, no. 2, 1989, pp. 181–203.

Carman, J. M., and E. Langeard: "Growth Strategies for Service Firms," *Strategic Management Journal,* vol. 1, no. 1, January–March 1980, pp. 7–22.

Chase, R. B., and R. H. Hayes: "Operations' Role in Service Firm Competitiveness," *Sloan Management Review,* vol. 33, no. 1, fall 1991, pp. 15–26.

Cowell, Donald: "Service Product Planning and Development," *The Marketing of Services,* Heinemann, London, 1984, chap. 7, pp. 115–146.

Haywood-Farmer, J., and J. Garcelon: "The Theoretical Issues Propagated by International Trade in Services," *Operations Management Review,* vol. 9, no. 1, 1992, pp. 18–27.

――― and J. Nollet: "Growth and Strategy," *Services PLUS,* G. Morin Publisher Ltd., Boucherville, Quebec, Canada, 1991, chap. 8, pp. 119–136.

Heskett, J. L.: "The Multinational Development of Service Industries," *Managing in the Service Economy,* Harvard Business School Press, Boston, 1986, chap. 8, pp. 135–152.

Ohmae, Kenichi: *The Borderless World,* Harper Business, New York, 1990.

Porter, Michael E.: "Competitive Strategy in Fragmented Industries," *Competitive Strategy,* Free Press, New York, 1980, chap. 9, pp. 191–215.

Sasser, W. E., R. P. Olsen, and D. D. Wyckoff: "The Multisite Service Firm Life Cycle," *Management of Service Operations,* Allyn and Bacon, Boston, 1978, pp. 534–566.

Shaw, John C.: "Competitive Strategy in Service Industries," *The Services Bulletin,* vol. 3, January 1987, pp. 3–4.

―――: *The Service Focus,* Dow Jones–Irwin, Homewood, Ill., 1990.

Stephenson, P. R., and R. G. House: "Perspective on Franchising," *Business Horizons,* vol. 14, no. 4, August 1971, pp. 35–42.

Thomas, Dan R. E.: "Strategy Is Different in Service Business," *Harvard Business Review,* July–August 1978, pp. 158–165.

QUANTITATIVE MODELS WITH SERVICE APPLICATIONS

This concluding part of the book contains a selection of quantitative and qualitative models that have found applications in service management. A forecast of service demand is information that is essential for planning new ventures, as well as for planning the hourly, daily, and even long-range activities of a service operation. In Chapter 14, we will look at several tools for making forecasts, including subjective, causal, and time series models.

Because some customer waiting is unavoidable in a service delivery system, the ability to predict the waiting experience of customers under various conditions is useful in the planning of capacity needs. Chapter 15 reviews the various analytical queuing models with service illustrations and applications to service capacity planning under different system performance criteria.

The final chapter, Chapter 16, introduces linear programming models with service applications and solutions using the personal-computer software called *QS: Quantitative Systems, Version 3.0.*

CHAPTER **14**

FORECASTING DEMAND
FOR SERVICES

Forecasting techniques allow us to translate the multitude of information available on data bases into strategies that can give a service a competitive advantage. The particular techniques we will describe are classified into three basic models: subjective, causal, and time series. It must be noted that while some services may use only one or another of these models, other services will make use of two or more models, depending on the application. For example, a fast-food restaurant may be interested in using a time series model to forecast the daily demand for menu items. The demand for hotel services, however, has both temporal and spatial characteristics, which will require the use of both time series models and causal models. Service firms may, on occasion, use subjective models to assess the future impact on their businesses from changing demographics, such as the aging of the general population. In general, as we move from subjective to causal to time series models, the forecast time horizon becomes shorter. The models, their characteristics, and possible applications are shown in Table 14.1.

CHAPTER PREVIEW

The chapter begins with subjective models because these methods are useful at the initial planning stage for service delivery systems when a long-time horizon is being considered. The Delphi technique is illustrated with an application to government policy planning for nuclear power. Causal models use regression analysis to form a linear relationship between independent variables and a dependent variable of interest. The site selection problem faced by a motel chain is used to illustrate the causal modeling approach to forecasting future occupancy of alternative sites.

The discussion of time series models begins with the common N-period moving

TABLE 14.1
CHARACTERISTICS OF FORECASTING METHODS

Method	Data required	Relative cost	Forecast horizon	Application
Subjective models:				
Delphi	Survey results	High	Long-term	Technological forecasting
Cross-impact analysis	Correlations between events	High	Long-term	Technological forecasting
Historical analogy	Several years of data for a similar situation	High	Medium- to long-term	General economic conditions
Causal models:				
Regression	All past data for all variables	Moderate	Medium-term	Demand forecasting
Econometric	All past data for all variables	Moderate to high	Medium- to long-term	Economic conditions
Time series models:				
Moving average	N most recent observations	Very low	Short-term (1 period)	Demand forecasting
Exponential smoothing	Smoothing constant, previous smoothed value, and most recent observation	Very low	Short-term (1 to 3 periods)	Demand forecasting

average. A more sophisticated time series model called exponential smoothing is then introduced and shown to accommodate trends and seasonal data.

SUBJECTIVE MODELS

Most of the forecasting techniques, such as time series and causal models, are based on data whose pattern is relatively stable over time so that we can reasonably expect to make useful forecasts. But in some cases we may have little data or no data with which to work. Or we may have data that exhibit patterns and relationships only over the short run and therefore are not useful for long-range forecasts.

When we lack sufficient or appropriate data, we must resort to forecast methods that are subjective or qualitative in nature. We will discuss three of these methods.

Delphi Method

The Delphi method, developed at the Rand Corporation by Olaf Helmer, is based on expert opinion. In its simplest form, questions are asked of persons with expertise in a given area, and these individuals are not permitted to interact with each other. Typically, the participants are asked to make numerical estimates. For example, they might be asked to predict the highest Dow Jones average for the coming year.

The test administrator tabulates the results into quartiles and supplies the findings to the experts, who are then asked to reconsider their answers in light of the new information. Additionally, those whose opinions are in the two outside quartiles are asked to justify their opinions. All the information from this round of questioning is then tabulated and once again returned to the participants. On this occasion, each participant who remains outside the middle two quartiles (interquartile range) may be asked to provide an argument on why he or she believes those who are at the opposite extreme are incorrect.

The process may continue through several more iterations with the intent of eventually having the experts arrive at a consensus that can be used for future planning. This method is very labor-intensive and requires input from persons with expert knowledge in the topic of interest. Obviously, Delphi is a very expensive, time-consuming method and is practical only for long-term forecasting.

An example of the application of the Delphi method can be seen in a study of the nuclear power industry.[1] Ninety-eight persons agreed to participate in the study. These people occupied key upper-level positions with architect-engineering firms, reactor manufacturers, and utility companies in the industrial sector concerned with nuclear power, as well as with state regulatory agencies, state energy commissions, congressional staffs, and nuclear regulatory agencies in the public sector.

The round-1 questionnaire that was sent to each participant contained 37 questions, 11 concerning the past evolution of the nuclear industry and 26 concerning the future. The questions were to be answered on a seven-point Likert scale ranging from "strongly agree" to "uncertain" to "strongly disagree," as shown below:

It is desirable *that utilities be permitted to integrate capital investment costs more aggressively into rate structures.*

No. jdgmt.	Strong. disagr.	Disagr.	Disagr. somewh.	Uncert.	Agree somewh.	Agree	Strong. agree

The questionnaire also asked for open-ended comments.

For round 2 of the study, the administrator provided a comprehensive summary of the first-round responses to the 11 questions concerning the past and a summary of the open-ended comments concerning the future. The number of responses to the above question are noted below, with the median (M) and interquartile range (designated by vertical bars) shown below the responses.

[1]C. H. Davis and J. A. Fitzsimmons, "The Future of Nuclear Power in the United States," *Technological Forecasting and Social Change,* Elsevier Science Publishing Co., Inc., New York, vol. 40, no. 2, September 1991, pp. 151–164.

No jdgmt.	Strong. disagr.	Disagr.	Disagr. somewh.	Uncert.	Agree somewh.	Agree	Strong. agree
1	6	5	6	15	35	8	

$$\vdash - \cdot\text{M}\cdot - \dashv$$

The 11 questions concerning the past were dropped from the round-2 questionnaire, and 11 new questions prompted by the open-ended comments from round 1 were added. The participants were invited to "defend" their positions with supporting comments if their opinions fell outside the interquartile range.

For round 3, which was the final round in this study, the administrator once again supplied the participants with feedback, this time from round 2, and invited the participants to "vote" again on the same questions. The following illustration of the resulting median and interquartile range after each round of voting demonstrates how the opinions of the experts shifted and finally arrived at a consensus for this particular question:

No jdgmt.	Strong. disagr.	Disagr.	Disagr. somewh.	Uncert.	Agree somewh.	Agree	Strong. agree
Round 1			$\vdash$ -M - -$\dashv$				
Round 2			$\vdash$ - - - - - - - -M - - - - - - - - -$\dashv$				
Round 3			$\vdash$ - - - - - - - -M - -$\dashv$				

Some of the questions in this study, as noted before, asked for assessments of where the industry has been and where it stands today. Other questions not only asked the experts where they think it should be headed but also asked them to address such issues as allocation of resources and the political realities that bear on the future of nuclear power. As we can see, the Delphi method is a useful tool in addressing situations where quantifiable data are not available.

Cross-Impact Analysis

Cross-impact analysis assumes that some future event is related to the occurrence of an earlier event. As in the Delphi method, a panel of experts studies a set of correlations between events presented in matrix form. These correlations are used as the basis for estimating the likelihood of the future event occurring.

As an example, consider a forecast conducted in 1992 that examines $3-per-gallon gasoline prices by 1993 (event A) and the commercial development of electric cars by 1997 (event B). By initial consensus, it might be determined that given A, the probability of B is .7, and given B, the probability of A is .6. These probabilities are shown below in a matrix:

	Probability of event	
Given event	A	B
A	—	.7
B	.6	—

Assume that the forecasted probability for commercial development of electric cars by 1997 is 1.0 and that the forecasted probability of $3 per gallon for gasoline by 1993 is .8. These new values are statistically inconsistent with the values in the matrix. The inconsistencies would be pointed out to the experts on the panel, who then would revise their estimates in a series of iterations. As with the Delphi method, an experienced administrator is needed to arrive at a satisfactory conditional probability matrix that can be used as a basis for generating a forecast.

Historical Analogy

Historical analogy assumes that the introduction and growth pattern of a new product or service will mimic the pattern established by a similar concept for which data are available. Historical analogy frequently is used to forecast the market penetration or life cycle of a new product or service. The concept of a product life cycle used in marketing involves stages, such as introduction, growth, maturity, and decline.

A famous use of historical analogy was the prediction of the market penetration of color television based on the experience with black-and-white television only a few years earlier. Of course, the appropriate analogy is not always so obvious. Because the pattern of previous product data can have many interpretations and the analogy can be questioned, the credibility of any forecast from this method is often suspect. The acceptance of a historical analogy forecast depends on making a convincing analogy.

CAUSAL MODELS

We know that it is fairly easy to make short-term forecasts when we are presented with uncomplicated data. But on occasion, a competitive service organization may have to deal with a wealth of statistical information, some of which may be relevant to making profitable forecasts and some of which may be extraneous. In these situations, also, it is more likely that the forecasts will need to be made for the next year—or for the next decade—rather than just for the next day, week, or month. Obviously, a long-term forecast has the potential of spelling success or devastation for the organization. Therefore, we need a way of separating out the critical information and processing it to help us make appropriate forecasts.

Causal models make assumptions similar to those of time series models (which we will consider later), i.e., that the data follow an identifiable pattern over time and that an identifiable relationship exists between the information we wish to forecast and other factors. These models range from very simple ones where the forecast is based on a technique called *regression analysis* to those known as *econometric models,* which use a system of equations.

Regression Models

The computer age has greatly simplified the use of regression models today. Now it is necessary only to collect the appropriate data and plug it into one of the many software programs available. A brief discussion of the mechanics of the models will suffice for an understanding of their application.

Each model involves the factor being forecast, which is designated as the *dependent variable,* or Y, and the factors that determine the value of Y, known as the *independent variables,* or X_i. If there are n independent variables, then the relationship between the dependent variable Y and the independent variables X is expressed as follows:

$$Y = a_0 + a_1X_1 + a_2X_2 + \cdots + a_nX_n \tag{1}$$

The values $a_0, a_1, a_2, \ldots, a_n$ are constant coefficients, which are determined by the computer program being used. If calculations are done by hand, the values are determined by using regression equations found in elementary statistics texts.

As an example, the management of La Quinta Inn, a national chain of hotels, commissioned a study to determine the direction of its expansion efforts.[2] It wanted to know what factors determined a profitable hotel location and thus would allow management to screen available real estate for new hotel sites. Investigators collected data on many factors at existing locations, such as traffic count, number of competitive rooms nearby, visibility of signs, local airport traffic, types of neighboring businesses, and distance to the central business district. In all, 35 factors, or independent variables, were considered, as shown in Table 14.2.

A preliminary statistical evaluation of the data for all those variables then allowed the investigators to identify four critical factors—STATE, PRICE, INCOME, and COLLEGE—to be used in the forecast model.

The firm's operating margin, obtained by adding depreciation and interest expenses to the profit and dividing by the total revenue, was chosen as the most reliable measure, or dependent variable Y, on which to base a forecast. For this case, the constant coefficients were calculated as $a_0 = 39.05$, $a_1 = -5.41$, $a_2 = +5.86$, $a_3 = -3.09$, and $a_4 = +1.75$. Substituting these coefficient values and the independent variables into equation (1) yields the regression forecasting model below:

Operating margin $Y = 39.05 + (-5.41)$STATE $+ (5.86)$PRICE $+$
$\qquad\qquad\qquad\qquad (-3.09)$INCOME $+ (1.75)$COLLEGE

[2]S. E. Kimes and J. A. Fitzsimmons, "Selecting Profitable Hotel Sites at La Quinta Motor Inns," *Interfaces,* vol. 20, no. 2, March–April 1990, pp. 12–20.

TABLE 14.2
INDEPENDENT VARIABLES FOR HOTEL LOCATION

Name	Description
	Competitive factors
INNRATE	Inn price
PRICE	Room rate for the inn
RATE	Average competitive room rate
RMS1	Hotel rooms within 1 mile
RMSTOTAL	Hotel rooms within 3 miles
ROOMSINN	Inn rooms
	Demand generators
CIVILIAN	Civilian personnel on base
COLLEGE	College enrollment
HOSP1	Hospital beds within 1 mile
HOSPTOTL	Hospital beds within 4 miles
HVYIND	Heavy industrial employment
LGTIND	Light industrial acreage
MALLS	Shopping mall square footage
MILBLKD	Military base blocked
MILITARY	Military personnel
MILTOT	MILITARY + CIVILIAN
OFC1	Office space within 1 mile
OFCTOTAL	Office space within 4 miles
OFCCBD	Office space in central business district
PASSENGR	Airport passengers enplaned
RETAIL	Scale ranking of retail activity
TOURISTS	Annual tourists
TRAFFIC	Traffic count
VAN	Airport van
	Area demographics
EMPLYPCT	Unemployment percentage
INCOME	Average family income
POPULACE	Residential population
	Market awareness
AGE	Years inn has been open
NEAREST	Distance to nearest inn
STATE	State population per inn
URBAN	Urban population per inn
	Physical attributes
ACCESS	Accessibility
ARTERY	Major traffic artery
DISTCBD	Distance to downtown
SIGNVIS	Sign visibility

Source: Reprinted by permission, "Selecting Profitable Hotel Sites at La Quinta Motor Inns," S. E. Kimes and J. A. Fitzsimmons, Interfaces, vol. 20, no. 2, March–April 1990, p.14. Copyright © 1990, the Operations Research Society of America and The Institute of Management Sciences, 290 Westminster Street, Providence, RI 02903.

By collecting data for the independent variables at a proposed hotel site and making appropriate transformations as needed, the operating margin can be forecasted. The results of this study proved the model to be very good in predicting the likelihood of success of a proposed location for a new inn.

As we can see, regression models require a relatively long history of data for both the dependent and independent variables. Most models give equal weight to all observations, but *discounted regression models* have been developed that will give more weight to more recent data when calculating the coefficients. Other special regression models known as *Fourier models* include adjustments for seasonality and cyclic influences.

Each regression model must be constructed to meet the needs of the individual organization, a process that often involves considerable time and expense. It also requires expertise in the selection of independent and dependent variables to ensure a relationship that has a logical and meaningful interpretation. For these reasons, regression models are appropriate only for making medium- and long-term forecasts.

Econometric Models

We noted above that econometric models are versions of regression models that involve a system of equations. The equations are related to each other, and the coefficients are determined as in the simpler regression models.

An econometric model consists of a set of simultaneous equations that expresses a dependent variable in terms of several different independent variables. Econometric models tend to be more expensive and sophisticated to use than other regression models; therefore, they are generally used only for long-range forecasts.

TIME SERIES MODELS

Time series models are applicable for making short-term forecasts when the values of observations occur in an identifiable pattern over time. These models range from the simple *N-period moving average* model to the more sophisticated and useful *exponential smoothing* models.

N-Period Moving Average

Sometimes observations made over a period of time appear to have a random pattern; consequently, we do not feel confident in basing forecasts for the future on them. Consider the data in Table 14.3 for a 100-room hotel located in a college town. We have decided to forecast only Saturday occupancy because the demand for each day of the week is influenced by different forces. For example, during the weekdays demand is generated by business travelers, but the weekend guest is often someone on vacation or visiting friends. Selection of the forecasting period is an important consideration and should be based on the nature of demand and the ability to use the information. For example, fast-food restaurants forecast demand by the hour of the day.

TABLE 14.3
SATURDAY OCCUPANCY AT A 100-ROOM HOTEL

Saturday	Period	Occupancy	Three-period moving average	Forecast
Aug. 1	1	79		
8	2	84		
15	3	83	82	
22	4	81	83	82
29	5	98	87	83
Sept. 5	6	100	93	87
12	7			93

The hotel owner above has noted an increase in occupancy for the last two Saturdays and wishes to prepare for the coming weekend (September 12), perhaps by discontinuing the practice of offering discount rates. Are the higher occupancy figures indicative of a change in the underlying average occupancy? To answer this question, we need a way of taking out the "noise" of occasional blips in the pattern so that we do not overreact to a change that is just random rather than permanent and significant.

The N-period moving-average method may be used in this simple example to smooth out the random variations and produce a reliable estimate of the underlying average occupancy. The method calculates a moving average MA_t for period t on the basis of selecting N of the most recent actual observations A_t, as shown in equation (2).

$$MA_t = \frac{A_t + A_{t-1} + A_{t-2} + \cdots + A_{t-N+1}}{N} \qquad (2)$$

If we select N equal to 3, we cannot begin our calculation until period 3 (August 15), at which time we add the occupancy figures for the three most recent Saturdays (August 1, 8, and 15) and divide the sum by 3 to arrive at a three-period moving average of $[(83 + 84 + 79)/3] = 82$. We use this value to forecast occupancy for the following Saturday, August 22. The moving-average forecast has smoothed out the random fluctuations to track better the average occupancy, which is then used to make a forecast for the next period. Each three-period moving-average forecast thus involves simply adding the three most recent occupancy values and dividing by 3. For example, to arrive at the moving average for August 22, we drop the value for August 1, add the value for August 22, and recalculate the average, getting 83. Continuing this iterative process for the remaining data, we can see how the moving-average occupancy of approximately 82 percent for Saturdays in August has recently increased, reflecting the near-capacity occupancy for the past two weekends. If the local college football team, after playing two consecutive home games, is scheduled for an away game on September 12, how confident are you in forecasting next Saturday's occupancy at 93 percent?

Although our N-period moving average has identified a change in the underlying average occupancy, the method is slow to react because old data are given equal weight (i.e., $1/N$) with new data in calculations of the averages. But more recent data may be better indicators of change; therefore, we may wish to assign more weight to recent observations. Rather than arbitrarily assigning weights to our moving-average data to fix the shortcoming, we will instead use a more sophisticated forecasting method that systematically ages the data. Our next topic, exponential smoothing, can also accommodate trends and seasonality in the data.

Simple Exponential Smoothing

Simple exponential smoothing is the time series method most frequently used for demand forecasting. Simple exponential smoothing also "smooths out" blips in the data, but its power over the N-period moving average is threefold: (1) old data are never dropped or lost; (2) older data are given progressively less weight; and (3) the calculation is simple and requires only the most recent data.

Simple exponential smoothing is based on the concept of feeding back the forecast error to correct the previous smoothed value. In equation (3) below, S_t is the smoothed value for period t, A_t is the actual observed value for period t, and α (alpha) is a smoothing constant usually assigned a value between 0.1 and 0.5.

$$S_t = S_{t-1} + \alpha(A_t - S_{t-1}) \tag{3}$$

The term $(A_t - S_{t-1})$ represents the forecast error because it is the difference between the actual observation and the smoothed value calculated in the prior period. A fraction α of this forecast error is added to the previous smoothed value to obtain the new smoothed value S_t. Notice how self-correcting this method is when you consider that forecast errors can be either positive or negative.

Our moving-average analysis of the occupancy data in Table 14.3 indicated that an actual increase in average occupancy occurred over the recent two Saturdays. These same occupancy data are repeated in Table 14.4, with the actual value for

TABLE 14.4
SIMPLE EXPONENTIAL SMOOTHING
Saturday Hotel Occupancy ($\alpha = 0.5$)

Saturday	Period t	Actual occupancy A_t	Smoothed value S_t	Forecast F_t	Forecast error $|A_t - F_t|$
Aug. 1	1	79	79.00		
8	2	84	81.50	79.00	5.00
15	3	83	82.25	81.50	1.50
22	4	81	81.63	82.25	1.25
29	5	98	89.81	81.63	16.38
Sept. 5	6	100	94.91	89.81	10.19
				MAD*	6.8625

*MAD = mean absolute deviation.

each period (A_t) shown in the third column. Using simple exponential smoothing, we will demonstrate again that a significant change in the mean occupancy has occurred.

Because we must start somewhere, let the first observed, or actual, value A_t in a series of data equal the first smoothed value S_t. Therefore, as shown in Table 14.4, S_1 for August 1 equals A_1 for August 1, or 79.00. The smoothed value for August 8 (S_2) may then be derived from the actual value for August 8 (A_2) and the previous smoothed value for August 1 (S_1) according to equation (3). We have selected an α equal to 0.5 because, as will be shown later, this results in a forecast that is similar to the one obtained by using a three-period moving average. For August 8:

$$S_2 = S_1 + \alpha(A_2 - S_1)$$
$$= 79.00 + 0.5(84 - 79.00)$$
$$= 81.50$$

Similar calculations are then made to determine the smoothed values (S_3, S_4, S_5, S_6) for successive periods.

Simple exponential smoothing assumes that the pattern of data is distributed about a constant mean. Thus, the smoothed value calculated in period t is used as the forecast for period $t + 1$, as shown below:

$$F_{t+1} = S_t \tag{4}$$

Our best estimate for August 15 occupancy will be 81.50, the most recent smoothed value at the end of August 8. Notice that the forecast error (84 – 79) was a positive 5 (i.e., we underestimated demand by 5) and that one-half of this error was added to the previous smoothed value to increase the new estimate of average occupancy. This concept of error feedback to correct an earlier estimate is an idea borrowed from control theory.

The smoothed values shown in Table 14.4 were calculated using an α value of 0.5. But, as noted above, if we wish to make the smoothed values less responsive to the latest data, we can assign α a smaller value. Figure 14.1 demonstrates graphically how an α of 0.1 and an α of 0.5 smooth the curve of the actual values. It is easily seen in this figure that the smoothed curve, particularly with $\alpha = 0.5$, has reduced the extremes (the dips and peak) and responded to the increased occupancy in the last two Saturdays. Therefore, basing forecasts on smoothed data helps prevent overreacting to the extremes in the actual observed values.

Equation (3) may be rewritten as follows:

$$S_t = \alpha(A_t) + (1 - \alpha)S_{t-1} \tag{5}$$

The basis for the name *exponential smoothing* can be observed in the weights given past data in equation (5). We see that A_t is given a weight α in determining S_t, and we can easily show by substitution that A_{t-1} is given a weight $\alpha(1 - \alpha)$. In

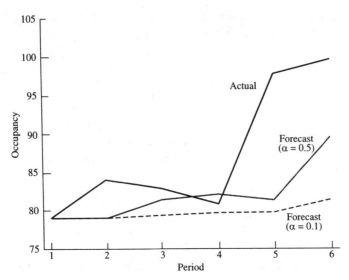

FIGURE 14.1
Simple exponential smoothing: Saturday hotel occupancy ($\alpha = 0.1$, and $\alpha = 0.5$).

general, actual value A_{t-n} is given a weight $\alpha(1 - \alpha)^n$, as shown in Figure 14.2, which graphs the exponential decay of weights, given a series of observations over time. Note that older observations never disappear entirely from the calculation of S_t as they would when the N-period moving average is used, but they do assume progressively decreasing importance.

Relationship between α and N

Selecting the value for α is a matter of judgment, often based on the pattern of historical data, with large values giving much weight to recent data in anticipation of changes. To help in the selection of α, a relationship can be made between the

FIGURE 14.2
Distribution of weight given past data in exponential smoothing ($\alpha = 0.3$).

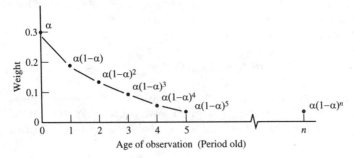

number of periods N in the moving-average method and the exponential smoothing constant α. If we assume that the two methods are similar when the average ages of past data are equal, then the following relationship results:

Moving average:

$$\text{Average age} = \frac{(0 + 1 + 2 + \cdots + N - 2 + N - 1)}{N}$$

$$= \frac{(N - 1)(N/2)}{N}$$

$$= \frac{N - 1}{2}$$

Exponential smoothing:

$$\text{Average age} = 0(\alpha) + 1(\alpha)(1 - \alpha) + 2(\alpha)(1 - \alpha)^2 + \cdots$$

$$= \frac{1 - \alpha}{\alpha}$$

The calculation above is a geometric series with the sum equal to

$$\frac{ar}{(1 - r)^2} \qquad \text{for } a = \alpha \text{ and } r = 1-\alpha$$

When the average ages are equated, the result is

$$\alpha = \frac{2}{(N + 1)} \qquad \text{or} \qquad N = \frac{(2 - \alpha)}{\alpha}$$

Using this relationship results in the following sample values for equating α and N:

α:	0.05	0.1	0.2	0.3	0.4	0.5	0.667
N:	39	19	9	5.7	4	3	2

As shown above, the usual assignment of a smoothing value between 0.1 and 0.5 is reasonable when compared with the number of periods in an equivalent moving-average forecast. The particular value assigned to α is a tradeoff between overreacting to random fluctuations about a constant mean and detecting a change in the mean value. Higher values of α are more responsive to change because of the greater weight given to recent data. In practice, the value of α is often selected on the basis of minimizing the forecast error measured by the mean absolute deviation (MAD).

Forecast Error

Although it is obvious in Figure 14.1 that the smoothed curves have evened out the peaks and valleys of the actual curve, how do we measure the accuracy of the forecasts? A common method of measuring forecast accuracy is the calculation of the *mean absolute deviation* (MAD). This is the calculation of the average value for the *absolute* values of forecast errors $A_t - F_t$ shown in Table 14.4. To calculate the MAD for this example, total the absolute differences and divide by the number of observations. The MAD value obtained is 6.8625.

Recall that the forecast values in this example were derived from smoothed values calculated with $\alpha = 0.5$, because this method is similar to a three-period moving-average method. For the three-period moving-average forecast developed earlier, the MAD value is 9.67. In this case simple exponential smoothing resulted in more accurate forecasts than the corresponding three-period moving-average method. However, if an α value of 0.1 is used, the MAD value is 9.18, reflecting the unresponsiveness to change of a small smoothing constant.

In any event, we desire an unbiased forecast with respect to its tracking of the actual mean for the data. Thus, the sum of the forecast errors should tend toward zero, taking into account positive and negative differences. If it does not, we should then look for underlying trends or seasonality and account for them explicitly. For the results shown in Table 14.4, the sum of forecast errors equals 34.32. This high positive sum suggests that an upward trend exists in the data.

Exponential Smoothing with Trend Adjustment

The *trend* in a set of data is the average rate at which the observed values change from one period to the next over time. The changes created by the trend can be treated using an extension of simple exponential smoothing.

In Table 14.5 we are following the experience of a new commuter airline during its first eight weeks of business. The average weekly load factors (percentages of seats sold) show a steady increase from approximately 30 percent for week 1 to approximately 70 percent for week 8. In this example the smoothed value S_t is calculated using equation (6), which is equation (5) modified by the addition of a

TABLE 14.5
EXPONENTIAL SMOOTHING WITH TREND ADJUSTMENT
Commuter Airline Load Factor ($\alpha = 0.5$, $\beta = 0.3$)

Week t	Actual occupancy A_t	Smoothed value S_t	Smoothed trend T_t	Forecast F_t	Forecast error $|A_t - F_t|$
1	31	31.00	0.00		
2	40	35.50	1.35	31.00	9.00
3	43	39.93	2.27	36.85	6.15
4	52	47.10	3.74	42.20	9.80
5	49	49.92	3.47	50.84	1.84
6	64	58.69	5.06	53.39	10.61
7	58	60.88	4.20	63.75	5.75
8	68	66.54	4.63	65.07	2.93
				MAD	6.58

trend value T_{t-1} to the previous smoothed value S_{t-1} in order to account for the weekly rate of increase in load factor.

$$S_t = \alpha(A_t) + (1 - \alpha) (S_{t-1} + T_{t-1}) \tag{6}$$

To incorporate a trend adjustment in our calculation, we will use β (beta) as a smoothing constant. This constant is usually assigned a value between 0.1 and 0.5 and may be the same as, or different from, α. The trend for a given period t is defined by $(S_t - S_{t-1})$, the rate of change in smoothed value from one period to the next (i.e., the slope of the demand curve). The smoothed trend T_t is then calculated at period t using equation (7), which is a modification of the basic exponential smoothing equation—equation (5)—with the observed trend $(S_t - S_{t-1})$ used in place of A_t.

$$T_t = \beta(S_t - S_{t-1}) + (1 - \beta)T_{t-1} \tag{7}$$

In order to anticipate cash flows during the business start-up period, the commuter airline owners are interested in forecasting future weekly load factors. After observing the first two weeks of activity, you are asked to provide a forecast for week 3. The smoothed values, trend figures, and forecasts in Table 14.5 are calculated in a stepwise manner. For the first observation in a series, week 1 in this instance, the smoothed value S_1 is equal to the actual value A_1, and the trend T_1 is set equal to 0.00. The forecast for week 2 is calculated using equation (8). In this case: $F_2 = 31 + 0.00 = 31.00$.

$$F_{t+1} = S_t + T_t \tag{8}$$

To compute the figures for week 2 and a forecast for week 3, we will use $\alpha = 0.5$ and $\beta = 0.3$. First, the smoothed value S_2 for week 2 is calculated using equation (6):

$$S_2 = (0.5)(31) + (1 - 0.5)(31 + 0.00)$$
$$= 35.50$$

Now we calculate the trend for week 2 with equation (7):

$$T_2 = (0.3)(35.50 - 31.00) + (1 - 0.3)0.00$$
$$= 1.35$$

The final step is to make a forecast for week 3 according to equation (8):

$$F_3 = 35.5 + 1.35 = 36.85$$

When the actual data for the following weeks are received, similar calculations can be made for the smoothed value, the trend, the forecast, and the forecast error. For all the forecasts shown in Table 14.5, the MAD is 6.58, and the sum of the real forecast error values is 30.9. In Figure 14.3 the actual load factors are plotted against the forecasts, using exponential smoothing with a trend adjustment.

Exponential Smoothing with Seasonal Adjustment

When we wish to account for seasonal effects on a set of data, we can use another extension of simple exponential smoothing. In simplest terms, we first remove the seasonality from the data and then smooth the data as we have already learned; finally, we put the seasonality back in to determine a forecast.

We will apply this seasonal adjustment to the data in Table 14.6, which reports the number of passengers per month taking a ferry to a resort island in the Caribbean for the years 1990 and 1991. In general, we denote a cycle, L, as the length of one season. L may be any length of time, but frequently, as in this case, it is 12 months. Note that we must have actual data for at least one full season before we can begin to start making smoothing and forecasting calculations.

A *seasonality index* I_t is used to deseasonalize the data in a given cycle L. Initially, I_t is estimated by calculating a ratio of the actual value for period t, A_t, divided by the average value $\bar{A}$ for all periods in cycle L, as shown in equation (9).

$$I_t = \frac{A_t}{\bar{A}} \tag{9}$$

where $\bar{A} = (A_1 + A_2 + \cdots + A_L)/L$.

In our passenger ferry example, $\bar{A} = 1971.83$, and by substituting this value into equation (9), we can calculate the index I_t for each period in the first season of L periods. The resulting indices for the months of 1990, shown in column 5 of Table 14.6, are then used to deseasonalize the data for the corresponding months in 1991 according to equation (10), which is a minor modification of our basic exponential

FIGURE 14.3
Exponential smoothing with trend adjustment: commuter airline load factors ($\alpha = 0.5$, $\beta = 0.3$).

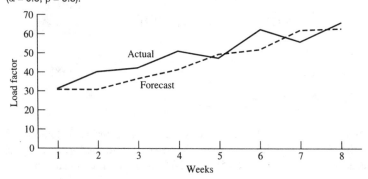

TABLE 14.6
EXPONENTIAL SMOOTHING WITH SEASONAL ADJUSTMENT
Ferry Passengers Taken to a Resort Island ($\alpha = 0.2$, $\gamma = 0.3$)

Period	t	Actual passengers A_t	Smoothed value S_t	Index I_t	Forecast F_t	$|A_t - F_t|$
			1990			
January	1	1651	. . . . .	0.837	. . . . .	
February	2	1305	. . . . .	0.662	. . . . .	
March	3	1617	. . . . .	0.820	. . . . .	
April	4	1721	. . . . .	0.873	. . . . .	
May	5	2015	. . . . .	1.022	. . . . .	
June	6	2297	. . . . .	1.165	. . . . .	
July	7	2606	. . . . .	1.322	. . . . .	
August	8	2687	. . . . .	1.363	. . . . .	
September	9	2292	. . . . .	1.162	. . . . .	
October	10	1981	. . . . .	1.005	. . . . .	
November	11	1696	. . . . .	0.860	. . . . .	
December	12	1794	1794.00	0.910	. . . . .	
			1991			
January	13	1806	1866.74	0.876	. . . . .	
February	14	1731	2016.35	0.721	1235.78	495.22
March	15	1733	2035.76	0.829	1653.41	79.57
April	16	1904	2064.81	0.888	1777.22	126.78
May	17	2036	2050.28	1.013	2110.24	74.24
June	18	2560	2079.71	1.185	2388.58	171.42
July	19	2679	2069.06	1.314	2749.38	70.38
August	20	2821	2069.19	1.363	2820.13	0.87
September	21	2359	2061.38	1.157	2404.40	45.40
October	22	2160	2078.95	1.015	2071.69	88.31
November	23	1802	2082.23	0.862	1787.90	14.10
December	24	1853	2073.04	0.905	1894.83	41.83
					MAD	100.68

smoothing equation—equation (5)—with A_t adjusted to account for seasonality using index I_{t-L}.

$$S_t = \alpha \frac{A_t}{I_{t-L}} + (1 - \alpha)S_{t-1} \tag{10}$$

For this example, the data for the 12 months in 1990 are used to give initial estimates of the seasonality indices. Therefore, we cannot begin to calculate new smoothed data until period 13 (January 1991). To begin the process, we assume that S_{12} equals A_{12}, as shown in Table 14.6 with a value of 1794. The smoothed value for January 1991 can now be calculated using equation (10), with $I_{t-L} = 0.837$ (i.e., the index I_t a year ago for January 1990) and $\alpha = 0.2$:

$$S_{13} = (0.2)\frac{1806}{0.837} + (1 - 0.2)1794$$

$$= 1866.74$$

The forecast for February (period $t + 1$) is then made by seasonalizing the smoothed value for January according to the following formula:

$$F_{t+1} = (S_t)(I_{t-L+1}) \tag{11}$$

Note that the seasonalizing factor I_{t-L+1} in this case is the index I_t for February 1990. Therefore, our forecast for February 1991 is

$$F_{14} = (1866.74)(0.662)$$
$$= 1235.78$$

If the seasonality indices are stable, forecasts based only on one cycle, L, will be reliable. If, however, the indices are not stable, they can be adjusted, or smoothed, as new data become available. After calculating the smoothed value S_t for an actual value A_t at the most recent period t, we can denote a new observation for a seasonality index at period t as (A_t/S_t). To apply the concept of exponential smoothing to the index, we use a new constant, gamma (γ), which is usually assigned a value between 0.1 and 0.5. The smoothed estimate of the seasonality index is then calculated from the following formula:

$$I_t = \gamma \frac{A_t}{S_t} + (1 - \gamma)I_{t-L} \tag{12}$$

We can now continue the calculations for 1991 in Table 14.6 by using equation (12) to update the seasonality indices for each month for future use. [Remember, in actual practice the smoothed values, indices, and forecasts for each period (month) in this new season of L periods would be calculated on a month-to-month basis as the most recent actual values became available.] According to equation (12), the new smoothed seasonality index for January 1991, I_{13}, using $\gamma = 0.3$ is

$$I_{13} = 0.3 \frac{1806}{1866.74} + (1 - 0.3)0.837$$

$$= 0.876$$

The mean absolute deviation (MAD) for February through December 1991 is 100.68. This indicates a very good fit of forecasts to actual data that exhibit a definite seasonality, but is it possible to make even more accurate forecasts?

Exponential Smoothing with Trend and Seasonal Adjustments

The answer to the question above is yes—sometimes. In some cases, adjusting only for trend or for seasonality will provide the current best estimate of the average, and at other times the forecast can be improved by considering all the factors together. We can include *both* trend and seasonal adjustments in exponential smoothing by weighting a *base* smoothed value with trend and seasonal indices to get a forecast for the following period. The appropriate equations follow:

$$S_t = \alpha \frac{A_t}{I_{t-L}} + (1 - \alpha)(S_{t-1} + T_{t-1}) \tag{13}$$

$$T_t = \beta(S_t - S_{t-1}) + (1 - \beta)T_{t-1} \tag{14}$$

$$I_t = \gamma \frac{A_t}{S_t} + (1 - \gamma)I_{t-L} \tag{15}$$

$$F_{t+1} = (S_t + T_t)I_{t-L+1} \tag{16}$$

The equations above can be applied to the data given in Table 14.7, and the resulting MAD of 159.89 for February through December 1991 tells us that in this case, we have not gained anything by adding a trend adjustment to the seasonal adjustment. Figure 14.4 demonstrates graphically the results of treating the actual data with a seasonal adjustment only and with both seasonal and trend adjustments.

FIGURE 14.4
Exponential smoothing with seasonal adjustment.

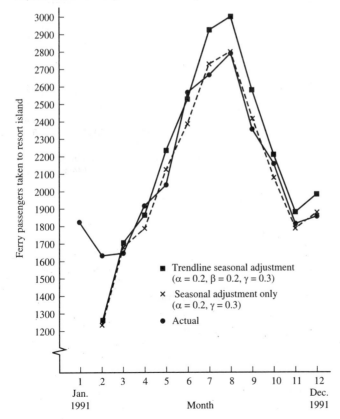

TABLE 14.7

EXPONENTIAL SMOOTHING WITH SEASONAL AND TREND ADJUSTMENTS

Ferry Passengers Taken to a Resort Island ($\alpha = 0.2$, $\beta = 0.2$, $\gamma = 0.3$)

Period	t	Actual passengers A_t	Smoothed value S_t	Trend T_t	Index I_t	Forecast F_t	$|A_t - F_t|$
			1990				
January	1	1651	. . . .	. . .	0.837	. . . .	
February	2	1305	. . . .	. . .	0.662	. . . .	
March	3	1617	. . . .	. . .	0.820	. . . .	
April	4	1721	. . . .	. . .	0.873	. . . .	
May	5	2015	. . . .	. . .	1.022	. . . .	
June	6	2297	. . . .	. . .	1.165	. . . .	
July	7	2606	. . . .	. . .	1.322	. . . .	
August	8	2687	. . . .	. . .	1.363	. . . .	
September	9	2292	. . . .	. . .	1.162	. . . .	
October	10	1981	. . . .	. . .	1.005	. . . .	
November	11	1696	. . . .	. . .	0.860	. . . .	
December	12	1794	1794.00	0.00	0.910	. . . .	
			1991				
January	13	1806	1866.59	14.52	0.876	. . . .	
February	14	1731	2027.99	43.89	0.719	1244.96	486.04
March	15	1733	2080.17	45.55	0.824	1699.05	33.95
April	16	1904	2136.87	47.78	0.878	1855.31	48.69
May	17	2036	2146.20	40.09	1.000	2232.48	196.48
June	18	2560	2188.55	40.54	1.166	2546.82	13.18
July	19	2679	2188.69	32.46	1.292	2946.00	267.00
August	20	2821	2190.96	26.42	1.340	3026.75	205.75
September	21	2359	2179.80	18.91	1.138	2577.42	218.42
October	22	2160	2188.97	16.96	0.999	2208.93	48.93
November	23	1802	2183.75	12.53	0.850	1897.35	95.35
December	24	1853	2164.36	6.14	0.894	1998.20	145.20
						MAD	159.89

Summary of Exponential Smoothing

Exponential smoothing is a relatively easy and straightforward way to make short-term forecasts. It has many attributes, including the following:

- All past data are considered in the smoothing process.
- Recent data are assigned more weight than older data.
- Only the most recent data are required to update a forecast.
- The model is easy to implement on a personal computer using spreadsheet software.
- Smoothing constants allow us to alter the rate at which the model responds to changes in the underlying pattern in the data.

SUMMARY

Decisions to embark on a new service concept often require subjective judgments about the future needs of customers. Subjective models like the Delphi method allow a panel of experts to defend their positions concerning the future, and through a number of iterations, they approach a consensus. Regression models have found application in service location analysis because of the need to account for several independent variables that contribute to demand generation. We ended our discussion of forecasting with an examination of time series models. Although the moving-average method is straightforward, we discovered that exponential smoothing has many superior qualities and has found wide acceptance in practice. Accounting for trends and seasonality is an important feature in forecasting service demand and is easily accommodated by means of exponential smoothing.

TOPICS FOR DISCUSSION

1. What characteristics of service organizations make forecast accuracy important?

2. For each of the three forecasting methods (time series, causal, and subjective), what costs are associated with the development and use of the forecast model? What costs are associated with forecast error?

3. The number of customers at a bank is likely to vary by the hour of the day and by the day of the month. What are the implications of this for choosing a forecasting model?

4. Compare N-period moving-average models with exponential smoothing models.

5. Suggest a number of independent variables for a regression model to predict the potential sales volume of a location for a retail store (e.g., a video rental store).

6. Suggest how the Delphi method can be incorporated into a cross-impact analysis.

EXERCISES

14.1 In September 1991, there were 1035 checking account customers at a neighborhood bank. The forecast for September (made in August) was for 1065 checking account customers. Use $\alpha = 0.1$ to update the forecast for October.

14.2. During the noon hour this past Wednesday at a fast-food restaurant, 72 hamburgers were sold. The smoothed value calculated the week before was 67. Update the forecast for next Wednesday, using simple exponential smoothing and $\alpha = 0.1$.

14.3. For the data in exercise 14.2, update the fast-food restaurant forecast if a trend value of 1.4 was calculated for the previous week. Use $\beta = 0.3$ to update the trend for this week, and determine the forecast for next Wednesday, using exponential smoothing with trend adjustment.

14.4. The demand for a certain drug in a hospital has been increasing. For the past six months we observed the following demand:

Month	Demand, units
January	15
February	18
March	22
April	23
May	27
June	26

Use a three-month moving average to make a forecast for July.

14.5. For the data in exercise 14.4, use $\alpha = 0.1$ to make a forecast for July.

14.6. For the data in exercise 14.4, use $\alpha = 0.1$ and $\beta = 0.2$ to make a forecast for July and August. Calculate the MAD for your January through June forecasts.

14.7. Prepare a spreadsheet model for the Saturday occupancy data in Table 14.4, and recalculate the forecasts, using $\alpha = 0.3$. What is the new MAD?

14.8. Prepare a spreadsheet model for the weekly load factor data in Table 14.5, and recalculate the forecasts, using $\alpha = 0.2$ and $\beta = 0.2$. Have you improved on the original MAD?

14.9. Prepare a spreadsheet model for the ferry passenger data in Table 14.6, and recalculate the forecasts, using $\alpha = 0.3$ and $\gamma = 0.2$. Has this change in the smoothing constants improved the MAD?

14.10. Prepare a spreadsheet model for the ferry passenger data in Table 14.6, and recalculate the forecasts, using $\alpha = 0.3$, $\beta = 0.1$, and $\gamma = 0.2$. Has this change in the smoothing constants improved the MAD?

CASE: OAK HOLLOW EVALUATION CENTER[3]

Oak Hollow Medical Evaluation Center is a nonprofit agency offering multidisciplinary diagnostic services to study children in the community who have disabilities or delays in development. The center can test each patient for physical, psychological, or social problems. Fees for services are based on an ability-to-pay schedule.

The evaluation center exists in a highly competitive environment. Many public-spirited organizations are competing for shrinking funds (Proposition 13 syndrome), and many groups, such as private physicians, private and school psychologists, and social service organizations, are also "competing" for the same patients.

As a result of the competitive situation that exists, the center finds itself in an increasingly vulnerable financial position.

Mr. Abel, the director of the center, is becoming increasingly concerned with the center's ability to attract adequate funding and serve community needs. Mr. Able must now develop an accurate estimate of the future patient load level,

---

[3]Prepared by Frank Krafka under the supervision of Professor James A. Fitzsimmons.

TABLE 14.8
ANNUAL NUMBER OF PATIENT TESTS PERFORMED*

Test	1990	1991	1992	1993	1994
Physical exam	390	468	509	490	582
Speech and hearing screening	102	124	180	148	204
Psychological testing	168	312	376	386	437
Social-worker interview	106	188	184	222	244

*All entering patients are given a physical examination. Patients are then scheduled for additional testing deemed appropriate.

TABLE 14.9
ANNUAL EXPENSES

Area	1990	1991	1992	1993	1994
Physical and neurological exams	$18,200	$24,960	$ 32,760	$ 31,500	$ 41,600
Speech and hearing tests	2,040	2,074	3,960	3,950	4,850
Psychological testing	6,720	12,480	16,450	16,870	20,202
Social work	3,320	3,948	4,416	5,550	7,592
Subtotal	$30,280	$43,462	$ 57,586	$ 57,870	$ 74,244
Other expenses	46,559	48,887	51,820	55,447	59,883
Total	$76,839	$92,349	$109,406	$113,317	$134,127

staffing requirements, and operating expenses as part of his effort to attract funding for the center. To this end, the director has approached an operations management professor at the local university for assistance in preparing a patient, staffing, and budget forecast for the coming year. The professor has asked you to aid her in this project. Tables 14.8 through 14.11 give you some pertinent information.

Assignments

1. Given the information available and your knowledge of different forecasting techniques, recommend a specific forecasting technique for the study. Consider the advantages and disadvantages of your preferred technique, and identify additional information, if any, that Mr. Abel would need.

2. Develop forecasts for patient, staffing, and budget levels for next year.

CASE: GNOMIAL FUNCTIONS, INC.[4]

Gnomial Functions, Inc. (GFI) is a medium-sized consulting firm in San Francisco that specializes in developing various forecasts of product demand, sales, consumption, or other information for its clients. To a lesser degree, it has also

[4]Prepared by Frank Krafka under the supervision of Professor James A. Fitzsimmons.

TABLE 14.10
MONTHLY PATIENT DEMAND, SEPTEMBER 1993–DECEMBER 1994

	Physical exam	Speech and hearing tests	Psychological testing	Social-worker interview
		1993		
September	54	16	42	24
October	67	21	54	31
November	74	22	48	33
December	29	9	23	13
		1994		
January	58	20	44	24
February	52	18	39	22
March	47	16	35	20
April	41	14	31	17
May	35	12	26	15
June	29	10	22	12
July	23	8	17	10
August	29	10	22	12
September	65	24	48	27
October	81	29	61	34
November	87	31	66	37
December	35	12	26	14

TABLE 14.11
CURRENT STAFFING LEVELS*

Physicians	2 part-time, 18 hours per week
Speech and hearing clinician	1 part-time, 20 hours per week
Psychologists	1 full-time, 38 hours per week
	1 part-time, 16 hours per week
Social worker	1 full-time, 40 hours per week

*The Oak Hollow Evaluation Center operates on a 50-week year.

developed ongoing models for internal use by client companies. When contacted by a potential client, GFI usually establishes a basic work agreement with the firm's top management that sets out the general goals of the end product, primary contact personnel in both firms, and an outline of the project's overall scope (including any necessary time constraints for intermediate and final completion and a rough price estimate for the contract). Following this step, a team of GFI personnel is assembled to determine the most appropriate forecasting technique and to develop a more detailed work program to be used as the basis for final contract negotiations. This team, which may vary in size according to the scope of the project and the client's needs, will perform the tasks established in the work program in conjunction with any personnel from the client firm who would be included in the team.

Recently, GFI was contacted by a rapidly growing regional firm that manufactures, sells, and installs active solar water-heating equipment for commercial and residential applications. DynaSol Industries has seen its sales increase by more than 200 percent during the past 18 months and wishes to obtain a reliable estimate of its sales during the next 18 months. The company management expects that sales should increase substantially because of competing energy costs, tax credit availability, and fundamental shifts in the attitudes of the regional population toward so-called exotic solar systems. The company also faces increasing competition within the burgeoning market. This situation requires major strategic decisions concerning the company's future. At the time when GFI was contacted, DynaSol had almost reached the manufacturing capacity of its present facility, and if it wishes to continue growing with the market, it will have to expand either by relocating to a new facility entirely or by developing a second manufacturing location. Each involves certain known costs, and each has its own advantages and disadvantages. The major unknown factors, as far as management is concerned, are the growth of the overall market for this type of product and how large a share the company would be able to capture.

Table 14.12 contains the preliminary information available to GFI on DynaSol's past sales.

TABLE 14.12

Month	DynaSol Industries sales, units	Sales, in thousands	Regional Market sales, units	Sales, in thousands
		1990		
September	24	$ 44.736	223	$ 396.048
October	28	52.192	228	404.928
November	31	59.517	230	408.480
December	32	61.437	231	422.564
		1991		
January	30	57.998	229	418.905
February	35	67.197	235	429.881
March	39	78.621	240	439.027
April	40	80.637	265	484.759
May	43	86.684	281	529.449
June	47	94.748	298	561.479
July	51	110.009	314	680.332
August	54	116.480	354	747.596
September	59	127.265	389	809.095
October	62	137.748	421	931.401
November	67	148.857	466	1001.356
December	69	153.300	501	1057.320
		1992		
January	74	161.121	529	1057.320
February	79	172.007	573	1145.264

Assignments

1. Given the information available and your knowledge of different forecasting techniques, you, as a team member, must develop a recommendation for utilizing a specific forecasting technique in the subsequent study. The final contract negotiations are pending, and so it is essential that you take into account the advantages and disadvantages of your preferred technique as they would apply to the problem at hand and point out any additional information you would like to have.

2. Assume that you are a member of DynaSol's small marketing department and that the contract negotiations with GFI have fallen through irrevocably. The company's top management has decided to use your expertise to develop a forecast for the next six months (and perhaps for the six-month period following that one as well), because it must have some information on which to base a decision to expand its operations. Develop such a forecast, and note, for the benefit of top management, any reservations or qualifications you feel are vital to its understanding and use of the information.

SELECTED BIBLIOGRAPHY

Box, G. E. P., and G. M. Jenkins: *Time Series Analysis: Forecasting and Control,* Holden-Day, Inc., San Francisco, 1970.

Brown, R. G.: *Smoothing, Forecasting and Prediction,* Prentice-Hall, Inc., Englewood Cliffs, N.J., 1963.

Chambers, J. C., S. K. Mullick, and D. D. Smith: "How to Choose the Right Forecasting Technique," *Harvard Business Review,* July–August 1971, pp. 45–74.

Chang, Yih-Long, and R. S. Sullivan: *QS: Quantitative Systems, Version 3.0,* Prentice-Hall, Inc., Englewood Cliffs, N.J., 1993.

Davis, C. H., and J. A. Fitzsimmons: "The Future of Nuclear Power in the United States," *Technological Forecasting and Social Change,* Elsevier Science Publishing Co., Inc., New York, vol. 40, no. 2, September 1991, pp. 151–164.

Kimes, S. E., and J. A. Fitzsimmons: "Selecting Profitable Hotel Sites at La Quinta Motor Inns," *Interfaces,* vol. 20, no. 2, March–April 1990, pp. 12–20.

Mabert, V. A.: "Forecast Modification Based upon Residual Analysis: A Case Study of Check Volume Estimation," *Decision Sciences,* vol. 9, no. 2, April 1978, pp. 285–296.

Wheelwright, S. C., and S. Makridakis: *Forecasting Methods for Management,* Wiley-Interscience, New York, 1973.

CHAPTER 15

QUEUING MODELS AND CAPACITY PLANNING

The capacity planning decision involves a tradeoff between the cost of providing service and the cost or inconvenience of customer waiting. The cost of service capacity is determined by the number of servers on duty, while customer inconvenience is measured by waiting time. Figure 15.1 illustrates this tradeoff, under the assumption that a monetary cost can be attributed to waiting. Increasing service capacity typically results in lower waiting costs and higher service costs. If the combined costs to the firm constitute our planning criterion, then an optimal service capacity minimizes these service-versus-waiting costs.

Xerox Corporation was faced with precisely such a dilemma when it introduced its Model 9200 Duplicating System.[1] On the one hand, its existing service and maintenance operation, which consisted of individual technical representatives serving individual territories, was no longer able to provide the level of service that gave the company its decisive competitive advantage. Compromising the level of service meant that customers would have to wait for service, which would translate, in this case, into lost revenue for the customer (and for Xerox indirectly). Xerox, consequently, turned to a queuing analysis to determine the best way to resolve its dilemma. Initial constraints, primarily involving human factors such as some loss of autonomy by the technical representatives and perceptions by the customer of less "personal" attention, led the company to consider establishing miniteams of service people who could provide faster service for more customers.

The cost to the Xerox customer above was straightforward because the Model 9200 was being used to replace a printer's previous offset system. Thus, a Xerox machine that was "down" meant lost income.

---

[1] W. H. Bleuel, "Management Science's Impact on Service Strategy," *Interfaces,* vol. 6, no. 1, November 1975, part 2, pp. 4–12.

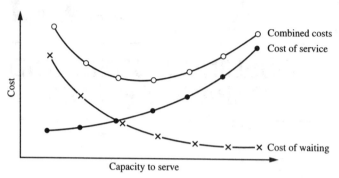

FIGURE 15.1
Economic tradeoff in capacity planning.

The problem Xerox faced at this point was to determine the appropriate number of members to assign to each team. The company used queuing analysis to minimize both customer waiting cost and Xerox service cost and arrived at an optimum result of three representatives per team.

The monetary cost of delaying a customer is usually more difficult to calculate than in the Xerox example, and sometimes it is impossible to determine. In a hospital, the cost of keeping a surgical team waiting for a pathologist's report could be the combined salaries of the team members plus the operating room cost. But the cost of keeping a patient waiting in a reception room for the physician is not easily calculated. Furthermore, as noted in Chapter 11, the circumstances affect the perception of waiting.

The tradeoff between customer waiting and service capacity can be seen in many everyday occurrences. For example, an emergency ambulance seldom is busy more than 30 percent of the time. Such low utilization is required in exchange for the ability to provide assistance on a moment's notice. Excess ambulance capacity is necessary because the implicit cost of waiting for this particular service may be exorbitant in terms of human lives. However, the usual scene at a post office is one of lines of impatient people waiting for service. Here a judgment has been made that the implicit cost of waiting is not critical, certainly not life-threatening, and besides, customers have few alternatives. Another result of the postal service strategy is harried employees, who may not be able to provide the best possible service under the pressure of demanding customers! The desire of customers to avoid waiting has not been lost on the Travis County, Texas, Tax Collector/Assessor's office. For an extra dollar, an automobile owner has the option of renewing his or her annual auto registration by mail, thus avoiding the necessity of appearing in person.

CHAPTER PREVIEW

It is necessary to predict the degree of customer waiting associated with different levels of capacity. A number of analytical queuing models are presented that can be used to make these waiting time predictions. The models are analytical in that for each case, a number of equations have been derived. Given a minimal amount of data—in particular, the mean arrival rate and mean service rate—the equations can generate characteristics of the system, such as the average time a customer should expect to wait. From these calculations, capacity planning decisions, such as determining the size of a parking lot, can be made, using a number of different criteria. In addition, the queuing models help explain the queuing phenomenon. For example, the models can predict the results of adding servers to a multiple-server system, as shown in the Xerox case above, or they can show the effect of reducing service time variation on waiting time.

Equations for selected queuing models are listed at the end of this chapter. One should be neither dismayed nor awed by these models. They are merely useful tools for the effective management of services and can be used easily, even scratched out "on the spot" on the back of an envelope, often to the amazement of those looking to you for answers to their situations.

ANALYTICAL QUEUING MODELS

On the basis of our discussion of queues in Chapter 11, it is evident that a large number of different queuing models exist. A popular system proposed by D. G. Kendall classifies parallel-server queuing models and uses the following notation, in which three features are identified: *A/B/C*. *A* represents the distribution of time between arrivals, *B* describes the distribution of service times, and *C* is the number of parallel servers. The descriptive symbols used for the arrival and service distributions include the following:

M = exponential interarrival or service time distribution (or the equivalent Poisson distribution of arrival or service rate).

D = deterministic interarrival or service time.

E_k = Erlang distribution with shape parameter k. (If $k = 1$, then Erlang is equivalent to exponential, and if $k = \infty$, then Erlang is equivalent to deterministic.)

G = general distribution (e.g., normal, uniform, or any empirical distribution).

Thus, $M/M/1$ designates a single-server queuing model with Poisson arrival rate and exponential service time distribution. The Kendall notation will be used to define the class to which a queuing model belongs. Further considerations will be noted that are particular to the model in question. For each queuing model, the assumptions underlying its derivation will be noted. The usefulness of an analytical model for a particular situation is limited by its assumptions. If the assumptions are invalid for a particular application, then one typically resorts to a computer simulation approach.

A final consideration involves the concepts of *transient state* and *steady state*. A system is in a transient state when the values of the operating characteristics depend on time. In a steady state, the system characteristics are independent of time, and the system is considered in statistical equilibrium. System characteristics are usually transient during the early stages of operation because of their dependence on initial conditions. For example, compare the initial conditions for a department store at opening time on a normal business day and on an end-of-year sale day, when crowds overwhelm clerks. The number in queue will initially be quite large, but given a long enough period of time, the system will eventually settle down. Once normal conditions have been reached, a statistical equilibrium is achieved in which the number in queue assumes a distribution independent of the starting condition. All the queuing model equations given at the end of the chapter assume that a steady state has been reached. As noted in Chapter 11, most service systems operate in a dynamic environment, with arrival rates sometimes changing every hour; thus, a steady state is seldom achieved. However, steady-state models can provide useful system performance projections for long-range capacity planning decisions.

Applications of these queuing models using both the equations and computer solutions will be illustrated in decision-making settings. All the computer solutions shown are output reports generated by using a popular software package for personal computers called *QS: Quantitative Systems, Version 3.0*.[2] The symbols used in these models and their definitions are listed below:

n = number of customers in the system

λ = [lambda] mean arrival rate (e.g., customer arrivals per hour)

μ = [mu] mean service rate per busy server (e.g., service capacity in customers per hour)

ρ = [rho] traffic intensity (λ / μ)

N = maximum number of customers allowed in the system

c = number of servers

P_n = probability of exactly n customers in the system

L_s = mean number of customers in the system

L_q = mean number of customers in queue

L_b = mean number of customers in queue for a busy system

W_s = mean time customer spends in the system

W_q = mean time customer spends in the queue

W_b = mean time customer spends in queue for a busy system

Standard *M/M/1* Model

Every queuing model requires specific assumptions with respect to the queuing system features discussed in Chapter 11 (i.e., calling population, arrival process, queue configuration, queue discipline, and service process). The application of any queuing model, therefore, should include validation with respect to these assumptions. The derivation of the standard *M/M/1* model requires the following set of assumptions about the queuing system:

1. *Calling population.* An infinite or very large population of callers arriving. The callers are independent of each other and not influenced by the queuing system (e.g., an appointment is not required).

[2]Yih-Long Chang and R. S. Sullivan, *QS: Quantitative Systems, Version 3.0*, Prentice-Hall, Englewood Cliffs, N.J., 1993.

2. *Arrival process.* Negative exponential distribution of interarrival times or Poisson distribution of arrival rate.

3. *Queue configuration.* Single waiting line with no restrictions on length and no balking or reneging.

4. *Queue discipline.* First-come, first-served (FCFS).

5. *Service process.* One server with negative exponential distribution of service times.

The selected equations given at the end of the chapter can be used to calculate performance characteristics on the basis of only the mean arrival rate λ and the mean service rate per server μ. These equations clearly indicate why the mean arrival rate (λ) must always be *less* than the mean service rate (μ) for a single-server model. If this condition were not true and λ were equal to μ, the mean values for the operating characteristics would be undefined because all the equations for mean values have the denominator ($\mu - \lambda$). The system would theoretically never reach a steady state. In general, the system's capacity to serve, represented by $c\mu$ (number of servers times service rate per server), must always exceed the demand rate λ.

Example 15.1: Boat Ramp

Lake Travis has one launching ramp near the dam for people who trailer their small boats to the recreational site. A study of cars arriving with boats in tow indicates a Poisson distribution with a mean rate of $\lambda = 6$ boats per hour during the morning launch. A test of the data collected on launch times suggests that an exponential distribution with a mean of 6 minutes per boat (equivalent service rate $\mu = 10$ boats launched per hour) is a good fit. If the other assumptions for an *M/M/*1 model apply (infinite calling population, no queue length restrictions, no balking or reneging, and FCFS queue discipline), then the equations found at the end of the chapter (and repeated below) may be used to calculate the system characteristics.

Probability that an arriving customer waits:

$$P(n > 0) = \rho = \frac{\lambda}{\mu} = 0.6 \qquad (I.2)$$

Probability of finding the ramp idle:

$$P_0 = 1 - \rho = 0.4 \qquad (I.1)$$

Mean number of boats in the system:

$$L_s = \frac{\lambda}{\mu - \lambda} = \frac{6}{10 - 6} = 1.5 \text{ boats} \qquad (I.4)$$

Mean number of boats in queue:

$$L_q = \frac{\rho\lambda}{\mu - \lambda} = \frac{(.6)(6)}{10 - 6} = 0.9 \text{ boat} \tag{I.5}$$

Mean time in system:

$$W_s = \frac{1}{\mu - \lambda} = \frac{1}{10 - 6} = 0.25 \text{ h (15 min)} \tag{I.7}$$

Mean time in the queue:

$$W_q = \frac{\rho}{\mu - \lambda} = \frac{.6}{10 - 6} = 0.15 \text{ h (9 min)} \tag{I.8}$$

These calculations are confirmed by the *QS: Quantitative Systems, Version 3.0* computer solution shown in the sidebar.

From our calculations we find that the boat ramp is busy 60 percent of the time. Thus, arrivals can expect immediate access to the ramp without delay 40 percent of the time, or when the ramp is idle. The calculations are internally consistent because the mean time in system (W_s) of 15 minutes is the sum of the mean time in queue (W_q) of 9 minutes and the mean service time of 6 minutes. Arrivals can expect to find the number in the system (L_s) to be 1.5 boats and the expected number in queue (L_q) to be 0.9 boat. The expected number of boats in queue plus the expected number being launched should add up to the expected number of boats in the system. However, the expected

---

FINAL SOLUTION FOR BOAT RAMP

M/M/1
WITH $\lambda = 6$ CUSTOMERS PER HOUR AND $\mu = 10$ CUSTOMERS PER HOUR

Overall system effective arrival rate = 6.000000 per hour
Overall system effective service rate = 6.000000 per hour
Overall system effective utilization factor = 0.600000
Average number of customers in the system (Ls) = 1.500000
Average number of customers in the queue (Lq) = 0.900000
Average time a customer in the system (Ws) = 0.250000 hour
Average time a customer in the queue (Wq) = 0.150000 hour
The probability that all servers are idle (P0) = 0.400000
The probability an arriving customer waits (PW) = 0.600000

Probability of *n* customers in the system

P(0) = 0.40000   P(1) = 0.24000   P(2) = 0.14400   P(3) = 0.08640
P(4) = 0.05184

$$\sum_{i=0}^{4} P(i) = 0.922240$$

---

number of boats being launched is not 1, the number of servers, but instead is calculated as follows:

$$\text{Expected number} \atop \text{being served} = \text{expected number} \atop \text{when idle} + \text{expected number} \atop \text{when busy}$$

$$= P_0(0) + P(n > 0)(1)$$
$$= (1 - \rho)(0) + \rho(1)$$
$$= \rho$$

Adding $\rho = 0.6$ person in the process of launching a boat and 0.9 boat on the average in queue, we get the expected 1.5 boats in the system.

Note that the number of customers in the system, n, is a random variable with a probability distribution given by equation (I.3), which is listed at the end of the chapter and repeated below in different form:

$$P_n = (1 - \rho)\rho^n \tag{I.3}$$

The number of customers in the system can also be used to identify states of the system. For example, when $n = 0$, the system is idle; for $n = 1$, the server is busy, but no queue exists; and for $n = 2$, the server is busy and a queue of 1 has formed. The probability distribution for n can be very useful for determining the size of a waiting room (number of chairs) required to accommodate arriving customers with a certain probability of assurance that each will find a vacant chair.

For the boat ramp example, let us determine the number of parking spaces needed to ensure that 90 percent of the time, a person arriving at the boat ramp will find a space to park while waiting to launch. Using the probability distribution for system states repeatedly for increasing values of n, we accumulate the system state probabilities until 90 percent assurance is exceeded. Table 15.1 and our computer solution in the sidebar above contain these calculations and indicate that a system state of $n = 4$ or less will occur 92 percent of the time. This suggests that room for four boat trailers should be provided because 92 percent of the time, arrivals will find three (four minus the one being served) or fewer people waiting in queue to launch.

TABLE 15.1
DETERMINING REQUIRED NUMBER OF PARKING SPACES

n	P_n	$P(\text{number of customers} \leq n)$
0	$(0.4)(0.6)^0 = 0.4$	0.4
1	$(0.4)(0.6)^1 = 0.24$	0.64
2	$(0.4)(0.6)^2 = 0.144$	0.784
3	$(0.4)(0.6)^3 = 0.0864$	0.8704
4	$(0.4)(0.6)^4 = 0.05184$	0.92224

Finite-Queue $M/M/1$ Model

A modification of the standard $M/M/1$ model may be made by introducing a restriction on the allowable number of customers in the system. Suppose that N represents the maximum number of customers allowed in the system or, in a single-server model, that $N - 1$ indicates the maximum number of customers in the queue. Thus, if a customer arrives at a point in time when N customers are already in the system, then the arrival departs without seeking service. An example of this type of finite queue is a telephone exchange in which callers are put on hold until all the trunk lines are in use; then any further callers receive a busy signal. Except for this one characteristic of finite capacity, all the assumptions of the standard $M/M/1$ model still hold. Note that the traffic intensity ρ can now exceed unity. Furthermore, P_N represents the probability of not joining the system, and λP_N is the expected number of customers lost.

This particular model is very useful in estimating expected lost sales due to an inadequate waiting area or an excessive queue length. In the boat ramp example, assume that the waiting area can accommodate only two boat trailers; thus, $N = 3$ for the system. Using equations (II.1) and (II.3) at the end of the chapter and repeated below, we can calculate the probabilities of 0, 1, 2, and 3 customers being in the system when $N = 3$ and $\rho = 0.6$.

$$P_0 = \frac{1 - \rho}{1 - \rho^{N+1}} \qquad \text{for } \lambda \neq \mu \tag{II.1}$$

$$P_n = P_0 \rho^n \qquad \text{for } n \leq N \tag{II.3}$$

n	Calculation	P_n
0	$\dfrac{1 - 0.6}{1 - 0.6^4}(0.6)^0$	0.46
1	$(0.46)(0.6)^1$	0.27
2	$(0.46)(0.6)^2$	0.17
3	$(0.46)(0.6)^3$	0.10
		1.00

Notice that the above distribution totals 1.00, which indicates that we have accounted for all possible system states. System state $n = 3$ occurs 10 percent of the time. With an arrival rate of 6 people per hour, 0.6 person per hour (6×0.10) will find inadequate waiting space and look elsewhere for a launching site. Using equation (II.4), repeated below, we can calculate the expected number in the system (L_s): 0.9. This figure is much smaller than the figure in the unlimited-queue case because, on the average, only 90 percent of the arrivals are processed.

$$L_s = \frac{\rho}{1 - \rho} - \frac{(N + 1)\rho^{N+1}}{1 - \rho^{N+1}} \qquad \text{for } \lambda \neq \mu \qquad \text{(II.4)}$$

$$= \frac{0.6}{1 - 0.6} - \frac{4(0.6)^4}{1 - (0.6)^4}$$

$$= 1.5 - 0.6 = 0.9$$

M/G/1 Model

For this model, any general service time distribution with mean $E(t)$ and variance $V(t)$ may be used. The condition that ρ be less than 1 still applies for the steady state, where ρ now equals $\lambda E(t)$. Except for the generality of the service time distribution, all the assumptions for the standard $M/M/1$ model apply. Unfortunately, an equation does not exist for determining the system state probabilities. However, the list of equations at the end of the chapter does contain equations for L_s, L_q, W_s, and W_q. Equation (III.2) is repeated below because the appearance of the service time variance term $V(t)$ provides some interesting insights.

$$L_q = \frac{\rho^2 + \lambda^2 V(t)}{2(1 - \rho)} \qquad \text{(III.2)}$$

Clearly, the expected number of customers waiting for service is directly related to the variability of service times. This suggests that customer waiting can be reduced by controlling the variability in service times. For example, the limited menu of fast-food restaurants contributes to their success because the reduction in the variety of meals they offer allows for standardization of service.

Recall from Chapter 11 that the variance of the exponential distribution is $1/\mu^2$, and notice that substituting this value for $V(t)$ in equation (III.2) yields $L_q = \rho^2/(1 - \rho)$, which is equivalent to equation (I.5) for the standard $M/M/1$ model. Now consider the $M/D/1$ model, with a deterministic service time and zero variance. Again, according to equation (III.2), when $V(t) = 0$, then $L_q = \rho^2/[2(1 - \rho)]$. Thus, one-half of the congestion measured by L_q is explained by the variation in service times. This implies that the variability in time between arrivals accounts for the other half of the congestion. Thus, considerable potential exists for reducing congestion simply by using appointments or reservations to control the variability in arrivals. Congestion in a queuing system is caused equally by variability in service times and in interarrival times, and so strategies for controlling congestion should address both sources.

Standard M/M/c Model

The assumptions for this model are the same as those for the standard $M/M/1$ model with the stipulation that service rates across channels be independent and equal; that is, all servers are considered identical. As before, $\rho = \lambda/\mu$; however, now ρ must be less than c, the number of servers, in order for steady-state results

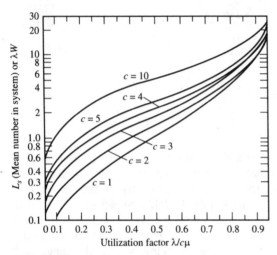

FIGURE 15.2
M/M/c model curves for L_s.

to occur. If we define the system utilization factor as $\lambda/c\mu$, then for any system in a steady state, the utilization factor must range between 0 and 1. Figure 15.2 illustrates the characteristic curves for L_s as a function of the utilization factor and c, the number of parallel servers. These curves graphically demonstrate the excessive congestion that occurs as one attempts to gain full utilization of service capacity.

The curves can also be used to demonstrate the disproportional gain that occurs when congestion is reduced by adding parallel servers. For example, consider a single-server system ($c = 1$) with a utilization factor of 0.8. From Figure 15.2, the value of L_s is 4. By adding another identical server, a two-channel system is created, and the utilization factor is reduced by one-half to 0.4. Figure 15.2 gives $L_s \approx 1$ [actually, $L_s = 0.95$, from equation IV.4]. A 400 percent reduction in congestion is achieved just by doubling the number of servers.

Now, instead of creating a two-channel system, just double the service rate of the single-server system and thus reduce the utilization factor to 0.4. Figure 15.2 gives $L_s \approx 0.67$ for this superserver system. However, this additional gain in reducing L_s is obtained at the cost of increasing the expected number in queue (from $L_q = 0.15$ to 0.27), as seen in Table 15.2. This is not surprising, because a single-server system would require more people to wait in line. In a multiple-server system of equal capacity, more people are able to be in service; thus, fewer wait in line. Therefore, the decision to use one superserver or the equivalent capacity with several servers in parallel depends on the concern for expected waiting time in queue (L_q/λ) or expected time in system (L_s/λ). As noted in Chapter 11 in our discussion of the psychology of waiting, a concern for reducing the waiting time in queue is usually advisable, particularly if people must physically wait in line. Furthermore, once service begins, the customer's attitude toward time changes

TABLE 15.2
EFFECTS OF DOUBLING SERVICE CAPACITY

System characteristic	Single-server baseline system	Two-server system	Single-superserver system
ρ	0.8	0.8	0.4
$(\lambda/c\mu)^*$	0.8	0.4	0.4
L_s	4.0	0.95	0.67
L_q	3.2	0.15	0.27

*Utilization factor.

because now the customer is the center of attention. However, the concept of using one large computer system to serve an entire university community is often justified because short turnaround time (time in system) and large memory are of primary importance.

Consolidating the entire service capacity into one superserver is one approach to achieving economies of scale in services. Another approach is the concept of pooling services. Pooling is accomplished by gathering together independent servers at one central location to form a single service facility with multiple servers.

Example 15.2: The Secretarial Pool

A small business school has assigned a secretary to each of its four departments: accounting, finance, marketing, and management. The secretaries type class materials and correspondence only for their own departmental faculty. The dean has received complaints from the faculty, particularly from the accounting faculty, about delays in getting work accomplished. The dean assigns an assistant to collect data on arrival rates and service times. After analyzing the data, the assistant reports that secretarial work arrives with a Poisson distribution at an average rate of $\lambda = 2$ requests per hour for all departments except accounting, which has an average rate of $\lambda = 3$ requests per hour. The average time to complete a piece of work is 15 minutes, regardless of its source, and the service times are exponentially distributed.

Because of budgeting limitations, no additional secretaries can be hired. However, the dean believes that service could be improved if all the secretaries were pooled and instructed to receive work from the entire business school faculty. All work requests would be received at one central location and processed on a first-come, first-served basis by the first secretary who became available, regardless of departmental affiliation. Before proposing the plan to the faculty, the dean asks the assistant who collected the data to analyze the performance of the existing system and compare it with the pooling alternative.

The present system is essentially four $M/M/1$ independent, single-channel queuing systems, each with a service rate of $\mu = 4$ requests per hour. The appropriate measure of system performance is the expected time in the system—or turnaround time, from the faculty viewpoint. The difference in arrival rates should explain why the accounting faculty is particularly concerned about delays. Using the $M/M/1$ equation $W_s = 1/(\mu - \lambda)$, we find for the present system of independent departmental secretaries that accounting faculty members experience an average turnaround time of $W_s = 1/(4 - 3) = 1.0$ hour, or 60 minutes, and the faculty members in the other departments experience an average turnaround time of $W_s = 1/(4 - 2) = 0.5$ hour, or 30 minutes.

The proposal to pool the secretarial staff creates a multiple-channel, single-queue system, or an $M/M/4$ system in this case. The arrival rate is the combined arrivals $(2 + 2 + 2 + 3)$ from all departments, or $\lambda = 9$ requests per hour. Equation (IV.1), repeated below with $c = 4$ and $\rho = 9/4$, is used to calculate the value of P_0:

$$P_0 = \frac{1}{\left(\displaystyle\sum_{i=0}^{c-1} \frac{\rho^i}{i!}\right) + \dfrac{\rho^c}{c!(1 - \rho/c)}} \tag{IV.1}$$

$$P_0 = \frac{1}{\dfrac{(9/4)^0}{0!} + \dfrac{(9/4)^1}{1!} + \dfrac{(9/4)^2}{2!} + \dfrac{(9/4)^3}{3!} + \dfrac{(9/4)^4}{4!(1 - 9/16)}}$$

$$= \frac{1}{1 + 9/4 + \dfrac{81/16}{2} + \dfrac{729/64}{6} + \dfrac{6561/256}{24(7/16)}}$$

$$= \frac{1}{7.68 + 2.44}$$

$$= 0.098$$

Equation (IV.4), repeated below, is used to calculate the value of L_s:

$$L_s = \frac{\rho^{c+1}}{(c-1)!(c-\rho)^2} P_0 + \rho \tag{IV.4}$$

$$= \frac{(9/4)^5}{(4-1)!(4-9/4)^2} (0.098) + 9/4$$

$$= \frac{59{,}049/1024}{6(1.75)^2} (0.098) + 2.25$$

$$= 0.31 + 2.25$$

$$= 2.56$$

$$W_s = \frac{L_s}{\lambda} = \frac{2.56}{9} = 0.28 \text{ hour, or 17 minutes}$$

The substantial reduction in expected turnaround time from 30 minutes (60 minutes for the accounting faculty) to 17 minutes should easily win faculty approval.

The benefits from pooling are achieved by better utilization of idle secretaries. Under the departmental system, four independent queues existed, which allowed situations to develop where a secretary in one department could be burdened with a long waiting line of work while a secretary in another department was idle. If a waiting request could be transferred to the idle secretary, then it would be immediately processed. Switching to a single queue avoids the utilization problem by not allowing a secretary to become idle until the waiting line of requests is empty.

Because the calculations for the *M/M/c* model are so tedious, we typically use the *QS: Quantitative Systems, Version 3.0* computer software to solve the model. The computer solution to the secretarial pool example is shown in the sidebar.

The success of pooling service resources comes from realizing that congestion results from variation in the rate of arrivals and variation in service times. If a total systems perspective of the process is taken, temporary idleness at one location can be used to reduce congestion at another location that has been caused by a temporary surge in demand or time-consuming requests. Furthermore, server

---

FINAL SOLUTION FOR SECRETARIAL POOL

M/M/4

WITH $\lambda = 9$ CUSTOMERS PER HOUR and $\mu = 4$ CUSTOMERS PER HOUR

Overall system effective arrival rate = 8.999999 per hour
Overall system effective service rate = 8.999999 per hour
Overall system effective utilization factor = 0.562500
Average number of customers in the system (Ls) = 2.560085
Average number of customers in the queue (Lq) = 0.310086
Average time a customer in the system (Ws) = 0.284454 hour
Average time a customer in the queue (Wq) = 0.034454 hour
The probability that all servers are idle (P0) = 0.098809
The probability an arriving customer waits (Pw) = 0.241178

Probability of *n* customers in the system

P(0) = 0.09881	P(1) = 0.22232	P(2) = 0.25011	P(3) = 0.18758
P(4) = 0.10552	P(5) = 0.05935	P(6) = 0.03339	P(7) = 0.01878
P(8) = 0.01056	P(9) = 0.00594	P(10) = 0.00334	

$$\sum_{i=0}^{10} P(i) = 0.995703$$

idleness that can be put to use but is not represents lost service capacity and results in a deterioration of service quality, as measured by customer waiting. The concept of pooling need not apply only to servers who are at different locations. The common practice in banks and post offices of having customers form a single queue rather than line up in front of the individual windows represents an application of the pooling concept. Theoretically, the average waiting time is reduced from that of multiple queues; however, the single long line may give arriving customers the impression of long waits. This is the reason McDonald's gave for abandoning the idea: it was feared that customers would balk upon seeing a long line.

Pooling service resources at one location should be undertaken with some caution if customers must travel to the facility. In this case, the expected travel time to the facility should be included with the expected waiting time in queue when the proposal is evaluated. For emergency services, dispersing the servers throughout the service area is generally preferred to assigning all services to one central location. An emergency ambulance system is a particularly good example of this need for physically dispersed servers in order to minimize response time.

Finite-Queue *M/M/c* Model

This model is similar to the finite-queue *M/M/*1 model with the exception that N, the maximum number in the system, must be equal to or greater than c, the number of servers. An arriving customer is rejected if the number in the system is equal to N or the length of the queue is $N - c$. All the other assumptions for the standard *M/M/c* model hold, except that ρ can now exceed c. Because excess customers are rejected, the system can reach a steady state, even when the capacity to serve is inadequate to meet total demand (i.e., $\lambda > c\mu$).

An interesting variation on this model is the no-queue situation, which occurs when no possibility exists for a customer to wait, because a waiting area is not provided. This situation can be modeled as a finite-queue system with $N = c$. A parking lot is an illustration of this no-queue situation. If we consider each parking space as a server, then at the point when the parking lot is completely full, an opportunity for further service no longer exists, and future arrivals must be rejected. If c equals the number of parking spaces, then the parking lot system can be modeled as a no-queue variation of the finite-queue *M/M/c* model.

General Self-Service *M/G/∞* Model

If there are an infinite number of servers in a multiple-server system or if arrivals serve themselves, a situation is created where no arriving customer must wait for service. This, of course, describes exactly the concept that has made the modern supermarket so popular. At least during the shopping portion (excluding check-out), customers do not experience waiting. The number of customers in the process of shopping does vary because of random arrivals and differing service times. The probability distribution of the number of customers in the system can be calculated by means of equation (VI.1), repeated below. Note that this distribution for P_n is, in fact, Poisson, with the mean, or L_s, equal to ρ. Furthermore, this model is not restricted to an exponential distribution of service times.

$$P_n = \frac{e^{-\rho}}{n!}\, \rho^n \qquad \text{where } L_s = \rho \qquad\qquad \text{(VI.1)}$$

The model is also useful as an approximation to describe circumstances where waiting may occur, but only rarely, as in emergency ambulance services. Using the Poisson distribution of the number of customers in the system, we can calculate the number of servers required to ensure that the probability of someone waiting is quite small.

Example 15.3: Supermarket

The typical supermarket can be viewed as two queuing systems in tandem. The arriving customer secures a shopping cart and proceeds to serve himself or herself by picking items from the shelves. Upon completing this task, the shopper joins a single queue (a new idea to reduce waiting caused by multiple queues) behind the checkout registers.

The checker tallies the bill, makes change, and sacks the groceries. The shopper then exits the system, perhaps with the assistance of a carryout person. T. L. Saaty's observation that departures from the standard $M/M/c$ queuing system are also Poisson-distributed suggests that the supermarket system can be analyzed as two independent systems in series.[3] The first is a self-service, or $M/M/\infty$, system, and the second (at the cash registers) is an $M/M/c$ system. Observation of customer behavior indicates that arrivals are Poisson-distributed, with a rate of 30 per hour, and shopping is completed in 20 minutes on the average, with exponential distribution. The shoppers then join the single queue behind the three checkout registers and wait until a register becomes available. The checkout process requires 5 minutes on the average, with exponential distribution.

For the shopping experience the $M/M/\infty$ model applies, with $\rho = 30/3$; thus $L_s = 10$ customers on the average engaged in the shopping activity. Using the *QS: Quantitative Systems, Version 3.0* software, we solve the $M/M/3$ checkout system with $\lambda = 30$ and $\mu = 12$. As shown in the sidebar, this yields $L_s = 6$ customers on the average in the checkout area. Thus, on the average there are 16 shoppers in the store. The expected time a customer spends in the supermarket is 20 minutes shopping plus 12 minutes (0.2 hour) checking out, for a total of 32 minutes.

GENERAL RELATIONSHIPS BETWEEN SYSTEM CHARACTERISTICS

In concluding the discussion of queuing models, it is necessary to point out that there are some general relationships between the average system characteristics that exist across all models. The first two relationships are definitional in nature.

---

[3]T. L. Saaty, *Elements of Queuing Theory with Applications,* McGraw-Hill, New York, 1961.

FINAL SOLUTION FOR SUPERMARKET

M/M/3

WITH $\lambda = 30$ CUSTOMERS PER HOUR AND $\mu = 12$ CUSTOMERS PER HOUR

Overall system effective arrival rate = 30.0000 per hour
Overall system effective service rate = 30.0000 per hour
Overall system effective utilization factor = 0.833333
Average number of customers in the system (Ls) = 6.011234
Average number of customers in the queue (Lq) = 3.511236
Average time a customer in the system (Ws) = 0.200375 hour
Average time a customer in the queue (Wq) = 0.117041 hour
The probability that all servers are idle (P0) = 0.044944
The probability an arriving customer waits (Pw) = 0.702247

Probability of n customers in the system

P(0) = 0.04494	P(1) = 0.11236	P(2) = 0.14045	P(3) = 0.11704
P(4) = 0.09753	P(5) = 0.08128	P(6) = 0.06773	P(7) = 0.05644
P(8) = 0.04704	P(9) = 0.03920	P(10) = 0.03266	

$$\sum_{i=0}^{10} P(i) = 0.836680$$

First, the expected number in the system should equal the expected number in queue plus the expected number in service, or

$$L_s = L_q + E \text{ (number in service)} \qquad (1)$$

Note that E (number in service) is not the number of servers; it equals ρ for all models except the finite-queue case.

Second, the expected time in the system should equal the expected time in queue plus the expected time in service, or

$$W_s = W_q + \frac{1}{\mu} \qquad (2)$$

where $1/\mu$ is the reciprocal of the service rate.

The characteristics for a busy system are conditional values based on the probability that the system is busy, or $P(n \geq c)$. Thus, the expected number in queue for a busy system is simply the expected number under all system states divided by the probability of the system being busy, or

$$L_b = \frac{L_q}{P(n \geq c)} \qquad (3)$$

Similarly, the expected waiting time in queue for a busy system is

$$W_b = \frac{W_q}{P(n \geq c)} \tag{4}$$

Furthermore, it has been shown that the following relationship exists between the expected number in the system and the expected time in the system:[4]

$$W_s = \frac{1}{\lambda} L_s \tag{5}$$

And the following relationship between the expected number in queue and the expected waiting time has also been shown to exist:

$$W_q = \frac{1}{\lambda} L_q \tag{6}$$

When equations (5) and (6) are applied for systems with a finite queue, an effective arrival rate must be used for λ. For a system with a finite queue, the effective arrival rate is $\lambda(1 - P_N)$.

These relationships are very useful because they permit derivation of all the average characteristics of a system from the knowledge of one characteristic obtained by analysis or by the collection of data on actual system performance.

CAPACITY PLANNING CRITERIA

Queuing theory indicates that in the long run, the capacity to serve must exceed the demand for service. If it does not meet that criterion, at least one of the following adjustments must occur:

1. Excessive waiting by customers will result in some reneging (i.e., a customer leaves the queue before being served) and thus in some reduction of demand.

2. Excessive waiting, if known or observed by potential customers, will cause them to reconsider their need for service and will reduce demand.

3. Under the pressure of long waiting lines, the servers may speed up, spend less time with each customer, and thus increase service capacity. However, a gracious and leisurely manner now becomes curt and impersonal.

4. Sustained pressure to hurry may result in eliminating time-consuming features and performing the bare minimum; thus, service capacity is increased.

These uncontrolled situations result from inadequate service capacity, which can be avoided through rational capacity planning.

Several approaches to capacity planning are explored on the basis of different criteria for evaluating service system performance. Determining the desired level of service capacity implies a tradeoff between the cost of service and the cost of customer waiting, as suggested by Figure 15.1. Thus, capacity analysis will utilize the queuing models to predict customer waiting for various levels of service.

[4] J. D. C. Little, "A Proof of the Queuing Formula: $L = \lambda W$," *Operations Research*, vol. 9, no. 3, May–June 1961, pp. 383–387. Also W. S. Jewell, "A Simple Proof of $L = \lambda W$," *Operations Research*, vol. 15, no. 6, November–December 1967, pp. 1109–1116, and S. Stidham, Jr., "A Last Word on $L = \lambda W$," *Operations Research*, vol. 22, no. 2, March–April 1974, pp. 417–421.

Average Consumer Waiting Time

This criterion for capacity planning can be appropriate in several circumstances. For example, a restaurant owner may wish to promote liquor sales in the bar and therefore stipulates that customers must be kept waiting for a table five minutes on the average. It has been suggested that because a watch face is typically divided into five-minute increments, people waiting in line may not realize how long they have been waiting until at least five minutes have passed. Therefore, in designing a drive-in bank facility, it may be advisable to have customers wait no more than five minutes on the average for service. In a study of a health clinic the appointment system was changed to meet increasing demand, but the same average waiting time for patients was maintained.[5] In these cases, the use of the *M/M/c* model would be appropriate to identify the service capacity in terms of the number of servers that would guarantee the desired expected customer waiting time.

Example 15.4: Drive-in Bank

Excessive congestion is a problem during the weekday noon hour at a downtown drive-in bank facility. Bank officials fear customers may take their accounts elsewhere unless service is improved. A study of customer arrivals during the noon hour indicates an average arrival rate of 30 per hour, with Poisson distribution. Banking transactions take three minutes on the average, with exponential distribution. Because of the layout of the drive-in facility, arriving customers must select one of the existing three lanes for service. Once a customer is in a lane, it is impossible for him or her to renege or jockey between lanes because of medians separating the lanes. Assuming that arriving customers select lanes at random, we can treat the system as parallel, independent, single-channel queuing systems with the arrival rate divided evenly among the tellers. If the bank officers agree to a criterion that customers should wait no more than five minutes on the average, how many drive-in tellers are required? Because we are concerned only with customers who actually wait, equation (I.9), repeated below, is appropriate.

$$W_b = \frac{1}{\mu - \lambda} \tag{I.9}$$

For the current three-teller system, arrivals per teller $\lambda = 30/3 = 10$ per hour. Thus, $W_b = 1/(20 - 10) = 0.1$ hour, or 6 minutes. Table 15.3 indicates that one additional teller is required to meet the service criterion.

Probability of Excessive Waiting

For public services that have difficulty identifying the economic cost of waiting, a service level is often specified. The service level is stated in a manner such that

---

[5]E. J. Rising, R. Baron, and B. Averill, "A Systems Analysis of a University Health-Service Outpatient Clinic," *Operations Research,* vol. 21, no. 5, September 1973, pp. 1030–1047.

TABLE 15.3
EXPECTED TIME IN QUEUE FOR BANK
TELLER ALTERNATIVES

No. tellers	λ per teller	μ	W_b, min
3	10	20	6
4	7.5	20	4.8

at least P or more percent of all customers should experience a delay less than T time units. For example, a federal guideline states that the response time for 95 percent of all ambulance calls should be less than 10 minutes for urban systems and less than 30 minutes for rural systems. The Public Utilities Commission gives a similar performance criterion for telephone service. The commission directs that telephone service must be provided at a resource level such that an incoming call can be answered within 10 seconds 89 percent of the time. A probability distribution of delays is required to identify service levels that will meet these probabilities of not exceeding a certain excessive delay. Equations for these delay probabilities are available for the standard $M/M/c$ model.[6] However, for the case when no delay is desired ($T = 0$), then equation (IV.3) for $P(n \geq c)$ can be used to find a value for c such that the probability of immediate service is at least P percent.

Example 15.5: Self-Serve Gas Station

A retail gasoline distributor plans to construct a self-service filling station on vacant property leading into a new housing development. On the basis of the traffic in the area, the distributor forecasts a demand of 48 cars per hour for a typical hour. The distributor believes that this demand is equally divided between those seeking regular fuels and those seeking unleaded fuels. Time studies conducted at other sites reveal an average self-service time of five minutes for a driver to fill the tank, pay the cashier, and drive away. The service times are exponentially distributed, and past experience justifies assuming an arrival rate with a Poisson distribution. Because of the two types of fuels, the queuing system can be modeled as two independent $M/M/c$ systems in parallel, each with a mean arrival rate of $\lambda = 24$ customers per hour. The distributor believes that the success of self-service stations is due to competitive gasoline prices and to the customers' desires for fast service. Therefore, the distributor would like to install enough regular and unleaded pumps to guarantee that arriving customers will find a free pump at least 95 percent of the time. Because equation (IV.3) is so tedious to apply, we have elected to use *QS: Quantitative Systems, Version 3.0* to calculate the probability that a customer waits for various values

[6]Saaty, op. cit.

TABLE 15.4
PROBABILITY OF FINDING ALL
GAS PUMPS IN USE

c	P_0	$P(n \geq c)$
3	0.11	0.44
4	0.13	0.27
5	0.134	0.06
6	0.135	0.02

of c. The results are summarized in Table 15.4, and a sample computer solution for the six-pump case is shown in the sidebar. Note from the sidebar that the probability P_w has reached a value of 0.018 and thus meets the criterion that less than 5 percent of arriving customers wait. This result suggests that six pumps should be installed for regular gas and six for unleaded.

Minimization of the Sum of Consumer Waiting Costs and Service Costs

If both customers and servers are members of the same organization, then the costs of providing service and employee waiting are of equal importance to the organization's effectiveness. This situation arises, for example, when organizations

---

FINAL SOLUTION FOR GAS STATION

M/M/6

WITH $\lambda = 24$ CUSTOMERS PER HOUR AND $\mu = 12$ CUSTOMERS PER HOUR

Overall system effective arrival rate = 24.0000 per hour
Overall system effective service rate = 24.0000 per hour
Overall system effective utilization factor = 0.333333
Average number of customers in the system (Ls) = 2.009009
Average number of customers in the queue (Lq) = 0.009009
Average time a customer in the system (Ws) = 0.083709 hour
Average time a customer in the queue (Wq) = 0.000375 hour
The probability that all servers are idle (Po) = 0.135135
The probability an arriving customer waits (Pw) = 0.018018

Probability of n customers in the system

P(0) = 0.13514   P(1) = 0.27027   P(2) = 0.27027   P(3) = 0.18018
P(4) = 0.09009   P(5) = 0.03604

$$\sum_{i=0}^{5} P(i) = 0.981982$$

---

rely on a captive service, such as a secretarial pool or computer service facility. In these cases the cost of employees' waiting time is at least equal to their average salary. In fact, the cost could be considerably more if all the implications of waiting were assessed, such as the frustration of not completing a task or the effect of delays on others in the organization.

The economic tradeoff depicted in Figure 15.1 best describes this situation where the capacity to serve may be increased by adding servers. As servers are added, the cost of service increases but is offset by a corresponding decrease in the cost of waiting. Adding both costs results in a convex total-cost curve for the organization that identifies a service capacity with minimum combined costs. The queuing models are used to predict the expected waiting time of employees for different levels of capacity, and the values are substituted in the total-cost function below.

Assuming linear cost functions for service and waiting and comparing alternatives based on steady-state performance, we calculate the total cost per unit of time (hour) as follows:

$$\text{Total cost per hour} = \text{hourly cost of service} + \text{hourly waiting cost}$$
$$TC = C_s C + C_w \lambda W_s$$
$$= C_s C + C_w L_s \qquad (7)$$

where C = number of servers
C_s = hourly cost per server
C_w = hourly cost of waiting customer

Recall that equation (5) converts λW_s, the number of arriving customers per hour times the average waiting time per customer, to its equivalent L_s. For equation (7), waiting is defined as time in system; however, if waiting in queue is more appropriate, then L_q is substituted for L_s. In situations where service is self-service, such as using a copying machine or a fax machine, waiting in queue might be justified.

Example 15.6: Computer Terminal Selection

The director of a large engineering staff is considering the rental of several computer terminals that will permit the staff to interact directly with the computer. On the basis of a survey of the staff, the director finds that the department will generate, on the average, eight requests per hour for service, and the engineers estimate that the average computer analysis will require 15 minutes. A computer terminal that is adequate for these needs rents for $10 per hour. When the average salary of the engineering staff is considered, the cost of keeping an engineer idle is $30 per hour. For the purpose of a "quick and dirty" analysis, the director assumes that the requests for service are Poisson-distributed and that user times are exponentially distributed. Furthermore, the engineering staff is large enough to assume an infinite calling population. Using

TABLE 15.5
TOTAL COST OF COMPUTER TERMINAL ALTERNATIVES

C	P_0	L_q	C_sC	C_wL_q	TC
3	0.11	0.88	$30	$26.4	$56.4
4	0.13	0.17	40	5.1	45.1
5	0.134	0.04	50	1.2	51.2
6	0.135	0.01	60	0.3	60.3

the *M/M/c* model and *QS: Quantitative Systems, Version 3.0* software to calculate L_q, the director performs calculations to get the results shown in Table 15.5.

Notice that L_q is used instead of L_s in the calculations because the computer terminals are self-serve devices. The results indicate that four terminals will minimize the combined costs of rent for the terminals and salary for the waiting engineers.

Our assumption of waiting costs being linear with time, as shown in equation (7), is suspect because as the delay increases, a larger percentage of customers become dissatisfied and vocal, possibly creating a mass exodus. Taguchi's concept of a quadratic quality loss function as described in Chapter 9 seems more appropriate, particularly when alternative service is available from a competitor. First, the longer the wait, the more irritated customers become and the greater the probability that they will take their future business elsewhere. In addition, they will tell friends and relatives of their bad experiences, which will also impact future sales. Finally, the loss of an immediate sale is small compared with the future stream of revenues forgone when a customer is lost forever. However, in practice, because of the difficulty of determining a customer waiting cost function, the linear assumption is usually made.

Probability of Sales Lost because of Inadequate Waiting Area

This planning criterion concerns the capacity of the waiting area rather than the capacity to serve. An inadequate waiting area may cause potential customers to balk and seek service elsewhere. This problem is of particular concern where arriving customers can see the waiting area, such as the parking lot at a restaurant or the driveway at a drive-in bank. Analysis of these systems uses the finite-queue *M/M/c* model to estimate the number of balking customers.

If N represents the maximum number of customers allowed in the system, then P_N is the probability of a customer arriving and finding the system full. Thus, P_N represents the probability of sales lost because of an inadequate waiting area, and λP_N represents the expected number of sales lost per unit of time. The cost of sales lost owing to an inadequate waiting area can now be compared with the possible investment in additional space.

Example 15.7: Downtown Parking Lot

A parking lot is a multiple-server queuing system without a queue; that is, the lot can be considered a service system in which each parking space is a server. After the lot is full, subsequent arrivals are rejected because the system has no provision for a queue. Thus, a parking lot is a finite-queuing system with a queue capacity of zero because N equals c. With this model in mind, an enterprising student notices the availability of a vacant lot in the central business district. The student learns from a real estate agent that the owner is willing to rent the property as a parking lot for $50 a day until a buyer is found. After making some observations of traffic in the area, the student finds that approximately ten cars per hour have difficulty finding space in the parking garage of the department store across the street from the vacant lot. The garage attendant reports that customers spend approximately one hour shopping in the store. For purposes of calculating the feasibility of this venture, the student assumes that the arrivals are Poisson-distributed and that shopping times are exponentially distributed. The student is interested in what potential business is being lost because the lot has room for only six cars.

This parking lot case can be considered an $M/M/c$ finite-queuing system with no provision for a queue. Therefore, the equations for the finite-queue $M/M/c$ model are calculated with $c = N$. Substituting for $c = N$ in equations (V.1), (V.2), (V.4), and (V.7) yields the following results for the no-queue case. No other equations are applicable.

$$P_0 = \frac{1}{\sum\limits_{i=0}^{N} \frac{\rho^i}{i!}} \tag{8}$$

$$P_n = \frac{\rho^n}{n!} P_0 \tag{9}$$

$$L_s = \rho(1 - P_N) \tag{10}$$

$$W_s = \frac{1}{\mu} \quad (\textit{Note: } L_q = 0) \tag{11}$$

With $\lambda = 10$ and $\mu = 1$ we see from the sidebar that *QS: Quantitative Systems, Version 3.0* has calculated $P_0 = 0.000349$ and $P_6 = 0.48$; thus, of the ten arriving customers per hour, approximately one-half ($10 \times 0.48 = 4.8$) find the lot full. Therefore, this lot with a capacity of six cars serves approximately one-half the demand.

Requirement that Expected Profit on Last Unit of Capacity Should Just Exceed Expected Loss

This capacity planning criterion does not rely on the use of queuing models; rather, it relies on an economic principle called *marginal analysis*. This approach is useful when a capacity decision must be made in which there are losses associated both

FINAL SOLUTION FOR PARKING LOT

M/M/6

WITH $\lambda = 10$ CUSTOMERS PER HOUR AND $\mu = 1$ CUSTOMER PER HOUR

Overall system effective arrival rate = 10.0000 per hour
Overall system effective service rate = 5.154851 per hour
Overall system effective utilization factor = 0.859142
Average number of customers in the system (Ls) = 5.154851
Average number of customers in the queue (Lq) = 0
Average time a customer in the system (Ws) = 0.515485 hour
Average time a customer in the queue (Wq) = 0 hour
The probability that all servers are idle (Po) = 0.000349
The probability an arriving customer waits (Pw) = 0.484515

Probability of *n* customers in the system

P(0) = 0.00035   P(1) = 0.00349   P(2) = 0.01744   P(3) = 0.05814
P(4) = 0.14535   P(5) = 0.29071   P(6) = 0.48451   P(7) = 0.00000
P(8) = 0.00000   P(9) = 0.00000   P(10) = 0.00000

$$\sum_{i=0}^{10} P(i) = 1.000000$$

with inadequate capacity and with excess capacity. This capacity problem typically arises during the facility design phase, such as when decisions are made concerning the seating capacity of a restaurant or movie theater. In addition to an estimate of the unit profit per customer and possible loss, the analysis requires a probability distribution for the service demand.

The marginal analysis criterion, as shown below, requires the expected revenue on the last sale to exceed the expected loss on the last sale.

$$E(\text{revenue on last sale}) \geq E(\text{loss on last sale})$$
$$(\text{unit revenue}) \cdot P(\text{revenue}) \geq (\text{unit loss}) \cdot P(\text{loss})$$
$$C_u \cdot P(d \geq x) \geq C_o \cdot P(d < x)$$
$$C_u \cdot [1 - P(d < x)] \geq C_o \cdot P(d < x)$$

$$P(d < x) \leq \frac{C_u}{C_u + C_o} \qquad (12)$$

where C_u = unit revenue from potential sale, cost of *underage* (inadequate capacity)
C_o = unit loss from idle capacity, cost of *overage* (excess capacity)
d = demand
x = capacity (e.g., airline seats, hotel rooms)

Given a probability distribution of demand, equation (12) suggests that capacity should just exceed the cumulative probability of demand that equals the ratio of unit revenue to the sum of unit revenue plus unit loss. This ratio is often called the *critical fractile*.

Example 15.8: Paradise Tours

Paradise Tours has been offering a Hawaiian adventure package each summer for the past several years that has attracted a good, though variable-sized, group of vacationers from the local university. A review of past records suggests that the demand for this tour is normally distributed, with a mean of 50, a standard deviation of 10, and no trend indicated. Paradise Tours reserves seats with a regularly scheduled airline at a special, reduced, affinity-group rate. This policy enables the airline to attract small groups not large enough to charter an entire plane. The airline also allows the travel agent to charge a $30 service fee in addition to the ticket price. However, a major concern of Paradise is the $10 charge by the airline for each unsold reserved seat. The airline is concerned about tying up seats during the peak season and also wants to prevent oversubscription by travel agents. Paradise has been reserving 50 seats and finds it has no record of ever paying the $10 overbooking charge. Should it continue this reservation policy?

Using equation (12), we calculate the following cumulative probability:

$$P(d < x) \leq \frac{30}{30 + 10} \leq 0.75$$

From the end-of-book Appendix table, Areas of a Standard Normal Distribution, the z value for 0.75 is 0.68. Thus, the number of seats to reserve is calculated as follows:

$$\text{Reserved seats} = \mu + z\sigma$$
$$= 50 + (0.68)(10)$$
$$= 56 \quad \text{(Rounded } down. \text{ Why?)}$$

SUMMARY

When the assumptions are met, analytical queuing models can help service system managers evaluate possible alternative courses of action by predicting waiting time statistics. The models also provide insights that help explain such queuing phenomena as pooling, the effect of finite queues on realized demand, the nonproportional effects of adding servers on waiting time, and the importance of controlling demand as seen by reducing service time variance. The approach to capacity planning is found to depend on the criterion of system performance used. Further, queuing models are useful in the analysis because of their ability to predict system performance. However, if the queuing model assumptions are not met or the system is too complex, then computer simulation modeling is required.

EQUATIONS FOR SELECTED QUEUING MODELS

Definition of Symbols

n = number of customers in the system

λ = [lambda] mean arrival rate (e.g., customer arrivals per hour)

μ = [mu] mean service rate per busy server (e.g., service capacity in customers per hour)

ρ = [rho] traffic intensity (λ/μ)

N = maximum number of customers allowed in the system

c = number of servers

P_n = probability of exactly n customers in the system

L_s = mean number of customers in the system

L_q = mean number of customers in queue

L_b = mean number of customers in queue for a busy system

W_s = mean time customer spends in the system

W_q = mean time customer spends in the queue

W_b = mean time customer spends in queue for a busy system

I. Standard M/M/1 Model[7]

$$P_0 = 1 - \rho \tag{I.1}$$

$$P(n > 0) = \rho \tag{I.2}$$

$$P_n = P_0 \rho^n \tag{I.3}$$

$$L_s = \frac{\lambda}{\mu - \lambda} \tag{I.4}$$

$$L_q = \frac{\rho\lambda}{\mu - \lambda} \tag{I.5}$$

$$L_b = \frac{\lambda}{\mu - \lambda} \tag{I.6}$$

$$W_s = \frac{1}{\mu - \lambda} \tag{I.7}$$

$$W_q = \frac{\rho}{\mu - \lambda} \tag{I.8}$$

$$W_b = \frac{1}{\mu - \lambda} \tag{I.9}$$

II. Finite-Queue M/M/1 Model

$$P_0 = \begin{cases} \dfrac{1 - \rho}{1 - \rho^{N+1}} & \text{for } \lambda \neq \mu \\[2ex] \dfrac{1}{N + 1} & \text{for } \lambda = \mu \end{cases} \tag{II.1}$$

[7]*Note:* $0 < \rho < 1.0$.

$$P(n > 0) = 1 - P_0 \tag{II.2}$$

$$P_n = P_0 \rho^n \quad \text{for } n \le N \tag{II.3}$$

$$L_s = \begin{cases} \dfrac{\rho}{1 - \rho} - \dfrac{(N + 1)\rho^{N+1}}{1 - \rho^{N+1}} & \text{for } \lambda \ne \mu \\[2ex] \dfrac{N}{2} & \text{for } \lambda = \mu \end{cases} \tag{II.4}$$

$$L_q = L_s - (1 - P_0) \tag{II.5}$$

$$L_b = \frac{L_q}{1 - P_0} \tag{II.6}$$

$$W_s = \frac{L_q}{\lambda (1 - P_N)} + \frac{1}{\mu} \tag{II.7}$$

$$W_q = W_s - \frac{1}{\mu} \tag{II.8}$$

$$W_b = \frac{W_q}{1 - P_0} \tag{II.9}$$

III. Standard *M/G/1* Model[8]

$$L_s = L_q + \rho \tag{III.1}$$

$$L_q = \frac{\rho^2 + \lambda^2 V(t)}{2(1 - \rho)} \tag{III.2}$$

$$W_s = \frac{L_s}{\lambda} \tag{III.3}$$

$$W_q = \frac{L_q}{\lambda} \tag{III.4}$$

IV. Standard *M/M/c* Model[9]

$$P_0 = \frac{1}{\left(\displaystyle\sum_{i=0}^{c-1} \dfrac{\rho^i}{i!} \right) + \dfrac{\rho^c}{c!(1 - \rho/c)}} \tag{IV.1}$$

$$P_n = \begin{cases} \dfrac{\rho^n}{n!} P_0 & \text{for } 0 \le n \le c \\[2ex] \dfrac{\rho^n}{c! c^{n-c}} P_0 & \text{for } n \ge c \end{cases} \tag{IV.2}$$

[8]*Note:* $V(t)$ = service time variance.
[9]*Note:* $0 < \rho < c$.

$$P(n \geq c) = \frac{\rho^c \mu c}{c!(\mu c - \lambda)} P_0 \tag{IV.3}$$

$$L_s = \frac{\rho^{c+1}}{(c-1)!(c-\rho)^2} P_0 + \rho \tag{IV.4}$$

$$L_q = L_s - \rho \tag{IV.5}$$

$$L_b = \frac{L_q}{P(n \geq c)} \tag{IV.6}$$

$$W_s = \frac{L_q}{\lambda} + \frac{1}{\mu} \tag{IV.7}$$

$$W_q = \frac{L_q}{\lambda} \tag{IV.8}$$

$$W_b = \frac{W_q}{P(n \geq c)} \tag{IV.9}$$

V. Finite-Queue *M/M/c* Model

$$P_0 = \frac{1}{\left(\displaystyle\sum_{i=0}^{c} \frac{\rho^i}{i!} \right) + \left(\frac{1}{c!} \right) \left(\displaystyle\sum_{i=c+1}^{N} \frac{\rho^i}{c^{i-c}} \right)} \tag{V.1}$$

$$P_n = \begin{cases} \dfrac{\rho^n}{n!} P_0 & \text{for } 0 \leq n \leq c \\[2ex] \dfrac{\rho^n}{c! c^{n-c}} P_0 & \text{for } c \leq n \leq N \end{cases} \tag{V.2}$$

$$P(n \geq c) = 1 - P_0 \sum_{i=0}^{c-1} \frac{\rho^i}{i!} \tag{V.3}$$

$$L_s = \frac{P_0 \rho^{c+1}}{(c-1)!(c-\rho)^2} \left[1 - \left(\frac{\rho}{c} \right)^{N-c} - (N-c) \left(\frac{\rho}{c} \right)^{N-c} \left(1 - \frac{\rho}{c} \right) \right] + \rho(1 - P_N) \tag{V.4}$$

$$L_q = L_s - \rho(1 - P_N) \tag{V.5}$$

$$L_b = \frac{L_q}{P(n \geq c)} \tag{V.6}$$

$$W_s = \frac{L_q}{\lambda(1 - P_N)} + \frac{1}{\mu} \tag{V.7}$$

$$W_q = W_s - \frac{1}{\mu} \tag{V.8}$$

$$W_b = \frac{W_q}{P(n \geq c)} \tag{V.9}$$

VI. Self-Service $M/G/\infty$ Model

$$P_n = \frac{e^{-\rho}}{n!} \rho^n \qquad \text{for } n \geq 0 \qquad \text{(VI.1)}$$

$$L_s = \rho \qquad \text{(VI.2)}$$

$$W_s = \frac{1}{\mu} \qquad \text{(VI.3)}$$

TOPICS FOR DISCUSSION

1. For a queuing system with a finite queue, the arrival rate can exceed the capacity to serve. Use an example to explain how this is feasible.

2. What are some disadvantages associated with the concept of pooling service resources?

3. Capacity planning using queuing models is usually applied to strategic decisions rather than to day-to-day operations. Explain.

4. Discuss how the $M/G/\infty$ model could be used to determine the number of emergency medical vehicles required to serve a community.

5. Discuss how one could determine the economic cost of keeping customers waiting.

EXERCISES

15.1. A general-purpose auto repair garage has one mechanic who specializes in muffler installations. Customers seeking service arrive at an average rate of two per hour, with Poisson distribution. The average time to install a muffler is 20 minutes, with negative exponential distribution.

  a. Upon arrival at the garage, how many customers should one expect to find in the system?

  b. The management is interested in adding another mechanic when the customer's average time in the system exceeds 90 minutes. If business continues to increase, at what arrival rate per hour will an additional mechanic be called for?

15.2. The business school is considering replacing the old minicomputer with a faster model. Past records show that the average student arrival rate is 24 per hour, Poisson-distributed, and that the service times are exponentially distributed. The computer selection committee has been instructed to consider only machines that will yield an average turnaround time (expected time in the system) of five minutes or less. What is the smallest computer processing rate per hour that can be considered?

15.3. The Lower Colorado River Authority (LCRA) has been studying the congestion at the boat-launching ramp near Mansfield Dam. On weekends the arrival rate averages five boaters per hour, Poisson-distributed. The average time to launch or to retrieve a boat is 10 minutes, with negative exponential distribution. Assume that only one boat can be launched or retrieved at a time.

  a. The LCRA plans to add another ramp when the average turnaround time (time in the system) exceeds 90 minutes. At what average arrival rate per hour should the LCRA begin to consider adding another ramp?

b. If there were room to park only two boats at the top of the ramp in preparation for launching, how often would an arrival find insufficient parking space?

15.4. On the average, four customers per hour use the public telephone in the sheriff's detention area, and the use has a Poisson distribution. The length of a phone call varies according to a negative exponential distribution, with a mean of five minutes. The sheriff will install a second telephone booth when an arrival can expect to wait three minutes or longer for the phone.

a. By how much must the arrival rate per hour increase to justify a second telephone booth?

b. Suppose the criterion for justifying a second booth is changed to the following: install a second booth when the probability of having to wait at all exceeds 0.6. By how much must the arrival rate per hour increase to justify a second booth?

15.5. A company has a central document-copying service. Arrivals are assumed to follow the Poisson probability distribution, with a mean rate of 15 per hour. Service times are assumed to follow the exponential distribution. With the present copying equipment the average service time is three minutes. A new machine is available that will have a mean service time of two minutes. The average wage of the people who bring the documents to be copied is $3 an hour.

a. If the new machine can be rented for $4 per hour *more* than the old machine, should the company rent the new machine? Consider lost productive time of employees as time spent waiting in queue *only* because the copying machine is a self-serve device.

b. For the *old* copying machine, when a person arrives, what is the probability that person will encounter people already *waiting in line* for service? (Be careful to identify properly the number of customers who might be present for this situation to arise.)

c. Suppose that the *new* copying machine is rented. How many chairs should be provided for those waiting in line if we are satisfied when at least 90 percent of the time there will be enough chairs?

15.6. Sea Dock, a private firm, operates an unloading facility located in the Gulf of Mexico for supertankers delivering crude oil for refineries in the Port Arthur area of Texas. Records show that on the average, two tankers arrive per day, with Poisson distribution. Supertankers are unloaded one at a time on a first-come, first-served (FCFS) basis. Unloading requires approximately 8 hours of a 24-hour working day, and unloading times have a negative exponential distribution.

a. Sea Dock has provided mooring space for three tankers. Is this sufficient to meet the U.S. Coast Guard requirement that at least 19 out of 20 arrivals should find mooring available?

b. Sea Dock can increase its unloading capacity to a rate of four ships per day through additional labor at a cost of $480 per day. Considering the $1000-per-day demurrage fee charged to Sea Dock for keeping a supertanker idle (this includes unloading time as well as time spent waiting in queue), should management consider this expansion opportunity?

15.7. Last National Bank is concerned about the level of service at its single drive-in window. A study of customer arrivals during the window's busy period revealed the following: on the average 20 customers per hour arrive, with Poisson distribution, and they are given FCFS service, requiring an average of two minutes, with service times having a negative exponential distribution.

a. What is the expected number of customers waiting in queue?

b. If Last National were using an ATM (automated teller machine) with a constant service time of two minutes, what would be the expected number of drive-in customers in the system?

c. There is space in the drive for three cars (including the one being served). What is the probability of traffic on the street being blocked by cars waiting to turn into the bank driveway?

d. Last National is considering adding teller stations at the current drive-in facility. It has decided on $5 per hour as the imputed cost of customer waiting time in the system. The hourly cost of a teller is $10. The average arrival rate of customers has reached 30 per hour. On the basis of the total hourly cost of tellers and customer waiting, how many tellers do you recommend? Assume that demand is equally divided among the tellers, that there are separate waiting lines, and that no customer jockeying is permitted.

15.8. Green Valley Airport has been in operation for several years and is beginning to experience flight congestion. A study of airport operations revealed that planes arrive at an average of 12 per hour, with Poisson distribution. On the single runway a plane can land and be cleared every four minutes on the average, and service times have a negative exponential distribution. Planes are processed on a FCFS basis, with takeoffs occurring between landings. Planes waiting to land are asked to circle the airport.

a. What is the expected number of airplanes circling the airport, waiting in queue for clearance to land?

b. A new ground-approach radar system approved by the FAA is being considered as a means of reducing congestion. Under this system, planes can be processed at a *constant* rate of 15 per hour (i.e., the variance is zero). What would be the expected number of airplanes circling the airport, waiting in queue for clearance to land, if the system were to be used?

c. Assume that the cost of keeping an airplane in the air is approximately $70 per hour. If the cost of the proposed radar system were $100 per hour, would you recommend its adoption?

15.9. Lakeside Community College has been using a medium-sized computer, donated by a local firm, to support its computer science program. The computer center director notes that students submit batch jobs at an average rate of 20 per hour, with Poisson distribution. Jobs are processed on a FCFS basis and take, on the average, two minutes of CPU time, with negative exponential distribution. Students are requested to remain in the ready room as their jobs are processed.

a. What is the expected number of students waiting in queue to have their jobs processed?

b. If only three chairs are provided in the ready room for students, what is the probability that an arriving student will find no chair available? (Assume that all students will sit given the opportunity.)

c. The college plans to consider replacing the computer when increases in demand result in an average waiting time in queue exceeding six minutes. If the computer center keeps track of the average arrival rate of students per hour, at what point should a new computer be considered?

d. Lakeside has an opportunity to get another computer, identical with the current one, for its computation center. Assume that the arrival rate is still 20 per hour, with Poisson distribution. What is the average number of jobs in the system if the computers operate in parallel to select jobs from a single queue?

e. As an alternative, the college decides to dedicate one computer to research computation and the other to teaching. If the demand of 20 jobs per hour were equally divided between research and teaching, on the average, how many jobs would be in the total system?

f. What savings in student waiting time could be achieved by pooling the computers?

15.10. Community Bank is planning the expansion of its drive-in facility. Observations of the existing single teller window reveal the following: customers arrive at an average rate of 10 per hour, with Poisson distribution, and they are given FCFS service, with an average transaction time of five minutes. Transaction times have a negative exponential distribution. Community Bank has decided to add another teller and install four remote stations with pneumatic tubes running from the stations to the tellers, who are located in a glassed-in building. The cost of keeping a customer waiting in the system is represented as a $5-per-hour loss of goodwill. The hourly cost of a teller is $10.

a. Assume that each teller is assigned two stations exclusively, that the demand is equally divided among the stations, and that no customer jockeying is permitted. What is the average number of customers waiting in the entire system?

b. If, instead, both tellers work all the stations and the customer waiting the longest is served by the next available teller, what is the average number of customers in the system?

c. What are the hourly savings achieved by pooling the tellers?

15.11. Consider a one-pump gas station that satisfies the assumptions for the $M/M/1$ model. It is estimated that on the average, customers arrive to buy gas when their tanks are one-eighth full. The mean time to service a customer is four minutes, and the arrival rate is six customers per hour.

a. Determine the expected length of the queue and the expected time in the system.

b. Suppose that customers perceive a gas shortage (when there is none) and respond by changing the fill-up criterion to more than one-eighth full on the average. Assuming that changes in λ are inversely proportional to changes in the fill-up criterion, compare results when the fill-up criterion is one-quarter full with the results in part **a**.

c. Make the same assumption as in part **b**, and compare the results obtained if the fill-up criterion is half full. Do we have the makings of a behaviorally induced gasoline panic?

d. It is reasonable to assume that the time to service a customer will decrease as the fill-up criterion increases. Under "normal" conditions it takes an average of two minutes to pump the gasoline and an average of two minutes to clean the windshield, check the oil, and collect the money. Rework parts **b** and **c** if the time to pump the gasoline changes proportionally to changes in the fill-up criterion.

CASE: HOUSTON PORT AUTHORITY

The Houston Port Authority has engaged you as a consultant to advise it on possible changes in the handling of wheat exports. At present a crew of dockworkers using conventional belt conveyors is assigned the task of unloading hopper cars containing wheat onto cargo ships bound for overseas destinations. The crew is known to take an average of $\frac{1}{2}$ hour to unload a car. The crew is paid a total wage of $10 per hour. Hopper car arrivals have averaged 12 per 8-hour shift. The railroad assesses a demurrage charge from time of arrival to release at a rate of $4 per hour on rolling stock not in service. Partially unloaded cars from one shift are first in line for the following shift.

A chi-square "goodness-of-fit" analysis of the arrival rates for the past months indicates a Poisson distribution. Data on unloading times for this period may be assumed to follow a negative exponential distribution.

Because of excessive demurrage charges, a proposal has been made to add another work crew. A visit to the work area indicates that both crews will be unable to work together on the same car because of congestion; however, two cars may be unloaded simultaneously with one crew per car.

During your deliberations, the industrial engineering staff reports that a pneumatic handling system has become available. This system can transfer wheat from cars to cargo ships at a constant rate of 3 cars per hour, 24 hours per day, with the assistance of a skilled operator earning $8 per hour. Such a system would cost $400,000 installed. The Port Authority uses a 10 percent discount rate for capital improvement projects. The port is in operation 24 hours a day, 365 days a year. For purposes of analysis, assume that there is a 10-year planning horizon. Prepare a recommendation for the Port Authority.

CASE: FREEDOM EXPRESS

Freedom Express, affectionately known as the Filibuster Fly, is a small commuter airline based in Washington, D.C., that serves the east coast. It runs nonstop flights between several cities and Washington National Airport (DCA).

DCA is frequently congested, and at such times planes are required to fly in a "stack" over the field; i.e., planes in the process of landing and those waiting for permission to land are deployed above the field.

FreeEx management is interested in determining the length of time its planes will have to wait so that an adequate amount of fuel can be loaded prior to departure from the outlying city to cover both the intercity flying time and the time in the stack. Excess fuel represents an unnecessary cost because it reduces the payload capacity. Equally important is the present cost of aviation fuel, $1.80 per gallon, and an average consumption rate of 20 gallons per minute.

The rate of arrival of all planes at DCA varies with the hour of the day. The arrival rate and the time in the stack are greatest each weekday between 4 and 5 p.m., and so FreeEx selected this time period for an initial study.

The study indicated that the mean arrival rate is 20 planes per hour, or one every three minutes. The variance about this mean, owing to flight cancellations and charter and private flights, is characterized by a Poisson distribution.

During clear weather, the DCA control tower can land one plane per minute, or 60 per hour. Landings cannot exceed this rate in the interest of air safety. When the weather is bad, the landing rate is 30 per hour. Both good- and bad-weather landing rates are mean rates with a Poisson distribution. FreeEx's flights are short enough that management can usually tell prior to takeoff in an outlying city whether or not the rate of landings in DCA will be reduced because of weather considerations.

When a plane runs short of fuel while in the stack, it is given priority to land out of order. DCA rules, however, make it clear that the airport will not tolerate abuse of this consideration. Therefore, FreeEx ensures that its planes carry enough fuel on flights so that it will take advantage of the policy no more than 1 time in 20.

Questions

1. During periods of bad weather as compared with periods of clear weather, how many additional gallons of fuel, on the average, should FreeEx expect its planes to consume owing to airport congestion?

2. Given FreeEx's policy of ensuring that its planes do not run out of fuel more than 1 in 20 times while waiting to land, how many reserve gallons (i.e., gallons over and above expected usage) should be provided for clear-weather flights? for bad-weather flights?

3. During bad weather, FreeEx has the option of instructing the Washington air controller to place its planes in a holding pattern from which planes are directed to land at either Washington National or Dulles International, whichever becomes available first. Assume that the Dulles landing rate in bad weather is also 30 per hour, Poisson-distributed, and that the combined arrival rate for both airports is 40 per hour. If FreeEx must pay $100 to have its passengers transported from Dulles to Washington National, should it exercise the option of permitting its aircraft to land at Dulles during bad weather? Assume that if the option is used, FreeEx's aircraft will be diverted to Dulles one-half of the time.

CASE: CEDAR VALLEY COMMUNITY COLLEGE

Cedar Valley Community College, founded only two years ago, has experienced enrollment beyond expectations. The large number of students in the computer science program has placed such demands on the college's small computer that complaints of excessive turnaround time have reached the president's office.[10]

As the computer center director, you have been asked to identify the new computer models that are available and to recommend a replacement for the existing batch processor. After talking to several computer hardware vendors, you have settled on a compatible system which has six models available that differ only in their processing speed and, of course, in price.

On the basis of historical records, you estimate that an average program can be processed in one, two, three, four, five, or six minutes, depending on whether model A, B, C, D, E, or F, respectively, is chosen. The rental cost of a particular model depends on its speed; the rental rate per minute is 90 cents/S, where S is the service time for the average program (e.g., model A, which completes a program in one minute, rents for 90 cents per minute; model B, for 45 cents per minute).

A statistical analysis of the distribution of the historical processing times reveals that they follow a negative exponential distribution. During the past month you

---

[10]Turnaround time for batch processing is the elapsed time from submitting a computer job to the time the output is available for pickup.

installed a time clock to gather information on the time of arrival of computer center users to plan the staffing of the ready desk. A study of the clock times indicates that on the average, 12 users arrive per hour, with Poisson distribution.

The president has suggested that a criterion of minimizing the average total cost per hour (rental plus waiting) be used in the analysis. For this analysis the cost of keeping a user waiting for output is estimated to be 50 cents per minute. At your suggestion, the president also agrees to an acceptable service level that does not exceed an average turnaround time of five minutes.

Which computer model(s) and configuration would you recommend?

CASE: PRONTO PIZZA

Pronto Pizza is a delivery-only pizza service that promises delivery within 40 minutes of receiving a call for an order or the customer gets $2 off the price. Pronto employs a single pizza maker, paid $10 per hour, who can make, on the average, one pizza every three minutes. This service time has a negative exponential distribution. Pizzas are placed in a large oven with a capacity for ten pizzas to bake for approximately 12 minutes. A team of six delivery persons serves the neighboring population within a maximum drive of 10 minutes from the store. The travel time to deliver a pizza in the market area and then return averages 10 minutes, with negative exponential distribution. Calls for pizza average one every five minutes, with negative exponential distribution. Pizzas are delivered one at a time to customers by drivers who use their own cars and are paid $8 per hour.

Assignments

1. Draw a process flow diagram, and identify the bottleneck operation.

2. Using the queuing equations, evaluate the delivery guarantee. What is the probability of paying off on the guarantee?

3. Determine the number of delivery persons required to ensure that the average waiting time for a completed pizza to be picked up for delivery is limited to one minute.

4. What do you think of this service guarantee policy?

5. What other design or operating suggestions could improve Pronto Pizza's performance and customer service?

SELECTED BIBLIOGRAPHY

Bleuel, W. H.: "Management Science's Impact on Service Strategy," *Interfaces,* vol. 6, no. 1, November 1975, part 2, pp. 4–12.

Budnick, F. S., D. McLeavey, and R. Mojena: *Principles of Operations Research for Management,* 2d ed., Richard D. Irwin, Inc., Homewood, Ill., 1988.

Crabill, T. B., D. Gross, and M. J. Magazine: "A Classified Bibliography of Research on Optimal Design and Control of Queues," *Operations Research,* vol. 25, no. 2, March–April 1977, pp. 219–232.

Drake, A. W., R. L. Keeney, and P. N. Morse (eds.): *Analysis of Public Systems,* M.I.T. Press, Cambridge, Mass., 1972.

Erikson, Warren J.: "Management Science and the Gas Shortage," *Interfaces,* vol. 4, no. 4, August 1974, pp. 47–51.

Foote, B. L.: "A Queuing Case Study of Drive-In Banking," *Interfaces,* vol. 6, no. 4, August 1976, pp. 31–37.

Grassman, W. K.: "Finding the Right Number of Servers in Real-World Queuing Systems," *Interfaces,* vol. 18, no. 2, 1988, pp. 94–104.

Hillier, F. S., and G. J. Lieberman: *Introduction to Operations Research,* 4th ed., Holden-Day, Inc., San Francisco, 1986.

Maggard, Michael J.: "Determining Electronic Point-of-Sale Cash Register Requirements," *Journal of Retailing,* vol. 57, no. 2, summer 1981, pp. 64–86.

Parikh, S. C.: "On a Fleet Sizing and Allocation Problem," *Management Science,* vol. 23, no. 9, May 1977, pp. 972–977.

Rising, E. J., R. Baron, and B. Averill: "A Systems Analysis of a University Health-Service Outpatient Clinic," *Operations Research,* vol. 21, no. 5, September 1973, pp. 1030–1047.

Rothkopf, M. H., and P. Rech: "Perspectives on Queues: Combining Queues Is Not Always Beneficial," *Operations Research,* vol. 35, no. 6, November–December 1987, pp. 906–909.

Saaty, T. L.: *Elements of Queuing Theory with Applications,* McGraw-Hill, New York, 1961.

CHAPTER 16

LINEAR PROGRAMMING MODELS IN SERVICES

Linear programming (LP) is a general computer-based modeling tool for making resource allocation decisions that transcend all aspects of service operations management. Linear programming is not computer programming. The programming refers to planning that uses mathematical models consisting of linear expressions.

A model is a selective abstraction of reality. Modeling is an art, because judgments are made in the selection of the important features of reality for the problem at hand. Modeling is also a science because data are collected to measure the relationship between decision variables, the objectives desired, and the resources available. The process of identifying decision variables and clarifying objectives imposes a discipline that is useful in itself.

The use of models such as linear programming springs from the belief that the decision-making process can be enhanced by applying the scientific method. Scientists study nature and conduct controlled experiments to understand better the phenomena of interest. Decision models are the laboratory of managers who are interested in testing the outcomes of decisions before their actual implementation. In this way potential disasters may be avoided, and the decision-making process may be improved through a better understanding of the environment.

CHAPTER PREVIEW

This chapter emphasizes the art of formulating linear programming models and interpreting computer output. The mathematical details involved in solving an LP model are not discussed. The availability of computer programs to solve LP models is extensive, and users need not be concerned about the mechanics of how optimal solutions are found, anymore than one needs to know the theory of the internal combustion engine to drive an automobile. The chapter concludes with a discussion of an extension of LP called *goal programming*. Goal programming is useful when one is dealing with the multiple objectives that are often present in service decision making. We begin by discussing the concept of an optimum solution to a constrained model.

CONSTRAINED OPTIMIZATION MODELS

In everyday life we are faced with making decisions in which the potential set of alternatives is restricted by money, time, physical limitations, or some other element. For example, suppose we wish to buy a car this week, we can qualify for a $10,000 loan, and we want a vehicle with an EPA rating of at least 30 miles per gallon. The set of possible cars is constrained by time, budget, and mileage performance. These constraints are restrictions that reduce the allowable set of solutions to our problem. Thus constraints actually help us make decisions by limiting our search for a solution to candidate cars that meet the stipulated requirements.

If economy were our goal, then we might measure this by calculating the cost per mile for each car meeting our constraints. The car with the lowest cost-per-mile value would be considered the optimum solution to our constrained decision problem.

Constrained optimization problems are common to service operations. For example, a potential location for a service facility is constrained by available sites. Scheduling telephone operators is constrained by the variations in demand for service and by the personnel policies regarding split shifts.

Linear programming models are a special class of constrained optimization models. In linear programming all relationships are expressed as linear functions. All linear programming models are of the following algebraic form:

Maximize (or minimize) $\qquad c_1 x_1 + c_2 x_2 + \cdots + c_n x_n$

subject to $\qquad a_{11} x_1 + a_{12} x_2 + \cdots + a_{1n} x_n \begin{cases} \leq \\ = \\ \geq \end{cases} b_1$

$$a_{21} x_1 + a_{22} x_2 + \cdots + a_{2n} x_n \begin{cases} \leq \\ = \\ \geq \end{cases} b_2$$

$$\vdots$$

$$a_{m1} x_1 + a_{m2} x_2 + \cdots + a_{mn} x_n \begin{cases} \leq \\ = \\ \geq \end{cases} b_m$$

and nonnegativity constraints

$$x_1, x_2, \ldots, x_n \geq 0$$

Note that each system constraint is limited to only one of the conditions $\leq$ or $=$ or $\geq$ (strictly $>$ or $<$ is not permitted). This problem structure contains the following characteristics:

1. *Decision variables.* The variables $x_1, x_2, \ldots, x_n$ are called decision variables that take on real values greater than or equal to zero. These variables represent actions the decision maker can take, such as assigning ten telephone operators to the Tuesday afternoon shift.

2. *Objective function.* The function $c_1x_1 + c_2x_2 + \ldots + c_nx_n$ is called the objective function, which is either maximized (e.g., profits) or minimized (e.g., costs), depending on the nature of the coefficients $c_1, c_2, \ldots, c_n$. The problem states that this function is made as large or small as possible, provided a system of constraints is met.

3. *Constraint functions.* As numerical values are assigned to the decision variables $x_1, x_2, \ldots, x_n$ to influence the objective function, these values are also assigned to each constraint function. The model requires that numerical values be assigned such that no constraint is violated. The numbers $b_1, b_2, \ldots, b_m$ taken together are called the *right-hand sides* (RHS). These numbers indirectly limit the possible values of the decision variables. For example, these RHS values could be resource constraints, such as total worker hours available.

4. *Parameters.* The coefficients in the objective function and the RHS values are parameters. Parameters are entities whose values remain fixed during the problem solution but could be changed later. Examples are unit profit contributions for the objective-function coefficients and the availability of resources for the RHS values.

5. *Constants.* The coefficients $a_{11}, a_{12}, \ldots, a_{1n}$ represent the consumption of the first RHS resource per unit of each decision variable. These coefficients reflect a constant rate of resource use—for example, the ounces of beef required to make a hamburger.

Example 16.1: Stereo Warehouse

The retail outlet of Stereo Warehouse, a discount audio components store, is planning a special clearance sale. The showroom has 400 square feet of floor space available for displaying this week's specials, a model X receiver and series Y speakers. Each receiver has a wholesale cost of $100, requires 2 square feet of display space, and will sell for $150. The wholesale cost for a pair of speakers is $50; the pair requires 4 square feet of display space and will sell for $70. The budget for stocking the stereo items is $8000. The sales potential for the receiver is considered to be no more than 60 units. However, the budget-priced speakers appear to have unlimited appeal. The store manager, desiring to maximize gross profit, must decide how many receivers and speakers to stock.

This problem can be formulated as an LP problem in the following manner:

Let x = number of receivers to stock
$\quad\ y$ = number of speakers to stock

Maximize	$50x + 20y$	gross profit
subject to	$2x + 4y \leq 400$	floor space
	$100x + 50y \leq 8000$	budget
	$x \leq 60$	sales limit
	$x, y \geq 0$	

The decision variables x and y appear in both the objective function and the constraint functions to ensure that the optimum solution does not violate the resource limits. The objective is to maximize gross profit, which represents the difference between the selling price and the wholesale cost for each receiver and speaker sold. Thus, the objective becomes maximize $(150 - 100)x + (70 - 50)y$, or $50x + 20y$. The first two constraints account for resources that cannot be exceeded, i.e., available floor space and budget dollars. Thus, the 400 square feet of floor space represents a less-than-or-equal-to constraint, with each receiver occupying 2 square feet and each speaker occupying 4 square feet. Likewise, the $8000 budget is consumed by the expenditure of $100 for each receiver stocked and $50 for each pair of speakers stocked. Finally, the sale of receivers is limited to 60 units.

The solution to this problem will increase the values of x and y until some of, but not necessarily all, the resources are depleted. The solution to the Stereo Warehouse example is deferred until a later section.

Before we leave the topic of constrained optimization models, a few caveats are in order. When a constrained optimization model is solved, the solution is called *optimal,* meaning that the best values for the decision variables have been found. However, this so-called optimal solution is optimal relative to the model and may not be optimal with regard to *reality.* Recall that the model is only an abstraction of reality and cannot include all the elements of reality. There can be a vast difference between the optimal solution of the model and what is finally implemented by the decision maker for reasons ranging from political considerations to personal preference. An optimal site selection for company headquarters could be vetoed by the corporate president, who refuses to live in the selected city. However, when used with care, linear programming models provide an excellent vehicle to structure a problem in explicit detail for all to see and to question. Constraints can be modified, added, or eliminated, and objective functions can be changed. Furthermore, the cost of pursuing a nonoptimal solution can be determined.

Next, we discuss the art of formulating LP models and consider examples of classic LP model structures applied to services.

FORMULATING LINEAR PROGRAMMING MODELS

The ability to recognize a potential linear programming problem and to structure it for computer solution is an art acquired from experience. However, some exposure to examples of classical forms of LP models can help. For example, recognizing that a problem is like the classical "diet problem" suggests the likely mathematical structure that will evolve. Experience with formulating LP problems suggests that the following strategy can be helpful.

1. Draw a diagram or construct a table showing the relationships in the problem, including the parameters and constraints.
2. Identify and invent symbolic notation for the decision variables.
3. State the objective in words.
4. Express each constraint in words, identify the right-hand-side values, and note the direction of the inequality.
5. Write out the complete model in algebraic form. Begin with the objective function; then list the right-hand sides, followed by the inequality signs; and finish by filling in the left-hand algebraic expressions for each constraint.
6. Note the nonnegativity conditions for the decision variables.
7. Using possible solutions, test the problem for internal consistency and completeness.

These guidelines are followed in formulating the example problems.

Diet Problem

This class of problems is illustrated by the selection of various food items for a meal that meets certain nutritional requirements. Given that each food item selected contributes to the nutritional requirements at different rates, the objective is to identify the food items and amounts that minimize costs.

Example 16.2: Lakeview Hospital

The dietitian at Lakeview is preparing a special milk shake as a "treat" for pediatric-care patients recovering from surgery. The dietitian wants to ensure that the level of cholesterol will not exceed 175 units and that the level of saturated fat will not exceed 150 units. The protein content should be at least 200 units, and the calorie content should exceed 100 units. The dietitian has selected three possible ingredients: an egg custard base, ice cream, and butterscotch-flavored syrup. One unit of the egg custard base costs 15 cents and contributes 50 units of cholesterol, no fat, 70 units of protein, and 30 calories. One unit of ice cream costs 25 cents and contributes 150 units of cholesterol, 100 units of fat, 10 units of protein, and 80 calories. One unit of butterscotch-flavored syrup costs 10 cents and contributes 90 units of cholesterol, 50 units of fat, no protein, and 200 calories. How many units of each ingredient should be included in the milk shake if costs are to be minimized?

The information from the problem statement is organized and displayed in Table 16.1.

The problem suggests the following decision variables:

Let E = units of egg custard base in the shake
   C = units of ice cream in the shake
   S = units of butterscotch syrup in the shake

TABLE 16.1
LAKEVIEW HOSPITAL DIET PROBLEM
Units of Nutritional Element per Unit of Ingredient

Nutritional element	Egg custard	Ice cream	Syrup	Nutritional requirement
Cholesterol	50	150	90	≤ 175
Fat	0	100	50	≤ 150
Protein	70	10	0	≥ 200
Calories	30	80	200	≥ 100
Cost per unit, cents	15	25	10	

The object is to minimize the total cost of the milk shake. Table 16.1 identifies the constraints as being cholesterol content less than or equal to 175 units, fat content less than or equal to 150 units, protein content equal to or more than 200 units, and calorie content equal to or more than 100 units. The algebraic expression of the model becomes:

Minimize $\qquad 0.15E + 0.25C + 0.10S$
subject to

$$50E + 150C + 90S \leq 175 \qquad \text{cholesterol}$$
$$100C + 50S \leq 150 \qquad \text{fat}$$
$$70E + 10C \qquad \geq 200 \qquad \text{protein}$$
$$30E + 80C + 200S \geq 100 \qquad \text{calories}$$
$$E, C, S \geq 0$$

Notice that the problem as formulated could yield a solution using egg custard base alone (i.e., $E = 3.5$, $C = 0$, and $S = 0$). Because such a solution would hardly be considered a milk shake, additional constraints should be added to the problem to preclude this from occurring.

Shift-Scheduling Problem

This problem arises when an operation must be staffed for a period of time during which the requirements for service vary. The objective is to schedule staff assignments to meet the requirements during the period, using the minimum number of people.

Example 16.3: Gotham City Police Patrol

Unable to hire new police officers because of budget limitations, the Gotham City police commissioner is trying to utilize the force better. The minimum requirements for police patrols for weekdays are noted below:

Time period	Patrol officers, minimum
Midnight–4 a.m.	6
4–8 a.m.	4
8–noon	14
12–4 p.m.	8
4–8 p.m.	12
8–midnight	16

Patrol officers are assigned in pairs to a patrol car, and they work an eight-hour shift. Currently, patrol officers report for duty at midnight, 8 a.m., and 4 p.m. The commissioner believes that a better use of officers could be achieved if they were also permitted to report for duty at 4 a.m., noon, and 8 p.m. Of course, this might require some patrol officers to switch partners after four hours of duty. How many patrol officers should report for their eight-hour shift at each of the six reporting times? The assignments must minimize the total number of officers and still meet the minimum staffing requirements.

The shaded areas in Figure 16.1 show the periods of overstaffing that result from the current practice of patrol officers reporting for eight-hour shifts at three reporting times (i.e., $x_1 = 6$, $x_3 = 14$, and $x_5 = 16$).

The decision variables for the staffing problem are defined as follows:

Let x_i = number of officers scheduled to report at reporting time i
for $i = 1, 2, 3, 4, 5, 6$

FIGURE 16.1
Gothham City Police shift-scheduling problem.

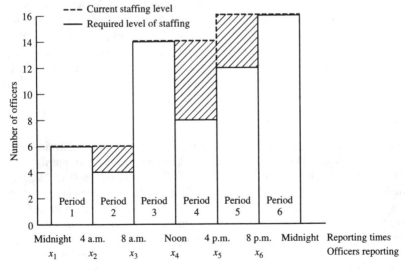

The problem is directed at minimizing the total number of patrol officers, with constraints on the minimum number required for each four-hour time interval during the day. The algebraic expression of the model also accounts for the implied constraint that once a patrol officer reports for duty, that officer remains on duty for a complete eight-hour shift.

$$
\begin{array}{lll}
\text{Minimize} & x_1 + x_2 + x_3 + x_4 + x_5 + x_6 & \\
\text{subject to} & x_1 \qquad\qquad\qquad\quad + x_6 \geq 6 & \text{period 1} \\
& x_1 + x_2 \qquad\qquad\qquad\ \geq 4 & \text{period 2} \\
& \quad\ \ x_2 + x_3 \qquad\qquad\ \geq 14 & \text{period 3} \\
& \qquad\quad x_3 + x_4 \qquad\quad\ \geq 8 & \text{period 4} \\
& \qquad\qquad\ x_4 + x_5 \quad\ \geq 12 & \text{period 5} \\
& \qquad\qquad\qquad x_5 + x_6 \geq 16 & \text{period 6}
\end{array}
$$

Notice that each decision variable appears in exactly two constraints to account for the eight-hour shift. For example, patrol officers reporting at 4 a.m. (i.e., x_2) contribute to the staffing requirements for both the second and third period because each period is four hours in duration. Because we are dealing with numbers of patrol officers, the decision variables must be restricted to integer values. Fortunately, because of the problem structure, the linear programming solution will be integer. In general, however, a linear programming solution yields nonnegative real (integer or fractional) numbers.

Workforce-Planning Problem

Employee turnover is common among service occupations; for example, bank tellers and airline attendants often leave their jobs. Furthermore, new employees require a training period before they are ready to meet the public. Also, the level of staff required varies in response to changes in consumer demand, such as during summer or holiday vacation periods for airlines. Workforce planning involves the identification of when and how many people to recruit to meet future staffing requirements and to replace employees who leave. The objective is to meet staff requirements in a dynamic setting at a minimum personnel cost.

Example 16.4: Last National Drive-In Bank

Last National must decide how many new bank tellers to hire and train over the next six months. The teller requirements, expressed as the number of teller-hours needed, are 1500 in January, 1800 in February, 1600 in March, 2000 in April, 1800 in May, and 2200 in June. One month of training is necessary before a teller can be assigned duty; thus, tellers must be hired one month before they are actually needed. Also, each trainee requires 80 hours of simulated job experience supervised by a regular teller during the month of training. Hence, for each trainee, 80 fewer hours are available from a regular teller. Each experienced teller works 160 hours per month, whether needed or not. Last National has 12 experienced tellers available at the beginning of January. Past

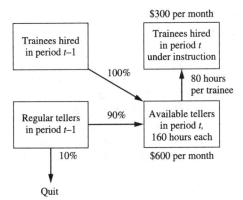

FIGURE 16.2
Monthly teller transition diagram.

experience has shown that by the end of each month, approximately 10 percent of the experienced tellers have quit their jobs. Regular tellers receive a salary of $600 per month, and trainees are paid $300 during their month of training. How many tellers should be hired for each of the next six months?

Figure 16.2 captures the essential relationships for this time-phased planning model. The decision variables are the number of trainees to hire for each period and the number of tellers available at the beginning of each period.

Let T_t = number of trainees hired at the beginning of period t
 for $t = 1, 2, 3, 4, 5, 6$
 A_t = number of tellers available at the beginning of period t
 for $t = 1, 2, 3, 4, 5, 6$

The objective is to minimize the total personnel costs for the six-month planning horizon. Two sets of constraints are required. One set represents the required teller-hours for each month. Another set keeps track of the number of available tellers from one month to the next, accounting for new hires and employee turnover. The following model makes use of some shorthand algebraic notations:

Minimize
$$\sum_{t=1}^{6} (600A_t + 300T_t)$$

subject to
$$160A_1 - 80T_1 \geq 1500 \quad \text{January}$$
$$160A_2 - 80T_2 \geq 1800 \quad \text{February}$$
$$160A_3 - 80T_3 \geq 1600 \quad \text{March}$$
$$160A_4 - 80T_4 \geq 2000 \quad \text{April}$$
$$160A_5 - 80T_5 \geq 1800 \quad \text{May}$$
$$160A_6 - 80T_6 \geq 2200 \quad \text{June}$$
$$A_1 = 12$$
$$0.9A_{t-1} + T_{t-1} - A_t = 0 \quad \text{for } t = 2, 3, 4, 5, 6$$
$$A_t, T_t \geq 0 \text{ and integer for } t = 1, 2, 3, 4, 5, 6$$

Note that when this model is used, only the value for January hiring is of immediate interest. The trainee hires for the other months can be treated as estimates for now. Prior to the start of February the model is run again, with the requirements for January dropped and the July requirements added. In this manner each hiring decision is based on a six-month projected requirement plan, which permits a gradual adjustment in the size of the workforce. Also, as in the police patrol example, the decision variables must be restricted to integers. Unfortunately, this problem structure does not necessarily yield integer results. This problem illustrates a special class of linear programming models called *integer programming,* which requires a special computer code that guarantees integer results.

Transportation Problem

Transportation problems are a special class of LP models called *networks.* The problem structure also ensures an integer solution. The problem is essentially one of shipping goods from origins, or supply points, to destinations, or demand points. Each destination has a particular demand and each origin a particular supply. The number of origins need not equal the number of destinations. To facilitate solution, a dummy origin or destination is added to balance the total demand and supply. Given a unit cost for shipping between each origin and destination pair, the objective is to minimize the total shipping cost. This problem structure also arises in nontransportation situations, such as assigning personnel to jobs.

Example 16.5: Lease-a-Lemon Car Rental

Lease-a-Lemon has discovered an imbalance in the distribution of rental cars in its northeast territory. The following surpluses of cars exist: 26 in New York, 43 in Washington, and 31 in Cleveland. Shortages of cars include 32 in Pittsburgh, 28 in Buffalo, and 26 in Philadelphia. The table below shows the distance in miles to transfer a car between each city:

	Pittsburgh	Buffalo	Philadelphia
New York	439	396	91
Washington	296	434	133
Cleveland	131	184	479

Develop a plan to redistribute the cars at a minimum cost on the basis of a transportation charge of $1 per mile.

Figure 16.3 is a network representation of the problem, with origin nodes showing positive supply and destination nodes showing negative demand. The supply and demand are balanced with the addition of a dummy destination node showing a −14 (i.e., 86 − 100) demand. The dummy represents cars not redistributed and thus has unit transportation costs of zero. The decision variables are the numbers of cars sent from the supply cities to the demand

Supplies   **Demands**

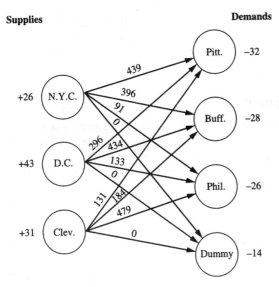

FIGURE 16.3
Lease-a-Lemon car redistribution network.

cities. To facilitate the model formulation, a unit transportation cost parameter is also defined below:

Let x_{ij} = number of cars sent from city i to city j for $i = 1, 2, 3$ and $j = 1, 2,$
3, 4
c_{ij} = unit cost in dollars to transport a car from city i to city j for $i = 1,$
2, 3 and $j = 1, 2, 3, 4$

The objective is to minimize the total redistribution cost. Two sets of constraints are required: one set limits the supply from each origin, and the other set limits the demand at each destination. The constraints will all be equalities because supply and demand are balanced.

Minimize $$\sum_{i=1}^{3}\sum_{j=1}^{4} c_{ij}x_{ij}$$

subject to

$$
\begin{array}{llll}
x_{11} + x_{12} + x_{13} + x_{14} & & & = 26 \\
\quad + x_{21} + x_{22} + x_{23} + x_{24} & & = 43 \\
\quad\quad x_{31} + x_{32} + x_{33} + x_{34} & = 31 \\
x_{11} \qquad\qquad + x_{21} \qquad\qquad + x_{31} & = 32 \\
\quad x_{12} \qquad\qquad + x_{22} \qquad\qquad + x_{32} & = 28 \\
\quad\quad x_{13} \qquad\qquad + x_{23} \qquad\qquad + x_{33} & = 26 \\
\quad\quad\quad x_{14} \qquad\qquad + x_{24} \qquad\qquad + x_{34} & = 14
\end{array}
$$

$$x_{ij} \geq 0 \qquad \text{for all } i, j$$

Notice the characteristic structure of the constraints that is common to all transportation problems. This structure and the appearance of only coefficients of 1 in the constraint equations assure an integer solution.

OPTIMAL SOLUTIONS AND COMPUTER ANALYSIS

The Stereo Warehouse problem (Example 16.1) is used to illustrate graphically the nature of LP models and their solutions. Because the problem has only the two decision variables x and y, we can draw a picture of the model and see how an optimal solution is achieved. This geometric representation of the model is also used to explain the computer-generated solution.

Graphical Solution of LP Models

Recall the formulation of the Stereo Warehouse model, where x and y represent the number of receivers and speakers to be stocked. In this formulation, Z represents the value of the objective function.

Maximize	$Z = 50x + 20y$	gross profit
subject to	$2x + 4y \leq 400$	floor space
	$100x + 50y \leq 8000$	budget
	$x \leq 60$	sales limit
	$x, y \geq 0$	nonnegativity

The set of inequalities or constraints defines a region of permissible values of x and y. Notice that letting $x = 0$ and $y = 0$ satisfies all the inequalities, as it should, because that is the "do-nothing" alternative. However, our interest is in finding the best, or optimal, values of x and y that maximize the objective function. For a two-variable problem, the permissible, or *feasible,* region can be identified if we plot each constraint inequality. The procedure for drawing the feasible region is as follows:

1. Assign one variable to the x axis and the other variable to the y axis.
2. Notice that the nonnegativity constraints on the variables limit the feasible region to the first quadrant (upper right-hand corner).
3. Temporarily change each inequality constraint to an equality.
4. Plot each constraint as an equation, using the x and y intercepts (i.e., assume that $x = 0$ and solve for the y intercept; then repeat for $y = 0$ to find the x intercept; finally, draw a straight line joining these two axis intercepts).
5. Identify the feasible side of the inequality. This can be accomplished by substituting $x = 0$ and $y = 0$ into the inequality constraint, unless (0, 0) happens to be on the line; then some other arbitrary point must be selected. If the inequality is satisfied, then the side containing $x = 0$ and $y = 0$ should be shaded; otherwise, the opposite side of the line is shaded (i.e., it represents a feasible region).

6. Notice that each constraint further reduces the feasible region into a geometric figure called a *convex polygon* (i.e., from inside the space looking outward, all the corners point outward).

The above procedure is followed for Stereo Warehouse to create the feasible region shown in Figure 16.4. Notice for the first constraint that the x intercept ($y = 0$) is $400/2 = 200$ and the y intercept ($x = 0$) is $400/4 = 100$. Also notice that the test point $x = 0$, $y = 0$ satisfies all three constraints; thus, the shaded area is either below or to the left of each constraint. Furthermore, notice that any point (combination of x and y values) within the feasible region simultaneously satisfies all three constraints and the nonnegativity condition.

The optimal solution to the problem can now be found graphically. Recall that the objective is to make Z as large as possible, provided the values of x and y are in the feasible region. If we let Z take on a trial value, say 2000, then we can plot Z as a straight line, using the intercept approach. For $Z = 2000$, the x intercept ($y = 0$) is $2000/50 = 40$ and the y intercept ($x = 0$) is $2000/20 = 100$. In Figure 16.5 we see the objective function $Z = 2000$ plotted on the graph of the feasible region. As the value of Z is increased to 3000, 3600, and finally 3800, we find that the objective function moves out from the origin in parallel lines, or contours. The maximum value of $Z = 3800$ occurs at point C (i.e., $x = 60$, $y = 40$), a corner of the polygon. If Z moves out any further, no point on the contour line will be common to the

FIGURE 16.4
Stereo Warehouse feasible region

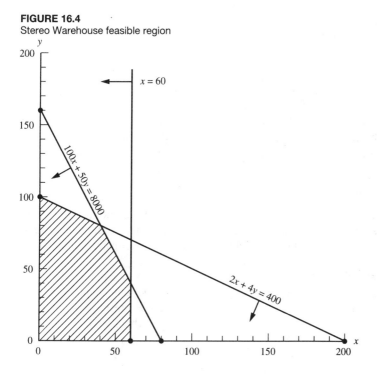

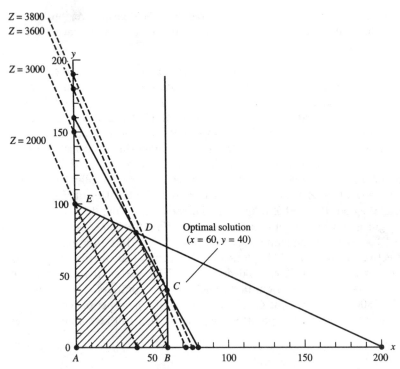

FIGURE 16.5
Stereo Warehouse optimal solution.

feasible region. We have just demonstrated an axiom of linear programming. An optimal solution to an LP model will always occur at a corner, or *extreme point,* of the feasible region. In the special case in which the slope of the objective function is identical to the slope of a constraint, the optimal solution will also include any point between the extreme points along the constraint line.

LP Model in Standard Form

Realizing that an optimal solution will be found at an extreme point reduces our search for a feasible region to a finite set of points. Furthermore, each extreme point is defined as the simultaneous solution of a pair of constraints stated as equations.

A formal way of restating an inequality constraint as an equation in linear programming models is accomplished with the use of a *slack* or *surplus* variable. For constraints of the $\leq$ variety, a nonnegative slack (i.e., resources not used) variable is added to the left-hand side. For example, the Stereo Warehouse floor-space constraint would be restated as

$$2x + 4y + s_1 = 400$$

The slack variable s_1 would represent available floor space not used by the receivers and speakers stocked. For constraints of the $\geq$ variety, a nonnegative surplus (i.e., results produced in excess of requirements) variable is subtracted from the left-hand side. For example, in the Gotham City Police Patrol problem, the first-period patrol officer requirement would be restated as

$$x_1 + x_6 - s_1 = 6$$

The surplus variable s_1 would represent the number of patrol officers assigned to the first period in excess of the requirement of six patrol officers.

The Stereo Warehouse model is reformulated below, using the following slack variables:

s_1 = square feet of floor space not used
s_2 = dollars of budget not allocated
s_3 = number of receivers that could have been sold

$$\begin{aligned}
\text{Maximize} \qquad & Z = 50x + 20y \\
\text{subject to} \qquad & 2x + 4y + s_1 && = 400 \\
& 100x + 50y \quad + s_2 && = 8000 \\
& x \qquad\qquad\quad + s_3 = 60 \\
& x, y, s_1, s_2, s_3 \geq 0
\end{aligned}$$

The Stereo Warehouse problem is solved by examining each extreme point, identified by the letters A, B, C, D, and E in Figure 16.5. Table 16.2 contains the analysis of these extreme points. At each extreme point, variables with positive

TABLE 16.2
STEREO WAREHOUSE EXTREME-POINT SOLUTIONS

Extreme point	Nonbasic variables	Basic variables	Variable value	Objective-function value Z
A	x, y	s_1	400	0
		s_2	8000	
		s_3	60	
B	s_3, y	s_1	280	3000
		s_2	2000	
		x	60	
C	s_3, s_2	s_1	120	3800
		y	40	
		x	60	
D	s_1, s_2	s_3	20	3600
		y	80	
		x	40	
E	s_1, x	s_3	60	2000
		y	100	
		s_2	3000	

TABLE 16.3 COMPUTER INPUT FOR STEREO WAREHOUSE

Free Format Model for STEREO WAREHOUSE

```
>> Max     50X+ 20Y
>>Subject to
>> (1)    2X+ 4Y <= 400
>> (2)    100X+ 50Y <= 8000
>> (3)    1X <= 60
```

---

values are labeled *basic,* and variables with zero values are labeled *nonbasic.* Notice that the number of basic variables equals the number of constraints in the problem. This result is always true for LP problems, except in the special case in which a basic variable is also zero-valued (a situation referred to as a *degenerate* solution). Also, notice that when a slack variable is nonbasic, its corresponding constraint is binding (i.e., all the resource is used).

The computer solution of LP problems evaluates the extreme points in a systematic way. This computer procedure is called the *simplex algorithm.* In our Stereo Warehouse example, the simplex algorithm starts at point A, proceeds to extreme point B (because variable x contributes more to the objective function than y), and stops at extreme point C, the optimum. The algorithm is able to identify optimality; thus, not all extreme points need be examined. The details of the simplex algorithm are not discussed here but can be found in any of the operations research texts listed in the Selected Bibliography at the end of this chapter.

Computer Analysis and Interpretation

All the illustrations of computer input and output reports that follow result from using the software package for personal computers called *QS: Quantitative Systems, Version 3.0.*[1]

The computer input for the Stereo Warehouse example is shown in Table 16.3. Using the free-format option, the input file looks identical to our earlier formulation of the problem.

The computer solution to the Stereo Warehouse problem is shown in Table 16.4. Each of the decision variables x and y and the slack variable s_1 have a nonzero solution value. The zero values for s_2 and s_3 indicate that these are nonbasic variables; thus, the corresponding constraints are binding. Also note that optimality was reached in two iterations, as expected from our graphical analysis above.

The opportunity cost has an important managerial interpretation. Recall that a nonbasic slack variable means that the corresponding constraint is binding at optimality. For the Stereo Warehouse problem, the budget constraint of $8000 (corresponding slack variable s_2) and the limit of 60 units for receiver sales (corresponding slack variable s_3) are restricting the profit to a maximum of $3800. The floor-space constraint is no problem, because at optimality 120 square feet (value of s_1) of the available 400 square feet are not being used. If profits are to be increased, more of the limiting resources must be obtained. The opportunity cost of $10 associated with the slack variable s_3 represents the increase in the objective-function value if one more receiver could be sold. Notice that if the limit on receiver sales is increased by 1, the budget constraint and the limit on x sales define the new extreme point:

$$100x + 50y = 8000$$
$$x = 61$$

The solution of the above simultaneous equations yields $x = 61$ and $y = 38$. Substituting these values into the objective function provides a revised profit of $3810, an increase of $10. A similar analysis explains the $0.40 increase in the objective-function value if the RHS of the budget constraint is increased by $1 to $8001 and the limit on x remains at 60 (the solution becomes $x = 60$ and $y = 40.02$).

The opportunity cost is often referred to as a *shadow price* because it represents the imputed price of a unit of the limited resource. Shadow prices can be used by a manager to decide on the value of securing more resources. For example, if money could be borrowed for less than 40 cents on the dollar during the period of the sale, the difference would become additional profit.

Most computer programs use the convention that if a unit increase in the RHS value improves the objective function (increases it for maximization or decreases it for minimization), then the shadow price is positive and represents the amount of objective-function change. However, in some problems increasing an RHS could result in impairing the objective function. For example, if the protein constraint in the Lakeview Hospital diet problem were increased, the objective function could increase, contrary to the minimization desired. The shadow price would be negative for this constraint if it were binding at optimality.

Finally, notice that the shadow price of a resource in excess (corresponding slack variable is basic) is considered zero. In the Stereo Warehouse problem the value to the manager of securing additional floor space is zero because not all the available floor space is used.

SENSITIVITY ANALYSIS

What happens to the optimal solution of an LP problem if the values of the model parameters change? This question is of great interest to a decision maker in an uncertain environment. Sensitivity of the solution with respect to the objective-function coefficients is discussed first, and then constraint RHS ranging is analyzed.

Objective-Function Coefficient Ranges

The permissible range of each objective-function coefficient is shown in Table 16.5. The coefficient for the y variable may range from a low of 0 to a high of 25. The x-variable coefficient has a range of 40 to infinity. Within these ranges the optimal solution remains at extreme point C, shown in Figure 16.6. As shown, the objective-function slope changes with different coefficient values and essentially pivots about extreme point C.

Notice that with a y coefficient of 0, the objective function lies along the line segment BC of constraint 3. When the y coefficient is 25, the objective function lies along the line segment DC, parallel to constraint 2. Notice, also, that if the coefficient of y exceeds 25, the optimal solution moves to the extreme point D. A similar analysis can be made for the x objective-function coefficient. The decision maker must be cautioned that the range for each coefficient is limited to changing one parameter at a time, holding all others fixed. Furthermore, the value of the objective function changes as these coefficients are changed.

Right-Hand-Side Ranging

The allowable RHS ranges for each of the constraints are shown in Table 16.6. The RHS for the second constraint ranges from 6000 to 9500. The RHS for the

FIGURE 16.6
Stereo Warehouse objective-function coefficient ranging.

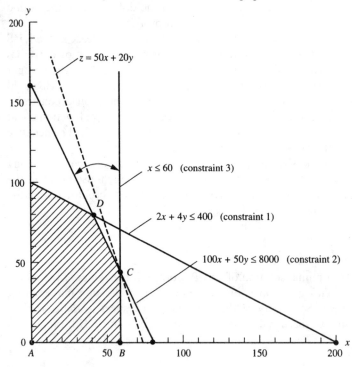

TABLE 16.4 COMPUTER RESULTS FOR STEREO WAREHOUSE

		Final Solution for STEREO WAREHOUSE				Page : 1	
Variable No.	Names	Solution	Opportunity Cost	Variable No.	Names	Solution	Opportunity Cost
1	X	+60.000000	0	4	S2	0	+.40000001
2	Y	+40.000000	0	5	S3	0	+10.000000
3	S1	+120.00000	0				

Maximized OBJ. = 3800 Iteration = 2 Elapsed CPU second = 5.078125E-02

TABLE 16.5 OBJECTIVE-FUNCTION COEFFICIENT SENSITIVITY RESULTS

		Sensitivity Analysis for Objective Coefficients			Page : 1		
Variable	Min. C(j)	Original	Max. C(j)	Variable	Min. C(j)	Original	Max. C(j)
X	+40.0000	+50.0000	+Infinity	Y	0	+20.0000	+25.0000

TABLE 16.6 RIGHT-HAND-SIDE RESULTS

		Sensitivity Analysis for RHS			Page : 1		
Constrnt	Min. B(i)	Original	Max. B(i)	Constrnt	Min. B(i)	Original	Max. B(i)
1	+280.000	+400.000	+Infinity	3	+40.0000	+60.0000	+80.0000
2	+6000.00	+8000.00	+9500.00				

429

third constraint ranges from 40 to 80. Within these ranges the optimal solution contains the same basic variables s_1, x, and y. The values of these variables will change, as well as the objective-function value. It should be noted that the shadow price for each resource applies *only* within these ranges. For example, recall that the shadow price for constraint 3 is a $10-per-unit increase in the RHS. Notice that the objective-function value increases from $3800 to $4000 when the RHS increases from 60 to 80 [i.e., $(80 - 60)(10) = 200$]. Likewise, the objective-function value is reduced by $200 when the RHS of constraint 3 decreases from 60 to 40.

Notice in Figure 16.7 what happens graphically when the RHS of constraint 3 is changed. As the RHS is increased, the extreme point C moves along the line segment CI until it becomes coincident with I at RHS = 80. The values of the basic variables at extreme point I are $s_1 = 240$, $x = 80$, and $y = 0$. This is a degenerate solution because variable $y = 0$ but still remains in the basis.

If the RHS of constraint 3 is reduced, the extreme point C moves along the line segment CD until it becomes coincident with D at RHS = 40. The values of the basic variables at extreme point D are $s_1 = 0$, $x = 40$, and $y = 80$. This is a degenerate solution because variable $s_1 = 0$ but still remains in the basis. A similar analysis for binding constraint 2 can be made to show graphically the movement of extreme point C along the line segment BII as the RHS is changed from 6000 to 9500.

FIGURE 16.7
Stereo Warehouse right-hand-side ranging.

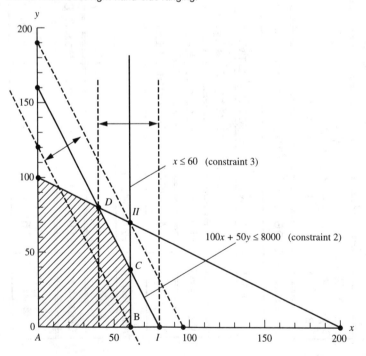

The concept that the resource shadow price is limited to the RHS range is important in *postoptimality analysis*. For example, in the Stereo Warehouse problem, suppose that additional money can be obtained at a cost less than the shadow price of 40 cents per dollar. The question of how much to obtain at this price is answered by the RHS range on the budget constraint. Secure $9500 – $8000, or $1500, in additional financing to maximize profits. The same caution raised earlier about treating the sensitivity analysis as being limited to changing one parameter at a time, holding all others fixed, is true for RHS ranging.

GOAL PROGRAMMING

Linear programming models allow for only one objective, and all constraints must be met absolutely. Many problems, particularly in the public sector, have multiple objectives in different units of measure. This makes the construction of a consolidated single objective difficult, if not impossible. For example, an emergency ambulance system could have the following objectives:

1. Maintain an average response time of approximately four minutes.
2. Ensure that 90 percent of all calls receive aid in less than 10 minutes.
3. Try not to exceed a budget of $100,000 per year.
4. Allocate calls to ambulance crews in an equitable manner.

Goal programming is a variation of linear programming that permits multiple and conflicting goals with different dimensions. Multiple goals are rank-ordered and treated as *preemptive priorities*. In the solution procedure, higher-ranked goals are not sacrificed to achieve lower-ranked goals. The solution approach is equivalent to solving a series of nested LP problems in which higher-ranked goals become constraints on lower-ranked goals. While linear programming optimizes a single objective, goal programming minimizes the deviations from goals. This solution approach is known as *satisficing* because not all goals will necessarily be met; instead, the goals will be achieved as closely as possible.

The objective function will contain only deviational variables (i.e., plus or minus deviations from goals), which can also be given *deviational weights* to distinguish relative importance within a priority level. The objective is always to minimize the sum of the deviations at each priority level, with consideration given to the hierarchy of preemptive priorities. All constraints are stated as equalities and contain both plus and minus deviational variables in addition to decision variables. To illustrate a goal programming model, the Stereo Warehouse example is reformulated as a goal program.

Example 16.6: Stereo Warehouse as a Goal Program

Let x = number of receivers to stock
  y = number of speakers to stock
  d_1^- = amount by which profit falls short of $999,999
  d_1^+ = amount by which profit exceeds $999,999

d_2^- = amount by which floor space used falls short of 400 square feet
d_2^+ = amount by which floor space used exceeds 400 square feet
d_3^- = amount by which budget falls short of $8000
d_3^+ = amount by which budget exceeds $8000
d_4^- = amount by which sales of receivers fall short of 60
d_4^+ = amount by which sales of receivers exceed 60
P_k = priority level with rank k

Minimize $\qquad\qquad Z = P_1 d_4^+ + P_2(d_1^- + 2d_3^+) + P_3(d_2^- + d_2^+)$
subject to

$$
\begin{aligned}
50x + 20y + d_1^- - d_1^+ &= 999{,}999 && \text{profit goal} \\
2x + 4y + d_2^- - d_2^+ &= 400 && \text{floor-space goal} \\
100x + 50y + d_3^- - d_3^+ &= 8000 && \text{budget goal} \\
x + d_4^- - d_4^+ &= 60 && \text{sales-limit goal}
\end{aligned}
$$

$$x, y, d_1^-, d_1^+, d_2^-, d_2^+, d_3^-, d_3^+, d_4^-, d_4^+ \geq 0$$

This formulation has translated the profit objective into a goal at the second priority level. Notice that only d_1^- is included in the objective function to be minimized. Minimizing d_1^-, the underachievement of the goal, forces the profit to approach 999,999, a very large number. The floor space used for display now becomes a third priority in which both deviational variables are minimized. In other words, we want to use approximately 400 square feet. The goal programming model permits a previous absolute constraint on available space to be treated as a more realistic approximate requirement. Exceeding the budget is to be avoided, and so only d_3^+ is found in the objective function. The deviational weight of 2 indicates that meeting the budget is twice as important as maximizing profit. Finally, exceeding the sales limit of 60 receivers is found at the first priority. This illustrates how system or physical constraints are treated in goal programming. Thus, the typical LP absolute constraints, such as $\leq$ or $\geq$, have their appropriate deviational variable at the first priority level. The goal hierarchy ensures that no solution will violate these system constraints.

Table 16.7 shows the computer input for the Stereo Warehouse goal programming model for solution using a regular LP program. To ensure that the goal hierarchy is not violated, the priority ranks have been given increasingly large weights (i.e., $P_1 = 1000$, $P_2 = 100$, and $P_3 = 1$). The variables labeled "DM" represent underachievement deviations (d^-), and the variables labeled "DP" represent overachievement deviations (d^+).

The goal programming solution to the Stereo Warehouse example is found in Table 16.8. Notice that the values for the decision variables x and y are identical to the values in the previous LP solution. When the value for DM1 is subtracted from its RHS of 999,999, the profit is found to be $3800, as before. The deviational variable DM2 takes on a value of 120, indicating the underachievement of our goal to use approximately 400 square feet of floor space. Our budget of $8000 is completely exhausted because DP3 = 0. The deviational variable DM4 is zero, as required to achieve the constraint on receiver sales.

TABLE 16.7 COMPUTER INPUT FOR STEREO WAREHOUSE
GOAL PROGRAMMING MODEL FOR SOLUTION USING LP

Free Format Model for STEREO WAREHOUSE

```
>> Min    100DM1+ 1DM2+ 1DP2+ 200DP3+ 1000DP4
>>Subject to
>> (1)    50X+ 20Y+ 1DM1-1DP1 = 999999
>> (2)    2X+ 4Y+ 1DM2-1DP2 = 400
>> (3)    100X+ 50Y+ 1DM3-1DP3 = 8000
>> (4)    1X+ 1DM4-1DP4 = 60
```

TABLE 16.8 COMPUTER RESULTS OF THE STEREO WAREHOUSE GOAL PROGRAMMING MODEL

Final Solution for STEREO WAREHOUSE   Page : 1

Variable No.	Names	Solution	Opportunity Cost	Variable No.	Names	Solution	Opportunity Cost
1	X	+60.000000	0	8	DP3		0 +159.92000
2	Y	+40.000000	0	9	DM4		0 +994.00024
3	DM1	+996199.06	0	10	DP4		0 +5.9997244
4	DP1	0	+100.00000	11	A1		0 -100.00000
5	DM2	+119.99999	0	12	A2		0 -1.0000000
6	DP2	0	+2.0000000	13	A3		0 +40.079998
7	DM3	0	+40.079998	14	A4		0 +994.00024

Minimized OBJ. = 9.962002E+07   Iteration = 7   Elapsed CPU second = .21875

In summary, all goals are met except the desire to utilize 400 square feet of floor space. The objective-function value is of little consequence because it is simply the sum of all weighted deviations. Unfortunately, the opportunity costs, or shadow prices, are of no interest because the objective function has no economic meaning.

SUMMARY

Linear programming is one of the most popular computer-based modeling techniques available to the modern service operations manager. The power of LP to find optimal solutions and to conduct sensitivity analyses is invaluable to the decision maker. Furthermore, the structure of the constrained optimization model fits well the real world of the service operations manager.

The art of formulating LP models is developed through examples and practice using a systematic approach. Many examples of LP models illustrate the general problem-solving nature of linear programming. We find that the discipline of formulating LP models helps decision makers clarify objectives and identify resource constraints.

The procedure for solving LP models was demonstrated by the use of graphics. Because no one solves real LP models by hand, the interpretation of computer solutions was stressed. Again, using graphics, the concepts of shadow prices and sensitivity analysis were demonstrated. Because many service operations managers are faced with multiple objectives, the concept of goal programming was introduced. With goal programming, the manager attempts to satisfy goals rather than optimize a single objective.

TOPICS FOR DISCUSSION

1. Give some everyday examples of constrained optimization problems.
2. How can the validity of linear programming models be evaluated?
3. Interpret the meaning of the opportunity cost for a nonbasic decision variable that did not appear in the LP solution.
4. Explain graphically what has happened when a degenerate solution occurs in an LP problem.
5. Using Figure 16.6, analyze the x objective-function coefficient that ranges from a value of 40 to infinity.
6. Using Figure 16.7, explain what happens to the LP solution as the RHS of binding constraint 2 ranges from $6000 to $9500.
7. Linear programming is a special case of goal programming. Explain.
8. What are some limitations to the use of linear programming?

EXERCISES

16.1. The Economy Cab Company wants to mix two fuels (A and B) for its taxicabs in order to minimize operating costs. The company needs at least 3000 gallons in order to operate its cabs next month. There are only 2000 gallons of fuel A available, and fuel B is unlimited in supply. The mixed fuel must have an octane rating of at least 80.

When fuels are mixed, the amount of fuel obtained is just equal to the sum of the amounts put in, assuming that no spillage or evaporation occurs. The resulting octane rating is just the average of the individual octanes, weighted in proportion to the respective volumes. Fuel A costs 20 cents per gallon and has an octane rating of 90; fuel B costs 10 cents per gallon and has an octane rating of 75.

a. Formulate this blending problem (a variation on the diet problem) as a linear programming model to minimize the cost of the blended fuel.

b. Using the graphical method, determine the amount of each fuel required for an optimum blend.

16.2. Springdale has been ordered by a federal district court to desegregate its school system. The city is divided into seven school districts and is served by three elementary schools, one junior high, and one high school. The table below gives the distance from each district to each elementary school and the number of minority and white children in each district. Ideally, minorities should represent 40 percent of the enrollment in each elementary school. However, achieving perfect desegregation is not practical; thus, the school board is willing to settle for a percentage of minorities in each school that is not less than 30 percent or more than 50 percent. Each school has a capacity of 400 students. Formulate a linear programming model to minimize the total number of student miles traveled by bus. Do not solve.

District	Distance to school, mi			Numbers in district	
	A	B	C	Minorities	Whites
1	10	18	32	90	40
2	0	25	38	110	20
3	20	13	24	50	60
4	8	22	33	70	70
5	35	0	16	40	130
6	26	14	24	30	120
7	38	7	0	10	160
Total				400	600

16.3. The computer input for the Lakeview Hospital example is shown in Table 16.9, with E, C, and S defined as units of egg custard base, ice cream, and butterscotch syrup. The results of the computer solutions are given in Tables 16.10 to 16.12.

TABLE 16.9
COMPUTER INPUT FOR LAKEVIEW HOSPITAL

Free Format Model for LAKEVIEW HOSPITAL

```
>> Min    .15E+ .25C+ .1S
>>Subject to
>> (1)    50E+ 150C+ 90S <= 175
>> (2)    100C+ 50S <= 150
>> (3)    70E+ 10C >= 200
>> (4)    30E+ 80C+ 200S >= 100
```

TABLE 16.10 LAKEVIEW HOSPITAL COMPUTER SOLUTION

Final Solution for LAKEVIEW HOSPITAL   Page : 1

Variable No.	Names	Solution	Opportunity Cost	Variable No.	Names	Solution	Opportunity Cost
1	E	+2.8571429	0	6	S3	0	+.00192857
2	C	0	+.19071429	7	A3	0	-.00192857
3	S	+.07142858	0	8	S4	0	+.00050000
4	S1	+25.714285	0	9	A4	0	-.00050000
5	S2	+146.42857	0				

Minimized OBJ. = .4357143   Iteration = 2   Elapsed CPU second = 5.078125E-02

TABLE 16.11 LAKEVIEW HOSPITAL OBJECTIVE-FUNCTION COEFFICIENT SENSITIVITY ANALYSIS

Sensitivity Analysis for Objective Coefficients   Page : 1

Variable	Min. C(j)	Original	Max. C(j)	Variable	Min. C(j)	Original	Max. C(j)
E	+.015000	+.150000	+1.48500	S	0	+.100000	+.603774
C	+.059286	+.250000	+Infinity				

TABLE 16.12 LAKEVIEW HOSPITAL RIGHT-HAND-SIDE SENSITIVITY ANALYSIS

Sensitivity Analysis for RHS   Page : 1

Constrnt	Min. B(i)	Original	Max. B(i)	Constrnt	Min. B(i)	Original	Max. B(i)
1	+149.286	+175.000	+Infinity	3	0	+200.000	+233.333
2	+3.57143	+150.000	+Infinity	4	+85.7143	+100.000	+157.143

a. What is the cost of the special milk shake?

b. How many units of each ingredient are required for this minimum-cost shake? If you feel that this mixture is unacceptable as a shake, suggest a constraint that would guarantee an acceptable shake.

c. What would be the cost of including one unit of ice cream in the mixture? Explain why this cost is less than 25 cents.

d. What is the cholesterol, fat, protein, and calorie content of this shake?

e. What are the ranges of acceptable unit costs for the egg custard base and butterscotch syrup for the computer solution to remain optimal?

f. What would the milk shake cost if the protein requirement were increased to its RHS limit?

g. Why are there no upper limits on the requirements for cholesterol and fat?

16.4. The computer input for the Gotham City Police Patrol example is shown in Table 16.13, with x_j defined as the number of patrol officers reporting for duty at the beginning of period j. The results of the computer solution are given in Table 16.14.

a. How many patrol officers are required to meet the staffing requirements? Is this solution an improvement over the current practice of patrol officers reporting at only three times during the day?

b. In what period is there an excess of patrol officers? As the police commissioner, how could you make full use of their time?

c. Using Figure 16.1 in the text, sketch in the results of this optimum staffing schedule.

d. What does an opportunity cost of zero for variable x_4 suggest to you?

e. A police officer, unhappy about reporting for duty at midnight, suggests the following schedule: $x_1 = 0$, $x_2 = 8$, $x_3 = 6$, $x_4 = 2$, $x_5 = 10$, and $x_6 = 6$. Show that this schedule is both feasible and optimal.

16.5. The computer input for the Last National Drive-In Bank example is shown in Table 16.15, with A_j and T_j representing the number of tellers available and trainees hired at the beginning of period j. The results of the computer solution are given in Table 16.16.

a. The solution did not result in integer values, as required. On the basis of the fractional solution, how many trainees would you recommend be hired in each of the coming six periods?

b. Is your recommendation in part **a** feasible?

c. Give a reason why you are not surprised to find that T_6 is nonbasic.

d. How much overstaffing results from your solution?

16.6. The computer input for the Lease-a-Lemon Car Rental example is shown in Table 16.17, with x_{ij} representing the number of cars to send from city i to city j. The results of the computer solution are given in Table 16.18.

a. What is the recommended schedule of car movements?

b. Is this solution degenerate?

16.7. A certain company is planning the introduction of a new product that will be promoted by specially trained agents. The new-product campaign is to be guided by the following considerations: (1) the training session for special agents should be as close to 20 working days as possible; (2) sales during the first quarter, it is hoped, will be near 5 million units;

TABLE 16.13 COMPUTER INPUT FOR GOTHAM CITY

Free Format Model for GOTHAM CITY

```
>> Min    1X1+ 1X2+ 1X3+ 1X4+ 1X5+ 1X6
>>Subject to
>> (1)   1X1+ 1X6  >= 6
>> (2)   1X1+ 1X2  >= 4
>> (3)   1X2+ 1X3  >= 14
>> (4)   1X3+ 1X4  >= 8
>> (5)   1X4+ 1X5  >= 12
>> (6)   1X5+ 1X6  >= 16
```

TABLE 16.14 GOTHAM CITY COMPUTER SOLUTION

Final Solution for GOTHAM CITY   Page : 1

Variable No.	Names	Solution	Opportunity Cost	Variable No.	Names	Solution	Opportunity Cost
1	X1	+2.0000000	0	10	A2	0	0
2	X2	+6.0000000	0	11	S3	0	+1.0000000
3	X3	+8.0000000	0	12	A3	0	-1.0000000
4	X4	0	0	13	S4	0	0
5	X5	+12.000000	0	14	A4	0	0
6	X6	+4.0000000	0	15	S5	0	0
7	S1	0	+1.0000000	16	A5	0	+1.0000000
8	A1	0	-1.0000000	17	S6	0	-1.0000000
9	S2	+4.0000000	0	18	A6	0	0

Minimized OBJ. = 32   Iteration = 6   Elapsed CPU second = .2734375

TABLE 16.15 COMPUTER INPUT FOR LAST NATIONAL BANK

```
Free Format Model for LAST NATIONAL BANK

>> Min      600A1+ 600A2+ 600A3+ 600A4+ 600A5+ 600A6+ 300T1+ 300T2+ 300T3+ 300T4+ 300T5+ 300T6
>>Subject to
>>  (1)    160A1-80T1  >=  1500
>>  (2)    160A2-80T2  >=  1800
>>  (3)    160A3-80T3  >=  1600
>>  (4)    160A4-80T4  >=  2000
>>  (5)    160A5-80T5  >=  1800
>>  (6)    160A6-80T6  >=  2200
>>  (7)    1A1 = 12
>>  (8)    .9A1-1A2+  1T1  =  0
>>  (9)    .9A2-1A3+  1T2  =  0
>>  (10)   .9A3-1A4+  1T3  =  0
>>  (11)   .9A4-1A5+  1T4  =  0
>>  (12)   .9A5-1A6+  1T5  =  0
```

439

TABLE 16.16 LAST NATIONAL BANK COMPUTER SOLUTION

Final Solution for LAST NATIONAL BANK   Page : 1

Variable No.	Names	Solution	Opportunity Cost	Variable No.	Names	Solution	Opportunity Cost
1	A1	+12.000000	0	16	A2	0	-2.7155173
2	A2	+11.674321	0	17	S3	0	+3.6519027
3	A3	+11.355530	0	18	A3	0	-3.6519027
4	A4	+12.931035	0	19	S4	0	+3.9747941
5	A5	+12.500001	0	20	A4	0	-3.9747941
6	A6	+13.750001	0	21	S5	0	+4.0861359
7	T1	+.87432152	0	22	A5	0	-4.0861359
8	T2	+.84864110	0	23	S6	0	+7.6680679
9	T3	+2.7110586	0	24	A6	0	-7.6680679
10	T4	+.86206907	0	25	A7	0	-330.00000
11	T5	+2.5000002	0	26	A8	0	-300.00000
12	T6	0	+913.44543	27	A9	0	-517.24139
13	S1	+350.05417	0	28	A10	0	-592.15222
14	A1	0	0	29	A11	0	-617.98352
15	S2	0	+2.7155173	30	A12	0	-626.89087

Minimized OBJ. = 46865.36   Iteration = 12   Elapsed CPU second = 1.039063

TABLE 16.17 COMPUTER INPUT FOR LEASE-A-LEMON

Free Format Model for LEASE-A-LEMON

```
>> Min   439X11+ 396X12+ 91X13+ 296X21+ 434X22+ 133X23+ 131X31+ 184X32+ 479X33
>>Subject to
>> (1)   1X11+ 1X12+ 1X13+ 1X14 = 26
>> (2)   1X21+ 1X22+ 1X23+ 1X24 = 43
>> (3)   1X31+ 1X32+ 1X33+ 1X34 = 31
>> (4)   1X11+ 1X21+ 1X31 = 32
>> (5)   1X12+ 1X22+ 1X32 = 28
>> (6)   1X13+ 1X23+ 1X33 = 26
>> (7)   1X14+ 1X24+ 1X34 = 14
```

TABLE 16.18 LEASE-A-LEMON COMPUTER SOLUTION

Final Solution for LEASE-A-LEMON   Page : 1

Variable No.	Names	Solution	Opportunity Cost	Variable No.	Names	Solution	Opportunity Cost
1	X11	0	+143.00002	11	X33	0	+553.00000
2	X12	0	+47.000027	12	X34	0	+165.00000
3	X13	+26.000000	0	13	A1	0	-349.00000
4	X14	0	0	14	A2	0	-349.00000
5	X21	+29.000000	0	15	A3	0	-184.00000
6	X22	0	+85.000015	16	A4	0	+52.999992
7	X23	0	+42.000000	17	A5	0	0
8	X24	+14.000000	0	18	A6	0	+258.00000
9	X31	+3.000000	0	19	A7	0	+349.00000
10	X32	+28.000000	0				

Minimized OBJ. = 16495   Iteration = 6   Elapsed CPU second = .390625

and (3) under no circumstances can training costs exceed $600,000. Write the objective function and constraints if the sales target is considered twice as important as the training time target. The training cost is $20,000 per day, and each day of training will produce 150,000 units of sales during the first quarter. The decision to be made concerns the number of days that should be spent on training sales agents.

Let x = the number of days devoted to training. Define other variables as necessary, and formulate a goal programming model.

16.8. Tennis World carries three lines of its Toe-brand tennis racket: the Student, the Weekender, and the Professional. The more expensive the line, the greater the markup, but the more expensive lines also require more floor space for increasingly elaborate displays. Pertinent data are summarized in the table below:

Tennis racket	Cost per racket to Tennis World	Tennis World markup, %	Display space per racket, ft^2
Student	$10	10	1
Weekender	15	20	2
Professional	30	50	5

In deciding on the optimal merchandising plan, the manager states the following goals in their order of preference: (1) avoid overrunning the purchasing budget of $2000; (2) achieve a gross margin (the sum of markups for each racket) of at least $500; (3) avoid using more than 300 square feet of floor space for displays; and (4) ensure that the entire purchasing budget is spent. Formulate a goal programming model to determine the number of each type of tennis racket to stock. Recall the following retailing relationship: selling price = cost + (markup) (cost).

CASE: MUNICH DELICATESSEN

Among the most popular items served by the Munich Deli is its bratwurst. This sausage is based on an original old-world recipe that combines beef, chicken, lamb, and assorted spices in a pure animal casing. By Department of Agriculture regulations, the Munich Deli must display on the sausage label certain content information and adhere to those content specifications in the processing and packaging of the sausage. Because of the popularity of its bratwurst, Munich Deli can sell all the bratwurst it can make. Potential variability of the costs of the major ingredients, however, causes a continuing problem for the processing manager, who must determine the amount of each ingredient to mix into the sausage.

Bratwurst is prepared in 100-pound batches. According to the label (which cannot be altered except through a lengthy and costly procedure), each batch consists of at least 30 percent lamb by weight, with no specific requirement on beef or chicken. Moreover, the label indicates that each batch, by weight, is at most 24 percent fat, at least 12 percent protein, and at most 64 percent water and other ingredients.

A recent Department of Agriculture study has shown that the major ingredients in bratwurst contain the label-controlled elements in the following proportions:

	Percentage of weight		
Element	Beef	Chicken	Lamb
Fat	20	15	25
Protein	20	15	15
Water and others	60	70	60

It can be reasonably assumed that the spices and casing add an insignificant amount to the total sausage weight and almost nothing in terms of the elements being controlled.

Currently, the costs of the principal ingredients are $1, $0.50, and $0.70 per pound for beef, chicken, and lamb, respectively. At these costs there seem to be unlimited supplies. Thus, the processing manager at Munich Deli must decide how much of each principal ingredient to mix into each batch of bratwurst to meet labeling requirements at the lowest cost.

A preliminary analysis suggests that this decision problem can be formulated as a linear programming model, with

x_1 = number of pounds of beef per batch
x_2 = number of pounds of chicken per batch
x_3 = number of pounds of lamb per batch

Formulate this problem as a linear programming problem and solve.

Questions

1. Suppose that the early, unseasonably cold weather reduces the production of lamb, and the price for new supplies of lamb rises to 85 cents per pound. What effect will this situation have on the optimum contents of the sausage found originally? What effect will this situation have on Munich Deli's production costs for each batch of bratwurst?

2. The Department of Agriculture is considering adopting new regulations that would restrict the water content in all sausage. For what range of values of water content would Munich Deli continue to use the same ingredients in its sausage as in the original optimum (i.e., the same basic variables)?

3. Suppose that a meat supplier advises Munich Deli of the availability of veal tongues. Referring to the original recipe for bratwurst reveals that veal tongues could be used, and technically this ingredient is already covered on the sausage label under the generic category "beef and beef by-products." Unlike the regular beef originally considered, these tongues are 30 percent fat, 15 percent protein, and 55 percent water, all by weight. The meat supplier is willing to sell Munich Deli these tongues for $0.40 per pound. Should this new ingredient be included in the optimal sausage composition? Why?

CASE: SEQUOIA AIRLINES

Sequoia Airlines is a well-established regional airline serving California, Nevada, Arizona, and Utah. Sequoia competes against much larger carriers in this regional market, and its management feels that the price, frequency of flight service, ability to meet schedules, baggage handling, and image projected by the flight attendants are the most important marketing factors airline passengers consider in deciding to use a particular carrier.

In every one of these areas, Sequoia is attaining its desired objectives. However, maintaining its flight attendant staff at desired levels has been difficult in the past, and many times it has had to ask flight attendants to work overtime because of worker shortages. This has resulted in excessive personnel costs and some morale problems among the flight attendants. One reason for the worker shortages is a higher-than-industry-average turnover rate, owing to experienced attendants being hired away by other airlines. This is not totally due to morale problems, as that cause seems to become important only during seasonal peak-demand periods, when shortages are particularly bad. By interviewing the existing personnel, Sequoia has discovered that competing regional carriers (whose training programs are not as highly developed) have been hiring away from Sequoia a significant proportion of its staff by offering slightly higher direct salaries, attractive indirect benefit packages, and a guarantee of a minimum number of flying hours in off-peak demand periods.

As a beginning, Sequoia's management has asked for a six-month hiring and training analysis of the flight attendant staff requirements, beginning next month (July). An investigation of the operations schedule indicates that 14,000 attendant-hours are needed in July; 16,000 in August; 13,000 in September; 12,000 in October; 18,000 in November; and 20,000 in December. Sequoia's training program for new personnel requires an entire month of classroom preparation before they are assigned to regular flight service. As junior flight attendants, they remain on probationary status for one additional month. Periodically, there is some personnel movement from the working flight attendant staff to the staff that supervises the training of new employees. Figure 16.8 shows the relationships and the percentages of interstaff movements that research has shown to be historically true.

Normally, when no personnel shortages occur, each junior flight attendant works an average of 140 hours per month and is paid a salary of $1050 during the probationary period. During the training period, each new employee is paid $750. The experienced flight attendants receive an average salary of $1400 per month, and they work an average of 125 hours per month. Each instructor receives a salary of $1500 per month.

The poorly kept secret of Sequoia's personalized training program is that the number of trainees is limited to no more than five per instructor. Instructors not needed in a particular month (surplus) may be used as flight attendants. To ensure a high level of quality in flight service, Sequoia requires that the proportion of junior flight attendant–hours not exceed 25 percent of any month's total (junior plus experienced) attendant-hours.

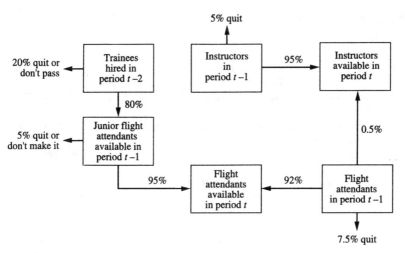

FIGURE 16.8
Sequoia Airlines flight attendant flows.

In May, Sequoia hired 10 new employees to enter the training program, and this month it hired 10 more. At the beginning of June there were 120 experienced flight attendants and 6 instructors on Sequoia's staff.

Let T_t = number of trainees hired at the beginning of period t,
 with $t = 1, 2, 3, 4, 5, 6$
 J_t = number of junior flight attendants available at the beginning of period t, with $t = 1, 2, 3, 4, 5, 6$
 F_t = number of experienced flight attendants available at the beginning of period t, with $t = 1, 2, 3, 4, 5, 6$
 I_t = number of instructors available at the beginning of period t, with $t = 1, 2, 3, 4, 5, 6$
 S_t = number of surplus instructors available as flight attendants at the beginning of period t, with $t = 1, 2, 3, 4, 5, 6$

Questions

1. For the forecast period (July–December), determine the number of new trainees who must be hired at the beginning of each month so that total personnel costs for the flight attendant staff and training program are minimized. Formulate the problem as a linear programming model and solve.

2. How would you deal with the noninteger results?

3. Discuss how you would use the LP model to make your hiring decision for the next six months.

SELECTED BIBLIOGRAPHY

Anderson, D. R., D. J. Sweeney, and T. A. Williams: *An Introduction to Management Science*, 6th ed., West Publishing Co., New York, 1991.

Budnick, F. S., D. McLeavey, and R. Mojena: *Principles of Operations Research for Management*, 2d ed., Richard D. Irwin, Inc., Homewood, Ill., 1988.

Chang, Yih-Long, and R. S. Sullivan: *QS: Quantitative Systems, Version 3.0*, Prentice-Hall, Englewood Cliffs, N.J., 1993.

Hillier, F. S., and G. J. Lieberman: *Introduction to Operations Research*, 4th ed., Holden-Day, Inc., San Francisco, 1986.

Lee, Sang M.: *Goal Programming for Decision Analysis*, Auerbach Publishers, Inc., Philadelphia, 1972.

Turban, E., and J. R. Meredith: *Fundamentals of Management Science*, 4th ed., Business Publications, Inc., Plano, Texas, 1988.

APPENDIX

Areas of a Standard Normal Distribution

An entry in the table is the proportion under the entire curve which is between $z = 0$ and a positive value of z. Areas for negative values of z are obtained by symmetry.

z	0.00	0.01	0.02	0.03	0.04	0.05	0.06	0.07	0.08	0.09
0.0	0.0000	0.0040	0.0080	0.0120	0.0160	0.0199	0.0239	0.0279	0.0319	0.0359
0.1	0.0398	0.0438	0.0478	0.0517	0.0557	0.0596	0.0636	0.0675	0.0714	0.0753
0.2	0.0793	0.0832	0.0871	0.0910	0.0948	0.0987	0.1026	0.1064	0.1103	0.1141
0.3	0.1179	0.1217	0.1255	0.1293	0.1331	0.1368	0.1406	0.1443	0.1480	0.1517
0.4	0.1554	0.1591	0.1628	0.1664	0.1700	0.1736	0.1772	0.1808	0.1844	0.1879
0.5	0.1915	0.1950	0.1985	0.2019	0.2054	0.2088	0.2123	0.2157	0.2190	0.2224
0.6	0.2257	0.2291	0.2324	0.2357	0.2389	0.2422	0.2454	0.2486	0.2517	0.2549
0.7	0.2580	0.2611	0.2642	0.2673	0.2703	0.2734	0.2764	0.2794	0.2823	0.2852
0.8	0.2881	0.2910	0.2939	0.2967	0.2995	0.3023	0.3051	0.3078	0.3106	0.3133
0.9	0.3159	0.3186	0.3212	0.3238	0.3264	0.3289	0.3315	0.3340	0.3365	0.3389
1.0	0.3413	0.3438	0.3461	0.3485	0.3508	0.3531	0.3554	0.3577	0.3599	0.3621
1.1	0.3643	0.3665	0.3686	0.3708	0.3729	0.3749	0.3770	0.3790	0.3810	0.3830
1.2	0.3849	0.3869	0.3888	0.3907	0.3925	0.3944	0.3962	0.3980	0.3997	0.4015
1.3	0.4032	0.4049	0.4066	0.4082	0.4099	0.4115	0.4131	0.4147	0.4162	0.4177
1.4	0.4192	0.4207	0.4222	0.4236	0.4251	0.4265	0.4279	0.4292	0.4306	0.4319
1.5	0.4332	0.4345	0.4357	0.4370	0.4382	0.4394	0.4406	0.4418	0.4429	0.4441
1.6	0.4452	0.4463	0.4474	0.4484	0.4495	0.4505	0.4515	0.4525	0.4535	0.4545
1.7	0.4554	0.4564	0.4573	0.4582	0.4591	0.4599	0.4608	0.4616	0.4625	0.4633
1.8	0.4641	0.4649	0.4656	0.4664	0.4671	0.4678	0.4686	0.4693	0.4699	0.4706
1.9	0.4713	0.4719	0.4726	0.4732	0.4738	0.4744	0.4750	0.4756	0.4761	0.4767
2.0	0.4772	0.4778	0.4783	0.4788	0.4793	0.4798	0.4803	0.4808	0.4812	0.4817
2.1	0.4821	0.4826	0.4830	0.4834	0.4838	0.4842	0.4846	0.4850	0.4854	0.4857
2.2	0.4861	0.4864	0.4868	0.4871	0.4875	0.4878	0.4881	0.4884	0.4887	0.4890
2.3	0.4893	0.4896	0.4898	0.4901	0.4904	0.4906	0.4909	0.4911	0.4913	0.4916
2.4	0.4918	0.4920	0.4922	0.4925	0.4927	0.4929	0.4931	0.4932	0.4934	0.4936
2.5	0.4938	0.4940	0.4941	0.4943	0.4945	0.4946	0.4948	0.4949	0.4951	0.4952
2.6	0.4953	0.4955	0.4956	0.4957	0.4959	0.4960	0.4961	0.4962	0.4963	0.4964
2.7	0.4965	0.4966	0.4967	0.4968	0.4969	0.4970	0.4971	0.4972	0.4973	0.4974
2.8	0.4974	0.4975	0.4976	0.4977	0.4977	0.4978	0.4979	0.4979	0.4980	0.4981
2.9	0.4981	0.4982	0.4982	0.4983	0.4984	0.4984	0.4985	0.4985	0.4986	0.4986
3.0	0.4987	0.4987	0.4987	0.4988	0.4988	0.4989	0.4989	0.4989	0.4990	0.4990

Source: Donald H. Sanders, A. Franklin Murph, and Robert J. Eng, *Statistics—A Fresh Approach,* McGraw-Hill Book Company, New York, 1976.

SUBJECT INDEX